"The Catholic Commentary on Sacred Sc____
in theological interpretation of Scripture i_ ___ ___ ___ ___ ___ ___
about it is inviting and edifying, from the format, photos, background notes, and cross-references (to Scripture and the Catechism) to the rich exposition of the text, quotations from the Church's living tradition, and reflections for contemporary life. It is a wonderful gift to the Catholic Church and a model for the rest of us. Highly recommended for all!"

—**Michael J. Gorman**, Ecumenical Institute of Theology,
St. Mary's Seminary and University, Baltimore

"This series corresponds perfectly to a pressing need in the Church. I am speaking about exegetical studies that are well grounded from a scholarly point of view but not overburdened with technical details, and at the same time related to the riches of ancient interpretation, nourishing for spiritual life, and useful for catechesis, preaching, evangelization, and other forms of pastoral ministry. Indeed, this is the kind of commentary for which the majority of readers have a great desire."

—**Cardinal Albert Vanhoye, SJ**, rector emeritus, Pontifical Biblical Institute;
former secretary of the Pontifical Biblical Commission

"There is a great hunger among Catholic laity for a deeper understanding of the Bible. The Catholic Commentary on Sacred Scripture fills the need for a more in-depth interpretation of Scripture. I am very excited to be able to recommend this series to our Bible Study groups around the world."

—**Gail Buckley**, founder and director, Catholic Scripture Study International
(www.cssprogram.net)

"This series represents a much-needed approach, based on good scholarship but not overloaded with it. The frequent references to the *Catechism of the Catholic Church* help us to read Holy Scripture with a vivid sense of the living tradition of the Church."

—**Christoph Cardinal Schönborn**, Archbishop of Vienna

"This could be the first commentary read by a pastor preparing a text and could be read easily by a Sunday school teacher preparing a text, and it would be an excellent commentary for a college Bible class. . . . The Catholic Commentary on Sacred Scripture will prove itself to be a reliable, Catholic—but ecumenically open and respectful—commentary."

—**Scot McKnight**, *Jesus Creed* blog

"The Word of God is the source of Christian life, and the Catholic Commentary on Sacred Scripture is an ideal tool for living our faith more deeply. This extraordinary resource combines superior scholarship and a vivid, accessible style that will serve the interested layperson and the serious scholar equally well. It feeds both the mind and the heart and should be on the shelf of every committed Catholic believer. I highly recommend it."

—**Charles J. Chaput, OFM Cap**, Archbishop of Philadelphia

"When the Scripture is read in the liturgy, it is heard as a living voice. But when expounded in a commentary, it is too often read as a document from the past. This fine series unites the ancient and the contemporary by offering insight into the biblical text—verse by verse—as well as spiritual application to the lives of Christians today."

—**Robert Louis Wilken**, University of Virginia

"This Bible commentary series is based on solid scholarship and enriched by the Church's long tradition of study and reflection. Enhanced by an attractive format, it provides an excellent resource for all who are serving in pastoral ministry and for the individual reader who searches the Scriptures for guidance in the Christian life."

—**Emil A. Wcela**, Auxiliary Bishop (retired), Diocese of Rockville Centre; past president, Catholic Biblical Association

The Gospel of
Luke

✝ Catholic Commentary on Sacred Scripture

The Gospel of Luke

Pablo T. Gadenz

Baker Academic
a division of Baker Publishing Group
Grand Rapids, Michigan

Published by Baker Academic
a division of Baker Publishing Group
PO Box 6287, Grand Rapids, MI 49516-6287
www.bakeracademic.com

Printed in the United States of America

ISBN 978-0-8010-3700-9

Library of Congress Cataloging-in-Publication Control Number: 2018009831

Nihil obstat:
Monsignor C. Anthony Ziccardi
Censor Librorum
January 16, 2018

Imprimatur:
Cardinal Joseph W. Tobin
Archbishop of Newark
January 24, 2018

The *nihil obstat* and *imprimatur* are official declarations that a book is free of doctrinal or moral error. No implication is contained therein that those who have granted the *nihil obstat* or *imprimatur* agree with the contents, opinions, or statements expressed.

Figure 1 is courtesy of the Israel Museum, collection of the Israel Museum, Jerusalem, and courtesy of the Israel Antiquities Authority, exhibited at the Israel Museum, Jerusalem.

Figure 21 is courtesy of the Israel Museum, collection of the Israel Museum, Jerusalem, and courtesy of the Israel Antiquities Authority, exhibited at the Israel Museum, Jerusalem.

18 19 20 21 22 23 24   7 6 5 4 3 2 1

Contents

Illustrations

Editors' Preface

> The Church has always venerated the divine Scriptures just as she venerates the body of the Lord. . . . All the preaching of the Church should be nourished and governed by Sacred Scripture. For in the sacred books, the Father who is in heaven meets His children with great love and speaks with them; and the power and goodness in the word of God is so great that it stands as the support and energy of the Church, the strength of faith for her sons and daughters, the food of the soul, a pure and perennial fountain of spiritual life.
>
> Second Vatican Council, *Dei Verbum* 21

> Were not our hearts burning [within us] while he spoke to us on the way and opened the scriptures to us?
>
> Luke 24:32

The Catholic Commentary on Sacred Scripture aims to serve the ministry of the Word of God in the life and mission of the Church. Since Vatican Council II, there has been an increasing hunger among Catholics to study Scripture in depth and in a way that reveals its relationship to liturgy, evangelization, catechesis, theology, and personal and communal life. This series responds to that desire by providing accessible yet substantive commentary on each book of the New Testament, drawn from the best of contemporary biblical scholarship as well as the rich treasury of the Church's tradition. These volumes seek to offer scholarship illumined by faith, in the conviction that the ultimate aim of biblical interpretation is to discover what God has revealed and is still speaking through the sacred text. Central to our approach are the principles taught by Vatican II: first, the use of historical and literary methods to discern what the biblical authors intended to express; second, prayerful theological reflection to understand the sacred text "in accord with the same Spirit by whom it was written"—that is, in light of the content and unity of the whole Scripture, the living tradition of the Church, and the analogy of faith (*Dei Verbum* 12).

The Catholic Commentary on Sacred Scripture is written for those engaged in or training for pastoral ministry and others interested in studying Scripture to understand their faith more deeply, to nourish their spiritual life, or to share the good news with others. With this in mind, the authors focus on the meaning of the text for faith and life rather than on the technical questions that occupy scholars, and they explain the Bible in ordinary language that does not require translation for preaching and catechesis. Although this series is written from the perspective of Catholic faith, its authors draw on the interpretation of Protestant and Orthodox scholars and hope these volumes will serve Christians of other traditions as well.

A variety of features are designed to make the commentary as useful as possible. Each volume includes the biblical text of the New American Bible, Revised Edition (NABRE), the translation approved for liturgical use in the United States. In order to serve readers who use other translations, the commentary notes and explains the most important differences between the NABRE and other widely used translations (e.g., RSV, NRSV, JB, NJB, and NIV). Each unit of the biblical text is followed by a list of references to relevant Scripture passages, Catechism sections, and uses in the Roman Lectionary. The exegesis that follows aims to explain in a clear and engaging way the meaning of the text in its original historical context as well as its perennial meaning for Christians. Reflection and Application sections help readers apply Scripture to Christian life today by responding to questions that the text raises, offering spiritual interpretations drawn from Christian tradition or providing suggestions for the use of the biblical text in catechesis, preaching, or other forms of pastoral ministry.

Interspersed throughout the commentary are Biblical Background sidebars that present historical, literary, or theological information, and Living Tradition sidebars that offer pertinent material from the postbiblical Christian tradition, including quotations from Church documents and from the writings of saints and Church Fathers. The Biblical Background sidebars are indicated by a photo of urns that were excavated in Jerusalem, signifying the importance of historical study in understanding the sacred text. The Living Tradition sidebars are indicated by an image of Eadwine, a twelfth-century monk and scribe, signifying the growth in the Church's understanding that comes by the grace of the

Holy Spirit as believers study and ponder the Word of God in their hearts (see *Dei Verbum* 8).

Maps and a glossary are included in each volume for easy reference. The glossary explains key terms from the biblical text as well as theological or exegetical terms, which are marked in the commentary with a cross (†). A list of suggested resources, an index of pastoral topics, and an index of sidebars are included to enhance the usefulness of these volumes. Further resources, including questions for reflection or discussion, can be found at the series website, www.CatholicScriptureCommentary.com.

It is our desire and prayer that these volumes be of service so that more and more "the word of the Lord may speed forward and be glorified" (2 Thess 3:1) in the Church and throughout the world.

Peter S. Williamson

Mary Healy

Kevin Perrotta

Note to Readers

The New American Bible, Revised Edition differs slightly from most English translations in its verse numbering of Psalms and certain other parts of the Old Testament. For instance, Ps 51:4 in the NABRE is Ps 51:2 in other translations; Mal 3:19 in the NABRE is Mal 4:1 in other translations. Readers who use different translations are advised to keep this in mind when looking up Old Testament references given in the commentary.

Abbreviations

†	Indicates that a definition of a term appears in the glossary
//	Indicates where a parallel account can be found in other Gospels
AB	Anchor Bible
ACW	Ancient Christian Writers
Catechism	*Catechism of the Catholic Church*, 2nd ed. (New York: Doubleday, 2003)
CCSL	Corpus Christianorum, Series Latina (Turnhout: Brepols, 1953–)
ch(s).	chapter(s)
Denzinger	H. Denzinger, *Compendium of Creeds, Definitions, and Declarations on Matters of Faith and Morals*, 43rd ed. Edited by Peter Hünermann. Latin-English (San Francisco: Ignatius, 2012)
ESV	English Standard Version
FC	Fathers of the Church
JBL	*Journal of Biblical Literature*
KJV	King James Version
LCL	Loeb Classical Library
Lectionary	*The Lectionary for Mass* (1998/2002 USA edition)
LXX	Septuagint
m.	Mishnah
NABRE	New American Bible (Revised Edition, 2011)
NET	New English Translation
NETS	A. Pietersma and B. G. Wright, eds., *A New English Translation of the Septuagint* (New York: Oxford University Press, 2007)
NIV	New International Version
NJB	New Jerusalem Bible
NRSV	New Revised Standard Version
NT	New Testament
NTS	*New Testament Studies*
OT	Old Testament
PNTC	Pillar New Testament Commentary
repr.	reprint
RSV	Revised Standard Version
SC	Sources chrétiennes (Paris: Cerf, 1943–)

v(v).   verse(s)
WBC   Word Biblical Commentary
WSA   The Works of Saint Augustine
ZECNT   Zondervan Exegetical Commentary on the New Testament

Books of the Old Testament

Gen	Genesis	Tob	Tobit	Ezek	Ezekiel
Exod	Exodus	Jdt	Judith	Dan	Daniel
Lev	Leviticus	Esther	Esther	Hosea	Hosea
Num	Numbers	1 Macc	1 Maccabees	Joel	Joel
Deut	Deuteronomy	2 Macc	2 Maccabees	Amos	Amos
Josh	Joshua	Job	Job	Obad	Obadiah
Judg	Judges	Ps(s)	Psalm(s)	Jon	Jonah
Ruth	Ruth	Prov	Proverbs	Mic	Micah
1 Sam	1 Samuel	Eccles	Ecclesiastes	Nah	Nahum
2 Sam	2 Samuel	Song	Song of Songs	Hab	Habakkuk
1 Kings	1 Kings	Wis	Wisdom	Zeph	Zephaniah
2 Kings	2 Kings	Sir	Sirach	Hag	Haggai
1 Chron	1 Chronicles	Isa	Isaiah	Zech	Zechariah
2 Chron	2 Chronicles	Jer	Jeremiah	Mal	Malachi
Ezra	Ezra	Lam	Lamentations		
Neh	Nehemiah	Bar	Baruch		

Books of the New Testament

Matt	Matthew	Eph	Ephesians	Heb	Hebrews
Mark	Mark	Phil	Philippians	James	James
Luke	Luke	Col	Colossians	1 Pet	1 Peter
John	John	1 Thess	1 Thessalonians	2 Pet	2 Peter
Acts	Acts	2 Thess	2 Thessalonians	1 John	1 John
Rom	Romans	1 Tim	1 Timothy	2 John	2 John
1 Cor	1 Corinthians	2 Tim	2 Timothy	3 John	3 John
2 Cor	2 Corinthians	Titus	Titus	Jude	Jude
Gal	Galatians	Philem	Philemon	Rev	Revelation

Introduction

In countless ways, Luke's Gospel has been the source of inspiration for Christians for almost two thousand years. Because of Luke, hymns of praise such as the Gloria and the Magnificat were introduced into Christian worship, prayers such as the Hail Mary were developed, St. Francis of Assisi began the custom of the Christmas manger, and painters such as Rembrandt and Caravaggio produced some of their great works of art.

Luke's Gospel is itself a great work of art, as the human author used all of his literary and narrative skills to write the longest of the four Gospels (over 19,000 words, about 1,100 more than Matthew). In telling us the life and teaching of Jesus Christ, Luke's Gospel is also a work of history, written down after careful investigation and on the basis of eyewitnesses and other reliable sources (1:1–3). Moreover, it is a work of theology, written so that readers may know that the teachings of Christianity are true (1:4): Jesus Christ is indeed Savior, Messiah, Lord, and Son of God (1:35; 2:11). Luke's Gospel is all these things, and it is also divinely inspired, communicating to us what God wanted written for the sake of our salvation (Catechism 107).

Authorship

The titles found at the beginning or end of the earliest extant manuscripts of the Gospel, including Papyrus 75, dated by scholars to around AD 200, attribute the work to "Luke."[1] Writing around AD 180, St. Irenaeus likewise ascribes it

---

1. Simon J. Gathercole, "The Titles of the Gospels in the Earliest New Testament Manuscripts," *Zeitschrift für die Neutestamentliche Wissenschaft* 104 (2013): 66–68.

to "Luke," who was "Paul's follower" and "set down in a book the Gospel that was preached by Paul."[2] Irenaeus says that Luke also wrote the Acts of the Apostles and that Luke even accompanied Paul on some of his journeys, which he indicated by writing in the first-person plural, the so-called "we" sections (Acts 16:10–17; 20:5–15; 21:1–18; 27:1–28:16).[3] In the same place, Irenaeus also refers to two verses in Paul's letters that mention Luke, one saying that Luke is with him (2 Tim 4:11) and one describing him as "the beloved physician" (Col 4:14). There is also a third (Philem 24), in which Luke is described as one of Paul's fellow workers. The Muratorian Fragment and Church Fathers such as Clement of Alexandria, Tertullian, Origen, Eusebius, Ambrose, Jerome, and Augustine similarly note such details.[4]

Among modern scholars, the view that the same author wrote both the Gospel and Acts is widely accepted. Also, the explanation considered most probable for the "we" sections in Acts is still the view that the author was present at the events narrated and so was a companion of Paul. Moreover, the traditional identification of this companion with the Luke mentioned in Paul's letters, though a contested issue, is still accepted by many.[5] Luke's relative obscurity also argues in favor of the traditional view; if the Gospel's author were really unknown, it would have been attributed to a more famous person such as an apostle. Moreover, since the Gospel was dedicated to a named person—Theophilus (1:3; see Acts 1:1)—it is implausible that it was written anonymously.[6]

There are other interesting but more speculative details about Luke suggested by some Church Fathers as well as some modern scholars. For example, since Luke (Greek *Loukas*) is a diminutive form of Lucius (*Loukios*), he has at times been identified with the Lucius mentioned by Paul (Rom 16:21)[7] and/or the Lucius of Cyrene who was with Paul and Barnabas in Antioch (Acts 13:1).[8] Moreover, Antioch is mentioned by some ancient sources as Luke's city of origin.[9] Luke has

2. Irenaeus, *Against the Heresies* 3.1.1, trans. Dominic J. Unger and M. C. Steenberg, ACW (New York: Newman, 2012), 30.

3. Irenaeus, *Against the Heresies* 3.14.1.

4. See the discussion in Rick Strelan, *Luke the Priest: The Authority of the Author of the Third Gospel* (Burlington, VT: Ashgate, 2006), 69–98.

5. See the discussion in Joseph A. Fitzmyer, *The Gospel according to Luke*, 2 vols., AB (New York: Doubleday, 1981–85), 1:40–51; and, more recently, Michael Wolter, *The Gospel according to Luke*, vol. 1, *Luke 1–9:50*, trans. Wayne Coppins and Christoph Heilig (Waco: Baylor University Press, 2016), 6–10.

6. Richard Bauckham, *Jesus and the Eyewitnesses: The Gospels as Eyewitness Testimony* (Grand Rapids: Eerdmans, 2006), 301.

7. Origen, *Commentary on Romans* 10.39.1–2.

8. See the discussion in Strelan, *Luke the Priest*, 71; Fitzmyer, *Luke*, 1:47.

9. *Anti-Marcionite Prologue* for Luke; Eusebius, *Ecclesiastical History* 3.4.6; Jerome, *Commentary on Matthew* Preface.2.

also been identified as the unnamed disciple "whose praise is in the gospel" (2 Cor 8:18 KJV).[10]

Also of interest is the question of Luke's ethnic background. Although it is often assumed that Luke was a Gentile, scholarly opinion on this question is actually divided,[11] and there is little support among the Church Fathers that he was a Gentile.[12] The main argument for considering Luke to be a Gentile comes from Colossians, where Luke (Col 4:14) is not included in the list of those like Mark "who are of the circumcision" (4:11). This is often interpreted as saying that Mark is Jewish and Luke is Gentile, but the phrase "of the circumcision" may instead refer to a subset of Jewish Christians—namely, the strict faction that was typically uncooperative with Paul (Gal 2:12). Paul would then be saying that from among this group, only a few, like Mark, are his coworkers.[13] Luke did not belong to this group, but could still have been Jewish. Indeed, Luke's extensive knowledge of the Old Testament and interest in the Jerusalem temple and Jewish priesthood suggest that he was Jewish. His good command of Greek is well explained if he was a *Hellenistic* Jew. Luke may thus have been like Paul, a Jew whose ministry was largely to the Gentiles. Likewise, his Gospel was probably written mainly for Gentile Christians.

Historical Context

Scholars who hold that Luke was indeed Paul's coworker (in the 50s AD) generally set the 80s as the upper limit for the writing of Luke's Gospel (or 90s at the latest).[14] Most modern scholars indeed favor a date for Luke in the 70s or 80s AD. One reason supporting this majority view is that it seems certain to most that Luke relied on Mark's Gospel, which is itself generally dated in the range AD 60 to 75. However, since Mark and Luke at times were coworkers

10. E.g., Origen, *Homilies on Luke* 1.6; Ambrose, *Exposition of the Gospel according to Luke* 1.11; Jerome, *Commentary on Matthew* Preface.2. These writers consider the "gospel" to which Paul is referring to be Luke's Gospel.

11. Among recent commentators who consider Luke to be Jewish, see, e.g., Wolter, *Luke 1–9:50*, 10–11, and James R. Edwards, *The Gospel according to Luke*, PNTC (Grand Rapids: Eerdmans, 2015), 8–10. On the other hand, John T. Carroll, *Luke: A Commentary*, New Testament Library (Louisville: Westminster John Knox, 2012), 2, considers it probable that he was a Gentile.

12. As mentioned, Origen identified Luke with the Lucius of Rom 16:21, who was a kinsman of Paul—i.e., Jewish. Epiphanius, *Panarion* 51.11.6, considered Luke to be one of the seventy(-two) disciples whom Jesus sent out on mission (Luke 10:1), and hence Jewish.

13. E. Earle Ellis, *The Gospel of Luke*, rev. ed., New Century Bible (Greenwood, SC: Attic, 1974), 52–53; David E. Garland, *Colossians and Philemon*, NIV Application Commentary (Grand Rapids: Zondervan, 1998), 278.

14. Wolter, *Luke 1–9:50*, 11–12; Craig S. Keener, *Acts: An Exegetical Commentary*, 4 vols. (Grand Rapids: Baker Academic, 2012–15), 1:400.

together with Paul (Col 4:10, 14; 2 Tim 4:11; Philem 24), it is not necessary to assume a long interval (of a decade or more) between the two Gospels.

Another reason for the majority position is that Luke's account of Jesus' prophecy about the fall of Jerusalem, an event that took place in AD 70, contains certain details (Luke 19:43; 21:20) that are more specific than Mark's version (Mark 13:14), suggesting to some scholars that Luke wrote it down after the fact. This reason, however, has been rejected by other scholars, since the details in Luke use vocabulary typical for a siege of a city such as is found in various Old Testament prophetic texts, especially those about the first destruction of Jerusalem by the Babylonians in 586 BC.[15] There is also no reason why Jesus himself could not have prophesied the fall of Jerusalem using such Old Testament prophecies.

Some scholars take the minority view that Luke's Gospel was written before AD 70.[16] In this regard, another factor to consider is the dating of Acts, which Luke wrote after his Gospel (Acts 1:1). Acts ends with Paul's two-year Roman imprisonment (AD 60–62; Acts 28:30), saying nothing about Paul's death (around AD 64 or 67). This seems surprising if Acts was written much later (in the 70s or 80s). The reason may be that the plan of Acts is to show that Christianity spread to "the ends of the earth" (Acts 1:8), and this plan reaches completion when Paul arrives in Rome, the capital of the empire (28:14). However, a good case can also be made that Paul's death had not yet occurred when Acts was written.[17] Considering the numerous parallels between Jesus' passion in Luke and Paul's imprisonment in Acts,[18] which illustrate the theological principle at work in Acts that the life of Jesus is the model for the life of the disciples (see the sidebar, "Parallels between Luke and Acts," p. 376), Luke would have included Paul's death if it had occurred before he wrote Acts. For scholars who accept this argument, Luke's Gospel would therefore also have been written while Paul was still alive. Several Church Fathers held this view—for example, the Church historian Eusebius.[19]

As for the location where the Gospel was written, modern scholars propose many different places. Since Luke was Paul's coworker, all of these proposals

15. Alexander Mittelstaedt, *Lukas als Historiker: Zur Datierung des lukanischen Doppelwerkes* (Tübingen: Francke, 2006), 131–59. Drawing on Mittelstaedt's work, Wolter, *Luke 1–9:50*, 11, concludes: "The announcements of the destruction of Jerusalem . . . cannot function as dating criteria."

16. E.g., Darrell L. Bock, *Luke 1:1–9:50*, Baker Exegetical Commentary on the New Testament (Grand Rapids: Baker Academic, 1994), 16–18. Bock dates Luke to the early to mid-60s.

17. See Colin J. Hemer, *The Book of Acts in the Setting of Hellenistic History* (Tübingen: Mohr Siebeck, 1989), 365–410.

18. Mittelstaedt, *Lukas als Historiker*, 170–71.

19. *Ecclesiastical History* 2.22.

have a connection to Paul: the city where Paul began his missionary career and from which Luke may have originated (Antioch in Syria), cities evangelized by Paul (Corinth[20] or Ephesus), or cities where Paul was imprisoned (Caesarea or Rome). Regardless of the place, the Gospel was probably originally intended for many church communities, in particular those that arose from Paul's missionary activity.

Genre

Over the last several decades, "it has become much clearer that the Gospels are in fact very similar in type to *ancient* biographies (Greek *bioi*; Latin *vitae*)."[21] This was the view of St. Justin Martyr in the second century, who referred to the Gospels as the "memoirs" of the apostles, using a term indicating a biography.[22]

More specifically, like other ancient biographies, Luke's Gospel (1) begins with a brief preface that mentions both written and oral sources (1:1–4); (2) focuses on one individual—Jesus—especially his public life and death; (3) is within the typical range of ten thousand to twenty thousand words; (4) follows a basic chronological structure but with other material—for example, some of Jesus' teaching and parables—arranged topically or thematically; (5) portrays the subject through a selection of his significant deeds and words (see 24:19); (6) includes information about his birth (Luke 1–2), ancestry (3:23–38), and one significant childhood event (2:41–52); and (7) has the purpose of confirming what has been taught about the subject (1:4) and of proposing him as an example to be imitated.[23]

As a kind of ancient biography, Luke's Gospel was written with the intention of writing a historical account. This is evident from the preface (1:1–4), which mentions how Luke is writing a narrative about events, based on the testimony of eyewitnesses, after careful investigation, and so that his readers can know the truth of what they have been taught. Luke's work continues in Acts, whose genre is not specifically biographical but more generally historical.

Of course, besides being historical narratives, the Gospels are also theological because of the unique Christian claims about Jesus, claims that are rooted in

20. The *Anti-Marcionite Prologue* mentions the region of Achaia, where Corinth was located. Jerome, *Commentary on Matthew* Preface.2, also mentions Achaia and nearby Boeotia.

21. James D. G. Dunn, *Jesus Remembered* (Grand Rapids: Eerdmans, 2003), 185 (emphasis in the original).

22. Michael F. Bird, *The Gospel of the Lord: How the Early Church Wrote the Story of Jesus* (Grand Rapids: Eerdmans, 2014), 249–52.

23. Richard A. Burridge, *What Are the Gospels? A Comparison with Graeco-Roman Biography*, 2nd ed. (Grand Rapids: Eerdmans, 2004), 185–212.

the Scriptures and bring them to fulfillment (see 24:27, 44). Jesus is not only someone about whom it is important to know, or even someone whom it is important to imitate. He is also someone in whom it is important to believe: "Everyone who believes in him will receive forgiveness of sins through his name" (Acts 10:43).

Structure and Literary Features

After the four-verse preface (1:1–4), Luke begins his account with a selection of events regarding the birth of Jesus, which is paired with the birth of John the Baptist (1:5–2:52). This "infancy narrative" is a fitting introduction to both Luke's Gospel and Acts—for example, through the titles used for Jesus that will be developed later: Son of God, Savior, Messiah, and Lord (1:35; 2:11). Also included in these two chapters are events that foreshadow Jesus' passion and resurrection and that announce the inclusion of the Gentiles in God's plan. The Gospel continues with Jesus' public ministry, following a general pattern similar to what is found in the Gospels of Matthew and Mark. A short section presents the ministry of John the Baptist and other events that prepare for Jesus' ministry (3:1–4:13). There follows a section of Jesus' teaching and healing ministry in Galilee (4:14–9:50). Unlike the other Gospels, Luke begins this section with Jesus' reading and sermon in the Nazareth synagogue, a passage that explains his mission (4:16–30). The main question in this section concerns the identity of Jesus, who is frequently presented using the technique of comparison—for example, with Old Testament prophets like Moses, Elijah, and Elisha—showing that Jesus is greater than these predecessors. The section culminates in Peter's confession of Jesus as the Messiah. The transition to the next section is made with Jesus' first passion prediction and the transfiguration, where Jesus' "exodus"—that is, death—in Jerusalem is announced. The long central section covers the journey to Jerusalem (9:51–19:44). This physical journey is the setting for the journey of discipleship of Jesus' followers, who learn from his teaching, including many of the famous parables found only in Luke. Jesus also teaches here about the kingdom of God, and indeed the section culminates with the acclamation of Jesus as king as he approaches Jerusalem. The ministry in the Jerusalem temple follows (19:45–21:38), in which opposition to Jesus intensifies, leading to the account of his passion and death (22:1–23:56) and then his resurrection, concluding with his ascension (24:1–53).

Luke is the most skilled Greek writer among the evangelists, using complex sentence constructions (e.g., the four-verse preface is one long sentence) and a wide vocabulary (e.g., words that occur only once in the New Testament). He can also write in different styles. For example, he writes the preface in classical Greek style, displaying his literary credentials, and then, beginning in 1:5, switches for the main story to a style typical of the †Septuagint, in order to show that the story of Jesus continues the story of God's people in the Old Testament.

Relationship to Other Biblical Writings

Luke's Gospel needs to be studied in relation to various other books or parts of the Bible.

Other Gospels. Luke says that many have already written a narrative about the events of Jesus' life (1:1). Most scholars would agree that among these written sources for Luke is Mark's Gospel. More than a third of the material in Luke is also found in Mark. Moreover, the outline of Luke largely follows the outline of Mark, except for the omission of some sections (such as Mark 6:45–8:26). Luke also interweaves other material into this basic outline (a large block of it, for example, in the central section). As for Matthew's Gospel, scholars are in less agreement regarding Luke's direct dependence on it. An additional quarter of material in Luke (i.e., not found in Mark) is also found in Matthew, but it usually occurs in different contexts. The remaining 40 percent or so of the material in Luke is unique, derived from his own sources. Besides the relationship between Luke and the other †synoptic Gospels, there may also be some kind of relationship between Luke and John's Gospel, written later. For example, only Luke and John mention the sisters Martha and Mary, Peter's running to inspect the empty tomb, and Jesus' resurrection appearance to the disciples in Jerusalem on the evening of Easter.

Acts. Luke is the only evangelist who provides a sequel to his Gospel—namely, the Acts of the Apostles. A common theological vision unifies the two works. Numerous parallels between them show that Luke presents the life of Jesus as the model for the life of the early Church, especially the lives of Peter and Paul. Moreover, passages in Acts may at times clarify or illustrate passages in Luke. For example, the Gospel's emphasis on God's salvation extending to the Gentiles (2:32; 24:47) becomes a reality through the apostles' mission in Acts (Acts 1:8; 11:18; 28:28).

Paul's Letters. Because Luke was Paul's coworker, it can also be helpful to consider the possible relationship of his Gospel to some of Paul's letters. One example that comes to mind is Luke's account of the institution of the Eucharist (Luke 22:19–20),[24] which is more similar to Paul's account (1 Cor 11:23–25)

---

24. Assuming, with most scholars, the authenticity of these verses.

than to those in Matthew and Mark. Moreover, with regard to their theology, some recent studies have emphasized what Luke and Paul share in common—for example, with regard to their understanding of Jesus as Lord and of justification.[25]

Old Testament. Luke's Gospel highlights that in Jesus the promises made in the Old Testament have come to fulfillment (18:31; 24:44), thus showing the continuity in God's plan of salvation. At times, this fulfillment is indicated by an explicit citation of an Old Testament passage (22:37, quoting Isa 53:12). However, many times Luke shows the fulfillment of the Old Testament by means of allusions (7:15, alluding to 1 Kings 17:23) and †typology. With the latter technique, he compares Old Testament figures like Elijah and Elisha (Luke 4:25–27) to Jesus, showing that Jesus' deeds are similar to but greater than those of his forerunners (7:1–17).

Theological Teachings and Themes

Among the theological teachings and themes of Luke are the following: the fulfillment in Jesus of God's plan of salvation announced in Scripture (4:18–21); the extension of the message of salvation to the Gentiles (7:1–10); the role of the Holy Spirit in disciples' lives (11:13; 12:12); the proclamation of good news to the poor and marginalized (4:18; 6:20); the prominence of women disciples (8:2–3), including Jesus' mother, Mary (1:26–56; 2:1–52); the recurrence of meal scenes (e.g., 14:1–24), which may point to the Eucharist (24:30–35) and the kingdom banquet (22:30); and the importance of the Jerusalem temple (1:9; 24:53).[26]

Like the other evangelists, Luke above all presents the figure of Jesus. Jesus is prophet (4:24), king (19:38), God's chosen †servant (23:35), the Son of Man (22:69), the Messiah (9:20), the son of David (18:38–39), and the Son of God (1:35). More than the other evangelists, Luke emphasizes that Jesus is the Savior, the one who brings God's salvation (2:11, 30; 19:9). Luke also emphasizes that Jesus is Lord (Greek *kyrios*, 2:11), the same title used for the Lord God of Israel in the †Septuagint and elsewhere in Luke (1:68). Thus, as recent scholarship has shown, Luke "does indeed portray Jesus as Israel's Lord and God."[27]

25. Stanley E. Porter, "Luke: Companion or Disciple of Paul?," in *Paul and the Gospels: Christologies, Conflicts, and Convergences*, ed. Michael F. Bird and Joel Willitts (London: T&T Clark, 2011), 146–68; Sigurd Grindheim, "Luke, Paul, and the Law," *Novum Testamentum* 56 (2014): 356.

26. The Church Fathers (e.g., Irenaeus, *Against the Heresies* 3.11.8; Augustine, *Harmony of the Gospels* 1.6.9) who compared the four evangelists to the four living creatures (Rev 4:7; see Ezek 1:10) consistently identified Luke with the calf on account of the Gospel's interest in the temple and its priestly sacrifices. They understood Luke's Gospel to have a priestly character.

27. Richard B. Hays, *Echoes of Scripture in the Gospels* (Waco: Baylor University Press, 2016), 243.

Reading Luke Today

In several ways, Luke's Gospel both invites and challenges today's readers. It invites them to answer Jesus' call to discipleship—"Follow me" (5:27; 9:23, 59; 18:22)—while challenging them to take seriously his words about detachment from material possessions and merciful care of the poor and needy (10:37; 12:15–21; 14:13, 33; 16:19–31). It invites them to develop a life of prayer (11:1–13) modeled after Jesus' own prayer (3:21; 5:16; 6:12; 22:40–46), while challenging them to persevere "without becoming weary" (18:1) when an answer to prayer seems a long time in coming. It invites them to be witnesses (24:48) to the risen Jesus by their words and deeds, while challenging them to maintain their testimony in the face of persecution (21:12–13). Despite the challenges, however, Luke invites readers to experience the joy of the gospel (2:10; 15:32; 24:52).

Finally, Luke's readers today can know that through an encounter with Jesus, liberty from the captivity (4:18) of sin and the new life of grace are available not just at some future time but at the present moment. "Today . . . a savior has been born for you" (2:11). "Today this scripture passage is fulfilled" (4:21). "Today salvation has come to this house" (19:9). So, start reading Luke's Gospel *today*!

Outline of the Gospel of Luke

I. Preface and Infancy Narrative (1:1–2:52)
   A. Preface (1:1–4)
   B. Announcement to Zechariah of the Birth of John (1:5–25)
   C. Announcement to Mary of the Birth of Jesus (1:26–38)
   D. Mary's Visitation to Elizabeth and Her Magnificat (1:39–56)
   E. Birth of John and Zechariah's Benedictus (1:57–80)
   F. Birth of Jesus (2:1–20)
   G. Presentation of Jesus in the Temple (2:21–40)
   H. Finding Jesus in the Temple (2:41–52)
II. Preparation for Jesus' Public Ministry (3:1–4:13)
   A. Preaching of John the Baptist (3:1–20)
   B. Baptism and Genealogy of Jesus, Son of God (3:21–38)
   C. Temptation of Jesus (4:1–13)
III. Jesus' Ministry in Galilee (4:14–9:50)
   A. Jubilee Proclamation in Nazareth (4:14–30)
   B. Miracles in Capernaum (4:31–44)
   C. Simon Peter and the Catch of Fish (5:1–11)
   D. Healing a Leper and a Paralyzed Man (First Controversy with Pharisees) (5:12–26)
   E. Call of Levi and Two Banquet Controversies (5:27–39)
   F. Two Sabbath Controversies (6:1–11)
   G. Choice of the Twelve (6:12–16)
   H. Sermon on the Plain (6:17–49)
   I. Miracles of Jesus the Prophet for a Centurion and the Widow of Nain (7:1–17)

J. John's Messengers and Jesus' Witness to John (7:18–35)

K. Pardoning a Sinful Woman in a Pharisee's House (7:36–50)

L. Women Disciples with Jesus and the Twelve (8:1–3)

M. Parables on Hearing the Word of God (8:4–18)

N. Jesus' New Family (8:19–21)

O. Jesus' Lake Trip: Calming the Storm and Healing a Possessed Man (8:22–39)

P. Healing a Woman with Hemorrhages and Raising Jairus's Daughter (8:40–56)

Q. Mission of the Twelve (9:1–6)

R. Herod's Perplexity about Jesus' Identity (9:7–9)

S. Feeding the Five Thousand (9:10–17)

T. Peter's Confession of Jesus as Messiah and Jesus' Revelation of the Cross (9:18–27)

U. Transfiguration of Jesus (9:28–36)

V. Healing a Father's Possessed Son and Instructions for the Disciples (9:37–50)

IV. Jesus' Journey to Jerusalem (9:51–19:44)

A. First Part of the Journey (9:51–13:21)

1. Beginning of the Journey: Facing Jerusalem (9:51–62)

2. Mission of the Seventy-Two (10:1–20)

3. The Father and the Son Who Reveals Him (10:21–24)

4. The Love Commandments and the Parable of the Good Samaritan (10:25–37)

5. Martha and Mary (10:38–42)

6. The Lord's Prayer and Other Teaching on Prayer (11:1–13)

7. God's Kingdom over Satan's Kingdom (11:14–26)

8. The Sign of Jonah and Sayings on Light (11:27–36)

9. Woes against the Pharisees and Law-Scholars (11:37–54)

10. Discourse on Authentic Discipleship, Treasure in Heaven, and Warnings to Repent (12:1–13:9)

11. Healing a Crippled Woman (13:10–17)

12. Kingdom Parables: Mustard Seed and Leaven (13:18–21)

B. Second Part of the Journey (13:22–17:10)

1. The Narrow Door into the Kingdom of God (13:22–30)

2. Herod's Wish to Kill Jesus and Jesus' Lament about Jerusalem (13:31–35)

3. Healing a Man with Dropsy (14:1–6)

4. Banquet Parables and Teaching on Discipleship (14:7–35)
5. Parables about Finding Lost Sinners (15:1–32)
6. Parables about Mammon and More Teaching on Discipleship (16:1–17:10)
C. Third Part of the Journey (17:11–18:30)
1. Healing Ten Lepers (17:11–19)
2. End Times: The Coming of the Kingdom and the Son of Man (17:20–37)
3. Parables about Prayer (18:1–14)
4. Teaching on Entering the Kingdom (18:15–30)
D. Fourth Part of the Journey (18:31–19:44)
1. Prediction of the Passion on the Way Up to Jerusalem (18:31–34)
2. Events in Jericho: Healing a Blind Man and Saving Zacchaeus (18:35–19:10)
3. Parable of the Returning King (Ten Gold Coins) (19:11–28)
4. Events on the Mount of Olives: Riding a Colt and Being Hailed as King (19:29–40)
5. Prediction of the Destruction of Jerusalem (19:41–44)
V. Jesus' Ministry in the Jerusalem Temple (19:45–21:38)
A. Cleansing the Temple and Teaching in the Temple (19:45–48)
B. Jesus' Authority Questioned (20:1–8)
C. Parable of the Tenant Farmers (20:9–19)
D. Question about Tribute to Caesar (20:20–26)
E. The Sadducees' Question about the Resurrection (20:27–40)
F. Jesus' Question about the Messiah and David (20:41–44)
G. Warning about the Scribes and Praise for a Widow (20:45–21:4)
H. End Times: The Destruction of Jerusalem and Coming of the Son of Man (21:5–38)
VI. The Passion and Resurrection of Jesus (22:1–24:53)
A. The Plot of Judas and the Chief Priests (22:1–6)
B. Preparations for Passover (22:7–13)
C. Last Supper: Institution of the Eucharist and Instructions for the Disciples (22:14–38)
D. Agony and Arrest on the Mount of Olives (22:39–53)
E. Peter's Three Denials (22:54–65)
F. Hearing before the Sanhedrin (22:66–71)
G. Trial before Pilate and Hearing before Herod (23:1–25)

Luke States His Purpose

Luke 1:1–4

Immediately sparking the reader's interest and displaying his own literary credentials, Luke begins his Gospel with a stately preface—brief but remarkably packed with meaning—in which he sets forth his intention of writing a historical account of the words and deeds of Jesus. His purpose is to assure his readers, schooled in the Old Testament and the Christian faith, of the truth of these words and deeds.

Preface (1:1–4)

¹Since many have undertaken to compile a narrative of the events that have been fulfilled among us, ²just as those who were eyewitnesses from the beginning and ministers of the word have handed them down to us, ³I too have decided, after investigating everything accurately anew, to write it down in an orderly sequence for you, most excellent Theophilus, ⁴so that you may realize the certainty of the teachings you have received.

OT: 2 Macc 2:19–32
NT: Luke 24:48; John 15:27; Acts 1:1–2, 21–22; 1 John 1:1–3
Catechism: three stages in the formation of the Gospels, 126; catechesis, 4–6
Lectionary: Third Sunday Ordinary Time (Year C)

1:1 Matthew and Mark directly introduce Jesus in the initial verses of their Gospels. Luke instead begins with the qualities and purpose of his Gospel about Jesus, writing a complex, one-sentence preface that extends for four verses. His Gospel is not the first, **since many have undertaken** to do what he is now doing. Luke likely refers both to written sources that still exist today (such as the Gospel of Mark) and to others no longer extant. He stands in the tradition of these earlier efforts and seeks to complement them.

What others have done and what he sets out to do is **to compile a narrative**. Since it is about past **events**—namely, those regarding the life of Jesus—Luke here signals that he is writing history, as the details in verses 2–3 further clarify.[1] Moreover, these events are not random happenings but **have been fulfilled among us**—that is, they are the fulfillment of God's plan, especially as foretold in the Old Testament. Indeed, at the end of the Gospel, Jesus will tell his disciples: "Everything written about me in the law of Moses and in the prophets and psalms must be fulfilled" (24:44; see 4:21; 9:30–31).

1:2 Another indicator that Luke is writing history is that these events were observed by **eyewitnesses**. They were present **from the beginning**, which may refer to the beginning of Jesus' public ministry (John 15:27; Acts 1:21–22) but also to the events surrounding his birth, with which the Gospel begins. Luke also mentions **ministers of the word**, who together with the eyewitnesses are the bearers of the traditions about Jesus and have **handed them down**.[2] Possible sources belonging to both categories are the twelve apostles (Luke 6:13–16; Acts 1:13, 26), eyewitnesses who became ministers of God's word (Acts 6:4; 10:39–42). Other eyewitness sources likely include named characters in the Gospel, such as Mary Magdalene and Joanna (Luke 8:2–3; 24:10); Martha and her sister, Mary (10:38–42); Zacchaeus (19:1–10); Cleopas (24:13–35);[3] and even Mary, the mother of Jesus, for the account of Jesus' birth (2:19, 51).[4] Luke's companion Paul would be a source who was a minister of the Word but not an eyewitness of Jesus' earthly life (1 Cor 15:3).

1:3 Luke's aim to write history is evident also in his emphasis on **investigating** (or "following") things **accurately** and **anew** (or "from the beginning" [NIV];

---

1. John Moles, "Luke's Preface: The Greek Decree, Classical Historiography and Christian Redefinitions," *NTS* 57 (2011): 462–63.

2. The verb *paradidōmi* is sometimes used as a technical term to refer to the handing down of traditions (Acts 16:4; 1 Cor 11:2, 23; 15:3). See also the related noun *paradosis* ("tradition") in 2 Thess 2:15; 3:6.

3. Richard Bauckham, *Jesus and the Eyewitnesses: The Gospels as Eyewitness Testimony* (Grand Rapids: Eerdmans, 2006), 29–30, 39–66, 117–19.

4. Richard Bauckham, "Luke's Infancy Narrative as Oral History in Scriptural Form," in *The Gospels: History and Christology*, ed. Bernardo Estrada, Ermenegildo Manicardi, and Armand Puig i Tàrrech, 2 vols. (Vatican City: Libreria Editrice Vaticana, 2013), 1:406–7.

see Acts 26:5), in order **to write** them **in an orderly sequence**. This last quality can mean chronological order (Acts 3:24), but also logical arrangement in narration (Acts 11:4). These qualities are meant to distinguish Luke's Gospel from its predecessors (e.g., Mark's Gospel does not recount Jesus' birth) and to present Luke as a trustworthy and capable writer.

Luke addresses one reader in particular, **Theophilus** (also Acts 1:1), a person of high standing since he is called **most excellent**. Perhaps he is Luke's patron, who financed the publication of the Gospel.[5] He may be a Roman official, like Felix or Festus (Acts 23:26; 24:3; 26:25), although there were also prominent Jews named Theophilus.[6] Probably he is already a Christian believer (see Luke 1:4). An actual person is meant, but the name—which in Greek literally means "God-loving" or "loved by God"—also takes on a symbolic meaning for any such reader of Luke's Gospel.

The Gospel's purpose is to give **certainty**[7] to Theophilus and all its readers.   **1:4**
Added emphasis is given in the Greek text since it is the last word of the sentence. Christian readers can have assurance of the truth of the **teachings** about Jesus they **have received**—literally, the things about which they have been instructed or "catechized" (verb *katēcheō*; see Acts 18:25).

Reflection and Application (1:1–4)

Reading like a "Theophilus." St. Ambrose comments, "The Gospel was written to Theophilus, i.e., to him whom God loves. If you love God, it was written to you. . . . Diligently preserve the pledge of a friend."[8] And Origen remarks, "Anyone who is 'Theophilus' is both 'excellent' and 'very strong.' . . . He has vigor and strength from both God and his Word. He can recognize the 'truth.'"[9]

Scripture and catechesis. Luke's Gospel was written in order to aid instruction in the Christian faith and has served that purpose ever since. Catechesis today

---

5. Similarly, the Jewish historian Josephus dedicates several of his works to a patron named Epaphroditus (*Jewish Antiquities* 1.8; *Life* 1.430; *Against Apion* 1.1).

6. Theophilus, son of Annas, was the Jewish high priest from AD 37 to 41. See James C. VanderKam, *From Joshua to Caiaphas: High Priests after the Exile* (Minneapolis: Fortress, 2004), 440–43. Some have argued that years later Luke writes his Gospel to this Theophilus, the former high priest; see, e.g., David L. Allen, *Lukan Authorship of Hebrews* (Nashville: B&H, 2010), 327–36.

7. The Greek word *asphaleia* (related to the word from which "asphalt" derives) indicates the firmness or stability of the teaching (see Ps 104:5 LXX).

8. Ambrose, *Exposition of the Holy Gospel according to Saint Luke* 1.12, trans. Theodosia Tomkinson (Etna, CA: Center for Traditionalist Orthodox Studies, 1998), 23 (translation adapted).

9. Origen, *Homilies on Luke* 1.6, trans. Joseph T. Lienhard, FC 94 (Washington, DC: Catholic University of America Press, 1996), 9. The word for "most excellent" is the superlative of "strong."

Luke the Historian and the Historicity of the Gospels

LIVING TRADITION

Commenting on the preface, St. Bonaventure notes that Luke's Gospel is historical: "Three attributes pertain to the narrative historian" (see 2 Macc 2:30): in composing his Gospel, Luke "took a sufficiency of material into account and was diligent and orderly."[a]

Similarly, Vatican II cites Luke's preface when affirming the historicity of the Gospels:

> Holy Mother Church has firmly and constantly held and continues to hold that the four Gospels . . . whose historicity the Church affirms without hesitation, faithfully hand on what Jesus . . . actually did and taught for their eternal salvation. . . . In composing the four Gospels, the sacred writers selected certain of the many traditions that had been handed on either orally or already in written form; others they summarized or explicated with an eye to the situation of the churches. Moreover, they retained the form and style of proclamation but always in such a fashion that they related to us an honest and true account of Jesus. For their intention in writing was that, either from their own memory and recollections or from the testimony of those "who from the beginning were eyewitnesses and ministers of the Word" we might know "the truth" concerning the things about which we have been instructed (cf. Luke 1:2–4).[b]

St. John Paul II likewise comments that "the Gospels do not claim to be a complete biography of Jesus in accordance with the canons of modern historical science. From them, nevertheless, *the face of the Nazarene emerges with a solid historical foundation.* The Evangelists took pains to represent him on the basis of trustworthy testimonies which they gathered (cf. Luke 1:3)."[c]

a. Bonaventure, *Commentary on the Gospel of Luke* 1.4, 6, ed. and trans. Robert J. Karris, 3 vols. (St. Bonaventure, NY: The Franciscan Institute, 2001–4), 1:27, 29.

b. Vatican II, *Dei Verbum* (Dogmatic Constitution on Divine Revelation) 19, from *The Scripture Documents: An Anthology of Official Catholic Teachings*, ed. Dean P. Béchard (Collegeville, MN: Liturgical Press, 2002), 27–28.

c. John Paul II, *Novo Millennio Ineunte* (At the Beginning of the New Millennium) 18 (emphasis in the original). Unless otherwise indicated, Church and papal documents are quoted from the Vatican website.

should thus be nourished through frequent contact with the Gospels (and the rest of the Scriptures), so as to lead people to a knowledge of the Church's faith and to a deeper personal relationship with Jesus.[10]

10. See Benedict XVI, *Verbum Domini* (On the Word of God in the Life and Mission of the Church) 72, 74.

God Visits His People

Luke 1:5–80

Luke's style changes as he begins the account of the events surrounding Jesus' birth, the infancy narrative (1:5–2:52). Whereas in the preface (1:1–4), Luke writes in classical Greek style, here he switches to using phrases and vocabulary typical of the †Septuagint. Indeed, the alert reader notices that the stories of John the Baptist and Jesus are written like stories in the Old Testament. Luke thus indicates that he is picking up where earlier biblical writers left off.[1] In the historical events that Luke records, God's plan of salvation first announced in the Old Testament continues to unfold. The Scriptures thus shed light on the meaning of the events, and conversely, those events bring the Scriptures to fulfillment.[2]

As in the days of old, God is again visiting his people (1:68, 78). He sends the angel Gabriel to Zechariah and Mary to announce the births of John the Baptist and Jesus and to explain their related missions as prophetic precursor and kingly Son of God. These two great figures come together in the meeting between their pregnant mothers, Elizabeth and Mary. In response to God's wondrous deeds, Mary and eventually Zechariah, after the birth of John, burst forth in songs of praise. By the end of the chapter, the stage is set for Jesus' birth.

1. François Bovon, *Luke*, trans. Christine M. Thomas, Donald S. Deer, and James Crouch, 3 vols., Hermeneia (Minneapolis: Fortress, 2002–13), 1:30: "The author intends to be counted among the legitimate successors of the Scriptures."
2. Benedict XVI, *Jesus of Nazareth: The Infancy Narratives*, trans. Philip J. Whitmore (New York: Image, 2012), 15, 17.

Announcement to Zechariah of the Birth of John (1:5–25)

[5]In the days of Herod, King of Judea, there was a priest named Zechariah of the priestly division of Abijah; his wife was from the daughters of Aaron, and her name was Elizabeth. [6]Both were righteous in the eyes of God, observing all the commandments and ordinances of the Lord blamelessly. [7]But they had no child, because Elizabeth was barren and both were advanced in years. [8]Once when he was serving as priest in his division's turn before God, [9]according to the practice of the priestly service, he was chosen by lot to enter the sanctuary of the Lord to burn incense. [10]Then, when the whole assembly of the people was praying outside at the hour of the incense offering, [11]the angel of the Lord appeared to him, standing at the right of the altar of incense. [12]Zechariah was troubled by what he saw, and fear came upon him. [13]But the angel said to him, "Do not be afraid, Zechariah, because your prayer has been heard. Your wife Elizabeth will bear you a son, and you shall name him John. [14]And you will have joy and gladness, and many will rejoice at his birth, [15]for he will be great in the sight of [the] Lord. He will drink neither wine nor strong drink. He will be filled with the holy Spirit even from his mother's womb, [16]and he will turn many of the children of Israel to the Lord their God. [17]He will go before him in the spirit and power of Elijah to turn the hearts of fathers toward children and the disobedient to the understanding of the righteous, to prepare a people fit for the Lord." [18]Then Zechariah said to the angel, "How shall I know this? For I am an old man, and my wife is advanced in years." [19]And the angel said to him in reply, "I am Gabriel, who stand before God. I was sent to speak to you and to announce to you this good news. [20]But now you will be speechless and unable to talk until the day these things take place, because you did not believe my words, which will be fulfilled at their proper time."

[21]Meanwhile the people were waiting for Zechariah and were amazed that he stayed so long in the sanctuary. [22]But when he came out, he was unable to speak to them, and they realized that he had seen a vision in the sanctuary. He was gesturing to them but remained mute. [23]Then, when his days of ministry were completed, he went home. [24]After this time his wife Elizabeth conceived, and she went into seclusion for five months, saying, [25]"So has the Lord done for me at a time when he has seen fit to take away my disgrace before others."

OT: Gen 17:1–3, 15–22; 18:9–15; Exod 30:7–8; Num 6:1–3; Judg 13:2–23; 1 Chron 24:10; Dan 8:16; 9:21; Mal 3:1, 23–24
NT: Luke 7:33

Catechism: angel Gabriel, 332; John the Baptist, 523, 696, 717–19; a people prepared, 716; spirit of Elijah, 2684; liturgy, 1070
Lectionary: December 19; Luke 1:5–17: Nativity of St. John the Baptist (Vigil)

In outline form, the infancy narrative (1:5–2:52) consists of two two-part panels or diptychs: first, the parallel announcements of the births of John the Baptist and Jesus, and second, the parallel birth narratives themselves. The message conveyed is that John the Baptist and Jesus are closely related: John prepares the way for Jesus, who is greater than John.[3] Several other episodes fill in the basic outline. The meeting between Elizabeth and Mary links the two announcements and serves as a bridge to the birth narratives. The two episodes after the birth of Jesus—the presentation of the infant Jesus and the finding of the twelve-year old Jesus—both occur in the temple and thus bring the infancy narrative, which begins in the temple, to its fulfillment (see Mal 3:1). They also look ahead to the rest of the Gospel, including Jesus' death and resurrection.

The two announcements (Luke 1:5–25 and 1:26–38) are themselves presented according to a pattern seen in Old Testament birth announcements of great figures like Isaac (Gen 17–18) and Samson (Judg 13). The similar pattern indicates that God's marvelous deeds in the Old Testament prefigure those happening now in the Gospel. The pattern has five steps, allowing for easy comparison of the related roles of John the Baptist and Jesus: (1) appearance of an angel (Luke 1:11, 26–28); (2) reaction of fear (1:12, 29); (3) message of the angel (1:13–17, 30–33); (4) response with a question (1:18, 34); and (5) giving of a sign (1:20, 36–37).[4]

Luke first situates his account in its historical context, as he will do twice more **1:5** (2:1–2; 3:1–2). The events surrounding Jesus' birth take place during the reign of **Herod, King of Judea** (see Matt 2:1). Among his many building projects, Herod had refurbished the Jerusalem temple and expanded its courts. It was there that an angel appeared to a Jewish **priest named Zechariah**, whose name means "†YHWH has remembered." Jewish priests belonged to the tribe of Levi and were descended from **Aaron**. They were organized in twenty-four groups (1 Chron 24:1–19; see Neh 12:1–7, 12–21), which served in the temple for a week at a time on a rotating basis.[5] The eighth group was Zechariah's **division of Abijah** (1 Chron 24:10). As was common, **his wife** was also from a priestly family. Her name was **Elizabeth**, like Aaron's wife Elisheba (Exod 6:23), a name derived from the Hebrew words "my God" and "oath."

---

3. Karl A. Kuhn, *Luke: The Elite Evangelist* (Collegeville, MN: Liturgical Press, 2010), 47–49.
4. Raymond E. Brown, *The Birth of the Messiah: A Commentary on the Infancy Narratives in the Gospels of Matthew and Luke*, rev. ed. (New York: Doubleday, 1993), 156.
5. Josephus, *Life* 1.2; *Jewish Antiquities* 7.365–66.

King Herod and Herod the Tetrarch

**BIBLICAL
BACKGROUND**

Herod the Great (Luke 1:5) was appointed king of the Jews by the Roman senate in 40 BC and took control of Jerusalem in 37 BC after defeating the †Hasmonean king Antigonus. He reigned for the rest of his life as a client-king of Caesar Augustus. Since he was the son of an Idumean father and an Arabian mother, he was considered a half Jew at best and certainly not a king in the line of David! Famous for his building projects, he expanded the Jerusalem temple complex; constructed the city of Caesarea, where Paul was later held in custody (Acts 25:4); and built or rebuilt fortresses such as Herodium near Bethlehem, Masada on the western shore of the Dead Sea, and Machaerus on its eastern shore, where John the Baptist was later imprisoned by Herod Antipas (Luke 3:19–20). Herod was notorious for his cruelty, killing three of his sons because of fear of conspiracies and uncertainty about his heir. When he died, his kingdom was divided among his sons Archelaus (Matt 2:22; deposed in AD 6 by the Romans), Herod Antipas, and Philip (Luke 3:1).

The consensus since the end of the nineteenth century for the date of Herod's death is 4 BC. However, several recent studies of the first-century Jewish historian Josephus's many references to Herod, as well as of ancient inscriptions and coins, propose that he died later, in 1 BC or AD 1.[a] The date has implications for dating Jesus' birth, which was one or two years earlier (Matt 2:16).

Throughout Jesus' public ministry, Herod Antipas was tetrarch of Galilee, a position he maintained until his exile in AD 39. "Herod" in Luke's Gospel refers to him, except the initial reference to King Herod (1:5). Like his father, Antipas engaged in building projects—for example, in his capitals Sepphoris and Tiberiàs. Since Antipas arrested and killed John the Baptist, Jesus had to be wary of him (9:7–9; 13:31–33). The two finally met during his trial in Jerusalem (23:6–15).

a. Jack Finegan, *Handbook of Biblical Chronology*, rev. ed. (Peabody, MA: Hendrickson, 1998), 298–301; Andrew E. Steinmann, "When Did Herod the Great Reign?," *Novum Testamentum* 51 (2009): 1–29; Bieke Mahieu, *Between Rome and Jerusalem: Herod the Great and His Sons in Their Struggle for Recognition* (Leuven: Peeters, 2012), 235–444.

1:6 Zechariah and Elizabeth are presented as model Jews: they are **righteous** before God, **observing** (or "walking in," RSV) **all the commandments and ordinances of the Lord blamelessly**. They do what God told Abraham: "Walk in my presence and be blameless" (Gen 17:1). Like the other characters encountered in these first two chapters (Mary, Joseph, Simeon, and Anna), they are obedient and devout.

Figure 1. A model of the temple sanctuary.

According to the law, such people are promised blessings from the Lord: **1:7**
they "will live and grow numerous" (Deut 30:16). In this case, however, **they
had no child, because Elizabeth was barren**. Moreover, they are **advanced
in years**, so there seems to be no more hope for children. The situation is like
that of Abraham and his wife, Sarah (Gen 11:30; 18:11). It also brings to mind
other Old Testament women like Rebekah (Gen 25:21), Rachel (Gen 29:31;
30:22–23), Manoah's wife (Judg 13:2–3), and Hannah (1 Sam 1:5, 19–20). All
these women were barren, but God remembered them and they conceived and
bore a son. Will God also remember Elizabeth?

The action now begins in the **sanctuary** (*naos*; 1:9, 21–22) of the temple **1:8–12**
complex (*hieron*; 2:27, 37, 46)—in other words, in the temple building. During
a week in which it is **his division's turn** of duty, **according to the practice** for
the assigning of priestly duties, Zechariah is **chosen by lot** (1 Chron 24:5; see
Acts 1:26) **to burn incense**, a task done twice daily (Exod 30:6–8) in association
with the morning and evening offerings (Exod 29:38–42). Here it is likely the
latter, around the ninth **hour** (three o'clock).[6] Zechariah thus enters the Holy
Place, the first room of the temple, where the **altar of incense** was located.

Meanwhile, **the whole assembly of the people was praying outside** in the
temple courts. Throughout Luke's Gospel, the people of Israel are often portrayed

6. Josephus, *Jewish Antiquities* 14.65.

37

as reverently attentive to God and to Jesus (7:29; 19:48; 21:38), in contrast with their leaders (7:30; 19:47; 20:19; 22:2). Their piety is here emphasized, as their "prayer" is as "incense before" God (Ps 141:2).

Suddenly, **the angel of the Lord** appears to Zechariah. Like others who experience such an angelic visitation (Luke 1:29; 2:9; 24:5), Zechariah is **troubled** and full of **fear**.

1:13–14   The angel's message begins with a word of reassurance: **Do not be afraid, Zechariah** (see 1:30; 2:10). His **prayer has been heard**! In words that echo the announcement to Abraham—"Your wife Sarah shall bear you a son, and you shall name him Isaac" (Gen 17:19 NRSV)—Zechariah is told: **your wife Elizabeth will bear you a son and you shall name him John**. The Hebrew name means "the Lord is gracious [or merciful]" (see Luke 1:58, 72; Exod 34:6). The **birth** will bring **joy and gladness** to his parents, and indeed **many** others **will rejoice** (see Luke 1:58). Throughout the first two chapters, the events recounted are "joyful mysteries."

1:15–17   The message continues with multiple references to the Old Testament, which help to show how John and his mission **will be great**. First, like the priestly sons of Aaron (Lev 10:9) and like Samson and Samuel, who were dedicated to God as †nazirites (Num 6:1–21; Judg 13:4–7; 1 Sam 1:11, 28), John **will drink neither wine nor strong drink** (see Luke 7:33). He will also **be filled with the holy Spirit even from his mother's womb** (see 1:41), as were various Old Testament prophets (see Isa 49:1; Jer 1:5). Moreover, John is the one who **will go before** the Lord **in the spirit and power of Elijah to turn the hearts of fathers toward children**. He will thus fulfill the prophecy of Malachi: "I am sending to you / Elijah the prophet. . . . / He will turn the heart of fathers to their sons" (Mal 3:23–24;[7] see also Mal 3:1; Luke 7:27). Prophecy in Israel, silent for centuries after Malachi (according to a common Jewish view of the time), will continue now with John, "prophet of the Most High" (Luke 1:76). John's mission is **to prepare a people fit for the Lord**. That is, **he will turn many of the children of Israel to the Lord their God** by his proclamation of repentance (3:3–4; 7:29). And as precursor of the Messiah (3:15–16), John will also prepare for the "Lord" Jesus (2:11).

1:18   Zechariah finds this wonderful news too incredible to believe: **How shall I know this?** He asks the same question that Abraham once did (Gen 15:8 LXX); yet unlike Abraham, who believed (Gen 15:6), Zechariah doubts. **For I am an old man, and my wife is advanced in years**. This again sounds like Abraham:

---

7. Mal 4:5–6 in the RSV and many other English versions. The NABRE instead follows the Hebrew numbering (as does the NJB).

"Can a child be born to a man who is a hundred years old? Can Sarah give birth at ninety?" (Gen 17:17; see 18:12). However, Zechariah knows that God fulfilled his promise to Abraham, so because of the precedent in Scripture he should believe the angel's message.[8]

The angel identifies himself as **Gabriel** (Luke 1:26), known from the book of Daniel (Dan 8:16). Gabriel once appeared to Daniel at the time of the "evening offering" (Dan 9:21), apparently the same time that he is now appearing to Zechariah (Luke 1:10). To Daniel, Gabriel prophesied regarding a period of "seventy weeks" until "a holy of holies will be anointed" (Dan 9:24). This prophecy is generally understood as referring to seventy weeks *of years* (490 years). However, it is possible that Luke presents the **proper time** for Gabriel's prophecies to **be fulfilled** as seventy weeks *of days* (490 days), beginning from this encounter. Luke tracks the time with various indicators: (1) in "the sixth month" of Elizabeth's pregnancy (Luke 1:26), Gabriel appears to Mary who becomes pregnant (1:38); (2) the birth of Jesus occurs nine months later, when "the time came for her to have her child" (2:6); and (3) Jesus is presented in the temple "when the days were completed for their purification" (2:22), forty days after his birth (Lev 12:1–4). The total is roughly fifteen months plus forty days—seventy weeks or 490 days—between the announcement to Zechariah in the temple and the appearance of Jesus the holy, anointed one (Luke 1:35; 2:11) in the same temple.[9]

1:19–20

Gabriel **was sent** precisely **to announce** to Zechariah **this good news** about John. For the first time Luke uses the verb *euangelizō* ("to announce good news"), which refers throughout Luke-Acts to the preaching of the gospel message (e.g., 4:18; Acts 5:42). The proper response to "good news" is to "believe" (see Acts 8:12). However, Zechariah **did not believe** and so is punished by becoming temporarily **speechless** (literally, "silent").

The people were waiting for Zechariah because the custom was for the priests to bless them after the incense offering (Num 6:24–26).[10] However, the sign indicated by Gabriel takes effect immediately: **he was unable to speak to them** and **remained mute** (*kōphos*, which can also mean "deaf"; Luke 7:22; see 1:62). Readers may perceive a further meaning to this sign: in God's plan, the priestly blessing will later come from Jesus instead (24:50).

1:21–25

In his mute condition, Zechariah finishes **his days of ministry** and then goes to his **home** outside of Jerusalem, as was typical for ordinary priests. In

---

8. Jean-Noël Aletti, *L'art de raconter Jésus Christ: L'écriture narrative de l'évangile de Luc* (Paris: Seuil, 1989), 70.

9. Andrés García Serrano, *The Presentation in the Temple: The Narrative Function of Lk 2:22–39 in Luke-Acts* (Rome: Gregorian & Biblical Press, 2012), 224–26.

10. *m. Tamid* 6:3; 7:2.

Angels

The Greek word *angelos* means "messenger" (Luke 7:24, 27; 9:52),
but in the announcements to Zechariah and Mary it refers not to a
human messenger but to an angel: a created, spiritual being. The
existence of angels is a truth of faith revealed in the Scriptures
(Catechism 328–30). In the Old Testament, the "angel of the Lᴏʀᴅ"
often brings important messages from God to chosen individuals
such as Abraham (Gen 22:11) and Moses (Exod 3:2). To the wife of
Manoah, the "angel of the Lᴏʀᴅ" announces that she will bear a son,
Samson (Judg 13:3). In Luke's Gospel, angels figure prominently.
The angel Gabriel (Luke 1:19, 26; see Dan 8:16; 9:21), who with Michael (Dan
10:13) and Raphael (Tob 3:17) is one of the three named angels in the Bible,
is one of those "who stand before God" (Luke 1:19; see Tob 12:15; Rev 8:2). In
addition, "the angel of the Lord" appears to the shepherds (Luke 2:9) along
with "a multitude of the heavenly host" (2:13). An angel appears to Jesus during his agony (22:43), and angels announce his resurrection (24:4, 23). Angels
are also often mentioned in Jesus' preaching (9:26; 12:8–9; 15:10; 16:22).

fulfillment of the angel's words, **Elizabeth** then **conceived**. She exclaims that
the Lord has taken away her **disgrace**, words that echo Rachel's response:
"God has removed my disgrace" (Gen 30:23). God has indeed remembered
Elizabeth!

Announcement to Mary of the Birth of Jesus (1:26–38)

²⁶In the sixth month, the angel Gabriel was sent from God to a town of
Galilee called Nazareth, ²⁷to a virgin betrothed to a man named Joseph,
of the house of David, and the virgin's name was Mary. ²⁸And coming
to her, he said, "Hail, favored one! The Lord is with you." ²⁹But she was
greatly troubled at what was said and pondered what sort of greeting this
might be. ³⁰Then the angel said to her, "Do not be afraid, Mary, for you
have found favor with God. ³¹Behold, you will conceive in your womb and
bear a son, and you shall name him Jesus. ³²He will be great and will be
called Son of the Most High, and the Lord God will give him the throne
of David his father, ³³and he will rule over the house of Jacob forever, and
of his kingdom there will be no end." ³⁴But Mary said to the angel, "How
can this be, since I have no relations with a man?" ³⁵And the angel said to
her in reply, "The holy Spirit will come upon you, and the power of the

Most High will overshadow you. Therefore the child to be born will be called holy, the Son of God. ³⁶And behold, Elizabeth, your relative, has also conceived a son in her old age, and this is the sixth month for her who was called barren; ³⁷for nothing will be impossible for God." ³⁸Mary said, "Behold, I am the handmaid of the Lord. May it be done to me according to your word." Then the angel departed from her.

OT: Gen 18:14; Exod 40:35; Judg 6:11–24; 2 Sam 7:8–16; Isa 7:14; 9:6; 11:1; Zeph 3:14–17
NT: Matt 1:18–25; Luke 2:4, 11; Rom 1:3
Catechism: Mary and Old Testament women, 64, 489; Immaculate Conception, 490–91, 722; the name "Jesus," 430, 2812; virginal conception of Jesus by the Holy Spirit, 484–88, 496–97, 505, 510, 695, 697, 723; nothing impossible with God, 269, 273; Mary's faith and *fiat*, 148, 494, 973, 2617, 2622, 2674; ecumenical councils on the incarnation, 456, 464–67; Hail Mary, 2676–77
Lectionary: Fourth Sunday Advent (Year B); Annunciation; Immaculate Conception; Our Lady of Guadalupe; December 20; Consecration of Virgins and Religious Profession

This passage follows not only the pattern seen in Old Testament birth announcements but also one found in Old Testament call narratives, such as the vocation of Gideon (Judg 6:11–24). For example, both Mary and Gideon are addressed with a title expressing their mission: "favored one" and "mighty warrior." Both are told: "The Lord is with you." Both are given a sign, and both accept their mission by giving consent. As a birth announcement, this passage is about Jesus, who will be born. As a call narrative, it is about Mary, who is given a mission.

The reference to **the sixth month** of Elizabeth's pregnancy and the appearance again of **the angel Gabriel** connect this passage to the previous one. Both announcements are part of one plan of God.   1:26–27

Nazareth in lower **Galilee** was a small village of several hundred inhabitants. It is not mentioned in the Old Testament, and a dismissive attitude toward it is found elsewhere in the New Testament (John 1:46). However, its residents apparently had a more positive outlook. According to the church historian Eusebius, descendants of David lived there.[11] The name of the town—from the Hebrew *netser*, meaning "branch" or "shoot"—may have reflected their hope for a messiah from the line of David: "There shall come forth a shoot from the stump of Jesse, and a *branch* shall grow out of his roots" (Isa 11:1 RSV [emphasis added]).

Thus, **Joseph** is fittingly introduced as being **of the house of David** (see Luke 2:4). He is **betrothed** to **Mary**, indicating the first stage of a Jewish marriage, in which a written document was presented by the groom to his bride but the bride remained in her family home until the wedding ceremony a year or so later,

11. *Ecclesiastical History* 1.7.14, citing the earlier historian Julius Africanus.

when she moved into her husband's home (see Matt 1:18).[12] The name "Mary" is the same as Miriam, the sister of Aaron and Moses (Exod 6:20). She is **a virgin**, a detail stated twice and whose significance will become clearer in verse 31.

The contrast in the settings of the two birth announcements is striking. The first occurs in the temple in Jerusalem, the second in an obscure village. The first occurs at the fixed hour of a liturgical celebration, the second at an unspecified time of day. The first occurs to an official priest, the second to a young maiden. Despite this contrast, the second announcement involves something greater than the first! This is in accord with the logic of a God who lifts up the lowly (Luke 1:52).

1:28   The angel's greeting, **Hail, favored one** (*chaire, kecharitōmene*), is a play on words—between the related Greek verbs *chairō* and *charitoō*. The word *chaire*, meaning "rejoice," is at times simply a greeting (Matt 26:49). However, in the †Septuagint, whose style Luke is imitating, it translates the summons for the people of Israel to rejoice: "Shout for joy, daughter Zion" (Zeph 3:14; Zech 9:9). What is the reason for such joy? **The Lord is with you**—that is, "The LORD is in your midst" (Zeph 3:15, 17), so "do not be afraid" (Luke 1:30) and "do not fear" (Zeph 3:16). If Zechariah's muteness represents the silence of prophecy in Israel until the time of fulfillment, by this call to joy Mary represents Israel as faithful "daughter Zion" to whom the Lord announces that the time of fulfillment has arrived.

Mary is the "favored one"—literally, "one who has been graced." The perfect tense of the verb *charitoō* indicates that this bestowing favor on Mary (making her full of grace, *gratia plena*, according to the †Vulgate) is not something that is about to happen to her as a result of the angel's message, but is rather an action completed in the past with effects that continue in the present. In view of the mission she is about to receive, Mary has already been transformed by grace. Mary's identity is defined by this transformation, so that the phrase becomes her title, replacing her name in the angel's greeting.

1:29   As Zechariah was troubled by the appearance of the angel (Luke 1:12), so Mary is **greatly troubled**. She **pondered** the meaning of the **greeting**, and she will continue to contemplate the extraordinary events taking place (2:19, 51).

1:30–31   As with Zechariah (1:13), the angel's message begins with a word of reassurance: **Do not be afraid**. The reason is that **Mary** has **found favor with God**. The noun "favor" (*charis*) can also be translated "grace" and is related to the verb *charitoō* in the greeting: the highly favored one found favor; the one full of grace found grace.

The angel's words—**Behold, you will conceive in your womb and bear a son, and you shall name him**—recall his similar words announcing John's

12. *m. Ketubbot* 4:4–12; 5:2.

The Immaculate Conception

LIVING TRADITION

St. Thomas Aquinas explains the phrase "Hail, full of grace" (Luke 1:28) by saying that "it is reasonable to believe that she who gave birth to 'the only Son of the Father, full of grace and truth' [John 1:14], had received greater gifts than any other." Since John the Baptist was sanctified in the womb (Luke 1:15), as was the prophet Jeremiah (Jer 1:5), all the more, "it is reasonable to believe that the blessed Virgin was sanctified before her birth."[a] Aquinas, however, thought that Mary contracted original sin at her conception but then was cleansed before her birth.[b] Shortly after him, Blessed John Duns Scotus instead explained that the grace of sanctification could be simultaneous with Mary's conception, so that she was "preserved from original sin" as "Christ showed the most perfect possible degree of mediating" with respect to Mary.[c] In 1854, Pope Pius IX defined Mary's Immaculate Conception as a dogma (Catechism 491), making reference to Luke 1:28.

a. Thomas Aquinas, *Summa Theologiae* IIIa.27.1, trans. Thomas R. Heath, vol. 51 (New York: McGraw-Hill, 1969), 7.

b. *Summa Theologiae* IIIa.27.2 (ad 2).

c. John Duns Scotus, *In Librum Tertium Sententiarum* 3.1, quoted in Luigi Gambero, *Mary in the Middle Ages*, trans. Thomas Buffer (San Francisco: Ignatius, 2005), 251.

birth (1:13) and echo the Old Testament announcement about the miraculous conception and birth of Isaac (Gen 17:19; 21:2). In addition, because of the emphasis (Luke 1:27) that Mary is a virgin, these words refer to the famous prophecy of Isaiah, which literally reads in the †Septuagint: "Behold, the virgin shall be with child and bear a son and you shall name him Emmanuel" (Isa 7:14 LXX; see Matt 1:21–23). This prophecy was a word "waiting" for its "owner":[13] the virgin Mary and her son **Jesus** are its ultimate fulfillment (Catechism 497). The name "Jesus" means "†YHWH saves" (see Matt 1:21). As "savior" (Luke 2:11), he will bring God's "salvation" (1:69; 2:30).

Whereas John the Baptist "will be great in the sight of [the] Lord" (1:15), Jesus   **1:32–33** **will be great** in an absolute sense. As **Son of the Most High**, he will surpass John, the "prophet of the Most High" (1:76).

Moreover, Jesus will possess **the throne of David his father**[14] and of **his kingdom there will be no end**. These words refer to God's promise to David spoken by the prophet Nathan: "Your house and your kingdom are firm forever

13. Benedict XVI, *Jesus of Nazareth: The Infancy Narratives*, 17.

14. Early Church Fathers considered Mary, like Joseph, to be in the line of David (see also Rom 1:3): perhaps already Ignatius of Antioch, *Ephesians* 18.2, and more clearly Justin Martyr, *Dialogue with*

before me; your throne shall be firmly established forever" (2 Sam 7:16). David ruled over all twelve tribes of Israel (see 2 Sam 5:1–5), but after the reign of his son Solomon, the kingdom was divided into two, with the northern kingdom eventually falling to the Assyrians (721 BC) and the southern kingdom to the Babylonians (586 BC). With the end of the Davidic monarchy and the scattering in exile of many of the tribes, God's promise seemed to have failed. However, expectation for a Davidic messiah who would restore Israel arose in the centuries before Jesus. The angel is here announcing the birth of this long-awaited Davidic Messiah (see Luke 2:11). He **will rule over the house of Jacob**, the regathered tribes of Israel (see Gen 49:28; Exod 19:3).

1:34   Like Zechariah, Mary asks a question of the angel regarding the fulfillment of the message: **How can this be?** A more literal rendering is "How will this be?" At first glance, it seems similar to Zechariah's question, "How shall I know this?" (Luke 1:18). Beneath the similarity in form, however, lies a greater dissimilarity in attitude. While Zechariah "did not believe" the words of the angel (1:20), Mary instead will be called "blessed" precisely for believing "what was spoken" by the angel (1:45). The difference is that whereas Zechariah "wanted proof," Mary "wants instructions."[15]

The reason for Mary's question is that she has **no relations with a man**. Mary's response is puzzling, since a betrothed woman would normally expect to begin sexual relations after the celebration of the second stage of marriage, when she moved into the home of her husband. One would think that after this delay the angel's words to her would be fulfilled, as they were for Zechariah following the delay of his remaining days of ministry (1:23–24). Some interpreters have therefore explained Mary's response as due to her interpreting the promise as having an immediate fulfillment, while she was still a virgin, although Gabriel's words do not say this. Another explanation, offered by Church Fathers such as Gregory of Nyssa and Augustine, is that Mary did not plan to have relations with Joseph, but had already dedicated herself to God as a virgin.[16] This idea is often dismissed as anachronistic, imposing a Christian ideal onto a Jewish context, since mainstream Jewish groups such as the Pharisees emphasized marriage. However, this possibility cannot be excluded, given the diversity of views in Judaism at the time (e.g., some Essenes practiced celibacy).[17]

Trypho 45.4, 100.3, and Irenaeus, *Against the Heresies* 3.16.3. As a relative of Elizabeth (Luke 1:36), she could also be from a priestly line.

15. Mitch Pacwa, *The Holy Land* (Cincinnati: Servant Books, 2013), 166.
16. See Luigi Gambero, *Mary and the Fathers of the Church*, trans. Thomas Buffer (San Francisco: Ignatius, 1999), 157, 221.
17. Bargil Pixner, *Paths of the Messiah*, ed. Rainer Riesner, trans. Keith Myrick, Sam Randall, and Miriam Randall (San Francisco: Ignatius, 2010), 24–26.

The angel explains that it will indeed be a virginal conception, occurring   1:35
through **the holy Spirit** (see Matt 1:18, 20) and by **the power of the Most High.**
The child, already called "Son of the Most High," will thus also **be called holy,**
the Son of God. The Davidic king was considered to be adopted as God's son
at his coronation (2 Sam 7:14; Ps 2:7), but the angel's explanation of Jesus' status
as God's Son is different and points to his divinity.

The verb **overshadow** (*episkiazō*), found in the Gospels only here and in the
description of the cloud at the transfiguration (Matt 17:5; Mark 9:7; Luke 9:34),
recalls how in Moses' day the cloud "settled down" (*episkiazō* in the LXX) over
the tent of meeting, the precursor to the temple (Exod 40:35). Here, the verb
suggests that Mary, who is about to become pregnant with Jesus, will thus become the new, living tent of meeting filled with God's holy presence. Gabriel's
first announcement took place in the temple, the place of God's presence. Now
in his second announcement, there is a new temple![18]

Just as a sign was given to Zechariah (his being made speechless), a sign is   1:36–37
now given to Mary: **Elizabeth** her **relative** has **conceived a son** despite **her old**
age. Through the kinship of the two women, the two announcements are also
connected. If God can make a **barren** womb fruitful, he can also make a virginal
womb fruitful, because **nothing will be impossible for God**, as the barren Sarah
had once discovered: "Is anything impossible for the LORD?" (Gen 18:14 NET).

Unlike the earlier announcement to Zechariah, who "did not believe" (Luke   1:38
1:20), this announcement ends with an act of faith. Mary is God's **handmaid,**
meaning "female servant or slave" (also 1:48; see 2:29 for Simeon a male servant).
She is one of the †*anawim*, the poor and lowly who put their trust in the Lord
(see Pss 10:17; 25:9; Zeph 2:3). She humbly expresses her consent to God's plan
through her *fiat*: **May it be done to me according to your word.** Corresponding
to her yes to God is the Son's yes to the Father: "Behold, I come to do your will"
(Heb 10:7). This is how the †incarnation of the Son of God takes place in the
womb of the Virgin Mary.

Reflection and Application (1:26–38)

Praying the Angelus. The Church daily reflects on the words of Scripture
announcing the †incarnation (1:26–38; John 1:14) in the Angelus prayer, traditionally said at morning, noon, and evening. St. John Paul II wrote, "I . . . came

---

18. Gary A. Anderson, "Mary in the Old Testament," *Pro Ecclesia* 16 (2007): 50: "Her body remains
holy forever thereafter as a result of housing the Holy One of Israel." Thus, "if one could turn to the
temple and say, 'how lovely is [your] dwelling place,' . . . why would one not do the same with" Mary?

Figure 2. *Annunciation of Cortona* by Fra Angelico. Words from Luke 1:35, 38 appear on the painting.

to understand why the Church says the Angelus three times a day. I realized how important are the words of that prayer. 'The Angel of the Lord declared unto Mary and she conceived of the Holy Spirit. . . . Behold the handmaid of the Lord: be it done unto me according to your word. . . . And the Word became flesh and dwelt among us. . . .' Such powerful words! They express the deepest reality of the greatest event ever to take place in human history."[19]

Mary's Visitation to Elizabeth and Her Magnificat (1:39–56)

[39]During those days Mary set out and traveled to the hill country in haste to a town of Judah, [40]where she entered the house of Zechariah and greeted Elizabeth. [41]When Elizabeth heard Mary's greeting, the infant leaped in her womb, and Elizabeth, filled with the holy Spirit, [42]cried out in a loud voice and said, "Most blessed are you among women, and blessed is the fruit of your womb. [43]And how does this happen to me, that the

19. John Paul II, *Gift and Mystery* (New York: Doubleday, 1996), 29.

Mary's Yes and the Incarnation

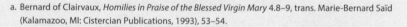

LIVING TRADITION

St. Bernard captures the drama of this crucial moment in salvation history by portraying the longing of the human race for Mary's response:

> Rejoice, O Daughter of Zion. . . . And since you have heard joyous and glad tidings, let us hear that joyous reply we long for. . . . The angel is waiting for your reply. . . . We, too, are waiting for this merciful word, my lady. . . . The price of our salvation is being offered to you. If you consent, we shall immediately be set free. . . . Doleful Adam and his unhappy offspring, exiled from Paradise, implore you, kind Virgin, to give this answer; David asks it, Abraham asks it; all the other holy patriarchs, your very own fathers beg it of you, as do those now dwelling in the region of the shadow of death. . . . Give your answer quickly, my Virgin. . . . The very King and Lord of all, he who has so desired your beauty, is waiting anxiously for your answer and assent, by which he proposes to save the world. . . . So, answer the angel quickly or rather, through the angel, answer God. Only say the word and receive the Word: give yours and conceive God's. Breathe one fleeting word and embrace the everlasting Word. Why do you delay? Why be afraid? Believe, give praise and receive. Let humility take courage and shyness confidence. . . . Blessed Virgin, open your heart to faith, your lips to consent and your womb to your Creator. Behold, the long-desired of all nations is standing at the door and knocking. . . . Get up, run, open! Get up by faith, run by prayer, open by consent! "Behold," she says, "I am the handmaiden of the Lord; let it be to me according to your word."[a]

a. Bernard of Clairvaux, *Homilies in Praise of the Blessed Virgin Mary* 4.8–9, trans. Marie-Bernard Saïd (Kalamazoo, MI: Cistercian Publications, 1993), 53–54.

mother of my Lord should come to me? [44]For at the moment the sound of your greeting reached my ears, the infant in my womb leaped for joy. [45]Blessed are you who believed that what was spoken to you by the Lord would be fulfilled."

[46]And Mary said:

> "My soul proclaims the greatness of the Lord;
> 　　[47]my spirit rejoices in God my savior.
> [48]For he has looked upon his handmaid's lowliness;
> 　　behold, from now on will all ages call me blessed.
> [49]The Mighty One has done great things for me,
> 　　and holy is his name.
> [50]His mercy is from age to age
> 　　to those who fear him.

⁵¹**He has shown might with his arm,**
    dispersed the arrogant of mind and heart.
⁵²**He has thrown down the rulers from their thrones**
    but lifted up the lowly.
⁵³**The hungry he has filled with good things;**
    the rich he has sent away empty.
⁵⁴**He has helped Israel his servant,**
    remembering his mercy,
⁵⁵**according to his promise to our fathers,**
    to Abraham and to his descendants forever."

⁵⁶**Mary remained with her about three months and then returned to her home.**

OT: Gen 17:7; 22:17–18; 25:22–23; Judg 5:24; 1 Sam 2:1–10; 2 Sam 6:1–15; 1 Chron 13:5–14; 15:25–28; Jdt 13:18

NT: Luke 6:21; 11:27–28

Catechism: visitation, 717; Mary, Mother of God, 495; Mary's faith, 148, 273; John the Baptist, 523; promise to Abraham, 422, 706; Marian devotion, 971; Magnificat and Hail Mary, 2097, 2619, 2622, 2675–77

Lectionary: Assumption; Visitation; Luke 1:39–45: Fourth Sunday Advent (Year C); December 21; Luke 1:39–47: Our Lady of Guadalupe; Luke 1:46–50, 53–54: Third Sunday Advent (Year B: Responsorial Psalm); Luke 1:46–56: December 22

1:39–40   The village of Ain Karim in **the hill country** near Jerusalem is the traditional site of **the house of Zechariah** and **Elizabeth**. It is located about five miles from the temple, a convenient distance for Zechariah's trips for priestly duty. For **Mary**, however, the journey from Nazareth would be about ninety miles, depending on the route, taking several days. There is no mention of Joseph accompanying her, unlike the later journey together to Bethlehem (2:4–5). She goes **in haste**, indicating her earnestness in fulfilling God's plan.

1:41–42   **Mary's greeting** provokes a reaction as Gabriel's greeting did before (1:29). **The infant** John **leaped** in his mother's **womb**, and **Elizabeth** herself was **filled with the holy Spirit**. The angel's words to Zechariah are being fulfilled, as the child is "filled with the holy Spirit even from his mother's womb" (1:15). The verb "leap" is used in the †Septuagint to describe how Esau and Jacob leaped or "jostled each other" in the womb of Rebekah, another once-barren woman (Gen 25:22). She was told that "the older will serve the younger" (Gen 25:23), which is the case here as well, as the older John already signals his role as precursor of the younger Jesus.

In the Spirit, Elizabeth says to Mary: **Most blessed are you among women**. The translation "most blessed" captures the superlative sense of the expression, which recalls Jewish heroines such as Jael and Judith: "Most blessed of women is Jael" (Judg 5:24), and "Blessed are you, daughter, by the Most High God, above all the women on earth" (Jdt 13:18). Like her forerunners, Mary has a mission to accomplish by which God will help Israel (see Luke 1:54). That mission involves bearing **the fruit** of her **womb**, Jesus. With these words, Elizabeth recognizes that Mary is with child, and like Mary, that child is **blessed**. The verb *eulogeō*, meaning "to invoke a blessing" on someone, appears here twice in passive form. What Elizabeth is saying is that Mary and Jesus have been blessed *by God*.

Elizabeth then asks a question: **How does this happen to me, that the mother**   1:43–44
of my Lord should come to me? In the Old Testament, the title "my lord" is frequently used for the Davidic king (e.g., 1 Kings 1:31; 2:38; Ps 110:1). In the Spirit, Elizabeth may thus recognize that Mary bears her king, the Messiah. Moreover, in the Old Testament, the Hebrew name of God, †YHWH, was translated in the †Septuagint as "Lord" (*kyrios*). So far in Luke, that word has thus been used to refer to the Lord God,[20] but now it is used for the first of many times for Jesus. Moreover, Luke has also just told his readers about Jesus' divinity as "Son of God" (Luke 1:35). Jesus can thus share with God the title "Lord" in its full sense (see the sidebar, "Jesus the Lord," p. 115). This affirmation about Jesus will also eventually lead to a deeper reflection on Mary's motherhood, culminating in a dogmatic definition at the Council of Ephesus. Since "the One whom she conceived as man by the Holy Spirit, who truly became her Son according to the flesh, was none other than the Father's eternal Son, the second person of the Holy Trinity . . . the Church confesses that Mary is truly 'Mother of God' (*Theotokos*)" (Catechism 495 [citing the Council of Ephesus, AD 431: Denzinger 251]).

Elizabeth's question also echoes the expression of awe of David when he was about to bring up the ark of the covenant to Jerusalem: "How can the ark of the LORD come to me?" (2 Sam 6:9). This suggests that Mary is being presented as the new ark of the covenant, an image or theme similar to her being presented as the new tent of meeting overshadowed by God's presence (Luke 1:35). Such a connection would also be a recurrence of references to this part of 2 Samuel (Luke 1:32; 2 Sam 7:12–16). There are also several other repeated words and phrases that serve to turn up the volume of this echo.[21] For example, verse 39 says that Mary "arose and went" (RSV) to the region of "Judah" (only here does Luke use the tribal name of the region, instead of "Judea" as in 1:65). Similarly,

---

20. Luke 1:6, 9, 11, 15–17, 25, 28, 32, 38.

21. See Richard B. Hays, *Echoes of Scripture in the Letters of Paul* (New Haven: Yale University Press, 1989), 29–32, for seven tests—including volume, recurrence, and thematic coherence—for evaluating possible allusions to Old Testament passages.

David "arose and went" to a village of "Judah" to retrieve the ark (2 Sam 6:2 LXX, the only other verse in Scripture that uses the same three Greek words in this way). Mary entered Zechariah's "house," as the ark entered the "house" of a certain Obed-edom (Luke 1:40; 2 Sam 6:10). The infant John **leaped** (*skirtaō*, Luke 1:41, 44) **for joy** when Mary arrived; so too David "danced" (*skirtaō* in one Greek version of 2 Sam 6:16) before the ark "with joy" (2 Sam 6:12). Elizabeth herself in verse 42 "cried out in a loud voice" (literally, "with a great *shout*"), like the people with their "shouts" before the ark (2 Sam 6:15 LXX). The Greek verb translated "cried out" (*anaphōneō*), found only here in the whole New Testament, is used in the parallel account of David's transport of the ark in 1 Chronicles (1 Chron 15:28 LXX); it only occurs five times in the Septuagint, always to describe liturgical singing and music before the ark (1 Chron 16:4–5, 42; 2 Chron 5:13). Finally, Mary stays with Elizabeth "about three months" (Luke 1:56), the same length of time that the ark remained in the house of Obed-edom before David brought it up to Jerusalem (2 Sam 6:11). In summary, "Luke, with various allusions, makes us understand that Mary is the true Ark of the Covenant, that the mystery of the temple—God's dwelling place here on earth—is fulfilled in Mary."[22]

1:45   Elizabeth concludes her Spirit-filled words by pronouncing the first beatitude in the Gospel: **Blessed are you who believed**. Unlike the word "blessed" found twice in verse 42 (a verb, *eulogeō*), here the word "blessed" translates the adjective *makarios*, referring to one who is "fortunate" or "happy" on account of receiving God's favor (see Luke 6:20–22). In contrast with Zechariah, who "did not believe" (1:20), Mary "believed" that God's word **spoken** to her **would be fulfilled**. In this way, she received the privilege of being the mother of the Son of God. She also became a model for all those who "hear" God's word and accept it (8:21; 11:28). Throughout the Gospel, not only God's words spoken through an angel but also those written in Scripture will be fulfilled (4:21; 18:31; 22:37; 24:44).

1:46–47   **My soul proclaims the greatness of the Lord**. In this first of the Lukan canticles—the Magnificat (the first word of the Latin translation)—Mary magnifies God for the blessings she has received, in words that echo the psalmist: "My soul will glory in the LORD. . . . / Magnify the LORD with me" (Ps 34:3–4). Earlier, Elizabeth commented briefly on what the Lord had done for her (Luke 1:25), but here Mary sings praise in an extended way. The Magnificat and the other canticles have been compared to opera arias, where the action of the story

22. Benedict XVI, homily, August 15, 2006, in *Maria: Pope Benedict XVI on the Mother of God* (San Francisco: Ignatius, 2009), 79.

The Assumption into Heaven of Mary, the Ark of the Covenant

LIVING TRADITION

St. John Damascene describes Mary as the new ark of the covenant when explaining her assumption into heaven, body and soul: "The company of Apostles lift you up on their shoulders, the true ark of the Lord God, as once the priests lifted up the †typological ark that pointed the way to you. . . . Your immaculate, completely spotless body was not left on earth, but you have been transported to the royal dwelling-place of heaven."[a]

In the readings for the feast of the Assumption (August 15), the Church similarly presents Mary as the ark of the covenant. At the Vigil Mass, the first reading recounts David's transfer of the ark to Jerusalem (1 Chron 15:3–4, 15; 16:1–2), suggesting a parallel to Mary's assumption, body and soul, to the heavenly Jerusalem. This idea receives emphasis in the psalm response: "Lord, go up to the place of your rest, you and the ark of your holiness" (Ps 132:8 Lectionary). At the Mass of the Day, the first reading juxtaposes the ark of the covenant in heaven with the woman clothed with the sun (Rev 11:19; 12:1–6, 10). The Gospel reading is the visitation (Luke 1:39–56), which itself echoes the Old Testament passages about the transfer of the ark.

a. John Damascene, *Homilies on the Dormition of the Holy Mother of God* 1.12, in *On the Dormition of Mary: Early Patristic Homilies*, trans. Brian E. Daley (Crestwood, NY: St. Vladimir's Seminary Press, 1998), 197–98.

comes to a halt for the purpose of entering more deeply into the significance of the events already recounted. As prophetic songs (see 1:67), they comment on the events of these first two chapters but also look forward to the whole of Luke's Gospel and Acts. In particular, Mary's song announces the great reversal that is unfolding as God raises up the lowly (v. 52).[23] This reversal will be seen later in the Beatitudes and woes (6:20–26) and in Jesus' teaching that "everyone who exalts himself will be humbled, but the one who humbles himself will be exalted" (14:11; also 18:14).

The Magnificat can be divided into two strophes, the first focusing on Mary's own reasons for praising God (Luke 1:46–50) and the second broadening to consider what God has done for Israel (vv. 51–55). The similar vocabulary suggests such a division: Mary is God's "handmaid" (v. 48), and Israel is "his servant"

23. Richard J. Dillon, *The Hymns of Saint Luke: Lyricism and Narrative Strategy in Luke 1–2* (Washington, DC: Catholic Biblical Association of America, 2013), 2–3, 13, 38–45.

(v. 54); God looks upon the "lowliness" of Mary (v. 48) and lifts up "the lowly" in general (v. 52); God's "mercy" extends "from age to age" to those (such as Mary) "who fear him" (v. 50), as also "his mercy" toward Israel is remembered "forever" (vv. 54–55). Mary thus stands as representative of her people Israel in singing praise to God.

Stylistically, the canticle has features often found in the psalms and other Hebrew poetry. The first two verses use synonymous parallelism—"my soul" and **my spirit**, "the Lord" and **God**—to twice express the same idea with similar words, as in the psalm: "Bless the Lord, my soul; / all my being, bless his holy name!" (Ps 103:1). Antithetical parallelism is later used to describe the reversal being worked by God, which contrasts "the rulers" with "the lowly" (Luke 1:52) and "the hungry" with "the rich" (vv. 52–53).

Mary's canticle echoes many Old Testament verses, especially from Hannah's canticle after the birth of Samuel (1 Sam 2:1–10), which begins, "My heart exults in the Lord, / my horn is exalted by my God" (1 Sam 2:1). Hannah continues, "I rejoice in your salvation" (1 Sam 2:1 ESV), as similarly Mary **rejoices** in her **savior** God. Indeed, as the angel will later say, Mary's son Jesus is this "savior," whose birth is a motive for "great joy" (Luke 2:10–11).

1:48–49   The Lord **has looked upon** Mary's **lowliness** (*tapeinōsis*) or "humble state" (NIV). Mary again refers to herself as a **handmaid**, a servant or slave (*doulē*, 1:38, 48), ready to do God's will. Hannah, before the birth of her child, had prayed in similar words: "Look on the humiliation [*tapeinōsis*] of your slave [*doulē*]" (1 Sam 1:11 NETS).

Mary also prophesies that **all ages** (literally, "all generations") will pronounce a beatitude on her by calling her **blessed**, recognizing God's favor to her, as indeed Elizabeth has just done (Luke 1:45). Thus, the person who says "Blessed Mary" or "Blessed Virgin Mary" (see 1:27) is fulfilling the inspired word of Scripture!

Mary uses titles for God that are familiar from the Old Testament: "savior" (v. 47) and **Mighty One**: "The Lord, your God, is in your midst, / a mighty savior" (Zeph 3:17). The reason for Mary's praise is **the great things** God **has done** for her personally, as the Lord did for Israel of old: "He is your God, who has done for you those great and awesome things" (Deut 10:21). She acknowledges that God's **name** is **holy**, for Scripture says that God acts for the sake of his "holy name" (Ezek 36:22).

1:50   Mary now speaks of God's **mercy** (also v. 54). Soon, Elizabeth and Zechariah will also experience God's mercy (1:58, 72, 78). Jesus will later speak about the importance of imitating God's mercy and compassion (6:36; 10:37). In the †Septuagint, the Greek word "mercy" (*eleos*) often translates the Hebrew *hesed*, referring to God's "steadfast love" that is "from everlasting to everlasting upon those who fear him" (Ps 103:17 RSV). The phrase **those who fear him** means especially the people of Israel in covenant with God (see Ps 111:5), but it will expand to include God-fearing people of every nation (see Acts 10:35).

Beginning the second part of the Magnificat, Mary recalls how God **has** **shown might with his arm**. In the exodus, God had displayed "the might" of his "arm" (Exod 15:16). Now, in fulfillment of the prophets, a new act of deliverance is taking place, one in which God will come "with power" to rule "by his strong arm" (Isa 40:10).   _{1:51–53}

God's looking on Mary's "lowliness" (Luke 1:48) is representative of how he has **lifted up the lowly**, Israel's †*anawim*. There is a great reversal at work, in which **the rulers** are not receiving favor but are **thrown down**. In a world dominated by Herods and Caesars (1:5; 2:1; 3:1), it is instead the child carried by the lowly handmaid from Nazareth whose kingdom will never end (1:33). Similarly, the Lord's blessings are upon those who fear him, not upon **the arrogant**; they are upon **the hungry**, not upon **the rich** (see Hannah's song, 1 Sam 2:3–8). This is because "the Lord resists the arrogant, / but he gives grace to the humble" (Prov 3:34 NETS; see James 4:6; 1 Pet 5:5), and because the rich are often "not rich in what matters to God" (Luke 12:21).

As Mary is the Lord's handmaid, so **Israel** is **his servant** whom he **has helped** (see Isa 41:8–10). The phrase **remembering his mercy** echoes the psalm: "He has remembered his mercy and faithfulness / toward the house of Israel" (Ps 98:3). Mary's life is thus situated within the larger context of the history of salvation of her people Israel, going all the way back to the patriarchs, or **fathers**, especially **Abraham**. God established a covenant with Abraham, swearing to him that in his "descendants all the nations of the earth will find blessing" (Gen 22:18; see also Gen 12:3; 26:3–4; 28:13–14). In Mary's offspring Jesus, who descends from Abraham (Luke 3:34), the oath to Abraham is now being fulfilled (1:73), and the blessing will be extended to all those who are reckoned Abraham's **descendants** (3:8; 13:16, 28–29; 19:9; Acts 3:25; 13:26).   _{1:54–55}

Mary remains with Elizabeth for **three months**—in other words, more or less until the birth of John. As Elizabeth's "relative" (Luke 1:36), Mary is perhaps still among the "relatives" (1:58) who celebrate John's birth. Since she is still only betrothed to Joseph, Mary then returns **to her home**. In this way, the narrative again emphasizes her virginal conception.   _{1:56}

Reflection and Application (1:39–56)

Celebrating the gospel of life. St. John Paul II wrote, "The value of the person from the moment of conception is celebrated in the meeting between the Virgin Mary and Elizabeth, and between the two children whom they are carrying in the womb."[24] The Gospel passage invites us to ask the question: How can we foster a culture of life that cares for children in the womb and for those who, like Elizabeth, are "advanced in years" (1:18)?

Familiarity with God's word. Pope Benedict XVI wrote, "The Magnificat . . . is entirely woven from threads of Holy Scripture, threads drawn from the Word of God. Here we see how completely at home Mary is with the Word of God, with ease she moves in and out of it. She speaks and thinks with the Word of God; the Word of God becomes her word, and her word issues from the Word of God. Here we see how her thoughts are attuned to the thoughts of God, how her will is one with the will of God. Since Mary is completely imbued with the Word of God, she is able to become the Mother of the Word Incarnate."[25] How about us? Are we completely imbued with God's Word? "Let the word of Christ dwell in you richly" (Col 3:16).

The Birth of John and Zechariah's Benedictus (1:57–80)

[57]When the time arrived for Elizabeth to have her child she gave birth to a son. [58]Her neighbors and relatives heard that the Lord had shown his great mercy toward her, and they rejoiced with her. [59]When they came on the eighth day to circumcise the child, they were going to call him Zechariah after his father, [60]but his mother said in reply, "No. He will be called John." [61]But they answered her, "There is no one among your relatives who has this name." [62]So they made signs, asking his father what he wished him to be called. [63]He asked for a tablet and wrote, "John is his name," and all were amazed. [64]Immediately his mouth was opened, his tongue freed, and he spoke blessing God. [65]Then fear came upon all their neighbors, and all these matters were discussed throughout the hill country of Judea. [66]All who heard these things took them to heart, saying, "What, then, will this child be?" For surely the hand of the Lord was with him.

[67]Then Zechariah his father, filled with the holy Spirit, prophesied, saying:

24. John Paul II, *Evangelium Vitae* (On the Value and Inviolability of Human Life) 45.
25. Benedict XVI, *Deus Caritas Est* (On Christian Love) 41.

[68]"Blessed be the Lord, the God of Israel,
>   for he has visited and brought redemption to his people.
[69]He has raised up a horn for our salvation
>   within the house of David his servant,
[70]even as he promised through the mouth of his holy prophets
>   from of old:
>>   [71]salvation from our enemies and from the hand of all who
>>   hate us,
[72]to show mercy to our fathers
>   and to be mindful of his holy covenant
[73]and of the oath he swore to Abraham our father,
>   and to grant us that, [74]rescued from the hand of enemies,
> without fear we might worship him [75]in holiness and
>   righteousness
>   before him all our days.
[76]And you, child, will be called prophet of the Most High,
>   for you will go before the Lord to prepare his ways,
[77]to give his people knowledge of salvation
>   through the forgiveness of their sins,
[78]because of the tender mercy of our God
>   by which the daybreak from on high will visit us
[79]to shine on those who sit in darkness and death's shadow,
>   to guide our feet into the path of peace."

[80]The child grew and became strong in spirit, and he was in the desert until the day of his manifestation to Israel.

OT: Gen 17:9–14; 22:16–18; 2 Sam 7:11–16; Isa 9:1; 40:3; Jer 23:5; Mal 3:1, 20
NT: Luke 2:21, 40, 52; 7:16; 19:44
Catechism: John the Baptist, 523–24; God visits his people, 422, 717; God's oath to Abraham, 706
Lectionary: Luke 1:57–66, 80: Nativity of St. John the Baptist; Luke 1:57–66: December 23; Luke 1:67–79: December 24

The second two-part panel in Luke's infancy narrative now begins with the birth stories of John and Jesus.

The time arrived for Elizabeth to have her child as it had come for once-barren Rebekah (Gen 25:24). **Elizabeth** is thus among the first to experience the **mercy** spoken about in the Magnificat (Luke 1:50, 54). Her **neighbors and relatives** fulfill the angel's words—"Many will rejoice at his birth" (1:14)—as **they rejoiced with her**.   **1:57–58**

God's covenant with Abraham stipulated **the eighth day** as the day **to circumcise** a boy (Gen 17:12). The dispute about what **to call him** leads to another   **1:59–61** fulfillment of the angel's words (Luke 1:13). Despite the objections raised by the others, Elizabeth calls him **John**, a fitting name since the Lord has been gracious and merciful to her (see Ps 116:5).

1:62–64   Not satisfied with Elizabeth's response, they ask **his father. They made signs** because Zechariah was not only mute but deaf as well.[26] This time Zechariah does not miss his opportunity. On a wooden **tablet** covered with wax, he writes **John is his name**. By his obedience to the angel's word, **his mouth was opened**, and he speaks, **blessing God** in the words of the Benedictus (see v. 68).

1:65–66   The **neighbors** are filled with **fear** in the presence of this sign from God (see 7:16). They recognize that the powerful **hand of the Lord was with** John, as it had been upon prophets like Elijah (1:17; 1 Kings 18:46). They wonder what the future of **this child** will hold.

1:67   As the third member of his family **filled with the holy Spirit** (Luke 1:15, 41), Zechariah then answered their question as he **prophesied** the words of the Benedictus (from the first word in Latin). The canticle is organized in two parts, referring first to God's salvation in the Messiah (vv. 68–75) and then to John's role as his precursor (vv. 76–79).

1:68   Zechariah's first words, **Blessed be the Lord, the God of Israel**, are basically the last words of several books of the psalter (Pss 41:14; 72:18; 106:48). They are also found in several prayers involving the royal succession from David to Solomon (1 Kings 1:48; 8:15; 2 Chron 2:11; 6:4). Here too the prayer involves a royal successor to David (Luke 1:69). Like a typical Jewish blessing, the initial statement is followed by phrases explaining the reasons for praising God.

The first reason is that God **has visited and brought redemption to his people**. God's visitation (1:78; 7:16; 19:44) means that he is present to bring assistance, such as when Sarah conceived (Gen 21:1) and in the exodus (Gen 50:24–25; Exod 3:16; 13:19). "Redeeming" means ransoming from captivity or slavery, and the redemption of individuals recalls God's redemption of his people at the exodus (Exod 6:6; 13:13–16; Lev 25:47–55). Jesus is the one through whom God will now bring redemption (Luke 2:38; 24:21) through a new exodus (9:31).

1:69–71   The second reason for Zechariah's praise of God is that **he has raised up a horn for our salvation**, which recalls David's song when he was delivered from his **enemies** (2 Sam 22:18; Ps 18:18): "The LORD is my rock, and my fortress, and my deliverer, . . . / my shield and the horn of my salvation" (2 Sam 22:2–3 RSV; see Ps 18:3). "Horn" is symbolic of God's power, like the powerful horns of a wild ox (Num 23:22; 24:8; Deut 33:17). Another verse, from Hannah's canticle, refers to the power of the messiah: "May he give strength to his king, /

---

26. Greek *kōphos*, Luke 1:22; 7:22.

and exalt the horn of his anointed!" (1 Sam 2:10). The "horn" here is **within the house of David** (see 2 Sam 7:11–16), so Zechariah is speaking about Jesus (Luke 1:27, 32), not about John, who is from the priestly line of Aaron. Like the **holy prophets from of old**, Zechariah is prophetically announcing that Jesus will be God's powerful agent of **salvation** (2:11, 30; 19:9–10).

Besides David, the fulfillment also involves **Abraham** and the patriarchs: **to show mercy** and **to be mindful of** (literally, "to remember") the **covenant** and **oath** by which God's blessings would extend to Abraham's descendants and all the nations (Gen 22:16–18). The significance of the names Zechariah ("†YHWH has remembered"), Elizabeth ("my God" and "oath"), and John ("YHWH is gracious [or merciful]") now becomes apparent. **1:72–73**

The purpose of being **rescued from the hand of enemies** (see Exod 14:30) is to **worship** (*latreuō*) God, as it was during the exodus: "Let my people go to serve me" (Exod 7:16; 8:16; 9:1; 10:3, where the verb "serve" is translated with *latreuō* in the †Septuagint). God's deliverance will also be transformative, leading to **holiness and righteousness**, as people "put on the new self, created in God's way in righteousness and holiness of truth" (Eph 4:24). **1:74–75**

The second half of the hymn (Luke 1:76–79) turns to Zechariah's **child** John, describing him with phrases that echo Gabriel's announcement and anticipate his mission. Whereas Jesus is "Son of the Most High" (1:32), John **will be called prophet of the Most High** (see 1:17). He **will go before the Lord to prepare his ways** through his proclamation of **forgiveness** (1:17; 3:3–4). Old Testament prophets spoke about preparing the way of the Lord God (Isa 40:3; Mal 3:1), but the "Lord" for whom John will prepare is Jesus as well (Luke 1:43; 2:11). **1:76–77**

The Greek word translated **daybreak**, *anatolē*, literally means "rising." It was also used in the †Septuagint to translate a Hebrew word meaning "branch" in prophecies that describe the messiah as a branch that sprouts up: "I will raise up a righteous branch for David" (Jer 23:5; see Zech 3:8; 6:12). Here, coupled with the image of light (Luke 1:79), it recalls messianic prophecies about the rising of "the sun of justice" (Mal 3:20) and "a star . . . from Jacob" (Num 24:17).[27] **1:78**

The coming messiah will **shine on those who sit in darkness and death's shadow**, in fulfillment of Isaiah's prophecy: "O you people who walk in darkness, . . . / and in the shadow of death, / light will shine on you!" (Isa 9:1 NETS; see Matt 4:16). He will bring **peace** (see Luke 2:14), as again Isaiah foretold about the "child" to be "born," who is the "Prince of Peace" (Isa 9:5). **1:79**

On the lips of the Jewish priest Zechariah, the conclusion of the Benedictus, with the words "shine" and "peace," may echo Aaron's priestly blessing, which

27. In the Septuagint, these two prophecies use the related verb *anatellō* ("rise").

he earlier was unable to pronounce (Luke 1:22): "The LORD bless you and keep you! / The LORD let his face *shine* upon you, and be gracious to you! / The LORD look upon you kindly and give you *peace!*" (Num 6:24–26 [emphasis added]). This peace is *shalom*, wholeness, resulting from harmony with God.

1:80   John **grew and became strong in spirit**, like Samson of old (Judg 13:24–25). His elderly parents may not have lived to see it, which may explain why John **was in the desert** though their home was in the "hill country" (Luke 1:39). He may even have spent some time at Qumran, with the Jewish community responsible for the †Dead Sea Scrolls. On **the day of his manifestation**, he will begin his ministry "in the desert" (3:2).

Reflection and Application (1:57–80)

Praying the Gospel canticles. Continuing the Jewish practice of prayer at regular hours (Ps 119:164), the Church unceasingly praises the Lord and sanctifies the whole day through the Liturgy of the Hours, consisting of psalms, Scripture readings, hymns, and prayers. The hinges of the day are Morning Prayer (Lauds) and Evening Prayer (Vespers), and the climax of these are the Benedictus and the Magnificat, respectively. This practice of praying the Gospel canticles is already attested in the sixth century in the Rule of St. Benedict (chs. 12, 13, 17). By praying the Gospel canticles, we join with Christians of all ages in praising the Lord unceasingly.

A Savior Is Born

Luke 2:1–52

Christians worldwide celebrate the birth of Jesus at Christmas, and it is Luke who relates many familiar details of the Christmas story: the swaddling clothes, the manger, shepherds keeping night watch, and angels singing "Gloria!" The historical setting during the reign of Caesar Augustus is significant, as there is an implicit comparison between the emperor and Jesus, whom the angels announce as Savior, Messiah, and Lord. After Luke recounts the birth of Jesus, he caps the infancy narrative with two events in which Jesus comes to the Jerusalem temple, where the story all began.

The Birth of Jesus (2:1–20)

¹In those days a decree went out from Caesar Augustus that the whole world should be enrolled. ²This was the first enrollment, when Quirinius was governor of Syria. ³So all went to be enrolled, each to his own town. ⁴And Joseph too went up from Galilee from the town of Nazareth to Judea, to the city of David that is called Bethlehem, because he was of the house and family of David, ⁵to be enrolled with Mary, his betrothed, who was with child. ⁶While they were there, the time came for her to have her child, ⁷and she gave birth to her firstborn son. She wrapped him in swaddling clothes and laid him in a manger, because there was no room for them in the inn.

⁸Now there were shepherds in that region living in the fields and keeping the night watch over their flock. ⁹The angel of the Lord appeared to

them and the glory of the Lord shone around them, and they were struck with great fear. [10]The angel said to them, "Do not be afraid; for behold, I proclaim to you good news of great joy that will be for all the people. [11]For today in the city of David a savior has been born for you who is Messiah and Lord. [12]And this will be a sign for you: you will find an infant wrapped in swaddling clothes and lying in a manger." [13]And suddenly there was a multitude of the heavenly host with the angel, praising God and saying:

> [14]"Glory to God in the highest
>   and on earth peace to those on whom his favor rests."

[15]When the angels went away from them to heaven, the shepherds said to one another, "Let us go, then, to Bethlehem to see this thing that has taken place, which the Lord has made known to us." [16]So they went in haste and found Mary and Joseph, and the infant lying in the manger. [17]When they saw this, they made known the message that had been told them about this child. [18]All who heard it were amazed by what had been told them by the shepherds. [19]And Mary kept all these things, reflecting on them in her heart. [20]Then the shepherds returned, glorifying and praising God for all they had heard and seen, just as it had been told to them.

OT: Gen 35:17–19, 21; Exod 13:2; 1 Sam 16:1–13; Isa 1:3; 7:14; 9:1–6; 40:9; 52:7; Mic 4:8; 5:1–4

NT: Matt 1:21; 2:1, 4–6; Luke 1:27, 32; 19:38; Acts 2:36; 5:37; Heb 1:6

Catechism: birth of Jesus, 423, 515, 525; angels, 333; shepherds, 486, 563, 724–25; Messiah, 437; Lord, 448; reflecting in the heart, 94

Lectionary: Luke 2:1–14: Christmas Mass during the Night; Luke 2:15–20: Christmas Mass at Dawn; Luke 2:16–21: Mary, Mother of God

2:1   As he does two other times (1:5; 3:1–2), Luke first situates events in their historical context (vv. 1–2). There has been much debate about how to understand his brief description here in relation to other available historical information. However, some recent studies have helped to clarify the issues.

The reference to **Caesar Augustus** introduces the delicate political situation that began in 63 BC when the Roman general Pompey invaded Jerusalem, leading to Roman control of the land of Israel. On the one hand, Rome represents a threat: Jesus will be put to death by the Roman prefect, Pontius Pilate. On the other, Rome represents an opportunity: Luke ends Acts with Paul proclaiming the gospel in Rome "without hindrance" (Acts 28:31). In all cases, however, it is not Roman might that determines the course of events, but rather God's plan coming to fulfillment. As already seen, that plan involves a great reversal between "the rulers" and "the lowly" (Luke 1:52).

Caesar Augustus

BIBLICAL
BACKGROUND

Following the assassination of Julius Caesar in 44 BC, his grand-nephew Octavian came to power as his adopted heir and assumed his name. In 31 BC, Octavian consolidated his rule with a victory at Actium over his rival Antony, and in 27 BC the Roman senate gave him the title Augustus ("revered" or "venerable"). His reign, until his death in AD 14, ushered in the long period of relative peace known as the *Pax Romana*. After Julius Caesar was declared a god by the Roman senate in 42 BC, Augustus referred to himself as "son of a god" (*divi filius*). He was hailed, for instance, in the calendar inscription from Priene (modern western Turkey) in 9 BC, as a "god" and "savior" who "established peace" and whose birth brought "good tidings" (noun *euangelion*).[a]

The reversal being worked by God (Luke 1:52) now emerges. The real "good news" (2:10; verb *euangelizō*) is the birth of an infant in a small village of an obscure province of the empire. Jesus is the true "Son of God" (1:35) and "savior" (2:11) who ushers in an era of God's "peace" (2:14). St. Ambrose perceptively comments, using Psalm 24: "For 'the earth is the Lord's,' and not Augustus.'"[b]

a. Quoted in Kazuhiko Yamazaki-Ransom, *The Roman Empire in Luke's Narrative* (London: T&T Clark, 2010), 82–83.

b. Ambrose, *Exposition of the Holy Gospel according to Saint Luke* 2.37, trans. Theodosia Tomkinson (Etna, CA: Center for Traditionalist Orthodox Studies, 1998), 58.

Caesar's **decree** that all **should be enrolled** refers to a census or registration, presumably taken for tax purposes.[1] **The whole world** means the Roman Empire, which would have been covered by various local censuses in Roman provinces and territories spread over a period of time. In the land of Israel, Herod collected taxes (e.g., to support his building projects) and, as a client-king of Rome, likely paid a percentage of the revenue to the emperor. A tax census seems to have been carried out toward the end of his reign, since Josephus mentions tax information for each region of Herod's kingdom when discussing its division among his sons after his death.[2]

1. Also suggested, and sometimes linked to a tax census, is a registration for the oath of loyalty that was sworn to Augustus throughout the Roman Empire in connection with his being awarded the title *pater patriae* ("father of the country"). See *Res gestae divi Augusti* (*The Deeds of the Divine Augustus*) 35; Josephus, *Jewish Antiquities* 17.42; Jack Finegan, *Handbook of Biblical Chronology*, rev. ed. (Peabody, MA: Hendrickson, 1998), 305–6; Armand Puig i Tàrrech, *Jesus: An Uncommon Journey* (Tübingen: Mohr Siebeck, 2010), 82; Bieke Mahieu, *Between Rome and Jerusalem: Herod the Great and His Sons in Their Struggle for Recognition* (Leuven: Peeters, 2012), 243–53, 261.

2. *Jewish War* 2.93–98; *Jewish Antiquities* 17.221–29, 317–21. See Mahieu, *Between Rome and Jerusalem*, 334–49.

2:2   The **enrollment** apparently occurred **when Quirinius was governor of Syria**. Josephus refers to a census conducted in Judea for tax purposes by the newly appointed Roman legate in the province of Syria, P. Sulpicius Quirinius, but this occurred later, in AD 6 or 7, after the Romans had deposed Herod's son Archelaus.[3] Luke is also familiar with this memorable census, as in Acts he mentions the revolt against it led by Judas the Galilean (Acts 5:37). Therefore, Luke's reference to Quirinius here seems intended to distinguish the enrollment at the time of Jesus' birth from the more well-known census some years later. However, it is difficult to explain what role Quirinius would have had in this earlier enrollment. Some have suggested that Quirinius was legate in Syria twice or that he earlier served in another administrative capacity.

A better approach is to reconsider the translation. The Greek word *prōtē*, translated **first**, can also mean "before" or "earlier" (see John 1:15, 30; Acts 1:1 NJB), so that the whole phrase is rendered: "This enrollment was *before* Quirinius was governor of Syria." Such a translation is already found in the Luke commentary by the great French Catholic biblical scholar M.-J. Lagrange in the early twentieth century, is currently given as an option in several Bible versions, and is well explained by various scholars.[4] In this reading, Luke clarifies that the census around the time of the birth of Christ was not the more well-known one under Quirinius that led to a revolt, but rather an earlier registration before the death of Herod, with which Jesus' family "peaceably complied."[5]

2:3–5   The reason for enrolling in one's **own town** could be to register property, as there is some evidence of such a practice, even for women.[6] Alternatively, the census may have been conducted according to Jewish custom, allowing for return to one's native city (see Ezra 2). Since **Joseph** is **of the house and family of David** (see Luke 1:27), he goes up from **Nazareth** in **Galilee** to **Bethlehem** in **Judea**, about six miles south of Jerusalem. Luke thus indicates that through the actions of Caesar Augustus, God arranged for the prophecy of Micah to be fulfilled: "But you, Bethlehem-Ephrathah / least among the clans of Judah, / From you shall come forth for me / one who is to be ruler in Israel" (Mic 5:1; see Matt 2:4–6).

---

3. *Jewish Antiquities* 18.1–10, 26.

4. M.-J. Lagrange, *Évangile selon Saint Luc*, 2nd ed. (Paris: Gabalda, 1921), 66–68. The NIV and ESV indicate, as an option for the translation, a census or registration "before" Quirinius. See also Stanley E. Porter, "The Witness of Extra-Gospel Literary Sources to the Infancy Narratives of the Synoptic Gospels," in *The Gospels: History and Christology*, ed. Bernardo Estrada, Ermenegildo Manicardi, and Armand Puig i Tàrrech, 2 vols. (Vatican City: Libreria Editrice Vaticana, 2013), 1:452–58; Puig i Tàrrech, *Jesus: An Uncommon Journey*, 89–91; Mahieu, *Between Rome and Jerusalem*, 447–64.

5. David E. Garland, *Luke*, ZECNT (Grand Rapids: Zondervan, 2011), 119.

6. Porter, "Witness of Extra-Gospel Literary Sources," 1:464.

© Baker Publishing Group

Figure 3. The traditional birth site of Jesus under the Church of the Nativity.

Though Luke's account of Jesus' birth is rather different from Matthew's, the two nonetheless agree in placing it in Bethlehem. Moreover, writing about AD 150, St. Justin Martyr, a native of Neapolis (modern Nablus) in Palestine, refers to a local tradition not found in either Gospel specifying that Jesus was born *in a cave* in Bethlehem.[7] As St. Jerome explains, the Romans unwittingly helped preserve this local tradition. Following the suppression of the Bar-Kokhba revolt under the emperor Hadrian in AD 135, the Romans erected pagan shrines at sites associated with Jewish and Christian veneration, such as the temple mount and Golgotha, while at the Bethlehem cave they planted a pagan grove dedicated to the god Adonis-Tammuz.[8] After the emperor Constantine embraced Christianity in the fourth century, the pagan shrine was

7. *Dialogue with Trypho* 78.5.
8. Jerome, *Epistle* 58.3.

taken down and the Church of the Nativity was built over the complex of caves.[9]

Bethlehem is **the city of David**, recalling how Samuel anointed the young David from among the sons of Jesse of Bethlehem (1 Sam 16:1–13). The connection reinforces Jesus' identity as son of David (Luke 1:32, 69). However, Jerusalem is called "the city of David" in the Old Testament (see 2 Sam 5:7, 9; 1 Kings 2:10). Jesus is thus associated with David's humble beginnings in Bethlehem rather than with his military might in Jerusalem. God's great reversal is again revealed.

Mary is **with child** but is described, as before (Luke 1:27), as Joseph's **betrothed**. This word again highlights the virginal conception of Jesus (see Matt 1:24–25).

2:6-7   The phrase **while they were there** indicates that Joseph and Mary have arrived in Bethlehem. Luke does not specify when during the last six months of Mary's pregnancy the trip there took place. Since Joseph is of David's family, it is possible that they are staying with extended family. The phrase **the time came** (literally, "the days were completed") and similar expressions are frequently repeated in these first two chapters (Luke 1:23, 57; 2:21–22). They mark human events and also the fulfillment of God's plan through those events.

Mary gives **birth to her firstborn son**, the one whom the angels worship (see Heb 1:6). The term "firstborn" expresses the rights of inheritance, as when Esau laments that he has lost the birthright and the blessing associated with being firstborn (Gen 27:36; see Deut 21:15–17). The firstborn in Israel had a sacred status (Exod 13:2; Num 3:13), and so the term here sets the stage for Jesus' presentation in the temple (Luke 2:23). It does not imply that Mary had other children.

Mary **wrapped him in swaddling clothes**, meaning the customary strips of cloth that provide warmth and also restrict movement of limbs, helping infants sleep. This detail again shows the humble beginnings of Jesus as son of David, as there is a similar description of David's son, Solomon, in the book of Wisdom: "In swaddling clothes and with constant care I was nurtured" (Wis 7:4). Mary also **laid him in a manger**, a feeding trough for animals. There may be an allusion here to the prophet Isaiah: "An ox knows its owner, / and an ass, its master's manger; / But Israel does not know, / my people has not understood" (Isa 1:3). These two details—the swaddling clothes and the manger—will be the sign given to the shepherds by the angel (Luke 2:12, 16). They may also be

9. See Rainer Riesner, "Bethlehem, the Birth Stories and Archaeology," in Estrada, Manicardi, and Puig i Tàrrech, *The Gospels: History and Christology*, 1:487–93.

The Birth of Jesus

LIVING TRADITION

According to Church Fathers such as Irenaeus, Clement of Alexandria, Tertullian, Origen, Eusebius, and Epiphanius, Jesus was born during the forty-first or forty-second year of the reign of Caesar Augustus—that is, in 3 or 2 BC.[a] This patristic view is in tension with the modern consensus that places Herod's death in 4 BC, with Jesus' birth shortly before it. However, some recent proposals date Herod's death to 1 BC or AD 1 (see the sidebar, "King Herod and Herod the Tetrarch," p. 36). The patristic view is also consistent with Luke's statement that Jesus is about thirty years old (3:23) during the fifteenth year (AD 28–29) of the reign of Tiberius Caesar (3:1). It finds expression in the optional chant from the *Roman Martyrology* before the Christmas Midnight Mass: "In the forty-second year in the reign of Caesar Octavian Augustus, the whole world being at peace, Jesus Christ . . . was born of the Virgin Mary in Bethlehem of Judah, and was made man: The Nativity of Our Lord Jesus Christ according to the flesh."[b]

a. Finegan, *Handbook of Biblical Chronology*, 288–91.
b. *The Roman Missal* (Totowa, NJ: Catholic Book Publishing, 2011), 1295.

a sign looking forward to Jesus' death, when his body will be "wrapped . . . in a linen shroud, and laid . . . in a rock-hewn tomb" (23:53 RSV).

The birth occurs where the animals are kept **because there was no room for them in the inn**. The Greek word *katalyma*, traditionally translated "inn," can indeed refer to a place of lodging for travelers (Exod 4:24 LXX). In Luke, however, the word appears only one other time, describing the "guest room" where Jesus eats the Last Supper (Luke 22:11; also Mark 14:14). Luke uses a different word, *pandocheion*, for the "inn" in the parable of the good Samaritan (Luke 10:34). Joseph and Mary may be staying in a Bethlehem home of Joseph's kin, but since the "guest room" is otherwise occupied, the birth takes place where the animals are kept at night, perhaps inside or attached to the house (see 13:15).[10] There is evidence that the caves under the Church of the Nativity were used as stables in the first century,[11] and houses were often built in front of such caves.

All these details of Jesus' birth help to show how the Son of God "emptied himself" (Phil 2:7) in assuming a human nature.

10. See Kenneth E. Bailey, *Jesus through Middle Eastern Eyes: Cultural Studies in the Gospel* (Downers Grove, IL: InterVarsity, 2008), 25–36.
11. See Riesner, "Bethlehem," 493.

2:8   Next, the news of Jesus' birth is announced to **shepherds** (Luke 2:8–14), people of lowly status in society but nonetheless positively regarded in Scripture, where even "the LORD" is a shepherd (Ps 23:1). The proximity to Jerusalem suggests that sheep from the **region** of Bethlehem were destined to be sacrificed in the temple.[12] One day, Jesus will similarly be "like a sheep . . . led to the slaughter" (Acts 8:32, citing Isa 53:7). The presence of shepherds in Bethlehem also recalls David the shepherd (1 Sam 16:11) and the promise of a new shepherd like him (Ezek 34:23). Jesus the son of David will be that shepherd, who goes in search of the lost sheep (see Luke 15:4–7; 19:10).

The shepherds were **keeping the night watch over their flock**. They were like "those who sit in darkness" (1:79; see Isa 9:1). The Lord's light, however, was about to "shine" on them (1:79), announcing that "a child is born to us, a son is given to us" (Isa 9:5).

2:9   For the third time (see Luke 1:11, 26), **the angel of the Lord** appears, but there is also something additional: **the glory of the Lord shone around** the shepherds. In the Old Testament, the "glory of the LORD" is the manifestation of his presence—for example, as a fire or cloud (Exod 24:16–17)—especially in the tabernacle and later the temple (Exod 40:34–35; 1 Kings 8:10–11). Here, the glory appears not in the temple but in a field on account of Jesus' birth nearby. As a result, the shepherds are **struck with great fear**—the typical human reaction to a heavenly visitation (Luke 1:12).

2:10   There follows the angel's message, beginning with the familiar word of assurance—**Do not be afraid!** (1:13, 30)—and marked by **great joy** (1:14). The angel's mission is to **proclaim . . . good news** (verb *euangelizō*, as in 1:19). The proclamation of the good news—that is, the gospel—will be the focal point of Jesus' own ministry[13] in fulfillment of the prophecies of Isaiah (Isa 40:9; 52:7; 61:1 LXX). Here, there is a contrast with Roman proclamations of good news issued, for instance, to honor the emperor or celebrate a military victory. The good news is **for all the people**: God's "people Israel" and "all the peoples" of every nation (Luke 2:31–32).

2:11   The message of Jesus' birth regards something happening **today**. Indeed, Luke frequently reminds readers that God's salvation is available "today" (4:21; 5:26; 19:5, 9; 23:43). Three titles are given to Jesus by the angel. First, Jesus (rather than Caesar Augustus) is the true **savior**. His very name means "†YHWH saves" (see Matt 1:21), and his mission is to bring salvation (Luke 1:69, 71; 2:30; 19:9–10).

---

12. See *m. Sheqalim* 7:4, which refers to Migdal-Eder ("tower of the flock") near Bethlehem (see Gen 35:19–21; Mic 4:8).

13. Luke 4:18, 43; 7:22; 8:1; 20:1.

Second, Jesus, who is born **in the city of David** (2:4), is the long-awaited Jewish **Messiah** (Greek *christos*)[14] in the line of David (see 1:32–33). Third, as already indicated by Elizabeth (1:43), Jesus is **Lord**. The use of the titles "Savior" and "Lord" for Jesus—titles also used for God (1:46–47)—points Luke's readers to the divinity of Jesus, the "Son of God" (1:35).

Before the shepherds can ask any questions (like Zechariah and Mary), they are given a **sign**, and indeed one more humble than even their own lowly status: **an infant wrapped in swaddling clothes and lying in a manger.**   2:12

Unlike the previous two angelic appearances, here the angel is **suddenly**   2:13–14 joined by **a multitude of the heavenly host**, the army of angelic beings who stand to the Lord's right and left and worship him (1 Kings 22:19; Neh 9:6). They are **praising God** in the words of the third Lukan canticle, the Gloria. This short canticle consists of two parallel phrases: **Glory to God** in heaven above and **on earth peace** "among people" (NET). In the Benedictus, Zechariah had prophesied concerning the gift of "peace" (Luke 1:79). Now, it is given, not on account of the emperor with his *Pax Romana*, but on account of Jesus. Receiving this peace are **those on whom his favor rests**, meaning people "of favor" or "of good will"—namely, those receiving God's favor.[15]

The shepherds' visit (2:15–20) is the third part of the passage. They go **in**   2:15–18 **haste**, just as Mary did when given her sign (1:39). Indeed, people respond with hurried excitement to a divine encounter, as Zacchaeus will also do when he meets Jesus (19:5–6). The shepherds find **Mary and Joseph,** and the sign they were looking for, **the infant lying in the manger.** As people were amazed at the events surrounding John's birth (1:63), so too **all** those hearing the shepherds' message are **amazed**.

Mary kept all these things—namely, the things and words (1:38, 65; 2:15,   2:19 17) recounted thus far. She was **reflecting on them in her heart**. Luke will essentially repeat this statement at the end of the chapter (2:51). These verses suggest that Mary is ultimately Luke's source for these events.[16]

The events of Christmas night conclude with **the shepherds** doing what the   2:20 angels did before them (vv. 13–14), **glorifying and praising God.**

14. In Luke's Gospel, the word *christos* is always translated "Messiah" by the NABRE since it retains its function as a title (e.g., 2:26; 3:15; 4:41; 9:20). Elsewhere in the New Testament, when it functions as another name for Jesus, it is generally translated "Christ."

15. Some later manuscripts have a slight variation at the end of the verse, leading to the translation familiar from Christmas carols: "peace on earth, good will to(wards) men."

16. Andrés García Serrano, *The Presentation in the Temple: The Narrative Function of Lk 2:22–39 in Luke-Acts* (Rome: Gregorian & Biblical Press, 2012), 35: "The possibility of Mary as eyewitness is still open. Luke could have received some information about Jesus' infancy from family traditions in the early Jewish Christian community in Jerusalem."

Reflection and Application (2:1–20)

Jesus' birth and the Eucharist. We celebrate the mystery of Jesus' birth every year at Christmas, but in a sense we can do so in every celebration of Mass. St. Gregory the Great is one of many saints who mention that since Bethlehem in Hebrew means "house of bread," it is a fitting birthplace for Jesus, who in the Eucharist becomes our "living bread" (John 6:51).[17] He also indicates that the manger points to the Eucharist, which St. Cyril of Alexandria also explains: Jesus is "placed like fodder in a manger. . . . By now approaching the manger, even his own table, we find no longer fodder, but the bread from heaven, which is the body of life."[18]

The Presentation of Jesus in the Temple (2:21–40)

[21]When eight days were completed for his circumcision, he was named Jesus, the name given him by the angel before he was conceived in the womb.

[22]When the days were completed for their purification according to the law of Moses, they took him up to Jerusalem to present him to the Lord, [23]just as it is written in the law of the Lord, "Every male that opens the womb shall be consecrated to the Lord," [24]and to offer the sacrifice of "a pair of turtledoves or two young pigeons," in accordance with the dictate in the law of the Lord.

[25]Now there was a man in Jerusalem whose name was Simeon. This man was righteous and devout, awaiting the consolation of Israel, and the holy Spirit was upon him. [26]It had been revealed to him by the holy Spirit that he should not see death before he had seen the Messiah of the Lord. [27]He came in the Spirit into the temple; and when the parents brought in the child Jesus to perform the custom of the law in regard to him, [28]he took him into his arms and blessed God, saying:

[29]"Now, Master, you may let your servant go
   in peace, according to your word,
[30]for my eyes have seen your salvation,
[31]which you prepared in sight of all the peoples,
[32]a light for revelation to the Gentiles,
   and glory for your people Israel."

17. Gregory the Great, *Homily* 7, in *Forty Gospel Homilies*, trans. David Hurst (Kalamazoo, MI: Cistercian Publications, 1990), 51.

18. Cyril of Alexandria, *Homilies on Luke* 2:7, in *Commentary on the Gospel of Saint Luke*, trans. R. Payne Smith (repr., Astoria, NY: Studion, 1983), 50.

[33] The child's father and mother were amazed at what was said about him; [34] and Simeon blessed them and said to Mary his mother, "Behold, this child is destined for the fall and rise of many in Israel, and to be a sign that will be contradicted [35] (and you yourself a sword will pierce) so that the thoughts of many hearts may be revealed." [36] There was also a prophetess, Anna, the daughter of Phanuel, of the tribe of Asher. She was advanced in years, having lived seven years with her husband after her marriage, [37] and then as a widow until she was eighty-four. She never left the temple, but worshiped night and day with fasting and prayer. [38] And coming forward at that very time, she gave thanks to God and spoke about the child to all who were awaiting the redemption of Jerusalem.

[39] When they had fulfilled all the prescriptions of the law of the Lord, they returned to Galilee, to their own town of Nazareth. [40] The child grew and became strong, filled with wisdom; and the favor of God was upon him.

OT: Exod 13:2, 12–15; Lev 12:2–8; Num 3:40; 18:15–16; 1 Sam 1:28; 2:26; Isa 40:1; 42:6; 46:13; 49:6; 52:9–10; Mal 3:1

NT: Matt 1:21; 2:23; Luke 1:31, 80; 3:6; Acts 28:28; Gal 4:4

Catechism: Jesus' circumcision, 527; presentation of Jesus, 529; consolation of Israel, 711; sign of contradiction, 575, 587; Jesus and the temple, 583; Mary's ordeal, 149

Lectionary: Luke 2:22–40: Holy Family (Year B); Presentation; Luke 2:22–35: December 29; Luke 2:33–35: Our Lady of Sorrows; Luke 2:36–40: December 30

The last two passages in the infancy narrative move beyond the parallelism between John and Jesus seen in the two angelic announcements and the two birth accounts. Both passages situate Jesus in the Jerusalem temple, so that the story that began with Zechariah's vision in the temple reaches a certain fulfillment with Jesus' arrival there.

Mary and Joseph are faithful observers of the law. Therefore, their child is **2:21** circumcised, like John (1:59), **when eight days were completed** (Gen 17:12; Lev 12:3). He is **named Jesus** in obedience to the words of **the angel** (Luke 1:31).

In Leviticus, the passage regarding circumcision continues by specifying **2:22–24** "thirty-three days more" for the mother, "till the days of her purification are fulfilled" (Lev 12:4). During this period following childbirth, she was considered ritually unclean and could not enter the temple. When forty **days were completed**, Mary and Joseph thus go **up to** the **Jerusalem** temple **for their purification.**[19] The journey also allows them to fulfill another Jewish observance: **to present** Jesus the firstborn **to the Lord.** Luke uses a ring structure

---

19. Luke writes "their" purification (Mary and Joseph), rather than "her" purification, probably because the stricter rabbis considered that a mother during this time would still be a source of ritual uncleanness for others (e.g., her husband) with whom she came in contact (*m. Niddah* 10:6). On this and

(A–B–B'–A'), introducing the purification (A) and presentation (B) and then giving the scriptural background of the presentation (B') and purification (A'). The emphasis falls in the middle on Jesus' presentation, in accord with Scripture: **"Every male that opens the womb shall be consecrated to the Lord"** (see Exod 13:2, 12–15; Num 18:15). For those living near Jerusalem, this observance, when the infant son was "a month old or more" (Num 3:40), took place in the temple: "We have agreed . . . as is prescribed in the law, to bring to the house of our God, to the priests who serve in the house of our God, the firstborn" (Neh 10:36–37). Scripture likewise indicates the sacrifices to be offered for the purification: **"a pair of turtledoves or two young pigeons"** (see Lev 12:8). This detail reveals their poverty; the regular offering, for those who could afford it, was one lamb and one pigeon or turtledove (Lev 12:6). The combination of poverty and pious observance of **the law** (Luke 2:22–24, 27, 39) highlights how Mary and Joseph are among the righteous †*anawim*.

On a larger scale, Luke's references to days being "completed" (see 2:6) show that God's plan of salvation as announced in Scripture is being fulfilled. Jesus the "Lord" (2:11) is brought to the temple, as Malachi had prophesied: "The lord whom you seek will come suddenly to his temple" (Mal 3:1). Also fulfilled are the seventy weeks prophesied by Gabriel (Dan 9:24), from Gabriel's appearance to Zechariah in the temple until Jesus' arrival in the temple (see comment on Luke 1:19–20).

2:25–27   In God's plan, the event also includes the meeting with **Simeon** (2:25–35) and Anna (vv. 36–38). Simeon, who bears the name of one of Jacob's sons (Gen 29:33), is described as **righteous**, like Zechariah and Elizabeth (Luke 1:6), and **devout** (see Acts 2:5; 8:2; 22:12). Moreover, he is **awaiting the consolation of Israel**—that is, the fulfillment of prophecies such as those in Isaiah: "'Console my people, console them,' says your God" (Isa 40:1 NJB; see Isa 49:13; 51:3; 61:2; 66:13). **The holy Spirit** is also **upon him**, as earlier with Mary (Luke 1:35). The **Spirit** indeed illuminates his thoughts, revealing the promise **that he should not see death before** seeing **the Messiah**, who is Jesus (2:11). The **Spirit** also guides Simeon's actions, inspiring him to go to **the temple** at the right time. He obeys the Spirit's promptings, like Mary and Joseph, who are obedient to the law. One might say that the law is fulfilled in them because they walk according to the Spirit (see Rom 8:4).

Meanwhile, Joseph and Mary bring in **the child Jesus to perform the custom of the law in regard to him**, presumably to pay the "redemption price" of

---

other points discussed here, see Richard Bauckham, "Luke's Infancy Narrative as Oral History in Scriptural Form," in Estrada, Manicardi, and Puig i Tàrrech, *The Gospels: History and Christology*, 1:410–17.

"five silver shekels" (Num 18:16) for the firstborn (see Exod 13:13, 15). Luke does not explicitly mention it, as his interest is more on the "redemption" to be wrought by Jesus himself (Luke 2:38).

Given the earlier connections between Mary's Magnificat and Hannah's canticle (1 Sam 2:1–10), there is a possible parallel here between Jesus' presentation and Samuel's dedication (1 Sam 1:28; compare 1 Sam 2:26 and Luke 2:52). This parallel suggests that, although Jesus returns to Nazareth with Mary and Joseph (Luke 2:39), he remains wholly dedicated to God, the "faithful priest" like Samuel (1 Sam 2:35; see Heb 2:17).

Simeon **took** or "received" Jesus **into his arms** and, as Zechariah had done   2:28–29
(1:64), **blessed God**. His canticle, the Nunc Dimittis, addresses God directly in the second person as **Master**, as Abram earlier did (Gen 15:2 LXX).

Now is the time of fulfillment, an emphasis on immediacy already seen in the angelic announcement: "*Today* . . . a savior has been born for you" (Luke 2:11 [emphasis added]). The time of waiting is over. Simeon is God's **servant** (*doulos*), like Mary the "handmaid" (*doulē*, 1:38, 48). Like Mary, he accepts God's plan for his life, revealed **according to** God's **word** (see 1:38). He **may** now **go**—that is, die—since God's promise to him has been fulfilled. Similarly, Abram wondered if he would go (i.e., die), but then God made a promise to him (Gen 15:2 LXX). The angels had sung of "peace to those on whom his favor rests" (Luke 2:14), and such a person is Simeon, who can now die **in peace**. The Church prays the words of the Nunc Dimittis in Night Prayer (Compline) every night, so that like Simeon, the faithful may end their days and their lives in God's peace.

Simeon's **eyes have seen** Jesus. Jesus will later tell his disciples: "Blessed are   2:30–32
the eyes that see what you see" (10:23); Simeon is among the first recipients of this beatitude. Jesus the Savior (2:11) is the means of God's **salvation**, a salvation that "all flesh shall see" (3:6, quoting Isa 40:5 LXX). This salvation was **prepared** of old by prophets like Isaiah and will now be prepared by John the Baptist (Luke 1:17, 76; 3:4). It is for **all the peoples**: God's **people Israel**—to whom it will bring glory (see Isa 46:13)—and **the Gentiles** as well. Indeed, Jesus will fulfill Isaiah's prophecy by bringing **light** even to the Gentiles: "I will also make you a light for the Gentiles, / that my salvation may reach to the ends of the earth" (Isa 49:6 NIV; see Isa 42:6). The universal scope of God's salvation, announced here, will be enacted in Acts in the progression from Jerusalem to Rome: "This salvation of God has been sent to the Gentiles" (Acts 28:28).

Joseph and Mary **were amazed** at Simeon's words, a typical reaction in Luke   2:33–35
to the marvels being worked by God (1:21, 63; 2:18). He **blessed them** and then

prophesied a specific word to **Mary his mother**: Jesus will be **a sign that will be contradicted**. He will have to suffer and die (9:22; 17:25; 24:26, 46), and even his followers will be contradicted (Acts 28:22). Moreover, Jesus' suffering will be associated with **the fall and rise of many in Israel**, indicating that though a remnant will accept him, others will stumble over him (see Rom 9:27, 32–33; 11:5, 7). In their response to Jesus, **the thoughts of many hearts** will **be revealed** (see Luke 5:22; 6:8; 9:47; 24:38), and the acceptance or rejection of Jesus will be a sign of one's acceptance or rejection of God (see 10:16).

Simeon also prophesies that **a sword will pierce** Mary's soul, as she personally shares in her son's sufferings (see John 19:25–27). Moreover, as a representative figure for Israel, Mary will experience sorrow at the division within Israel over her son: "Let a sword pass through the land" (Ezek 14:17 NETS; the same Greek word is used for "pass through" and "pierce").

2:36–38   Besides the inspired Simeon, there is another devout individual, **a prophetess, Anna**, who **worshiped night and day with fasting and prayer**. A typical Lukan emphasis is seen here—namely, the pairing of male and female characters, showing that the gospel message is for all (see Gal 3:28). However, whereas Simeon is characterized mainly by the words he speaks, Anna is characterized by an unusually long description.[20] Her name Anna (Hannah in Hebrew) recalls Hannah the mother of Samuel. Besides the information about her family and clan, Luke writes that **she was advanced in years, having lived seven years with her husband after her marriage, and then as a widow until she was eighty-four.** This description suggests that if Mary represents Israel as virgin, Anna represents Israel primarily as widow ("eighty-four"[21] equals twelve times seven—i.e., the number of Israel's tribes times the number of perfection). Isaiah's prophecy is being fulfilled: "The reproach of your widowhood no longer remember. / For your husband is your Maker; / the LORD of hosts is his name, / Your redeemer, the Holy One of Israel" (Isa 54:4–5; see 62:4–5, 12). Isaiah is portraying the Lord God as Israel's bridegroom redeemer—that is, the kinsman who redeems a childless widow by marrying her (see Ruth 4:5–6, 14). Anna speaks about Jesus to those longing for **the redemption of Jerusalem**. Jesus is this awaited redeemer of the people (see Luke 1:68), and he refers to himself later as the "bridegroom" (5:34).

2:39–40   After fulfilling **all the prescriptions of the law of the Lord** (noted for the fifth time; see 2:22, 23, 24, 27), the family returns **to their own town of Nazareth**

20. The following discussion draws on Andrés García Serrano, "Anna's Characterization in Luke 2:36–38: A Case of Conceptual Allusion?," *Catholic Biblical Quarterly* 76 (2014): 464–80.

21. The 84 years may refer instead to the length of her widowhood, making her about 105 years old (about 14 years of virginity, 7 years of married life, 84 years of widowhood). This was the age attained by Judith, who like Anna was a widow noted for her fasting (Jdt 8:6; 16:23).

(see 1:26; 2:4). There, **the child grew and became strong**, exactly as was noted for John (1:80). Since Jesus is greater than John, his **wisdom** is also noted. Moreover, God's **favor** rests **upon him**, as it does with his mother (1:30).

In summary, the presentation of Jesus brings readers back to the temple to announce Jesus' future suffering and universal mission.

Reflection and Application (2:21–40)

Sign of contradiction. Karol Wojtyła, the future Pope John Paul II, wrote that "Jesus is both the light that shines . . . and at the same time a sign of contradiction,"[22]—in other words, one who is opposed. Do I let the light of Jesus shine, or do I instead oppose or resist him?

The Finding of Jesus in the Temple (2:41–52)

[41]**Each year his parents went to Jerusalem for the feast of Passover,** [42]**and when he was twelve years old, they went up according to festival custom.** [43]**After they had completed its days, as they were returning, the boy Jesus remained behind in Jerusalem, but his parents did not know it.** [44]**Thinking that he was in the caravan, they journeyed for a day and looked for him among their relatives and acquaintances,** [45]**but not finding him, they returned to Jerusalem to look for him.** [46]**After three days they found him in the temple, sitting in the midst of the teachers, listening to them and asking them questions,** [47]**and all who heard him were astounded at his understanding and his answers.** [48]**When his parents saw him, they were astonished, and his mother said to him, "Son, why have you done this to us? Your father and I have been looking for you with great anxiety."** [49]**And he said to them, "Why were you looking for me? Did you not know that I must be in my Father's house?"** [50]**But they did not understand what he said to them.** [51]**He went down with them and came to Nazareth, and was obedient to them; and his mother kept all these things in her heart.** [52]**And Jesus advanced [in] wisdom and age and favor before God and man.**

OT: Exod 12; Lev 23:5–8; Deut 16:1–8; 1 Sam 2:26; Isa 11:1–3
NT: Luke 19:47; 24:5
Catechism: Jesus the Son, 503, 2599; Jesus' human knowledge, 472; Jesus' obedience and hidden life, 517, 531–32, 564; finding of Jesus, 534; Jesus and the temple, 583; reflecting in the heart, 94
Lectionary: Holy Family (Year C); Luke 2:41–51: St. Joseph; Immaculate Heart of Mary

22. Karol Wojtyła, *Sign of Contradiction* (New York: Seabury, 1979), 198.

Luke bridges the thirty-year gap between Jesus' infancy and public ministry by recounting an event from Jesus' boyhood. Such accounts occur in both the Old Testament and ancient Hellenistic biographies, highlighting a hero's qualities and anticipating his future greatness. The account here, again situated in the temple, emphasizes Jesus' wisdom and understanding. It also looks forward to his teaching ministry in the temple and to his death and resurrection.

2:41–42   Joseph and Mary are again presented as faithful observers of the law: **each year his parents went to Jerusalem for the feast of Passover**. Passover was one of the three great pilgrimage feasts (see Exod 23:14), celebrating the liberation of Israel from slavery in Egypt (Exod 12; Lev 23:5–8; Deut 16:1–8). Israel, God's firstborn son (Exod 4:22), was freed, while the firstborn in Egypt were struck down (Exod 4:23; 11:5; 12:29–30). When Jesus **was twelve years old**, his family **went up** as usual. This Passover pilgrimage foreshadows his future journey as an adult, when he who is the firstborn (Luke 2:7) goes up to Jerusalem (9:51; 18:31; 19:28) and celebrates the Passover (22:7–15) before his death. Moreover, Jesus' age may recall Samuel. Though the biblical text is silent about Samuel's age when the Lord called him (1 Sam 3:1–10), one Jewish tradition considered him to be twelve years old at the time.[23]

2:43–45   At the end of the feast, **the boy Jesus remained behind in Jerusalem**. This is the result of his decision (see Luke 2:49), about which **his parents did not know**. The trip back to Nazareth took several days, and Mary and Joseph **journeyed for a day**, imagining him to be **in the caravan** of travelers **among their relatives and acquaintances**, perhaps as he had done in earlier pilgrimages. **Not finding him**, they travel another day back **to Jerusalem to look for him**.

2:46–47   **After three days**, they finally **found** Jesus. The mention of "three days" naturally suggests a connection to Jesus' resurrection. The expression itself is not conclusive, since Luke refers to the resurrection with the slightly different phrase "on the third day" (9:22; 18:33; 24:7, 46). However, other elements indicate that Luke may indeed be foreshadowing the resurrection here.[24] For example, the place (Jerusalem) and time of year (Passover) are the same. Also, the experience of not finding Jesus occurs again in the resurrection narrative (24:3, 23). Moreover, the journey of two people (Mary and Joseph) away from and back to Jerusalem while Jesus is missing is like the journey away from and back to Jerusalem of the two disciples on the road to Emmaus (24:13, 33). Another connection to the resurrection is evident later in the passage (2:49).

23. Josephus, *Jewish Antiquities* 5.348.
24. Luke Timothy Johnson, *The Gospel of Luke*, Sacra Pagina 3 (Collegeville, MN: Liturgical Press, 1991), 61–62.

Jesus is found **in the temple**, the point of departure and point of arrival of Luke's account in these first two chapters. He is **sitting in the midst of the teachers**, recalling how the young boy Daniel sat in the midst of the elders in the story of Susanna (Dan 13:50). He is **listening**, but because he is also **asking questions**—a typical teaching method of the rabbis—and because of **his understanding** and **his answers**, clearly he is also there as a teacher himself. Since sitting is the position for teaching (Luke 4:20; 5:3; Matt 5:1), the scene looks forward to Jesus' teaching ministry, especially in the temple (Luke 19:47; 20:1; 21:37–38).

The people were "astounded" at Jesus' answers (2:47), but now his **mother**   2:48
Mary and **father** Joseph are **astonished** (see 2:18, 33) on account of the **great anxiety** they have experienced. Perhaps the sword prophesied by Simeon includes suffering caused by not fully understanding Jesus' mission. Mary asks Jesus, **Son, why have you done this to us?**

In his first spoken words in the Gospel, Jesus answers with a question: **Why**   2:49
were you looking for me? The same verb "look for, seek" is also used in the question posed to the women at the empty tomb: "Why do you seek the living one among the dead?" (24:5). In both cases, the question implies that if the people understood earlier events (Jesus' presentation) or words (his resurrection predictions), they would not be looking for him. Jesus then explains: **I must be in my Father's house.** In Luke, the verb *dei* ("must") is used to convey divine necessity—that is, what Jesus must do in fulfillment of God's plan.[25] Jesus' answer also contrasts his "father" Joseph with his heavenly Father, showing that he is conscious of his identity (1:32, 35). Ultimately, Jesus must be about his Father's affairs or "business"[26] (KJV), obeying his will (see 22:42).

Mary and Joseph do not **understand** his reply. Their experience will later   2:50
be repeated by the disciples, who, despite having the privilege of seeing and hearing Jesus (10:23–24), will also fail to understand his sayings (9:45; 18:34). Mysteries of faith, even when revealed, are still only known partially (1 Cor 13:12). One's understanding can always grow.

Afterward, Jesus returns with Mary and Joseph to **Nazareth**, where he **was**   2:51
obedient or "subject" **to them.** For her part, Mary **kept all these things in her heart**, seeking to understand them better, as she did after the shepherds' visit (Luke 2:19).

In conclusion, Jesus' increase in **wisdom** and **favor** is again highlighted (2:40).   2:52
Since Jesus' "understanding" has also just been mentioned (v. 47), there may be an allusion here to the qualities of the messiah, as prophesied by Isaiah: "The

---

25. Luke 4:43; 9:22; 13:33; 17:25; 19:5; 22:37; 24:7, 26, 44.
26. The word "house" is not found in Jesus' reply, though it is implied by the temple context.

The Joyful Mysteries

The messianic joy foretold by the prophets (Isa 49:13; Zeph 3:14) has arrived in the events recounted in Luke's first two chapters. They bring "joy" (Luke 1:14; 2:10) and "gladness" (1:14, 44)[a] as Mary, Elizabeth, and others "rejoice" and "exult" (1:14, 28, 47, 58). For centuries, Christians have meditated on these texts as they pray the Joyful Mysteries of the Rosary. St. John Paul II explains:

> The first five decades . . . are marked by *the joy radiating from the event of the Incarnation*. This is clear from the very first mystery, the Annunciation, where Gabriel's greeting to the Virgin of Nazareth is linked to an invitation to messianic joy: "Rejoice, Mary." . . . Exultation is the keynote of the encounter with Elizabeth, where the sound of Mary's voice and the presence of Christ in her womb cause John to "leap for joy" (see 1:44). Gladness also fills the scene in Bethlehem, when the birth of the divine Child, the Savior of the world, is announced by the song of the angels and proclaimed to the shepherds as "news of great joy" (2:10). The final two mysteries, while preserving this climate of joy, already point to the drama yet to come. . . . To meditate upon the "joyful" mysteries, then, is to enter into the ultimate causes and the deepest meaning of Christian joy. . . . Mary leads us to discover the secret of Christian joy, reminding us that Christianity is, first and foremost, *euangelion*, "good news," which has as its heart and its whole content the person of Jesus Christ, the Word made flesh, the one Savior of the world.[b]

a. The Greek word that the NABRE translates "joy" in 1:44 is translated "gladness" in 1:14.
b. John Paul II, *Rosarium Virginis Mariae* (On the Most Holy Rosary) 20 (emphasis in the original).

spirit of the LORD shall rest upon him: / a spirit of wisdom and of understanding" (Isa 11:2). Jesus also increases in **age**, meaning growth in stature and maturity as well. When he next appears in Luke's narrative, he will no longer be twelve, but about thirty years old (Luke 3:23).

Reflection and Application (2:41–52)

Obedience. St. Maximilian Kolbe writes:

Obedience is the one and the only way of wisdom and prudence for us to offer glory to God. If there were another, Christ would certainly have shown it to us by word and example. Scripture, however, summed up his entire life at Nazareth in the words: "He was subject to them" [2:51]; Scripture set obedience as the theme of the rest of his life, repeatedly declaring that he came into the world to do his Father's will. Let us love our loving Father with all our hearts. Let our obedience increase that love, above all when it requires us to surrender our own will. Jesus Christ crucified is our sublime guide toward growth in God's love.[27]

The sanctifying value of ordinary life. St. Josemaría Escrivá invites us to meditate on Jesus' hidden life in Nazareth: "Of Jesus' thirty-three years, thirty were spent in silence and obscurity, submission and work."[28]

27. Maximilian M. Kolbe, from his *Letters*, quoted in *The Liturgy of the Hours: Supplement* (New York: Catholic Book Publishing, 1992), 11.
28. Josemaría Escrivá, *Furrow* (New York: Scepter, 1987), §485.

The Precursor and the Son of God

Luke 3:1–4:13

Some eighteen years after the previous scene, John's prophetic mission begins. John prepares the way for Jesus with his baptism of repentance for the forgiveness of sins. When Jesus himself is baptized, the Father's voice acknowledges him as the beloved Son and the Holy Spirit descends upon him, signaling the beginning of his mission. To understand that mission, Jesus' genealogy is presented, going back to Adam. Like Adam, Jesus is tempted by the devil. Unlike Adam, Jesus is victorious over temptation, thus revealing that he is the one who can save humanity from sin.

The Preaching of John the Baptist (3:1–20)

[1]In the fifteenth year of the reign of Tiberius Caesar, when Pontius Pilate was governor of Judea, and Herod was tetrarch of Galilee, and his brother Philip tetrarch of the region of Ituraea and Trachonitis, and Lysanias was tetrarch of Abilene, [2]during the high priesthood of Annas and Caiaphas, the word of God came to John the son of Zechariah in the desert. [3]He went throughout [the] whole region of the Jordan, proclaiming a baptism of repentance for the forgiveness of sins, [4]as it is written in the book of the words of the prophet Isaiah:

> "A voice of one crying out in the desert:
> 'Prepare the way of the Lord,
>   make straight his paths.

⁵Every valley shall be filled
    and every mountain and hill shall be made low.
The winding roads shall be made straight,
    and the rough ways made smooth,
⁶and all flesh shall see the salvation of God.'"

⁷He said to the crowds who came out to be baptized by him, "You brood of vipers! Who warned you to flee from the coming wrath? ⁸Produce good fruits as evidence of your repentance; and do not begin to say to yourselves, 'We have Abraham as our father,' for I tell you, God can raise up children to Abraham from these stones. ⁹Even now the ax lies at the root of the trees. Therefore every tree that does not produce good fruit will be cut down and thrown into the fire."

¹⁰And the crowds asked him, "What then should we do?" ¹¹He said to them in reply, "Whoever has two tunics should share with the person who has none. And whoever has food should do likewise." ¹²Even tax collectors came to be baptized and they said to him, "Teacher, what should we do?" ¹³He answered them, "Stop collecting more than what is prescribed." ¹⁴Soldiers also asked him, "And what is it that we should do?" He told them, "Do not practice extortion, do not falsely accuse anyone, and be satisfied with your wages."

¹⁵Now the people were filled with expectation, and all were asking in their hearts whether John might be the Messiah. ¹⁶John answered them all, saying, "I am baptizing you with water, but one mightier than I is coming. I am not worthy to loosen the thongs of his sandals. He will baptize you with the holy Spirit and fire. ¹⁷His winnowing fan is in his hand to clear his threshing floor and to gather the wheat into his barn, but the chaff he will burn with unquenchable fire." ¹⁸Exhorting them in many other ways, he preached good news to the people. ¹⁹Now Herod the tetrarch, who had been censured by him because of Herodias, his brother's wife, and because of all the evil deeds Herod had committed, ²⁰added still another to these by [also] putting John in prison.

OT: Isa 40:3–5

NT: Luke 1:17, 76–77, 80; 7:19–20; 9:9; John 1:15, 19–28; 3:28; Acts 1:5; 10:37; 11:16; 13:24–25; 19:4. // Matt 3:1–12; 14:3–4; Mark 1:2–8; 6:17–18

Catechism: John the Baptist, 535, 696; fruits of repentance, 1460; works of mercy, 2447

Lectionary: Luke 3:1–6: Second Sunday Advent (Year C); Luke 3:10–18: Third Sunday Advent (Year C)

Beginning here, there are often parallels to Luke's account in Matthew or Mark or both. At times, therefore, Luke's theological message can be better understood by comparing accounts, noting especially his distinctive elements.

3:1   Luke's third correlation between the events he recounts and world history is the most detailed (see 1:5; 2:1). Thirty years or so (3:23) have passed since the events of Jesus' birth. **Tiberius Caesar** has succeeded his stepfather Augustus as Roman emperor, reigning from AD 14 to 37. Roman-Jewish relations in the land of Israel are relatively calm during this period: "under Tiberius all was quiet."[1] **The fifteenth year** of his **reign** corresponds to AD 28–29, which is consistent with the other information provided here. **Pontius Pilate was governor**, specifically prefect, **of Judea** from AD 26 to 36, when he was suspended by Vitellius, the Roman legate in Syria. **Herod** Antipas **was tetrarch of Galilee** and Perea from the death of his father until AD 39, when he was exiled by the emperor Gaius (Caligula). Pilate and Herod will come together at Jesus' trial (23:12; Acts 4:27). Herod's half **brother Philip** was **tetrarch of the region of Ituraea and Trachonitis**, northeast of the Sea of Galilee, until his death around AD 34. He rebuilt Caesarea Philippi (Matt 16:13; Mark 8:27). **Lysanias** was **tetrarch of Abilene**, northwest of Damascus. All three of these tetrarchies were later ruled by King Herod Agrippa I (see Acts 12), a grandson of Herod the Great.[2]

3:2–3   Besides civic leaders, Luke also lists two Jewish high priests. **Annas** was appointed high priest by Quirinius (Luke 2:2) in AD 6, and deposed by the Roman prefect Gratus in AD 15[3]—a good example of how Rome controlled the high priesthood. Luke mentions him because he continued to exercise influence (see John 18:13, 24; Acts 4:6), as five of his sons and his son-in-law **Caiaphas** became high priest after him. Caiaphas was high priest from AD 18 to 36 or 37, when he was deposed by Vitellius. These two high priests are among the unnamed "chief priests" mentioned later (e.g., Luke 22:66).

In the days of all these leaders, **the word of God came to John the son of Zechariah**. John is presented exactly like Old Testament prophets who received the word of God at specific historical moments.[4] John is still **in the desert** (1:80), and this too is part of God's plan (see v. 4). The desert is the Judean wilderness (see Matt 3:1) in the **whole region of the Jordan** River, northwest of the Dead Sea. Since Qumran was nearby, the young John, a priest's son, may have had some contact with that priestly community. The Jordan was also the place where Elijah was taken up to heaven in a whirlwind (2 Kings 2:6–14). It is now the place where John appears as a prophet "in the spirit and power of Elijah" (Luke 1:17).

1. Tacitus, *Histories* 5.9, trans. Clifford H. Moore, 4 vols., LCL (Cambridge, MA: Harvard University Press, 1925–37), 2:191.
2. Josephus, *Jewish Antiquities* 18.237, 252.
3. Josephus, *Jewish Antiquities* 18.26, 34.
4. Jer 1:1–3; Ezek 1:1–3; Hosea 1:1; Mic 1:1; Zeph 1:1; Hag 1:1; Zech 1:1.

Silvano Kim

Figure 4. The baptismal site Qasr al-Yahud on the Jordan River.

John's prophetic mission, already announced by Zechariah (1:77), involves **proclaiming a baptism of repentance for the forgiveness of sins** (see Mark 1:4). This is the legacy for which he will be remembered in the early Church (Acts 10:37; 13:24; 19:4). John's preaching prepares for Jesus' own mission of calling people to repentance (Luke 5:32; 13:3, 5) and forgiving their sins (5:20; 7:48). Jesus will also instruct his disciples to proclaim "repentance, for the forgiveness of sins . . . to all the nations" (24:47). "Repentance" (*metanoia*)—literally, a "change of mind"—leads to a change of behavior: a conversion or turning away from sin (3:8; 15:7, 10; Acts 26:20).

John's ministry of baptizing, which gave him the title "the Baptist" (Luke 7:20, 33; 9:19), can be considered against the background of Jewish ritual washings and immersions that are prescribed for ritual cleansing (e.g., Lev 15). One had to wash in a *mikveh* (pool for ritual bathing) before entering the temple courts.

Jewish Groups and Leaders

BIBLICAL BACKGROUND

In the first century, high priests like Annas and Caiaphas (Luke 3:2) led the Jerusalem †Sanhedrin (22:66), the Jewish people's supreme judicial council or "senate" (Acts 5:21) with seventy other members (see Num 11:16, 24–25). The council handled internal Jewish affairs, interacting with the Roman authorities when necessary (Luke 23:1; Acts 22:30). The general terms "leaders" and "rulers" are also used to refer to its members or those associated with them (e.g., Luke 19:47; 23:35; Acts 4:5–6). More specifically, the Sanhedrin included chief priests, elders, and scribes (Luke 9:22; 20:1; Mark 15:1). The "chief priests" (Luke 22:4; 23:4) included the high priest plus former high priests and other members of the high priest's family (Acts 4:6). For the most part they belonged to the Sadducee party (Acts 5:17), which denied the resurrection of the dead (Luke 20:27; Acts 23:8) since they accepted only those doctrines clearly found in the five books of Moses (see Luke 20:37). Also among the Sadducees were the "elders" (22:52), wealthy members of the Jerusalem aristocracy (different from village "elders," 7:3).

On the other hand, the "scribes" (22:2; 23:10) belonged mainly to the party of the Pharisees (Acts 23:9). Beyond the Sanhedrin, there were many scribes and Pharisees, and the two are often mentioned together (Luke 5:21, 30; 6:7; 11:53; 15:2). They were teachers (5:17) and scholars of the law (7:30; 14:3). They also had seats of honor in synagogues (11:43; 20:46). The Pharisees accepted not only the whole written law (the Torah and the other parts of the Hebrew Bible) but also the oral traditions (see Gal 1:14) that would later find expression, for instance, in the †Mishnah. They zealously observed laws regarding table fellowship (Luke 5:30; 15:2), the sabbath (6:2, 7; 14:3), ritual purity (11:38), and tithing (11:42).

The Jewish historian Josephus discusses the Pharisees and Sadducees along with a third party, the Essenes, for whom he expresses admiration. This ascetical group, which included priests, participated only to a limited extent in temple sacrifices, as they were even more concerned with ritual purity than the Pharisees and viewed the Jerusalem priesthood as corrupt. Not explicitly mentioned in the New Testament, the Essenes had various communities, perhaps including one in Jerusalem, as there was an Essene gate in the southwest corner of the city.[a] Most scholars think that Qumran was a community of Essenes, to whom belonged the †Dead Sea Scrolls.

a. Josephus, *Jewish War* 2.119–66; 5.145; *Jewish Antiquities* 18.19.

Other washings were practiced by groups such as the Pharisees on the basis of ancestral traditions (Luke 11:38; Mark 7:1–5). In contrast with these ritual washings, however, John's baptism was specifically connected to his call to repentance, echoing Isaiah: "Wash yourselves clean! / Put away your misdeeds from before my eyes; / cease doing evil" (Isa 1:16). Proselytes converting to Judaism would undergo such a ritual washing that also implied a turning away from sinful ways, but this may be a later practice. John's proximity to Qumran suggests a parallel to the ritual washings there, which also entailed reforming one's life: "One is not cleansed unless one turns away from one's wickedness."[5] However, whereas most of these ritual washings were done repeatedly, a person apparently received John's baptism only once, and received it from him personally (Luke 7:29–30; 20:4) or later from his disciples (Acts 18:25; 19:3).

All four Gospels quote the words of the prophet Isaiah (Isa 40:3) to describe **3:4–6** John the Baptist (Matt 3:3; Mark 1:2–3; John 1:23). Zechariah's canticle has already alluded to this verse (Luke 1:76). John is literally a voice of one crying out in the desert (1:80; 3:2). His mission is to prepare the way of the Lord, make straight his paths. In Isaiah, these two parallel phrases refer to the Lord God: "Prepare the way of the Lord! / Make straight . . . a highway for our God!" (Isa 40:3).[6] John, however, is also preparing the way for Jesus, who indeed is the Lord (Luke 1:43; 2:11).

Unlike the other Gospels, Luke lengthens the Isaiah quotation to include two more verses, thus announcing **the salvation of God** (see Isa 40:5 NETS). Hence, the quotation provides a key for understanding not just John's ministry but also God's plan of salvation through Jesus, as it will unfold in the Gospel and in Acts. Moreover, this salvation is universal in scope: **all flesh shall see** it, including the Gentiles (Luke 2:30–32; Acts 28:28). A great reversal is taking place, as God levels the playing field: **every valley shall be filled and every mountain and hill shall be made low** (see Luke 1:52; 13:28–30; 14:11; 18:14).

Whereas John summons people to "prepare the way of the Lord, / make **3:7–9** straight his paths" (v. 4), the wicked do just the opposite: "The way of peace they know not. . . . / Their roads they have made crooked" (Isa 59:8). By their evil deeds, "they hatch adders' eggs. . . . / If one of them is crushed, it will hatch a viper" (Isa 59:5). This may be the text that stands behind John's words **to the crowds: You brood of vipers!** He sternly reproves the sinful dispositions of those who come **to be baptized** and exhorts them to **produce good fruits**—good deeds—**as evidence of** their **repentance**. Otherwise, they will be **cut down** like a **tree**. According to an interpretation of Isaiah at Qumran, the one who wields

---

5. 1QS (*Rule of the Community*) V, 13–14, in *The Dead Sea Scrolls Study Edition*, ed. Florentino García Martínez and Eibert J. C. Tigchelaar, 2 vols. (Leiden: Brill; Grand Rapids: Eerdmans, 2000), 1:81.
6. See 1QS VIII, 14, which cites Isa 40:3.

Isaiah's New Exodus Fulfilled in Luke-Acts

BIBLICAL BACKGROUND

Luke's quotation (3:4–6) from Isaiah 40:3–5 not only explains John's mission but serves as one of the keys for understanding Jesus' mission. This passage from the beginning of the second part of Isaiah (Isa 40–66) announces that God will bring about Israel's restoration from exile. Isaiah presents this new saving intervention by God using images drawn from Israel's foundational saving event, the exodus. For example, the "way of the LORD" being prepared (40:3) is later described like the crossing of the sea in Exodus 14:

> Thus says the LORD,
> who opens a way in the sea,
> a path in the mighty waters,
> Who leads out chariots and horsemen,
> a powerful army,
> Till they lie prostrate together, never to rise . . .
> See, I am doing something new! . . .
> In the wilderness I make a way. (Isa 43:16–17, 19; see also 48:20–21;
> 51:10–11; 63:7–14)

In the years leading up to the birth of Jesus, there was widespread hope for Israel's restoration. Though the Jewish people had long been allowed to return from Babylon, it seemed that the exile had only partially come to an end: the Davidic kingdom had not yet been restored, the twelve tribes of Israel were still scattered among the nations, and Gentile powers like the Romans continued to oppress Israel. The people thus looked for God to send the messiah to restore the kingdom (see Acts 1:6), to gather the twelve tribes (see Luke 22:30; Acts 26:6–7), and to bring even the Gentiles under God's rule (see Acts 11:18; 15:12–18).

Luke presents Jesus' mission as fulfilling the prophecies that portray Israel's restoration as a new exodus.[a] For example, the "way" (*hodos*) that is being prepared will become an image, in Luke's long travel narrative (Luke 9:51–19:44), of the "journey" (*hodos*) of discipleship (9:57). In Acts, Luke will continue this perspective by referring to the Church community, made up of both Jews and Gentiles, as "the Way" (Acts 9:2; 19:9, 23; 24:14, 22). On account of Jesus, God's "salvation" will be seen by "all flesh" (Luke 3:6; Isa 40:5 LXX), including the Gentiles (Luke 2:30–32; Acts 28:28). At his transfiguration, Jesus will speak with Moses and Elijah about his "exodus" (Luke 9:31) that will take place in Jerusalem. At the Last Supper in Jerusalem, Jesus will celebrate the Passover where he establishes a "new covenant" (22:20), recalling how God established the Sinai covenant after the exodus.

a. David W. Pao, *Acts and the Isaianic New Exodus* (Tübingen: Mohr Siebeck, 2000), 37–69; Richard B. Hays, *Reading Backwards: Figural Christology and the Fourfold Gospel Witness* (Waco: Baylor University Press, 2014), 62–64.

the ax is the messiah (see Isa 10:34–11:1),[7] so John may be referring to Jesus by these words. Indeed, the same image is used by Jesus later in his parable of the fig tree (Luke 13:6–9). John thus warns them about **the coming wrath**, when God will mete out punishment to evildoers (see Mal 3:19).

Like all Jews, those who come to John consider **Abraham** to be their **father** (see Gen 17:5; Isa 51:2; Luke 1:55, 73). However, he cautions them not to be presumptuous. Not all who regard Abraham as father will be saved (16:24), whereas others, such as tax collectors (19:9) and even Gentiles (13:28–29), will unexpectedly be reckoned **children to Abraham**.

In a question-and-answer dialogue unique to Luke (3:10–14), **the crowds,**   3:10–11 having been challenged to produce "good fruits," ask for advice about how to express their repentance: **"What then should we do?"** Like prophets of old, John instructs them to give to those in need (Isa 58:7; Ezek 18:7). Those with **two tunics** and **food** ought to **share** with those who lack these basic necessities (see Luke 12:22–23, 33; 1 Tim 6:8). If such radical sharing was required as evidence of repentance for John's listeners, what ought repentance to look like for people today?

As a **teacher**, John gives added instructions to two groups who also ask: 3:12–13 **What should we do?** First, he tells **tax collectors** to **stop collecting more than what is prescribed**. He is aware of the widespread corruption that existed in their profession. Indeed, tax collectors were often equated with sinners (Luke 5:30; 15:1–2; 18:11). However, Luke will give several examples of *repentant* tax collectors. Besides Levi (5:27–32), whose call is also found in Matthew and Mark (Matt 9:9–13; Mark 2:13–17), there is the tax collector in the parable (Luke 18:9–14) and Zacchaeus the chief tax collector (19:1–10), both unique to Luke.

Second, John instructs **soldiers** (either Roman or serving Herod Antipas)   3:14 not to **practice extortion**, abusing their power by taking money through threats and violence. They should also **not falsely accuse anyone, and be satisfied with** their **wages**, thus avoiding dishonesty (see Lev 19:11) and greed (see Luke 12:15). Although soldiers will later arrest John (3:20) and mistreat and crucify Jesus (23:11, 36), Luke will portray several soldiers in a positive light: the centurion in Capernaum (7:1–10), the centurion at the cross (23:47), the centurion Cornelius and his devout soldier (Acts 10:1–8), and the centurion Julius who treats Paul kindly (Acts 27:1, 3, 43). The message is that the occupations of tax

---

7. Richard Bauckham, "The Messianic Interpretation of Isaiah 10:34," in *The Jewish World around the New Testament* (Grand Rapids: Baker Academic, 2010), 193–205, referring to 4Q161 8–10 III, 2–18, and 4Q285 5.

collector and soldier are not wrong in themselves; rather, the behavior that typically characterized those occupations is.

3:15–16   **The people** wonder **whether John might be the Messiah**, though the reader already knows that Jesus is the Messiah (Luke 2:11). John denies the claim by referring to **one mightier** than he, who **will baptize** not just with water but **with the holy Spirit and fire**. As John's baptism was distinct from the ritual washings of his Jewish contemporaries, so also Jesus' baptism will be distinct from John's. This is seen in Acts, where Peter does everything John did and more. When asked the same question as John—"What should we do?" (Acts 2:37 NRSV)—Peter answers with an exhortation to repentance and baptism *in Jesus' name* for the forgiveness of sins *and* for the receiving of the Holy Spirit (Acts 2:38).

Compared to Jesus, John does not feel **worthy** to perform even a menial service of untying **the thongs** (literally, in the singular, "the strap") **of his sandals**. In some form, this saying appears in all four Gospels as well as Acts (Matt 3:11; Mark 1:7; John 1:27; Acts 13:25). Clearly, early Christians considered it important for properly understanding the relationship between John the herald and Jesus the Messiah.[8]

3:17   The Messiah will be **winnowing** at the **threshing floor**, separating the **wheat** from the **chaff**. With this agricultural image, John explains the separation that will take place with the "coming wrath" (Luke 3:7). A forklike shovel is used to toss threshed wheat into the air so that the wind can blow aside the lighter chaff, while the heavier wheat kernels fall to the ground. The wheat can then be gathered in a **barn**, while the chaff, a symbol for the wicked (Ps 1:4; Hosea 13:3), is burned in **fire**. Simeon had already announced such a separation in Israel on account of the Messiah (Luke 2:34).

3:18   Despite this prospect of judgment for those not heeding the message of repentance, Luke summarizes John's ministry as one of **exhorting** the people as he **preached good news** (1:19; 2:10), the good news of God's unfolding plan of salvation (3:6).

3:19–20   Preaching repentance can get a person into trouble. Indeed, **Herod the tetrarch** put **John in prison** in the Machaerus fortress on the eastern side of the Dead Sea. The reasons were that Herod had married **Herodias, his brother's**

---

8. Several Church Fathers (e.g., Jerome, *Commentary on Matthew* 3.11) also understood John's saying at a symbolic level as referring to the custom of removing a sandal when someone relinquished the opportunity to marry a widow (see Deut 25:8–10; Ruth 4:5–8). John would be saying that not he but his kinsman Jesus is the bridegroom (see Luke 5:34; John 3:29). See Luis Alonso Schökel, *Símbolos matrimoniales en la Biblia* (Estella, Spain: Verbo Divino, 1997), 114–18; David Lyle Jeffrey, *Luke*, Brazos Theological Commentary on the Bible (Grand Rapids: Brazos, 2012), 59–62.

wife,[9] and **committed** other **evil deeds**, and thus was **censured** by John. This marriage caused difficulties with the Nabatean king Aretas IV, the father of Herod's first wife, who waged war on Herod and destroyed his army. According to Josephus, some Jews saw this as God's punishment on Herod for killing John the Baptist.[10] Herod's persecution of John presages his hostile attitude toward Jesus (9:7–9; 13:31).

Reflection and Application (3:1–20)

Courageously speaking the truth. The ascetical English bishop St. John Fisher greatly identified with his patron saint, John the Baptist. In 1529, he gave a speech defending the marriage of Henry VIII to Catherine of Aragon against the king's wish to have that marriage declared null so that he could marry Anne Boleyn. Fisher said that like John the Baptist he was willing to "lay down his life" for "the cause of marriage."[11] Fisher was later imprisoned in the Tower of London and condemned to death for not recognizing the king as the head of the Church in England. He was beheaded on Henry's orders, as centuries before Herod had beheaded John the Baptist (Luke 9:9). Like John the Baptist and John Fisher, many other martyrs throughout history have courageously defended the truth against the errors of their time. How are we responding today?

The Baptism of Jesus (3:21–22)

[21]**After all the people had been baptized and Jesus also had been baptized and was praying, heaven was opened** [22]**and the holy Spirit descended upon him in bodily form like a dove. And a voice came from heaven, "You are my beloved Son; with you I am well pleased."**

OT: Gen 1:2; Ps 2:7; Isa 11:2; 42:1; 61:1
NT: // Matt 3:13–17; Mark 1:9–11; John 1:32–34
Catechism: Jesus' baptism, 535–37, 565, 608, 1223–25; Jesus at prayer, 2600; descent of the Spirit, 701, 1286; beloved Son, 444
Lectionary: Luke 3:15–16, 21–22: Baptism of the Lord (Year C)

9. Matthew and Mark call this half brother "Philip" (Matt 14:3; Mark 6:17), but Josephus, *Jewish Antiquities* 18.109–10, 136–37, identifies him as another half brother named Herod, not Philip the tetrarch (Luke 3:1). Some have proposed that he was called Herod Philip, "Herod" being the dynastic name common to various sons of Herod the Great.
10. *Jewish Antiquities* 18.109–19.
11. Quoted in Maria Dowling, *Fisher of Men: A Life of John Fisher, 1469–1535* (New York: St. Martin's Press, 1999), 138.

3:21   Since Luke has just mentioned John's imprisonment, John's role in baptizing Jesus is not explicitly mentioned (compare Matt 3:13–15; Mark 1:9–11). All attention is focused on Jesus, the "one mightier" than John (Luke 3:16). Luke associates Jesus' baptism with that of others: **all the people had been baptized and Jesus also had been baptized**. Though he is holy (1:35) and without sin, Jesus is in solidarity with the crowds (3:10) of sinners. These include the tax collectors (3:12) who acknowledge "the righteousness of God" by listening to John and being baptized by him (7:29).

Jesus also **was praying**. Throughout the Gospel, besides teaching about prayer, Jesus is frequently presented at prayer.[12] While he was praying, **heaven was opened**, indicating his communication with the "Father, Lord of heaven" (10:21).

3:22   Moreover, **the holy Spirit descended upon him**, in connection with his prayer. A similar connection is seen later when Jesus exhorts his disciples to pray to receive the Holy Spirit (11:13). Here the Messiah (2:11, 26), who will baptize with the Holy Spirit (3:16), has the Holy Spirit come *upon him*, in fulfillment of Isaiah's prophecies: "The Spirit of the LORD shall rest upon him" (Isa 11:2) and "Upon him I have put my spirit" (Isa 42:1). Jesus is filled with the power of the Holy Spirit (Luke 4:1, 14) and will soon refer back to his baptism, applying to himself a similar passage from Isaiah: "The Spirit of the Lord is upon me, / because he has anointed me" (4:18; Isa 61:1). Peter will also refer to Jesus' baptism and explain "how God anointed Jesus of Nazareth with the holy Spirit and power" (Acts 10:38). The Spirit's action at Jesus' baptism is thus a public manifestation that formally inaugurates his mission as Messiah (see Catechism 536).[13]

The Spirit appeared **in bodily form like a dove**. This image may recall the "Spirit of God . . . hovering" over creation (Gen 1:2 NIV; see Deut 32:11, where a bird likewise "hovers"). The meaning is then that in Jesus there is a new beginning, a new creation (see 2 Cor 5:17). In Acts, the Spirit will appear again at Pentecost, but as tongues of fire (Acts 2:3), fulfilling what John the Baptist had said: "He will baptize you with the holy Spirit and fire" (Luke 3:16).

Completing the trinitarian manifestation, **a voice came from heaven**, the voice of God the Father: **"You are my beloved Son; with you I am well pleased."** At Jesus' transfiguration, the Trinity will similarly be revealed with cloud and voice (9:34–35). The voice from heaven confirms more publicly the angel's message to Mary that Jesus is the Son of God (1:32, 35). The words recall the

12. Luke 5:16; 6:12; 9:18, 28–29; 11:1; 22:41–45.
13. Benedict XVI, *Jesus of Nazareth: From the Baptism in the Jordan to the Transfiguration*, trans. Adrian J. Walker (New York: Doubleday, 2007), 25–26.

psalmist's declaration of divine sonship of God's "anointed one" (Ps 2:2): "You are my son; / today I have begotten you" (Ps 2:7). In Acts, this Davidic, messianic psalm is explicitly applied to Jesus (Acts 4:25–27; 13:33). The reference to Jesus as "beloved Son" also recalls the sacrifice of Isaac, where he is called Abraham's "beloved son" three times (Gen 22:2, 12, 16 LXX). In the second part of the heavenly message there is an allusion to Isaiah's †servant of the Lord: "Here is my servant whom I uphold, / my chosen one with whom I am *pleased*" (Isa 42:1 [emphasis added]). These allusions hint at his mission as †suffering servant (see Acts 8:32–33, citing Isa 53:7–8).[14] In sum, Jesus the Davidic Messiah is the Son of God and the servant of the Lord.

The Genealogy of Jesus, the New Adam (3:23–38)

[23]When Jesus began his ministry he was about thirty years of age. He was the son, as was thought, of Joseph, the son of Heli, [24]the son of Matthat, the son of Levi, the son of Melchi, the son of Jannai, the son of Joseph, [25]the son of Mattathias, the son of Amos, the son of Nahum, the son of Esli, the son of Naggai, [26]the son of Maath, the son of Mattathias, the son of Semein, the son of Josech, the son of Joda, [27]the son of Joanan, the son of Rhesa, the son of Zerubbabel, the son of Shealtiel, the son of Neri, [28]the son of Melchi, the son of Addi, the son of Cosam, the son of Elmadam, the son of Er, [29]the son of Joshua, the son of Eliezer, the son of Jorim, the son of Matthat, the son of Levi, [30]the son of Simeon, the son of Judah, the son of Joseph, the son of Jonam, the son of Eliakim, [31]the son of Melea, the son of Menna, the son of Mattatha, the son of Nathan, the son of David, [32]the son of Jesse, the son of Obed, the son of Boaz, the son of Sala, the son of Nahshon, [33]the son of Amminadab, the son of Admin, the son of Arni, the son of Hezron, the son of Perez, the son of Judah, [34]the son of Jacob, the son of Isaac, the son of Abraham, the son of Terah, the son of Nahor, [35]the son of Serug, the son of Reu, the son of Peleg, the son of Eber, the son of Shelah, [36]the son of Cainan, the son of Arphaxad, the son of Shem, the son of Noah, the son of Lamech, [37]the son of Methuselah, the son of Enoch, the son of Jared, the son of Mahalaleel, the son of Cainan, [38]the son of Enos, the son of Seth, the son of Adam, the son of God.

OT: Gen 5:1–32; 11:10–27; Ruth 4:18–22; 1 Chron 1:1–34; 2:1–15; 3:1–5
NT: Matt 1:1–16

14. Jon D. Levenson, *The Death and Resurrection of the Beloved Son: The Transformation of Child Sacrifice in Judaism and Christianity* (New Haven: Yale University Press, 1993), 200–202.

Catechism: Jesus' public life begins, 535
Lectionary: January 6 (option)

3:23 Following his baptism, **Jesus began his ministry**. The word "ministry" does not appear in the Greek text, which says simply that Jesus "was beginning." Something new is indeed beginning in salvation history (see Acts 10:37). Jesus **was about thirty years of age**, which in the fifteenth year of the reign of Tiberius (Luke 3:1), AD 28–29, would place Jesus' birth in 3–2 BC, if "about" is understood narrowly.[15] The age of thirty is significant in the Old Testament: David began to reign at thirty (2 Sam 5:4), and Levites also began their ministry at that age (Num 4:2–3, 46–47).

Luke's genealogy of Jesus is carefully situated between the baptism and temptation narratives. Unlike Matthew's genealogy (Matt 1:2–16) that moves forward from Abraham to Jesus, Luke begins with Jesus and goes backward (see Ezra 7:1–5) all the way to Adam. In this way, he emphasizes how Jesus fulfills human history by coming to save all people (Luke 2:30–32; 3:6). He also presents Jesus the Son of God as a new Adam, who conquers temptation instead of giving in to it.

Luke's genealogy, like Matthew's (see Matt 1:16), points out the virginal conception of Jesus. **He was the son, as was thought, of Joseph**. The reader knows that Mary has conceived through the Holy Spirit (Luke 1:35), but characters in the narrative are unaware of this. The people in his hometown of Nazareth will thus ask: "Isn't this the son of Joseph?" (4:22).

Joseph was **the son of Heli**.[16] Since Matthew gives Joseph's father as Jacob (Matt 1:16), right away there are difficulties comparing the two genealogies. One explanation, which goes back at least to the fourth century[17] and eventually became common up until the early twentieth century, is that Luke is giving Jesus' genealogy through Mary. Joseph would thus be the son-in-law of Heli, the father of Mary.[18] Another explanation, which goes back to the early third century, is that the difference is due to the practice of levirate marriage (Deut 25:5–6), in which a brother of a man who died without children would marry the widow and raise up children for the deceased (see Luke 20:27–33). Eusebius

15. See the sidebars, "King Herod and Herod the Tetrarch," p. 36, and "The Birth of Jesus," p. 65.
16. The word "son" actually does not occur here nor in the remainder of the genealogy, but it is implied throughout from its use at the beginning of the genealogy.
17. Fortunatianus of Aquileia, *Commentary on the Gospels*, trans. H. A. G. Houghton (Berlin: de Gruyter, 2017), 6–7.
18. For the suggested reasons explaining this, see John Nolland, *Luke 1–9:20*, WBC 35A (Dallas: Word, 1989), 169–70. Joachim, the name of Mary's father from the second-century *Protevangelium of James*, is often then explained as another name for Heli.

draws on the earlier historian Julius Africanus to explain that Heli and Jacob were half brothers (having the same mother but different fathers, descending from two different sons of David). When Heli died childless, Jacob married his widow with Joseph as the offspring. Luke gives the legal father, Heli, and Matthew gives the biological father, Jacob.[19]

Genealogies often convey a theological message through the use of numerical symbolism, and one could shape the genealogy accordingly (e.g., by skipping generations). Matthew's genealogy is organized in three groups of fourteen generations (Matt 1:17), emphasizing Jesus' Davidic lineage, since fourteen is the numerical equivalent of the name "David" in Hebrew. Luke's genealogy emphasizes the number seven, the number of perfection. **Enoch**, who "walked with God" (Gen 5:22, 24), was known to be "seventh" from Adam (Jude 14; see Gen 5:3–18; 1 Chron 1:1–3). However, of greater perfection is Jesus, presented by Luke as the seventy-seventh from Adam (see Gen 4:24; Matt 18:22). Several key figures occupy the position of a multiple of seven in the list: **Abraham** (twenty-first), **David** (thirty-fifth), and someone named **Joshua**, which in Greek is the same as Jesus (forty-ninth = seven times seven).[20] *(margin: 3:24–37)*

Like Matthew, Luke highlights that Jesus is a descendant of David (1:27, 32, 69; 2:4). Aware of the expectation of a Davidic messiah, families in the Davidic line carefully preserved their genealogical records in the first century,[21] so Luke probably based his genealogy on records from Jesus' family. Unlike Matthew, who traces Jesus' Davidic lineage through Solomon (Matt 1:6–7), Luke does so through **Nathan**. This "Nathan" is not the prophet (2 Sam 7:2) but a little-known son of David (2 Sam 5:14; 1 Chron 3:5; 14:4). A reference in Zechariah to the "house of Nathan" right after a reference to the "house of David" (Zech 12:12) suggests that there was an expectation that the line of Davidic descent would pass not through Solomon but through Nathan. The reversal theme again appears: Jesus descends not through the line of Davidic kings, but rather from an obscure line, thus "making a fresh start, comparable with God's original choice of David himself."[22]

At Jesus' baptism, a heavenly voice announced Jesus as God's "Son" (Luke 3:22). Here, at the end of the genealogy, there is **Adam, the son of God** (see *(margin: 3:38)*

19. Eusebius, *Ecclesiastical History* 1.7; 6.31.
20. Richard Bauckham, *Jude and the Relatives of Jesus in the Early Church* (Edinburgh: T&T Clark, 1990), 315–78. See also Christophe Guignard, "Jesus' Family and Their Genealogy according to the Testimony of Julius Africanus," in *Infancy Gospels: Stories and Identities*, ed. Claire Clivaz et al. (Tübingen: Mohr Siebeck, 2011), 67–93.
21. Eusebius, *Ecclesiastical History* 3.12, 20, 32. A first-century ossuary referring to the "house of David" provides corroborating evidence.
22. Bauckham, *Jude*, 335.

Gen 1:26–27; 5:1). There is a parallel between Adam and Jesus, though Jesus' divine sonship is of another order (Luke 1:35). In the temptation passage that follows, Jesus as the new Adam will be victorious over the devil, unlike the first Adam who fell (Gen 3). The comparison will continue in Luke's passion narrative.[23] As Paul does in his letters (Rom 5:12–19; 1 Cor 15:21–22, 45–49), Luke teaches a theology of Adam as a †type of Jesus. In the second century, St. Irenaeus comments on the Adam-Christ †typology, explaining that Jesus, "receiving the ancient fathers, . . . regenerated them to the life of God. . . . For this reason Luke, when he began the genealogy of the Lord, carried it back to Adam, pointing out that they did not regenerate him for the Gospel of life, but he them." Irenaeus continues with Eve-Mary typology: "The knot of Eve's disobedience was untied by Mary's obedience. For what the virgin Eve tied by her unbelief, this Mary untied by her belief."[24]

The Temptation of Jesus (4:1–13)

[1]Filled with the holy Spirit, Jesus returned from the Jordan and was led by the Spirit into the desert [2]for forty days, to be tempted by the devil. He ate nothing during those days, and when they were over he was hungry. [3]The devil said to him, "If you are the Son of God, command this stone to become bread." [4]Jesus answered him, "It is written, 'One does not live by bread alone.'" [5]Then he took him up and showed him all the kingdoms of the world in a single instant. [6]The devil said to him, "I shall give to you all this power and their glory; for it has been handed over to me, and I may give it to whomever I wish. [7]All this will be yours, if you worship me." [8]Jesus said to him in reply, "It is written:

'You shall worship the Lord, your God,
    and him alone shall you serve.'"

[9]Then he led him to Jerusalem, made him stand on the parapet of the temple, and said to him, "If you are the Son of God, throw yourself down from here, [10]for it is written:

'He will command his angels concerning you,
    to guard you,'

23. Jerome Neyrey, *The Passion according to Luke: A Redaction Study of Luke's Soteriology* (Mahwah, NJ: Paulist Press, 1985), 165–92.

24. Irenaeus, *Against the Heresies* 3.22.4, trans. Dominic J. Unger and M. C. Steenberg, ACW (New York: Newman, 2012), 105.

¹¹and:

> 'With their hands they will support you,
>   lest you dash your foot against a stone.'"

¹²Jesus said to him in reply, "It also says, 'You shall not put the Lord, your God, to the test.'" ¹³When the devil had finished every temptation, he departed from him for a time.

OT: Deut 6:13, 16; 8:2–3; Ps 91:11–12
NT: Heb 2:18; 4:15. // Matt 4:1–11; Mark 1:12–13
Catechism: Jesus filled with the Spirit, 695; Jesus' temptations, 538–40, 566, 2119; the devil's claim to kingdoms, power, and glory, 2855; first commandment, 2084, 2096
Lectionary: First Sunday Lent (Year C)

The temptation narrative in Luke 4 continues the sequence of episodes from **4:1** Luke 3. Although there is a shift from John to Jesus, the location is basically the same: **the Jordan** and **the desert** (see 3:2–3). Moreover, the Spirit descended upon Jesus at his baptism, so now Jesus is **filled with the holy Spirit** and **led by the Spirit**.

As the "son of Adam" (3:38), Jesus is **tempted by the devil** as was Adam **4:2** (Gen 3). The word "devil" (*diabolos*), meaning "slanderer," is used in the †Septuagint to translate the Hebrew *satan*, meaning "adversary" (e.g., 1 Chron 21:1). With the article, it here refers to the chief adversary, the fallen angel (Luke 10:18), "the ancient serpent, who is called the Devil and Satan" (Rev 12:9, referring to Gen 3). Elsewhere in Luke, Jesus frequently mentions him and his nefarious activity (8:12; 11:18; 13:16; 22:31, 53), and his role in Jesus' betrayal will specifically be noted (22:3).

Besides recalling Adam's temptation, the passage echoes Israel's exodus and desert experience. All three—Adam, Israel, and Jesus—are tested as God's firstborn son (for Israel, see Exod 4:22; Deut 8:5). Having passed through water like Israel in the exodus, Jesus is tested throughout **forty days** in the desert, as the people of Israel were tested for forty years (Num 14:33–34; Deut 8:2).[25] Israel, like Adam in the garden, failed the test. Specifically, the three temptations over which Jesus is triumphant echo three failures of Israel: (1) when "in the desert they gave in to their cravings" (Ps 106:14) in their demands for food (Exod 16:3); (2) when "they forgot the God who had saved them" (Ps 106:21) and practiced idolatry (Exod 32:1–6); and (3) when they "tested" God

---

25. The verb *peirazō* (Luke 4:2) means both "tempt" and "test." God "tempts no one" (James 1:13) and does not let us be tested beyond our strength (1 Cor 10:13 NRSV). However, God tests individuals—e.g., by allowing them to be tempted by the devil.

(Ps 95:9; Exod 17:7).[26] Therefore, Jesus, who has come for Israel's consolation and redemption (Luke 2:25, 38) and is in solidarity with the people (3:21), fasts for forty days, eating **nothing during those days**, like Moses before him (Exod 34:28; Deut 9:18, 25; 10:10).

4:3   The first temptation, to **command this stone to become bread**, addresses Jesus' physical need for food. However, it runs deeper since it also regards Jesus' identity as **the Son of God** (see Luke 3:22). Will Jesus use his divine sonship to serve his own needs or those of others? Clearly, Jesus' mission is directed toward others: "He has sent me to proclaim liberty to captives" (4:18). His mission includes satisfying the hungry (6:21), multiplying bread (9:16–17), and, ultimately, changing bread into his body (22:19).

4:4   Jesus responds by quoting Scripture—**One does not live by bread alone** (see Deut 8:3)—a verse that recalls God's gift of manna to the Israelites in response to their hunger (Exod 16:4–35). Literally, the word translated "one" is a "human being" (*anthrōpos*). Jesus is indeed "Son of God," but he experienced temptation in the human nature he shares with all of humanity (Heb 2:14). The result is that because he was "tested . . . yet without sin" (Heb 4:15), "he is able to help those who are being tested" (Heb 2:18).

4:5–7   The devil then tempts Jesus with a vision of **all the kingdoms of the world** (*oikoumenē*), whose **power** (or "authority," RSV) and **glory** he promises to **give** to Jesus on condition that he **worship** him.[27] Jesus will indeed receive power, glory, and more (see Luke 21:27; 22:69), not from the devil but from God the Father (see 10:22), and his kingdom will last forever (see 1:32–33). However, in God's plan of salvation, Jesus must first experience the suffering of the cross (24:26). The temptation thus attempts to shortcut Jesus' mission. Moreover, it focuses on power understood in a worldly sense, like that of Caesar Augustus, who can issue decrees concerning the whole "world" (*oikoumenē*, 2:1). However, Jesus is not a king like these earthly rulers but one who proclaims the kingdom of God (4:43). He has an authority more far-reaching than theirs (4:32, 36; 5:24; 20:8). His glory will be that of God the Father (9:26).

4:8   Again, Jesus replies quoting Deuteronomy: **You shall worship the Lord, your God, / and him alone shall you serve** (see Deut 6:13). The word "worship" answers the devil's temptation. Jesus quotes from the same chapter in which is found the †*Shema* prayer recited twice daily by devout Jews: "Hear,

---

26. David E. Garland, *Luke*, ZECNT (Grand Rapids: Zondervan, 2011), 178.

27. The devil claims that this power **has been handed over** to him. In God's plan to bring good even out of evil (see Rom 8:28), the devil has been permitted a measure of power, and Scripture refers to him as the ruler of this world (see John 12:31; 14:30; 16:11; Eph 2:2; 6:12; 1 John 5:19). However, he remains a creature subject to God's power (Catechism 395), which overcomes him (John 16:33; 1 John 4:4).

O Israel! The Lord is our God, the Lord alone!" (Deut 6:4). Since Jesus is the Son of God (Luke 1:32, 35; 3:22) and has already been identified as Lord (1:43; 2:11), he can indeed be "worshiped," as the disciples will do at the end of the Gospel (24:52 NRSV).

Luke has the same three temptations as Matthew, but recounts them in a differ- **4:9** ent order because of the different role the passage has in the overall Gospel narrative. In Matthew, the third and climactic temptation is the one just considered, which takes place on a mountain (Matt 4:8) and finds its answer in Matthew's concluding mountain scene, where Jesus is worshiped (28:16–17). In Luke, the climactic temptation occurs in **the temple** in **Jerusalem**, the place where Luke's Gospel both begins (Luke 1:9) and ends (24:53). Rather than throwing himself **down** from the temple's highest point, **the parapet**,[28] Jesus at the end of the Gospel is "taken up to heaven" (24:51). The temptation involves his identity as **Son of God**, and with his ascension Jesus is vindicated as "Son of the Most High" (1:32).

In order to bolster his third temptation, the devil tries Jesus' tactic of quoting **4:10–11** Scripture, citing two consecutive verses of a psalm (Ps 91:11–12). However, the devil has chosen the wrong psalm, as its following verse predicts his own demise: "You can tread upon the asp and the viper, / trample the lion and the dragon" (Ps 91:13). Jesus not only fulfills this verse, which recalls the promise of victory after the fall (Gen 3:15), but will refer to it when he shares with his disciples this "power 'to tread upon serpents' . . . and upon the full force of the enemy" (Luke 10:19).

Not engaging the devil's misinterpretation of the psalm, Jesus again replies **4:12** quoting Deuteronomy: **You shall not put the Lord, your God, to the test** (see Deut 6:16). Israel had tested the Lord God at Massah (Deut 6:16; see Exod 17:7). However, Jesus is the Lord (Luke 1:43; 2:11) being put to the test here, so with these words, he puts an end to the devil's temptations.

The devil, thwarted three times by Jesus, thus **departed** from him. Jesus' **4:13** experience provides a lesson to his followers: "Resist the devil, and he will flee from you" (James 4:7). However, the devil will have his opportunity after **a time**, when he enters into Judas (Luke 22:3) at the dark "hour" of Jesus' passion (22:53).

Reflection and Application (4:1–13)

Spiritual training. Jesus' three temptations have been compared[29] to the three temptations—for sensual gratification (gluttony, lust), for power and riches

---

28. "The parapet" may refer to the temple's southeastern corner. Josephus, *Jewish Antiquities* 15.412, comments on the dizzying height of the royal portico over the deep Kidron Valley below.

29. E.g., Bonaventure, *Commentary on the Gospel of Luke* 4.8, 23, ed. and trans. Robert J. Karris, 3 vols. (St. Bonaventure, NY: The Franciscan Institute, 2001–4), 1:296–97, 311.

(avarice), and for ostentatious display (pride, vainglory)—against which Christians are warned in 1 John: "the lust of the flesh and the lust of the eyes and the pride of life" (1 John 2:16 RSV). These correspond to the original temptations in Genesis: "The woman saw that the tree was good for food, and that it was a delight to the eyes, and that the tree was to be desired to make one wise" (Gen 3:6 RSV). Remedies for these three temptations are the three practices especially observed during Lent: fasting, almsgiving, and prayer. Scripture commends such exercises of spiritual training (Matt 6:1–18; 1 Cor 9:25–27; 1 Tim 4:7–8). By fasting and other acts of self-denial, we learn self-control. By almsgiving, we practice detachment from material things and avoid creating false needs for ourselves. By prayer, especially using the Scriptures as Jesus did, we humble ourselves before God, relying on his grace.

Jesus' Mission as Messiah

Luke 4:14–44

Jesus' public ministry in Galilee now begins, introducing a large section of Luke's Gospel (4:14–9:50). At the beginning of this section, Luke presents a two-part panel or diptych: Jesus' ministry in Nazareth (4:16–30) and Capernaum (4:31–43). Similar introductory and concluding verses frame the two passages (4:14–15, 44). The focus in Nazareth is on Jesus' words, and in Capernaum on his deeds. Jesus' proclamation in Nazareth is the mission statement that provides the key for understanding his mission as Messiah. In fulfillment of Isaiah's prophecies, Jesus proclaims a jubilee that brings liberty from the power of evil. This mission then begins to unfold through his healing miracles in Capernaum. However, the reactions to Jesus differ: he is driven out of Nazareth (4:24, 29), but the people of Capernaum seek to keep him from leaving (4:42).

Jesus Proclaims the Jubilee in Nazareth (4:14–30)

¹⁴Jesus returned to Galilee in the power of the Spirit, and news of him spread throughout the whole region. ¹⁵He taught in their synagogues and was praised by all.
   ¹⁶He came to Nazareth, where he had grown up, and went according to his custom into the synagogue on the sabbath day. He stood up to read ¹⁷and was handed a scroll of the prophet Isaiah. He unrolled the scroll and found the passage where it was written:

> [18]"The Spirit of the Lord is upon me,
>   because he has anointed me
>   to bring glad tidings to the poor.
> He has sent me to proclaim liberty to captives
>   and recovery of sight to the blind,
>   to let the oppressed go free,
> [19]and to proclaim a year acceptable to the Lord."

[20]Rolling up the scroll, he handed it back to the attendant and sat down, and the eyes of all in the synagogue looked intently at him. [21]He said to them, "Today this scripture passage is fulfilled in your hearing." [22]And all spoke highly of him and were amazed at the gracious words that came from his mouth. They also asked, "Isn't this the son of Joseph?" [23]He said to them, "Surely you will quote me this proverb, 'Physician, cure yourself,' and say, 'Do here in your native place the things that we heard were done in Capernaum.'" [24]And he said, "Amen, I say to you, no prophet is accepted in his own native place. [25]Indeed, I tell you, there were many widows in Israel in the days of Elijah when the sky was closed for three and a half years and a severe famine spread over the entire land. [26]It was to none of these that Elijah was sent, but only to a widow in Zarephath in the land of Sidon. [27]Again, there were many lepers in Israel during the time of Elisha the prophet; yet not one of them was cleansed, but only Naaman the Syrian." [28]When the people in the synagogue heard this, they were all filled with fury. [29]They rose up, drove him out of the town, and led him to the brow of the hill on which their town had been built, to hurl him down headlong. [30]But he passed through the midst of them and went away.

OT: Lev 25:8–55; 1 Kings 17:8–24; 2 Kings 5:1–15; Isa 58:6; 61:1–2

NT: Luke 3:22–23; James 5:17. // Matt 4:12; 13:54–58; Mark 1:14; 6:1–6; John 4:43–44

Catechism: Messiah, 436, 695, 1286; good news to the poor, 544, 714, 2443; the liturgical year, 1168

Lectionary: Luke 4:16–21: Chrism Mass; Institution of Readers; Luke 4:14–21: Third Sunday Ordinary Time (Year C); Luke 4:21–30: Fourth Sunday Ordinary Time (Year C); Luke 4:14–22: Thursday after Epiphany; Luke 4:24–30: Monday Third Week of Lent; Luke 4:16–22: Confirmation

4:14–15   **In the power of the Spirit** (see 3:22; 4:1), Jesus travels back north from Judea to **Galilee**. He begins his public ministry by teaching in the Jewish **synagogues**. He quickly draws attention, and **news** of his activity goes out **throughout the whole region** (also 4:37; 5:15; 7:17).

4:16   Jesus returns to **Nazareth** and, **according to his custom**, goes **into the synagogue on the sabbath**. Luke places this visit right at the beginning of his account of Jesus' public ministry (compare Matt 13:54–58; Mark 6:1–6) because Jesus' proclamation in the synagogue sets the program for the rest of his ministry.

In the town **where he had grown up** and the synagogue where he had studied Scripture, Jesus now stands up during the service **to read** from the Scriptures.

Luke captures the drama of the moment, lingering over each of Jesus' actions. **4:17** After "he stood up," Jesus **was handed a scroll**, then **unrolled the scroll**. After the reading, these three actions will be reversed (Luke 4:20). The effect is to highlight the reading, which stands in the center. The scroll is of **the prophet Isaiah**, and Jesus finds **the passage** (Isa 61:1–2) that explains his mission. John the Baptist's mission was similarly explained using Isaiah (Luke 3:4–6).

Applying the first-person text to himself (see v. 21), Jesus confirms with his **4:18–19** own words what earlier events had revealed about his *identity*: **The Spirit of the Lord is upon me / because he has anointed me** (see Isa 61:1). At his baptism, the Spirit had indeed descended "upon him" (Luke 3:22). Jesus the Spirit-filled Messiah is thus like David (see 1:32, 69; 2:4): "Samuel, with the horn of oil in hand, anointed him in the midst of his brothers, and from that day on, the spirit of the LORD rushed upon David" (1 Sam 16:13).

The rest of the Isaiah passage regards Jesus' *mission*, which involves both *words* and *deeds*. Regarding his *words*, Jesus has been **sent** in order **to bring glad tidings** (verb *euangelizō*) and **to proclaim** (verb *kēryssō* in Luke 4:18 and 19, sometimes translated "preach"). At the end of the chapter, as Jesus goes around "preaching," he will repeat that he has been sent to "proclaim the good news" (4:43–44; see 7:22; 8:1; 20:1). These key verbs are related to the nouns "gospel" (*euangelion*) and "gospel proclamation" (*kērygma*) (see Rom 16:25). The book of Isaiah is thus fittingly called the "Old Testament Gospel" because of its proclamation of good news (Isa 40:9; 52:7; 61:1 LXX; see comment on Luke 2:10).

The privileged recipients of Jesus' proclamation will be **the poor** (6:20; 7:22). These are the †*anawim* (Isa 61:1), who are materially poor (Luke 16:20; 21:2) and humbly look to God—and now to Jesus—to provide what they need. However, Jesus will also reach out to those who are spiritually poor but perhaps materially wealthy: tax collectors and sinners (5:27–32; 7:29; 15:1; 19:1–10).

The content of Jesus' preaching is his proclamation of **liberty** (*aphesis*). This phrase from the Isaiah passage points back to an important verse in Leviticus: "You shall *proclaim liberty* in the land for all its inhabitants. It shall be a jubilee for you" (Lev 25:10 [emphasis added]). During a jubilee year (see the sidebar, "Jubilee Year," p. 101), those in debt-slavery were set free. Thus, what Jesus is announcing in Nazareth is the definitive time of jubilee! His ministry will be one of granting liberty to those "in debt" on account of their "sins" (see Luke 7:41–48). Indeed, Jesus will especially set people free through the forgiveness (same word *aphesis*) of their sins (24:47; also 5:20; 7:48, which use the related verb *aphiēmi*, "forgive").

Moreover, regarding Jesus' *deeds*, Jesus will set people free by physical healings—for example, Peter's mother-in-law (see comment on Luke 4:39). Powerful miracles will bring liberty to the **captives**—for instance, the woman who is set free by Jesus from her bondage to Satan (13:16; see 4:35, 41). Jesus will thus bring about Israel's restoration from its true exile, in fulfillment of Isaiah's prophecies: "Loose the bonds from your neck, / captive daughter Zion!" (Isa 52:2). Other healing miracles will include giving **sight to the blind** (Luke 7:21–22; 18:35–43; see Isa 35:5).

The next phrase is inserted from another chapter of Isaiah: **to let the oppressed go free** (see Isa 58:6). It is better rendered "to set at liberty those who are oppressed" (Luke 4:18 RSV), so as to show the repetition of the word "liberty" (*aphesis*). This is an example of what the rabbis would later call the rule of *gezerah shawah*, by which two similar texts linked by a common word could be used to interpret one another. The word "liberty" (*aphesis*) links the two passages—Isa 61:1 and 58:6—as found in the †Septuagint of Isaiah. The Hebrew text of Isaiah has two different words, but nonetheless the two passages may have been associated with one another because of common themes.[1]

The end of the reading goes back to Isaiah 61 and again refers to the jubilee, the **year acceptable to the Lord** (Isa 61:2 LXX).

4:20   After the reading, the three actions before the reading are reversed: **rolling up the scroll, he handed it back to the attendant and sat down**. By sitting, Jesus prepares to teach the people (see Luke 5:3; Matt 5:1), and they in turn fix their **eyes** on him as they await his words. Earlier, the elderly Simeon understood that his "eyes" had seen God's salvation (Luke 2:30). Will the people of Nazareth likewise understand?

4:21   Jesus makes a bombshell announcement: **Today this scripture passage is fulfilled in your hearing**. With Jesus, the time of waiting for the fulfillment of God's promises in the Scriptures is over (see 24:27, 44). The messianic jubilee announced by Isaiah is at hand! "Behold, now is the acceptable time" (2 Cor 6:2 RSV). Here and later in his ministry, Jesus will emphasize that God's blessings are available "today" (see Luke 19:5, 9; 23:43). Moreover, the fulfillment takes place, literally, in their "ears" (KJV). The people should thus consider themselves "blessed" (see 10:23–24) for seeing Jesus with their "eyes" (4:20)

1. François Bovon, *Luke*, trans. Christine M. Thomas, Donald S. Deer, and James Crouch, 3 vols., Hermeneia (Minneapolis: Fortress, 2002–13), 1:153.

Jubilee Year

In the exodus, God freed the people of Israel from *slavery* in Egypt and gave them the promised *land*. So that Israelites might continue living in this freedom (see Lev 25:38, 42, 55), the Torah provided a way for those who sold their ancestral *land* and were reduced to *slavery* because of debts to regain their property and liberty (Lev 25:8–55). The fiftieth year, following seven weeks of years, was this year of jubilee: "You shall proclaim liberty in the land for all its inhabitants. It shall be a jubilee for you, when each of you shall return to your own property, each of you to your own family" (Lev 25:10). An indentured Israelite could also be liberated by being redeemed by a kinsman (Hebrew *go'el*, Lev 25:25–26). There was in addition a year of remission of debts for the poor every seven years (Deut 15:1–11).

In the second part of Isaiah (Isa 40–66), the jubilee concept is applied to the people as a whole to describe the return of Israel's exiles to the land. The Lord God is portrayed as Israel's kinsman redeemer (*go'el*) who frees Israel from the slavery caused by debts—that is, the exile caused by sins (Isa 49:7–9; 50:1). It is also applied to individuals: the jubilee is a time for "releasing those bound unjustly" and "setting free the oppressed" (Isa 58:6). Moreover, Isaiah interprets the jubilee in connection with the messiah: the Lord's "anointed" is the one who will "proclaim liberty" and "announce a year of favor from the LORD" (Isa 61:1–2). The jubilee law thus becomes a prophecy for Israel's future restoration: the messiah will come as the kinsman who redeems the enslaved people, ushering in a jubilee age of liberty. For example, a document found at Qumran combines the jubilee (Lev 25) and the year of remission (Deut 15), interpreting debts spiritually in terms of sins; a priest-king Melchizedek (see Gen 14; Ps 110) will come to proclaim "liberty" and "to free them from . . . all their iniquities."[a] This background helps to understand how Luke presents Jesus, in his reading of Isaiah in Nazareth, as the fulfillment of these expectations of a messiah-redeemer who proclaims the jubilee.[b]

a. 11Q13 (*Melchizedek*) II, 1–6, in *The Dead Sea Scrolls Study Edition*, ed. Florentino García Martínez and Eibert J. C. Tigchelaar, 2 vols. (Leiden: Brill; Grand Rapids: Eerdmans, 2000), 2:1207.

b. For the ideas in this sidebar, see John Sietze Bergsma, *The Jubilee from Leviticus to Qumran: A History of Interpretation* (Leiden: Brill, 2007), 104–5, 191–203, 277–304.

and hearing him with their ears. However, Jesus will twice warn that those with "ears to hear ought to hear" (8:8; 14:35). Will the people of Nazareth take heed?

Initially, they do: **all spoke highly of him**. The verb *martyreō* here, meaning **4:22** "bear witness, testify," is used frequently in Acts when referring to individuals who are "well-spoken of" by the people (see Acts 6:3; 10:22; 16:2; 22:12). The people are **amazed at the gracious words** of Jesus, witnessing to the power of his preached word (see Luke 4:32).

However, the people are also perplexed: **Isn't this the son of Joseph?** This is what "was thought" (3:23), though the reader knows quite well that Jesus is the Son of God (1:32, 35; 3:22). Despite the Davidic lineage of people in Nazareth (see comment on 1:26–27), perhaps Jesus' origins were simply too humble for him to be considered the Messiah. The parallel passages say that "they took offense at him" (Matt 13:57; Mark 6:3).

4:23   Only Luke the physician (Col 4:14) records Jesus' **proverb, "Physician, cure yourself."** Jesus interprets the people's reaction as a demand for a sign from him, like those that **were done in Capernaum**. Unlike Matthew and Mark, Luke has not yet specifically recounted **the things** Jesus did in Capernaum (see Luke 4:31–41; 7:1–10), although Jesus has already been active in many towns of Galilee (4:14–15). Luke recounts this Nazareth scene first because it provides the key for understanding the events of Jesus' ministry.

4:24   Jesus continues with the first of his six **Amen** sayings in Luke (12:37; 18:17, 29; 21:32; 23:43). Beginning a sentence with this Hebrew word emphasizes the truth of the statement that follows. Jesus gives a general principle that **no prophet is accepted** (or "acceptable," RSV) in his hometown, implying that he is himself a prophet (see 7:16, 39; 9:8, 19; 13:33; 24:19). Jesus has just proclaimed the jubilee, the year "acceptable" (4:19) to the Lord, but now he is the one not "acceptable." This occurs **in his own native place**, precisely where the law said that one returns during a jubilee (Lev 25:10 LXX). With this ironic play on words, Jesus is about to issue his Jewish listeners "a prophetic challenge"[2] regarding the scope of the jubilee.

4:25–26   Calling on two Old Testament prophets as supporting witnesses (see Deut 19:15), Jesus the prophet explains that the blessings of the messianic jubilee apply not only to Israel but also to the Gentiles (see Luke 2:32). First, **Elijah** worked a miracle for a Gentile **widow in Zarephath in the land of Sidon**, enabling her and her son to survive a **famine** (1 Kings 17:8–16).

4:27   Second, **Elisha** worked a miracle for the Gentile **Naaman the Syrian**, who was **cleansed** of his leprosy (2 Kings 5:1–14). These two Gentiles—a woman and a man in typically Lukan fashion—even end up acknowledging the God of Israel (1 Kings 17:24; 2 Kings 5:15), foreshadowing how in Jesus the Gentiles will be led to worship the one true God. Indeed, at the end of the Gospel, Jesus

---

2. Craig A. Evans and James A. Sanders, *Luke and Scripture: The Function of Sacred Tradition in Luke-Acts* (Minneapolis: Fortress, 1993), 23, 69, 76.

will commission his disciples to extend the jubilee proclamation of forgiveness (*aphesis*) "to all the nations" (Luke 24:47).

Jesus' comparison with Elijah and Elisha also sets the stage for understanding his later deeds in light of these two Old Testament prophets (e.g., 5:12–14; 7:1–10, 11–17; 17:11–19). Thus, Jesus fulfills not only prophetic *texts* such as Isaiah 61 (Luke 4:21) but also prophetic †*types* such as Elijah and Elisha.

Jesus' scriptural argument for inclusion of the Gentiles **filled** his listeners **with**   4:28
fury, since it challenged their understanding of Israel's status as God's chosen people. Certainly, various Old Testament texts promised that the Gentiles would be included in God's plan of salvation (e.g., Isa 2:2–4) and even that Israel's restoration would occur with the help of Gentiles (e.g., Isa 60:1–9). However, the experience of oppression by Gentiles, such as the Romans, led many to expect that the Gentiles would not be saved but rather would be crushed in the coming "day of vindication" of God (Isa 61:2), a phrase Jesus did not include in his reading (Luke 4:19).

Perhaps considering Jesus to be a false prophet who must die (see Deut   4:29
18:20), the people sought **to hurl him down headlong** from **the brow of the hill**. Though Jesus' public ministry has just begun, his death is already foreshadowed. Simeon had indeed predicted that Jesus would be "a sign that will be contradicted" (Luke 2:34). The power of evil stands behind such opposition: the devil had told Jesus, "throw yourself down" (4:9), and now the people try to do just that to him.

Since Jesus the prophet can only die in Jerusalem (13:33), he escapes this   4:30
attempt on his life. **He passed through the midst of them and went away**, apparently never to return to Nazareth.

In summary, Jesus' Nazareth discourse is indeed a mission statement that sets the program of his ministry of preaching and healing. It presents the gospel in miniature: Jesus the Messiah fulfills Scripture, preaches good news to the poor, gives sight to the blind, proclaims liberty to usher in the jubilee, restores Israel's captives, reaches out to the Gentiles, and finally experiences rejection but escapes, thus foreshadowing his death and resurrection.

Reflection and Application (4:18–21)

Proclaiming liberty. St. John Paul II led the Church in celebrating the Great Jubilee of the year 2000. Pope Francis called an Extraordinary Jubilee of Mercy for 2016. The Church's celebration of jubilee years reminds us that the jubilee proclaimed by Jesus is ongoing. Jesus is still bringing liberty to captives and forgiveness of sins to those who repent and believe in him (Acts 2:38; 10:43; 13:38–39).

Jesus Works Miracles in Capernaum (4:31–44)

---

³¹Jesus then went down to Capernaum, a town of Galilee. He taught them on the sabbath, ³²and they were astonished at his teaching because he spoke with authority. ³³In the synagogue there was a man with the spirit of an unclean demon, and he cried out in a loud voice, ³⁴"Ha! What have you to do with us, Jesus of Nazareth? Have you come to destroy us? I know who you are—the Holy One of God!" ³⁵Jesus rebuked him and said, "Be quiet! Come out of him!" Then the demon threw the man down in front of them and came out of him without doing him any harm. ³⁶They were all amazed and said to one another, "What is there about his word? For with authority and power he commands the unclean spirits, and they come out." ³⁷And news of him spread everywhere in the surrounding region.

³⁸After he left the synagogue, he entered the house of Simon. Simon's mother-in-law was afflicted with a severe fever, and they interceded with him about her. ³⁹He stood over her, rebuked the fever, and it left her. She got up immediately and waited on them.

⁴⁰At sunset, all who had people sick with various diseases brought them to him. He laid his hands on each of them and cured them. ⁴¹And demons also came out from many, shouting, "You are the Son of God." But he rebuked them and did not allow them to speak because they knew that he was the Messiah.

⁴²At daybreak, Jesus left and went to a deserted place. The crowds went looking for him, and when they came to him, they tried to prevent him from leaving them. ⁴³But he said to them, "To the other towns also I must proclaim the good news of the kingdom of God, because for this purpose I have been sent." ⁴⁴And he was preaching in the synagogues of Judea.

NT: Matt 4:13; 7:28–29; Luke 8:28; John 2:12; Acts 16:16–18. // Matt 4:23; 8:14–17; Mark 1:21–39
Catechism: exorcisms 550, 1673; laying on of hands, 1519

The last part of Luke 4 closely parallels Mark's Gospel (Mark 1:21–39), yet the context for understanding it is unique to Luke—namely, Jesus' preceding discourse in Nazareth. The mission outlined in Nazareth begins to unfold through Jesus' healing ministry in Capernaum.

4:31–32   **Capernaum** (see 4:23; 7:1; 10:15), in Herod's region of **Galilee** (3:1), was a small fishing **town** on the northwestern shore of the Sea of Galilee, about a twenty-five-mile walk from Nazareth.[3] **On the sabbath**, Jesus continues his customary practice of **teaching** (4:15–16). Like the residents of Nazareth who were "amazed" at Jesus' "words" (4:22), the people of Capernaum are **astonished** because **he spoke with authority** (literally, "his word" had authority). Jesus' word has authority even to expel unclean spirits (vv. 35–36), heal the sick (v. 39), and forgive sins (5:24). This "authority" was obviously not given to him by the devil (see 4:6 RSV) but is being used *against* the forces of the devil.

In Capernaum, under the ruins of a fifth-century white limestone **synagogue**, one can see the foundation of a first-century black basalt synagogue, perhaps the one built by the local centurion (7:5). $\qquad$ 4:33–34

The recollected atmosphere of the synagogue on this sabbath is disturbed by the cries of **a man with the spirit of an unclean demon**. In this first of Jesus' exorcisms, Luke uses a redundant expression to clarify for his Gentile readers that *daimonion* ("demon") here refers not to a deity (see Acts 17:18) but to an evil spirit. The demon responds with an idiomatic phrase—**What have you to do with us?** (see Luke 8:28)—which in this case means, "Leave us alone!" (NET). Though powerless before Jesus, the demon expresses awareness of Jesus' mission—**Have you come to destroy us?**—and of his identity as **the Holy One of God** (see 1:35). Elisha was called "a holy man of God" (2 Kings 4:9), and Jesus has just compared himself to Elisha (Luke 4:27). The title may therefore highlight Jesus' role as a *prophet* (4:24). Another possibility is that Jesus is implicitly presented as a *priest*, like Aaron, "the holy one of the LORD" (Ps 106:16; see Exod 28:36; Num 16:7).[4] Indeed, the high priest Aaron is responsible for separating the clean from the unclean (Lev 10:10), as Jesus will do in expelling the unclean demon.

Jesus **rebuked** the evil spirit, restoring the man not with a magical incantation (see Acts 8:9–11; 13:6; 19:19) but by the authority of his word. His commands— **Be quiet! Come out of him!**—expel the demon and also impose silence (see Luke 4:41), so that Jesus' identity may be revealed in a fitting manner and at the proper time. $\qquad$ 4:35

The people, again **amazed** by **his word** that has both **authority and power** (v. 32), continue to **spread** reports about Jesus (see 4:14; 5:15; 7:17). $\qquad$ 4:36–37

---

3. Capernaum (estimated population 1,000) was larger than Nazareth (400), but smaller than cities like Tiberias and Sepphoris (8,000). See Sharon Lea Mattila, "Revisiting Jesus' Capernaum: A Village of Only Subsistence-Level Fishers and Farmers?," in *The Galilean Economy in the Time of Jesus*, ed. David A. Fiensy and Ralph K. Hawkins (Atlanta: Society of Biblical Literature, 2013), 85.

4. On the parallel in Mark 1:24, see Joel Marcus, *Mark*, 2 vols., AB (New York: Doubleday, 2000–2009), 1:188.

Synagogues

BIBLICAL BACKGROUND

Besides the synagogues in Nazareth (Luke 4:16) and Capernaum (4:33), Jesus taught in other synagogues (4:15, 44; 6:6; 13:10). Some possibilities are Magdala (8:2), where the ruins of a first-century synagogue have been discovered, and Chorazin (10:13). A synagogue was a multipurpose gathering place for the Jewish people of a town. On the sabbath and feast days, they gathered for Scripture reading and prayer, sitting on tiered benches along the walls. The sabbath service included readings from the Torah and the prophets (Acts 13:15, 27; 15:21), followed by a teaching explaining the Scriptures (Luke 4:20–22; Acts 13:15–16). The services were organized by a synagogue official (*archisynagōgos*, Luke 8:49; 13:14; Acts 18:8, 17), who might also be a priest. He was assisted in his duties by elders (Luke 7:3) and an attendant (4:20). Prayer in the synagogue was spiritually united to the central worship in the Jerusalem temple, with its animal sacrifices (2:24; 22:7), incense offerings (1:8–10), and pilgrimages for the feasts of Passover (2:41; 22:7), Pentecost (Acts 2:1; 20:16), and Tabernacles (John 7:2).[a]

a. For many of the ideas in this sidebar, see Rachel Hachlili, *Ancient Synagogues—Archaeology and Art: New Discoveries and Current Research* (Leiden: Brill, 2013), 5–54.

4:38   The exorcism is followed by a related healing miracle. Jesus **left the synagogue** or, more literally, "arose and left." He then entered **the house of Simon** nearby. The Simon mentioned here for the first time is of course Simon Peter (5:8) or simply "Peter" (8:45). Archaeologists have uncovered what was possibly his house in a group of basalt homes only thirty yards away from the synagogue.[5] Simon's call will be recounted in the next chapter (5:1–11), unlike in Matthew and Mark, where it precedes the healing of his **mother-in-law** who is ill with **a severe fever**. Those in the house **interceded** with Jesus, expressing in this way their faith in his ability to heal.

4:39   Jesus **rebuked the fever** as he had "rebuked" the demon (4:35) (a detail not found in the †synoptic parallels), indicating that the two miracles should be considered together. Illness, whether physical or psychological, is very different from demonic possession (see Catechism 1673). The oppression caused by evil spirits can, however, have harmful effects on the body, as indicated later in the story of the crippled woman (13:11, 16; see Catechism 395). Moreover, illness, with its ultimate consequence, death, is an evil from which Jesus the "physician"

5. Mattila, "Revisiting Jesus' Capernaum," 79, 82.

(4:23) liberates human beings. In this case, again in response to Jesus' powerful word, **it left her**. The verb here is *aphiēmi*, related to the "liberty" (*aphesis*) proclaimed by Jesus "to captives" (4:18).[6] With these miracles on a sabbath (v. 31), which free people from captivity to both demons and diseases, Jesus is advancing his program of jubilee liberation, announced on a sabbath (4:16–19).

The healing occurs **immediately** (see 5:25; 8:44, 55; 13:13; 18:43). **She got up** or, more literally, "she arose" (*anistēmi*, just as in v. 38 for Jesus), the same verb used later for Jesus' resurrection (18:33; 24:7, 46). Like Jesus and because of Jesus, his followers will experience a resurrected new life, as the woman did. In gratitude, she **waited on them**. Her response is one of service (see 8:3), by which she also imitates Jesus (22:27).

The exorcism of the man and the healing of the woman are just a sample **4:40–41** of Jesus' wider ministry of healing and exorcisms. Once the sabbath is over **at sunset**, people are permitted to carry things and travel greater distances (see Acts 1:12), so they bring to Jesus those who are **sick with various diseases**. Giving **each of them** personalized attention, he **cured them** as **he laid his hands on** them. He uses this gesture again later in his healing ministry (Luke 13:13), as do his disciples (Acts 9:12, 17; 28:8). There are also more exorcisms of **demons**. The same pattern occurs as in the synagogue: **because they knew** his identity, Jesus **rebuked** them and silenced them. The demons—fallen angels—call Jesus **Son of God** and **Messiah**, the same titles that angels have earlier revealed (Luke 1:35; 2:11), but which will be revealed later to the people.

The next morning, **at daybreak**, Jesus leaves Capernaum for **a deserted** **4:42** **place**. In the parallel verse, Mark indicates that Jesus went to pray (Mark 1:35). In the next chapter, Luke will explain that it was Jesus' custom to "withdraw to deserted places to pray" (Luke 5:16). Undoubtedly because of the many miracles they have seen, **the crowds** seek **to prevent him from leaving**. Their reaction is just the opposite of that of the people of Nazareth.

However, neither rejection nor popularity determines Jesus' actions. Rather, **4:43–44** he **must** (see comment on 2:49) carry out the mission for which he was **sent**, as described in his mission statement in Nazareth: to **proclaim the good news** by **preaching** (see 4:18–19). Jesus continues to preach **in the synagogues**, a comment that echoes the earlier remark (4:15) and thus serves to frame these passages (4:14–44). Whereas the parallel verse indicates Jesus' preaching in *Galilee* (Mark 1:39), Luke writes **Judea**, probably using the word here in its

---

6. In the parallels, the explicit subject of the verb *aphiēmi* is "the fever" (Matt 8:15; Mark 1:31). However, it is not explicit in Luke, so grammatically it could be the same subject ("Jesus") as the previous phrase: "He rebuked the fever and set her free" (see Ps 105:20 LXX).

broader sense (inclusive of Galilee) as a general designation for the land of the Jews (see Luke 23:5; Acts 10:37).

The content of the gospel message that Jesus preaches is **the kingdom of God**. This kingdom counters the devil and his temptation regarding "all the kingdoms of the world" (Luke 4:5). As Jesus' ministry of exorcism and healing unfolds, the kingdom of God advances and the devil's dominion must retreat.

Calling Disciples and Answering Pharisees

Luke 5:1–6:11

As his mission unfolds through his teaching and miracles, Jesus calls disciples to join him: Simon Peter, James, John, and Levi. They respond in a radical way, leaving everything to follow him. However, not everyone responds so favorably. In five consecutive controversies, Pharisees question Jesus' words and actions. In his responses, Jesus provides glimpses of his identity, referring to himself as Son of Man, physician, and bridegroom. Others express insight about Jesus as they begin to address him as Lord.

Simon Peter and the Catch of Fish (5:1–11)

¹While the crowd was pressing in on Jesus and listening to the word of God, he was standing by the Lake of Gennesaret. ²He saw two boats there alongside the lake; the fishermen had disembarked and were washing their nets. ³Getting into one of the boats, the one belonging to Simon, he asked him to put out a short distance from the shore. Then he sat down and taught the crowds from the boat. ⁴After he had finished speaking, he said to Simon, "Put out into deep water and lower your nets for a catch." ⁵Simon said in reply, "Master, we have worked hard all night and have caught nothing, but at your command I will lower the nets." ⁶When they had done this, they caught a great number of fish and their nets were tearing. ⁷They signaled to their partners in the other boat to come to help them. They came and filled both boats so that they were in danger of sinking. ⁸When Simon Peter saw this, he fell at the knees of Jesus and said,

"Depart from me, Lord, for I am a sinful man." [9]For astonishment at the catch of fish they had made seized him and all those with him, [10]and likewise James and John, the sons of Zebedee, who were partners of Simon. Jesus said to Simon, "Do not be afraid; from now on you will be catching men." [11]When they brought their boats to the shore, they left everything and followed him.

OT: Isa 6:1–8; Jer 16:16
NT: John 1:41–42; 21:1–19. // Matt 4:18–22; Mark 1:16–20
Catechism: God's presence in Jesus, 208; the Church is apostolic, 863
Lectionary: Fifth Sunday Ordinary Time (Year C); Admission to Candidacy for Diaconate and Priesthood

5:1–3   Jesus is again teaching, but this time not in a synagogue (4:15–16, 31–33, 44). Rather, he is by the **Lake of Gennesaret**, with **two boats** and **fishermen** nearby. The **crowd** is **listening** to Jesus preach **the word of God**. The frequent combination of the verb "listen, hear" with the phrase "the word of God" emphasizes that listening is the first step in the human response to God (8:11–15, 21; 11:28; Acts 13:7).[1] Among the bystanders is **Simon**, who has already hosted Jesus at his house (Luke 4:38) and is now in the midst of his work as a fisherman. Since the crowd is **pressing in** on Jesus, he gets into Simon's boat in order to be seen and heard more easily **a short distance from the shore** (Matt 13:1–2; Mark 4:1). Jesus **sat down**, the traditional posture for teaching (Luke 4:20; Matt 5:1).

5:4–5   Jesus has a further reason for getting into Simon's boat. He tells him: **put out into deep water** (literally, "put out into the deep," RSV). The accompanying instruction to **lower your nets for a catch** is in the plural and so includes others in Simon's boat (perhaps his brother Andrew; see Matt 4:18; Mark 1:16). Simon's experience of a **night** of fruitless toil—catching **nothing**—would suggest to him that it is pointless to try again. Nonetheless, he obeys: **at your command I will lower the nets**. Simon is thus one of the first to listen to Jesus' words and act on them (see Luke 6:47). His response is one of trusting faith in Jesus' "command" (literally, "word"). Earlier in the Gospel, Mary accepted in faith the "word" spoken to her by the angel (1:38). Now, Simon similarly accepts the "word" of Jesus.

5:6–7   Simon's obedient response leads to an abundant yield: **they caught a great number of fish**, filling **both boats**. The miracle looks ahead to the missionary task of Peter and the Church (see v. 10).[2] Moreover, the two boats may refer to

---

1. On listening to Jesus' words, see Luke 6:47; 10:39.
2. Markus Bockmuehl, *Simon Peter in Scripture and Memory: The New Testament Apostle in the Early Church* (Grand Rapids: Baker Academic, 2012), 116–17. John's Gospel recounts a post-resurrection miraculous catch of fish, which similarly points to the mission of Peter and the Church (John 21:1–19).

Duc in Altum! "Put Out into the Deep!"

The words of Jesus to Peter are still relevant today, as recent successors of Peter have explained. After the Jubilee Year 2000, St. John Paul II wrote:

> At the beginning of the new millennium . . . our hearts ring out with the words of Jesus when one day, after speaking to the crowds from Simon's boat, he invited the Apostle to "put out into the deep" for a catch: "*Duc in altum*" (Luke 5:4). Peter and his first companions trusted Christ's words, and cast the nets. . . . Now we must look ahead, we must "put out into the deep," trusting in Christ's words: *Duc in altum!* . . . This is the moment of faith . . . in order to open our hearts to the tide of grace and allow the word of Christ to pass through us in all its power: *Duc in altum!*[a]

In his inaugural homily, Pope Benedict XVI similarly commented:

> Today, too, the Church and the successors of the apostles are told to put out into the deep sea of history and to let down the nets, so as to win men and women over to the gospel—to God, to Christ, to true life. . . . There is nothing more beautiful than to be surprised by the gospel, by the encounter with Christ. There is nothing more beautiful than to know him and to speak to others of our friendship with him.[b]

a. John Paul II, *Novo Millennio Ineunte* 1, 15, 38.
b. Benedict XVI, homily for the inauguration of his pontificate, April 24, 2005, in *The Essential Pope Benedict XVI: His Central Writings and Speeches*, ed. John F. Thornton and Susan B. Varenne (New York: HarperCollins, 2007), 35.

"the twofold character of the Christian church as Jewish and Gentile."[3] At the end of the Gospel, Jesus will tell Peter and the other apostles that their mission begins "from Jerusalem" at the heart of the people of Israel and extends from there "to all the nations" (24:47; see Acts 1:8). However, already in the next chapter, the missionary meaning of catching a "great number" (*plēthos . . . poly*) of fish becomes evident, as Jesus—just after choosing the twelve apostles—preaches to a "large number" (*plēthos poly*) of people "from all Judea and Jerusalem and the coastal region of Tyre and Sidon" (Luke 6:17)—that is, from both Jewish and Gentile territory.

The full name **Simon Peter** is therefore used here in view of his selection and future mission as an apostle (Luke 6:14). Also introduced are **James and John, the sons of Zebedee**, who as apostles together with Peter are about to embark

5:8–10

3. François Bovon, *Luke*, trans. Christine M. Thomas, Donald S. Deer, and James Crouch, 3 vols., Hermeneia (Minneapolis: Fortress, 2002–13), 1:171–72.

Fishing on the Lake of Gennesaret

BIBLICAL BACKGROUND

Luke uses the name "Lake of Gennesaret"[a] (5:1; see 8:22–23, 33) for the seven-by-thirteen-mile body of freshwater that the other Gospels call the "Sea of Galilee" (Matt 4:18; 15:29; Mark 1:16; 7:31) or the "Sea of Tiberias" (John 6:1; 21:1). In the Old Testament, it is called the "Sea of Chinnereth" (e.g., Num 34:11; Josh 12:3; 13:27). Gennesaret is the fertile area bordering the northwestern shore of the lake, south of Capernaum (Matt 14:34; Mark 6:53).

The names of villages along the lake are one indication that fishing was an important industry (and remains so today). Bethsaida (Luke 9:10) can mean "house of fishing,"[b] and the Greek name for Magdala (8:2) was Taricheae, meaning a center for salting fish. Fishermen might work together as partners (5:10) in a cooperative. However, their business was heavily taxed, and they had to purchase fishing rights from the local tax collector.[c] The Gospels describe fishing with a hook (Matt 17:27) and nets (e.g., Mark 1:18; John 21:6), such as a casting net (Matt 4:18) and a dragnet (Matt 13:47–48). In Luke 5, certain details—nighttime fishing, two boats, washing the nets—suggest the use of trammel nets (three-layer nets that trap fish swimming through the coarser mesh of the outer layers and into the finer mesh of the middle layer).[d] The boats were probably like the first-century boat found in the muddy shore in 1986, when a drought lowered the water level. This twenty-seven-by-eight-foot wooden boat with mast and sail had a crew of five or more (see Mark 1:19–21), and is similar to the boat depicted in a first-century mosaic found at Magdala.[e]

a. See 1 Macc 11:67; Josephus, *Jewish War* 3.463, 506, 516.
b. Joseph A. Fitzmyer, *The Gospel according to Luke*, 2 vols., AB (New York: Doubleday, 1981–85), 1:765.
c. K. C. Hanson and Douglas E. Oakman, *Palestine in the Time of Jesus: Social Structures and Social Conflicts*, 2nd ed. (Minneapolis: Fortress, 2008), 99.
d. Mendel Nun, *The Sea of Galilee and Its Fishermen in the New Testament* (Ein-Gev: Kinnereth Sailing Company, 1989), 28–40.
e. Shelley Wachsmann, *The Sea of Galilee Boat: A 2000 Year Old Discovery from the Sea of Legends*, 2nd ed. (Cambridge, MA: Perseus, 2000), 302–22.

on a totally new kind of fishing partnership, and who as a trio will accompany Jesus at certain key moments in his ministry (8:51; 9:28).

Simon's reaction is one of **astonishment** at this sudden experience of the awesome power and presence of God. Whereas earlier he called him "Master" (5:5), recognizing his authority as a teacher (v. 3), he now goes a step further and addresses Jesus as **Lord** (1:43; 2:11)—the first person in the Gospel to call him by this important title (see the sidebar, "Jesus the Lord," p. 115). He confesses that he is **a sinful man**, not unlike Isaiah who, after seeing a vision

Figure 5. Magdala boat mosaic (first century AD).

of the Lord God, recognized that he was "a man of unclean lips" (Isa 6:5).[4] **Depart from me**, Simon tells Jesus, acutely aware of his own unworthiness. However, it is precisely individuals who recognize their sinfulness that Jesus has come to call (Luke 5:32). **Do not be afraid**, he tells Simon, in words previously addressed by angels to human beings (1:13, 30; 2:10), words that Jesus will frequently address to people in the Gospel (8:50; 12:7, 32). Jesus then explains what Peter's future mission involves: **From now on you will be catching men**. Fishing is an image of the work of evangelization, like the "fishers of men" phrase found in the parallel verses (Matt 4:19; Mark 1:17). However, the verb that Luke uses emphasizes that Peter and the other fishermen will be catching people *alive*. Their mission will be to lead people to new *life* (see Acts 5:20; 11:18).

4. The German philosopher Rudolf Otto insightfully recognized the similar response of Isaiah and Peter to the awesome divine presence; see Otto, *The Idea of the Holy*, trans. John W. Harvey, 2nd ed. (1917; repr., Oxford: Oxford University Press, 1958), 50. See also Catechism 208.

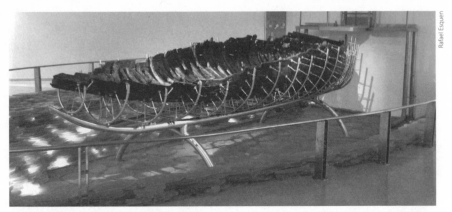

Figure 6. Galilee boat (first century BC or AD).

5:11   Luke highlights how Peter and the others **followed** Jesus *after* seeing his miracles and hearing his preaching (compare Matt 4:18–22; Mark 1:16–20). Rather than specifying what they left in following Jesus (e.g., their nets, their boat, their father Zebedee), Luke simply says that **they left everything**, emphasizing the radical nature of Christian discipleship (see Luke 5:28; 14:33).

Cleansing of a Leper (5:12–16)

¹²Now there was a man full of leprosy in one of the towns where he was; and when he saw Jesus, he fell prostrate, pleaded with him, and said, "Lord, if you wish, you can make me clean." ¹³Jesus stretched out his hand, touched him, and said, "I do will it. Be made clean." And the leprosy left him immediately. ¹⁴Then he ordered him not to tell anyone, but "Go, show yourself to the priest and offer for your cleansing what Moses prescribed; that will be proof for them." ¹⁵The report about him spread all the more, and great crowds assembled to listen to him and to be cured of their ailments, ¹⁶but he would withdraw to deserted places to pray.

OT: Lev 13–14; Num 5:2–3; 2 Kings 5:1–15
NT: Luke 4:27; 7:22; 17:11–19. // Matt 8:1–4; Mark 1:40–45
Catechism: Jesus as Lord, 448; Jesus hears the prayer of faith, 2616; Jesus withdraws to pray, 2602
Lectionary: Friday after Epiphany

The following block of six passages (5:12–6:11) closely parallels Mark's Gospel (Mark 1:40–3:6) in content, order, and even wording at times. There nonetheless are elements unique to Luke that highlight aspects of his message. For example, the earlier reference to Elisha's healing of Naaman the Syrian (Luke 4:27) has prepared readers for the cleansing of the leper here (see also 17:11–19).

Jesus the Lord

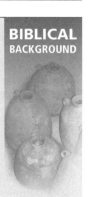

The Hebrew name of God, †YHWH (Exod 3:14–15; 6:2–3), was translated in the †Septuagint as *kyrios*, "Lord," and is generally rendered with small capitals—"LORD"—in English versions of the Old Testament. In Luke, the word *kyrios* occurs about a hundred times, many more than in the other Gospels. About forty of these refer to God (e.g., Luke 1:6; 2:22; 10:21; 20:37). Another forty or so (which the NABRE also translates as "Lord" in almost all cases) refer to Jesus (e.g., 6:46; 7:6; 9:54; 10:39; 24:3), including cases where the †synoptic Gospel parallels lack the title (7:19; 22:61). The approximately twenty remaining occurrences are mainly in parables, where the word is translated "sir," "master," or "owner" (14:22; 16:3; 20:13), and the character so called may represent God (20:15) or Jesus (12:36).

At times, there is an overlap in the title's application to God and Jesus. For example, Isaiah foretells one who will "prepare the way of the LORD" (Isa 40:3), meaning the Lord God of Israel. However, since Jesus is also called "Lord" in the Gospel's early chapters (Luke 1:43; 2:11), when Luke later quotes this Isaiah passage to describe John the Baptist, the term "Lord" points to Jesus as well (3:4; also 1:76). Also important are the occurrences where people like Peter, the leper, the centurion, and Zacchaeus address Jesus as "Lord" (5:8, 12; 7:6; 19:8). Regardless of what these individuals understood about Jesus at the time—that is, whether *kyrios* was simply a polite address: "Sir"—the title carries a deeper meaning in Luke's narrative, since the Gospel was written at a time when Christians were already worshiping Jesus as "Lord" (e.g., Rom 10:9; 1 Cor 12:3; Phil 2:11). In summary, Luke's intention with his almost equal use of the word *kyrios* for God and for Jesus is to lead his readers to understand the divine identity of Jesus.[a]

a. C. Kavin Rowe, *Early Narrative Christology: The Lord in the Gospel of Luke* (Berlin: de Gruyter, 2006; Grand Rapids: Baker Academic, 2009), 34–117, 147, 208–18; Richard B. Hays, *Reading Backwards: Figural Christology and the Fourfold Gospel Witness* (Waco: Baylor University Press, 2014), 63–66.

What will happen when **a man full of leprosy** encounters Jesus who is full **5:12** of the Holy Spirit (4:1)? "Leprosy" can refer to many kinds of skin diseases, not just the medical condition of leprosy (Hansen's disease). People with such skin diseases were considered ritually unclean and had to live separately, so that others would not touch them and become unclean themselves (Lev 13:45–46). The man therefore comes to Jesus in need of physical healing but also ritual cleansing in order to be restored to the community. He takes a risk by meeting Jesus not outside but **in one of the towns**. Like Peter in the previous passage (Luke 5:8), the leper falls before Jesus and addresses him as **Lord**. As in many other miracle stories, he makes an act of faith in Jesus' ability to heal him: **if you wish, you can make me clean.**

5:13–14   Because Jesus' mission is to "let the oppressed go free" (4:18), he replies, **I do will it,** using the same word translated "wish" in the leper's request. However, Jesus here does not accomplish the healing simply by his word—**Be made clean**—as on other occasions (4:35; 5:24). Instead, a gesture accompanies the words: **Jesus stretched out his hand** and **touched him.** As a result, **the leprosy left him immediately.** The significance of Jesus' gesture is that rather than becoming unclean, Jesus by his touch both heals and cleanses. Here and also later in other miracles involving cases of ritual impurity (Num 5:2)—the healing of the woman with hemorrhages and the raising of Jairus's dead daughter (Luke 8:40–56)—Jesus displays "a contagious purity"[5] through touch, as power goes forth from him (see 6:19; 8:46). His command, **Go, show yourself to the priest,** is the concrete way for the cleansed man to be readmitted to the community, by offering the sacrifice prescribed in the law of Moses (Lev 14:1–20) and having his cleansed status publicly recognized.

What does all this say about Jesus? Certainly, as later miracles will also show, he is a *prophetic* figure like Elisha, who healed Naaman the leper (Luke 4:27). Jesus refers to himself as a "prophet" (4:24; 13:33), as do others (7:16; 9:8, 19; 24:19). The contagious purity manifested by Jesus' touch is distinctive, however, and suggests that he is also a *priestly* figure who is the means of cleansing and source of holiness, analogous to the temple, the altar, and the high priest.[6]

5:15–16   Jesus' fame continues to **spread all the more,** as many others come **to listen** and **to be cured.** Jesus, however, **would withdraw to deserted places to pray.** The Greek verb forms indicate that going off to pray was his customary behavior. Indeed, Luke frequently mentions Jesus at prayer, often in places of solitude (see comment on 3:21). Therefore, before teaching his disciples about prayer with his *words* (11:1–4), Jesus does so by his *example.*

Healing of a Paralyzed Man (5:17–26)

> [17]**One day as Jesus was teaching, Pharisees and teachers of the law were sitting there who had come from every village of Galilee and Judea and**

5. Tom Holmén, "A Contagious Purity: Jesus' Inverse Strategy for Eschatological Cleanliness," in *Jesus Research: An International Perspective*, ed. James H. Charlesworth with Petr Pokorný (Grand Rapids: Eerdmans, 2009), 199–229.

6. Holmén, "Contagious Purity," 211, 222–23, 225; Crispin H. T. Fletcher-Louis, "Jesus as the High Priestly Messiah: Part 2," *Journal for the Study of the Historical Jesus* 5 (2007): 64–70.

The Priesthood of Jesus

In commenting on Jesus' command to the leper, the early Church writer Origen speaks of him as high priest: "Go, therefore, show yourself to the priest, that seeing you he may know that you were made clean, not through the observances of the Law, but by the operation of grace; not by the shadow that is the earthly priest, but by the heavenly splendor of the High Priest."[a] Similarly, St. Bon-aventure gives as one of the reasons for Jesus' command "that the priestly dignity of Christ and the grace of the . . . new priesthood may be made known to them, a grace that not only can declare that someone has been cured, but also can cure."[b] Whereas modern biblical scholarship has generally been skeptical that Christ is portrayed as a priest in this and other Gospel passages, the increased study of first-century Juda-ism in recent years has led to a rediscovery of this idea: for instance, "Jesus' touching a leper without incurring uncleanness (5:12–16), his forgiving sins (5:17–26), his assumption of Davidic priestly status (6:1–10)—all these are symbolic indicators that Luke thought of Jesus as a kind of high priest. . . . The Gospel closes . . . with an account of Jesus' ascension, where Jesus takes on a benedictory and therefore high-priestly posture."[c]

a. Origen, *Fragments on Matthew*, in *The Sunday Sermons of the Great Fathers*, ed. and trans. M. F. Toal, 4 vols. (repr., Swedesboro, NJ: Preservation Press, 1996), 1:302 (translation adapted).

b. Bonaventure, *Commentary on the Gospel of Luke* 5.31, ed. and trans. Robert J. Karris, 3 vols. (St. Bon-aventure, NY: The Franciscan Institute, 2001–4), 1:407 (translation adapted).

c. Nicholas Perrin, *Jesus the Temple* (Grand Rapids: Baker Academic, 2010), 62–63. See also Vernon K. Robbins, "Priestly Discourse in Luke and Acts," in *Jesus and Mary Reimagined in Early Christian Literature*, ed. Vernon K. Robbins and Jonathan M. Potter (Atlanta: SBL Press, 2015), 28–33.

Jerusalem, and the power of the Lord was with him for healing. [18]And some men brought on a stretcher a man who was paralyzed; they were trying to bring him in and set [him] in his presence. [19]But not finding a way to bring him in because of the crowd, they went up on the roof and lowered him on the stretcher through the tiles into the middle in front of Jesus. [20]When he saw their faith, he said, "As for you, your sins are forgiven." [21]Then the scribes and Pharisees began to ask themselves, "Who is this who speaks blasphemies? Who but God alone can forgive sins?" [22]Jesus knew their thoughts and said to them in reply, "What are you thinking in your hearts? [23]Which is easier, to say, 'Your sins are forgiven,' or to say, 'Rise and walk'? [24]But that you may know that the Son of Man has authority on earth to for-give sins"—he said to the man who was paralyzed, "I say to you, rise, pick up your stretcher, and go home." [25]He stood up immediately before them, picked up what he had been lying on, and went home, glorifying God.

²⁶Then astonishment seized them all and they glorified God, and, struck with awe, they said, "We have seen incredible things today."

OT: Isa 35:6; 43:25
NT: Luke 4:18; 7:22, 48–50; John 5:1–18; Acts 3:1–10; 14:8–13. // Matt 9:1–8; Mark 2:1–12
Catechism: Pharisees, 574–76; sacraments as powers from Christ, 1116; Son of Man, 440; Jesus heals and forgives, 589, 1421, 1503; sacrament of forgiveness, 1441, 1484; silent prayer, 2616
Lectionary: Monday Second Week of Advent

5:17   In this first of a series of five controversies (5:17–6:11; compare Mark 2:1–3:6), the **Pharisees**, strict observers of the law (Acts 26:5), make their first appearance in the Gospel. They are Jesus' opponents in this whole series (Luke 5:21, 30, 33; 6:2, 7) and later as well. They have come from the whole land of Israel together with **teachers of the law**, perhaps to investigate the reports they have heard. In their presence, Jesus' **teaching** becomes the context for a **healing** miracle, a manifestation of **the power of the Lord** that is **with him** (see 4:14).

5:18–19   Whereas the leper approached Jesus on his own initiative, **some men** now bring to Jesus **a man who was paralyzed**. By his words, the leper expressed his faith that Jesus could heal him. These men express their faith by their undaunted efforts **to bring him in** through the **roof**.

5:20   Jesus sees **their faith** but also perceives that the man is in need of more than physical healing. The consequences of sin are more serious than those of illness (see 12:4–5), so Jesus addresses that condition: **As for you, your sins are forgiven**. The verb "forgive" (*aphiēmi*) corresponds to the noun "liberty" (*aphesis*) proclaimed by Jesus in Nazareth (4:18). Moreover, the phrase "as for you" is literally "man" or "human being" (*anthrōpos*). In a sense, the man's situation of sin and illness represents that of all human beings, children of Adam (a name that means "man," "human being"). Although sin can result in bodily sickness (Ps 38:4), there is no explicit indication that the man's illness was caused by his personal sins (see Luke 13:1–5; John 9:1–3). Still, illness and death, like personal sins, stem from the fallen human condition after the sin of Adam (see Catechism 1008, 1505). However, human beings are now being liberated by Jesus, the new Adam (see comment on Luke 3:38).

5:21–24   The controversy begins as **the scribes and Pharisees** think he is speaking **blasphemies**, equating himself with God. However, from the readers' vantage point, they are ironically speaking the truth about Jesus' divinity: **Who but God alone can forgive sins?** Reading **their thoughts**, Jesus responds with a pronouncement that his **authority** (*exousia*) includes the ability **to forgive sins**. He demonstrates this by healing the **paralyzed** man, using a simple command: **Rise and walk**. He also for the first time refers to himself as **the Son of Man**.

The divine authority that Jesus here displays already points to the "son of man" in Daniel who receives "dominion" (*exousia*) from God (Dan 7:13–14 LXX). Several of Jesus' later "Son of Man" sayings will clearly allude to this figure (Luke 9:26; 21:27; see the sidebar, "The Son of Man," p. 181).

As with Peter's mother-in-law, the healing works **immediately**. The verb **5:25–26** **stood up** (like the verb "rise" in 5:23–24) is also used later for Jesus' resurrection (see comment on 4:39). The man responds to his gift of new life by **glorifying God**, and everyone else likewise **glorified God**. By his life and mission, Jesus leads others to glorify God (see 7:16; 13:13; 17:15; 18:43) as they experience God's saving action **today** (see 2:11; 4:21; 19:5, 9; 23:43).

The Call of Levi and the Bridegroom's Banquet (5:27–39)

[27]After this he went out and saw a tax collector named Levi sitting at the customs post. He said to him, "Follow me." [28]And leaving everything behind, he got up and followed him. [29]Then Levi gave a great banquet for him in his house, and a large crowd of tax collectors and others were at table with them. [30]The Pharisees and their scribes complained to his disciples, saying, "Why do you eat and drink with tax collectors and sinners?" [31]Jesus said to them in reply, "Those who are healthy do not need a physician, but the sick do. [32]I have not come to call the righteous to repentance but sinners."

[33]And they said to him, "The disciples of John fast often and offer prayers, and the disciples of the Pharisees do the same; but yours eat and drink." [34]Jesus answered them, "Can you make the wedding guests fast while the bridegroom is with them? [35]But the days will come, and when the bridegroom is taken away from them, then they will fast in those days." [36]And he also told them a parable. "No one tears a piece from a new cloak to patch an old one. Otherwise, he will tear the new and the piece from it will not match the old cloak. [37]Likewise, no one pours new wine into old wineskins. Otherwise, the new wine will burst the skins, and it will be spilled, and the skins will be ruined. [38]Rather, new wine must be poured into fresh wineskins. [39][And] no one who has been drinking old wine desires new, for he says, 'The old is good.'"

OT: Isa 54:5–8; 62:4–5
NT: Luke 7:34; 15:1–2; John 3:29; Rev 19:7, 9. // Matt 9:9–17; Mark 2:13–22
Catechism: Jesus eats with sinners, calling them to repentance, 545, 574, 588, 1443; detachment from riches, 2544, 2556; fasting, 1430, 1438, 2043; Jesus the physician and bridegroom, 1503, 796
Lectionary: Luke 5:27–32: Saturday after Ash Wednesday

5:27–28   Jesus calls **a tax collector** to become his disciple. Tax collectors were agents of
a "chief tax collector" (19:2) and in Galilee were under the tax administration
of Herod Antipas. Since Capernaum was near the border with Philip's territory and by the lake, it had a **customs post** for collecting tolls as well as taxes
associated with fishing. Herod also collected taxes on the land and its produce.
The overall tax burden, including the Roman tribute (20:22) and the temple
tax (Matt 17:24), was probably a third or more of a person's income.[7] Since
the collection system encouraged corruption, tax collectors were generally
despised and considered sinners (Luke 5:30), though Luke often depicts them
as repentant (see comment on 3:12–13).

The tax collector's name in Luke and Mark is **Levi** but "Matthew" in Matthew.
It is generally agreed that they are two names for the same individual. The name
"Matthew" appears in Luke's list of the twelve apostles (6:15).

Levi responds wholeheartedly to Jesus' invitation to **follow** him, **leaving**
everything behind as the first disciples did (5:11). Jesus will later summon
all his disciples to this radical detachment: "Everyone of you who does not
renounce all his possessions cannot be my disciple" (14:33).

5:29–32   Levi gives **a great banquet** for Jesus, the first of many meal scenes in Luke
that point ahead (or back) to the Last Supper. Another controversy with the
Pharisees surfaces, because Jesus is eating **with tax collectors and sinners**. In
response, he compares himself to a **physician** (4:23). This implies that sin is the
real illness and that "tax collectors and sinners" are **the sick** who **need** healing:
"I saw their ways, / but I will heal them" (Isa 57:18). Jesus has just taught this
lesson by forgiving the paralyzed man's sins before healing him physically. By
eating with tax collectors and sinners (see Luke 7:34; 15:1–2; 19:5), Jesus does
not condone their sins but calls them to **repentance**. At the end of the Gospel,
Jesus will commission his disciples to continue this mission by proclaiming
repentance and forgiveness of sins (24:47).

5:33–35   A further controversy arises in the same setting, as Jesus is asked why his disciples **eat and drink**, rather than **fast often and offer prayers** like **the disciples**
of John and **of the Pharisees** (see 18:12). Jesus responds by describing himself
as **the bridegroom** (see John 3:29). The combination of "fasting and prayer"
was seen earlier with the widow Anna (Luke 2:37), who was a representative
figure for Israel awaiting redemption. There, Jesus was implicitly presented as
the kinsman redeemer who becomes Israel's bridegroom (see comment on
2:36–38). The same background clarifies this passage. Jesus is the bridegroom
redeemer foretold by Isaiah: "As a bridegroom rejoices in his bride / so shall

---

7. James D. G. Dunn, *Jesus Remembered* (Grand Rapids: Eerdmans, 2003), 311.

your God rejoice in you" (Isa 62:5; see 54:5–8). The wait is over, so it is time not to fast but to feast. Indeed, the context of Levi's "great banquet" suggests that with Jesus the time for the messianic wedding banquet has arrived (see Isa 25:6–8; 55:1–3; Rev 19:7, 9)!

However, alluding to his death, Jesus says that there will come a time **when the bridegroom** will be **taken away** (see Isa 53:8; Acts 8:33). **Then they will fast**. Indeed, after Jesus' death, resurrection, and ascension, early Christians practiced fasting (Acts 13:2–3; 14:23).[8] Contemporary Christians can thus ask themselves: "What role should fasting or other acts of self-denial play in my life?"

Jesus continues with a **parable**, a comparison that teaches spiritual truths   **5:36–39** using an image or story drawn from daily life. Here there is a double parable with two images—**a new cloak** and **new wine**—which illustrate Jesus' reply to the question of fasting. The spiritual truth is that with the coming of Jesus, something new is happening. Specifically, at the Last Supper, Jesus will take the cup (with *wine*) and establish the "*new* covenant" in his blood that will be "shed" (22:20).[9] Therefore, a new response is required; **fresh wineskins** are needed. One cannot simply continue with the old ways.

After this emphasis on the **new**, the curious remark that **the old is good**, not found in the †synoptic parallels, seems at first glance to say instead that the **old wine** and the old ways that go with it are to be preferred. Rather, the point of this saying is that people, such as the Pharisees, who are satisfied with the good things of the old, such as the law, are not very willing to accept the fulfillment of those things in the New Covenant that Jesus establishes.

Reflection and Application (5:27–39)

Going forth to the outskirts. Jesus reached out to "tax collectors and sinners." The Church must do likewise, as Pope Francis explains: "In fidelity to the example of the Master, it is vitally important for the Church today to go forth and preach the Gospel to all: to all places, on all occasions, without hesitation, reluctance or fear." And again: "All of us are asked to obey his call to go forth from our own comfort zone in order to reach all the 'peripheries' in need of the light of the Gospel."[10]

---

8. According to the *Didache*, a manual of Christian instruction generally dated to the first century, Christians fasted on Wednesdays and Fridays (*Didache* 8.1).

9. Apart from the current passage, this is the only other occurrence of the word "new" in Luke's Gospel. Moreover, the verb for "shed" is the same verb as the **spilled** wine here.

10. Francis, *Evangelii Gaudium* (On the Proclamation of the Gospel in Today's World) 23, 20.

Two Sabbath Controversies (6:1–11)

¹While he was going through a field of grain on a sabbath, his disciples were picking the heads of grain, rubbing them in their hands, and eating them. ²Some Pharisees said, "Why are you doing what is unlawful on the sabbath?" ³Jesus said to them in reply, "Have you not read what David did when he and those [who were] with him were hungry? ⁴[How] he went into the house of God, took the bread of offering, which only the priests could lawfully eat, ate of it, and shared it with his companions." ⁵Then he said to them, "The Son of Man is lord of the sabbath."

⁶On another sabbath he went into the synagogue and taught, and there was a man there whose right hand was withered. ⁷The scribes and the Pharisees watched him closely to see if he would cure on the sabbath so that they might discover a reason to accuse him. ⁸But he realized their intentions and said to the man with the withered hand, "Come up and stand before us." And he rose and stood there. ⁹Then Jesus said to them, "I ask you, is it lawful to do good on the sabbath rather than to do evil, to save life rather than to destroy it?" ¹⁰Looking around at them all, he then said to him, "Stretch out your hand." He did so and his hand was restored. ¹¹But they became enraged and discussed together what they might do to Jesus.

OT: Exod 20:8–11; 34:21; Lev 24:5–9; Deut 5:12–15; 23:26; 1 Sam 21:2–7; 1 Kings 13:4, 6
NT: Luke 13:10–17; 14:1–6. // Matt 12:1–14; Mark 2:23–3:6
Catechism: Jesus and the sabbath, 581–82, 2173

6:1–2   The last two controversies involve the **sabbath**. In the first (vv. 1–5), Jesus' disciples are **picking the heads of grain** as they walk **through a field**, something permitted in the Torah: "When you go through your neighbor's grainfield, you may pluck some of the ears with your hand" (Deut 23:26). They are **rubbing them in their hands** in order to remove the husk around the grain. However, since it is the sabbath, **some Pharisees** object that the disciples' actions amount to **unlawful** harvesting (Exod 34:21).[11]

The Pharisees' zeal for sabbath observance was motivated by the belief that disobedience would lead to disaster for the whole nation. Indeed, as punishment for disobedience (Deut 28:15, 36–37, 63–64), Israel had gone into exile and Jerusalem had been destroyed: "If you do not obey me and keep holy the sabbath day . . . I will set fire to its gates . . . and it will consume the palaces of Jerusalem" (Jer 17:27). In Jesus' time, the effects of exile still continued, since

11. *m. Shabbat* 7:2.

Israel's tribes were scattered and the land was controlled by a Gentile oppressor. In order to hasten Israel's restoration, therefore, obedience was necessary, especially with regard to observances like the sabbath that safeguarded Israel's identity. However, these Pharisees failed to see that in Jesus the time of restoration was at hand.

Jesus comes to his disciples' defense by referring to the time when **David,** **6:3–4** who was fleeing from King Saul, **went into the house of God**, **took the bread of offering** (1 Sam 21:2–7), and **shared it with his companions** who **were hungry**. On one level, the lesson seems to be that tending to human need takes precedence over sabbath regulations. Although this is true, as the rabbis would explain for cases where life is in danger,[12] there is also a deeper lesson about Jesus' identity.

What David did apparently happened *on a sabbath*, when fresh loaves of this bread of the presence (also known as "showbread," Exod 25:30) were set out on the gold-plated table in the tent of meeting, replacing the old loaves (Lev 24:8; 1 Sam 21:7). The comparison suggests that if David **ate** the priests' bread on the sabbath, so can Jesus, the son of David (Luke 1:32; 18:38–39), do what he is doing on the sabbath. Jesus thus points to his identity as the Davidic Messiah, whose authority surpasses David's, as he will later explain by quoting Psalm 110 (see Luke 20:41–44). Moreover, **only the priests could lawfully eat** the loaves (Lev 24:9), but according to Psalm 110, the king in the line of David was also a type of priest (Ps 110:4; see 2 Sam 6:13–14), like Melchizedek who foreshadowed him (Gen 14:18).[13] Jesus similarly unites the dignity of priest and king.[14]

There may also be a subtle eucharistic allusion in the passage. The combination here of "bread" with the verbs "took" and "shared" (literally, "gave") occurs again at the feeding of the five thousand and the Last Supper (Luke 9:16; 22:19).

Jesus' final pronouncement also indicates that the main lesson regards his **6:5** identity: **The Son of Man is lord of the sabbath**. Like his first use of the "Son of Man" title when he forgave sins (5:24), this second occurrence involving the sabbath highlights Jesus' *divine* authority: Who but God alone has authority over the sabbath (Gen 2:2–3)? Later uses of the title (e.g., Luke 21:27; 22:69) will clarify that Jesus has this divine authority as the "son of man" prophesied by Daniel (Dan 7:13–14).

The next **sabbath** controversy (Luke 6:6–11) involves a healing (see 13:10–17; **6:6–7** 14:1–6) and occurs back in **the synagogue**, where there is **a man** with a **hand** that

---

12. *m. Yoma* 8:6.

13. Joseph Lozovyy, *Saul, Doeg, Nabal, and the "Son of Jesse": Readings in 1 Samuel 16–25* (New York: T&T Clark, 2009), 181–82.

14. Origen, *Homilies on Samuel* fragment 10, in SC 328:166–67.

is **withered**. Only Luke mentions that it is the **right** hand, perhaps to show that the man represents Israel waiting to be "restored" (6:10), still languishing in exile "by the rivers of Babylon": "If I forget you, O Jerusalem, / let my right hand wither!" (Ps 137:1, 5 NRSV). Jesus' opponents, **the scribes and the Pharisees** (Luke 5:21, 30), **watched him closely** (14:1; 20:20), ironically fulfilling Scripture: "The sinner will closely watch the righteous" (Ps 37:12 NETS). Their concern for sabbath observance has degenerated into observing their neighbor so as **to accuse him**.

6:8–9   Jesus again **realized their intentions** (see Luke 5:22). Addressing their hypocrisy head on, he tells the man to **come up and stand** in the sight of everyone. He asks a question that reveals his intentions and exposes those of his opponents. Jesus the Savior (2:11) has clearly come **to do good** and **save life**. His opponents, however, have come **to do evil** and **destroy** life, hardly a fitting way to observe the sabbath!

6:10   "**Stretch out your hand**": Jesus again heals by his word of command. The man obeys and his hand is **restored**. For Jesus, who has come to proclaim the jubilee time of liberty for the oppressed (4:18), there is no better day for restoration than the sabbath, the weekly jubilee day of rest (see 13:16). Moreover, the verb "restore" (with its related noun form) is often used to refer to divided Israel's restoration and regathering (Hosea 11:11 LXX; Jer 16:15 LXX; Acts 1:6; 3:21). The division of the tribes of Israel had begun with the separation into the northern and southern kingdoms. At that time, the king of the northern kingdom, Jeroboam, told the people to forget Jerusalem and its temple, and he set up his own rival sanctuaries (1 Kings 12:28–30). However, when he then stretched out his hand, it withered, until a prophet interceded for him that it be restored (1 Kings 13:4, 6). Now, with the healing of the man who stretches out his withered hand, Jesus gives a sign that his jubilee program of Israel's restoration has begun.[15]

6:11   However, Jesus' opponents view things differently and become **enraged** (literally, "filled with fury" [NRSV]) as they consider **what they might do to Jesus**. In Nazareth, the people were similarly "filled with rage" (4:28 NRSV). Jesus' words continue to provoke opposition that foreshadows his passion.

In summary, these two sabbath controversies primarily concern Jesus' identity rather than merely sabbath observance. "Jesus was not just another reforming rabbi, out to make life 'easier' for people. . . . The issue is another one altogether."[16]

15. Michael E. Fuller, *The Restoration of Israel: Israel's Re-gathering and the Fate of the Nations in Early Jewish Literature and Luke-Acts* (Berlin: de Gruyter, 2006), 243–44; Scott W. Hahn, *Kinship by Covenant: A Canonical Approach to the Fulfillment of God's Saving Promises* (New Haven: Yale University Press, 2009), 450n27.

16. Bruce Chilton and Jacob Neusner, *Judaism in the New Testament: Practices and Beliefs* (London: Routledge, 1995), 143.

Reflection and Application (6:1–11)

The real presence. "You are to set the Bread of the Presence on the table before me continually" (Exod 25:30 NET). These "loaves," explains St. Cyril of Alexandria, foreshadowed the Eucharist, "the bread that comes down from heaven to be set forth upon the holy tables of the churches."[17] "In his Eucharistic presence [Jesus] remains mysteriously in our midst as the one who loved us and gave himself up for us" (Catechism 1380 [citing Gal 2:20]). Catholics express their faith in Jesus' eucharistic presence among them, for example, by genuflecting toward the tabernacle upon entering a church or making the sign of the cross when passing a church. How conscious am I of Jesus' real presence in the Eucharist?

---

17. Cyril of Alexandria, *Homilies on Luke* 6:3, in *Commentary on the Gospel of Saint Luke*, trans. R. Payne Smith (repr., Astoria, NY: Studion, 1983), 121 (translation adapted).

The Twelve and the Sermon on the Plain

Luke 6:12–49

The restoration of Israel with its twelve tribes is now officially instituted with Jesus' choice of the twelve apostles. Jesus then teaches the law for the renewed Israel in the Sermon on the Plain, instructing the Twelve and many others about the kingdom of God and the way of discipleship.

Jesus Chooses the Twelve Apostles (6:12–16)

---

¹²In those days he departed to the mountain to pray, and he spent the night in prayer to God. ¹³When day came, he called his disciples to himself, and from them he chose Twelve, whom he also named apostles: ¹⁴Simon, whom he named Peter, and his brother Andrew, James, John, Philip, Bartholomew, ¹⁵Matthew, Thomas, James the son of Alphaeus, Simon who was called a Zealot, ¹⁶and Judas the son of James, and Judas Iscariot, who became a traitor.

OT: Exod 19:3
NT: Acts 1:13, 26. // Matt 10:1–4; Mark 3:13–19
Catechism: Jesus at prayer, 2600; twelve apostles, 551, 765, 880, 1577
Lectionary: Saints Simon and Jude

6:12 As he will do at the transfiguration (9:28), Jesus goes up **the mountain**, though in neither case is the mountain specified. At the transfiguration, Moses appears (9:30) and Jesus is presented as the prophet like Moses to whom people should listen (9:35; Deut 18:15). Here there is a similar comparison. Moses would go up

Mount Sinai to speak with God (Exod 19:3; 24:12–18; 34:1–4) and then would come down the mountain to speak to the people (19:25; 32:15; 34:29–32); he also set up twelve stones for the twelve tribes of Israel (24:4). Jesus now similarly goes up the mountain **to pray** and comes down to teach (Luke 6:17); he also chooses the twelve apostles (v. 13).

On this occasion (see 3:21; 5:16), the extent of Jesus' prayer is emphasized: **he spent the night in prayer to God.** His choice of the Twelve is thus the fruit of prayer and also serves as a lesson for Christians making important decisions (see Acts 1:24).

The night of prayer is followed by a **day** of action. From among his many **dis-**   6:13
ciples, Jesus chooses **Twelve**. The number has a symbolic significance: through the Twelve, Jesus is regathering the twelve tribes of Israel in fulfillment of Israel's hope for restoration.[1] This connection is made explicit at the Last Supper where Jesus says that they "will sit on thrones judging the twelve tribes of Israel" (Luke 22:30). In Acts, Matthias will be chosen as a replacement for Judas, in order to maintain twelve as the foundational number (Acts 1:26). The Twelve are **named apostles.** The word "apostle" means "one who is sent." As Jesus has been sent by God (Luke 4:43), so will he soon send out the apostles on a mission (9:2).

The lists of the Twelve always begin with **Simon, whom he named Peter**   6:14–16
(see Matt 10:2; Mark 3:16; Acts 1:13). Luke has already recounted his call (Luke 5:1–11). The new name *petros*, meaning "rock," indicates Peter's specific mission (see Matt 16:18; John 1:42). Listed second is Peter's **brother Andrew**, otherwise unmentioned in Luke. Next are the other brothers, **James** and **John,** Zebedee's sons and Simon's fishing partners (Luke 5:10). Peter, James, and John will form an inner circle of the Twelve in key episodes (8:51; 9:28). Peter and John also appear together in another episode in Luke (22:8) and various times in Acts (3:1–4:23; 8:14–25). Most of the other apostles are mentioned in Luke only here, since they function more as a group than as individuals. **Bartholomew** is identified in Christian tradition with Nathanael (John 1:45–49; 21:2), and **Judas the son of James** with Thaddeus (Matt 10:3; Mark 3:18). The tax collector Levi (Luke 5:27) is here called **Matthew,** as in all lists of the Twelve. **Simon who was called a Zealot** refers to "the Cananean" (Matt 10:4; Mark 3:18), an epithet derived from the Hebrew root *qana',* meaning "to be zealous." This could simply mean that he was zealous for God and the law (Acts 21:20; 22:3), or it may identify him with the nationalists who harbored sentiments of revolution

---

1. Michael E. Fuller, *The Restoration of Israel: Israel's Re-gathering and the Fate of the Nations in Early Jewish Literature and Luke-Acts* (Berlin: de Gruyter, 2006), 239–45; Richard Bauckham, "The Restoration of Israel in Luke-Acts," in *The Jewish World around the New Testament* (Grand Rapids: Baker Academic, 2010), 354–61.

against Rome, even though such Zealots were apparently not an organized movement until the years leading up to the Jewish revolt in AD 66. As always, listed last is **Judas Iscariot**, whose surname may indicate his family's town of origin (Kerioth: Josh 15:25; Jer 48:24; see John 6:71). He is identified as the future **traitor** (Luke 22:3, 47–48).

Sermon on the Plain, Part 1: Beatitudes and Woes (6:17–26)

¹⁷And he came down with them and stood on a stretch of level ground. A great crowd of his disciples and a large number of the people from all Judea and Jerusalem and the coastal region of Tyre and Sidon ¹⁸came to hear him and to be healed of their diseases; and even those who were tormented by unclean spirits were cured. ¹⁹Everyone in the crowd sought to touch him because power came forth from him and healed them all.
²⁰And raising his eyes toward his disciples he said:

> "Blessed are you who are poor,
>   for the kingdom of God is yours.
> ²¹Blessed are you who are now hungry,
>   for you will be satisfied.
> Blessed are you who are now weeping,
>   for you will laugh.
> ²²Blessed are you when people hate you,
>   and when they exclude and insult you,
>   and denounce your name as evil
>   on account of the Son of Man.

²³Rejoice and leap for joy on that day! Behold, your reward will be great in heaven. For their ancestors treated the prophets in the same way.

> ²⁴But woe to you who are rich,
>   for you have received your consolation.
> ²⁵But woe to you who are filled now,
>   for you will be hungry.
> Woe to you who laugh now,
>   for you will grieve and weep.
> ²⁶Woe to you when all speak well of you,
>   for their ancestors treated the false prophets in this way.

OT: Isa 61:1–2
NT: Matt 4:24–25; Mark 3:7–10; 6:56. // Matt 5:3–12

Catechism: power from Christ, 695, 1116, 1504; beatitudes, 2444; blessed are the poor, 2546;
   woe to the rich, 2547
Lectionary: Luke 6:17, 20–26: Sixth Sunday Ordinary Time (Year C)

Jesus comes **down** the mountain **with** the Twelve and proceeds to teach them,   6:17
as well as many other **disciples** and **people.** The setting for his discourse is **a
stretch of level ground,** hence the name "Sermon on the Plain." The crowds
have come not only from the whole land of Israel (**all Judea** in the broad sense,
4:44), but also from Gentile territory: **the coastal region of Tyre and Sidon**
(modern-day Lebanon). The mention of these two cities, historically enemies
of Israel (1 Macc 5:15; Isa 23; Ezek 26–28), foreshadows the apostles' later mission to the Gentiles.

As before, the crowds come not only **to hear** Jesus but also **to be healed**   6:18–19
(Luke 5:15), both of **diseases** and **unclean spirits** (4:40–41). Jesus' **touch** communicates **power** for healing **them all,** as it did for the leper (5:13).

Jesus has been teaching frequently (4:15, 31; 5:3, 17; 6:6), but only now   6:20, 24
does Luke present in an extended way the content of his teaching. The Sermon
on the Plain (6:20–49)[2] can be divided into three parts: beatitudes and woes
(6:20–26), commands on love and mercy (6:27–38), and teaching on the two
ways (6:39–49).[3] The discourse has many parallels to Matthew's Sermon on the
Mount (Matt 5–7), though it is much shorter. Both begin with a set of beatitudes,
but Luke's list has only four and is immediately followed by a corresponding set
of woes. Moreover, the context is rather different, with Luke's sermon coming
after the choice of the Twelve.

The Beatitudes are directed **toward his disciples,** providing instruction on
what it means to follow Jesus. One can try to imagine the expectation of the
disciples who had witnessed his healings and perhaps understood the symbolism of the Twelve. Jesus had already spoken about **the kingdom of God** (Luke
4:43). Did that mean that he was about to restore the Davidic kingdom of Israel
(see Acts 1:6), overthrowing the yoke of the Romans?[4]

Blessed are you who are poor. Jesus' first words are hardly those of one fo-
menting a rebellion (see Luke 23:19)! His words are nonetheless revolutionary
as they involve a reversal of values regarding what constitutes true happiness.
Indeed, the word "blessed" refers to those who are "happy" or "fortunate" in
God's sight (see comment on 1:45). Some measure of economic poverty, not
necessarily destitution, was a familiar reality for most people in Galilee at the

---

2. The material in Luke 6:20–8:3 is largely absent from Mark.
3. François Bovon, *Luke,* trans. Christine M. Thomas, Donald S. Deer, and James Crouch, 3 vols.,
Hermeneia (Minneapolis: Fortress, 2002–13), 1:216.
4. Tim Gray, *Mission of the Messiah* (Steubenville, OH: Emmaus Road, 1998), 63.

Blessed Poverty

"Holy Poverty puts to shame all greed, avarice, and all the anxieties of this life."[a] St. Francis of Assisi not only wrote about evangelical poverty but lived it. Commenting on the beatitude about the poor, Pope Benedict XVI singles out St. Francis as "the figure whom the history of faith offers . . . as the most intensely lived illustration of this Beatitude." He continues with a lesson on biblical interpretation:

> The saints are the true interpreters of Holy Scripture. The meaning of a given passage of the Bible becomes most intelligible in those human beings who have been totally transfixed by it and have lived it out. . . . Francis of Assisi was gripped in an utterly radical way by the promise of the first Beatitude, to the point that he even gave away his garments. . . . For Francis, this extreme humility was above all freedom for service, freedom for mission, ultimate trust in God. . . . It is above all by looking at Francis of Assisi that we see clearly what the words 'Kingdom of God' mean. . . . It is in figures such as he that the Church grows toward the goal that lies in the future, and yet is already present.[b]

a. Francis of Assisi, *The Praises of the Virtues*, in *St. Francis of Assisi: Writings and Early Biographies*, ed. Marion A. Habig (Chicago: Franciscan Herald Press, 1973), 133.

b. Benedict XVI, *Jesus of Nazareth: From the Baptism in the Jordan to the Transfiguration*, trans. Adrian J. Walker (New York: Doubleday, 2007), 78–79. See also Benedict XVI, *Verbum Domini* 48.

time.[5] The lack of material resources would typically lead the poor to greater reliance on God (hence, the "poor in spirit" of Matt 5:3). These pious poor, or †*anawim* (Isa 61:1), are those to whom Jesus comes to bring glad tidings (see comment on Luke 4:18–19). Their closer relationship with God is what makes them **blessed**. True happiness does not come from possessing the kingdoms offered by the devil (4:5–6) but from the kingdom of God, which Jesus says is theirs at the present time. In particular, this kingdom belongs to disciples like Peter, James, John, and Levi, who leave "everything" (5:11, 28)—that is, who voluntarily become poor—in order to follow Jesus.

The beatitude is better understood by considering its opposite: **woe to you who are rich**. A "woe" is a warning of coming judgment. The one who finds **consolation** now in earthly riches typically does not rely on God. Thus, it is difficult for the rich to enter the kingdom (18:24–25), though with God it is possible (18:27; 19:2, 9). For example, among the early Christians, those with wealth came to the aid of those in need (Acts 2:45; 4:34–35).

5. David A. Fiensy, *Christian Origins and the Ancient Economy* (Eugene, OR: Cascade, 2014), 23.

The next two beatitudes further describe the poor and the happiness that **6:21, 25**
will be theirs through their reliance on God. They include those **who are
now hungry**, since Jesus promises that they **will be satisfied**. Jesus himself
experienced hunger (Luke 4:2) but resisted the devil's temptation. Mary,
who put her trust in God, expresses this beatitude in her Magnificat: "The
hungry he has filled with good things" (1:53). In some cases, such as that
of the poor Lazarus, "who longed to satisfy his hunger" (16:21 NRSV), the
promise is fulfilled only in the afterlife (16:22). However, Jesus will provide
a sign of this heavenly banquet by feeding the five thousand so that all are
"satisfied" (9:17).

The poor are also those **who are now weeping** on account of their difficult
situation. This promise also looks to the future: they **will laugh**. Nevertheless,
Jesus will again provide a present sign of the promise when he brings the
weeping of mourners to an end by raising their loved ones from the dead
(7:13–16; 8:52–56).

The second and third woes correspond to these two beatitudes. Those **who
are filled now** and **laugh now**, but rely on themselves and live for themselves,
will in the future **be hungry**, **grieve and weep** (see 12:15–21; 16:19–31). This
reversal was already announced in the Magnificat: "The rich he has sent away
empty" (1:53).

The last beatitude concerns the persecution that Jesus' disciples will experi- **6:22–23,
26**
ence from those who **hate** them **on account of the Son of Man** (see 21:17).
Jesus, who has likened himself to a rejected prophet (4:24), similarly compares
his disciples to the **prophets** who were mistreated. In response, they should
rejoice because of the **reward** they will receive **in heaven**. The apostles will
later fulfill this command: "They left the presence of the Sanhedrin, rejoicing
that they had been found worthy to suffer dishonor for the sake of the name"
(Acts 5:41). Others, like Stephen, will experience martyrdom and so win their
heavenly reward (Acts 7:54–60).

The corresponding **woe** warns that when **all speak well of** individuals, it
is because, like **the false prophets**, they are not truly speaking God's word,
preferring "human praise to the glory of God" (John 12:43).

As a whole, the Beatitudes reverse the world's understanding of true happiness, showing that it is found not in riches, gratification, entertainment, and
fame, but in God. Learning this lesson on discipleship requires *faith*, since the
promises and rewards may not be experienced until the heavenly kingdom. It
also requires *charity*, as those with economic means are exhorted to tend to
the needs of the poor, the hungry, and the weeping.

Reflection and Application (6:17–26)

Beatitudes and Christian life. The Second Vatican Council called for a renewal of moral theology, saying that instruction on Christian living should draw more on the Scriptures.[6] One fruit of this renewal is the retrieval of the teaching that the Beatitudes reveal God's plan for our eternal beatitude, happiness in the life to come (Catechism 1716–29).[7] A person learns to live the Beatitudes by practicing, with the aid of God's grace, the theological virtues (faith, hope, and charity; see 1 Cor 13:13) and the moral virtues (prudence, justice, fortitude, and temperance; see Wis 8:7), and by being empowered by the Holy Spirit's gifts (see Isa 11:1–2), so that the fruits of the Spirit, such as love, joy, and peace (see Gal 5:22), become manifest in one's life.

Sermon on the Plain, Part 2: Love and Be Merciful (6:27–38)

[27]"But to you who hear I say, love your enemies, do good to those who hate you, [28]bless those who curse you, pray for those who mistreat you. [29]To the person who strikes you on one cheek, offer the other one as well, and from the person who takes your cloak, do not withhold even your tunic. [30]Give to everyone who asks of you, and from the one who takes what is yours do not demand it back. [31]Do to others as you would have them do to you. [32]For if you love those who love you, what credit is that to you? Even sinners love those who love them. [33]And if you do good to those who do good to you, what credit is that to you? Even sinners do the same. [34]If you lend money to those from whom you expect repayment, what credit [is] that to you? Even sinners lend to sinners, and get back the same amount. [35]But rather, love your enemies and do good to them, and lend expecting nothing back; then your reward will be great and you will be children of the Most High, for he himself is kind to the ungrateful and the wicked. [36]Be merciful, just as [also] your Father is merciful.

[37]"Stop judging and you will not be judged. Stop condemning and you will not be condemned. Forgive and you will be forgiven. [38]Give and gifts will be given to you; a good measure, packed together, shaken down, and overflowing, will be poured into your lap. For the measure with which you measure will in return be measured out to you."

---

6. Vatican II, *Optatam Totius* (Decree on the Training of Priests) 16.

7. Servais Pinckaers, *The Pinckaers Reader: Renewing Thomistic Moral Theology*, ed. John Berkman and Craig Steven Titus (Washington, DC: Catholic University of America Press, 2005), 129.

OT: Exod 34:6; Lev 19:2, 18
NT: Mark 4:24; Acts 20:35; Rom 12:14, 20–21. // Matt 5:38–48; 7:1–2, 12
Catechism: Golden Rule, 1789, 1970; the sacrament of mercy, 1458; forgiveness and mercy, 2842
Lectionary: Luke 6:27–38: Seventh Sunday Ordinary Time (Year C); Luke 6:36–38: Monday Second
 Week of Lent

With a series of imperatives, Jesus now addresses all those **who hear** him. As **6:27–28**
with the Beatitudes, his commands would have unsettled his listeners: **Love your
enemies**. To those who may have expected Jesus to lead a revolt against Rome,
Jesus was in effect saying: "Love the Romans." This was and remains a difficult
message. It also expands the scope of the law of Moses: "You shall love your neighbor as yourself" (Lev 19:18). Jesus will similarly interpret this commandment of
Moses to include love of enemies in the parable of the good Samaritan (see Luke
10:25–37). Of course, Jesus' message also means loving enemies within the community. Even among the apostles there was probably a need for this instruction,
since the Twelve included both a tax collector and someone zealous for the law.

 Three more commands give concrete examples of what it means to love one's
enemies: **do good** to them, **bless** them, **pray** for them. Jesus is again further
developing Old Testament teaching (Exod 23:4–5; Prov 25:21–22; see Rom
12:20). He himself will set the standard by praying for those who crucify him
(Luke 23:34). The early Christians will follow Jesus' teaching and example (see
Acts 7:60; Rom 12:14; 1 Pet 3:9).

 Examples of nonretaliation further explain love of enemies. By turning the **6:29–30**
other **cheek** or giving one's **tunic** (the inner garment) to someone who **takes** the
outer **cloak**, one refuses to "be conquered by evil" and instead conquers "evil
with good" (Rom 12:21). At the individual level, a person thus trusts in God to
settle accounts, relatively unconcerned about preserving one's own honor and
reputation. Such selfless behavior is also marked by a magnanimous attitude:
one is ready to **give to everyone who asks** and **not demand** things **back**.

 Summarizing the foregoing instructions is the Golden Rule: **Do to others** **6:31**
as you would have them do to you. Again, Jesus' teaching extends beyond
a typical Jewish formulation (which is therefore sometimes called the Silver
Rule): "Do to no one what you yourself hate" (Tob 4:15). One should do good
to others and not only abstain from mistreating them. This rule applies even
when they do not reciprocate.

 Jesus argues from the lesser to the greater to show the reasonableness of his **6:32–35**
high standard of ethical behavior. If **even sinners love those who love them**, how
much greater love should those trying to avoid sin have? Thus, if people like the
Pharisees who look down on "sinners" (5:30) fail to accept Jesus' command—**love
your enemies**—they ironically remain at the same level as sinners. Jesus' Golden

Rule is likewise a challenge to rise above the reciprocity of **sinners** who only **do good to those who do good to** them. The same applies for his command to **lend expecting nothing back**. In all these cases, there is not much **credit** (literally, "grace") otherwise. The standard that Jesus proposes is one of imitating God, who **himself is kind** to those who are evil: "Good and upright is the Lord, / therefore he shows sinners the way" (Ps 25:8). Those who do so become **children of the Most High**, hence also imitating Jesus, who is "Son of the Most High" (Luke 1:32). The **reward** (literally, "wage"; see 10:7) for those who follow such a standard **will be great**, not necessarily in this life but "in heaven" (6:23).

6:36   The imitation of God also requires disciples to **be merciful, just as** God the **Father is merciful**: "The Lord, the Lord, / a God merciful and gracious, / slow to anger, / and abounding in steadfast love and faithfulness" (Exod 34:6 NRSV; see Pss 86:15; 103:8). With this imperative, Jesus is interpreting another Torah commandment—"Be holy, for I, the Lord your God, am holy" (Lev 19:2)—in terms of the divine attribute of mercy. God's mercy was emphasized earlier in Luke (see 1:50, 54, 58, 72, 78). Later, Jesus will illustrate the command to be merciful, like his teaching on love of enemies, in the parable of the good Samaritan (10:33, 37). By contrast, for the Pharisees (in Hebrew, *perushim*, meaning "separatists"), holiness meant separation from anything that could render a person unclean. Such a difference underlies the controversies over table fellowship with tax collectors and sinners (5:30; 7:39; 15:2; 19:7), where Jesus, by being merciful, leads sinners back to God.

6:37–38   Concretely, being merciful means that one will **stop judging, stop condemning**, and **forgive**. The result for behaving in this way is that a person **will not be judged** or **condemned** but rather **forgiven**—*by God*. This teaching is similarly expressed in the Lord's Prayer: "Forgive us our sins / for we ourselves forgive everyone in debt to us" (11:4).

Give is repeated as the last command in this series (see v. 30). By giving to others, a person will receive **gifts** back from God in recompense (see v. 35), indeed to an **overflowing** degree. Jesus summarizes his teaching with a corollary, as it were, of the Golden Rule: **the measure with which you measure will in return be measured out to you**.

Reflection and Application (6:27–38)

Be merciful. St. John Paul II explains that Luke's "Gospel has earned the title of 'the Gospel of mercy.'"[8] The merciful Jesus (7:13) reveals the Father's mercy

---

8. John Paul II, *Dives in Misericordia* (On the Mercy of God) 3.

(15:20) and calls us likewise to be merciful (6:36; 10:37). How can I better live out this call to mercy? *Hear Ejekwon's Phone Call*

Sermon on the Plain, Part 3: The Two Ways (6:39–49)

³⁹And he told them a parable, "Can a blind person guide a blind person? Will not both fall into a pit? ⁴⁰No disciple is superior to the teacher; but when fully trained, every disciple will be like his teacher. ⁴¹Why do you notice the splinter in your brother's eye, but do not perceive the wooden beam in your own? ⁴²How can you say to your brother, 'Brother, let me remove that splinter in your eye,' when you do not even notice the wooden beam in your own eye? You hypocrite! Remove the wooden beam from your eye first; then you will see clearly to remove the splinter in your brother's eye.

⁴³"A good tree does not bear rotten fruit, nor does a rotten tree bear good fruit. ⁴⁴For every tree is known by its own fruit. For people do not pick figs from thornbushes, nor do they gather grapes from brambles. ⁴⁵A good person out of the store of goodness in his heart produces good, but an evil person out of a store of evil produces evil; for from the fullness of the heart the mouth speaks.

⁴⁶"Why do you call me, 'Lord, Lord,' but not do what I command? ⁴⁷I will show you what someone is like who comes to me, listens to my words, and acts on them. ⁴⁸That one is like a person building a house, who dug deeply and laid the foundation on rock; when the flood came, the river burst against that house but could not shake it because it had been well built. ⁴⁹But the one who listens and does not act is like a person who built a house on the ground without a foundation. When the river burst against it, it collapsed at once and was completely destroyed."

NT: Luke 8:21; James 1:22–25. // Matt 7:3–5, 16–27; 10:24–25; 12:33–35; 15:14
Catechism: the two ways, 1696, 1970; fruits of grace, 2005
Lectionary: Luke 6:39–45: Eighth Sunday Ordinary Time (Year C)

In this last passage of the sermon, Jesus teaches in **parable** style using a variety of vivid images. In the first, he points out that **a blind person** cannot **guide a blind person**, since **both** will **fall into a pit**. Jesus is metaphorically speaking about a **teacher** and **disciple** relationship. The parallel saying in Matthew specifically applies to the Pharisees as false teachers (Matt 15:12, 14). The same is likely true here, in view of the series of five controversies with the Pharisees (Luke 5:17–6:11), which also mentioned the "teachers of the law" (5:17). Jesus

6:39–40

himself will be called "teacher" about a dozen times in Luke (e.g., 7:40; 9:38; 10:25). Since **every disciple will be like his teacher,** Jesus is setting before his listeners the choice between following him as teacher or following others.

6:41–42   The image of the **splinter** in a **brother's eye** and the **wooden beam** in one's own eye teaches the lesson of not judging others' faults without first addressing our own worse faults (see 6:37; Matt 7:1–5). Otherwise, one is a **hypocrite.** Jesus is ruling out not fraternal correction (see Luke 17:3) but rather a critical spirit. The context suggests a specific reference to those Pharisees who are on the lookout so as to accuse others (6:7).

6:43–45   The choice between two ways of living, one **good** and one **evil,** is now set forth with the image of a **tree** that **is known** either by its **good fruit** or its **rotten fruit.** The early Christians used this biblical theme of two ways as a means of instruction in moral conduct.[9] It is rooted in Old Testament passages that similarly contrast the ways of life and death (Deut 30:15–20), even using the imagery of a tree with its fruit (Ps 1).

6:46–49   However, whereas Old Testament teaching on the two ways involves doing what God has commanded, now Jesus says: **do what I command.** Teaching with such authority is only possible for one who is **Lord, Lord,** like the God who revealed himself to Moses (Exod 34:6). The focus on Jesus in these concluding verses (indicated also by the pronouns **me** and **my**) thus reminds readers that the sermon is more than a collection of moral teachings. It involves a way of discipleship in obedience to a divine teacher, so as to become like him (Luke 6:40).

A final image of two people **building a house** illustrates this way of discipleship and its opposite. A true disciple of Jesus is one who **listens to his words, and acts on them,** not like the one who **listens** but **does not act.** The first is like one who lays **the foundation on rock,**[10] whereas the second is like one who builds **without a foundation.** Only the first **house** can withstand the torrential **flood** of the overflowing **river** (see Rev 12:15); the other is **completely destroyed.** With this image in mind, all disciples of Jesus can consider their own response to Jesus' words.

Reflection and Application (6:39–49)

Building our lives on rock. Do I listen to Jesus' words—the Word of God in Scripture—and act accordingly (see 6:47; 8:21; 11:28)? Pope Benedict XVI

---

9. *Didache* 1–6; *Barnabas* 18–20.
10. The word "rock" (*petra*) may be linked to the name Peter (*Petros*) at the beginning of this section (Luke 6:14). See, e.g., David E. Garland, *Luke,* ZECNT (Grand Rapids: Zondervan, 2011), 273. Despite his denials of Jesus in the hour of trial, Peter will return and strengthen the others (22:31–34).

writes that "those who build their lives on his word build in a truly sound and lasting way. . . . Many things in which we trust for building our lives . . . prove ephemeral. Possessions, pleasure, and power show themselves sooner or later to be incapable of fulfilling the deepest yearnings of the human heart. In building our lives we need solid foundations."[11] God's word gives us this firm foundation: "Your word, LORD, stands forever; / it is firm as the heavens" (Ps 119:89).

11. Benedict XVI, *Verbum Domini* 10.

Jesus the Great Prophet

Luke 7:1–50

After Jesus' teaching in the Sermon on the Plain, the focus turns to Jesus' deeds, which reveal that he is a great prophet. His miracles (7:1–17) recall those of the prophets Elijah and Elisha, mentioned by him at Nazareth. Jesus also discusses the prophetic role of John the Baptist in relationship to himself (7:18–35). A Pharisee with whom he dines wonders whether Jesus is really a prophet when a woman anoints his feet (7:36–50). Actually, Jesus is more than a prophet. Whereas some come to faith in him (7:9, 50), others have questions about his deeper identity (7:19–20, 49). These questions, like earlier ones (4:36; 5:21), push the Gospel narrative forward in this lengthy section (4:14–9:50) toward an answer in Peter's confession of Jesus as Messiah (9:20).

Jesus Heals the Centurion's Servant (7:1–10)

¹When he had finished all his words to the people, he entered Capernaum. ²A centurion there had a slave who was ill and about to die, and he was valuable to him. ³When he heard about Jesus, he sent elders of the Jews to him, asking him to come and save the life of his slave. ⁴They approached Jesus and strongly urged him to come, saying, "He deserves to have you do this for him, ⁵for he loves our nation and he built the synagogue for us." ⁶And Jesus went with them, but when he was only a short distance from the house, the centurion sent friends to tell him, "Lord, do not trouble yourself, for I am not worthy to have you enter under my roof. ⁷Therefore, I did not consider myself worthy to come to you; but say the word

and let my servant be healed. [8]For I too am a person subject to authority, with soldiers subject to me. And I say to one, 'Go,' and he goes; and to another, 'Come here,' and he comes; and to my slave, 'Do this,' and he does it." [9]When Jesus heard this he was amazed at him and, turning, said to the crowd following him, "I tell you, not even in Israel have I found such faith." [10]When the messengers returned to the house, they found the slave in good health.

OT: 2 Kings 5:1–15
NT: Luke 23:47; Acts 10. // Matt 8:5–13; John 4:46–54
Catechism: preparation for Communion, 1386; faith, 2610
Lectionary: Ninth Sunday Ordinary Time (Year C)

After his preaching tour, Jesus returns to **Capernaum** (4:31, 42). Because it was　7:1–2 a border town with a customs post (5:27), it may have had a garrison under the command of a **centurion**.[1] Centurions, who oversaw up to one hundred soldiers, are often favorably portrayed by Luke (23:47; Acts 10:1–2, 22; 27:1, 3, 43). Whereas those encountered in the New Testament are generally Roman centurions, this one likely served instead under Herod Antipas, the tetrarch who ruled Galilee as a client of Rome. In any case, he is a Gentile, and his **slave**,[2] whom he holds in high regard, is **ill and about to die**.

The centurion, who has a good relationship with the Jews, sends the vil-　7:3–5 lage **elders** to **Jesus** to intercede on his behalf. These are local Jewish leaders, distinct from the elders who are members of the Jerusalem †Sanhedrin (Luke 9:22; 20:1; 22:52, 66). They present two reasons why **he deserves** or "is worthy of" the favor: **he loves** the Jewish **nation** and **built** the Jewish **synagogue** in Capernaum (4:33). Their remarks indicate his relative wealth compared to the townspeople, but also show that Jews and Gentiles, traditionally enemies, can love each other, as Jesus has just taught (6:27, 35). In Acts, Luke will describe another centurion, Cornelius, "respected by the whole Jewish nation" (Acts 10:22), whose baptism leads to peaceful coexistence between Jews and Gentiles in the Church (Acts 11:18; 15:7–11). God's universal plan of salvation thus unfolds through these two centurions (see Luke 2:30–32; 3:6), as Jesus had earlier foretold by mentioning Naaman, the Gentile officer healed by Elisha (4:27; 2 Kings 5:1–15).

As **Jesus** approaches **the house**, more envoys from **the centurion** relay a　7:6–8 message. No doubt the centurion is aware of the traditional prohibition for a

1. James D. G. Dunn, *Jesus Remembered* (Grand Rapids: Eerdmans, 2003), 310.
2. A similar passage in John's Gospel (John 4:46–54) concerns the sick son of a royal official.

Figure 7. Synagogue in Capernaum (fifth century AD), built over a first-century synagogue.

Jew to visit a Gentile (Acts 10:28; 11:3).[3] Addressing Jesus respectfully as **Lord** (Luke 5:8, 12), he humbly says, through his **friends**, that he is **not worthy** or fit to have Jesus **enter** his home. He then reiterates that he **did not consider** himself **worthy** to approach Jesus (despite what the elders said about him, v. 4). However, as a military man, he understands **authority**. He therefore suggests that his **servant** be **healed** simply by the authority of Jesus' **word** (4:32, 36).

7:9   Jesus praises the centurion's **faith** as greater than anything he has seen **in Israel**. Jesus had witnessed the faith of the men carrying the paralyzed man (5:20), so how is the centurion's faith greater? Perhaps his faith goes beyond belief in Jesus' healing power (even when not physically present) to a deeper recognition of Jesus' "authority" (7:8; see 5:24) and identity. Since the centurion is not Jewish, his faith also shows that God has "opened a door of faith to the Gentiles" (Acts 14:27 RSV), one that will continue to open wider in the course of Luke-Acts.

7:10   On their return, **the messengers** find **the slave in good health**. Like Elisha, who sent a message to Naaman regarding his healing (2 Kings 5:10), Jesus has healed from a distance, without even meeting the centurion. However, as the

3. *Jubilees* 22.16.

next passage will show, Jesus is even greater than Elisha and other Old Testament prophets.

Reflection and Application (7:1–10)

Receiving Jesus under our roof. The centurion's words are paraphrased in the prayer recited by the faithful just before receiving Communion (Catechism 1386): "Lord, I am not worthy that you should enter under my roof, but only say the word and my soul shall be healed" (see Matt 8:8; Luke 7:6–7).[4] Do I receive Communion with a faith in Jesus like that of the centurion (7:9)?

Raising the Son of the Widow of Nain (7:11–17)

¹¹Soon afterward he journeyed to a city called Nain, and his disciples and a large crowd accompanied him. ¹²As he drew near to the gate of the city, a man who had died was being carried out, the only son of his mother, and she was a widow. A large crowd from the city was with her. ¹³When the Lord saw her, he was moved with pity for her and said to her, "Do not weep." ¹⁴He stepped forward and touched the coffin; at this the bearers halted, and he said, "Young man, I tell you, arise!" ¹⁵The dead man sat up and began to speak, and Jesus gave him to his mother. ¹⁶Fear seized them all, and they glorified God, exclaiming, "A great prophet has arisen in our midst," and "God has visited his people." ¹⁷This report about him spread through the whole of Judea and in all the surrounding region.

OT: 1 Kings 17:10, 17–24; 2 Kings 4:32–37
NT: Luke 1:68, 78; Acts 9:39–42; 20:9–12
Catechism: pledge of the resurrection, 994; God's visitation, 1503
Lectionary: Tenth Sunday Ordinary Time (Year C); All Souls; Masses for the Dead; St. Monica (optional)

Luke's penchant for grouping stories about men and women is seen here. After healing the almost-dead slave of the centurion, Jesus raises the dead son of **a widow**, a miracle that only Luke recounts. The setting is a small village about six miles southeast of Nazareth called **Nain**, a journey of some twenty-five miles southwest from Capernaum (7:1). The meeting at **the gate of the city** recalls a similar episode with Elijah and a widow at the gate of a city (4:26; 1 Kings 17:10 RSV).

7:11–12

---

4. *The Roman Missal* (Totowa, NJ: Catholic Book Publishing, 2011), Communion Rite.

The Tears of a Mother

LIVING
TRADITION

The raising of the widow's son (7:11–17) is an optional reading at Mass on the memorial of St. Monica (August 27), whose persistent prayers for her son, St. Augustine, led to his conversion. Augustine later wrote: "While she constantly wept over me in your sight as over a dead man, it was over one who though dead could still be raised to life again; she offered me to you upon the bier of her meditation, begging you to say to this widow's son, 'Young man, arise, I tell you,' that he might live again and begin to speak, so that you could restore him to his mother."[a]

St. Augustine's mentor, St. Ambrose, understands the widow as Mother Church: "Let the Mother of the Church weep for you, she who intercedes for all as a widowed mother for only sons, for she suffers with the spiritual grief of nature when she perceives her children urged on to death by mortal sins."[b] St. Augustine himself makes this interpretation: "His widowed mother rejoiced over that young man brought back to life. About people daily restored to life in the spirit their mother the Church rejoices."[c]

a. Augustine, *Confessions* 6.1.1, trans. Maria Boulding, WSA I/1 (Hyde Park, NY: New City Press, 1997), 135.

b. Ambrose, *Exposition of the Holy Gospel according to Saint Luke* 5.92, trans. Theodosia Tomkinson (Etna, CA: Center for Traditionalist Orthodox Studies, 1998), 186–87.

c. Augustine, *Sermon* 98.2, in *Sermons*, trans. Edmund Hill, 11 vols., WSA III/4 (Hyde Park, NY: New City Press, 1990–97), 4:43.

The scene is a confrontation between life and death.[5] Jesus, full of power (Luke 4:14; 5:17; 6:19), is headed into the town, together with **his disciples and a large crowd**, while the dead **man** is **being carried out** of the town, accompanied by **his mother** and **a large crowd**. Without a husband and now without her **only son**, the woman has also lost her means of support. Perhaps Jesus sees in the situation a foreshadowing of the sorrow of his own widowed mother at the death of her only son.

7:13–15   As **the Lord** of life (see 24:34), Jesus takes the initiative and springs into manifold action: he sees the woman, is **moved with pity**, tells her not to **weep**, comes **forward**, touches the open **coffin**, and tells the **young man** to **arise**. His outreach is in keeping with the spirit of Old Testament commandments regarding care for widows (Deut 14:28–29; 24:17, 19–21; 26:12–13), but by showing pity (or "compassion," RSV), he also fulfills his own command: "Be merciful"

5. The commentary on this passage and the next draws on Jean-Noël Aletti, *Le Jésus de Luc* (Paris: Mame-Desclée, 2010), 111–22.

Elijah and Elisha Prefigure John, Jesus, and the Apostles

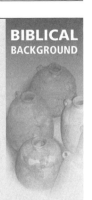

All four Gospels mention Elijah, and two of them present John the Baptist as the fulfillment of Elijah's promised return (Mal 3:23–24).[a] Only Luke mentions Elisha (Luke 4:27), the prophet who succeeded Elijah and received a double portion of his spirit when he was taken away into heaven (1 Kings 19:16, 19–21; 2 Kings 2:8–15). On one level, these two prophets prefigure the relationship between John and Jesus. John goes "in the spirit and power of Elijah" (Luke 1:17) to prepare the way for Jesus (7:27, quoting Mal 3:1). The Spirit descends upon Jesus at his baptism, and John is taken away (Luke 3:20–22). On another level, the two prophets prefigure the relationship between Jesus and the apostles. After Jesus ascends to heaven, the apostles receive his Spirit at Pentecost (Acts 1–2).

Thus, Jesus is like *both* Elijah and Elisha (Luke 4:25–27),[b] two prophets who performed miracles and ministered to Gentiles (7:1–10; 1 Kings 17:8–16; 2 Kings 5:1–14). Like Elijah, Jesus spends forty days in the desert (Luke 4:2; 1 Kings 19:8) and raises a widow's son from the dead (Luke 7:11–17; 1 Kings 17:17–24). Jesus is thought to be Elijah (Luke 9:8, 19), and Elijah appears with him on the mount of transfiguration (9:30). Jesus is also contrasted with Elijah: he does not call down fire from heaven (9:54–55; 2 Kings 1:10, 12) and gives opposite instructions regarding discipleship (Luke 9:62; 1 Kings 19:20).

Like Elisha, Jesus heals lepers (Luke 5:12–16; 17:11–19; 2 Kings 5:1–14), raises the dead (Luke 7:11–17; 2 Kings 4:32–37), saves debtors (Luke 7:36–50; 2 Kings 4:1–7), and feeds a multitude (Luke 9:10–17; 2 Kings 4:42–44). Besides being a worker of miracles, Elisha is a model for Jesus because he was a prophet who was *anointed* (1 Kings 19:16). Being a prophet is thus part of Jesus' mission as *Messiah*, as he announced in Nazareth, quoting the prophet Isaiah: "The Spirit of the Lord is upon me, / because he has anointed me" (Luke 4:18; Isa 61:1).

a. Matt 11:13–14; 17:11–13; Mark 9:12–13; see Mark 1:6; 2 Kings 1:8.
b. Richard B. Hays, *Echoes of Scripture in the Gospels* (Waco: Baylor University Press, 2016), 237–43.

(Luke 6:36). His compassionate care includes one extra detail: after raising the son, **Jesus gave him to his mother**, exactly as Elijah had done (1 Kings 17:23). The promise of Jesus' beatitude is thus fulfilled: "Blessed are you who are now weeping, / for you will laugh" (Luke 6:21).

All in the two originally separate crowds are now united in a response of **7:16–17** praise, as **they glorified God** (see 5:26). Jesus, who had implicitly referred to himself as a prophet (4:24), is now publicly recognized as **a great prophet**, suggesting the prophet like Moses that God promised to raise up (Deut 18:15). Indeed, Jesus **has arisen**. This verb, the same as in Jesus' command to the dead man to "arise" (Luke 7:14), foreshadows his own resurrection from death (24:6, 34). As a prophet, Jesus is like Elijah, who raised the son of the widow of Zarephath (1 Kings 17:17–24), and Elisha, who raised the son of the Shunammite woman (2 Kings 4:32–37). As "Lord" (Luke 7:13), Jesus is greater than these prophets, healing by his own word rather than by praying to God. In the saving help that Jesus brings, **God has visited his people**, as in the days of Moses (Exod 4:31; 13:19 RSV) and as prophesied earlier in the Gospel (Luke 1:68, 78). Because of the miracle, Jesus' fame continues to **spread** (4:14, 37; 5:15).

Reflection and Application (7:11–17)

Bereavement ministry. In the Psalms, we read: "The LORD . . . comes to the aid of the orphan and the widow" (Ps 146:9). Jesus the "Lord" (Luke 7:13) aided a widow and had compassion on her. How can we extend Jesus' compassion to the widows and widowers in our communities, especially those left alone or with limited means of support?

John the Baptist's Messengers and Jesus' Witness to John (7:18–35)

---

¹⁸The disciples of John told him about all these things. John summoned two of his disciples ¹⁹and sent them to the Lord to ask, "Are you the one who is to come, or should we look for another?" ²⁰When the men came to him, they said, "John the Baptist has sent us to you to ask, 'Are you the one who is to come, or should we look for another?'" ²¹At that time he cured many of their diseases, sufferings, and evil spirits; he also granted sight to many who were blind. ²²And he said to them in reply, "Go and tell John what you have seen and heard: the blind regain their sight, the lame walk, lepers are cleansed, the deaf hear, the dead are raised, the poor have the good news proclaimed to them. ²³And blessed is the one who takes no offense at me."
   ²⁴When the messengers of John had left, Jesus began to speak to the crowds about John. "What did you go out to the desert to see—a reed swayed by the wind? ²⁵Then what did you go out to see? Someone dressed in fine garments? Those who dress luxuriously and live sumptuously are found in royal palaces. ²⁶Then what did you go out to see? A prophet? Yes,

I tell you, and more than a prophet. [27]This is the one about whom scripture says:

> 'Behold, I am sending my messenger ahead of you,
> he will prepare your way before you.'

[28]I tell you, among those born of women, no one is greater than John; yet the least in the kingdom of God is greater than he." [29](All the people who listened, including the tax collectors, and who were baptized with the baptism of John, acknowledged the righteousness of God; [30]but the Pharisees and scholars of the law, who were not baptized by him, rejected the plan of God for themselves.)

[31]"Then to what shall I compare the people of this generation? What are they like? [32]They are like children who sit in the marketplace and call to one another,

> 'We played the flute for you, but you did not dance.
> We sang a dirge, but you did not weep.'

[33]For John the Baptist came neither eating food nor drinking wine, and you said, 'He is possessed by a demon.' [34]The Son of Man came eating and drinking and you said, 'Look, he is a glutton and a drunkard, a friend of tax collectors and sinners.' [35]But wisdom is vindicated by all her children."

OT: Exod 23:20; Isa 35:5–6; 61:1; Mal 3:1–2, 23
NT: Matt 21:31–32; Mark 1:2; Luke 1:17, 76; 3:4, 16; 4:18; 16:16. // Matt 11:2–19
Catechism: the one who is to come, 453; John the Baptist, 523, 719; good news to the poor, 544; Jesus' signs, 547
Lectionary: Luke 7:18–23: Wednesday Third Week of Advent; Anointing of the Sick; Luke 7:24–30: Thursday Third Week of Advent

The two miracles involving people who were about to die or died (7:2, 12) set **7:18–20** the stage for a discussion of Jesus and his mission ("the dead are raised," v. 22). First, **disciples of John** ask Jesus about his identity (vv. 18–23). Next, Jesus explains John's role in God's plan, thus indirectly indicating who he himself is (vv. 24–28). Finally, Jesus reflects on the divided response to John and himself (vv. 29–35).

In prison (3:20), **John** is informed **about all these things** Jesus is doing. Perhaps he is wondering if he will experience the "liberty to captives" proclaimed by Jesus in Nazareth (4:18). Accordingly, he sends **two of his disciples** to ask **the Lord** a question about his identity: **Are you the one who is to come, or should we look for another?** John himself had referred to one mightier than he who was coming (3:16), but it appears that he now has doubts whether Jesus is the one. His question asks whether Jesus is the Messiah whom the Jewish people were expecting to come, in fulfillment of Old Testament promises (see the sidebar, "Messianic Expectations," p. 179). Jesus is indeed the Messiah, as Peter will later recognize (9:20), but he does not come in the manner that some expected—for example, as a conquering king. In response, Jesus clarifies his identity and mission as Messiah.

7:21–23   Jesus responds first with deeds—that is, his miracles—not so much ones done earlier but those he did **at that time** (literally, "in that hour"): **he cured many of their diseases** (as in 4:40; 6:18) and **evil spirits** (4:31–37; 6:18), and **he also granted sight to many who were blind**. Jesus then adds his verbal response, so that the two disciples, having both **seen and heard**, can return as witnesses to **tell John**. Jesus' words echo his reading from Isaiah in Nazareth and summarize his miracles: **the blind regain their sight** (4:18; 7:21; Isa 61:1 LXX), **the lame walk** (Luke 5:17–26), **lepers are cleansed** (5:12–16), **the deaf hear** (see comment on 11:14), **the dead are raised** (7:11–17), and **the poor have the good news proclaimed to them** (4:18; 6:20). Jesus' words also refer to various prophecies of Isaiah, which he is now fulfilling: "Then the eyes of the blind shall see, / and the ears of the deaf be opened; / Then the lame shall leap like a stag, / and the mute tongue sing for joy" (Isa 35:5–6; also Isa 26:19; 29:18–19; 42:7). All of these things are happening *at the present time*. Therefore, there is no need to look for another. The Messiah, the one who is to come, has already arrived!

Jesus' response has striking similarities to a manuscript fragment found at Qumran that mentions the "anointed one" and then lists the Lord's marvelous deeds: to give "sight to the blind," "make the dead live," and "proclaim good news to the poor."[6] Jesus' answer is thus consistent with certain other Jewish expectations of the signs that would accompany messianic times.

Jesus concludes with a beatitude: **blessed is the one who takes no offense at me**. It could also be translated: "Blessed is anyone who does not stumble on account of me" (NIV). Perhaps John had "stumbled" in his expectation. He had announced "the coming wrath" of the one who would burn the chaff in fire (Luke 3:7, 16–17). Jesus will indeed speak about wrath and fire, but later (12:49; 17:29–30; 21:23). For now, John must understand, as Elijah before him, that the "Lord" (7:19) is not always to be found in fire (see 1 Kings 19:12).

7:24–25   After explaining his own identity, Jesus clarifies John's role. He asks several rhetorical questions: Is John **a reed swayed by the wind?** Is he **someone dressed in fine garments?** Clearly not, since John was just the opposite. John was not

6. 4Q521 (*Messianic Apocalypse*) 2 II, 1–12, in *The Dead Sea Scrolls Study Edition*, ed. Florentino García Martínez and Eibert J. C. Tigchelaar, 2 vols. (Leiden: Brill; Grand Rapids: Eerdmans, 2000), 2:1045.

Figure 8. Coin with reed of Herod Antipas.

swayed by political pressure when it came to censuring Herod (Luke 3:19). His ascetical life in the desert was well known (7:33), even if Luke does not mention John's rough clothing of camel's hair (Mark 1:6). With these questions, Jesus is likely contrasting John with his enemy, Herod Antipas. Around AD 20, the tetrarch of Galilee had minted coins to mark the founding of his capital city, Tiberias, where he built one of his **royal palaces**. The coins had the image of a reed, which were common to the area by the Sea of Galilee. To his critics, however, a reed could easily describe the wavering character of Herod.[7] Moreover, the Gospel later records the fine garments associated with Herod when he mockingly clothes Jesus with "resplendent garb" (Luke 23:11).

With the third rhetorical question—is John **a prophet?**—Jesus affirms who   **7:26–27** John really is (see 20:6). However, John is also **more than a prophet** because of his unique role as precursor to the Messiah. Just as Jesus explained his own identity by alluding to Scripture (7:22), so now he combines two texts from Scripture to explain John's role as **messenger** (Exod 23:20; Mal 3:1). By recalling the journey to the promised land, the Exodus text suggests that John announced the **way** leading to a new exodus (see Luke 3:4–6; the sidebar, "Isaiah's New Exodus Fulfilled in Luke-Acts," p. 84). The context of the passage from Malachi recalls the figure of Elijah (Mal 3:23), in whose spirit and power John was sent to **prepare** for the Messiah (see Luke 1:17, 76). The **you** mentioned in these texts, for whom John is preparing, is now understood to be Jesus himself. Indirectly, Jesus thus reaffirms that he is the Messiah.

Jesus continues with a paradox. In view of John's unique role, **no one is**   **7:28** **greater than John**—that is, during the age of "the law and the prophets" (16:16). However, with the advent in Jesus of **the kingdom of God** (4:43; 16:16), people

7. Gerd Theissen, *The Gospels in Context: Social and Political History in the Synoptic Tradition*, trans. Linda M. Maloney (Minneapolis: Fortress, 1991), 26–42; Morten Hørning Jensen, *Herod Antipas in Galilee*, 2nd ed. (Tübingen: Mohr Siebeck, 2010), 205–6, 231–32, 297.

are, as Paul says, "not under law but under grace" (Rom 6:14 RSV). They are "a new creation" (2 Cor 5:17) and "children of God" (Luke 20:36; Rom 8:14, 16). Therefore, **the least** in the new **is greater than** John, the greatest of the old. John is a bridge figure in salvation history, at the head of those "prophets and kings" of the past who longed to see the Messiah (Luke 10:24) but entering as just one more among many into the "kingdom of God" (13:28–29).

7:29–30   Luke adds a parenthetical remark explaining how the response to John has been divided. Those **who listened** to him, including **tax collectors** (see 3:12), **acknowledged the righteousness of God**. Literally, they "justified" or "vindicated" God, recognizing God's righteous plan at work in John and responding to his call to repentance (3:3). Hence, they **were baptized**. In contrast, **the Pharisees and scholars of the law**, like Jewish leaders later in the Gospel (20:1–8), **rejected the plan of God** manifested in John. They thus refused to be **baptized by him**.

7:31–34   With a short parable, Jesus explains that those like the Pharisees who rejected John are also rejecting him. He refers to them as **the people of this generation**, a phrase with negative connotations (see 9:41; 11:29–32, 50–51; 17:25; Acts 2:40), which also recalls the evil generation that rejected God in the wilderness following the exodus (Num 32:13; Deut 1:35; 32:5, 20). They are compared to **children** who are supposed to be playing, but who neither **dance** (A)[8] as at a wedding nor **weep** (B) as at a funeral. In other words, they respond neither to **John the Baptist** (B'), who fasted from **food** and **wine** (Luke 1:15; 5:33), nor to Jesus **the Son of Man** (A'), who comes like a bridegroom **eating and drinking** with **tax collectors and sinners** (5:30, 34). Though there is "a time to weep . . . and a time to dance" (Eccles 3:4), the opponents of John and Jesus do neither; they do "not know how to interpret the present time" (Luke 12:56).

7:35   In contrast, Jesus will likely find a favorable hearing from "all the people who listened" to John and vindicated God (7:29). Using a proverb, he explains that they will be counted among **all** the **children** of **wisdom**, which likewise is **vindicated**. God's wisdom, personified here as in the Old Testament, invites her "children" to "listen" (Prov 8:32). She "teaches her children" (Sir 4:11) now through Jesus, who is filled with wisdom (Luke 2:40, 52). He comes "eating and drinking" (7:34) so as to issue wisdom's invitation: "Come, eat of my food, / and drink of the wine I have mixed" (Prov 9:5). Readers are also included in this invitation; they can thus ask themselves whether they are listening and responding to Jesus' message and his messengers.

8. David E. Garland, *Luke*, ZECNT (Grand Rapids: Zondervan, 2011), 316.

Jesus Pardons a Sinful Woman in a Pharisee's House (7:36–50)

³⁶A Pharisee invited him to dine with him, and he entered the Pharisee's house and reclined at table. ³⁷Now there was a sinful woman in the city who learned that he was at table in the house of the Pharisee. Bringing an alabaster flask of ointment, ³⁸she stood behind him at his feet weeping and began to bathe his feet with her tears. Then she wiped them with her hair, kissed them, and anointed them with the ointment. ³⁹When the Pharisee who had invited him saw this he said to himself, "If this man were a prophet, he would know who and what sort of woman this is who is touching him, that she is a sinner." ⁴⁰Jesus said to him in reply, "Simon, I have something to say to you." "Tell me, teacher," he said. ⁴¹"Two people were in debt to a certain creditor; one owed five hundred days' wages and the other owed fifty. ⁴²Since they were unable to repay the debt, he forgave it for both. Which of them will love him more?" ⁴³Simon said in reply, "The one, I suppose, whose larger debt was forgiven." He said to him, "You have judged rightly." ⁴⁴Then he turned to the woman and said to Simon, "Do you see this woman? When I entered your house, you did not give me water for my feet, but she has bathed them with her tears and wiped them with her hair. ⁴⁵You did not give me a kiss, but she has not ceased kissing my feet since the time I entered. ⁴⁶You did not anoint my head with oil, but she anointed my feet with ointment. ⁴⁷So I tell you, her many sins have been forgiven; hence, she has shown great love. But the one to whom little is forgiven, loves little." ⁴⁸He said to her, "Your sins are forgiven." ⁴⁹The others at table said to themselves, "Who is this who even forgives sins?" ⁵⁰But he said to the woman, "Your faith has saved you; go in peace."

OT: 2 Kings 4:1–7
NT: Matt 26:6–13; Mark 14:3–9; Luke 5:20; 8:48; John 11:2; 12:1–8
Catechism: Jesus dines with Pharisees, 575, 588; prayer of the forgiven sinner, 2616, 2712; sacrament of forgiveness, 1441, 1481
Lectionary: Luke 7:36–8:3: Eleventh Sunday Ordinary Time (Year C)

7:36–38 The unexpected role reversal just described, where sinners listen but religious leaders reject God's plan (7:29–35), is now illustrated in another meal scene (see 5:29–39). **A Pharisee** invites Jesus **to dine** at his **house** (see 11:37–54; 14:1–24). Such a scene would have recalled for Gentile readers the Hellenistic *symposium*, in which a distinguished host invited guests to a banquet, including a chief guest known for wisdom. Something would then trigger a discussion, in which the chief guest would have the last word.[9] Here the actions of **a sinful**

9. E. Springs Steele, "Luke 11:37–54—A Modified Hellenistic Symposium?," *JBL* 103 (1984): 379–94.

woman prompt the discussion. Why would such a woman drop in uninvited? Possibly, it was a public event where people could come just to listen to the guest teacher. Since Jesus was known to be a friend of sinners (7:34), the woman may have dared to seek him out. She may also have known others who were present.[10] The banquet was served on low tables and the guests **reclined** on their sides with their feet behind them, such that the woman **stood behind** Jesus **at his feet**. She had brought **an alabaster flask of ointment**, a hint of what she would do.

The woman's actions are more startling than her surprising entrance. Luke focuses attention on her actions by stringing them together using the conjunction "and" (partially lost in most translations): **weeping** she began to wet **his feet with her tears** *and* **she wiped them with her hair** *and* **kissed** his feet *and* **anointed them with the ointment**. The verb tenses also indicate ongoing actions—in other words, she *kept on doing* these things. Also surprising, however, is what **the Pharisee** was *not doing*. The word "Pharisee" occurs four times (vv. 36–39), each time connected either with his invitation or his house, as if to suggest what he *should be doing*—namely, offering the gestures of hospitality expected of a host toward an honored guest. As Jesus will explain (vv. 44–46), she makes up for what he failed to do in hospitality. Moreover, though her actions are often interpreted as immodest (e.g., letting her hair down in public in order to dry Jesus' feet), her gestures are, on account of her weeping, more likely those of "grief, supplication, and gratitude."[11]

7:39   The reader is now given an insider's view of the reaction of the **Pharisee**. He has already judged **what sort of woman this is**—namely, **a sinner**—and now he passes judgment on Jesus, who despite his reputation as **a prophet** (7:16) seems unable to perceive the woman as he does. Through the Pharisee's wrong judgment, the question of Jesus' identity is again raised (see 7:19).

7:40–43   Ironically, Jesus demonstrates that he is a prophet by perceiving the thoughts of **Simon** the Pharisee (see John 4:16–19). As the honored guest, he now exercises his role of **teacher** by telling a parable, an indirect way for him to address the situation. In the parable, a **creditor** cancels the unequal **debt** of **two people**

10. In John 12:1–8, the woman anointing Jesus is Mary, the sister of Lazarus, who is at table, and of Martha, who is serving. The event occurs in Bethany shortly before Passover (see Matt 26:6–13; Mark 14:3–9). Luke omits an anointing scene in his passion narrative in favor of this one here, situated in an unnamed city and having a different narrative purpose. Despite the different contexts, there are interesting similarities. Luke and John both say that the woman *anointed* Jesus' *feet* (Matthew and Mark say *head*) and *wiped* them with *her hair* (John 11:2; 12:3 RSV). Moreover, Luke later mentions Martha's sister Mary, and like the woman here, she is at Jesus' feet (Luke 10:39).

11. Charles H. Cosgrove, "A Woman's Unbound Hair in the Greco-Roman World, with Special Reference to the Story of the 'Sinful Woman' in Luke 7:36–50," *JBL* 124 (2005): 689.

(**five hundred days' wages** and **fifty**). In saying that the creditor **forgave** the **debt**, the verb *charizomai* is used, which can mean remitting debts, as here, or forgiving sins (2 Cor 2:10; Eph 4:32; Col 2:13; 3:13). As used in the parable, the word is a synonym for *aphiēmi*, "forgive" (Luke 7:47–49). In view of Jesus' jubilee mission of proclaiming liberty (4:18; Lev 25:10), the parable is thus declaring the remission of the debt of sin![12]

Jesus lets Simon draw the lesson of the parable by asking him which debtor would **love** the creditor **more**. With his answer about the person **whose larger debt was forgiven**, Simon shows that he has now **judged rightly**, although he does not yet grasp the parable's application.

Jesus bluntly clarifies its application, explaining how the two debtors represent **the woman** and **Simon**. Jesus details the Pharisee's omissions of hospitality by comparing them to the woman's acts of devotion. She in effect behaved as the true host. Whereas he provided no **water** for washing, no **kiss**, and no **oil** to **anoint** his **head**, she did more than the equivalent of these, as she **bathed** his **feet**, did not cease **kissing** them, and **anointed** them.

7:44–46

The emphasis on Jesus' **feet** is noteworthy. In the Greek text, the word occurs seven times in the passage. It calls to mind a text from Isaiah: "How beautiful . . . are the *feet* of the one bringing good news, / Announcing peace, bearing good news, / announcing salvation, saying to Zion, / 'Your God is King!'" (Isa 52:7 [emphasis added]).[13] Jesus is the one who will announce *peace* and *salvation* to the woman (see Luke 7:50). His jubilee proclamation of liberty again provides the key for understanding (4:18–19; Isa 61:1–2).[14] By liberating the woman from her sins, Jesus will bring her salvation.

Jesus explains that the forgiveness of *debts* in the parable refers to **sins** that are **forgiven** (verb *aphiēmi*, four times in Luke 7:47–49; see 5:20–24). By forgiving sins, Jesus is carrying out his jubilee mission of proclaiming "liberty" (noun *aphesis*, 4:18; 24:47).

7:47

The next part of the verse has been interpreted in two different ways. The NABRE translation, **hence, she has shown great love**, implies that her love is the *result* of forgiveness received. However, the word "hence" can also be translated "because" (NJB), which seems to say just the opposite, that her love was the *cause* of forgiveness. The first view is the one supported by the parable,

---

12. James A. Sanders, "Sins, Debts, and Jubilee Release," in *Luke and Scripture: The Function of Sacred Tradition in Luke-Acts*, by Craig A. Evans and James A. Sanders (Minneapolis: Fortress, 1993), 84–92.

13. Garland, *Luke*, 325–26.

14. According to Jewish expectation at Qumran (11Q13 II, 15–25), the messianic figure who proclaims the jubilee in Isa 61 was identified with the messenger of Isa 52 who announces redemption (Isa 52:7–10). See John Sietze Bergsma, *The Jubilee from Leviticus to Qumran: A History of Interpretation* (Leiden: Brill, 2007), 289.

Giving Jesus Good Hospitality

LIVING TRADITION

St. Teresa of Ávila (speaking of herself in the third person) explains that receiving the Eucharist is like having Jesus enter our house:

> When she received Communion, this person . . . strove to strengthen her faith so that in receiving her Lord it was as if, with her bodily eyes, she saw him enter her house. Since she believed that this Lord truly entered her poor home, she freed herself from all exterior things. . . . She strove to recollect the senses so that all of them would take notice of so great a good. . . . She considered she was at his feet and wept with the Magdalene,[a] no more nor less than if she were seeing him with her bodily eyes in the house of the Pharisee. And even though she didn't feel devotion, faith told her that he was indeed there. . . . Receiving Communion is not like picturing with the imagination, as when we reflect upon the Lord on the cross . . . when we picture within ourselves how things happened to him in the past. In Communion the event is happening now, and it is entirely true. There's no reason to go looking for him in some other place farther away. . . . Now, then, if when he went about in the world the mere touch of his robes cured the sick [Luke 6:19; 8:43–48], why doubt, if we have faith, that miracles will be worked while he is within us and that he will give what we ask of him, since he is in our house? His Majesty is not accustomed to paying poorly for his lodging if the hospitality is good.[b]

a. In the past, the unnamed sinful woman was often identified with Mary Magdalene (see Luke 8:2).

b. Teresa of Ávila, *The Way of Perfection* 34.7–8, in *The Collected Works of Saint Teresa of Avila*, trans. Kieran Kavanaugh and Otilio Rodriguez, 3 vols. (Washington, DC: ICS Publications, 1976–85), 2:171–72.

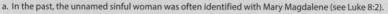

where love follows as a response to debt-forgiveness. The end of the verse also supports this view: **the one to whom little is forgiven, loves little**.

Earlier, Jesus said that he came to call "sinners" to "repentance" (5:32), and later he will send his disciples to preach "repentance, for the forgiveness of sins" (24:47). The woman, despite being known as a sinner (7:37, 39), is one of those who listened (see 7:29) and repented. Her conversion included her coming to faith (v. 50). Her tears and loving actions are then the fruit that give evidence of her repentance (3:8). In contrast, the Pharisee, like those mentioned earlier who rejected God's plan (7:30), did not think he needed to repent. Consequently, he could be forgiven little and, as a result, showed little love.

7:48–50   In words that echo those spoken to the paralyzed man (5:20, 23), Jesus gives assurance to the woman that her **sins are forgiven**.[15] As before, the people

15. The verb form in v. 48 is the same as in v. 47, where the NABRE translates "have been forgiven."

question: **Who is this who even forgives sin?** Though "God alone can forgive sins" (5:21), readers already know that Jesus is the "Son of God" (1:35). The question can thus be left unanswered. Jesus lets the woman go: **Your faith has saved you; go in peace**. He will say exactly the same words in the next chapter to a woman whom he heals (8:48). Here, as with the paralyzed man and his friends (5:20), it is faith that leads to forgiveness and salvation. In sum, Jesus praises both the woman's faith and her love. As Paul teaches: "in Christ Jesus," what counts is "faith working through love" (Gal 5:6).

The chapter began with stories of a man with faith (into whose house Jesus *does not* enter) and a weeping woman, leading to the recognition that Jesus is a prophet. The chapter now ends with a story of a man (into whose house Jesus *does* enter) and a weeping woman with faith, leading to the recognition that Jesus is a prophet. Amid questions about his identity, Jesus is vindicated as a prophet and, indeed, more than a prophet.

Reflection and Application (7:36–50)

Pride and humility. St. Augustine explains the contrast between the end and the beginning of Luke 7: "The teacher of humility . . . sat down in the house of a certain proud Pharisee called Simon. And though he was sitting in his house, there wasn't anywhere in his heart where the Son of Man might lay his head. . . . Into the centurion's house, on the other hand, he never entered, and he took possession of his heart. . . . This man's faith is discerned and praised in an act of humility."[16] Am I humble like the centurion or proud like the Pharisee? Is there room in my heart for Jesus?

Go in peace. In the sacrament of penance, Jesus forgives a person's sins through the ministry of a priest. To conclude the celebration of the sacrament, the priest says to the penitent Jesus' final words to the woman, after he had forgiven her sins: "Go in peace" (Luke 7:50).

---

16. Augustine, *Sermon* 62.1, in *Sermons*, trans. Edmund Hill, 11 vols., WSA III/3 (Hyde Park, NY: New City Press, 1990–97), 3:156–57.

Jesus' Parables and Power

Luke 8:1–56

With parables and powerful miracles, Jesus continues his ministry in and near Galilee. Accompanying him are the apostles and also a group of women disciples (8:1–3). In his teaching (8:4–21), Jesus insists on the importance of properly hearing the word of God. In his miracles (8:22–56), he manifests extraordinary power over the forces of nature, evil, sickness, and death. There is an emphasis on responding to Jesus with faith (8:12–13, 25, 48, 50). The miracles again raise questions of Jesus' identity (8:25, 28), pointing ahead to Peter's confession in Luke 9.

Women Journey with Jesus and the Twelve (8:1–3)

¹Afterward he journeyed from one town and village to another, preaching and proclaiming the good news of the kingdom of God. Accompanying him were the Twelve ²and some women who had been cured of evil spirits and infirmities, Mary, called Magdalene, from whom seven demons had gone out, ³Joanna, the wife of Herod's steward Chuza, Susanna, and many others who provided for them out of their resources.

NT: Matt 27:55–56; Mark 15:40–41; 16:9; Luke 23:49, 55–56; 24:1–11; Acts 13:1
Lectionary: Luke 7:36–8:3: Eleventh Sunday Ordinary Time (Year C)

8:1 As in an earlier summary (4:43–44), Luke reminds readers that Jesus' mission is **preaching and proclaiming the good news**, as he defined it in his Nazareth discourse (4:18–19). The content of his preaching continues to be **the kingdom of God** (4:43). With him are **the Twelve** apostles (6:13–16).

Also with Jesus are **some women** who have benefited from his healings and   8:2–3
now express their gratitude in service. These women "from Galilee" will follow Jesus even to his death and burial (23:49, 55–56) and will be the ones who discover the empty tomb, hear the announcement of the resurrection, and report it to the apostles (24:1–11). Three are named here, though there are **many others**. Most familiar is **Mary, called Magdalene**, who is mentioned again in Luke's resurrection narrative (24:10) and frequently in the other Gospels.[1] She is from Magdala, a fishing town on the western shore of the lake. Jesus had freed her from a severe case of possession by **seven demons** (see 11:26).

The two other named women are **Joanna** and **Susanna**. Joanna is also mentioned in Luke's resurrection narrative (24:10). Since she and Mary Magdalene thus accompany Jesus for a good portion of his public ministry, they may well be among Luke's "eyewitnesses" (1:2) on whose testimony his Gospel is based, especially Joanna, who is mentioned only by Luke.[2] In particular, since she is **the wife of Herod's steward Chuza**, she may be—like Manaen, "a close friend of Herod the tetrarch" (Acts 13:1)—a source of Luke's special passages about Herod (Luke 13:31–33; 23:6–15). Her association with Herod's household also indicates that Jesus' followers included people of high social and economic standing. Hence, with **their resources**, she and the other women **provided for them**. What is emphasized here is their financial support.

Luke's complementary depictions of men and women include even the itinerant groups of disciples that accompany Jesus. As Paul says, "There is neither Jew nor Greek, there is neither slave nor free person, there is not male and female; for you are all one in Christ Jesus" (Gal 3:28). By reaching out to Gentiles, the poor, and women, Jesus challenged the social conventions of his time.

The Parables of the Sower and of the Lamp (8:4–18)

[4]**When a large crowd gathered, with people from one town after another journeying to him, he spoke in a parable.** [5]**"A sower went out to sow his seed. And as he sowed, some seed fell on the path and was trampled, and the birds of the sky ate it up.** [6]**Some seed fell on rocky ground, and when it grew, it withered for lack of moisture.** [7]**Some seed fell among thorns, and**

1. Matt 27:56, 61; 28:1; Mark 15:40, 47; 16:1, 9; John 19:25; 20:1, 18.
2. Richard Bauckham, *Jesus and the Eyewitnesses: The Gospels as Eyewitness Testimony* (Grand Rapids: Eerdmans, 2006), 131.

the thorns grew with it and choked it. [8]And some seed fell on good soil, and when it grew, it produced fruit a hundredfold." After saying this, he called out, "Whoever has ears to hear ought to hear."

[9]Then his disciples asked him what the meaning of this parable might be. [10]He answered, "Knowledge of the mysteries of the kingdom of God has been granted to you; but to the rest, they are made known through parables so that 'they may look but not see, and hear but not understand.'

[11]"This is the meaning of the parable. The seed is the word of God. [12]Those on the path are the ones who have heard, but the devil comes and takes away the word from their hearts that they may not believe and be saved. [13]Those on rocky ground are the ones who, when they hear, receive the word with joy, but they have no root; they believe only for a time and fall away in time of trial. [14]As for the seed that fell among thorns, they are the ones who have heard, but as they go along, they are choked by the anxieties and riches and pleasures of life, and they fail to produce mature fruit. [15]But as for the seed that fell on rich soil, they are the ones who, when they have heard the word, embrace it with a generous and good heart, and bear fruit through perseverance.

[16]"No one who lights a lamp conceals it with a vessel or sets it under a bed; rather, he places it on a lampstand so that those who enter may see the light. [17]For there is nothing hidden that will not become visible, and nothing secret that will not be known and come to light. [18]Take care, then, how you hear. To anyone who has, more will be given, and from the one who has not, even what he seems to have will be taken away."

OT: Ps 119:105; Isa 6:9–10; 55:10–11
NT: Luke 11:33; 12:2; 19:26; John 12:39–40; Acts 28:26–27; 1 Pet 1:23. // Matt 13:1–23; Mark 4:1–25
Catechism: parables reveal the kingdom, 546, 1151; prayer that bears fruit, 368, 2668, 2707, 2731
Lectionary: Luke 8:4–10, 11–15: Confirmation

The parables and miracles in the rest of Luke 8 closely parallel those found in Mark 4–5.

8:4–5, 11–12   A **large crowd** gathers again to hear Jesus (5:15; 6:17), who now teaches in parables. The **parable** of the **sower** (8:5–8) serves as a model, since Jesus gives its explanation (vv. 11–15) and his reason for teaching in parables (v. 10). It is also one of several parables using agricultural imagery. The parable portrays a farmer who generously casts **his seed**, aware that **some** will fall in less productive areas but nevertheless trying to use all the land available. **The seed** sown represents **the word of God**, which is preached now by Jesus (8:1), and

Parables in Luke

A parable (Greek *parabolē*) is a figure of speech comparing two things—literally, placing them alongside each other. Occasionally, the Greek term is translated with other words such as "proverb" (4:23) or "lesson" (21:29). Similarly in the †Septuagint, *parabolē* often translates the Hebrew *mashal*, which can mean "proverb" (1 Kings 5:12)[a] or refer to another figurative saying that teaches an object lesson (Num 24:21; Mic 2:4).

Some of Jesus' parables are very brief comparisons—that is, similes or similitudes; for example, the kingdom of God "is like" a mustard seed or yeast (Luke 13:18–21). Others are short narratives, complete with a plot, several characters, and dialogue—for example, the great banquet (14:16–24) or the rich man and Lazarus (16:19–31). The parables are characteristic of Jesus' teaching—for example, about the kingdom of God (13:18–21; 19:11–27; 21:29–31). Besides conveying Jesus' teaching, parables can also explain his mission; for example, the parables of the lost sheep, lost coin, and prodigal son justify his outreach to sinners (15:1–32). Many parables are somewhat allegorical—for example, the sower (8:4–15) and the wicked tenants (20:9–19)—with each detail signifying some reality. Their interpretation thus involves another level of meaning, though one should not press the details too far.[b]

The vivid imagery of the parables is drawn from daily life: household tasks (8:16; 11:33; 13:20–21; 15:8–10), banquets (14:7–11, 16–24), and shepherding (15:4–7). Not surprisingly for an agrarian society with crops such as wheat, barley, grapes, figs, and olives (see Deut 8:8),[c] several parables use farming imagery: the sower (Luke 8:4–15), the rich fool who needs bigger barns (12:16–21), the barren fig tree (13:6–9), the mustard seed (13:18–19), the dishonest steward who reduces debts on olive oil and wheat (16:1–8), the wicked tenant farmers (20:9–19), and the budding fig tree (21:29–31).

a. 1 Kings 4:32 RSV.
b. Craig L. Blomberg, *Interpreting the Parables*, 2nd ed. (Downers Grove, IL: IVP Academic, 2012), 19–25, 33–81.
c. On the fruitfulness of the land near Capernaum, see Josephus, *Jewish War* 3.516–19.

later by his followers.[3] The proper response to the word is to hear or listen (see 5:1). Indeed, there is great emphasis in the first part of this chapter on hearing God's word (8:8, 10–15, 18, 21). Not all hearing is the same, however, so the parable details four kinds of response. These refer to four kinds of people, but can also be applied to the varying responses of the same person at different

3. Luke 9:2; 10:1, 9; 24:47; Acts 4:31; 8:4, 14, 25; 11:1; 13:5, 46; 15:35; 17:13; 18:11.

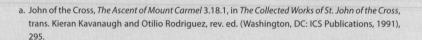

The Thorns of Riches

LIVING TRADITION

St. John of the Cross offers sober advice regarding worldly riches:

> The vanity of rejoicing over riches, titles, status, positions, and other similar goods after which people usually strive is clear. . . . Though it is true that temporal goods of themselves are not necessarily the cause of sin, yet, because of the weakness of its tendencies, the human heart usually becomes attached to them and fails God, which is sin. . . . This is why the Lord in the Gospel calls them thorns; the one who willfully handles them will be wounded with some sin [Matt 13:22; Luke 8:14]. In St. Luke's Gospel the exclamation—which ought to be greatly feared—asserts: "How difficult will it be for those who have riches to enter the kingdom of heaven" (those who have joy in them), and demonstrates clearly a person's obligation not to rejoice in riches, since one is thereby exposed to so much danger [Luke 18:24; see Matt 19:23].[a]

a. John of the Cross, *The Ascent of Mount Carmel* 3.18.1, in *The Collected Works of St. John of the Cross*, trans. Kieran Kavanaugh and Otilio Rodriguez, rev. ed. (Washington, DC: ICS Publications, 1991), 295.

times. First, **those on the path** represent those who **heard** only superficially. **The devil** carries off the **word** so that it does not enter **their hearts**, like **the birds** that eat the seed that remains on the surface without sinking into the soil. The limited response of such people does not lead them to **believe and be saved** (see 7:50), which are the goals of hearing the word. Those who exhibit such an unbelieving response include the Pharisees who do not listen to John (7:30) and the elders, chief priests, and scribes who do not believe either John or Jesus (20:5; 22:67).

8:6, 13   Second, **those on rocky ground** represent those who **believe**, unlike the first group, but **fall away** when they experience **trial** (*peirasmos*). Jesus himself withstood every "temptation" (*peirasmos*) of the devil (4:13). He later remarks that the apostles have stood by him in his "trials" (22:28) but also prays that they may not "undergo the test" (*peirasmos*, 22:40, 46). Similarly, all believers ask in the Lord's Prayer not to be led into "temptation" (11:4 RSV), so as not to risk falling away. However, those who **have no root** eventually fall away. Like the house built without a foundation (6:49), their belief does not go deep: when a trial comes ("the river burst against it"), the house collapses.

8:7, 14   Third, those **among thorns** represent those whose faith is **choked** by various worldly cares, so that it does not **produce mature fruit** (see 6:44). Three examples are given, which are echoed later in the Gospel. Jesus tells his disciples not to let **anxieties** weigh down their hearts (21:34). He also teaches about the danger of **riches** and the need for detachment (12:15–21; 14:33; 16:13, 19–31; 18:18–25). He similarly warns against the pursuit of hedonistic **pleasures** (12:19; 16:19).

Finally, what falls on **good** or **rich soil** represents those who **have heard**   8:8, 15
the word and responded properly. Unlike the first group, they believe and are saved, as they **embrace it with a generous and good heart**. In contrast to the second group, who fall away amid trial, these are the ones marked by **perseverance** (see Luke 21:19). Whereas those in the third group fail to produce mature fruit, these are the ones who **bear fruit** and are blessed with a **hundredfold** yield.[4] This abundant yield is seen in Acts, as the seed of the word of God grows through the increase in the number of believers (Acts 6:7; 12:24; 13:49; 19:20).

The parable concludes with an exhortation: **Whoever has ears to hear ought to hear** (see Luke 14:35). When heard, the word achieves the end for which it was sent (see Isa 55:11).

Besides explaining **the meaning of this parable**, Jesus gives a reason why   8:9–10
he often teaches **through parables**. In the previous chapter, Jesus' *miracles* were described in comparison with the prophets Elijah and Elisha. Similarly, Jesus presents his *teaching* in light of Israel's prophetic tradition, alluding to the prophet Isaiah: **they may look but not see, and hear but not understand** (see Isa 6:9). In other words, Jesus is aware that like the prophets before him who met with rejection, he is "a sign that will be contradicted" (Luke 2:34), one who brings "division" (12:51). The meaning of Jesus' parables will hence be perceived by those whose hearts are "generous and good" (8:15), but not by those with a "sluggish" heart (Isa 6:10).[5] While **disciples** are **granted** this **knowledge, the rest** remain on the surface rather than attaining **the mysteries of the kingdom of God** hidden in the parables. The word "mysteries" refers to God's unfolding plan of salvation: "There is a God in heaven who reveals mysteries" (Dan 2:28). Jesus is the one who is now revealing God's plan of salvation.

The passage concludes with the brief parable of the lighted **lamp** placed **on**   8:16–18
a lampstand (see Luke 11:33–34). Like the seed, the lamp is an image for God's word: "Your word is a lamp for my feet, / a light for my path" (Ps 119:105). Thus, the person who, when hearing God's word, embraces and understands it (Luke 8:10, 15) is filled with light and becomes a **visible** lamp so that others **may see the light**. Those who have been granted knowledge of the mysteries

---

4. The biblical precedent is Isaac's "hundredfold" yield (Gen 26:12), which was recounted in other Jewish literature: *Jubilees* 24.15; Philo, *On the Change of Names* 1.268.

5. At the end of Acts, Paul similarly quotes Isaiah to explain the divided reception his preaching receives (Acts 28:24–27, citing Isa 6:9–10).

Figure 9. Carved lampstand (temple menorah) from the Magdala synagogue.

of the kingdom must make them **known**. Hence, this parable complements the previous one: a person receives the word in order to believe and be saved (v. 12), thus becoming a lamp that enlightens others so that they too may be saved. So much depends on **how you hear** the word of God.

Reflection and Application (8:4–18)

Responding to God's word. The two parables of the sower and the lamp encourage both preachers and hearers of God's word to reflect on what they are doing. For preachers, the message of these parables is captured well by the threefold exhortation that a bishop addresses to newly ordained deacons in the Rite of Ordination: "Believe what you read, teach what you believe, and practice what you teach."[6] For those hearing God's word preached—in homilies, conferences, retreats, and so on—one could similarly say: Believe what you hear, share what you believe, and practice what you share. Regarding the first step, Paul says, "Faith comes from what is heard" (Rom 10:17). For the second step, Peter in Acts declares, "It is impossible for us not to speak about what we have seen and

6. *The Roman Pontifical*, Ordination of Deacons (Vatican City: Vox Clara Committee, 2012), 120.

heard" (Acts 4:20). For the third, James writes, "Be doers of the word and not hearers only" (James 1:22).

The New Family of Jesus (8:19–21)

> ¹⁹Then his mother and his brothers came to him but were unable to join him because of the crowd. ²⁰He was told, "Your mother and your brothers are standing outside and they wish to see you." ²¹He said to them in reply, "My mother and my brothers are those who hear the word of God and act on it."

NT: Luke 11:27–28; 18:29–30. // Matt 12:46–50; Mark 3:31–35
Catechism: brothers of Jesus, 500; Jesus' true family, 764, 2233

Jesus' teaching on hearing the word continues, but the arrival of **his mother and his brothers** leads him to teach also about his true family.[7] **Because of the crowd**, his relatives cannot reach him. In effect, Jesus is surrounded not by his natural family but by his new family of disciples, those like the Twelve and the women (8:1–3) who have heard his word and responded.

In Jesus' **reply**, the phrase **my mother and my brothers** refers to the members of this new family, made up of **those who hear the word of God and act on it**. Earlier, Jesus said something similar about hearing and acting on *his* words (6:47). God's word and Jesus' word both require the same response, suggesting Jesus' divine authority.

Membership in Jesus' natural family is not incompatible with membership in his new family. In Acts, the family of disciples that gathers after Jesus' ascension includes both groups: the apostles and "some women," but also "Mary the mother of Jesus, and his brothers" (Acts 1:13–14). Moreover, Mary herself has already provided the model of hearing and doing the word of God with her *fiat*: "May it be done to me according to your word" (Luke 1:38; see 11:28).

Jesus will later indicate that the demands of discipleship in his new family can create tensions with a person's natural family (12:51–53; 14:26; 21:16). However, he also promises abundant rewards for those who have "given up" natural family "for the sake of the kingdom of God" (18:29–30).

7. In the †Septuagint, the term *adelphos* is used not only for "brother" but also for extended family members such as a cousin (1 Chron 23:21–22) and a nephew (Gen 13:8). The Catholic Church similarly understands the New Testament references to Jesus' brothers. They are not children of Mary, who remained a virgin, but other close relatives of Jesus such as cousins or children of Joseph by a prior marriage. See Catechism 500.

Reflection and Application (8:19–21)

Experiencing the Church as a family. How can we better live the reality of the *family of God* (see Eph 2:19) in our parishes, seminaries, church groups, organizations, and movements? We can try doing what loving Christian families do: we can pray together, eat meals together, care for one another, visit and support those who are alone or in need, share our faith with each other, study God's word together, and so forth.

Jesus Calms a Storm at Sea (8:22–25)

²²One day he got into a boat with his disciples and said to them, "Let us cross to the other side of the lake." So they set sail, ²³and while they were sailing he fell asleep. A squall blew over the lake, and they were taking in water and were in danger. ²⁴They came and woke him saying, "Master, master, we are perishing!" He awakened, rebuked the wind and the waves, and they subsided and there was a calm. ²⁵Then he asked them, "Where is your faith?" But they were filled with awe and amazed and said to one another, "Who then is this, who commands even the winds and the sea, and they obey him?"

OT: Ps 107:28–30; Isa 51:9–10; Jon 1
NT: // Matt 8:23–27; Mark 4:35–41
Catechism: praying in the tempest, 2743; faith, 2610

Four miracle stories, organized in groups of two, make up the rest of the chapter. The first two miracles occur during a round-trip sea voyage, while the last two are sandwiched together. The miracles demonstrate the extent of Jesus' power and invite responses of faith.

8:22   Jesus gets **into a boat**[8] (see 5:3) in order to head over **to the other side of the lake** of Gennesaret **with his disciples**. From a town such as Capernaum (7:1) or Magdala (8:2) on the western shore of the lake, he crosses over to the eastern side (see 8:26).

8:23   During the crossing, Jesus falls **asleep**. Because Jesus shared in flesh and blood (Heb 2:14), he experienced tiredness as human beings do (see John 4:6). However, his sleeping also recalls the prophet Jonah, who fell asleep during a sea voyage, when a storm arose that created **danger** (Jon 1:4–5), precisely the

8. Tertullian, *Concerning Baptism* 12, sees the boat in the storm as representing the Church, buffeted by the waves of trials and persecutions but protected by Jesus.

Figure 10. Mount Arbel and the Sea of Galilee.

situation here! Indeed, because of the mountains and cliffs surrounding the Sea of Galilee (e.g., Mount Arbel on the western coast near Magdala), **a squall** or windstorm can quickly funnel down on the lake.

In the book of Jonah,[9] the sailors turn in prayer to God to keep from **per-** **8:24** **ishing** (Jon 1:6, 14), but here the fearful disciples turn to Jesus. Addressing him as **Master**, the title used by Peter before the miraculous catch (Luke 5:5), they **woke** Jesus and **he awakened**. There are similar Old Testament passages where God is apparently asleep and needs to be awakened to save his people (e.g., Pss 35:23; 44:24). One example comes from Isaiah: "Awake, awake, put on strength, / arm of the LORD!" (Isa 51:9). In the next verse, Isaiah refers to the foundational Old Testament event of salvation, the exodus *crossing of the sea*: "Was it not you who dried up the sea, / the waters of the great deep, / You who made the depths of the sea into a way / for the redeemed to pass through?" (Isa 51:10). As Jesus crosses the sea with his disciples, he symbolizes the new exodus (see the sidebar, "Isaiah's New Exodus Fulfilled in Luke-Acts," p. 84), in which he is now the one who saves his people. He acts as God does, exercising authority over **the wind and the waves** and restoring **calm** (see Ps 107:28–30). Jesus **rebuked** the elements of nature, as he had earlier rebuked demons and a fever (Luke 4:35, 39, 41). He is more than a prophet; he is Lord!

---

9. The comparison to Jonah becomes explicit later, when Jesus speaks of "the sign of Jonah" and claims to be "greater than Jonah" (Luke 11:29–30, 32).

Two Natures United in One Person

LIVING
TRADITION

Commenting on this passage, St. Bede expresses the Church's teaching on the union of Jesus' divine and human natures in his one divine person: "In this voyage, the Lord deigns to show each nature of his one and the same person. He who as man sleeps in the boat then as God tames with a word the fury of the sea."[a] Most famous for teaching these truths about Jesus is Pope St. Leo the Great, in his letter to Flavian:

> The character of each nature, therefore, being preserved and united in one person, humility was assumed by majesty, weakness by strength, mortality by eternity.... Each nature does what is proper to each in communion with the other: the Word does what pertains to the Word, and the flesh to what pertains to the flesh. One shines forth with miracles; the other succumbs to injuries. And just as the Word does not depart from equality with the Father's glory, just so the flesh does not abandon the nature of our race.[b]

a. Bede, *Commentary on Luke's Gospel* 8:23, translated from CCSL 120:180.
b. Denzinger 293–94. See Catechism 467.

8:25 Jesus asks: **Where is your faith?** His question highlights once again the importance of believing (5:20; 7:9, 50). The disciples ask one another: **Who then is this**? Earlier, others asked similar questions about Jesus' identity (4:36; 5:21; 7:19–20, 49). In the next chapter, the disciples will have the chance to answer their own question when Jesus poses it to them (9:20).

Jesus Heals the Man Possessed by Demons (8:26–39)

[26]Then they sailed to the territory of the Gerasenes, which is opposite Galilee. [27]When he came ashore a man from the town who was possessed by demons met him. For a long time he had not worn clothes; he did not live in a house, but lived among the tombs. [28]When he saw Jesus, he cried out and fell down before him; in a loud voice he shouted, "What have you to do with me, Jesus, son of the Most High God? I beg you, do not torment me!" [29]For he had ordered the unclean spirit to come out of the man. (It had taken hold of him many times, and he used to be bound with chains and shackles as a restraint, but he would break his bonds and be driven by the demon into deserted places.) [30]Then Jesus asked him, "What is your name?" He replied, "Legion," because many demons had entered him. [31]And they pleaded with him not to order them to depart to the abyss.

164

[32]A herd of many swine was feeding there on the hillside, and they pleaded with him to allow them to enter those swine; and he let them. [33]The demons came out of the man and entered the swine, and the herd rushed down the steep bank into the lake and was drowned. [34]When the swineherds saw what had happened, they ran away and reported the incident in the town and throughout the countryside. [35]People came out to see what had happened and, when they approached Jesus, they discovered the man from whom the demons had come out sitting at his feet. He was clothed and in his right mind, and they were seized with fear. [36]Those who witnessed it told them how the possessed man had been saved. [37]The entire population of the region of the Gerasenes asked Jesus to leave them because they were seized with great fear. So he got into a boat and returned. [38]The man from whom the demons had come out begged to remain with him, but he sent him away, saying, [39]"Return home and recount what God has done for you." The man went off and proclaimed throughout the whole town what Jesus had done for him.

OT: Lev 11:7; Num 19:16; Deut 14:8; Isa 65:1, 4
NT: Luke 4:33–35, 41; Acts 16:16–18, 39. // Matt 8:28–34; Mark 5:1–20
Catechism: Jesus' exorcisms, 550, 1673

The crossing is completed as they reach **the territory of the Gerasenes**.[10] Jesus   **8:26** is now **opposite Galilee**, in the district of the Decapolis. The herding of unclean animals ("swine," v. 32; see Deut 14:8) is an indicator that this is a *Gentile* rather than Jewish area. Though Gentiles may have previously gone to Jesus in Galilee (e.g., people from Tyre and Sidon, Luke 6:17), here it is Jesus who goes to them in Gentile land, the only such visit in Luke. This may explain the allusion to Jonah in the previous passage. Jonah was the prophet sent to Gentiles in Nineveh, as Jesus now goes to Gentiles in foreign land. Jesus' visit is aptly described by Isaiah: "I was ready to respond to those who did not ask, / to be found by those who did not seek me. / I said: Here I am! Here I am! / To a nation that did not invoke my name" (Isa 65:1).

    A man who is **possessed by demons** meets Jesus. Luke describes his terrible   **8:27–29** situation: the man does not wear **clothes**, does not **live in a house** (and so is isolated from others), and is **driven** about since no **restraint** is effective. He is

---

10. The Greek manuscripts have three readings for the location of this event near the lake. "Gerasenes" is better attested here and in Mark 5:1, but "Gadarenes" in Matt 8:28. Gerasa and Gadara were cities in the Decapolis, but the first (Jerash) is more than thirty miles from the lake and the second (Umm Qais) is about five miles away. The evangelists may be referring to the location only in a general way (e.g., "territory," Luke 8:26). However, a local tradition of a site near the lake (Kursi) has led some scholars, from Origen in the third century till the present day, to opt for "Gergesenes" as the original reading. Scribes unfamiliar with the geography may have changed the text because the other cities were better known.

possessed by an **unclean spirit** and lives **among the tombs**, an unclean place (Num 19:16). Once again Isaiah describes the situation: "Sitting in tombs . . . eating the flesh of pigs" (Isa 65:4).[11] However, like others possessed by demons (Luke 4:34, 41), he perceives Jesus' identity as **son of the Most High God** (1:32). In Acts, Paul and his companions will similarly be addressed by a possessed girl as "slaves of the Most High God" (Acts 16:17).

8:30–33   In response, Jesus asks the demon's **name**. The reply is a Latin military word, **Legion**, indicating a case of possession by an army of several thousand **demons**—much worse than Mary Magdalene's seven (Luke 8:2)![12] The demons negotiate with Jesus not to be sent to the **abyss** (literally, the "bottomless" place), understood as their place of confinement (see Rev 20:1, 3) and often associated with deep *waters* (Gen 7:11). Jesus allows them to enter **a herd of many swine**, which, when seized by the demons, **rushed down** the hill into the water and **drowned**. Despite their tactic, the demons end up in the watery abyss. Together with the previous passage, Jesus' new exodus is unfolding, bringing salvation to his people in their crossing of the sea, but destruction to the enemy army in their drowning in the sea (see Exod 14:28–29; 15:4).

The miracle again shows how Jesus brings liberty to those who are captive to the devil (Luke 4:18, 35), so that they might "turn from darkness to light and from the power of Satan to God" (Acts 26:18).

8:34–37   In the exorcism's aftermath, the **people** of the area and indeed **the entire population** are **seized with fear** and ask Jesus **to leave**. He gets back into the **boat** and returns to Jewish territory, completing the journey begun in the previous passage (8:22). Jesus has indeed come as a light to the Gentiles (2:32), but acceptance of him requires turning away from evil ways,[13] even when this involves economic loss. Gentiles here resist Jesus, just as Gentiles will similarly resist Paul after he performs an exorcism that leads to economic loss, eventually asking him to leave their city (Acts 16:18–21, 39).

However, there is one person who responds positively—**the man from whom the demons had come out**. He is completely restored, as a point-by-point comparison with his previous condition makes clear. He is no longer naked but **clothed**. He is no longer possessed but **in his right mind**. He no longer needs

11. The previous verse in the †Septuagint also mentions demons (Isa 65:3 LXX).

12. Some scholars (e.g., Gerd Theissen, *The Gospels in Context: Social and Political History in the Synoptic Tradition*, trans. Linda M. Maloney [Minneapolis: Fortress, 1991], 109–11) also interpret the term "Legion" as a reference to Roman soldiers, who protected the cities of the Decapolis. In particular, the tenth Roman legion, which was stationed in Syria and put down the Jewish revolt in AD 66–73, had an image of a boar on its standards.

13. The pigs may indicate pagan sacrifices (see 2 Macc 6:18–21). For example, the Romans sacrificed pigs in their religious rites at tombs (Cicero, *On the Laws* 2.57).

to be restrained but sits at Jesus' **feet** like a disciple (see Luke 10:39; Acts 22:3). All these things indicate that, like the woman who stood at Jesus' feet (Luke 7:38), this man has been **saved** (7:50).

Though the man **begged** to go with him, Jesus tells him to **return home**, thus restoring him also to his family and community. The man is instructed to **recount what God has done** for him. He instead goes and tells **what Jesus had done** for him, since for him Jesus does the work of God. The reader well understands that this is because Jesus is the Son of God (1:32, 35; 3:22; 4:41; 8:28). As with the stilling of the storm, Jesus here manifests divine power, doing what God does. And even though Jesus goes away, the news about him is **proclaimed** by the man, the first person besides John (3:3) and Jesus (4:18–19, 44; 8:1) to "proclaim." In the next chapter, Jesus will send out the Twelve on a mission to "proclaim" (9:2). Here, a Gentile becomes the first missionary bringing the good news of Jesus to others.

8:38–39

Jesus Heals the Woman with Hemorrhages and Raises Jairus's Daughter (8:40–56)

---

⁴⁰When Jesus returned, the crowd welcomed him, for they were all waiting for him. ⁴¹And a man named Jairus, an official of the synagogue, came forward. He fell at the feet of Jesus and begged him to come to his house, ⁴²because he had an only daughter, about twelve years old, and she was dying. As he went, the crowds almost crushed him. ⁴³And a woman afflicted with hemorrhages for twelve years, who [had spent her whole livelihood on doctors and] was unable to be cured by anyone, ⁴⁴came up behind him and touched the tassel on his cloak. Immediately her bleeding stopped. ⁴⁵Jesus then asked, "Who touched me?" While all were denying it, Peter said, "Master, the crowds are pushing and pressing in upon you." ⁴⁶But Jesus said, "Someone has touched me; for I know that power has gone out from me." ⁴⁷When the woman realized that she had not escaped notice, she came forward trembling. Falling down before him, she explained in the presence of all the people why she had touched him and how she had been healed immediately. ⁴⁸He said to her, "Daughter, your faith has saved you; go in peace."

⁴⁹While he was still speaking, someone from the synagogue official's house arrived and said, "Your daughter is dead; do not trouble the teacher any longer." ⁵⁰On hearing this, Jesus answered him, "Do not be afraid; just have faith and she will be saved." ⁵¹When he arrived at the house he allowed no one to enter with him except Peter and John and James, and the

child's father and mother. [52]All were weeping and mourning for her, when he said, "Do not weep any longer, for she is not dead, but sleeping." [53]And they ridiculed him, because they knew that she was dead. [54]But he took her by the hand and called to her, "Child, arise!" [55]Her breath returned and she immediately arose. He then directed that she should be given something to eat. [56]Her parents were astounded, and he instructed them to tell no one what had happened.

OT: Lev 15:25–30; Num 5:2–3; 15:38–40; 1 Kings 17:17–24; 2 Kings 4:30–37

NT: Luke 5:13; 6:19; 7:13–14, 50; Acts 9:39–42; 19:11–12. // Matt 9:18–26; Mark 5:21–43

Catechism: power from Christ, 695, 1116, 1504; faith and miracles, 548; pledge of the resurrection, 994; prayer of faith, 2616

Two miracles now unfold in sandwich fashion, as one story falls in the middle of the other. Various details also link the two miracles, both of which teach the necessity and power of faith.

8:40–42   Upon Jesus' return from the eastern side of the lake, he is **welcomed** by **the crowd. Jairus, an official of the synagogue**, perhaps from Capernaum, humbly approaches Jesus, falling at his **feet** (7:38). Jairus (Mark 5:22) is one of the few petitioners for a miracle who are named, possibly indicating that he was well known in the early Church and handed on his eyewitness account of this event.[14] Like the Jewish elders sent by the centurion who urged Jesus to come (Luke 7:4), Jairus also **begged him to come to his house**. His **daughter**, who is **about twelve**, is **dying**. She is his **only** daughter, like the "only son" of the widow of Nain who had died (7:12). Jesus goes with Jairus, but **the crowds** are pressing upon him.

8:43–44   The sandwiched miracle story now begins as **a woman afflicted with hemorrhages** approaches. Her condition has lasted **twelve years**, the same as the age of Jairus's daughter. Besides the physical suffering, it also renders her perpetually "unclean" (Lev 15:25), separating her from the community (Num 5:2).[15] Believing that Jesus can heal her, she courageously but stealthily approached from **behind**, and **touched the tassel on his cloak**. In obedience to the Mosaic law, Jesus, like other Jewish men, wore tassels on the corners of his garments as a reminder to do "all the commandments" and "be holy" to God (Num 15:38–40). Her plan works, as she is healed **immediately**.

8:45–46   However, Jesus asks a question—**Who touched me?**—in order to have a personal encounter with the person healed. Addressing Jesus as **Master** once again (Luke 5:5), Peter thinks Jesus' question is unreasonable because the people

---

14. Bauckham, *Jesus and the Eyewitnesses*, 53–55.

15. 11Q19 (*Temple*[a]) XLVIII 14–17.

in the surrounding **crowds** are bumping into them. Jesus therefore explains that **power** went out from him when he was **touched** (see 6:19). This power has previously been identified as the "power of the Spirit" and the "power of the Lord" (4:14; 5:17). Because of this power, the touch both physically heals her and renders her ritually clean. Moreover, Jesus is not made unclean by the touch (see Lev 15:19). It is rather his holiness that is contagious (see comment on Luke 5:13–14).

Having been discovered, **the woman** comes forth **trembling, falling down**   8:47
before Jesus, as Jairus did (8:41). Words of Isaiah aptly describe her: "This is the one whom I approve: / the afflicted one, crushed in spirit, / who *trembles* at my word" (Isa 66:2 [emphasis added]).

Jesus calls her **Daughter**, recalling Jairus's daughter—yet another link helping   8:48
the reader understand the two miracles together. He lets her go with the same consoling words he spoke to the woman whose sins he forgave (Luke 7:50): **your faith has saved you; go in peace**. Though the word "save" here points to her physical healing (the verb, *sōzō*, can mean both "save" and "heal"), the phrase in general emphasizes the connection between faith and salvation. Jesus will again repeat the exact phrase "your faith has saved you" in later healing miracles (17:19; 18:42).

The story shifts back to the **daughter** of Jairus, with the news that she is **dead**.   8:49–50
Jesus gives reassurance: **do not be afraid** (see 5:10). He also instructs Jairus with words echoing what he just told the woman: **have faith and she will be saved**. Thus again the connection is made, which applies to all readers: have faith and you will be saved (see Rom 10:9).

At the house, Jesus takes inside the girl's parents and three of the apostles,   8:51–53
Peter and John and James, who form an inner circle among the Twelve (see Luke 9:28). He tells the people who are **weeping and mourning** outside: **Do not weep**. He similarly told the widow of Nain not to weep before he raised her son (7:13). He will tell the same thing to the women of Jerusalem who are mourning over his imminent death (23:27–28). Although he is **ridiculed**, he explains that the girl **is not dead, but sleeping** (see John 11:11–14). On the practical level, this explanation prepares for his injunction to secrecy (Luke 8:56).

Touching **her by the hand**, he calls her to **arise**. The girl's spirit or **breath**   8:54–55
returned[16] and she **arose**. The miracle happens **immediately**, yet another link to the woman's healing (vv. 44, 47). Moreover, as with earlier healings (4:39; 5:23–25; 6:8; 7:14), the two verbs translated as "arise" (*egeirō*) and "arose" (*anistēmi*)

---

16. This phrase may recall 1 Kings 17:21, where Elijah prays that the widow's son's life breath may return. Jesus' earlier raising of the widow's son at Nain alludes to the same passage.

are later used to describe Jesus' resurrection (24:6–7, 34, 46). He also directs that the girl **be given something to eat**, an indication that she has returned to ordinary human life. In his appearance to the disciples in Jerusalem, Jesus will similarly ask for something to eat (24:41), not however because he needs food, but as proof of the reality of his risen body. At his resurrection, Jesus passes to a glorified existence in which he dies no more.

8:56   The miracle concludes with the instruction **to tell no one what had happened**— echoing his command to the healed leper (5:14). After Peter's confession, Jesus will similarly direct his disciples not to tell anyone that he is the Messiah (9:21). Beyond miracles and titles, the full truth about Jesus and his mission first needs to be revealed.

The four consecutive miracle stories repeatedly emphasize the importance of faith and show Jesus' great power over nature, evil, sickness, and death. His power over death looks ahead to his own resurrection. As he was sleeping but then arose to calm the storm, and as he raised the "sleeping" girl, so too will he rise from the sleep of death, so that all those who have faith in him may be saved and share in his resurrection.

The Messiah and Suffering Son of Man

Luke 9:1–50

Jesus now begins to give the Twelve a share in his mission of healing and teaching. Moreover, his spreading fame again raises the question of his identity, even with Herod. After miraculously feeding five thousand, Jesus poses this question to his disciples, and Peter makes his confession that Jesus is the Messiah. This marks a turning point in the Gospel, as Jesus begins to announce that as the Son of Man, he must suffer and be killed. Those who wish to follow him must likewise take up their cross. The disciples struggle to understand this new dimension of his and their mission. Three of them—Peter, John, and James—are privileged to witness the transfiguration to help them realize that the suffering Son of Man is also the glorious Son of God. When the Galilean ministry (4:14–9:50) comes to an end, Jesus will begin the journey to Jerusalem.

The Twelve Sent on Mission (9:1–6)

[1]He summoned the Twelve and gave them power and authority over all demons and to cure diseases, [2]and he sent them to proclaim the kingdom of God and to heal [the sick]. [3]He said to them, "Take nothing for the journey, neither walking stick, nor sack, nor food, nor money, and let no one take a second tunic. [4]Whatever house you enter, stay there and leave from there. [5]And as for those who do not welcome you, when you leave that town, shake the dust from your feet in testimony against them." [6]Then they set out and went from village to village proclaiming the good news and curing diseases everywhere.

NT: Luke 10:1–12; Acts 13:51; 18:6. // Matt 10:1, 5–14; Mark 6:7–13
Catechism: mission of the Twelve, 551

9:1–2   Jesus equips **the Twelve** (6:13; 8:1) to share in his ministry, thus multiplying his outreach and training them for their future mission. He gives them the **power and authority** by which he performs exorcisms and healing miracles (see 4:36; 5:17, 24; 8:46), so that they may similarly expel **demons** and **cure diseases**. The significance of their being called "apostles" (6:13) becomes clear, as they are **sent** (verb *apostellō*) by Jesus. Extending his mission, they go forth **to proclaim the kingdom of God** (see 8:1) **and to heal [the sick]** (see 6:18–19).

9:3   Jesus gives them specific directions. They are to **take nothing for the journey**, leaving everything behind (see 5:11, 28). Those sent on mission have to travel light and not be weighed down by excess baggage. They must forgo not only nonessential things like a **walking stick** (see Matt 10:10; Mark 6:8) but also basic necessities such as **food, money**, and **a second tunic** (a change of shirt). Neither do they need a **sack** in which to carry such things. Through this radical simplicity, Jesus is teaching them to rely more on God than on their own resources. The apostles will be stepping out in faith, trusting that they will receive what they need. In the next chapter, Jesus will give similar instructions to a larger group of disciples whom he sends out (Luke 10:4). Later in the passion narrative, however, Jesus will instead tell his disciples to take a sack and a money bag (22:35–36) on account of the more hostile circumstances that the disciples will face.

9:4   Wherever they go, they are to find a **house** as their base and **stay there** until they move on. This practice is intended to ensure an upright intention, avoiding any semblance of pandering to the wealthy, who could give more comfortable hospitality (see 1 Pet 5:2).

9:5   It is to be expected that, like those who reject Jesus (Luke 4:28–29; 6:11), some will **not welcome** the apostles. In this case, they are to **shake the dust** off their **feet** as they **leave that town** (see Acts 13:51; 18:6). This action gives **testimony** of God's coming judgment unless such people repent (see Luke 10:10–14).

9:6   The apostles obediently **set out** on their mission, **curing diseases** and **proclaiming the good news** (verb *euangelizō*). An equivalent expression for their preaching task occurs earlier in the passage: "Proclaim the kingdom of God" (v. 2, verb *kēryssō*). These two verbs—from which come English words like "evangelization" and "kerygma"—were used earlier to describe Jesus' ministry of preaching (see 4:18–19, 43–44; 8:1). They are applied to the apostles' mission here and later in Acts (Acts 8:4–5; 28:31). They continue to apply to the Church's mission today.

Herod Inquires about Jesus (9:7–9)

---

[7]Herod the tetrarch heard about all that was happening, and he was greatly perplexed because some were saying, "John has been raised from the dead"; [8]others were saying, "Elijah has appeared"; still others, "One of the ancient prophets has arisen." [9]But Herod said, "John I beheaded. Who then is this about whom I hear such things?" And he kept trying to see him.

OT: Mal 3:23
NT: Luke 13:31; 23:8. // Matt 14:1–2; Mark 6:14–16

Hearing **all** the news, **Herod** raises the question of Jesus' identity that has frequently appeared throughout the Galilean ministry (5:21; 7:19–20, 49; 8:25): **Who then is this?** The reports he gets are the same as those given later by the disciples (9:19). **Some** think that Jesus is **John** the Baptist **raised from the dead**. When readers last heard about **John** (7:18–19), he was still in prison (3:20), but since then he has been **beheaded** by **Herod** (Matt 14:3–12; Mark 6:17–29), adding to the list of Herod's "evil deeds" (Luke 3:19). **Others**—perhaps linking Jesus' miracles to Old Testament precedent—think that Jesus is **Elijah**, who was foretold to appear again (Mal 3:23). Another opinion is that he is **one of the ancient prophets** who **has arisen**, perhaps even the prophet like Moses who is supposed to arise (Deut 18:15, 18; 34:10). Although these reports are inaccurate or incomplete, they correctly recognize that Jesus is a prophetic figure (Luke 4:24; 7:16, 39). Ironically, he is the one who will rise from the dead.

Herod is **trying to see him**, perhaps for evil intent (13:31) or out of idle curiosity (23:8). Knowing the fate of John, Jesus is not so eager to see Herod. It is probably no coincidence that the New Testament never mentions a visit by Jesus to Herod's two capital cities, Sepphoris and Tiberias. Jesus sought to avoid him.

9:7–9

The Feeding of the Five Thousand (9:10–17)

---

[10]When the apostles returned, they explained to him what they had done. He took them and withdrew in private to a town called Bethsaida. [11]The crowds, meanwhile, learned of this and followed him. He received them and spoke to them about the kingdom of God, and he healed those who needed to be cured. [12]As the day was drawing to a close, the Twelve approached him and said, "Dismiss the crowd so that they can go to the surrounding villages and farms and find lodging and provisions; for we are

in a deserted place here." [13]He said to them, "Give them some food yourselves." They replied, "Five loaves and two fish are all we have, unless we
ourselves go and buy food for all these people." [14]Now the men there numbered about five thousand. Then he said to his disciples, "Have them sit
down in groups of [about] fifty." [15]They did so and made them all sit down.
[16]Then taking the five loaves and the two fish, and looking up to heaven, he
said the blessing over them, broke them, and gave them to the disciples to
set before the crowd. [17]They all ate and were satisfied. And when the leftover fragments were picked up, they filled twelve wicker baskets.

OT: Exod 16; Num 11; 1 Sam 21:4; 1 Kings 17:8–16; 2 Kings 4:42–44
NT: Luke 6:4; 22:19; 24:30, 35. // Matt 14:13–21; Mark 6:30–44; John 6:1–13
Catechism: prefiguring the Eucharist, 1335
Lectionary: Luke 9:11–17: Corpus Christi (Year C); Institution of Acolytes

9:10–11   **When the apostles returned** from their mission, Jesus **took them and withdrew**
from public view. The purpose, according to Mark, was so that they might rest
from their labors (Mark 6:31). However, the reference to Herod (Luke 9:7–9),
which Luke has so compactly sandwiched between the apostles' setting out and
their returning (9:6, 10), suggests that Jesus may have withdrawn because of the
threat posed by Herod (see Matt 14:12–13). His aim in going toward **Bethsaida** is
to get out of Herod's territory. Bethsaida (see Luke 10:13) was a fishing village at the
northern end of the Sea of Galilee, but east of the Jordan River and hence in Philip's
tetrarchy. It was also the town of origin of Peter, Andrew, and Philip (John 1:44).
    What was intended as a retreat **in private** soon became known, and **the crowds**
followed Jesus and his apostles. **He received** or welcomed them, as they had
welcomed him (Luke 8:40), and proceeds to minister to them in word and deed.

9:12–15   A complication arises when the **day** is far spent. They are **in a deserted place**
(erēmos), so **the Twelve** want Jesus to let the people **go to the surrounding**
villages for **provisions**. The mention of a "deserted" (i.e., uninhabited) place
and nearby "villages" (as in Matt 14:13, 15; Mark 6:31–32, 35–36) indicates that
they have not yet arrived at Bethsaida. Some scholars say the feeding miracle
took place in its vicinity, but a better explanation is that they have just begun
withdrawing "towards" Bethsaida (Luke 9:10 NJB).[1] Indeed, Mark mentions
Bethsaida as the destination to which the disciples are headed by boat *after* the
miracle (Mark 6:45). The miracle could then have occurred where early Christian tradition situates it, Tabgha, a little southwest of Capernaum.[2]

    1. A similar phrase occurs when Jesus is going "toward Jerusalem" (Luke 9:53 NRSV). See also
Acts 21:3.
    2. Also relevant is Luke's omission of the material found in Mark 6:45–8:26, a section beginning with
the disciples going toward Bethsaida (Mark 6:45) and ending with them actually in Bethsaida (Mark

Figure 11. Mosaic of loaves and fish (fifth or sixth century) in the Tabgha Church of the Multiplication.

Rather than **dismiss the crowd**, however, Jesus tells the Twelve to return the favor of hospitality that they received during their mission: **give them some food yourselves**. They take stock of the little they have—**five loaves** (*artos*) **and two fish**—and so wonder if they need to **buy food for all these people**. Jesus instead has them make the people **sit down in groups of [about] fifty**. **The men** are **about five thousand** in number. These details allude to several biblical passages, thus presenting Jesus as the one prefigured by various Old Testament people and events.

1. In the time of Moses, when the people needed food in the "wilderness" (*erēmos*, Exod 16:3, 14, 32 LXX), God gave them manna—namely, "bread" (*artos*, Exod 16:4, 12, 15, 32 LXX). When the people were also clamoring for the *fish* they ate in Egypt (Num 11:5, 22), God gave them quail (Exod 16:13; Num 11:31–32).[3] Moreover, Moses like the apostles was concerned about the burden of feeding "all this people" (Num 11:12–13). The arrangement in groups of "fifty" may also recall Israel in the wilderness (Exod 18:21, 25; Deut 1:15; see

---

8:22). This suggests that Luke's mention of their going to Bethsaida is a shorthand way of telescoping a longer journey. See Heinz-Wolfgang Kuhn, "Bethsaida in the Gospel of Mark," in *Bethsaida: A City by the North Shore of the Sea of Galilee*, ed. Rami Arav and Richard A. Freund, 4 vols. (Kirksville, MO: Truman State University Press, 1995–2009), 3:117–19.

3. "Quail came to them *from the sea*" (Wis 19:12 [emphasis added]). François Bovon, *Luke*, trans. Christine M. Thomas, Donald S. Deer, and James Crouch, 3 vols., Hermeneia (Minneapolis: Fortress, 2002–13), 1:359: "In this context they are like flying fish."

Mark 6:40). The similarities suggest that Jesus is the prophet like Moses (Luke 7:16; 9:8; Deut 18:15) who is bringing about a new exodus (see the sidebar, "Isaiah's New Exodus Fulfilled in Luke-Acts," p. 84). Shortly, Moses will appear with Jesus at the transfiguration, where indeed they will converse about Jesus' "exodus" (Luke 9:30–31). In the intervening passage, Jesus will be identified as the Messiah (9:20). In Jewish literature of the time, there was the expectation that the manna would return in the days of the Messiah: "And it shall come to pass when all is accomplished . . . that the Messiah shall then begin to be revealed. . . . And it shall come to pass at that self-same time that the treasury of manna shall again descend from on high, and they will eat of it in those years."[4]

2. As Jesus told the apostles to "give" the people to eat, so did the prophet Elisha in a similar case where there were twenty loaves to feed a hundred men, yet they ate and had some left over (2 Kings 4:42–44). Jesus has already compared himself to Elisha by his words and deeds (Luke 4:27; 7:1–17). He now works a greater miracle than Elisha, with fewer loaves for more men. Elisha was himself recognized as a great miracle worker, performing "twice as many marvels" as Elijah (Sir 48:12), one way of interpreting his receiving a double portion of his spirit (2 Kings 2:9). Jesus is compared with both Elijah (Luke 9:8, 19, 30) and Elisha but is greater than both.

3. The phrase "five loaves" occurs in the Old Testament only when David asks Ahimelech for "five loaves" (1 Sam 21:4), the passage to which Jesus referred in the incident of picking grain on the sabbath (Luke 6:3–4). Unlike Matthew and Mark, Luke links the feeding miracle to this sabbath controversy by refer- ring to bread that is taken and given (6:4 NRSV; 9:16). David, who was run- ning from Saul, took five loaves and gave them to his men, much as now Jesus, who is avoiding Herod, takes five loaves and gives them to his apostles. In this way, Jesus nourishes his flock, as Ezekiel foretold: "I will set up over them one shepherd, my servant David, and he shall feed them" (Ezek 34:23 RSV).[5] Jesus will presently be identified as the "Messiah" (Luke 9:20), a Davidic title (2:11).

9:16   The miracle itself occurs through a simple series of actions. **Taking** the **loaves and fish** and while **looking up to heaven**, Jesus **said the blessing** and **broke them**. He then **gave them to his disciples**, who thus play an intermediary role in distributing the food to the people. Jesus' action of "looking to heaven" is typical for a person praying (18:13; Mark 7:34; John 17:1; Acts 7:55). His other four actions—taking, blessing, breaking, and giving the bread—are all found

---

4. *2 Baruch* 29.3, 8, in *The Old Testament Pseudepigrapha*, ed. James H. Charlesworth, 2 vols., Anchor Bible Reference Library (New York: Doubleday, 1983–85), 1:630–31.

5. Roger David Aus, *Feeding the Five Thousand: Studies in the Judaic Background of Mark 6:30–44 par. and John 6:1–15* (Lanham, MD: University Press of America, 2010), 157–59.

in accounts of the institution of the Eucharist at the Last Supper (Matt 26:26; Mark 14:22). For "bless," Luke's account substitutes the equivalent "give thanks" (*eucharisteō* in Luke 22:19; see Matt 15:36; Mark 8:6), as is also found in Paul's account (1 Cor 11:24). The feeding miracle thus points forward to the greater miracle of the Eucharist. The meal scene at Emmaus likewise has the same four actions—"He took bread, said the blessing, broke it, and gave it to them"—by which Jesus is "recognized" (Luke 24:30–31). Here too, following "the breaking of the bread," Jesus is "made known" (24:35) as Messiah (9:20).

Like the people in the days of Moses who ate their "fill of bread" (Exod 16:8, 12), here too **all ate and were satisfied**. In this sign of the messianic banquet, the promise of the beatitude is thus fulfilled: "Blessed are you who are now hungry, / for you will be satisfied" (Luke 6:21). Moreover, like the miracle of Elisha where there was "some left over" (2 Kings 4:43–44), here too there are plenty of **leftover fragments**. The **twelve wicker baskets** that they fill—one for each of the "Twelve" (Luke 9:12)—is another sign that Jesus is bringing about the restoration of Israel by regathering the twelve tribes.

9:17

Reflection and Application (9:10–17)

Looking up to heaven. An echo of Jesus' action in the feeding miracle is found in the First Eucharistic Prayer (Roman Canon), highlighting the connection between the miracle, the Last Supper, and the Eucharist: "He took bread in his holy and venerable hands, and with eyes raised to heaven to you, O God, his almighty Father, giving you thanks, he said the blessing, broke the bread and gave it to his disciples, saying: Take this, all of you, and eat of it, for this is my Body, which will be given up for you."[6]

Peter's Messianic Confession
and Jesus' First Passion Prediction (9:18–27)

[18]Once when Jesus was praying in solitude, and the disciples were with him, he asked them, "Who do the crowds say that I am?" [19]They said in reply, "John the Baptist; others, Elijah; still others, 'One of the ancient prophets has arisen.'" [20]Then he said to them, "But who do you say that I am?" Peter said in reply, "The Messiah of God." [21]He rebuked them and directed them not to tell this to anyone.

6. *The Roman Missal* (Totowa, NJ: Catholic Book Publishing, 2011), Eucharistic Prayer I.

²²He said, "The Son of Man must suffer greatly and be rejected by the elders, the chief priests, and the scribes, and be killed and on the third day be raised."

²³Then he said to all, "If anyone wishes to come after me, he must deny himself and take up his cross daily and follow me. ²⁴For whoever wishes to save his life will lose it, but whoever loses his life for my sake will save it. ²⁵What profit is there for one to gain the whole world yet lose or forfeit himself? ²⁶Whoever is ashamed of me and of my words, the Son of Man will be ashamed of when he comes in his glory and in the glory of the Father and of the holy angels. ²⁷Truly I say to you, there are some standing here who will not taste death until they see the kingdom of God."

OT: 2 Sam 7:12–16; Ps 118:22; Dan 7:13–14; 9:26; Hosea 6:2
NT: Luke 2:11; 12:9; 14:27; 17:25, 33; 18:31–33; 20:17; 24:7; Rom 1:16. // Matt 16:13–28; Mark 8:27–9:1
Catechism: Jesus at prayer, 2600; Peter's confession, 552; passion prediction, 557; the daily cross, 1435
Lectionary: Luke 9:18–24: Twelfth Sunday Ordinary Time (Year C); Luke 9:22–25: Thursday after Ash Wednesday

9:18–19 As at other significant moments in the Gospel, Jesus is **praying** (see comment on 3:21). The time has now come to address the question of his identity directly. He therefore asks **the disciples: Who do the crowds say that I am?** Their response is the same as what Herod has been hearing (9:7–8): **John the Baptist** or **Elijah** or **one of the ancient prophets.** All of these suggestions recognize Jesus as some kind of prophet (see 7:16). As there is consensus on this point, Jesus can go further and begin a new stage of revelation regarding his identity.

9:20 He thus asks a second question: **Who do you say that I am?** The one who answers is **Peter**, who identifies Jesus as **the Messiah of God.** This truth was earlier announced by an angel (2:11), revealed to Simeon (2:26), and known by demons (4:41). However, Peter, the first in the list of apostles (6:14), is the first human being who, in response to Jesus' public ministry, confesses him as the awaited Messiah (*christos*, "anointed one"). Jesus himself had indirectly referred to this title in the Nazareth synagogue, when he applied to himself the words of the prophet Isaiah: "The Spirit of the Lord is upon me, / because he has *anointed* me" (Luke 4:18 [emphasis added]). Moreover, after being recognized as a prophet (7:16), Jesus had prepared for this further recognition of his identity by explaining John's role as a prophet who prepares for the Messiah (7:26–27).

In addition, the immediate context in Luke sheds light on this title. Only in Luke is the multiplication of the loaves (9:10–17) tightly sandwiched between the questions of his identity (9:7–9, 18–20) that receive their answer in Peter's

Messianic Expectations

BIBLICAL BACKGROUND

Among the Jewish people, there emerged by the †Hasmonean era, a century or so before Jesus' birth, expectations for a messiah (Hebrew *mashiah*, "anointed one"; Greek *christos*).[a] God would raise up a leader who would restore Israel (Ezek 37:21–25), overthrow (Ps 2) or convert the Gentiles (Isa 49:6), renew temple worship (Zech 6:12–13), and bring about an era of peace (Isa 9:5–6) and righteousness (Jer 23:5–6). In the Old Testament, an "anointed" figure could be a king (1 Sam 16:13; 2 Sam 2:4; 5:3; 1 Kings 1:39), a priest (Exod 28:41; 30:30; 40:13, 15), or even a prophet (1 Kings 19:16). Messianic hopes thus looked for a king, specifically one in the line of David, in fulfillment of Old Testament promises (2 Sam 7:11–16; Ps 132:10–11; Isa 11:1–4; Ezek 34:23–24). The *Psalms of Solomon*, written in the first century BC and not part of the Bible, witness to these hopes: "See, O Lord, and raise up for them their king, the son of [David] . . . / to rule over Israel, your servant. . . . And he shall be a righteous king . . . / and there shall be no injustice in his days . . . / for all shall be holy, and their king the anointed of the Lord."[b] Moreover, based on biblical texts that speak of "the anointed priest" (Lev 4:3, 5, 16; 6:15) and of dual leadership (Zech 4:14; 6:11), some Qumran documents speak of two messiahs, with precedence seemingly given to the priestly messiah of Aaron.[c] Since other biblical texts speak of a prophet to come like Moses (Deut 18:15, 18), the return of Elijah (Mal 3:23), and an anointed prophet (Isa 61:1), some Qumran documents also speak of a prophetic messiah.[d] In Luke, Jesus fulfills these diverse expectations of a messiah who is priest, prophet, and king.

a. For the ideas in this sidebar, see Michael F. Bird, *Are You the One Who Is to Come? The Historical Jesus and the Messianic Question* (Grand Rapids: Baker Academic, 2009), 31–62; John J. Collins, *The Scepter and the Star: Messianism in Light of the Dead Sea Scrolls*, 2nd ed. (Grand Rapids: Eerdmans, 2010), 79–148.

b. *Psalms of Solomon* 17.21, 32 (NETS).

c. 1QS IX, 11; 1Q28a II, 11–21.

d. 4Q521 2 II, 1–12; 11Q13 II, 15–20.

confession. "In the time between Herod's question and Peter's answer (you are 'the Messiah of God,' 9:20), Jesus acts out his identity"[7] as Messiah. In other words, the recognition of his messianic identity is connected to the feeding miracle, just as later at the Last Supper (22:19) and at Emmaus, he will be "made known to them in the breaking of the bread" (24:35).[8] Therefore, the Old

7. Bovon, *Luke*, 1:359–60.

8. John Nolland, *Luke 1–9:20*, WBC 35A (Dallas: Word, 1989), 443: "In this experience the disciples became aware of the identity of Jesus in much the same way that the Christian of Luke's day knew Jesus in the eucharistic meal."

Testament allusions found in the miracle of the loaves and fishes also help readers understand aspects of his messianic identity. For example, Jesus as Messiah is like a new Moses who brings back the treasury of manna (see comment on 9:12–15). He is a prophetic Messiah who works miracles like Elisha, who was an anointed prophet (1 Kings 19:16). He is, of course, also a kingly Messiah in the line of David (see Luke 1:32–33; 2:11). In this regard, Jesus' preaching on the *kingdom* of God (4:43; 8:1, 10), mentioned again in the immediate context (9:11), is also part of his mission as a kingly Messiah. Both Jesus' words and deeds thus prepare for Peter's confession.

9:21 In response, Jesus **rebuked** or, rather, ordered his disciples forcefully, commanding **them not to tell this to anyone**. He did not reprimand them for confessing him as Messiah but instead indicated that this truth could not yet be proclaimed openly. Apparently, Jesus has more to reveal regarding his messianic identity. The disciples comply with this order, as no one again speaks of him as Messiah until Jesus himself raises the issue after the long journey to Jerusalem (Luke 20:41).

9:22 The further revelation (which in the Greek text continues the same sentence without interruption) is that the Messiah **must suffer greatly**. The verb "must," as elsewhere in Luke (see comment on 2:49), expresses what is necessary to fulfill God's plan. However, the Messiah's suffering will be difficult for the disciples to understand (9:45; 18:34). Only after his death and resurrection will Jesus be able to explain to them, from the Scriptures, that it was "necessary that the Messiah should suffer" (24:26) because it was "written that the Messiah would suffer" (24:46). Later in Acts, equipped with this deeper understanding of God's plan (Acts 2:23), Peter will renew his confession of Jesus as the Messiah, a Messiah whom the Scriptures predicted "would suffer" (Acts 3:18; also Paul in Acts 17:3; 26:23).

In introducing his sufferings in this first passion prediction, Jesus refers to himself again as **the Son of Man** (Luke 5:24; 6:5, 22; 7:34), a title that appears in his other predictions that he will **be rejected** and **killed** (17:24–25; 18:31–33). The ones who will reject Jesus are the Jewish leaders of the Jerusalem †Sanhedrin (22:66): **the elders, the chief priests, and the scribes** (see 20:1, 19). Jesus will also allude to his passion in other sayings and a parable (12:50; 13:33; 20:9–18).

Jesus' further revelation concerns not just his death but also his resurrection: **on the third day** he will **be raised** (18:33). After the resurrection, the angels at the tomb will recall this prediction (24:7). The risen Jesus will then explain to his disciples that this too was foretold in the Scriptures (24:25–27, 46; e.g.,

The Son of Man

BIBLICAL BACKGROUND

In Luke, Jesus refers to himself as "the Son of Man" twenty-five times (including 24:7, where the two men at the tomb quote his earlier words). Like the occurrences in the other Gospels, these fall roughly into three categories, referring to his public ministry (e.g., 5:24; 6:5; 9:58; 19:10), his suffering (e.g., 9:22, 44; 18:31), or his glorification and future coming (e.g., 9:26; 17:30; 21:27; 22:69). In the Old Testament, the phrase "son of man" (Hebrew *ben-'adam*) often refers to humanity in general or to some mortal human being—in other words, a descendant of Adam (e.g., Num 23:19; Pss 8:5; 146:3). The prophet Ezekiel is addressed in this way almost a hundred times (e.g., Ezek 2:1). Hence, even though the phrase is also used for the Davidic king (Ps 80:18), it lacked the overt political implications of a title like "Messiah." Jesus could thus safely use the phrase to speak about himself. However, some of Jesus' "Son of Man" sayings (e.g., Luke 9:26; 21:27; 22:69) clearly allude to the book of Daniel:

> I saw coming with the clouds of heaven
>
>> One like a son of man.
>> When he reached the Ancient of Days
>>   and was presented before him,
>> He received dominion, splendor, and kingship. (Dan 7:13–14)

At times, such occurrences imply that Jesus has divine authority—for example, to forgive sins (see Luke 5:21, 24). Moreover, in Jewish writings of the period, the figure from Daniel 7 was understood to be a kingly messiah[a] or a priestly figure (see Rev 1:13),[b] both of which also shed light on Jesus' use of the title.

a. *1 Enoch* 46–52; 61–62; *4 Ezra* 13. See John J. Collins, "The Son of Man in Ancient Judaism," in *Handbook for the Study of the Historical Jesus*, ed. Tom Holmén and Stanley E. Porter, 4 vols. (Leiden: Brill, 2011), 2:1552–61.

b. *1 Enoch* 14. See Crispin H. T. Fletcher-Louis, "Jewish Apocalyptic and Apocalypticism," in Holmén and Porter, *Handbook for the Study of the Historical Jesus*, 2:1598–1600. See also Fletcher-Louis, "Jesus as the High Priestly Messiah: Part 2," *Journal for the Study of the Historical Jesus* 5 (2007): 57–60, 71–77.

Hosea 6:2). Jesus' clarification regarding what kind of Messiah he is thus sets the stage for the rest of the Gospel.

Not surprisingly, the revelation of Jesus' sufferings has implications for **all**   9:23 disciples. The one who **wishes to come after** (*opisō*) a suffering Messiah can hardly expect to escape suffering. Rather than pursue their own selfish ambitions, his followers should **deny** themselves and even **take up** their **cross** (see

Taking Up the Cross

LIVING TRADITION

Thomas à Kempis gives readers of *The Imitation of Christ* a powerful exhortation to heed Jesus' teaching about the cross:

> Why then are you afraid to take up the cross, the way that leads to the kingdom of God? In the cross is salvation; in the cross is life; in the cross is protection; in the cross is heavenly sweetness; in the cross is strength of mind; in the cross is spiritual joy; in the cross is supreme virtue; in the cross is perfect holiness. There is no salvation for the soul nor hope for eternal life, except in the cross. So take up your cross and follow Jesus, and you will go on to eternal life. He went before you carrying his cross, and on the cross he died for you, that you too may carry your cross, and that you too may die on the cross. If you die with him, you will live with him. If you join him in suffering, you will join him in glory. . . .
>
> If there had been anything better, anything more suited or more useful to our salvation than suffering, Christ surely would have pointed it out to us by his word and example. For the disciples who followed him and for all those who wish to follow him, he clearly urges carrying the cross, saying: "If anyone would come after me, let him deny himself and take up his cross and follow me" [Matt 16:24; Luke 9:23].[a]

a. Thomas à Kempis, *The Imitation of Christ* 2.12, trans. William C. Creasy (Macon, GA: Mercer University Press, 2015), 48, 51.

Luke 14:27). Jesus' hearers would have been familiar with this image in light of the Roman practice of crucifixion, in which a condemned person often carried the crossbeam to the site of execution. However, they could hardly have grasped its full significance until Jesus was himself put to death on a cross. As Jesus was being led away to be crucified, Simon of Cyrene literally fulfilled this command, as "the cross" was laid on him so that he could "carry it behind" (*opisthen*) Jesus (23:26). Nevertheless, carrying the cross is not reserved for such exceptional moments or for cases of martyrdom but is a **daily** task—an emphasis found only in Luke—involving dying to one's desires so as to belong to Christ more completely (see Gal 2:19–20; 5:24).

9:24   Three explanatory phrases develop this teaching (Luke 9:24–26). First, those who avoid the cross, wishing **to save** their lives, will **lose** them, but paradoxically those who embrace the cross, thereby losing their lives **for** the **sake** of the Messiah, **will save** them (17:33). This paradox recalls the promise of great reward in heaven to those who are hated for the sake of the Son of Man (6:22–23). Jesus later gives more examples of what it means to lose one's life, indicating that those who give up relationships or material things "for the sake of the kingdom of God" will receive back from God "an overabundant return" (18:29–30).

Second, it does not matter if those who avoid the cross are otherwise so **9:25** successful as **to gain the whole world** (see 4:5–6). Since "life does not consist of possessions" (12:15), they will still **lose or forfeit** themselves.

Third, some avoid the cross because they are **ashamed** of a suffering Messiah **9:26** and his **words**. This is because "the word of the cross is folly to those who are perishing" (1 Cor 1:18 RSV). However, true disciples, such as Paul, are "not ashamed of the gospel" (Rom 1:16). They recognize "the power of God" (1 Cor 1:18) in Jesus' message of the cross and hence even make the cross their "boast" (Gal 6:14). Jesus here warns those who are ashamed of him that **the Son of Man will be ashamed of** them **when he comes in his glory** (Luke 12:9). This is the first time that Jesus mentions his second coming (12:40; 17:24; 18:8; 21:27). It is also the clearest allusion so far to the figure mentioned in Daniel: "There came one like a son of man. . . . / And to him was given dominion / and glory and kingdom" (Dan 7:13–14 RSV). This appearance of the glory of the Son together with **the glory of** God **the Father and of the holy angels** was already anticipated at Jesus' birth (Luke 2:9–14).

As all three explanatory phrases make clear, therefore, the decision to follow Jesus by taking up one's cross is something of no little importance. One's salvation depends on it!

After the radical demands of the foregoing verses, Jesus ends with a consol- **9:27** ing promise: **there are some** present who will **see the kingdom of God** before they **taste death**. As with other sayings about the kingdom, this one spans the present and the future. On the one hand, the kingdom has already come with Jesus (6:20; 10:9–11; 11:20; 17:21). On the other hand, the kingdom will come more fully in the future (21:31; 22:16, 18), beginning with Jesus' resurrection and ascension. The statement may thus refer to those **standing** there, especially the apostles, who after Jesus' resurrection will see him and hear him speak about the kingdom of God and will become witnesses of these events (Acts 1:3, 9, 22; 10:41). The saying here also leads directly into the passage about the transfiguration, where three of the apostles who will become witnesses of the resurrection—Peter, John, and James—will immediately get a glimpse of the kingdom as they see Jesus' glory (Luke 9:32).

In the few verses following Peter's confession, Jesus has thus laid out the principal elements of the rest of his messianic mission: his suffering, death, resurrection, and coming in glory.

Reflection and Application (9:18–27)

Who do you say that I am? Jesus asks each of us this question today. It is a question we cannot ignore, because our eternal salvation depends on how we respond, both with our words and with our lives. Pope Benedict XVI suggests a response for us: "Say to him: 'Jesus, I know that you are the Son of God who have given your life for me. I want to follow you faithfully and to be led by your word. You know me, and you love me. I place my trust in you, and I put my whole life into your hands. I want you to be the power that strengthens me and the joy that never leaves me.'"[9]

The Transfiguration of Jesus (9:28–36)

[28]About eight days after he said this, he took Peter, John, and James and went up the mountain to pray. [29]While he was praying his face changed in appearance and his clothing became dazzling white. [30]And behold, two men were conversing with him, Moses and Elijah, [31]who appeared in glory and spoke of his exodus that he was going to accomplish in Jerusalem. [32]Peter and his companions had been overcome by sleep, but becoming fully awake, they saw his glory and the two men standing with him. [33]As they were about to part from him, Peter said to Jesus, "Master, it is good that we are here; let us make three tents, one for you, one for Moses, and one for Elijah." But he did not know what he was saying. [34]While he was still speaking, a cloud came and cast a shadow over them, and they became frightened when they entered the cloud. [35]Then from the cloud came a voice that said, "This is my chosen Son; listen to him." [36]After the voice had spoken, Jesus was found alone. They fell silent and did not at that time tell anyone what they had seen.

OT: Exod 24:9–18; 34:29–35; 40:34–35; Deut 18:15; Ps 2:7; Isa 42:1; Dan 7:9, 13–14

NT: Luke 3:21–22; 24:4; John 1:14; Acts 1:10; 3:22–23; 7:37; 2 Pet 1:15–18. // Matt 17:1–9; Mark 9:2–10

Catechism: Jesus at prayer, 2600; transfiguration, 554–56; Moses and Elijah, 2583; new exodus, 1151; cloud manifests the Holy Spirit, 697; Jesus reveals the Father, 516

Lectionary: Second Sunday Lent (Year C); Transfiguration

9:28   The transfiguration occurs **about eight days** later. Matthew and Mark say "after six days" (Matt 17:1; Mark 9:2), so Luke is indicating the same period in an

9. Benedict XVI, homily at World Youth Day in Madrid, August 21, 2011, in *Let Us Become Friends of Jesus: Meditations on Prayer*, ed. Jeanne Kun (Frederick, MD: The Word Among Us, 2013), 52–53.

inclusive way. This perhaps alludes to the feast of Tabernacles, in which not only the first day but also the eighth had special significance (Lev 23:35–36, 39).[10] During the feast, the people of Israel dwelt in booths or tents—Peter refers to tents in Luke 9:33—recalling how they lived in tents in the wilderness (Lev 23:42–43). Back then, God's glory filled the tabernacle and a cloud overshadowed the tent of meeting (Exod 40:35). Now this is all fulfilled in Jesus who appears in glory (Luke 9:32), overshadowed by a cloud (v. 34).

Jesus takes with him **Peter, John, and James**—those whose call is recounted first (5:10–11) and who form an inner circle among the apostles (8:51). Except in the initial list of the Twelve (6:14), Luke inverts the typical order of James and John (8:51; Acts 1:13), reflecting the importance and collaboration of Peter and John in the early Church (Luke 22:8; Acts 3:1–4:19; 8:14). They go **up the mountain**,[11] the privileged place **to pray** to God (Luke 6:12).

That Jesus is **praying** suggests that something momentous is about to happen **9:29** (3:21; 9:18). Earlier, when Jesus went up the mountain to pray before choosing the Twelve, there were echoes of Moses similarly going up the mountain as he gathered the twelve tribes at Mount Sinai (see comment on 6:12). Here, the allusions to Moses are even more numerous. For example, Jesus is accompanied by three apostles, as Moses was accompanied by Aaron, Nadab, and Abihu (Exod 24:1, 9). Moreover, Jesus' **face** is **changed**, recalling how Moses' "face shone because he had been talking with God" (Exod 34:29 RSV). However, since Jesus is greater than Moses, his changed **appearance** also recalls "the appearance of the Lord's glory" (Exod 24:17 NETS) when Moses ascended Mount Sinai with his companions and saw the God of Israel. Jesus' **clothing** becomes **dazzling white**, which likewise is similar to an Old Testament portrayal of God, from the book of Daniel: "The Ancient of Days took his throne. / His clothing was white as snow" (Dan 7:9). Jesus just referred to himself three verses earlier (Luke 9:26) as coming in glory like Daniel's Son of Man, the one who is presented to the Ancient of Days (Dan 7:13–14). Jesus now appears in "glory" (Luke 9:32) as the Son of Man[12] and Son of God (v. 35).

The allusions become explicit as **Moses** himself appears with Jesus, **and** **9:30–31** **Elijah** too. Elijah had been taken up to heaven (2 Kings 2:11) but was destined

10. Among early Christians (e.g., *Barnabas* 15.8–9), the phrase "eighth day" was also used to refer to Jesus' resurrection, which took place on the first day after the sabbath (Luke 23:56–24:1). The detail may thus be one of various ways in which Luke indicates that the transfiguration is an anticipation of the resurrection.

11. By the fourth century, the mountain of the transfiguration was identified as Mount Tabor; see, e.g., Cyril of Jerusalem, *Catecheses* 12.16.

12. As the Son of Man, Jesus is the son of Adam who receives the glory that Adam lost by his sin, with the dazzling clothes replacing the clothes of Adam (Gen 3:7, 21). See Bovon, *Luke*, 1:375.

to appear again, according to Malachi (Mal 3:23–24). Moses, mentioned in the same prophecy (Mal 3:22), had died in the land of Moab, but the mystery surrounding his burial place (Deut 34:5–6; Jude 9) led to speculation that he also had been taken to heaven.[13] Here, Moses and Elijah, as two witnesses (Deut 19:15), represent the law and the prophets testifying to Jesus (see Luke 16:16; 24:27, 44), indicating that his life and mission are the fulfillment of God's plan in the Scriptures. Luke introduces them saying **behold, two men**, adding that they **appeared in glory**. Thus he connects this event with the resurrection, where "*behold, two men* in dazzling garments" (24:4) testify that Jesus has been raised. At the ascension as well, "*behold, two men* . . . in white" garments (Acts 1:10 RSV [emphasis added]) testify that the ascended Jesus will come again. The transfiguration thus provides a glimpse of Jesus' future glorification (Luke 24:26) in his resurrection and ascension.

As Matthew and Mark also note (Matt 17:3; Mark 9:4), Moses and Elijah are **conversing with** Jesus. However, only Luke indicates the topic: **his exodus**. The term refers to his "departure"—that is, his death (see 2 Pet 1:15), which he just predicted (Luke 9:22)—but it also communicates the deeper significance of his death. Like a new Moses, Jesus is bringing about a new exodus. The place where this will occur is not Egypt, but **Jerusalem**, the city toward which Jesus is about to journey (9:51) and in which he will die (13:33). In his exodus, he will pass from death to his resurrection and ascension, with his point of arrival in heaven (24:51; Acts 1:9–11). He will thus open up the way to heaven for his followers, such as Stephen, who at his martyrdom experiences Jesus in heavenly glory (Acts 7:55–60).[14] By his exodus, Jesus will also **accomplish**, or fulfill, God's plan in the Scriptures (see Luke 24:26–27, 44).

9:32   The scene shifts now to the other trio, **Peter and his companions**. Despite being chosen witnesses of the event, they are **overcome by sleep**! This is actually not surprising since, in Scripture, sleep sometimes accompanies a heavenly encounter or vision (Gen 15:12; Dan 8:18). Only Luke notes this detail, perhaps to link the scene to the only other passage in Luke where Jesus takes along Peter, John, and James—namely, the raising of Jairus's daughter, whom Jesus said was merely sleeping (Luke 8:51–52). One thus wonders whether the three apostles' sleep is a taste of death (see 9:27), so that, becoming **fully awake** and seeing **his glory**, they have a taste of their future share in his resurrection. What they briefly witness by way of anticipation is what Stephen will later experience as

13. Josephus, *Jewish Antiquities* 4.326.
14. Simon S. Lee, *Jesus' Transfiguration and the Believers' Transformation* (Tübingen: Mohr Siebeck, 2009), 117–18, 123–24.

he "fell asleep" at his martyrdom (Acts 7:60). This image can be applied to all Christians: "Awake, O sleeper, / and arise from the dead, / and Christ will give you light" (Eph 5:14).

As **Moses** and **Elijah** begin to leave, **Peter** expresses his contentment: **it is   9:33 good that we are here**. Because he recently heard Jesus' message about the cross, he would rather hold on to this fleeting moment of glory. Hence, he suggests making **three tents**, perhaps like Moses, who set up the tent of meeting where God's glory came to dwell (Exod 40:34–35). However, Peter **did not know what he was saying,** perhaps thinking that the time of fulfillment had already come, prior to Jesus' suffering. Moreover, **Jesus** is greater than Moses and Elijah, yet Peter seems to be treating them all on the same level.

A cloud came as if interrupting Peter's **speaking**. It clearly alludes to Moses,   9:34 recalling "the cloud" that "covered the tent of meeting" (Exod 40:34). The cloud **cast a shadow over them** (verb *episkiazō*), like the cloud that overshadowed the tent of meeting (*episkiazō*, Exod 40:35 LXX). Jesus' glorified body is now the living tent of meeting, the new temple wherein God dwells with his presence. Jesus does not need Peter to build him a tent, because he is the tent! Moreover, the angel Gabriel earlier announced that the Holy Spirit would come upon Mary and the power of the Most High would "overshadow" (*episkiazō*) her (Luke 1:35). The overshadowing cloud here is similarly a sign of the Holy Spirit, like the dove at Jesus' baptism (3:22). The apostles **became frightened when they entered the cloud,** a typical reaction to God's glorious presence (2:9).

As at the baptism (3:22), the **voice** of God the Father is heard, completing   9:35 the manifestation of the Trinity. It echoes the second psalm: **This is my chosen Son**. Jesus is greater than Moses, Elijah, and any of the ancient prophets (see 9:8, 19) because he is the Son of God (1:32, 35), a truth now revealed to the three apostles. However, just as the declaration of Jesus as Messiah (9:20) was accompanied by the revelation of his suffering as the Son of Man (9:22), so too with the word "chosen" here, Jesus' presentation as God's Son is combined with that of the †suffering servant (see 23:35): "Here is my servant whom I uphold, / my *chosen* one with whom I am pleased" (Isa 42:1 [emphasis added]; see comment on Luke 3:22).

The last words spoken by the voice—**listen to him**—complete the comparison here between Moses and Jesus, as they echo the promise of a prophet like Moses that God will raise up: "That is the one to whom you shall listen" (Deut 18:15). For the apostles, the divine command ratifies Jesus' difficult sayings regarding his own death and a disciple's cross (Luke 9:22–23). Even though they struggle to understand, they will stay on the right path by listening to Jesus.

9:36   The extraordinary experience quickly comes to an end as **Jesus** is **found alone**. The stunned disciples are **silent** and do not **tell anyone**. Similarly, Jesus had just enjoined them "not to tell" that he was the Messiah "to anyone" (9:21). For the **time** being, they should just listen to Jesus, having been informed of his identity as God's Son and reassured that glorification will follow suffering. The time for speaking will come after the resurrection (24:44–48).

Reflection and Application (9:28–36)

Participating in Jesus' prayer. Key events in Jesus' life take place in the context of his prayer: his baptism (3:21), the calling of the Twelve (6:12–13), Peter's confession (9:18–20), and the transfiguration (9:28–29). Thus

> prayer was the central act of the person of Jesus and, indeed . . . [he] is constituted by the act of prayer, of unbroken communication with the one he calls "Father." If this is the case, it is only possible really to understand this person by entering into this act of prayer, by participating in it. . . . Therefore a participation in the mind of Jesus, i.e., in his prayer . . . is not some kind of pious supplement to reading the Gospels, adding nothing to knowledge of him or even being an obstacle to the rigorous purity of critical knowing. On the contrary, it is the basic precondition if real understanding . . . is to take place. . . . The person who prays begins to see.[15]

The Disciples' Inability and Incomprehension (9:37–50)

[37]On the next day, when they came down from the mountain, a large crowd met him. [38]There was a man in the crowd who cried out, "Teacher, I beg you, look at my son; he is my only child. [39]For a spirit seizes him and he suddenly screams and it convulses him until he foams at the mouth; it releases him only with difficulty, wearing him out. [40]I begged your disciples to cast it out but they could not." [41]Jesus said in reply, "O faithless and perverse generation, how long will I be with you and endure you? Bring your son here." [42]As he was coming forward, the demon threw him to the ground in a convulsion; but Jesus rebuked the unclean spirit, healed the boy, and returned him to his father. [43]And all were astonished by the majesty of God.

While they were all amazed at his every deed, he said to his disciples, [44]"Pay attention to what I am telling you. The Son of Man is to be handed

---

15. Joseph Ratzinger, *Behold the Pierced One: An Approach to a Spiritual Christology*, trans. Graham Harrison (San Francisco: Ignatius, 1986), 26–27.

over to men." [45]But they did not understand this saying; its meaning was hidden from them so that they should not understand it, and they were afraid to ask him about this saying.

[46]An argument arose among the disciples about which of them was the greatest. [47]Jesus realized the intention of their hearts and took a child and placed it by his side [48]and said to them, "Whoever receives this child in my name receives me, and whoever receives me receives the one who sent me. For the one who is least among all of you is the one who is the greatest."

[49]Then John said in reply, "Master, we saw someone casting out demons in your name and we tried to prevent him because he does not follow in our company." [50]Jesus said to him, "Do not prevent him, for whoever is not against you is for you."

OT: Num 11:26–30; Deut 32:5, 20
NT: Matt 10:40; Luke 10:16; 18:16, 32, 34; 22:24; John 13:20. // Matt 17:14–23; 18:1–5; Mark 9:14–40
Catechism: passion prediction, 557; the disciples' misunderstanding, 554

The disciples' need for further growth and training is emphasized in four related incidents, which highlight their present inability to fulfill their mission and their incomprehension of Jesus' mission.

First, Jesus once again finds **a large crowd** (7:11), as he returns **from the mountain** of transfiguration. Like the encounters with the widow of Nain and Jairus, the situation here involves a parent with an **only child** (7:12; 8:42). A father begs Jesus to **look at**—that is, care for (see 1:48)—his **son** who is tormented by an unclean **spirit** that causes epileptic symptoms (see Matt 17:15 RSV). Before turning to Jesus, the father **begged** his **disciples to cast it out**. Earlier, Jesus had indeed given the Twelve power (*dynamis*) over demons (9:1). However, here **they could not** (verb *dynamai*) drive it out.   **9:37–40**

Jesus' response echoes the words of Moses to the generation of Israelites who wandered in the wilderness (Deut 32:5): **O faithless and perverse generation**. The point is that the disciples have to continue growing in faith (see Luke 8:25; Matt 17:20), so as to be able to use the power Jesus has given them. Their time of training is not unlimited, however, since he will not be with them for very **long** before his death (Luke 9:44). For the moment, **Jesus rebuked** the demon (4:35, 41) and **returned** the **healed** son **to his father**, as at Nain he gave the son back to his mother (7:15).   **9:41–42**

Unlike in Matthew and Mark, the next incident is recounted without mentioning any change in location, thus stressing the connection between events. Precisely while **all** are **astonished** and **amazed** at the miracle, Jesus makes his second passion prediction **to his disciples**. Because they still need to grow   **9:43–44** in faith, Jesus tells them to **pay attention** to—literally, to put into their ears (see 8:8; 14:35)—these words: **The Son of Man is to be handed over to men** (18:32). This prediction uses the language of an important Old Testament text for understanding Jesus' sufferings—namely, Isaiah's fourth †servant song (Isa 52:13–53:12); for example, "on account of their sins he was *handed over*" (Isa 53:12 LXX, author's translation). Jesus will later quote another phrase from the same verse: "This scripture must be fulfilled in me, namely, 'He was counted among the wicked'" (Luke 22:37, quoting Isa 53:12). Coming at the end of the section of Galilean ministry (Luke 4:14–9:50), the first two passion predictions (9:22, 44) recall Jesus' experience of rejection in Nazareth at the beginning (4:24, 29) and look forward to the long section in Luke in which Jesus will journey toward his passion in Jerusalem (9:51–19:44).

9:45   However, to the disciples' earlier lack of faith is now added their incomprehension as they fail to **understand** the prediction. This is due to their weakness (see v. 46), but it is also part of God's plan, since **its meaning was hidden from them** (18:34). Only after the resurrection will their minds be opened by Jesus (24:45). Out of fear of further reproof (9:41), they do not **ask him about this saying**.

9:46–48   Instead, in the third incident, the disciples argue about who is **the greatest** (see 22:24). They have not yet learned the lesson of reversal expressed in the Magnificat and the Beatitudes. **Jesus** corrects them with an illustration, as he places **a child** next to him (18:16). The one who **receives** such lowly and weak members in society receives Jesus and the Father **who sent** him. Moreover, becoming the **least** through service of others is the true indicator of who is **greatest** (22:26–27).

9:49–50   The passage began with the disciples' failure to cast out a demon (9:37–43), and it ends with an incident involving **someone** successfully **casting out demons**. Because he is not of the disciples' **company**, this situation is unacceptable to **John**, so they try to **prevent** or stop him, as Joshua similarly wished to stop some men who were prophesying (Num 11:28). Like Moses correcting Joshua (Num 11:29), **Jesus** corrects John's jealousy and tells them not to **prevent** him. The general principle is that **whoever is not against you is for you**. God works in ways that go beyond the limits of one's own group. The disciples will grasp this lesson later in Acts when the Holy Spirit descends even upon Gentiles, demonstrating that no one should *prevent* them (Acts 10:47; 11:17) from being baptized.

As the Galilean ministry comes to a close, it is evident from these four incidents that the disciples need more formation in order to understand the way of discipleship and so be equipped for their eventual mission. This will be one of Jesus' principal tasks during the long journey to Jerusalem.

Reflection and Application (9:50)

Communion not competition. "Whoever is not against you is for you." Jesus' words encourage a spirit of communion among different groups in the Church, including traditional institutions like the parish, diocese, and religious orders, as well as the new organizations, movements, and communities that the Holy Spirit has raised up in recent times. Moreover, Catholics should recognize how the Holy Spirit is also at work among other Christians, and thus promote the unity of Christians through prayer and collaboration (Catechism 819, 821).

The Journey to Jerusalem Begins

Luke 9:51–10:42

Now begins the large central section of Luke's Gospel, the so-called travel narrative (9:51–19:44).[1] In the solemn first verse, Jesus firmly begins his journey to Jerusalem (9:51), the city where he will accomplish his "exodus" (9:31). Ten chapters later, he finally arrives when he enters the temple (19:45), marking the start of the section dedicated to the Jerusalem ministry (19:45–21:38).

Jesus' journey is mentioned several times toward the beginning of the central section (9:51–53, 56–57; 10:38). Thereafter, there are only a few reminders about the journey (13:22; 17:11; 18:31), but these notices divide the travel narrative into smaller parts.[2] As Jesus draws closer and begins the immediate ascent ("going up to Jerusalem," 18:31) from Jericho (18:35; 19:1), there are more frequent travel notices mentioning locations along the way, such as Bethphage, Bethany, and the Mount of Olives (19:11, 28–29, 36–37, 41).

During the journey, those accompanying Jesus are almost always described using the word "crowd" (*ochlos*).[3] However, once he enters the temple, this word is replaced by the more specific "people"—in other words, of Israel (*laos*)[4]— which is almost completely absent from the central section (except 18:43). The term "crowd" (*ochlos*) anticipates the disciples' later mission in Acts by suggesting the presence during the journey of non-Jews—that is, Samaritans (Acts 8:6) and Gentiles (Acts 11:24, 26).

1. Many ideas in this introduction depend on Jean-Noël Aletti, *L'art de raconter Jésus Christ: L'écriture narrative de l'évangile de Luc* (Paris: Seuil, 1989), 111–23, 134–36.
2. Luke 9:51–13:21; 13:22–17:10; 17:11–18:30; 18:31–19:44.
3. Luke 11:14, 27, 29; 12:1, 13, 54; 13:14, 17; 14:25; 18:36; 19:3, 39.
4. Luke 19:47–48; 20:1, 6, 9, 19, 26, 45; 21:23, 38; 22:2.

Indeed, Jesus meets Samaritans as he journeys toward Jerusalem, traversing all the regions that make up the land of Israel, from locations in or near Galilee (Luke 10:13, 15; 17:11) through ones in Samaria (9:52; 17:11) to Judea. All the Lukan references to Samaritans occur in this central section (9:52–55; 10:33–37; 17:15–19). In contrast to the typical hostility between Jews and Samaritans, Jesus displays a positive attitude, thus anticipating the disciples' later mission to Samaria (Acts 8:4–25). Since Samaria had been the capital of the northern kingdom and the Samaritans descended from some of the northern tribes, the references to Samaria and the Samaritans may illustrate Jesus' plan for Israel's restoration, by which he regathers the tribes under one king.[5]

Along these lines, whereas in the Galilean section Jesus is highlighted as prophet, here in the travel narrative there is a growing emphasis on Jesus as *king*: "Blessed is the king who comes / in the name of the Lord" (Luke 19:38). Moreover, most of Jesus' teaching about the *kingdom* of God occurs in this central section,[6] including the announcement that the kingdom is "at hand" (10:9, 11) and several kingdom parables (13:18–21; 19:11–27).

Whether in parables, sayings, or discourses, the material in the central section consists mostly of Jesus' teaching.[7] By contrast, there are fewer miracle stories here (five) than in the Galilean section (seventeen, including summaries). These observations suggest that the physical journey to Jerusalem serves as a general framework for Jesus' teaching, especially regarding the journey of discipleship, which consists in taking up one's cross and following after Jesus (9:23). The Galilean ministry ended with various failures of the disciples (9:37–50), showing how they needed more training. Hence, in this section, Jesus will instruct the disciples—for example, on prayer (11:1–13), on not being afraid or worrying (12:1–12, 22–34), on being vigilant (12:35–48), on being trustworthy (16:1–13), on forgiveness and avoiding sin (17:1–4), on faith (17:5–6), and on accepting the kingdom like children (18:15–17). He will also speak to the crowds on the radical commitment involved in being a disciple (14:26–27, 33). Jesus also continues to teach through parables, and many famous parables that are unique to Luke occur in this section—for example, the good Samaritan (10:29–37), the rich fool (12:16–21), the prodigal son (15:11–32), the dishonest steward

---

5. V. J. Samkutty, *The Samaritan Mission in Acts* (London: T&T Clark, 2006), 113–21, 203. In Acts, when the disciples ask Jesus when he is "going to restore the kingdom to Israel" (Acts 1:6), he explains that Israel's restoration is tied up with their mission first "in Jerusalem," then "throughout Judea and Samaria," and finally to the nations, "the ends of the earth" (Acts 1:8).

6. Luke 9:60, 62; 11:2, 20; 12:31–32; 13:18–21, 28–29; 16:16; 17:20–21; 18:16–17, 24–30; 19:11.

7. The teaching material in the central section is either unique to Luke or also found in Matthew, in contrast with much of the material in the Galilean section, which closely parallels Mark.

(16:1–8), the rich man and Lazarus (16:19–31), the persistent widow (18:1–8), and the Pharisee and tax collector (18:9–14).

Finally, the drama of the central section unfolds with the repeated statements that Jesus is being rejected and will be put to death in Jerusalem (13:33–34; 17:25; 18:31–33). As he approaches the city, he thus repeatedly warns of its impending judgment (11:49–51; 13:6–9, 35; 19:41–44), "because you did not recognize the time of your visitation" (19:44).

Jesus Sets His Face toward Jerusalem (9:51–62)

---

⁵¹When the days for his being taken up were fulfilled, he resolutely determined to journey to Jerusalem, ⁵²and he sent messengers ahead of him. On the way they entered a Samaritan village to prepare for his reception there, ⁵³but they would not welcome him because the destination of his journey was Jerusalem. ⁵⁴When the disciples James and John saw this they asked, "Lord, do you want us to call down fire from heaven to consume them?" ⁵⁵Jesus turned and rebuked them, ⁵⁶and they journeyed to another village.

⁵⁷As they were proceeding on their journey someone said to him, "I will follow you wherever you go." ⁵⁸Jesus answered him, "Foxes have dens and birds of the sky have nests, but the Son of Man has nowhere to rest his head." ⁵⁹And to another he said, "Follow me." But he replied, "[Lord,] let me go first and bury my father." ⁶⁰But he answered him, "Let the dead bury their dead. But you, go and proclaim the kingdom of God." ⁶¹And another said, "I will follow you, Lord, but first let me say farewell to my family at home." ⁶²[To him] Jesus said, "No one who sets a hand to the plow and looks to what was left behind is fit for the kingdom of God."

OT: 1 Kings 19:19–21; 2 Kings 1:9–12; 2:9–11; Isa 50:7; Mal 3:1
NT: Luke 13:22; 17:11; 19:28; Acts 19:21. // Matt 8:19–22
Catechism: Jesus' journey to Jerusalem, 557; Jesus has nowhere to rest, 544
Lectionary: Thirteenth Sunday Ordinary Time (Year C); Luke 9:57–62: Consecration of Virgins and Religious Profession

9:51 Significant events in Jesus' life happen at appointed times in accord with God's plan (see 2:6, 21–22). Here, a turning point occurs **when the days** are **fulfilled** (*symplēroō*) for the events regarding his exodus from death to glory (9:22, 31, 44) to begin to unfold. These events are described now as **his being taken up**, a reference to his ascension to heaven (see Acts 1:2, 11, 22). The phrase recalls how Elijah—who just appeared with Jesus at the transfiguration—was himself taken up into heaven (2 Kings 2:9–11). Elisha then received a double portion of Elijah's spirit, and Jesus after his ascension will similarly grant his disciples a share in his Holy Spirit when the day of Pentecost is "fulfilled" (*symplēroō*, Acts 2:1).

Jesus **resolutely determined** (literally, "set his face") **to journey to Jerusalem**. A verse from the third †servant song of Isaiah provides key background: "I have set my face like flint, / knowing that I shall not be put to shame" (Isa 50:7). Jesus, God's chosen †servant (Luke 9:35; Isa 42:1), is firmly setting out on his journey toward Jerusalem, aware that it is the place where he will die, like prophets before him (Luke 13:33–34). Another, related meaning of setting one's face is the prophetic resolve needed to preach judgment:[8] "Son of man, turn your face toward Jerusalem: preach against its sanctuary, prophesy against the land of Israel" (Ezek 21:7).[9] As Ezekiel prophesied regarding the destruction of Jerusalem (586 BC), so Jesus will prophesy against the city and its temple, foretelling its destruction (Luke 13:35; 19:41–44; 21:6, 20–24), which the Romans carried out in AD 70.

Jesus **sent messengers ahead of him** (literally, "before his face"), thus echoing   **9:52–53**
the phrase in the previous verse. In a sense, these messengers are continuing the ministry of John the Baptist: "Behold, I am sending my messenger ahead of you, / he will prepare your way before you" (7:27; see Exod 23:20; Mal 3:1), and "Prepare the way of the Lord" (Luke 3:4; Isa 40:3). The messengers indeed go **to prepare for his reception**.

Setting off from Galilee going south toward Jerusalem, they cross into the region of Samaria and enter a **village**. However, the **Samaritan** villagers do not **welcome** Jesus. **Because the destination of his journey was Jerusalem,**[10] they do not accept him since they considered Mount Gerizim to be the proper place to worship. Hence, the rejection is not directed against Jesus personally but is rather motivated by the general enmity between Jews and Samaritans (see the sidebar, "Samaritans," p. 212). That the Samaritans do not "welcome" Jesus (verb *dechomai*) at the beginning of this central section also recalls how Jesus was not "accepted" (adjective *dektos*, Luke 4:24) in Nazareth, at the beginning of the Galilean section. However, Jesus does not reject the Samaritans and will indeed display a positive attitude toward them (10:33–37; 17:15–19).

---

8. Craig A. Evans, "'He Set His Face': On the Meaning of Luke 9:51," in *Luke and Scripture: The Function of Sacred Tradition in Luke-Acts*, by Craig A. Evans and James A. Sanders (Minneapolis: Fortress, 1993), 93–105.

9. Ezek 21:2 RSV. See also Ezek 6:2; 13:17; 21:2 (20:46 RSV).

10. Literally, "because *his face* was going toward Jerusalem," thus highlighting Jesus' firm resolve for the third time in as many verses.

Eventually, with the disciples' mission, Samaritans will accept the gospel (*dechomai*, Acts 8:14).

9:54   Filled with indignation at seeing Jesus rejected, **James and John** ask whether they should **call down fire from heaven to consume them**. John the Baptist had spoken about the Messiah as one who brings fire (3:16–17). Now that John has been killed, these two **disciples**—aptly called "sons of thunder" (Mark 3:17) for such impetuous zeal—may want to take upon themselves his role of going before Jesus "in the spirit and power of Elijah" (Luke 1:17). Elijah had indeed called down fire from heaven to consume his enemies, sent against him by the king of *Samaria* (2 Kings 1:9–12).[11]

9:55–56   However, their suggestion shows that they have misunderstood Jesus' mission yet again (Luke 9:45–46, 49), perhaps like John the Baptist himself (7:18–23). **Jesus** is indeed like Elijah in many ways, but he is also greater than Elijah. He thus **rebuked them**. If even *Jewish* leaders will reject him (9:22), it is to be expected that *Samaritans* will reject him, so he counsels forbearance, allowing for the possibility of their turning later to the gospel (Acts 8:5–6). Jesus had also instructed his disciples to love their enemies and be merciful (Luke 6:27, 35–36). He will soon teach in parable form that such love and mercy extends even to traditional enemies such as Samaritans (10:29–37). Therefore, a warning is acceptable (see 9:5; 10:10–11), but a violent response is ruled out. Jesus and his disciples simply leave and journey **to another village**.

9:57–58   The misunderstanding of James and John shows their need for further training in the way of discipleship, and the **journey** to Jerusalem provides the perfect setting for it. The word "journey" or "way" is later used figuratively in Acts to signify the Christian way of life, "the Way of the Lord" (Acts 18:25).[12] Here, as they all make their way, Luke presents three sayings of Jesus on discipleship. They occur in distinct dialogues between Jesus and unnamed individuals who are potential followers. Indeed, the verb "follow" occurs in each of the three dialogues. The individuals' final responses are not given, leaving the dialogues open-ended. The effect is to invite readers—other (potential) followers—to apply the sayings to their lives.[13]

In the first dialogue, **someone** tells Jesus, **I will follow you wherever you go**. In reply to this idealistic but perhaps naive statement, **Jesus** challenges the person to be aware of the sacrifices involved in being his disciple. If **the Son of Man has nowhere to rest his head**, the disciple should likewise be prepared even

11. A variant reading for Luke 9:54 even includes the phrase "as also Elijah did."
12. Also, Acts 9:2; 18:26; 19:9, 23; 22:4; 24:14, 22.
13. Daniel Marguerat and Yvan Bourquin, *How to Read Bible Stories: An Introduction to Narrative Criticism*, trans. John Bowden (London: SCM, 1999), 171.

to give up house and home (Luke 18:29). In contrast, even **foxes** and **birds** have their homes in **dens** or **nests**. Jesus certainly does not preach a prosperity gospel!

In the second dialogue, Jesus takes the initiative of calling someone to **fol-**   9:59–60
low him, as he earlier did with Levi (5:27). The individual seems willing but delays his response, asking Jesus instead to **let** him **go first and bury** his **father**. Burying the dead was understood to be a religious duty (Tob 1:17–19; 2:3–8), especially serious for one's parents (Tob 4:3–4; 6:15; 14:10–13). Burial typically occurred the very day of death (Luke 23:53; Acts 5:5–10). It is not stated whether the individual's father has already died, in which case the delay would be rather brief. If not, the request may be more of an excuse, under the guise of religious obligations toward one's family, to delay indefinitely the response to Jesus' call.

Jesus' response permits no delay: **Let the dead bury their dead**. This apparently severe rejoinder is a way of indicating that following Jesus should be the top priority. Delaying one's response might indicate failure to appreciate the radical nature of the commitment. Even family obligations have to be put in proper perspective and at times set aside (Luke 8:19–21; 14:26; 18:29) or left for others who are still "dead"—in other words, those who have not yet answered Jesus' call to discipleship (see 15:24, 32).

Moreover, one who follows Jesus also shares in his mission: **go and pro-claim the kingdom of God**. Jesus has just sent the Twelve on such a mission (9:1–2), and he will soon send out other disciples (10:9, 11). Delaying one's response would therefore also mean shirking another serious obligation, that of proclaiming the kingdom.

In context, Jesus' words about burying the dead may also be a sign of the judgment that he is about to prophesy, since he has "set his face" toward Jerusalem (see v. 51). When the prophet Jeremiah prophesied the coming destruction of Jerusalem and its temple by the Babylonians (586 BC), a similar sign was given: "They shall die, the great and the lowly, in this land, unburied and unlamented" (Jer 16:6).[14] Since Jesus will likewise prophesy the coming destruction of Jerusalem and its temple (Luke 13:35; 19:41–44), besides preaching judgment on other unrepentant towns (10:10–16), his words indicate the urgency of responding to his call.

A third potential disciple says: **I will follow you, Lord**. Like the previous   9:61–62
individual, however, following Jesus is not **first** in his priorities, as he asks Jesus to **let** him **say farewell** to those **at home**. In response, Jesus again insists on the radical commitment required to be his follower: **No one who sets a hand to**

---

14. Markus Bockmuehl, "'Let the Dead Bury Their Dead' (Matt 8:22 / Luke 9:60): Jesus and the Halakhah," *Journal of Theological Studies* 49 (1998): 564.

the plow and looks to what was left behind is fit for the kingdom of God.[15]
The request and the response recall Elisha's request to Elijah—to which he
assented—to take leave of his parents before following him, when Elijah called
him as he was *plowing* (1 Kings 19:19–21). Like his refusal to call down fire
from heaven, Jesus' response here thus contrasts with Elijah's. As the Messiah
and Son of God (Luke 9:20, 35), Jesus is greater than Old Testament prophets
(11:32). Therefore, the commitment required of disciples is greater. Those who
follow him must do so unconditionally.

Mission of the Seventy-Two (10:1–20)

[1]After this the Lord appointed seventy[-two] others whom he sent ahead
of him in pairs to every town and place he intended to visit. [2]He said to
them, "The harvest is abundant but the laborers are few; so ask the master of the harvest to send out laborers for his harvest. [3]Go on your way;
behold, I am sending you like lambs among wolves. [4]Carry no money bag,
no sack, no sandals; and greet no one along the way. [5]Into whatever house
you enter, first say, 'Peace to this household.' [6]If a peaceful person lives
there, your peace will rest on him; but if not, it will return to you. [7]Stay in
the same house and eat and drink what is offered to you, for the laborer
deserves his payment. Do not move about from one house to another.
[8]Whatever town you enter and they welcome you, eat what is set before
you, [9]cure the sick in it and say to them, 'The kingdom of God is at hand
for you.' [10]Whatever town you enter and they do not receive you, go out
into the streets and say, [11]'The dust of your town that clings to our feet,
even that we shake off against you.' Yet know this: the kingdom of God is
at hand. [12]I tell you, it will be more tolerable for Sodom on that day than
for that town.

[13]"Woe to you, Chorazin! Woe to you, Bethsaida! For if the mighty
deeds done in your midst had been done in Tyre and Sidon, they would
long ago have repented, sitting in sackcloth and ashes. [14]But it will be
more tolerable for Tyre and Sidon at the judgment than for you. [15]And as
for you, Capernaum, 'Will you be exalted to heaven? You will go down to
the netherworld.'" [16]Whoever listens to you listens to me. Whoever rejects
you rejects me. And whoever rejects me rejects the one who sent me."

[17]The seventy[-two] returned rejoicing, and said, "Lord, even the
demons are subject to us because of your name." [18]Jesus said, "I have

15. The point of the image is that one has to keep looking forward so that the furrow made by the
plow may come out straight.

observed Satan fall like lightning from the sky. [19]Behold, I have given you
the power 'to tread upon serpents' and scorpions and upon the full force
of the enemy and nothing will harm you. [20]Nevertheless, do not rejoice
because the spirits are subject to you, but rejoice because your names are
written in heaven."

OT: Gen 10; Num 11:16–30; 2 Kings 4:29; Ps 91:13; Isa 14:12–15

NT: Matt 10:7–16; Mark 6:8–11; Luke 9:1–6, 48; John 4:35; 1 Cor 9:14; 10:27; 1 Tim 5:18. // Matt 9:37–38; 11:20–24

Catechism: the disciples continue Jesus' mission, 765, 787, 858; praying for laborers, 2611; laborers deserve payment, 2122; listening to the Church's teaching, 87

Lectionary: Luke 10:1–12, 17–20: Fourteenth Sunday Ordinary Time (Year C); Luke 10:1–9: St. Luke; Holy Orders; Luke 10:5–6, 8–9: Anointing of the Sick

Jesus gives another group of disciples the opportunity to share in his mission. **10:1**
Continuing his journey to Jerusalem, **the Lord** again **sent ahead of him** ("before
his face," as in 9:52) some disciples whom he had **appointed** (verb *anadeiknymi*),
so that they might prepare for his arrival in **every town and place** where he
was about to go. They are doing what was done by John the Baptist, whose
"manifestation" or commissioning (noun *anadeixis*, 1:80) was for the purpose
of going "ahead of" (literally, "before the face of") him (7:27) to prepare his way.

Their mission recalls that of the Twelve (9:1–6), but their number is larger:
seventy[-two]. Whereas the mission of the Twelve points to the regathering
of the twelve tribes of Israel, the sending out of this second group anticipates
the mission to the Gentiles since seventy or seventy-two was the number of
the Gentile nations (Gen 10; see Exod 1:5; Deut 32:8 NIV).[16] Jesus has come as
God's salvation for both Israel and the nations (Luke 2:32). After his ascension,
his disciples' mission begins in Israel but will then extend to "all the nations"
(24:47; see Acts 10:35; 11:18). Interestingly, the mission to Samaria will be a step
linking the two (Acts 1:8; 8:5). Since Jesus has recently entered into Samaritan
territory (Luke 9:52), the pattern of the later mission is thus anticipated here.

The disciples are sent out **in pairs**, perhaps for mutual support, a practice
that Jesus and the early Church will continue later.[17]

Before they leave, Jesus gives them extended instructions (10:2–12). First, they **10:2**
are to **ask** the **master of the harvest** for more **laborers**. The image of a **harvest**
that **is abundant** signifies their mission and recalls the hundredfold yield (8:8;
also John 4:35–38). Earlier, Jesus had similarly used the image of catching a

16. The Greek manuscripts are divided between "seventy" and "seventy-two" disciples. This likely reflects a similar variation in the table of nations in Gen 10: whereas the Hebrew text lists seventy nations, the †Septuagint has seventy-two. See also Num 11:24–26.

17. Luke 19:29; 22:8; Acts 8:14; 11:30; 13:2; 15:27, 39–40; 19:22.

great number of fish (Luke 5:6–10). Elsewhere in the Bible, the harvest image connotes God's judgment (Joel 4:13;[18] Rev 14:15). Though the accent here is on mission, Jesus will soon speak of judgment (Luke 10:14) for those who do not accept him and his disciples.

The word rendered "master" is *kyrios*, often translated "Lord." The idea is that the disciples are to pray to God the Father **to send out** more workers, though Jesus is the one *sending* them out (10:1). Jesus will himself soon pray to the "Father, *Lord* of heaven and earth" (10:21 [emphasis added]). Also, a Scripture passage will be quoted referring to God as "Lord" (10:27). On the other hand, Jesus has himself just been called "Lord" (*kyrios*) by the evangelist (10:1; see 10:39, 41). In context, the disciples also repeatedly address Jesus as "Lord" (e.g., 9:54; 10:17; 11:1). Because of this double use of "Lord" for the Father and for Jesus,[19] readers of the Gospel are led to recognize Jesus' divinity and therefore the fittingness of praying also to him.

10:3 Jesus is aware of the dangers that lie ahead. The disciples will be **like lambs among wolves.** They may have thus wondered about their prospects for survival, let alone success: "Is a wolf ever allied with a lamb? / So the sinner with the righteous" (Sir 13:17; see Ezek 22:27; Acts 20:29). The comparison to lambs also indicates that the disciples are not being sent out as warriors to establish the kingdom of God (Luke 10:9) by force. Rather, they **go** bringing greetings of peace (v. 5).

10:4 Like the Twelve sent out earlier (9:3), these disciples are to leave behind all unnecessary possessions. They are to rely on divine providence at work through those who offer them hospitality. Therefore, they will **carry no money bag** and **no sack** to hold provisions. They also are to carry **no sandals,** probably meaning a second pair besides those one would wear. Jesus later recalls these instructions but alters them in light of new circumstances (22:35–36). The final instruction, to **greet no one along the way,** recalls the word of Elisha to his servant Gehazi: "If you meet anyone, give no greeting, and if anyone greets you, do not answer" (2 Kings 4:29). The reason was that Elisha was sending Gehazi on an urgent mission. Likewise, the mission of proclaiming the kingdom requires a sense of urgency, so the disciples should remain focused and avoid lengthy delays and distractions (see Luke 9:59–62).

10:5–6 When the disciples reach their destination and enter a **house,** then they can extend a true greeting: **Peace to this household.** "Peace" is a traditional

18. Joel 3:13 RSV.
19. C. Kavin Rowe, *Early Narrative Christology: The Lord in the Gospel of Luke* (Berlin: de Gruyter, 2006; Grand Rapids: Baker Academic, 2009), 134.

greeting (Hebrew *shalom*; e.g., 1 Chron 12:19) but it is also the blessing that accompanies the birth of the Messiah (Luke 2:14). When Jesus is recognized as "king" as he approaches Jerusalem, "peace" is again proclaimed (19:38). "Peace" will also be Jesus' own greeting after the resurrection (24:36). The "peace" that the disciples extend is thus a blessing associated with "the kingdom of God" (10:9) that comes in Jesus.

Someone who accepts this gift is **a peaceful person**—literally, "a son of peace," using a biblical way of speaking that characterizes someone by a particular quality.[20] Such a peaceable person would be open to hearing the disciples' message and allowing them to use the house as a base for their mission (Acts 16:14–15, 40).

Like the Twelve (Luke 9:4), the disciples are to **stay in the same house** rather **10:7** than **move about** looking for a better place. The food and drink **offered** to them are their recompense for preaching the gospel, **for the laborer deserves his payment** ("wages," RSV). This principle has its biblical roots in the tithes of produce given to the Levites as "recompense in exchange for labor in the tent of meeting" (Num 18:31). Paul applies this and similar Old Testament laws (Num 18:8; Deut 18:1–5) to those who preach the gospel, on the basis of Jesus' teaching: "Do you not know that those who perform the temple services eat [what] belongs to the temple, and those who minister at the altar share in the sacrificial offerings? In the same way, the Lord ordered that those who preach the gospel should live by the gospel" (1 Cor 9:13–14). Moreover, in one of Paul's pastoral letters, the principle recorded here appears verbatim: "The laborer deserves his wages" (1 Tim 5:18 RSV). These comparisons with the Levites suggest, as Paul says elsewhere, that those who preach the gospel carry out a "priestly service" (Rom 15:16).

Staying in one house provides a base for evangelizing a **town** that extends a **10:8** **welcome** to the disciples. While in the town, they are to **eat what is set before** them. In contrast to the Pharisees' restrictive customs regarding table fellowship, Jesus' own practice of eating with tax collectors and sinners is the model for his disciples (Luke 5:29–30; 7:34; 15:1–2; 19:5–7). They will likely enter Samaritan villages (as in 9:52), where the issue of Jews eating with Samaritans would arise (John 4:9).[21] Moreover, looking ahead to the Gentile mission, this instruction is helpful for overcoming the resistance of Jewish Christians to associating with Gentiles (see Acts 10:28; 11:3).[22] Indeed, Paul seems to rely on a tradition

---

20. For example, wisdom's "children" (Luke 7:35), "children of light" (16:8), and "son of encouragement" (Acts 4:36).

21. *m. Shevi'it* 8:10.

22. *Jubilees* 22.16.

handing down this teaching of Jesus, when he explains: "If an unbeliever invites you to a meal . . . eat whatever is set before you" (1 Cor 10:27 NRSV).[23]

10:9 Jesus also states what activities the disciples will carry out: **cure the sick** and proclaim that **the kingdom of God is at hand**. This is the same combination of deed and word seen in Jesus' own ministry (Luke 6:18; 8:1–2; 9:11) and in the mission of the Twelve (9:1–2, 6). The same combination will also be seen in the Church's mission later (Acts 8:7, 12), even down to the present time. The kingdom ushered in by Jesus, through his word and mighty deeds, is extended through the mission of those he sends out.

10:10–12 However, when a **town** does not **receive** the disciples, they are to **shake off** (or "wipe off," a different verb than in Luke 9:5) **the dust** from their **feet**. Earlier, it was explained that this action signifies a "testimony against them" (9:5). This may be another reason why the disciples here go out in pairs (10:1), so that their message may be confirmed by the testimony of at least two witnesses (Deut 19:15). The action is accompanied by a warning: **the kingdom of God is at hand**. The drawing near of the kingdom is a word of salvation for those who receive it but a word of judgment to those who refuse to repent and believe. Indeed, on that coming **day** of judgment (Luke 10:14; 17:29–30), **that town** will fare worse than **Sodom**, the proverbial place of wickedness and perversion of hospitality.[24]

10:13–14 Jesus singles out three such towns associated with his ministry in and near Galilee. He pronounces a **woe** on the first two: **Chorazin** and **Bethsaida**. Besides the parallel verse (Matt 11:21), Chorazin is not otherwise mentioned in the Bible. It has been identified with the ruins at a site about two and a half miles from Capernaum, and was probably visited by Jesus on his preaching tours (Luke 4:15, 43–44; 8:1). Bethsaida (9:10) likewise had witnessed some of his **mighty deeds** (see Mark 8:22–26). However, at about the same time (AD 30), Philip the tetrarch had raised its status to a city,[25] renamed it Julias (after Livia-Julia, mother of the emperor Tiberius), and apparently introduced there the Roman imperial religion. Jesus laments that these towns have not **repented** in response to his ministry. He compares them to **Tyre and Sidon**, Phoenician cities from which people had earlier come to listen to Jesus (Luke 6:17). Despite those cities' past oppression of the people of Israel (Joel 4:4–8;[26] 1 Macc 5:15), under the same circumstances they would have manifested their repentance even by wearing rough **sackcloth** and sprinkling themselves with

23. David J. Rudolph, *A Jew to the Jews: Jewish Contours of Pauline Flexibility in 1 Corinthians 9:19–23* (Tübingen: Mohr Siebeck, 2011), 183–90.

24. See Gen 13:13; 19:1–28; Isa 1:7, 9; Lam 4:6; Ezek 16:46–52; Amos 4:11.

25. Josephus, *Jewish War* 2.168; *Jewish Antiquities* 18.28.

26. Joel 3:4–8 RSV.

The Kingdom of God

BIBLICAL BACKGROUND

David's kingdom was considered to be that "of the LORD's kingship" (1 Chron 28:5; see 2 Chron 13:8). Thus as son of David (Luke 1:32; 18:38–39) but even more as Son of God (1:35),[a] Jesus the *king* ushers in the *kingdom* of God.

During the Galilean ministry, Jesus and his apostles begin proclaiming the good news of God's kingdom.[b] However, most of Jesus' teaching about the kingdom of God appears on the journey to Jerusalem—which culminates in his being acclaimed king (19:38). There are more than twenty references to the kingdom in this central section. Proclaiming God's kingdom now becomes an urgent priority (9:60, 62). With Jesus' coming, the kingdom is "at hand" in the midst of the people (10:9, 11; see 11:20; 17:21). However, one must also seek it and pray for its coming in fullness (11:2; 12:31). As the kingdom of God advances, Satan's kingdom is in retreat (11:17–20; see 10:18). Jesus also uses parables to explain the kingdom (13:18–21; 19:11–27). He describes the great banquet that will take place in the kingdom (13:28–29; 14:15–24; see 22:16, 18), to which the poor and the sick are invited (14:21). He gives the conditions for entering the kingdom, indicating that it reverses worldly values (18:16–17, 24–25, 29–30). He promises the kingdom to his followers (12:32; see 22:29–30; 23:42, 51).[c]

Though it may seem weak when compared to the kingdoms of the world (4:5), such as the mighty Roman Empire, the kingdom of God transcends earthly armies (21:20, 31). Paradoxically, Luke's story ends in Rome, with Paul "with complete assurance and without hindrance" proclaiming "the kingdom of God" (Acts 28:31). Daniel's prophecy is thus being brought to fulfillment: "The God of heaven will set up a kingdom that shall never be destroyed" (Dan 2:44).

a. Costantino Antonio Ziccardi, *The Relationship of Jesus and the Kingdom of God according to Luke-Acts* (Rome: Editrice Pontificia Università Gregoriana, 2008), 501–3.
b. Luke 4:43; 6:20; 7:28; 8:1, 10; 9:2, 11, 27.
c. See Aletti, *L'art de raconter Jésus Christ*, 121–22.

ashes, traditional disciplines associated with fasting and penitential prayer that seeks God's mercy (Dan 9:3–5; Jon 3:5–9). Therefore, **the judgment** on those ancient enemies of Israel will be less severe than for Chorazin and Bethsaida. This comparison anticipates the situation in Acts, where there will be resistance to the gospel among many Jews but reception of the gospel among many Gentiles (Acts 13:45–46; 18:5–6; 28:24–28).

A third city in a similar situation is **Capernaum**. Although the people there 10:15 were amazed at his miracles and tried to prevent him from leaving (Luke

4:31–42), they too must not have repented and shown true faith in Jesus (see 7:9). At the judgment, the town will thus not **be exalted to heaven** but will **go down to the netherworld**. The language echoes the judgment on Babylon found in Isaiah: "You said in your heart, / 'I will ascend to heaven.' . . . / But you are brought down to Sheol" (Isa 14:13, 15 RSV). The "netherworld" (*hadēs* in the †Septuagint and the New Testament) corresponds to the Hebrew *she'ol*, referring in general to the abode of the dead (Gen 37:35). In Luke's Gospel, the word occurs only one other time, where it indicates more specifically a place of torment for the wicked after death (Luke 16:23), a meaning also found in some Jewish sources.[27] Here, the word may have a similar meaning and is hence sometimes translated "hell" (e.g., NJB).

By means of these comparisons with wicked cities and enemies of Israel—Sodom, Tyre, Sidon, and Babylon—Jesus shows that the stakes are high if one rejects him and his message.

10:16   After this aside in which Jesus speaks rhetorically to the towns, he again speaks to those he is sending out: **whoever listens to you listens to me**. This is what apostolic authority means: there is a certain identification between Jesus and those whom he sends. This is true for better or for worse: **whoever rejects you rejects me**. Indeed, ever since the beginning of the journey to Jerusalem, the emphasis has been on rejection (see 9:53). The link extends even further, since the one who rejects the disciples and Jesus also **rejects the one who sent** him—namely, God the Father. This is the inverse of the earlier statement: "Whoever receives me receives the one who sent me" (9:48). The stakes are indeed high!

10:17   The return of **the seventy[-two]** is recounted without any break. Considering their prospects of rejection (10:16), one would expect them to come back discouraged, but instead they are **rejoicing**. Addressing Jesus as **Lord**, they specify the reason for their joy: **even the demons are subject to us**. Jesus had presumably given them, like the Twelve, "power and authority over all demons and to cure diseases" (9:1). Through their ministry of curing the sick and preaching the kingdom of God (10:9), the kingdom of the evil one is in retreat (see 11:20). Sent out by Jesus, they are successful **because** they invoke the **name** of Jesus (see Acts 3:6; 16:18). Indeed, "at the name of Jesus / every knee should bend" (Phil 2:10).

10:18   **Jesus** confirms what they say, explaining that he **observed Satan fall like lightning** from heaven.[28] Jesus' words apply to the devil the judgment in Isaiah against the king of Babylon: "How you have fallen from the heavens, / O Morning

27. E.g., *Jubilees* 7.29.
28. The name "Satan" for the devil (see comment on Luke 4:2) appears here for the first time in Luke.

Apostolic Tradition

LIVING
TRADITION

In Luke 9 and 10, Jesus gives his apostles and disciples a share in his authority as he sends them out on mission. St. Irenaeus, the second-century Church Father and bishop in what is now France, cites Luke 10 as he explains how Jesus' teaching authority has been handed down in the Church through the apostles and their successors:

> The Lord of all things gave to his apostles the power of the gospel, and through them we, too, know the truth, that is, the doctrine of God's Son. To them the Lord also said, "He who hears you hears me; and he who despises you, despises me and him who sent me" [10:16]. . . .
>
> In point of fact, we received the knowledge of the economy of our salvation through no others than those through whom the gospel has come down to us. This gospel they first preached orally, but later by God's will they handed it on to us in the Scriptures. . . .
>
> All, therefore, who wish to see the truth can view in the whole Church the tradition of the apostles that has been manifested in the whole world. Further, we are able to enumerate the bishops who were established in the Churches by the apostles, and their successions even to ourselves. . . . Since, however, . . . it would be too long to list the successions of all the Churches, we shall here address the tradition of the greatest and most ancient Church, known to all, founded and built up at Rome by the two most glorious apostles, Peter and Paul—the tradition received from the apostles . . . which has come down even to us through the successions of the bishops. . . . For with this Church, because of her greater authority, it is necessary that every Church, that is, the faithful who are everywhere, should agree, because in her the apostolic tradition has always been safeguarded.[a]

a. Irenaeus, *Against the Heresies* 3, Preface, 3.1.1, and 3.3.1–2, trans. Dominic J. Unger and M. C. Steenberg, ACW (New York: Newman, 2012), 29–30, 32–33.

Star, son of the dawn!" (Isa 14:12).[29] The devil seeks to "scale the heavens" in order to make himself "like the Most High" (Isa 14:13–14). However, through their mission, the disciples are contributing to the devil's downfall. Certainly, the struggle is not over yet, as is evident from the diabolic activity mentioned later in the Gospel and Acts[30] as well as that seen throughout history. Nevertheless, by his words Jesus anticipates the ultimate victory over Satan.

Therefore, there is nothing to fear because Jesus has given the disciples **power** ("authority," RSV) over **the full force of the enemy**. Jesus describes this authority   **10:19**

29. The Isaiah passage is similarly used to describe the fall of Satan in nonbiblical Jewish literature; see, e.g., *Life of Adam and Eve* 12–16.
30. Luke 11:14; 22:3, 31, 53; Acts 5:16; 8:7; 16:16; 26:18.

as the ability **to tread upon serpents and scorpions** (alluding to Ps 91:13; see comment on Luke 4:10–11). The image suggests a text from Deuteronomy: as God guided the people of Israel "through the vast and terrible wilderness with its saraph serpents and scorpions" (Deut 8:15), so too Jesus' disciples will be protected from lasting **harm**. Therefore, they should not be afraid.

10:20   To those who have ministered in his "name" (Luke 10:17), Jesus clarifies the real reason to **rejoice**: their **names are written in heaven**. This refers to "the book of life" (Ps 69:29; Phil 4:3; Rev 3:5; 21:27), a familiar biblical image for those who will be saved.

In summary, the mission of the seventy-two, as an anticipation of the Gentile mission in Acts, provides a model for the Church's ongoing mission to advance the kingdom of God through word and deed. Amid the dangers posed by the forces of evil, Jesus continues to send out his disciples, empowering them for the task and promising them a heavenly reward.

Reflection and Application (10:1–20)

Vocation. Laborers are needed because "the harvest is abundant" (Luke 10:2). Though all Christians share in Jesus' mission on account of their baptism, it "is carried out above all by men and women" who make "a full and lifelong commitment" to mission and "are prepared to go forth into the whole world to bring salvation."[31] Is the Lord calling me or someone I know to such a commitment?

Missionary joy. "The Gospel joy which enlivens the community of disciples is a missionary joy. The seventy-two disciples felt it as they returned from their mission."[32] How often do I experience this joy that comes from sharing my faith?

The Son Reveals the Father (10:21–24)

---

[21]At that very moment he rejoiced [in] the holy Spirit and said, "I give you praise, Father, Lord of heaven and earth, for although you have hidden these things from the wise and the learned you have revealed them to the childlike. Yes, Father, such has been your gracious will. [22]All things have been handed over to me by my Father. No one knows who the Son is except the Father, and who the Father is except the Son and anyone to whom the Son wishes to reveal him."

---

31. John Paul II, *Redemptoris Missio* (On the Permanent Validity of the Church's Missionary Mandate) 79.

32. Francis, *Evangelii Gaudium* (On the Proclamation of the Gospel in Today's World) 21.

²³Turning to the disciples in private he said, "Blessed are the eyes that see what you see. ²⁴For I say to you, many prophets and kings desired to see what you see, but did not see it, and to hear what you hear, but did not hear it."

OT: Isa 29:14
NT: John 3:35; 10:15; 13:3; 1 Cor 1:19, 21, 26–28. // Matt 11:25–27; 13:16–17
Catechism: Jesus' prayer, 2603
Lectionary: Tuesday First Week of Advent; Confirmation

Jesus turns now to address the **Father**. He is still reflecting on the disciples'   **10:21** mission, but his words now focus at a higher level on what that mission reveals about God's plan of salvation and his own relationship as Son to the Father. Whereas in the Galilean section, people frequently asked about Jesus' identity in response to his miracles, here it is Jesus himself who reveals who he is through his teaching (11:29–32).

As the disciples returned rejoicing (10:17), so too Jesus **rejoiced**, exulting in **the holy Spirit**. This verb for "rejoice" or "exult" is found elsewhere in Luke only in the Magnificat, where Mary's "spirit rejoices in God" (1:47). In a cry of jubilation, Jesus gives **praise** and thanks to God, **Lord of heaven and earth**, in words typical of Jewish thanksgiving prayers, which often also give a reason **for** the praise (2 Sam 22:48–50; Ps 136:26; Sir 51:1–2; Dan 2:23).[33] He directly addresses God as "Father" in his prayer, something not common for individuals in the Old Testament (see Ps 89:27). This points to his status as Son (Luke 10:22) and complements the earlier words of the Father about the Son (3:22; 9:35). It also prepares for the Lord's Prayer in the next chapter (11:2). Jesus will also address God as "Father" in his prayers in the garden and on the cross (22:42; 23:34, 46).

As in Mary's Magnificat (1:51–52), so also the reason here for Jesus' praise is the great reversal being worked by God, who has **hidden these things from the wise and the learned** but **revealed them to the childlike**. Jesus is referring to everything associated with the mission of the disciples. They are the humble souls (see 14:11; 18:14) to whom God has revealed the mysteries of his kingdom (8:10), in contrast to the trained religious leaders, who may be puffed up with pride (see 14:7; 18:11). Isaiah had prophesied this reversal (Isa 29:14), and Paul takes it up in 1 Corinthians. First quoting the verse from Isaiah—"For it is written: / 'I will destroy the wisdom of the *wise*, / and the learning of the *learned* I will set aside'" (1 Cor 1:19 [emphasis added])—Paul

---

33. See also the Qumran thanksgiving hymns: 1QHª (*Hodayotᵃ*) XV, 26–27.

then comments, in words similar to this Gospel passage: "Not many of you were wise by human standards.... Rather, God chose the foolish of the world to shame the wise" (1 Cor 1:26–27). He further notes that this was "the will of God" (1 Cor 1:21; verb *eudokeō*), similar to Jesus' words that **such has been your gracious will** (noun *eudokia*).[34] Like the lowly shepherds to whom Jesus' birth was revealed, the disciples are those "on whom his favor rests" (Luke 2:14; noun *eudokia*).

10:22   In language that sounds like phrases in John's Gospel (John 3:35; 10:15; 13:3), Jesus develops the connection earlier expressed between the Father, the Son, and the disciples (see Luke 9:48; 10:16). First, he notes the authority given to him: **All things have been handed over to me by my Father**. In contrast, one recalls the devil's claim to the authority "handed over" to him (4:6). Second, Jesus reflects on his relationship as Son to the Father: **No one knows who the Son is except the Father, and who the Father is except the Son**. Already at the age of twelve, he had expressed awareness of his identity as Son (2:49). He now expresses it more fully—the words "Father" and "Son" occur a total of eight times in verses 21–22—and he does so in "the holy Spirit" (v. 21), giving a glimpse of the life of the Trinity. He thus reveals to the larger group of disciples what Peter, John, and James found out on the mountain (9:35) and Mary had been told by the angel (1:32, 35). Third, as **Son**, Jesus is the one who reveals the Father to **anyone to whom** he **wishes**—namely, his disciples. Thus in teaching his disciples and sending them on their mission, Jesus is making known to them the *Father's* plan of salvation. Such is the connection between the sending Father, the sent Son who sends, and the sent disciples (see 4:18, 43; 9:2, 48; 10:1, 16).

10:23–24   Having revealed his identity as Son, Jesus expresses with a beatitude the unique privilege that **the disciples** have been given: **Blessed are the eyes that see what you see** (8:10). They, like Simeon, have received the blessing of seeing God's salvation with their own eyes (2:26, 30). The theme of reversal appears again (see v. 21), since **many prophets and kings** were not given this opportunity. Indeed, the prophets Moses and Elijah finally saw at the transfiguration (9:30) and King David only "foresaw" it (Acts 2:31). Moreover, the disciples, like the three apostles on the mountain who were reminded to "listen" to Jesus (*akouō*, Luke 9:35), are told how fortunate they are **to hear** (*akouō*) Jesus, who is both "prophet" (7:16) and "king" (19:38).

---

34. Peter Richardson, "The Thunderbolt in Q and the Wise Man in Corinth," in *From Jesus to Paul*, ed. Peter Richardson and John C. Hurd (Waterloo, ON: Wilfrid Laurier University Press, 1984), 91–101.

Doing the Love Commandments and the Parable of the Good Samaritan (10:25–37)

²⁵There was a scholar of the law who stood up to test him and said, "Teacher, what must I do to inherit eternal life?" ²⁶Jesus said to him, "What is written in the law? How do you read it?" ²⁷He said in reply, "You shall love the Lord, your God, with all your heart, with all your being, with all your strength, and with all your mind, and your neighbor as yourself." ²⁸He replied to him, "You have answered correctly; do this and you will live."

²⁹But because he wished to justify himself, he said to Jesus, "And who is my neighbor?" ³⁰Jesus replied, "A man fell victim to robbers as he went down from Jerusalem to Jericho. They stripped and beat him and went off leaving him half-dead. ³¹A priest happened to be going down that road, but when he saw him, he passed by on the opposite side. ³²Likewise a Levite came to the place, and when he saw him, he passed by on the opposite side. ³³But a Samaritan traveler who came upon him was moved with compassion at the sight. ³⁴He approached the victim, poured oil and wine over his wounds and bandaged them. Then he lifted him up on his own animal, took him to an inn and cared for him. ³⁵The next day he took out two silver coins and gave them to the innkeeper with the instruction, 'Take care of him. If you spend more than what I have given you, I shall repay you on my way back.' ³⁶Which of these three, in your opinion, was neighbor to the robbers' victim?" ³⁷He answered, "The one who treated him with mercy." Jesus said to him, "Go and do likewise."

OT: Lev 18:5; 19:16, 18; Deut 6:5; 2 Chron 28:5–15; Dan 12:2
NT: Luke 18:18; Rom 13:9; Gal 5:14; James 2:8. // Matt 22:34–40; Mark 12:28–34
Catechism: love God, 2083; love your neighbor, 1825, 2822; oil a sign of healing, 1293; the priest in the sacrament of penance bandages wounds, 1465
Lectionary: Fifteenth Sunday Ordinary Time (Year C); Anointing of the Sick

Just after Jesus' words about things being hidden from the learned (10:21), such **10:25** a learned person appears: **a scholar of the law**—that is, a scribe and teacher of the Torah. Such scholars in Luke are always portrayed negatively (7:30; 11:45–52; 14:3), and this one is no exception, since he wants **to test** Jesus (see 4:2, 12). Addressing Jesus as **Teacher**, he asks a question typical of the late Old Testament period (see Dan 12:2; 2 Macc 7:9) that would continue to occupy the rabbis:³⁵ **what must I do to inherit eternal life?** The rich official will later ask Jesus exactly the same question (Luke 18:18).

35. On inheriting life in the world to come, see *m. Avot* 2:7; 4:16; 5:19; *Sanhedrin* 10:1–4.

10:26   **Jesus** turns the question around, asking the "scholar of the law" to answer from **the law** itself. For Jesus, the answer is to be found in Scripture. He also asks—**How do you read it?**—referring to the interpretation of Scripture, which will be taken up in the parable.

10:27   In response, the scholar combines the two Old Testament verses that contain the phrase **You shall love** (Lev 19:18; Deut 6:5).[36] The Deuteronomy text comes first, since it involves loving **the Lord, your God, with all your heart, with all your being** (or "soul," RSV), **with all your strength, and with all your mind**. This verse forms part of the †*Shema* prayer recited twice daily by Jews (see Deut 6:4–9).[37] The Hebrew text of Deuteronomy has three elements rather than Luke's four: "heart," "being" ("soul," RSV), and "strength" (Deut 6:5). However, since the Hebrew word "heart" can also refer to the seat of understanding, the †Septuagint sometimes translates it as "mind" (Lev 19:17 LXX; Deut 4:39 LXX), and some manuscripts of the Septuagint even have "mind" in the *Shema* also. Thus it is not surprising that Luke has the fourth element "mind." The idea is that the commandment to love God embraces every aspect of one's being.

The Leviticus text follows immediately: **and your neighbor as yourself**. It is possible that the combination of love of God and neighbor had already been made by the time of Jesus, since it appears in nonbiblical Jewish literature (without the quotations of the biblical texts), although the dating of these texts is uncertain.[38]

10:28   Jesus affirms that the scholar has **answered correctly**. However, knowing the right answer (see 7:43) and doing the right thing are two different matters, and indeed the original question asked what he needed to "do" (*poieō*, v. 25). This emphasis on doing is also found in Jesus' teaching (6:47; 8:21), so he continues: **do this and you will live**. These words echo another passage from Leviticus: "By doing so one shall live" (Lev 18:5 NRSV). This stress on what one needs to "do" will be repeated at the end of the passage (twice in Luke 10:37).

10:29   The scholar, seeking to **justify** why he asked the first question if he already knew its answer, asks a second question: **Who is my neighbor?** The context in Leviticus indeed suggested a range of options. "Neighbor" could be understood more narrowly as a relative or a member of one's people (Lev 19:17–18). It could also be understood more broadly to include the foreigner sojourning in the land: "You shall treat the alien who resides with you no differently than the natives born among you; you shall love the alien as yourself" (Lev 19:34).

---

36. There are actually two others (Lev 19:34; Deut 11:1), but these refer back to the two verses quoted. The combination of verses is another example of the *gezerah shawah* technique (see comment on Luke 4:18–19).

37. *m. Berakhot* 1:1–4.

38. *Testament of Issachar* 5:2; *Testament of Dan* 5:3.

This second question regards the interpretation of Scripture. As with other **10:30** such matters (e.g., the sabbath, Luke 6:9; 13:15–16; 14:3), Jesus is the one who gives Scripture its authoritative interpretation since "all things have been handed over" to him by the Father (10:22). Here, he interprets the commandment by telling a parable.

The setting of the parable is the steeply descending road about seventeen miles long **from Jerusalem to Jericho**, a drop in elevation of about 3,300 feet. **A man** (presumably a Jew) **went down** on this road and **fell victim to robbers** (a realistic scenario), who **stripped and beat him**, **leaving him half-dead**.

Three individuals encounter the half-dead man. First, there is **a priest** who is **10:31–32** similarly **going down** from Jerusalem, probably returning home after finishing his time of ministry in the temple, and then **likewise a Levite**.[39] They behave in the same manner: they both **saw** the man, but **passed by on the opposite side**. Although no reason is stated, they, especially the priest, may have been motivated by concerns for ritual purity, thinking that the man was already dead or about to die (Num 5:2). The law taught that, except for close relatives, even apart from priestly service in the temple, no priest "shall make himself unclean for any dead person" (Lev 21:1–2).[40] However, the end of the parable will indicate that whatever reasons they had were insufficient. They passed by "idly" when their "neighbor's life" was "at stake" (Lev 19:16), and hence by their omission they failed to love their neighbor (Lev 19:18).

A third passerby is now introduced. Following typical order, one would expect **10:33–35** a common Israelite (see Ezra 2:70; 6:16),[41] but surprisingly it is a **Samaritan**, one who was considered an enemy. However, he too knows the Torah, and in contrast to the first two, he helps the man. For someone like the scholar who is familiar with Scripture, all this should sound familiar on account of the passage (to which the parable alludes) that recounts how leaders of Samaria helped a group of captives of Judah: "All of them who were naked they clothed, . . . gave them food and drink, anointed them, and all who were weak they set on donkeys. They brought them to Jericho" (2 Chron 28:15). There is thus a biblical precedent for showing love to one's enemies.

The Samaritan **was moved with compassion at the sight** and **approached the victim**. The phrase "moved with compassion" translates the verb *splanchnizomai*, which up to this point has only occurred in Luke to describe Jesus' reaction

---

39. The Levites assisted the priests in the temple (see Num 3:9–10).
40. The oral law, as formulated later in the †Mishnah (*m. Nazir* 7:1), indicates that a priest may bury a neglected corpse, even though he becomes ritually unclean by doing so. In part, Jesus may here be teaching a similar lesson, indicating that the commandment to love one's neighbor takes precedence.
41. *m. Gittin* 5:8.

Samaritans

BIBLICAL BACKGROUND

The Samaritans descended from the Israelites of the northern tribes of Ephraim and Manasseh. However, Jews regarded them as having doubtful lineage on account of intermarriage with the Gentile peoples imported by the Assyrians after they conquered the northern kingdom in 721 BC and sent some Israelites into exile (2 Kings 17:6–24; 2 Chron 30:6–11).[a] Besides these ethnic tensions, there was an enduring religious rift associated with the Samaritans' worship on Mount Gerizim[b] rather than at the Jerusalem temple (John 4:20). The †Hasmonean Jewish ruler John Hyrcanus destroyed the Samaritan temple on Mount Gerizim around 111 BC. Later, under the Roman prefect Coponius (AD 6–9), some Samaritans struck back by littering the Jerusalem temple with human bones at Passover, thus defiling it.[c] Moreover, when Cumanus was the Roman procurator (AD 48–52), Samaritans from the border village of Ginae killed a group of Galileans passing through Samaria on the way to Jerusalem for a feast.[d]

This background of hostility explains the rejection of Jesus by the Samaritan villagers (Luke 9:53) but also makes the parable of the good Samaritan (10:29–37) particularly effective for teaching love of neighbor. Jesus' healing of ten lepers also breaks down the enmity, as one of them—a Samaritan—returns to thank him (17:11–19). These passages set the stage for the Acts of the Apostles, where the gospel is proclaimed to Samaria (Acts 1:8; 8:4–25). In the new community that emerges in the land of Israel, the long-standing animosity can be overcome: "The church throughout all Judea, Galilee, and Samaria was at peace" (Acts 9:31). The regathering of the Samaritans thus forms part of the program of Israel's restoration in Luke-Acts.[e]

a. Josephus, *Jewish Antiquities* 9.277–80, 288–91. See Gary N. Knoppers, *Jews and Samaritans: The Origins and History of Their Early Relations* (Oxford: Oxford University Press, 2013), 1–101.
b. Knoppers, *Jews and Samaritans*, 184, 202.
c. Josephus, *Jewish Antiquities* 18.29–30.
d. Josephus, *Jewish Antiquities* 20.118.
e. David Ravens, *Luke and the Restoration of Israel* (Sheffield: Sheffield Academic, 1995), 92–106; Richard Bauckham, "The Restoration of Israel in Luke-Acts," in *The Jewish World around the New Testament* (Grand Rapids: Baker Academic, 2010), 356.

to the widow's dead son (Luke 7:13).[42] Actually, this is just one of three action verbs linking this passage to that one: both Jesus at Nain and the Samaritan in the parable "see" the problem, "are moved with compassion," and "approach" the dead or half-dead individual (see 7:13–14). Thus the model behavior of the

42. It occurs once more, in the parable of the prodigal son, to describe the father's compassionate response (Luke 15:20).

Jesus the Good Samaritan

Ever since the second century, the obvious ethical meaning of the parable as an injunction to love one's neighbor has been complemented by an allegorical interpretation in which the good Samaritan represents Jesus. For example, Irenaeus writes that human nature "had fallen in with robbers, but he had pity on it and bound its wounds." Origen adds: "The man who was going down is Adam. . . . The Samaritan is Christ. . . . He carries the half-dead man, and brings him to . . . the Church." Origen does not ignore the ethical lesson: "It is possible for us to imitate Christ. . . . He is speaking not so much to the teacher of the Law as to us . . . when he says, 'Go and do likewise.'"

Augustine also uses the allegorical interpretation: "The whole human race, you see, is that man who was lying in the road, left there by bandits half dead, who was ignored by the passing priest and Levite, while the passing Samaritan stopped by him to take care of him and help him. . . . In this Samaritan the Lord Jesus Christ wanted us to understand himself." And again: "Robbers have left you half-dead on the road; but you've been found lying there by the passing and kindly Samaritan. Wine and oil have been poured into you, you have received the sacrament of the Only-begotten Son; you have been lifted onto his mule, you have believed that Christ became flesh; you have been brought to the inn, you are being cured in the Church."[a]

a. Irenaeus, *Against the Heresies* 3.17.3 (trans. Unger and Steenberg, 86); Origen, *Homilies on Luke* 34.3–9, trans. Joseph T. Lienhard, FC 94 (Washington, DC: Catholic University of America Press, 1996), 138–41; Augustine, *Sermons* 171.2 and 179A.7, in *Sermons*, trans. Edmund Hill, 11 vols., WSA III/5 (Hyde Park, NY: New City Press, 1990–97), 5:247–48, 312.

Samaritan has already and only been demonstrated by Jesus himself. On this basis, it is possible that Luke intends the reader to understand the Samaritan as a figure of Jesus. From here, it is just a small step to the common identification of the Samaritan with Christ that is found among the Church Fathers (see the sidebar, "Jesus the Good Samaritan").

The Samaritan's compassion is manifested in a series of actions by which he **cared** for the man. He uses the resources he has available (**oil and wine, his own animal**), including his own money (**two silver coins**—i.e., two days' wages). He gives of his own time (**the next day**). He gets other people to help (**the innkeeper**). He promises to follow up (**on my way back**).

Finishing the parable, Jesus invites the scholar to draw his own conclusion: **10:36** Who **was neighbor to the robbers' victim?** It is important to note the change of perspective. The scholar had asked about the neighbor as the *object* who is to receive his love. Jesus instead presents the neighbor as the *subject* who gives love. However, this neighbor is a Samaritan, with whom the scholar does not readily identify, even though the Samaritan has kept the commandment better than the priest and Levite.[43] Can the scholar at least acknowledge love received from a neighbor like the Samaritan whom he considers his enemy?

10:37   Still finding it difficult to say "the Samaritan," the scholar replies: **The one who treated him with mercy**. His answer is again correct. Literally, it is the one who "did" (*poieō*) mercy. And, as earlier, Jesus' words challenge the man not just to know the right answers, but also to *do* the right things, identifying even with the Samaritan: **Go and do** (*poieō*) **likewise**. If he does, then he too will become a neighbor who gives love, even to his enemies.

In summary, Jesus' teaching in the parable hearkens back to his earlier teaching: "Love your enemies" (Luke 6:27, 35) and "be merciful" (6:36). Readers are summoned to become neighbors even to their enemies, by "doing" mercy to them. In that way, they will do the commandment and live.

Reflection and Application (10:25-37)

Go and do likewise. The good Samaritan showed mercy by caring for the sick man. Catholic tradition has highlighted such corporal works of mercy, which also include feeding the hungry, sheltering the homeless, clothing the naked, welcoming the stranger, and visiting the imprisoned (see Isa 58:6-7; Matt 25:31-46). Also emphasized are the spiritual works of mercy, which include instructing others in the faith, practicing fraternal correction, giving advice or consolation to those who need it, forgiving and bearing with those who wrong us, and praying for the living and the dead (see Catechism 2447). What works of mercy can I carry out in order to love my neighbor?

Martha and Mary (10:38-42)

---

[38]**As they continued their journey he entered a village where a woman whose name was Martha welcomed him.** [39]**She had a sister named Mary [who] sat beside the Lord at his feet listening to him speak.** [40]**Martha, burdened with much serving, came to him and said, "Lord, do you not care that my sister has left me by myself to do the serving? Tell her to help**

---

43. Several Church Fathers indicate that the Samaritans considered themselves to be the guardians of the law, deriving their name from the Hebrew verb *shamar*, meaning "keep, guard." In 2 Chron 13:11, a Jewish king seemingly mocks this idea. See Knoppers, *Jews and Samaritans*, 16.

me." [41]The Lord said to her in reply, "Martha, Martha, you are anxious and worried about many things. [42]There is need of only one thing. Mary has chosen the better part and it will not be taken from her."

NT: John 11:1–2; 12:2–3
Lectionary: Sixteenth Sunday Ordinary Time (Year C); St. Martha; Consecration of Virgins and
   Religious Profession

Since the parable of the good Samaritan emphasizes love of neighbor, many   10:38
scholars suggest that this next passage instead highlights love of "the Lord,
your God" (10:27; see vv. 39–41, where the title "Lord" is again used for Jesus).
Moreover, like the earlier list of women who followed Jesus along with the Twelve
(8:1–3), this passage highlights women disciples, **Martha** and Mary, who happen to be siblings. In typical Lukan fashion, they complement James and John,
siblings as well, who appeared at the beginning of the **journey** (9:54) that now
continues. Martha **welcomed** Jesus, and so the passage further explains what
it means to welcome Jesus and his gospel message (10:8).

The **village** of Martha and Mary, unspecified by Luke, is Bethany, according
to John's Gospel (John 11:1). Bethany is near Jerusalem ("about two miles away,"
John 11:18), so Luke fittingly mentions it toward the end of the journey there
(Luke 19:29). However, the mention of Bethany here near the beginning of the
central section, when Jesus is presumably still some distance from Jerusalem,
would not fit the geographic framework. The "orderly sequence" of Luke's narrative can be logical rather than chronological (1:3).

Mary assumes the posture of a disciple, by sitting **beside the Lord at his**   10:39
feet (8:35; Acts 22:3).[44] Her focus is on **listening to him speak**—literally, "to
his word." She is doing exactly what the voice at the transfiguration said to do:
"Listen to him" (Luke 9:35). She realizes what a blessed opportunity it is to hear
what she hears (10:23–24).

Martha, on the other hand, is **burdened** or "distracted" (RSV) on account   10:40
of **much serving**. Certainly, Martha's efforts to serve her special guest are all
well and good (see 4:39; 8:3). Indeed, she is following Old Testament precedent:
the widow of Zarephath and the woman of Shunem gave such hospitality to the
prophets Elijah and Elisha (1 Kings 17:10–16; 2 Kings 4:8). However, there is
already a hint of her shortcoming in the description. Since there is so "much"
to do, she is distracted and too busy to pay attention to Jesus' words. Her concern also leads her to want to take her sister away from Jesus, whom she asks

---

44. Earlier, a woman stood at Jesus' *feet* and anointed them (7:36–50). As already noted, John's Gospel
identifies Mary the sister of Martha as someone who anointed Jesus' feet (John 11:2; 12:3).

to intervene: **Lord, do you not care that my sister has left me by myself to do the serving?** She follows up her question, which expects a yes answer, with a command: **tell her to help me.**

10:41–42   In response, Jesus corrects her as earlier he corrected James and John (Luke 9:55). Affectionately repeating her name (see 22:31)[45]—**Martha, Martha**—he points out what is wrong with her fretful activity: **you are anxious and worried.** In the parable of the sower, Jesus had warned that anxieties can, like thorns, choke a person's response to the word (8:14). He later cautions against being anxious (12:22, 25–26) and allowing oneself to be weighed down with the anxieties of life (21:34). Certainly, Martha's anxieties spring from her desire to serve Jesus, not from the pursuit of sinful pleasures also mentioned in these other verses. However, Jesus' teaching about not being anxious has general application.

Second, he explains why Mary's behavior is proper. Whereas Martha is concerned **about many things**, Jesus explains that **only one thing** is necessary: listening to him. In other words, the aspect that takes priority when Jesus is "welcomed" (10:38) is welcoming—in other words, listening to—his message of salvation, as Mary was doing. This is **the better part** ("the good portion," RSV) that **Mary**, like "good soil" (8:8, 15), **has chosen** (see 9:35).

Interestingly, Lydia in Acts makes the right combination, responding like both Mary and Martha. First, she "listened" to the gospel message preached by Paul and then offered hospitality to him and his companions (Acts 16:14–15).

Reflection and Application (10:38–42)

Active and contemplative. From early on in Christian history, Martha and Mary have been understood as signifying the active life and the contemplative life.[46] For contemporary Christians, it is helpful to emphasize the unity of these two dimensions of their lives: union with God through prayer overflows into all one's activities, so that they bear fruit (see John 15:5).

---

45. François Bovon, *Luke*, trans. Christine M. Thomas, Donald S. Deer, and James Crouch, 3 vols., Hermeneia (Minneapolis: Fortress, 2002–13), 1:253–54n57.

46. E.g., Origen, *Fragments on Luke* 171 (trans. Lienhard, 192).

Prayer and Almsgiving

Luke 11:1–54

The topic of Jesus' earlier conversation with the scholar of the law—loving God and neighbor (10:27)—is further explained in Luke 11. At the beginning of the chapter, Jesus teaches his disciples about prayer (11:1–13), including the Lord's Prayer, so that they can grow in love of God, sharing in Jesus' own intimate relationship with the Father (see 10:21–22). At the end of the chapter (11:37–54), Jesus strongly corrects the Pharisees and scholars of the law for their preoccupation with ritual washings (11:38), urging that instead they love their neighbor by giving alms (11:41). In the middle section, Jesus addresses the crowds (11:14, 27, 29), revealing to them more about who he is in response to some who accuse him of being guided by evil spirits (11:14–15, 17–26) and to others who are seeking a sign (11:16, 29–32). At the very center of the chapter, Jesus explains the key to loving God and neighbor: hearing the word of God and keeping it (11:27–28).

Jesus Teaches the Disciples to Pray (11:1–13)

¹He was praying in a certain place, and when he had finished, one of his disciples said to him, "Lord, teach us to pray just as John taught his disciples." ²He said to them, "When you pray, say:

> Father, hallowed be your name,
>   your kingdom come.
> ³Give us each day our daily bread

⁴and forgive us our sins
for we ourselves forgive everyone in debt to us,
and do not subject us to the final test."

⁵And he said to them, "Suppose one of you has a friend to whom he goes at midnight and says, 'Friend, lend me three loaves of bread, ⁶for a friend of mine has arrived at my house from a journey and I have nothing to offer him,' ⁷and he says in reply from within, 'Do not bother me; the door has already been locked and my children and I are already in bed. I cannot get up to give you anything.' ⁸I tell you, if he does not get up to give him the loaves because of their friendship, he will get up to give him whatever he needs because of his persistence.

⁹"And I tell you, ask and you will receive; seek and you will find; knock and the door will be opened to you. ¹⁰For everyone who asks, receives; and the one who seeks, finds; and to the one who knocks, the door will be opened. ¹¹What father among you would hand his son a snake when he asks for a fish? ¹²Or hand him a scorpion when he asks for an egg? ¹³If you then, who are wicked, know how to give good gifts to your children, how much more will the Father in heaven give the holy Spirit to those who ask him?"

OT: Exod 16:4–5; Isa 63:16; 64:7; Jer 3:19; Ezek 36:23

NT: Mark 14:36; Luke 10:21–22; 12:22–32; 22:42; 23:34, 46; Rom 8:15; Gal 4:6. // Matt 6:9–13; 7:7–11

Catechism: Jesus a model of prayer, 520, 2601; Lord's Prayer, 2759, 2773; Father, 2779; your kingdom come, 2632; daily bread, 2837; forgiveness, 1425, 2845; prayer of petition, 2613, 2761; prayer for the Holy Spirit, 728, 2671

Lectionary: Seventeenth Sunday Ordinary Time (Year C); Luke 11:5–13: Anointing of the Sick

11:1 The previous passage took place in "a certain village" (10:38 NRSV), and this one occurs in **a certain place**. Luke again does not specify the exact location. The focus is not on *where* it happened but on *what* Jesus was doing: **he was praying**. The disciples, who are by now accustomed to seeing Jesus praying, are inspired to enter more deeply into prayer themselves. So **one of his disciples** asks him, **Lord, teach us to pray**, as **John** did with **his disciples** (see 5:33). The rabbis of the time typically gave instruction on prayer to their disciples. In response to the request, Jesus teaches a new prayer, brief but profound, which changes the very way of praying.

Luke's version of the Lord's Prayer is shorter than the one in Matthew (Matt 6:9–13), containing five petitions instead of seven. Like the variations in the accounts of Jesus' institution of the Eucharist, the differences here may reflect

218

how the Lord's Prayer was used in prayer and worship in the early Church.[1] Matthew's version became the one commonly adopted for liturgical, devotional, and catechetical use.[2]

Earlier in his own prayer, Jesus addressed God as "Father" (Luke 10:21).   **11:2** He also explained that as the Son he could reveal the Father to whomever he wished (10:22). Thus he now reveals that **when you pray**, it is good to begin by addressing God as **Father**. Whereas the title "Father" for God is typically used in the Old Testament in relation to the people of Israel as a whole (Deut 32:6; Mal 2:10) or to Israel's king as a special case (2 Sam 7:14; Ps 89:27),[3] Jesus is distinctive in teaching that ordinary individuals can regularly address God as "Father." In this way, Jesus invites disciples to share in the deep intimacy of his own relationship with the Father, whom elsewhere he describes as merciful (Luke 6:36; 15:20), giving (11:13; 12:32), attentive to human needs (12:30), and forgiving (23:34). Jesus may have taught the prayer in Aramaic,[4] saying *Abba*, a word preserved in its original form elsewhere in the New Testament (Mark 14:36; Rom 8:15; Gal 4:6). To name God *Abba* or "Father" in prayer expresses a family bond, indicating that "we may be called the children of God" (1 John 3:1). It is with such "childlike" (Luke 10:21; see 18:17) trust and simplicity that one should daringly pray the petitions of the Lord's Prayer.

The first two petitions focus on things of God (**your**) and the last three on the needs of those praying ("us"). The passive form of the petition that God's **name** be **hallowed**—honored as holy—recognizes that God alone can make it happen: "I will sanctify my great name" (Ezek 36:23 NRSV). Empowered by God, human beings, such as Mary, can hold God's name in reverence: "Holy is his name" (Luke 1:49). The petition also asks for assistance so that one's life may not profane God's name (see Exod 20:7; Deut 5:11) but rather reflect his holiness: "Be holy, for I, the LORD your God, am holy" (Lev 19:2).

The second petition, **your kingdom come**, recalls the preaching of Jesus (Luke 4:43; 6:20; 8:1; 9:11) and of his disciples (9:2; 10:9) about the kingdom. Though the kingdom is already at hand with Jesus (11:20; 17:21), one must also fervently pray for its future coming in power (12:31; 23:42, 51). The petition implicitly asks that God's kingdom rather than Satan's kingdom rule in one's own life (see 11:18–20).

1. James D. G. Dunn, *Jesus Remembered* (Grand Rapids: Eerdmans, 2003), 227–28.
2. A form similar to Matthew's is found in *Didache* 8.2.
3. God is also addressed as "Father" in some later Old Testament texts (e.g., Wis 14:3; Sir 51:10) and as "my Father" at Qumran (4Q372 I, 16).
4. Or Hebrew. See James R. Edwards, *The Gospel according to Luke*, PNTC (Grand Rapids: Eerdmans, 2015), 331.

Daily Bread

LIVING TRADITION

The petition "Give us each day our daily bread" (Luke 11:3) was interpreted in various ways by the Church Fathers, thus shedding light on the meanings it can have for contemporary Christians. St. Cyprian (third century), following Tertullian, explains that the petition "may be understood both spiritually and literally." By the spiritual meaning, he refers to Christ as "the bread of life" (John 6:48) and to the practice of receiving "his Eucharist daily as the food of salvation."[a] St. Augustine gives the literal meaning and two spiritual meanings: "'Daily bread' represents all that is necessary to sustain us in this life. . . . It may also refer to the sacrament of the body of Christ, which we receive daily. . . . [We can also] interpret 'daily bread' in a spiritual sense, as meaning the divine precepts, which we should daily reflect on and put into practice."[b]

The word "daily" in Luke 11:3 (and in the parallel verse, Matt 6:11) translates *epiousios*, which does not elsewhere occur in any prior Greek literature. Origen and Jerome after him relate it to the word "essence" or "substance" (*ousia*) and interpret it as referring to the Eucharist. They both also relate *epiousios* to a similar word, *periousios*, meaning "special" (Exod 19:5 LXX). Moreover, they are both familiar with another interpretation referring to tomorrow's bread—that is, bread for the age to come in the heavenly banquet, of which the Eucharist is a foretaste.[c]

a. Cyprian, *On the Lord's Prayer* 18, trans. Alistair Stewart-Sykes (Crestwood, NY: St. Vladimir's Seminary Press, 2004), 78.
b. Augustine, *The Lord's Sermon on the Mount* 2.7.25–27, in *New Testament I and II*, trans. Michael G. Campbell, WSA I/15–1/16 (Hyde Park, NY: New City Press, 2014), 80–82.
c. Origen, *On Prayer* 27, trans. Alistair Stewart-Sykes (Crestwood, NY: St. Vladimir's Seminary Press, 2004), 175–86; Jerome, *Commentary on Matthew* 1.6.11, trans. Thomas P. Scheck, FC 117 (Washington, DC: Catholic University of America Press, 2008), 88–89.

11:3   The petition for **bread** (*artos*) functions at several levels. First, it is a prayer—made with confidence in God (see 12:22–24)—that life's basic needs may be met, that those "who are now hungry . . . will be satisfied" (6:21). Indeed, the disciples, sent out on mission with no "food" (*artos*, 9:3), trusted that God would supply what they needed. Jesus had also multiplied the "loaves" (*artos*), and all who ate were satisfied (9:16–17).

In the verses that follow (11:5, 11–12), "loaves of bread" (*artos*) and other items of food are used to illustrate Jesus' teaching on prayer. These examples point to gifts from God of a higher order than physical food—for example, the gift of "the holy Spirit" (v. 13). This context suggests that the request for bread is also open to spiritual interpretation. For example, recalling the first temptation, it is a reminder that "one does not live by bread alone" (4:4; see Matt 4:4) since one also needs the "word of God" (Luke 11:28). Again, the multiplication of the loaves not only signified the feeding of the hungry crowds but also recalled the manna in the wilderness and pointed ahead to the Eucharist (see comment on 9:12–16). So too, as the Church Fathers taught, the petition for bread is a prayer for the new manna of the Eucharist. In particular, the words **give us each day** and **daily** (an unusual word; see the sidebar, "Daily Bread," p. 220) allude to the manna, the day's amount of "bread" that was "given" by God "each day" (Exod 16:4–5, 15 LXX) during the Israelites' journey to the promised land. Jesus will institute the Eucharist as the bread for the disciples' journey to the kingdom, which is already present but still awaited in its fullness. The petition for bread thus fittingly follows the petition for the coming of the kingdom.

11:4   The petition **forgive us our sins** has a reason attached to it: **for we ourselves forgive everyone in debt to us**. Thus the prayer is also a constant reminder to forgive others, indeed "everyone" (a word not found in the parallel, Matt 6:12). Moreover, the verb "forgive" (*aphiēmi*) and the use of the word "debts" for sins (see Luke 7:41–48) recall Old Testament legislation regarding the jubilee (Lev 25:10) and "remission of debts" (Deut 15:1; noun *aphesis* in the LXX). In Nazareth, Jesus had announced his jubilee mission of proclaiming "liberty" (noun *aphesis*, Luke 4:18). He now includes the jubilee in his model prayer, indicating that it is a permanent aspect of his mission.[5]

The final petition in Luke's version is **do not subject us to the final test**. The NABRE translates the Greek word *peirasmos* as "final test," such that the petition asks that one be spared the great tribulation that was expected to accompany the coming of the messiah and the end of the age. The word may also refer to any "trial" (8:13) or "test" (22:40, 46) that is willed or permitted by God, such as when God tested the Israelites after the exodus (verb *peirazō*, Exod 16:4; 20:20 LXX). Here, the word is generally translated "temptation" (RSV). Indeed, the same word is used for the devil's temptation of Jesus (Luke 4:13).[6] The petition thus beseeches the Father for protection from the evil one (see Matt 6:13) and for strength to bear trials and resist temptations (see 1 Cor 10:13).

---

5. This idea and some others in this chapter are indebted to Tim Gray, private communication.

6. God "himself tempts no one" (James 1:13), but God may lead someone into temptation in the sense of allowing that person to be tempted by the devil (see Luke 4:1–2). See Joseph A. Fitzmyer, "And Lead Us Not into Temptation," *Biblica* 84 (2003): 262–65.

The Lord's "New Exodus" Prayer

What could Jesus have meant in teaching the Lord's Prayer to the disciples, and how might they as first-century Jews have understood it?[a] At his transfiguration, Jesus had spoken with Moses and Elijah about his death and resurrection as his "exodus" (Luke 9:31). This idea of the new exodus provides a key for understanding the phrases of the Lord's Prayer. When Christians pray it, they are in a sense asking that God's great act of salvation through Jesus' death and resurrection be accomplished in their lives, as the Israelites experienced God's salvation in the original exodus.

Addressing God as "Father" recalls those verses where God is described as father when referring to Israel's exodus: "Israel is my son, my firstborn. . . . Let my son go" (Exod 4:22–23); and "Out of Egypt I called my son" (Hosea 11:1). God's children yearn for freedom (see Rom 8:19–23)—freedom even from the slavery of sin and death. The first petition, "Hallowed be your name," echoes a text from Ezekiel, where the hope for Israel's restoration from exile is described using the exodus theme of entry into the land: "I will sanctify my great name. . . . I will take you from the nations . . . and bring you into your own land" (Ezek 36:23–24 NRSV). The petition "Your kingdom come" may draw on Micah 4:8, another text for the return of the exiles. In these petitions, Christians thus pray that after this exile on earth they may together reach the promised land of God's heavenly kingdom. The petition about "daily bread" recalls the manna given each day during the journey toward the earthly promised land (Exod 16), thus pointing to the Eucharist, which is similarly food for the journey to heaven. The petition about forgiving debts recalls the jubilee, which itself was based on the liberty won in the exodus (see Lev 25:54–55). The end of the prayer asks for God's deliverance—despite the times of testing (see Luke 22:40, 46) that recall the testings that occurred in the exodus (Deut 4:34; 7:19; 29:2)—so as safely to enter God's kingdom.

a. For the ideas in this sidebar, see Brant Pitre, *Jesus and the Last Supper* (Grand Rapids: Eerdmans, 2015), 161–93.

11:5–8   After the prayer itself, Jesus continues teaching about prayer, so that the disciples can learn not only what to say but also how to say it. The parable about the **friend** to whom a person **goes at midnight** instructs disciples to pray with persistence, expecting God to hear and answer their prayers. The request for **three loaves of bread** connects the parable to the Lord's Prayer with its petition for bread (Luke 11:3). The form of the reply—**do not bother me**—is a command prohibiting an action that is already ongoing. The person outside is being told to stop because he keeps bothering the friend, like the widow in

The Holy Spirit in Luke-Acts

BIBLICAL BACKGROUND

As the author of both his Gospel and the Acts of the Apostles, Luke highlights the Holy Spirit and his work more than any other evangelist. At the Gospel's beginning, the Spirit raises up a prophet, John the Baptist (Luke 1:15), and inspires prophetic words from Elizabeth (1:41–42), Zechariah (1:67), and Simeon (2:25–28). The Spirit also comes upon Mary (1:35) in a unique way so that she conceives Jesus. The beginning of Jesus' public ministry is also marked by the action of the Holy Spirit. At Jesus' baptism (3:22), his temptation (4:1–2), and in his preaching ministry (4:14, 18), Luke relates how Jesus is filled with the Spirit and acts in the power of the Spirit. Moreover, Jesus' prayer to the Father is a prayer in the Spirit (10:21). Since Jesus is also the one who baptizes with the Holy Spirit (3:16), the Spirit is active in the lives of his disciples (11:13; 12:12).

Indeed, the Gospel ends and Acts begins with references to the Spirit's coming in power to enable the disciples to witness to Jesus (Luke 24:48–49; Acts 1:8). At Pentecost, the Spirit dramatically empowers them to proclaim the gospel (Acts 2:1–4) and then continues to guide the expanding mission of the Church (Acts 8:15; 13:2), even in unexpected ways (Acts 10:44). The same Spirit also inspired the authors of Scripture (Acts 1:16; 4:25). The Spirit fills Peter and the other disciples so that they give courageous witness to Jesus in the face of persecution (Acts 4:8; 5:32) and even martyrdom (Acts 7:55). The apostles impart the Spirit to others through baptism and the laying on of hands (Acts 2:38; 8:17; 19:6). The Spirit also guides Church leaders in their deliberations (Acts 15:28) and makes them overseers over the flock (Acts 20:28). Moreover, the Spirit pours out his various gifts for the building up of the Church (Acts 11:28; 19:6). From the evangelist's teaching on the Spirit, Christians can thus learn the manifold ways that the Holy Spirit continues to work in their lives and in the life of the Church.

---

the parable who "keeps bothering" the judge (18:5). Jesus then explains—**I tell you**—that even if **friendship** does not motivate the person inside to **get up to give him the loaves,** he will do so on account of the **persistence** (*anaideia*) of the one asking. The meaning of *anaideia* is closer to "shamelessness"[7] or "shameless audacity" (NIV). The lesson is that the person in need can boldly keep asking God without embarrassment, confident that God will respond and provide help.

---

7. Klyne R. Snodgrass, *Stories with Intent: A Comprehensive Guide to the Parables of Jesus* (Grand Rapids: Eerdmans, 2008), 437–45.

11:9-10   Jesus repeats the phrase **I tell you**—often used to introduce the meaning of a parable[8]—in order to emphasize his point. Disciples, filled with confidence in God (see 1 John 5:14), can pray with daring, not hesitating to **ask**, **seek**, and **knock**. The threefold progression and the form of the verbs, indicating continuous action—asking, seeking, knocking—highlight perseverance in prayer. **Everyone** who prays in this way **receives**, **finds**, and has **the door** (Luke 11:7) **opened**.

11:11-13   What makes such bold and unrelenting prayer possible is an attitude of filial trust in the Father. Jesus illustrates the point with a comparison: a **father**, whose **son** needs food (see v. 3) and **asks for a fish** or **an egg**, will not give him something harmful. Both the parable (vv. 5–8) and the sayings (vv. 11–13) teach about prayer using a **how much more** argument that moves from lesser to greater. If someone will get up in the middle of the night to give a friend who is shamelessly bothering him whatever he needs, *how much more* will God answer prayer. If parents despite their faults give **good gifts** to their **children**, *how much more* **will the Father in heaven give** better gifts, even the "gift" of **the holy Spirit** (Acts 2:38), **to those who ask him**! Jesus himself prays in the Spirit to the Father (Luke 10:21), so his disciples who imitate him in prayer (11:1) can similarly share in the life of God.

Reflection and Application (11:1–13)

Praying the Lord's Prayer. Since Christians pray the Our Father frequently, there is a risk of reciting it routinely and without sufficient recollection. It is thus helpful every so often to ponder it slowly during an extended time of quiet prayer (e.g., thirty minutes). In this way, one can contemplate each of its phrases and petitions, applying them to one's life and accompanying them with one's own prayer. "We can be aware that we are with him, of what we are asking him, of his willingness to give to us, and how eagerly he remains with us."[9]

God's Kingdom Overcomes Satan's Kingdom (11:14–26)

---

[14]He was driving out a demon [that was] mute, and when the demon had gone out, the mute person spoke and the crowds were amazed. [15]Some of

---

8. Luke 15:7, 10; 16:9; 18:8, 14; 19:26.
9. Teresa of Ávila, *The Way of Perfection* 29.6, in *The Collected Works of Saint Teresa of Avila*, trans. Kieran Kavanaugh and Otilio Rodriguez, 3 vols. (Washington, DC: ICS Publications, 1976–85), 2:148.

them said, "By the power of Beelzebul, the prince of demons, he drives out demons." ¹⁶Others, to test him, asked him for a sign from heaven. ¹⁷But he knew their thoughts and said to them, "Every kingdom divided against itself will be laid waste and house will fall against house. ¹⁸And if Satan is divided against himself, how will his kingdom stand? For you say that it is by Beelzebul that I drive out demons. ¹⁹If I, then, drive out demons by Beelzebul, by whom do your own people drive them out? Therefore they will be your judges. ²⁰But if it is by the finger of God that [I] drive out demons, then the kingdom of God has come upon you. ²¹When a strong man fully armed guards his palace, his possessions are safe. ²²But when one stronger than he attacks and overcomes him, he takes away the armor on which he relied and distributes the spoils. ²³Whoever is not with me is against me, and whoever does not gather with me scatters.

²⁴"When an unclean spirit goes out of someone, it roams through arid regions searching for rest but, finding none, it says, 'I shall return to my home from which I came.' ²⁵But upon returning, it finds it swept clean and put in order. ²⁶Then it goes and brings back seven other spirits more wicked than itself who move in and dwell there, and the last condition of that person is worse than the first."

OT: Exod 8:15; Isa 49:24–25; 53:12
NT: Matt 9:32–34; 16:1; Mark 8:11; Luke 9:50. // Matt 12:22–30, 38, 43–45; Mark 3:22–27
Catechism: the finger of God, the Holy Spirit, 700; God's kingdom conquers Satan's, 385, 539, 550; Jesus' absolute claims, 590
Lectionary: Luke 11:14–23: Thursday Third Week of Lent

Jesus expels **a demon**, healing a **mute person**. The word Luke uses, *kōphos*, **11:14** can also refer to a deaf person (7:22) or to one who is both deaf and mute (like Zechariah, 1:22, 62; also Mark 7:32). This miracle is the first of only five in the central section (see Luke 13:10–17; 14:1–6; 17:11–19; 18:35–43), much fewer than the seventeen during the Galilean ministry (including three summary accounts of multiple healings). Many of those earlier miracles led people to wonder about Jesus' identity (e.g., 4:36; 7:16; 8:25). Here, the miracle is instead recounted with more attention to the ensuing dispute, thus highlighting the increasing rejection that Jesus faces as he journeys toward Jerusalem.[10] In response, **the crowds** are **amazed**—similar to earlier reactions to Jesus' miracles (4:36; 8:25; 9:43).

However, two related objections are raised. First, **some** say that by **Beelze- 11:15–16 bul, the prince of demons, he drives out demons**. Second, **to test him** (verb

---

10. Jean-Noël Aletti, *L'art de raconter Jésus Christ: L'écriture narrative de l'évangile de Luc* (Paris: Seuil, 1989), 116–17.

peirazō, as when the devil "tempted" Jesus, 4:2), **others** ask **for a sign from heaven**. Jesus will answer the objections one at a time (11:17–26 and 29–32). The name "Beelzebul" means something like "master of the exalted house" (see Matt 10:25), apparently deriving from the pagan god *Baal* ("master" or "lord") and the word *zebul* (an exalted dwelling; see 1 Kings 8:13 RSV; Isa 63:15). The name is mocked as "Baalzebub" ("lord of the flies") in the passage where Elijah called down fire from heaven (2 Kings 1:2–16; see Luke 9:54). Pagan gods were considered to be demons (Deut 32:17; Ps 96:5 LXX), so "Beelzebul" refers either to a chief demon or to Satan himself (see Luke 11:18).

11:17–19 To accuse Jesus of casting out demons by Satan's power shows the level of resistance against him; it also reveals the lack of "sound" judgment of his opponents (see v. 34). Their faulty reasoning is pointed out by Jesus with a saying about a **kingdom divided: if Satan is divided against himself, how will his kingdom stand?** Moreover, knowing that others are also casting out demons (9:49; see Acts 19:13), he asks a rhetorical question: **by whom do your own people drive them out?**

11:20 Rather, Jesus casts out evil spirits **by the finger of God**.[11] This phrase recalls the words of Pharaoh's magicians after the plague of gnats, shortly before the exodus. Up to this third plague, they had imitated by their sorcery the signs and wonders of Moses and Aaron. Unable to do so any longer, they recognize that the power at work is "the finger of God" (Exod 8:15).[12] Similarly, Jesus indicates that God's power is at work in his miracles before his own exodus takes place in Jerusalem (Luke 9:31). Hence, **the kingdom of God has come upon** them, and the kingdom of Satan is in retreat.

11:21–22 A short parable provides an explanation. Though Satan is like **a strong man**, Jesus is **one stronger** (see 4:2–13). Using the same word, John the Baptist had similarly described him as "one mightier," because he comes with the power of "the holy Spirit" (3:16). Jesus thus **overcomes** Satan and divides **the spoils**, in fulfillment of Isaiah (Isa 49:24–25; 53:12).

11:23 A choice is therefore set before his listeners. Jesus warns that a person cannot remain neutral but must either stand **with** or **against** him (see Luke 9:50). Jesus has come to re-**gather** the people, but the one who rejects him **scatters**.

11:24–26 Jesus gives a further warning with a saying about **an unclean spirit**. Though it was driven **out of someone**, it may eventually try to **return**, even bringing along **seven other spirits**, so that the person ends up in a **worse** condition. This story recalls the "unclean spirit"—or rather, the "Legion" of demons—who

---

11. The parallel verse says "by the Spirit of God" (Matt 12:28).
12. Exod 8:19 RSV.

pleaded with Jesus not to be sent into the watery abyss and instead enter the swine (8:29–33). The meaning is again that one cannot remain neutral, as a **home** cannot remain unoccupied for long. One should pray to "the Father" to "give the holy Spirit" (11:13) so that, "filled with the holy Spirit" like Jesus (4:1), one can resist the devil. If "the Spirit of God dwells in" a person (1 Cor 3:16), there will be no room for evil spirits to **dwell there**.

Hearing God's Word through Jesus' Preaching and Wisdom (11:27–36)

²⁷While he was speaking, a woman from the crowd called out and said to him, "Blessed is the womb that carried you and the breasts at which you nursed." ²⁸He replied, "Rather, blessed are those who hear the word of God and observe it."

²⁹While still more people gathered in the crowd, he said to them, "This generation is an evil generation; it seeks a sign, but no sign will be given it, except the sign of Jonah. ³⁰Just as Jonah became a sign to the Ninevites, so will the Son of Man be to this generation. ³¹At the judgment the queen of the south will rise with the men of this generation and she will condemn them, because she came from the ends of the earth to hear the wisdom of Solomon, and there is something greater than Solomon here. ³²At the judgment the men of Nineveh will arise with this generation and condemn it, because at the preaching of Jonah they repented, and there is something greater than Jonah here.

³³"No one who lights a lamp hides it away or places it [under a bushel basket], but on a lampstand so that those who enter might see the light. ³⁴The lamp of the body is your eye. When your eye is sound, then your whole body is filled with light, but when it is bad, then your body is in darkness. ³⁵Take care, then, that the light in you not become darkness. ³⁶If your whole body is full of light, and no part of it is in darkness, then it will be as full of light as a lamp illuminating you with its brightness."

OT: 1 Kings 10:1–10; Ps 119:105; Jon 3:1–10
NT: Matt 16:4; Mark 8:12; Luke 1:28; 6:47; 8:15–16, 21; 1 Cor 1:22. // Matt 5:15; 6:22–23; 12:39–42
Catechism: Jesus greater than Solomon and Jonah, 590
Lectionary: Luke 11:29–32: Wednesday First Week of Lent; Luke 11:27–28: Assumption (Vigil); Consecration of Virgins and Religious Profession

A common emphasis on the word of God links the three seemingly unrelated parts of this passage. True blessing comes from hearing and keeping God's word (vv. 27-28), communicated of old by Jonah's preaching and Solomon's wisdom and now by Jesus (vv. 29-32) and filling with light those who receive it (vv. 33-36).

11:27-28   After Jesus deals with the objection about Beelzebul but before he can reply to the other objection, about a sign (11:16), **a woman** interrupts him with a beatitude intended to praise him by honoring his mother: **Blessed is the womb that carried you and the breasts at which you nursed**. In a sense, she is fulfilling Mary's own prophecy that "all ages" will call her "blessed" (1:48). However, the fundamental reason that she is blessed, as Elizabeth had said in her beatitude, is Mary's *belief* in the Lord's message through the angel (1:45). Jesus replies to the woman with a beatitude that echoes Elizabeth's, specifying this more basic reason for blessedness: **Blessed are those who hear the word of God and observe it**. Indeed, Mary gave a model response to God's word (1:38), and thus she is the *blessed* Virgin Mary. She sets an example for other disciples to follow on the way to beatitude: hear the word and act on it (see 6:47; 8:21).

11:29-32   As **the crowd** continues to grow, Jesus addresses the objection about **a sign** (11:16). Seeking a sign is an indication that **this generation is an evil generation**. The phrase likens the Israelites of his day who reject him (see 17:25) to the evil generation that wandered in the wilderness and failed to enter the promised land (Num 32:13; Deut 1:35). Earlier, Jesus had criticized "this generation" of his contemporaries for failing to respond to him and John (Luke 7:31; see 9:41). Here Jesus speaks six times against **this generation** (11:29-32, 50-51). Because he is being rejected, Jesus frequently warns **this generation** about the coming **judgment** (see 10:13-14; 11:19), when others will join together to **condemn it** for failing to hear and repent.

Hence, the only **sign** that **will be given it** is **the sign of Jonah**. In the parallel passage in Matthew, the sign of the prophet Jonah is explained as a reference to Jesus' death and resurrection, since "Jonah was in the belly of the whale three days and three nights" (Matt 12:40) before being returned to land (Jon 2:11). Implicitly, this may be the meaning here also because the mention of **the Son of Man** who will become a sign recalls Jesus' passion prediction: "The Son of Man must . . . be killed and on the third day be raised" (Luke 9:22). However, in the immediate context about hearing "the word of God" (11:28), the reference is more to **the preaching of Jonah** than to his sojourn in the whale's belly. In response, **the Ninevites** surprisingly **repented** (Jon 3:1-10). Hence, the *preaching* of Jesus—and then about Jesus by his disciples—is the sign, which eventually will lead even the Gentiles to repent (Acts 11:18), as did the Gentile people of **Nineveh**.

There is a similar emphasis on a Gentile hearing the word of God in the reference to **the queen of the south** (i.e., of Sheba), who came **to hear the wisdom of Solomon** (see 1 Kings 10:1–10). Jesus is now the one whose wisdom (Luke 2:40, 52) people need to hear, as he is the personification of wisdom (see 7:35), a wisdom that goes beyond "the wise" of this world (10:21). Paul sums up the message nicely: "Jews demand signs and Greeks look for wisdom, but we proclaim Christ . . . the wisdom of God" (1 Cor 1:22–24).

With these comparisons to a prophet (**Jonah**) and a king (**Solomon**), readers are reminded that Jesus is both prophet and king (Luke 7:16; 19:38). Indeed, he is **greater than** these forerunners, and the "prophets and kings" who came before him would have wished to see and hear him (10:24).

The emphasis on hearing the word of God continues with Jesus' sayings about **11:33** a **lamp** and **light** (11:33–36). The connection between God's word and light, seen earlier in Jesus' teaching (8:15–16), is rooted in Scripture: "Your word is a lamp for my feet, / a light for my path" (Ps 119:105). Jesus, who is "light" (Luke 2:32), is the one who communicates the word of God that must be heard (see 5:1; 6:47; 10:39; 11:28).

The light image shifts to one's ability to see through one's **eye**, which is **the 11:34–36 lamp of the body**. When the **eye is sound** (*haplous*), there is no difficulty and a person becomes **full of light, but when it is bad** (*ponēros*), then that person remains **in darkness**. This observation, coming shortly after Jesus' comment about "this generation" being "evil" (*ponēros*, v. 29), suggests that his opponents are not making sound or sincere judgments about him (see 11:15), precisely because they have an "evil" eye, such that **the light** in them has **become darkness**.

The scriptural background is helpful for understanding the image's ethical meaning.[13] Having a good eye ("bountiful eye") is a biblical idiom for a person who is generous, one who shares "bread with the poor" (Prov 22:9 RSV).[14] On the other hand, one whose "eye" is "evil" (Deut 15:9 KJV) gives nothing to a neighbor in need (see Prov 28:22 KJV). Such an interpretation builds on Jesus' recent parable about the good Samaritan, who knew how to look upon his neighbor (Luke 10:33) with mercy. Moreover, in the next passage, Jesus will admonish the Pharisees to give alms (11:41), an activity associated with having a good eye (Tob 4:7, 16).

---

13. Dale C. Allison Jr., "The Eye Is the Lamp of the Body (Matthew 6:22–23 = Luke 11:34–36)," *NTS* 33 (1987): 76–77.

14. Indeed, "generous" is a possible meaning of the adjective *haplous* (Luke 11:34), translated by the NABRE as "sound." In Rom 12:8 and 2 Cor 9:13, the related noun *haplotēs* is translated "generosity."

Woes against the Pharisees and Law-Scholars (11:37–54)

[37]After he had spoken, a Pharisee invited him to dine at his home. He entered and reclined at table to eat. [38]The Pharisee was amazed to see that he did not observe the prescribed washing before the meal. [39]The Lord said to him, "Oh you Pharisees! Although you cleanse the outside of the cup and the dish, inside you are filled with plunder and evil. [40]You fools! Did not the maker of the outside also make the inside? [41]But as to what is within, give alms, and behold, everything will be clean for you. [42]Woe to you Pharisees! You pay tithes of mint and of rue and of every garden herb, but you pay no attention to judgment and to love for God. These you should have done, without overlooking the others. [43]Woe to you Pharisees! You love the seat of honor in synagogues and greetings in marketplaces. [44]Woe to you! You are like unseen graves over which people unknowingly walk."

[45]Then one of the scholars of the law said to him in reply, "Teacher, by saying this you are insulting us too." [46]And he said, "Woe also to you scholars of the law! You impose on people burdens hard to carry, but you yourselves do not lift one finger to touch them. [47]Woe to you! You build the memorials of the prophets whom your ancestors killed. [48]Consequently, you bear witness and give consent to the deeds of your ancestors, for they killed them and you do the building. [49]Therefore, the wisdom of God said, 'I will send to them prophets and apostles; some of them they will kill and persecute' [50]in order that this generation might be charged with the blood of all the prophets shed since the foundation of the world, [51]from the blood of Abel to the blood of Zechariah who died between the altar and the temple building. Yes, I tell you, this generation will be charged with their blood! [52]Woe to you, scholars of the law! You have taken away the key of knowledge. You yourselves did not enter and you stopped those trying to enter." [53]When he left, the scribes and Pharisees began to act with hostility toward him and to interrogate him about many things, [54]for they were plotting to catch him at something he might say.

OT: Gen 4:8–11; Lev 27:30; Num 19:16; Deut 14:22; 2 Chron 24:19–22; Jer 26:4–9
NT: Matt 15:1–2; Mark 7:1–5, 15; Luke 7:36; 12:33; 14:1; 20:46. // Matt 23:4–7, 13, 23–36
Catechism: Jesus and the Pharisees, 575, 579, 588; almsgiving, 2447

11:37　**A Pharisee** invites Jesus **to dine** with him, the second of three such occurrences in Luke (7:36; 14:1). The first time, Jesus taught a lesson to his host about forgiveness and love. Here Jesus similarly emphasizes important matters of the law, but his tone is more severe as he strongly reprimands the Pharisees and scholars of the law gathered **at table**.

The Pharisee is **amazed** that Jesus does not **observe the prescribed washing**   11:38
before the meal, a custom of ritual purity not required by the law of Moses but
added by later traditions (see Mark 7:3–5).[15] The Pharisee's consternation—
rather different from the marveling amazement of the crowds after Jesus' recent miracle (Luke 11:14)—suggests that his "eye" is not "sound" (11:34). His
reaction triggers Jesus' teaching, as did the reaction of Simon the Pharisee at
the first meal (7:36–40).

However, Jesus' teaching now takes the form of denunciation. He reproves   11:39–41
the Pharisees, calling them **fools**, a term often applied to the wicked (e.g.,
Ps 94:8). With their ritual observances, they are concerned with **the outside**.
However, they neglect **the inside**, where moral contamination originates. An
external washing is useless if **inside** they **are filled with plunder and evil**. In
order to cleanse **what is within**, Jesus instructs them to **give alms**, so that they
may store up treasure in heaven (Luke 12:33; see the sidebar, "Almsgiving and
Treasure in Heaven," p. 241). Scripture speaks of the blessings that come from
giving alms: "Almsgiving saves from death, and purges all sin" (Tob 12:9).[16] In
Acts, the almsgiving of the Gentile Cornelius is remembered before God (Acts
10:4, 31), eventually leading to his receiving the gift of the Holy Spirit (Acts
10:44–48) and the blessings of repentance and faith (Acts 11:18; 15:9).

Like an Old Testament prophet (e.g., Isa 5:8–24), Jesus now pronounces   11:42
a series of woes or warnings of impending judgment, three directed against
the **Pharisees** (Luke 11:42–44) and three against the scholars of the law (vv.
45–52). In the Sermon on the Plain, four woes contrasted with four beatitudes
(6:20–26). Here, the woes contrast with the beatitude pronounced on those
who hear and keep God's word (11:28). The first **woe** denounces the Pharisees
for focusing on slight matters such as paying **tithes** on each **herb**[17] but neglect-
ing weighty matters such as **judgment** or justice and **love for God** (see 10:27;
Deut 6:5). Isaiah similarly had pronounced a woe on those who deprive "the
needy of judgment" and make "widows their plunder" (Isa 10:1–2), and Micah
had likewise counseled people "to do justice and to love goodness" (Mic 6:8).

Micah also had counseled them "to walk humbly" with God (Mic 6:8), pre-   11:43
cisely what the **Pharisees** are not doing. In the second **woe**, Jesus thus warns
them about their taking pride in status by seeking **the seat of honor in synagogues** and delighting in public **greetings**.

---

15. *m. Yadayim* 1:1–2:4.
16. See also Prov 19:17; Sir 3:30; Dan 4:24 (4:27 RSV). Giving alms (*eleēmosynē*, also Luke 12:33) is
thus a key element in Jesus' ethic of mercy (*eleos*, 10:37).
17. The biblical laws on tithing (e.g., Deut 14:22) were specified in further detail by the rabbis (see,
e.g., *m. Maʿaserot*).

11:44   The third **woe** is full of irony. The Pharisees, so careful to avoid becoming ritually contaminated, are in reality the ones who contaminate others, like **graves** that render unclean those who touch them (see Num 19:16).

11:45–46   **One of the scholars of the law** (see Luke 10:25) takes umbrage at Jesus' words, leading to three more woes directed against them. The first **woe** chastises them for the heavy **burdens** they **impose on people**—for instance, through their detailed interpretations of the requirements of Torah. In Acts, Peter comments that the "yoke" of the Mosaic law is difficult to bear (Acts 15:10); consequently, the scholars should not make it even more difficult. Moreover, they **do not lift one finger** to help people fulfill the laws. Jesus' words thus serve as a reminder for those who teach in his name that they must also assist and accompany those whom they teach.

11:47–51   The second **woe** warns the scholars that they are following in the footsteps of their **ancestors** who **killed** the many **prophets** sent by God. **Abel** and **Zechariah** run the gamut of Old Testament examples, from the first murder in Genesis to a murder in 2 Chronicles, which eventually became the last book in the Jewish canon (Gen 4:8–11; 2 Chron 24:19–22). Though the scholars seem to honor these prophets by **building** their **memorials**, they in fact prefer to keep them dead and buried. Indeed, they will continue to **kill and persecute** those sent by **God**, including Jesus himself (see Acts 7:52), as well as **some** of the **prophets and apostles** in the early Church (see Luke 21:12; Acts 8:1; 12:2).

Not just the scholars but **this generation** receives this warning (see Luke 11:29–32). Jeremiah had prophesied to his generation the destruction of the temple and the city of Jerusalem (by the Babylonians in 586 BC) because the people had not listened to the prophets whom God kept sending (Jer 26:4–9). Similarly, Jesus with these words begins to warn that "this generation will not pass away" (Luke 21:32) until the temple and Jerusalem itself are destroyed (see 21:5–6, 20–24), which indeed occurred at the Romans' hands in AD 70.

11:52   The last **woe** is again ironic. The **scholars of the law**, who should not only hear and keep God's word (see 11:28) but also teach it to others, actually **have taken away the key to knowledge**—that is, about God's word and hence about the kingdom (see 8:10). In their teaching, they may have focused, like the Pharisees, on slight matters and neglected important matters (11:42). As a result, they **did not enter** the kingdom and have **stopped those trying to enter** (see 18:16–17, 24–25; Matt 23:13).

11:53–54   Jesus' strong words end Luke's account of the meal, as he then **left** the Pharisee's home. Rather than heed his warnings as a call to conversion, **the scribes** (i.e., scholars of the law) **and Pharisees** react with **hostility**. They will thus

interrogate him further, trying **to catch him** in his speech so as to accuse him (Luke 6:7). For his part, Jesus will continue teaching his followers and the crowds the nature of true discipleship.

Reflection and Application (11:52)

Teaching theology and the Church's mission. Jesus' last rebuke of the scholars of the law (11:52) is a reminder that theological teaching at every level must not hinder but rather serve the Church's mission of proclaiming the kingdom of God so as to lead people to salvation.

Genuine Disciples in a Growing Kingdom

Luke 12:1–13:21

In a long, interactive sermon (12:1–13:9), Jesus teaches about genuine discipleship in contrast to the hypocrisy of the Pharisees (12:1), whom he has just denounced. The Pharisees are not present, so Jesus' words are addressed alternately to his disciples and the crowds (12:1, 13, 22, 54) and include replies to three interruptions (12:13, 41; 13:1). He teaches his disciples to be fearless in the face of persecution (12:1–12). Moreover, they should not be worried about possessions but instead should seek God's kingdom and give alms (12:13–34). Jesus also teaches about discipleship and its opposite through parables: the rich fool (12:16–21) and the servants awaiting their master (12:35–48).

When speaking to the crowds, Jesus warns them to discern the signs of the time (12:56) and to repent (13:1–5) in view of the coming judgment (12:58–59). The parable of the barren fig tree (13:6–9) similarly warns of the impending judgment on Jerusalem and its leaders, a message often repeated throughout the central section (11:49–51; 13:34–35; 19:41–44). Jesus also refers to his upcoming suffering in Jerusalem (12:50).

Jesus' words are accompanied by deeds. Hence, after the sermon, he heals a crippled woman on the sabbath. His adversaries' negative reaction further illustrates the contrast between Jesus and the "hypocrites" (13:15). The healing is a sign of the kingdom, which he then explains in two kingdom parables. The parable about the mustard seed highlights the growth of the kingdom, evident by the growing crowds, and the one about the yeast or leaven contrasts the kingdom with the different kind of "leaven" of the Pharisees (12:1; 13:21).

Fearless in the Face of Persecution (12:1–12)

¹Meanwhile, so many people were crowding together that they were trampling one another underfoot. He began to speak, first to his disciples, "Beware of the leaven—that is, the hypocrisy—of the Pharisees.

²"There is nothing concealed that will not be revealed, nor secret that will not be known. ³Therefore whatever you have said in the darkness will be heard in the light, and what you have whispered behind closed doors will be proclaimed on the housetops. ⁴I tell you, my friends, do not be afraid of those who kill the body but after that can do no more. ⁵I shall show you whom to fear. Be afraid of the one who after killing has the power to cast into Gehenna; yes, I tell you, be afraid of that one. ⁶Are not five sparrows sold for two small coins? Yet not one of them has escaped the notice of God. ⁷Even the hairs of your head have all been counted. Do not be afraid. You are worth more than many sparrows. ⁸I tell you, everyone who acknowledges me before others the Son of Man will acknowledge before the angels of God. ⁹But whoever denies me before others will be denied before the angels of God.

¹⁰"Everyone who speaks a word against the Son of Man will be forgiven, but the one who blasphemes against the holy Spirit will not be forgiven. ¹¹When they take you before synagogues and before rulers and authorities, do not worry about how or what your defense will be or about what you are to say. ¹²For the holy Spirit will teach you at that moment what you should say."

NT: Matt 12:31–32; 16:6; Mark 3:29; 8:15; 13:11; Luke 8:17; 9:26; 21:14–15; 2 Tim 2:12. // Matt 10:19–20, 26–33

Catechism: secrets revealed at the judgment, 678; Gehenna, 1034; hierarchy of creatures, 342; angels serve at the judgment, 333; Holy Spirit, 1287, 1864

News about Jesus has spread widely (5:15; 7:17), so that more **people** are **crowd-**   12:1
ing together to hear him. He will soon address them (12:13–14), but **first**[1] he
speaks to **his disciples: Beware of the leaven—that is, the hypocrisy—of the
Pharisees**. These Pharisees were hypocrites because on the outside they acted
as if they were upright, but inside they were full of evil (see 11:39). They were
quick to point out what they perceived as the faults of others but did not see their
own (see 6:42). Jesus associates their hypocrisy with leaven, which the Israelites
were told to remove from their houses at the time of the exodus (Exod 12:15).
Moreover, "a little leaven leavens the whole lump" (1 Cor 5:6; Gal 5:9 RSV).
With this image, Jesus indicates that the Pharisees are a corrupting influence

---

1. This adverb could also be read as part of Jesus' statement: "First of all, beware . . ."

on the people.[2] They are thus poor leaders. Jesus instead will teach his followers how to be genuine disciples and good leaders, so that they become a *positive* influence or leaven, as coworkers for the kingdom (see Luke 13:21; Col 4:11).

12:2-3   With a series of contrasting statements, Jesus explains that no one will get away with hypocrisy. Such inconsistency between external appearance and **concealed** reality will eventually be **revealed** or exposed. Earlier, a similar set of contrasts regarding what is **secret** coming to **light** was applied in a positive sense to the spread of God's word from the believer's heart to others (Luke 8:17). Similarly, Jesus' words here can also be understood as referring to the disciples' witness to Jesus and the gospel,[3] as it would be another form of hypocrisy to believe in Jesus in one's heart but deny him in public (see 12:8–9).

12:4-5   What might lead disciples to deny Jesus is fear of being persecuted (see 11:49). However, Jesus tells them, his **friends** (see John 15:15), that they should **not be afraid of those who** can only **kill the body**. Rather, the one to **be afraid of** is God, who **has the power to cast into Gehenna**. The word derives from the "Valley of Hinnom" (Hebrew *ge-hinnom*, Josh 15:8), located south of Jerusalem. Idolatrous sacrifices of children by fire were carried out there under the evil kings Ahaz and Manasseh (2 Chron 28:3; 33:6) before Josiah's reform (2 Kings 23:10). Jeremiah prophesied that because of God's judgment the valley's future would also be marked by death and defilement (Jer 7:31–33; 19:2–13). The valley thus became an image for the place of final punishment of the wicked, described as a place of unquenchable fire (see Isa 66:24).[4] This is the sense of "Gehenna" in the New Testament (Matt 5:22; 23:33; Mark 9:43; James 3:6), and hence it is translated "hell" in many English versions.

With these words, Jesus is putting the life of the body in relative perspective, since the inheritance of eternal life must be the ultimate concern of disciples (Luke 10:25; 18:18, 30). Hence, "the beginning of wisdom is fear of the LORD" (Prov 9:10). Such reverential fear guides believers to do what is right in obedience to God, without caving in. In Acts, Peter and the apostles, despite having been thrown in jail for the gospel, show that they have learned this lesson about **whom to fear**: "We must obey God rather than men" (Acts 5:29; see 4:19).

12:6-7   Fearing the Lord also means trusting in his providential care (Luke 12:22–32), so there is no reason to **be afraid** of persecutors. Jesus reasons from the lesser to the greater. If God cares even for **sparrows**—so cheap that **five** of them are **sold for two small coins** totaling about one hour's wage—how much more

2. In Matthew, the Pharisees' corrupting influence is specified as their "teaching" (Matt 16:12).

3. François Bovon, *Luke*, trans. Christine M. Thomas, Donald S. Deer, and James Crouch, 3 vols., Hermeneia (Minneapolis: Fortress, 2002–13), 2:178.

4. See *1 Enoch* 27:1–3; 54:1–6.

must he care for people, who **are worth more than many sparrows**? If God knows even the number of **hairs** on someone's **head**, will he not also know and be attentive to that individual's more serious concerns?

Rather than fear, a disciple should focus on being a witness **who acknowl-** **12:8–9** **edges** or confesses Jesus (Rom 10:9–10) **before** men and women in this life. In this way, Jesus promises that, as the glorified **Son of Man**, he **will acknowledge** such disciples **before the angels of God** in the judgment in the next life. Along with the promise comes a warning that **whoever denies** Jesus now **will be denied before the angels of God** later (Luke 9:26; 2 Tim 2:12).

Nevertheless, the one **who speaks a word against the Son of Man** can still **be** **12:10** **forgiven**, such as Peter, who indeed denied Jesus (Luke 22:57–60). Even those responsible for putting Jesus to death can be forgiven if they repent (23:34; Acts 3:17–19). However, **the one who blasphemes against the holy Spirit will not be forgiven**. This difficult saying seems to refer to the obstinate refusal to repent, which involves lying to, testing, or opposing the Holy Spirit (Acts 5:3, 9; 7:51). The Holy Spirit's grace brings about the forgiveness of sins, so there can be no forgiveness when the offer is deliberately rejected by a refusal to repent (see Catechism 1864). Jesus thus gives a warning to those who resist the Holy Spirit, thinking that they "have no need of repentance" (Luke 15:7).

Still advising his disciples about coming persecutions (see v. 4), Jesus tells **12:11–12** them: **do not worry** about **your defense**. When they are put on trial, **the holy Spirit will teach** them the things they **should say** (see 21:14–15). The Spirit is indeed "the Advocate" who teaches everything needed in such situations (John 14:26). Disciples should thus keep asking "the Father in heaven" to "give the holy Spirit" (Luke 11:13)!

Reflection and Application (12:1)

Avoiding hypocrisy. Blessed John Henry Newman powerfully preaches against hypocrisy in one of his sermons:

> How seasonable is our Lord's warning to us . . . to beware of the leaven of the Pharisees, which is hypocrisy: professing without practicing. He warns us against it as *leaven*, as a subtle insinuating evil which will silently spread itself throughout the whole character. . . . He warns us that the pretense of religion never deceives beyond a little time. . . . Let us ever remember that all who follow God with but a half heart, strengthen the hands of his enemies, . . . perplex inquirers after truth, and bring reproach upon their Savior's name. . . . Woe unto the deceiver and self-deceived! . . . God give us grace to flee from this woe while we have time!

Let us examine ourselves, to see if there be any wicked way in us. . . . And let us pray God to enlighten us, and to guide us, and to give us the will to please him, and the power.[5]

Parable of the Rich Fool and Treasure in Heaven (12:13–34)

[13]Someone in the crowd said to him, "Teacher, tell my brother to share the inheritance wit me." [14]He replied to him, "Friend, who appointed me as your judge and arbitrator?" [15]Then he said to the crowd, "Take care to guard against all greed, for though one may be rich, one's life does not consist of possessions."

[16]Then he told them a parable. "There was a rich man whose land produced a bountiful harvest. [17]He asked himself, 'What shall I do, for I do not have space to store my harvest?' [18]And he said, 'This is what I shall do: I shall tear down my barns and build larger ones. There I shall store all my grain and other goods [19]and I shall say to myself, "Now as for you, you have so many good things stored up for many years, rest, eat, drink, be merry!"' [20]But God said to him, 'You fool, this night your life will be demanded of you; and the things you have prepared, to whom will they belong?' [21]Thus will it be for the one who stores up treasure for himself but is not rich in what matters to God."

[22]He said to [his] disciples, "Therefore I tell you, do not worry about your life and what you will eat, or about your body and what you will wear. [23]For life is more than food and the body more than clothing. [24]Notice the ravens: they do not sow or reap; they have neither storehouse nor barn, yet God feeds them. How much more important are you than birds! [25]Can any of you by worrying add a moment to your lifespan? [26]If even the smallest things are beyond your control, why are you anxious about the rest? [27]Notice how the flowers grow. They do not toil or spin. But I tell you, not even Solomon in all his splendor was dressed like one of them. [28]If God so clothes the grass in the field that grows today and is thrown into the oven tomorrow, will he not much more provide for you, O you of little faith? [29]As for you, do not seek what you are to eat and what you are to drink, and do not worry anymore. [30]All the nations of the world seek for these things, and your Father knows that you need them. [31]Instead, seek his kingdom, and these other things will be given you besides. [32]Do not be afraid any longer, little flock, for your Father is pleased to give you the kingdom. [33]Sell your belongings and give alms. Provide money bags for

5. John Henry Newman, "Profession without Practice," in *Parochial and Plain Sermons* (repr., San Francisco: Ignatius, 1997), 89–91.

**yourselves that do not wear out, an inexhaustible treasure in heaven that
no thief can reach nor moth destroy. [34]For where your treasure is, there
also will your heart be.**

OT: Tob 4:7–11; Prov 10:2; Sir 11:18–19; 29:12
NT: Luke 9:25; 11:41; 18:22; 1 Tim 6:18–19. // Matt 6:19–21, 25–33
Catechism: the focus of Jesus' mission, 549; avoiding greed in the heart, 2534, 2536; trust in divine providence, 305; little flock, 543, 764; almsgiving, 2447; the Church's treasury, 1475–77
Lectionary: Luke 12:13–21: Eighteenth Sunday Ordinary Time (Year C); Luke 12:32–48: Nineteenth Sunday Ordinary Time (Year C)

An interruption from **someone in the crowd** leads to a change of subject. From   **12:13–15**
teaching the disciples not to "worry" or "be afraid" about facing persecution,
Jesus now instructs the crowd and his disciples not to "worry" or "be afraid"
about lacking material necessities (12:4, 7, 11, 22, 29, 32).

In response to the man's demand that Jesus settle an inheritance dispute, Jesus
declines with a question that hints at his identity: **who appointed me as your
judge and arbitrator?** The question echoes the one put to Moses: "Who has
appointed you ruler and judge over us?" (Exod 2:14), which Luke includes twice
in Stephen's speech in Acts in showing that, although some Israelites rejected
Moses, God appointed him as their redeemer (Acts 7:27, 35). Similarly, Jesus will
be rejected but will bring about God's redemption (Luke 21:28; Acts 3:13–14).

Rather than resolve the dispute, Jesus uses the occasion to instruct **the crowd**
to be on **guard against all greed**. As he just did with regard to bodily life (see
Luke 12:4–5), so now he puts **possessions** in relative perspective by speaking
about treasure in heaven (vv. 21, 33–34).[6]

He makes his point with the **parable** of the **rich** fool (vv. 16–21), unique to   **12:16–19**
Luke. The man's obsession with his material **goods** leads to self-absorption. He
is only concerned about "me": **my harvest, my barns, my grain.** The problem is
not what he thinks it is—where to **store** his **bountiful harvest**—but rather his
selfish greed. In contrast, Joseph in Genesis also "collected grain" abundantly
(Gen 41:49), but the purpose was to feed others in time of famine. Here, the
man's focus on **himself** even extends into the future: **I shall say to myself.**
The Greek word for "self" (in "myself") is *psychē*, which refers to a person's
"life" (Luke 6:9). The man thinks he is in control of his life.

He also congratulates himself on having **so many good things stored up.** He
can therefore **rest, eat, drink,** and **be merry.** It seems that he has misinterpreted
the similar words of the teacher in Ecclesiastes, who advised finding joy despite
life's toil: "There is nothing better for a person under the sun than to eat and

6. This idea and some others in this chapter are indebted to Tim Gray, private communication.

drink and be glad" (Eccles 8:15 NIV). Forgetting also the end of Ecclesiastes (see Eccles 12:5–7), the rich man thinks that his possessions give him security now and **for many years** to come.

12:20   However, **God** calls him a **fool**, a term Jesus earlier applied to the Pharisees (Luke 11:40). "The fool says in his heart, / 'There is no God'" (Ps 14:1). Effectively, the rich man behaved as if there is no God, since he put his trust in his possessions rather than in God. He is an atheist in practice. However, his plans come to naught, because that very **night** his **life** (*psychē*) is **demanded of** him. The Greek word rendered "demanded" is used to call in a debt (Luke 6:30; Deut 15:2–3 LXX). The "life" that the man considered to be his own was really on loan from God. Though he wished "to save his life," he ended up losing it (Luke 9:24).

12:21   The lesson of the parable is thus similar to what Jesus said earlier about persecution (12:4–5): keep God in the picture. One should view earthly things, whether negative or positive, from the perspective of eternity (*sub specie aeternitatis*, as the Latin phrase goes). This is precisely what the man did not do. He was too busy thinking about himself to think of God and to thank God for blessing him with a rich harvest. Thus he was also too busy hoarding his wealth rather than sharing it with the poor (see 18:22–23). He stored up **treasure for himself** rather than "treasure in heaven" (12:33; 18:22), and so was **not rich** toward **God**.

12:22–30   Addressing now the **disciples**, Jesus returns to the subject of God's providential care (see 12:6–7), but considered now with regard to material goods rather than persecution. This is really the flip side of the same coin as the parable: the rich man had an abundance of goods and so could "eat" and "drink" (v. 19), and Jesus now speaks to those who lack material goods and so **worry** about what to **eat** and **drink** and **wear**. In both cases, it is a matter of entrusting one's **life** (*psychē*) to God. Once again Jesus reasons from the lesser to the greater: if **God feeds** the **birds** and **clothes the grass** and **flowers** with **splendor** beyond that of **Solomon, will he not much more provide** for human beings, who are **much more important**? Therefore, disciples are called to put **worrying** aside and not be **anxious**, a message repeated four times (vv. 22, 25, 26, 29). Such worrying is a sign of **little faith**, with one's behavior differing little from that of the unbelieving **nations**, or Gentiles, who **seek** after **these things**. One can thus fall into the same trap as the rich man: looking to possessions to provide security. God the **Father knows** what people **need**, so disciples should trustingly pray to the "Father" for their "daily bread," as Jesus taught them (11:2–3).

12:31–32   Rather than worry, disciples should **seek** God's **kingdom**. Those who strive to live "for the sake of the kingdom of God" will "receive [back] an

Almsgiving and Treasure in Heaven

BIBLICAL BACKGROUND

"Treasures gained by wickedness do not profit, / but righteousness delivers from death" (Prov 10:2 NRSV). The parallelism between the two halves of this proverb suggests that the reference to "righteousness" refers to treasures of righteous deeds like almsgiving.[a] This is how later Old Testament books understood the proverb. For example, Sirach says: "Store up almsgiving in your treasury, / and it will save you from every evil" (Sir 29:12). And Tobit says: "Give alms from your possessions. . . . Give in proportion to what you own. If you have great wealth, give alms out of your abundance; if you have but little, do not be afraid to give alms even of that little. You will be storing up a goodly treasure for yourself against the day of adversity. For almsgiving delivers from death" (Tob 4:7–10).

Jesus' teaching in Luke builds on these Old Testament texts. He refers to the cleansing power of almsgiving (Luke 11:41) and twice connects giving alms to the poor with storing up lasting "treasure in heaven" (12:33; 18:22). Such teaching is often misunderstood, as if self-interested people are presuming to tell God to save them for their good works. Rather, "the reason that scripture attaches a reward to charity is not simply to appeal to self-interest (though an element of that remains) but to make a statement about the nature of the world."[b] To behave in this way is thus to act with *faith* (the opposite is "little faith," 12:28). "Charity, in short, is not just a good deed *but a declaration of belief about the world and the God who created it.*"[c] "The economy of the Kingdom of Heaven, Jesus teaches, reflects the type of world God has created. Showing mercy to the poor taps into the larger font of mercy that governs God's providential hand. It is for this reason and this reason alone that funding such a treasury leads to unimagined compensation."[d]

a. Gary A. Anderson, *Charity: The Place of the Poor in the Biblical Tradition* (New Haven: Yale University Press, 2013), 54–55.
b. Anderson, *Charity*, 108.
c. Anderson, *Charity*, 4 (emphasis in the original).
d. Anderson, *Charity*, 159.

overabundant return in this present age" (18:29–30), as **these other things will be given** them. Moreover, the **Father is pleased to give** such as these **the kingdom**, already now in this life and in its fullness in "eternal life in the age to come" (18:30). By focusing on this "kingdom" perspective, disciples can learn **not** to **be afraid**, even if they remain **little** in the eyes of the world. Jesus here refers to the disciples as a **flock** (see 15:4–7), using the imagery of sheep and shepherd so beloved elsewhere in Scripture (Ps 23; John 10:1–18).

This kingdom perspective answers the possible objection to Jesus' teaching—namely, that God has seemingly *not* provided food for all those who have died and continue to die of famine. As the parable of the poor Lazarus also shows (Luke 16:20–22), not every situation of need is rectified in this life, yet God's providential care nonetheless extends into the next life. Of course, that does not remove the responsibility of the rich man in that parable, or of the rich man in the parable just considered, or of people today who possess more than they need.

12:33–34   Hence, Jesus continues with the exhortation: **sell your belongings and give alms** (see 11:41; 18:22). Whereas those who worry reveal their lack of faith (12:28–29), those instead who are generous in giving alms step out in faith. Almsgiving thus serves "as a *diagnostic* of faith."[7] Paradoxically, by giving alms one also stores up **treasure in heaven**, in contrast to the rich fool who stored up "treasure for himself" (v. 21). Earthly treasures can be stolen by a **thief** or destroyed by a **moth**, but these heavenly treasures are secure.

Jesus now sums up his teaching about trusting in God's providence rather than in possessions: **Where your treasure is**—either on earth or in heaven—**there also will your heart be**. The "heart" represents the center of a person's inner life. Whereas the Pharisees concentrate on external appearance but are not clean on the inside (11:39; 16:15), Jesus is interested in the attitude of the heart (see 6:45; 8:15).

Reflection and Application (12:22–34)

Fear of the Lord. Scripture frequently reminds us that "the fear of the LORD is the beginning of wisdom."[8] Such fear is also numbered among the gifts of the Holy Spirit (Isa 11:2). To those who have this reverential fear (see Luke 12:5), Jesus says, "Do not be afraid" (12:32). Commenting on this verse, Blaise Pascal writes: "Fear not, provided you fear; but if you fear not, then fear."[9]

Treasure in heaven. The almsgiving and other charitable deeds that we carry out by God's grace have a durable quality since they are "remembered before God" (Acts 10:31). They make up a treasure in heaven (Luke 12:33; 18:22) that can later benefit us and others. This biblical concept of charitable deeds as a "storable commodity" provides the foundation for the Church's teaching on the "treasury of merits"[10] (see Catechism 1475–77).

7. Anderson, *Charity*, 65.
8. Ps 111:10; see Job 28:28; Prov 1:7; 9:10; 15:33; Sir 1:14–27.
9. Blaise Pascal, *Pensées*, 775, trans. William F. Trotter (New York: E. P. Dutton, 1958; repr., Mineola, NY: Dover, 2003), 230.
10. Anderson, *Charity*, 33, 113.

Vigilant Servants Awaiting Their Master's Coming (12:35–48)

---

[35]"Gird your loins and light your lamps [36]and be like servants who await their master's return from a wedding, ready to open immediately when he comes and knocks. [37]Blessed are those servants whom the master finds vigilant on his arrival. Amen, I say to you, he will gird himself, have them recline at table, and proceed to wait on them. [38]And should he come in the second or third watch and find them prepared in this way, blessed are those servants. [39]Be sure of this: if the master of the house had known the hour when the thief was coming, he would not have let his house be broken into. [40]You also must be prepared, for at an hour you do not expect, the Son of Man will come."

[41]Then Peter said, "Lord, is this parable meant for us or for everyone?" [42]And the Lord replied, "Who, then, is the faithful and prudent steward whom the master will put in charge of his servants to distribute [the] food allowance at the proper time? [43]Blessed is that servant whom his master on arrival finds doing so. [44]Truly, I say to you, he will put him in charge of all his property. [45]But if that servant says to himself, 'My master is delayed in coming,' and begins to beat the menservants and the maidservants, to eat and drink and get drunk, [46]then that servant's master will come on an unexpected day and at an unknown hour and will punish him severely and assign him a place with the unfaithful. [47]That servant who knew his master's will but did not make preparations nor act in accord with his will shall be beaten severely; [48]and the servant who was ignorant of his master's will but acted in a way deserving of a severe beating shall be beaten only lightly. Much will be required of the person entrusted with much, and still more will be demanded of the person entrusted with more."

OT: Exod 12:11; Hab 2:3
NT: Mark 13:33–37; Luke 22:27; John 13:4–5. // Matt 24:43–51
Catechism: vigilance, 2849
Lectionary: Luke 12:32–48: Nineteenth Sunday Ordinary Time (Year C); Luke 12:35–40: Masses for the Dead; Luke 12:35–44: Holy Orders; Blessing of Abbots and Abbesses; Anointing of the Sick

The topic changes as Jesus now instructs his disciples to be alert for his coming. **12:35–38**
He makes his point with short parables about **servants** awaiting the **arrival**
of **the master** (vv. 35–38), a household owner not knowing when the thief is
coming (vv. 39–40), and—after Peter's interruption (v. 41)—a steward in charge
of his absent master's servants (vv. 42–48).

The phrase **gird your loins** expresses the stance of readiness disciples should
have. It means to gather up one's ankle-length robe and tuck it in at the waist

with a belt, so as to be dressed for service (17:8) or travel (1 Kings 18:46). The wording here more specifically alludes to the command given to Israel regarding the Passover meal before the exodus: "This is how you are to eat it: with your loins girt" (Exod 12:11). Jesus' accompanying command to **light your lamps** (see Luke 8:16; 11:33–36) also fits this connection, since the Passover meal and ensuing flight in the exodus took place at night.[11] That night "was a night of vigil for the LORD, when he brought them out of the land of Egypt; so on this night all Israelites must keep a vigil for the LORD throughout their generations" (Exod 12:42). So too Jesus' disciples must now be **vigilant**, even **in the second or third watch**—in other words, the middle or latter part of the night. The Passover imagery used to describe waiting for the **master's return** is consistent with Jewish expectation that the messiah would come during the meal on Passover night.[12]

Thus, not surprisingly, when the master comes there is a meal, and the watchful servants **recline at table**. This refers to the messianic banquet, when people "will recline at table in the kingdom of God" (Luke 13:29). The context of a **wedding** may also suggest the messianic banquet (see comment on 5:33–35). What is surprising, however, is the role reversal, as the master comes not to be served[13] but to serve (see Matt 20:28; Mark 10:45)—that is, **to wait on** (*diakoneō*)—these doubly **blessed** servants. At the Last Supper, these words will have an initial fulfillment as Jesus sits "to eat this Passover" meal with his apostles (Luke 22:15), telling them: "I am among you as the one who serves" (*diakoneō*, 22:27). The Eucharist, which Jesus establishes at that meal after his *coming* to Jerusalem, thus becomes the foretaste and anticipation of the messianic banquet in the kingdom (22:30) at his *second coming*.

12:39–40   **The Son of Man will come**, however, at an unknown **hour** (Acts 1:7), so disciples **must be prepared**. The mention here of the "Son of Man" as an explanation of the preceding sayings identifies Jesus with the "master" (*kyrios*) whose arrival the servants are awaiting (Luke 12:36–38). In another role reversal, the passage also describes the Son of Man as **the thief** (see Rev 3:3; 16:15), **the hour** of whose coming is not **known** by "the owner of the house" (NRSV, NIV).[14]

---

11. Bovon, *Luke*, 2:231: "The allusion to the Passover is undeniable." It is thus helpful to recall Jesus' warning to guard against the Pharisees' "leaven" (12:1), like the command to Israel to remove "leaven" for the Passover (Exod 12:15).

12. Dale C. Allison Jr., *The Intertextual Jesus: Scripture in Q* (Harrisburg, PA: Trinity Press International, 2000), 59–62.

13. In Luke 17:7–8, a master instead comes to be served, but there Jesus is teaching his apostles (17:5) a lesson on servant leadership.

14. Translating "owner" distinguishes this **master of the house** (*oikodespotēs*) from the "master" (*kyrios*) in verses 36–38, who represents Jesus.

Peter interrupts Jesus with a question: **is this parable meant for us** (i.e., the   12:41
Twelve) **or for everyone?** He addresses Jesus as **Lord** (*kyrios*), and "the Lord"
(*kyrios*) replies in the following verse (Luke 12:42). In context, this title again
identifies Jesus with the returning "master" (*kyrios*) in the preceding parable
(vv. 36–38) as well as the one following (vv. 42–48).[15]

The Lord answers with a question of his own: **Who, then, is the faithful**   12:42–44
[*pistos*] **and prudent steward whom the master will put in charge?** This is an
indirect way of saying that he is especially addressing Peter and the Twelve,
whom he has chosen for leadership positions in the restored Israel (6:13;
22:29–30). They and those who come after them must serve as "trustworthy"
(*pistos*) stewards (1 Cor 4:1–2). Like the vigilant servants (Luke 12:37–38),
such a responsible **servant** leader is **blessed**, and **his master on arrival** puts
him in charge of all his property. In the Old Testament, Joseph is an example
of such a wise servant who was put "in charge" (Gen 39:4–5; 41:33, 41; Acts
7:10). Joseph stored up grain beyond measure and distributed rations in time
of famine (Gen 41:49, 56). Similarly, the wise steward's task is **to distribute**
[the] food allowance (literally, "measure of grain") **at the proper time**, unlike
the rich fool who kept the grain for himself (Luke 12:18). The Twelve literally carry out this task in the early Church and then appoint others to do so
(Acts 6:1–6). Spiritually, this task of Church leaders refers to nourishing the
faithful in a fitting way with the word (see 1 Cor 3:2; Heb 5:12)[16] and with the
Eucharist.[17]

The opposite of the "faithful" (*pistos*, Luke 12:42) steward is the **servant**   12:45–46
who **begins to beat** the other servants, **to eat and drink** like the rich fool
(12:19), and even **get drunk**. The **master** who arrives unexpectedly **will pun-**
ish him severely—literally, "cut him in two" (NET; see Exod 29:17)—and
will then put him **with the unfaithful** (*apistos*). This two-step punishment
ultimately refers to the judgment of the wicked at Jesus' second **coming**, which
seems **delayed** but **will come** (see Hab 2:3; Heb 10:37). However, it also can
refer to the judgment at the end of a person's life (as with the rich fool, Luke
12:20), involving the death of the body and the casting of the soul into Gehenna (12:5). In the context of Jesus' coming to Jerusalem with his frequent
words of judgment (11:50–51; 13:35; 19:43–44), the warning of punishment
here applies more directly to the failed leadership in Israel, who will beat

---

15. See C. Kavin Rowe, *Early Narrative Christology: The Lord in the Gospel of Luke* (Berlin: de Gruyter,
2006; Grand Rapids: Baker Academic, 2009), 151–57.

16. E.g., Gregory the Great, *Pastoral Rule* 3.39.

17. *The Roman Missal* (Totowa, NJ: Catholic Book Publishing, 2011), Communion Antiphon (option) for the Common of Pastors (For One Pastor).

the apostles (11:49; Acts 5:40; 23:2) before Jerusalem itself is destroyed by the Romans. These words also serve as a warning to Church leaders in every generation, who must not abuse the flock (Luke 12:32; see 1 Pet 5:2) in their charge.

12:47–48 **The servant** who is derelict in responsibility is punished in proportion to culpability (see Num 15:27–30). The one who knowingly fails to do the **master's will** is **beaten severely**, while the **ignorant** one who is negligent is **beaten only lightly**. Hence, to whom **more** is **entrusted, more** is **demanded**.

Those in positions of leadership have therefore even more reason to fear God (Luke 12:5)! As St. Augustine says: "I'm terrified by what I am for you, [but] I am given comfort by what I am with you. For you I am a bishop, with you . . . I am a Christian. The first is the name of an office undertaken, the second a name of grace; that one means danger, this one salvation."[18] And commenting on this passage in Luke, St. Ambrose writes: "It seems to be set before priests, whereby they know that they will suffer severe punishment in the future, if, intent on worldly pleasure, they have neglected to govern the Lord's household and the people entrusted to them."[19]

Jesus Comes to Cast Fire on the Earth (12:49–59)

[49]"I have come to set the earth on fire, and how I wish it were already blazing! [50]There is a baptism with which I must be baptized, and how great is my anguish until it is accomplished! [51]Do you think that I have come to establish peace on the earth? No, I tell you, but rather division. [52]From now on a household of five will be divided, three against two and two against three; [53]a father will be divided against his son and a son against his father, a mother against her daughter and a daughter against her mother, a mother-in-law against her daughter-in-law and a daughter-in-law against her mother-in-law."

[54]He also said to the crowds, "When you see [a] cloud rising in the west you say immediately that it is going to rain—and so it does; [55]and when you notice that the wind is blowing from the south you say that it is going to be hot—and so it is. [56]You hypocrites! You know how to interpret the appearance of the earth and the sky; why do you not know how to interpret the present time?

18. Augustine, *Sermon* 340.1, in *Sermons*, trans. Edmund Hill, 11 vols., WSA III/9 (Hyde Park, NY: New City Press, 1990–97), 9:292.
19. Ambrose, *Exposition of the Holy Gospel according to Saint Luke* 7.131, trans. Theodosia Tomkinson (Etna, CA: Center for Traditionalist Orthodox Studies, 1998), 289.

⁵⁷"Why do you not judge for yourselves what is right? ⁵⁸If you are to go
with your opponent before a magistrate, make an effort to settle the matter on the way; otherwise your opponent will turn you over to the judge,
and the judge hand you over to the constable, and the constable throw you
into prison. ⁵⁹I say to you, you will not be released until you have paid the
last penny."

OT: Mic 7:6
NT: Matt 16:2–3; Mark 10:38–39; Luke 2:34; 3:16. // Matt 5:25–26; 10:34–35
Catechism: fire of the Holy Spirit, 696; baptism of Jesus' redeeming death, 536, 607, 1225,
  2804
Lectionary: Luke 12:49–53: Twentieth Sunday Ordinary Time (Year C)

Jesus continues the focus on his coming: **I have come to set the earth on**   12:49–50
fire. This fire is different from what Elijah called down from heaven (9:54–55;
2 Kings 1:10). It is associated with **a baptism** that Jesus still has to receive: the
words "fire" and "baptism" are emphasized in the Greek text as the first words
in the two parallel sentences. John the Baptist had prophesied regarding one
who was "coming" who would "baptize . . . with the holy Spirit and fire" (Luke
3:16). The combination here of fire and baptism therefore looks forward to
Jesus' sending (24:49) the tongues of fire at Pentecost (Acts 2:3–4), when the
disciples will be baptized—that is, filled with the Holy Spirit (Acts 1:5). In the
Father's plan, this is the fire that will come down from heaven (see Luke 9:54),
which Jesus longs to see **blazing**. Before the Spirit can be given in this way,
however, Jesus must suffer the "baptism" of his passion and death (see Mark
10:38–39), in order to fulfill the Scriptures (see Luke 18:31). Having set his
face toward Jerusalem (9:51), Jesus is hard-pressed with this mission **until it
is accomplished**.

John the Baptist, however, had also warned of a punishment by "fire" (3:9,
17). The image thus signifies as well the judgment that will occur at the Son of
Man's coming (see 17:29–30).

These two different aspects—the giving of the Spirit and judgment—are not   12:51–53
surprising since Jesus has **come** as a sign of contradiction (2:34). He comes offering **peace** to those who accept it (see 2:14; 19:42), but since some reject that
offer, he brings **division**. This division will even affect **household** relationships
(see 14:26; 18:29): **father** and **son**, **mother** and **daughter**, **mother-in-law** and
daughter-in-law. Such was foretold by the prophet Micah:

  For the son belittles his father,
    the daughter rises up against her mother,

> The daughter-in-law against her mother-in-law,
>   and your enemies are members of your household. (Mic 7:6)

However, after this description of family strife, the prophet goes on to describe Israel's regathering and restoration (Mic 7:12–15). Jesus thus foretells that there will be a time of tribulation in which Israel is divided over him. This will be followed by the time of restoration[20] at his second coming (see Acts 1:6; 3:18–21; Rom 11:7, 25–26). Jesus' words also apply to people of every nation. In choosing to follow Jesus, disciples must be willing to bear with the divisions that may result among family and friends who do not share their commitment.

12:54–56   Turning now to the **crowds** (see Luke 12:13), Jesus notes that they are able **to interpret the appearance** of external weather-related phenomena—**rain** coming from the Mediterranean in the **west** or a heat wave from the desert in the **south**—but not the inner meaning of **the present time**, which is an opportune time (*kairos*) for repenting (see 13:3, 5) and recognizing the Messiah. Because of this disparity between the outside and the inside, Jesus calls them **hypocrites**. When Jesus reaches Jerusalem, he will lament that it likewise "did not recognize the time" (*kairos*) of its "visitation" (19:44).

12:57–59   Jesus urges the crowd to **judge** for themselves **what is right** in the looming crisis of which they are hardly aware. As he travels on the way to Jerusalem, the city that is coming under judgment, he uses a courtroom image involving a case of debt in order to exhort them to waste no time but **to settle the matter** while still **on the way** to court. Otherwise, they will face the **judge**, who represents God, and be thrown into debtor's **prison**, from which no one is **released** without paying **the last penny**.[21] Debts represent sins (see 7:40–43, 47; 11:4), and Jesus' mission is precisely to proclaim the jubilee year of remission of such debts (4:18–19). However, these debts will not be forgiven without repentance—the sooner, the better. Jesus will now take up this message by issuing an urgent summons to repentance (13:3, 5).

Reflection and Application (12:49)

On fire with zeal. Inspired by Jesus' words about his mission (12:49), St. Ignatius of Loyola told departing missionaries like St. Francis Xavier: "Go, set the world on fire!" Zeal for the mission of spreading the gospel is a hallmark of saints.

---

20. Brant Pitre, *Jesus, the Tribulation, and the End of the Exile: Restoration Eschatology and the Origin of the Atonement* (Tübingen: Mohr Siebeck, 2005), 209–10.

21. This small, copper coin is the *lepton* (also Luke 21:2); 128 of them made up a day's wage (*denarius*).

Repentance and Its Fruits: Parable of the Fig Tree (13:1–9)

¹At that time some people who were present there told him about the
Galileans whose blood Pilate had mingled with the blood of their sacrifices. ²He said to them in reply, "Do you think that because these Galileans
suffered in this way they were greater sinners than all other Galileans? ³By
no means! But I tell you, if you do not repent, you will all perish as they
did! ⁴Or those eighteen people who were killed when the tower at Siloam
fell on them—do you think they were more guilty than everyone else who
lived in Jerusalem? ⁵By no means! But I tell you, if you do not repent, you
will all perish as they did!"

⁶And he told them this parable: "There once was a person who had a fig
tree planted in his orchard, and when he came in search of fruit on it but
found none, ⁷he said to the gardener, 'For three years now I have come in
search of fruit on this fig tree but have found none. [So] cut it down. Why
should it exhaust the soil?' ⁸He said to him in reply, 'Sir, leave it for this
year also, and I shall cultivate the ground around it and fertilize it; ⁹it may
bear fruit in the future. If not you can cut it down.'"

OT: Isa 5:1–7; Jer 8:13
NT: Matt 21:19; Mark 11:13–14, 20; John 5:14; 8:24; 9:2–3
Catechism: punishments of sin, 1472–73; repentance, 1430–31
Lectionary: Third Sunday Lent (Year C)

Some people in the crowd now tell Jesus **about the Galileans** who had gone   13:1–3
up to Jerusalem to offer **sacrifices** but were killed by **Pilate**. This incident is
not recorded elsewhere but is consistent with other descriptions of Pilate's
brutality.[22] The interlocutors' intention was probably to elicit Jesus' opinion
about the Roman occupation. Jesus rather uses the interruption, like the two
previous ones (12:13, 41), to develop his teaching further. He first clarifies that
those who **suffered** this fate were not **greater sinners** than the rest, as was commonly thought of people who experienced misfortune (Job 4:7–9; John 9:2).
Jesus instead broadens the perspective by calling everyone to settle accounts
with God (Luke 12:58): **repent** or else **you will all perish**, not just in this life
but in the next (see 12:5). Rather than being afraid of someone like Pilate, who
can only "kill the body" (12:4), they should fear God.

Jesus reiterates the message by providing another example from current   13:4–5
events, involving **eighteen people who were killed** by a falling **tower at Siloam**,
near the "Pool of Siloam" **in Jerusalem** (John 9:7). Like the Galileans, these

22. Philo, *Embassy* 299–305; Josephus, *Jewish Antiquities* 18.55–62, 85–89.

were not **guilty** (literally, "debtors") to a greater degree **than everyone else**. Hence, everyone must **repent** or else **perish**. Jesus' words serve as a summons to repentance and readiness for people of every age, who do not know when their "life will be demanded" of them (Luke 12:20), whether because of accident, human malice, or other reason.

These two examples—Romans killing Jews and falling buildings in Jerusalem— take on a particular vividness in the context of the impending destruction of Jerusalem and its temple by the Romans (AD 70). The people and leaders are therefore urged to repent; otherwise they will literally perish **as they** (those in the examples) **did**.[23] Jesus first spoke about "repentance" at Levi's banquet (5:32), but ever since he began the journey to Jerusalem, he insists on the need to "repent" (10:13; 11:32) and will continue to do so (15:7, 10; 16:30).

13:6–9   Jesus illustrates the urgency of his message of repentance with the **parable** of the **fig tree** that produces no **fruit**. The ethical application of the parable for the modern reader is clear: God patiently waits to see if a person will repent and **bear fruit in the future** (see Rom 2:4–5; 2 Pet 3:9–10, 15). **If not**, however, the owner will **cut** the tree **down**: one's individual "life will be demanded" of a person (Luke 12:20), or the day of judgment will arrive with Christ's second coming. The parable's message recalls John the Baptist's words about the fruits of repentance: "Every tree that does not produce good fruit will be cut down and thrown into the fire" (3:9).

However, in the context of Jesus' journey to Jerusalem and in view of the biblical background, the parable first of all refers to Israel.[24] The tree is planted in an **orchard**—that is, a "vineyard" (NRSV and other versions), a common image for Israel in the Old Testament (see Isa 5:1–7, which also mentions a tower and inhabitants of Jerusalem, as Jesus just did in Luke 13:4). The owner may represent God, but since the **gardener** addresses him as **sir** (*kyrios*), he may also represent Jesus the "Lord" (*kyrios*, 12:41–42; 13:15). The **three years** may even refer to the length of Jesus' public ministry (see the sidebar, "The Duration of Jesus' Public Ministry," p. 261).[25] Identifying Jesus with the one who comes **in search of fruit on** a **fig tree** also correlates with the tradition of Jesus actually doing such a thing (Matt 21:19; Mark 11:13), at the time that he cleansed the temple. Luke is undoubtedly familiar with this tradition but instead includes the similar parable to teach the same lesson about the impending judgment on

23. N. T. Wright, *Jesus and the Victory of God* (Minneapolis: Fortress, 1996), 331.

24. Klyne R. Snodgrass, *Stories with Intent: A Comprehensive Guide to the Parables of Jesus* (Grand Rapids: Eerdmans, 2008), 255–65.

25. Ambrose, *Luke* 7.165 (trans. Tomkinson, 303). Among modern scholars, see Arthur A. Just Jr., *Luke 9:51–24:53: A Theological Exposition of Sacred Scripture* (St. Louis: Concordia, 1997), 536.

Figure 12. Fig tree.

Jerusalem and its temple.[26] Here, the gardener's intervention to **leave it for this year also** so that he can **fertilize it** offers hope that there is one last chance for repentance, but clearly time is running out.

Reflection and Application (13:1–5)

Wake-up call. Tragedies that occur, whether far away or close to home, can alert us to turn away from sin and destructive behaviors. One of God's purposes in permitting them is to call us to repentance. "Suffering must serve *for conversion.*"[27]

26. A tower (see Luke 13:4; 14:28) often represents the Jerusalem temple (see Matt 21:33; Mark 12:1) on account of Isaiah's song of the vineyard (Isa 5:1–2), the details of which were already interpreted at Qumran in reference to Jerusalem and its temple (4Q500).

27. John Paul II, *Salvifici Doloris* (On the Christian Meaning of Human Suffering) 12 (emphasis in the original).

Jesus Frees a Crippled Woman on the Sabbath (13:10–17)

---

[10]He was teaching in a synagogue on the sabbath. [11]And a woman was there who for eighteen years had been crippled by a spirit; she was bent over, completely incapable of standing erect. [12]When Jesus saw her, he called to her and said, "Woman, you are set free of your infirmity." [13]He laid his hands on her, and she at once stood up straight and glorified God. [14]But the leader of the synagogue, indignant that Jesus had cured on the sabbath, said to the crowd in reply, "There are six days when work should be done. Come on those days to be cured, not on the sabbath day." [15]The Lord said to him in reply, "Hypocrites! Does not each one of you on the sabbath untie his ox or his ass from the manger and lead it out for watering? [16]This daughter of Abraham, whom Satan has bound for eighteen years now, ought she not to have been set free on the sabbath day from this bondage?" [17]When he said this, all his adversaries were humiliated; and the whole crowd rejoiced at all the splendid deeds done by him.

OT: Exod 20:8–11; Deut 5:12–15; Isa 40:2; 42:7; 45:16
NT: Luke 5:20; 6:7; 14:3, 5; 19:9
Catechism: sabbath healing, 582

A miracle story that also involves a controversy now illustrates the contrast between Jesus and Israel's religious leaders, whose hypocrisy has been criticized in the preceding discourse (12:1). The crowd can decide for themselves which of the two to follow.

13:10–11   Jesus moves to a familiar setting, **teaching in a synagogue on the sabbath** (4:15–16, 31–33; 6:6). However, **a woman** is **there who** is **crippled by a spirit**.[28] Like the woman afflicted with hemorrhages for twelve years (8:43), this woman has suffered for a long time—**eighteen years**.[29]

13:12–13   **Jesus** directly addresses her—**Woman**—and adds: **you are set free** (see the related verb in 13:15–16). The verb is passive, implying that God is the one who has acted. Jesus then **laid his hands on her** in a gesture often used for healing (4:40). God is working through Jesus in a way similar to the earlier healing of the paralyzed man (i.e., the direct address and passive verb): "Man, your sins are forgiven you" (5:20 RSV). The woman is cured **at once**, or "immediately," as was the man (5:25) and others healed by Jesus (8:44, 47, 55). She **stood up straight**, or rather "she was made straight" (RSV), the passive form again suggesting that

---

28. On the physical effects of demonic oppression, see comment on Luke 4:39.

29. Some scholars suggest a link to the "eighteen" in the previous passage (Luke 13:4). Jesus will himself refer to the "eighteen years" (v. 16), revealing special knowledge about the woman's situation.

God is the one acting through Jesus. Recognizing this, the woman **glorified God**, as the man also did (5:25).

However, **the leader of the synagogue** objects to the **work** that was **done**.   **13:14**
To him, this is a clear violation of **the sabbath** precept that limits work to the other **six days** (Exod 20:8–11; Deut 5:12–15). Directing his comments **to the crowd**, he instructs them to **come** on any day other than **the sabbath** in order **to be cured**. He thinks that God is on his side, but the irony is that God is the one who has "worked" to heal the woman.

In response, Jesus, who is **the Lord** even "of the sabbath" (Luke 6:5), gives   **13:15–16**
the sabbath its authoritative interpretation. As before, he reasons from the lesser to the greater by discussing animals and human beings (see 12:6–7, 24). The sabbath precept against work also forbids work that one does with animals such as an "ox or donkey" (Deut 5:14; see Exod 20:10). Nonetheless, everyone **on the sabbath** would **untie** (or "set free") **his ox or his ass from the manger and lead it out for watering.**[30] How much more then **ought**[31] the woman to be **set free on the sabbath**! Because of their double standard, Jesus calls his opponents **hypocrites** (Luke 12:1). By focusing on the external observance of the sabbath, they miss its inner, twofold meaning.

First, the sabbath was a reminder about creation: "For in six days the LORD made the heavens and the earth . . . but on the seventh day he rested. That is why the LORD has blessed the sabbath day and made it holy" (Exod 20:11). Through this sabbath healing, Jesus gives a glimpse of the new creation (with its new "Paradise," Luke 23:43). Earlier, he rescued the paralyzed "Man" (5:20 RSV), Adam, from his sins, and now he heals the crippled "Woman" (13:12), Eve, oppressed by **Satan**.[32]

Second, the sabbath recalled Israel's exodus: "Remember that you too were once slaves in the land of Egypt, and the LORD, your God, brought you out from there. . . . That is why the LORD, your God, has commanded you to observe the sabbath day" (Deut 5:15). The sabbath healing of the woman who was **bound** signals that Jesus' mission is to lead Israel in a new exodus (Luke 9:31) from the **bondage** not of Pharaoh but of Satan. Jesus is thus fulfilling his mission, announced on a sabbath (4:16), of bringing "liberty to captives" (4:18–19). Moreover, Jesus calls the woman a **daughter of Abraham**—as later he will call

---

30. The rabbis later detailed what was permitted or forbidden for one's animals on the sabbath: *m. Shabbat* 5:1–4; 7:2; 15:1–2; *Eruvin* 2:1–4.

31. The Greek verb *dei* ("must") again here indicates what is necessary according to God's plan (see comment on Luke 2:49), which differs from what the synagogue leader believes "ought" to happen (*dei*, v. 14).

32. Bovon, *Luke*, 2:292: the woman is "like a regenerated Eve."

Zacchaeus a "son of Abraham" (19:9 NRSV)—since she too is a member of God's chosen people, Israel, set free to worship him (see 1:73–74).

13:17   As a result, the leader of the synagogue and **all** Jesus' **adversaries** are **humiliated**. This phrase alludes to a verse from Isaiah: "All who oppose him shall be ashamed and disgraced" (Isa 45:16 LXX, NETS). This is said about opposition to "the God of Israel, the savior" (Isa 45:15). The echo thus suggests that "Jesus *is* the God of Israel, the Savior . . . whom these opponents have failed to know."[33]

For their part, **the whole crowd** sides with Jesus rather than with the hypocritical leaders. They therefore **rejoiced at** Jesus' **deeds** (see Luke 19:37).

Kingdom Parables: Mustard Seed and Yeast (13:18–21)

---

[18]Then he said, "What is the kingdom of God like? To what can I compare it? [19]It is like a mustard seed that a person took and planted in the garden. When it was fully grown, it became a large bush and 'the birds of the sky dwelt in its branches.'"

[20]Again he said, "To what shall I compare the kingdom of God? [21]It is like yeast that a woman took and mixed [in] with three measures of wheat flour until the whole batch of dough was leavened."

OT: Ezek 17:22–24
NT: Luke 12:1; 17:6. // Matt 13:31–33; Mark 4:30–32
Catechism: prayer as leaven, 2660; leaven that makes society rise, 2832

13:18–19   Still in the synagogue and drawing a lesson from the miracle, Jesus **then** (or "therefore," NRSV) recounts two parables of **the kingdom of God**. The arrival of "the kingdom of God" was earlier announced by Jesus in connection with his driving out demons (11:20). This is precisely what has happened here with the woman set free from the bondage of Satan.

The first parable involves **a person** (or "man" [NIV], to pair with the "woman" in v. 21) who sows **a mustard seed**. The plant grows so much that **"the birds of the sky dwelt in its branches."** This phrase refers to several Old Testament passages (e.g., Ezek 17:23; 31:6) that describe earthly kingdoms as mighty trees. These are cut down and replaced by "a tender shoot" (Ezek 17:22) that then becomes a majestic tree: "I bring low the high tree, / lift high the lowly tree" (Ezek 17:24). This is the great reversal announced in Mary's Magnificat: God

---

33. Richard B. Hays, *Reading Backwards: Figural Christology and the Fourfold Gospel Witness* (Waco: Baylor University Press, 2014), 69. Luke's text and the verse from Isaiah (LXX) have four consecutive Greek words in common (a string found nowhere else in the Bible) plus related forms of a verb.

Pairing of Men and Women in Luke

BIBLICAL BACKGROUND

Luke frequently pairs passages involving male and female characters. For example, the angel appears to Zechariah and Mary (1:11–20, 26–38); Simeon and Anna encounter Jesus in the temple (2:25–38); Jesus rebukes the demon possessing a man and the fever afflicting Peter's mother-in-law (4:33–39); he heals the centurion's dying slave and raises the widow's dead son (7:2–15); and Simon of Cyrene and the women of Jerusalem meet Jesus on his way to Calvary (23:26–31). Such pairings also occur in Jesus' teaching—for example, the widow of Zarephath and Naaman the Syrian (4:26–27); the queen of the south and the men of Nineveh (11:31–32); the man who plants a mustard seed and the woman who mixes leaven (13:18–21); and the man who finds the lost sheep and the woman the lost coin (15:4–10). A passage can sometimes be paired with more than one passage; for example, the raising of the widow's son also relates to the raising of Jairus's daughter (8:49–56). Thus, paired passages need not be adjacent—for example, the twelve apostles (6:13–16) and the women disciples (8:2–3).

The pairings are not simply a stylistic feature but have a theological purpose.[a] They show that, amid human diversity, God's salvation in Jesus overcomes division: "There is neither Jew nor Greek, there is neither slave nor free person, there is not male and female; for you are all one in Christ Jesus. And if you belong to Christ, then you are *Abraham's descendant*" (Gal 3:28–29 [emphasis added]). Indeed, the crippled woman healed on a sabbath is a "*daughter of Abraham*" (Luke 13:16 [emphasis added]) and Zacchaeus is a "*son of Abraham*" (19:9 NRSV [emphasis added]). The pairings also show how Jesus brings fulfillment to Old Testament prophecies involving God's sons and daughters (e.g., Isa 43:6; 49:22; 60:4), as Peter explains on the day of Pentecost: "Your sons and your daughters shall prophesy, . . . / even on my male servants and female servants / in those days I will pour out my Spirit" (Acts 2:17–18 ESV, citing Joel 3:1–2).[b] Moreover, "just as the fall was both theirs, so redemption was both theirs."[c] Jesus thus brings healing to both "Man" (Luke 5:20 RSV) and "Woman" (13:12).

a. Allen Black, "'Your Sons and Your Daughters Will Prophesy . . .': Pairings of Men and Women in Luke-Acts," in *Scripture and Traditions: Essays on Early Judaism and Christianity*, ed. Patrick Gray and Gail R. O'Day (Leiden: Brill, 2008), 193–206.
b. Joel 2:28–29 RSV.
c. Bonaventure, *Commentary on the Gospel of Luke* 4.80, ed. and trans. Robert J. Karris, 3 vols. (St. Bonaventure, NY: The Franciscan Institute, 2001–4), 1:358 (translation adapted).

has "lifted up the lowly" (Luke 1:52). God's kingdom is revealed in apparently insignificant people like the woman, healed from Satan's bondage. Moreover, as the kingdom becomes **fully grown**, many will make their home there, like the growing crowds who are following Jesus now and those who will be added later, both from the Jews (Acts 6:7) and from the Gentiles (Acts 11:24).

The mustard seed is sown not "in a field" or "in the ground" (Matt 13:31; Mark 4:31), but **in the garden**. The word "garden" may be an allusion to the garden of Eden (see John 18:1; 19:41), which is described in one of the passages just mentioned from Ezekiel (Ezek 31:8–9; also 36:35). That is why the seed grows into a "tree" (NRSV and other versions, whereas the NABRE translates **bush**). When fully established in the new creation, the kingdom of God becomes like the tree of life![34]

13:20–21   In the second parable, **a woman** takes **yeast** or "leaven" (RSV), so that the whole unit (Luke 12:1–13:21) is framed by contrasting references to the "leaven" of the Pharisees (12:1) and the "leaven" of the kingdom. The Pharisees' leaven represented their hidden (adjective *kryptos*, 12:2) hypocrisy, soon to be exposed. Similarly, **the kingdom of God** is hidden at first, like leaven **mixed [in]** or "hidden in" (verb *enkryptō*) the **flour**, but its all-pervading effect is soon manifested. The **three measures** of flour is a large amount that can feed more than a hundred people. Therefore, from inconspicuous beginnings, the kingdom of God grows to embrace even **the whole** world.

---

34. On the link between the "kingdom" and the new creation ("Paradise"), see Luke 23:42–43.

The Last Are First
at God's Kingdom Banquet

Luke 13:22–14:35

Jesus continues his journey to Jerusalem in the next part (13:22–17:10) of the travel narrative. As before, he is accompanied by crowds (14:25) and teaches about discipleship. More specifically, this next unit (13:22–14:35) focuses on parables and events involving meals, through which Jesus teaches about the banquet in the kingdom of God. This banquet involves a reversal: those considered "last" will become "first" (13:29–30; 14:10–11, 13, 21).

The Narrow Door into the Kingdom of God (13:22–30)

²²He passed through towns and villages, teaching as he went and making his way to Jerusalem. ²³Someone asked him, "Lord, will only a few people be saved?" He answered them, ²⁴"Strive to enter through the narrow door, for many, I tell you, will attempt to enter but will not be strong enough. ²⁵After the master of the house has arisen and locked the door, then will you stand outside knocking and saying, 'Lord, open the door for us.' He will say to you in reply, 'I do not know where you are from.' ²⁶And you will say, 'We ate and drank in your company and you taught in our streets.' ²⁷Then he will say to you, 'I do not know where [you] are from. Depart from me, all you evildoers!' ²⁸And there will be wailing and grinding of teeth when you see Abraham, Isaac, and Jacob and all the prophets in the kingdom of God and you yourselves cast out. ²⁹And people will come from the east and the west and from the north and the south and will recline at

table in the kingdom of God. ³⁰For behold, some are last who will be first, and some are first who will be last."

OT: Ps 6:9; 107:3; Isa 25:6–9; 43:5–6
NT: Matt 25:10–12. // Matt 7:13–14, 22–23; 8:11–12; 19:30; 20:16; Mark 10:31
Catechism: call to conversion, 1036; people of all nations enter the kingdom, 543
Lectionary: Twenty-First Sunday Ordinary Time (Year C)

13:22   The reminder that Jesus is **making his way to Jerusalem** begins the next part (13:22–17:10) of the central section. Along the journey, he visits **towns and villages** as before (9:52, 56; 10:1, 38), and his main activity continues to be **teaching** (see 11:1–2; 13:10).

13:23–24   **Someone** asks, **"Lord, will only a few people be saved?"**[1] Others will later ask a related question—"Who can be saved?" (18:26)—and twice Jesus is similarly asked about "eternal life" (10:25; 18:18). All these questions refer to life "in the age to come" (18:30).

Jesus does not give numbers or percentages, but he does indirectly contrast the "few" in the question with the **many** who are unsuccessful in their **attempt** to be saved. Jesus' words serve as a warning to the "great" (14:25, same Greek word as "many") crowds following him. They are also echoed in his parable about the "many" guests invited to a dinner (14:16), none of whom actually gets to taste it (14:24).

The image Jesus uses here is that of entering **through the narrow door**. One must **strive** or struggle to do so. Using the same Greek verb, Paul writes, "Fight the good fight of the faith" (1 Tim 6:12 NRSV). Many are not able or **strong enough**. Despite God's universal saving will (1 Tim 2:4), salvation should not be taken for granted!

13:25–27   Jesus develops the image further: the narrow **door** is now **locked** from the inside by **the master of the house** (see Luke 14:21). Those **outside** try **knocking** to get in: **Lord, open the door for us.** Once again, the nearby use of the title "Lord" (*kyrios*) in the narrative (13:23) and then in the parable suggests that Jesus is the Lord and master of the house. This identification is confirmed by their plea—**We ate and drank in your company and you taught in our streets**—which refers precisely to what Jesus has been doing (11:37; 13:22).

Twice they are rebuffed with the phrase: **I do not know where you are from.** Although they *know* Jesus, they have not *acknowledged* him but rather denied him; now it is their turn to be denied (12:8–9): **Depart from me, all you evildoers!** These words echo those of the psalmist—"Away from me, all

1. A Jewish work from around AD 100 expresses such a view: *4 Ezra* 7.47; 8.1, 3; 9.15.

who do evil!" (Ps 6:9). Now it is too late to knock (Luke 11:10). The evildoers have missed their chance to repent (13:1–9).

All that is left for those excluded is **wailing and grinding of teeth** (see Ps   13:28–29
112:10), a combined image often found in Matthew and associated with the outer darkness and fiery furnace of hell (Matt 8:12; 13:42, 50; 22:13; 25:30).

However, those who are saved will enter into **the kingdom of God** with the patriarchs **Abraham, Isaac, and Jacob** as well as **all the prophets.** They come from **east, west, north,** and **south,** referring at one level to the restoration of Israel (Isa 43:5–6), and specifically to the reuniting of Samaritans and Jews, descendants of the northern kingdom of "Ephraim" and the southern king-dom of "Judah," gathered "from the four corners of the earth" (Isa 11:12–13).[2] At another level, the phrase refers to the inclusion of the Gentiles (see Isa 49:6).

In **the kingdom,** they **recline at table** (Luke 12:37), in a banquet that has already been prefigured in earlier meal scenes in Luke (see 9:17) and explained by Jesus in his parable of the servants awaiting their master's return (12:35–38). Jesus thus answers the question about salvation (13:23) by discussing entrance into the kingdom banquet.[3]

In the banquet, **some are last** [*eschatos*] **who will be first** [*prōtos*]**, and some**   13:30
are first who will be last. For example, some who are Gentiles will enter into eternal life in the kingdom, whereas some in Israel may be judged unworthy to enter (see Acts 13:46–48). This message of reversal will be developed in two upcoming parables, where Jesus contrasts the leaders in Israel with the poor (Luke 14:13, 21). In one parable, the person who goes to the "lowest" or last (*eschatos*) place is then invited higher, whereas the one who went to the seat of honor ends up in the "lowest" (i.e., last) place (14:9–10). In the other parable, the one invited "first" (*prōtos*, 14:18) ends up not even tasting the dinner (14:24).

Jesus' Death Foreshadowed (13:31–35)

---

[31]**At that time some Pharisees came to him and said, "Go away, leave this area because Herod wants to kill you." [32]He replied, "Go and tell that fox, 'Behold, I cast out demons and I perform healings today and tomorrow,**

---

2. David Ravens, *Luke and the Restoration of Israel* (Sheffield: Sheffield Academic, 1995), 100–102, notes that the parallel passage in Matthew only mentions east and west (Matt 8:11), whereas Luke also includes north and south. See Jer 3:11–12; 16:15.

3. Jewish sources similarly use a banquet to describe life in the age to come; see, e.g., *m. Avot* 4:16.

and on the third day I accomplish my purpose. ³³Yet I must continue on my way today, tomorrow, and the following day, for it is impossible that a prophet should die outside of Jerusalem.'

³⁴"Jerusalem, Jerusalem, you who kill the prophets and stone those sent to you, how many times I yearned to gather your children together as a hen gathers her brood under her wings, but you were unwilling! ³⁵Behold, your house will be abandoned. [But] I tell you, you will not see me until [the time comes when] you say, 'Blessed is he who comes in the name of the Lord.'"

OT: Deut 32:11; Ps 118:26

NT: Luke 19:38–46. // Matt 23:37–39

Catechism: Jesus and the Pharisees, 575; passion in Jerusalem, 557–58; announcement of the temple's destruction, 585

13:31   The **Pharisees** are typically Jesus' foes, yet here **some** of them try to help him, unless they are acting from a hypocritical motive (12:1). Since Jesus sends them back to **Herod** (13:32), they are certainly in touch if not in league with him (see Mark 3:6; 8:15; 12:13). As tetrarch, Herod governed not only Galilee but also Perea[4] east of the Jordan. The other Gospels record that Jesus spent some time "across the Jordan" (Matt 19:1; Mark 10:1; John 10:40) before his final arrival in Jerusalem. Whether he is there now or still in Galilee (see Luke 17:11), he is advised to **leave**. Herod's wish **to kill** Jesus—as he had killed John the Baptist—was already implied by his earlier efforts to see him (9:9), leading Jesus to move toward Bethsaida, outside of Herod's jurisdiction (9:10).

13:32–33   Ultimately, however, it is not Herod's scheming that determines Jesus' movement but rather God's plan, according to which Jesus **must** (see 2:49) go to **Jerusalem**. That is the city where **a prophet** like him (4:24; 7:16, 39) **should die** (18:31–33). For the time being (**today and tomorrow**), he can continue the activities that characterize his mission: to **cast out demons** (11:14–20) and **perform healings** (14:4). In a short time—**the third day** (which elsewhere refers to his resurrection 9:22; 18:33; 24:7, 46)—Jesus will **accomplish** his **purpose** by completing his mission.

Jesus calls Herod a **fox**, perhaps a reference to Herod's crafty[5] or destructive character (Song 2:15) but also to his relative insignificance (Neh 3:35)[6]—he is no kingly lion (Prov 20:2). However, there may be a subtle wordplay in

---

4. Josephus, *Jewish Antiquities* 17.188, 318.

5. Plato, *Republic* 2.8 (365c).

6. Neh 4:3 RSV.

The Duration of Jesus' Public Ministry

BIBLICAL BACKGROUND

Like Matthew and Mark, Luke presents only one journey of Jesus as an adult to Jerusalem, for the feast of Passover (Luke 22:1–15), at which he is put to death. As a result, the duration of Jesus' public ministry as portrayed by the †synoptic Gospels is typically described as about one year, though nothing in them requires such a limit. On the other hand, John's Gospel presents Jesus going up to Jerusalem for many feasts spread over at least two-plus years but as many as three and a half years.[a] In fact, there seem to be indications in the synoptic Gospels that the evangelists are aware that Jesus' public ministry lasted several years and involved various trips to Jerusalem. Jesus' lament over Jerusalem is one example: "Jerusalem, Jerusalem . . . *how many times* I yearned to gather your children together" (Luke 13:34 [emphasis added]; also Matt 23:37). For Jesus' listeners, the natural way to understand these words would be to conclude that Jesus had made multiple trips to Jerusalem.[b] Another example that some have interpreted as pointing to Jesus' multiyear ministry is the phrase "for three years" in the parable of the barren fig tree (Luke 13:7). Despite the awareness of a Judean and multiyear ministry suggested by these texts, Luke retains the framework of describing one journey of Jesus from Galilee to Jerusalem. He is perhaps thus indicating Jesus' definitive departure from Galilee; even in John's Gospel, Jesus does not return to Galilee between his later visits to Jerusalem (John 7:9–10; 10:40; 11:54). The journey framework is also due to Luke's "theological geography" that moves *toward* Jerusalem in the Gospel (for Jesus' death and resurrection) and then *from* Jerusalem in Acts (for the mission to the Gentiles). Luke thus tends to omit precise details of place when recounting, on the one hand, events occurring in Gentile territory north of Galilee, such as Peter's confession in Caesarea Philippi (Luke 9:18; see Matt 16:13; Mark 8:27), and on the other, events (perhaps from previous trips to Jerusalem) occurring in or near Jerusalem but which are recounted long before Jesus' arrival in the city (e.g., Luke 10:38–42).[c]

a. Harold W. Hoehner, "The Chronology of Jesus," in *Handbook for the Study of the Historical Jesus*, ed. Tom Holmén and Stanley E. Porter, 4 vols. (Leiden: Brill, 2011), 3:2336–37.
b. John P. Meier, *A Marginal Jew: Rethinking the Historical Jesus*, 5 vols. (New Haven: Yale University Press, 1991–2016), 1:404. Meier also mentions Luke 4:44, which says that Jesus preached in the synagogues of *Judea*; see Mark 1:39.
c. See Raymond E. Brown, *The Gospel according to John*, 2 vols., AB (New York: Doubleday, 1966–70), 1:422.

the epithet, since in Hebrew the word "fox" (*shuʿal*) sounds similar to Saul (*shaʾul*).[7] As Saul wanted to kill David, but David was warned to escape (e.g., 1 Sam 19:1–2; 22:5), so now Herod wants to kill Jesus, the son of David who

7. James R. Edwards, *The Gospel according to Luke*, PNTC (Grand Rapids: Eerdmans, 2015), 405.

inherits David's throne (Luke 1:32; 18:38–39).[8] Indeed, Jesus earlier recalled a passage about David's flight from Saul (6:3–4) and later, as he was evading Herod (9:9–10), used "five loaves" to feed the people as David had done (see comment on 9:12–15).

13:34   **Jerusalem**—the city where Jesus will die—is now twice addressed in a lament that recalls Jesus' earlier words: **you who kill the prophets and stone those sent to you** (11:47–51). Jesus' mission is to **gather** Jerusalem's **children** and bring about Israel's restoration, like **a hen** gathering **her brood under her wings**. The image portrays Jesus in the same role as God toward the wilderness generation: "Like an eagle to protect his brood, / he too yearned for his young; / spreading his wings, he received them / and bore them aloft on his back" (Deut 32:11 NETS). Jesus **yearned** to do this (literally, "was willing"), but they **were unwilling**.

13:35   Like Jeremiah (see Jer 7:6, 13–15), Jesus warns that the consequence for Jerusalem of its leaders' continuing to shed innocent blood—not just his own but also that of his disciples (Acts 7:59–60; 12:2)[9]—will be judgment on the city. Earlier, the image was that of the fig tree to be cut down (Luke 13:6–9). Now Jesus prophesies using another image with similar meaning: **your house will be abandoned** (see Jer 12:7). These words refer to the destruction of Jerusalem and its temple, which the Romans carried out in AD 70.

Nonetheless, in interpreting this and similar sayings, it is important to remember that "God has not rejected his people" (Rom 11:2)[10]—the people of Israel—"for the gifts and the call of God are irrevocable" (Rom 11:29). Resistance to Jesus from part of Israel is included in God's plan, a divine mystery that allows for the gospel message to go to the Gentiles (Rom 11:25; see Acts 28:28).

The following words, **'Blessed is he who comes in the name of the Lord'** (from Ps 118:26), look forward to Jesus' arrival in Jerusalem, when he will be hailed with the acclamation: "Blessed is the king / who comes in the name of the Lord" (Luke 19:38; see Matt 21:9; Mark 11:9; John 12:13). Though the people of Jerusalem will respond favorably (Luke 19:48), its leaders will not join in that chorus of praise (19:39, 47), so Jesus will again warn about its coming destruction (19:41–44; 21:6, 20). Only at his second coming in glory, which is the emphasis in the parallel verse (Matt 23:39), will all of Jerusalem proclaim this blessing.

---

8. See Yuzuru Miura, *David in Luke-Acts: His Portrayal in Light of Early Judaism* (Tübingen: Mohr Siebeck, 2007), 216–25.

9. Josephus, *Jewish Antiquities* 20.200.

10. See Vatican II, *Nostra Aetate* (Declaration on the Relation of the Church to Non-Christian Religions) 4.

Sabbath Healing and Banquet Parables in a Pharisee's House (14:1–24)

¹On a sabbath he went to dine at the home of one of the leading Pharisees, and the people there were observing him carefully. ²In front of him there was a man suffering from dropsy. ³Jesus spoke to the scholars of the law and Pharisees in reply, asking, "Is it lawful to cure on the sabbath or not?" ⁴But they kept silent; so he took the man and, after he had healed him, dismissed him. ⁵Then he said to them, "Who among you, if your son or ox falls into a cistern, would not immediately pull him out on the sabbath day?" ⁶But they were unable to answer his question.

⁷He told a parable to those who had been invited, noticing how they were choosing the places of honor at the table. ⁸"When you are invited by someone to a wedding banquet, do not recline at table in the place of honor. A more distinguished guest than you may have been invited by him, ⁹and the host who invited both of you may approach you and say, 'Give your place to this man,' and then you would proceed with embarrassment to take the lowest place. ¹⁰Rather, when you are invited, go and take the lowest place so that when the host comes to you he may say, 'My friend, move up to a higher position.' Then you will enjoy the esteem of your companions at the table. ¹¹For everyone who exalts himself will be humbled, but the one who humbles himself will be exalted." ¹²Then he said to the host who invited him, "When you hold a lunch or a dinner, do not invite your friends or your brothers or your relatives or your wealthy neighbors, in case they may invite you back and you have repayment. ¹³Rather, when you hold a banquet, invite the poor, the crippled, the lame, the blind; ¹⁴blessed indeed will you be because of their inability to repay you. For you will be repaid at the resurrection of the righteous."

¹⁵One of his fellow guests on hearing this said to him, "Blessed is the one who will dine in the kingdom of God." ¹⁶He replied to him, "A man gave a great dinner to which he invited many. ¹⁷When the time for the dinner came, he dispatched his servant to say to those invited, 'Come, everything is now ready.' ¹⁸But one by one, they all began to excuse themselves. The first said to him, 'I have purchased a field and must go to examine it; I ask you, consider me excused.' ¹⁹And another said, 'I have purchased five yoke of oxen and am on my way to evaluate them; I ask you, consider me excused.' ²⁰And another said, 'I have just married a woman, and therefore I cannot come.' ²¹The servant went and reported this to his master. Then the master of the house in a rage commanded his servant, 'Go out quickly into the streets and alleys of the town and bring in here the poor and the crippled, the blind and the lame.' ²²The servant reported, 'Sir, your orders

have been carried out and still there is room.' ²³The master then ordered the servant, 'Go out to the highways and hedgerows and make people come in that my home may be filled. ²⁴For, I tell you, none of those men who were invited will taste my dinner.'"

OT: Deut 22:4; Prov 25:6–7

NT: Matt 12:11; 22:1–10; 23:6, 12; Mark 12:39; Luke 6:6–11; 11:37, 43; 13:10–17; 18:14; 20:46

Catechism: Jesus dines with Pharisees, 575, 588; sabbath healing, 582; parables about the king-dom feast, 546

Lectionary: Luke 14:1, 7–14: Twenty-Second Sunday Ordinary Time (Year C)

14:1–3   For the third time, Jesus goes **to dine** (literally, "eat bread," as in v. 15) in **the home** of **one** of the **Pharisees** (see 7:36; 11:37). Similarly, for the third time, a controversy arises about healing on the **sabbath** (see 6:6; 13:10–11). The **scholars of the law and Pharisees** present at the meal are **observing him carefully** (same verb as in 6:7), undoubtedly ready again to accuse him. Right **in front of** Jesus is **a man suffering from dropsy**—that is, edema or swelling caused by excess fluid. Because this condition may be accompanied by thirst, but satisfying the thirst only makes it worse, ancient writers compared dropsy to greed.[11] Thus it is often suggested that Luke specifies the man's illness so that it may serve as a metaphor for these Pharisees' insatiable craving for honor (14:7).

The scene contrasts the **leading** Pharisee with this sick man, setting up an example of the reversal between first and last that was recently announced (13:30). The man's presence triggers what follows. As before, Jesus asks if it is **lawful to cure on the sabbath** (6:9).

14:4   Although **they kept silent**, the reader by now knows that the answer is yes. It is not only lawful but most fitting: it "ought" to be done (13:16). Therefore, Jesus **healed** and then **dismissed him**, which suggests that the man was not one of those invited. The verb "dismiss" is the same verb used when the crippled woman was "set free" (13:12), also on a sabbath. Jesus is thus continuing the jubilee program he announced on a sabbath of bringing "liberty to captives" (4:18).

14:5–6   Jesus again justifies his action by appealing to the Pharisees' own sabbath activities (13:15) and by reasoning from the lesser to the greater (see 12:6–7, 24; 13:15–16). Alluding to one of the laws in the Torah—"You shall not see your neighbor's donkey or ox fallen on the road and ignore it; you must help in lift-ing it up" (Deut 22:4)—Jesus gives an example of a **son or ox**[12] that **falls into a cistern. Would not** everyone **immediately pull him out on the sabbath day?** Of course. If this is done even for an animal, how much more ought the man

---

11. E.g., Polybius, *Histories* 13.2.2.

12. Some manuscripts read "ass or ox," the same animals as in 13:15.

be healed on the sabbath! However, **they were unable to answer his question**. They seem to be like those who "ate and drank" in his company (Luke 13:26) but nevertheless find themselves excluded from God's kingdom (13:28).

The "no comment" response by the **invited** guests, who instead are focused on **choosing the places of honor** (see 11:43; 20:46), now prompts Jesus to teach in parables. Eating bread (14:1) is not sufficient, as they also need God's word spoken through Jesus (see Deut 8:3). Just as in his first two visits to Pharisees' homes, Jesus ends up teaching about what happens there (Luke 7:36–40; 11:37–39).   **14:7–11**

In the first parable, Jesus instructs the guests to do the opposite of what they are doing, lest they be forced to **give** their **place** to **a more distinguished guest** and **with embarrassment** go to **the lowest** [*eschatos*] **place** (see Prov 25:6–7). Rather, by choosing **the lowest place** for themselves, they may be invited **to a higher position** and thus be held in **esteem** or honor by the others. At a practical level, this is good advice for those concerned precisely about honor and shame. More importantly, at the level of the gospel message, the teaching indicates the great reversal being worked by God between first and last (*eschatos*, Luke 13:30).

In other words, **everyone who exalts himself will be humbled**—that is, by God—**but the one who humbles himself will be exalted**, also by God (see Ezek 17:24; 21:31).[13] This message is so important that it is repeated verbatim later (Luke 18:14). Earlier, Mary also proclaimed the same message in her Magnificat: God "has looked upon his handmaid's lowliness" (1:48) and "has lifted up the lowly" (1:52). Jesus preached this message because he lived it: "He humbled himself. . . . Because of this, God greatly exalted him" (Phil 2:8–9).

In the parable, the meal is described as **a wedding banquet**, just as in Jesus' parable about the servants awaiting their master's return (Luke 12:36). Earlier, at Levi's banquet (5:34), Jesus referred to himself as the bridegroom and his disciples as wedding guests. Therefore, the parable here, which superficially appears to be a lesson about social etiquette, is ultimately about how to enter and **recline at table** (12:37; 13:29–30) at the messianic wedding banquet in the kingdom.

Having instructed the guests, Jesus now teaches **the host** about entrance into the kingdom banquet. With that goal in mind, the host should follow these rules about guests at **a lunch or a dinner**: **invite** no one (e.g., **relatives**, **friends**, **wealthy neighbors**) who might return the favor, thus giving **repayment** (see 6:34). Rather, **invite** to a **banquet** those like the man with dropsy: **the poor, the crippled, the lame, the blind** (see v. 21)—in other words, people who cannot   **14:12–14**

---

13. Ezek 21:26 RSV.

repay. Doing so extends Jesus' own mission of proclaiming good news to "the poor," recovery of sight to "the blind," and healing for "the lame" (4:18; 7:22). Jesus pronounces a beatitude on those doing so, who become **blessed** like the poor themselves (6:20). They **will be repaid**, by God, **at the resurrection of the righteous** from the dead in the age to come (see 20:35–36; Acts 24:15; Rom 6:5).

14:15   One of Jesus' **fellow guests**, realizing that he is speaking about the heavenly banquet, interjects with a beatitude of his own: **Blessed is the one who will dine** (literally, "eat bread," as in Luke 14:1) **in the kingdom of God**. Earlier, Jesus had similarly declared "blessed" those servants who were vigilant for their master's arrival, promising that they would "recline at table" (12:37). He had also just spoken about those who "will recline at table in the kingdom of God" (13:29).

14:16–17   Jesus again uses the interruption to develop his teaching further (see 11:45; 12:13, 41; 13:1). With another parable, he clarifies his fellow guest's beatitude as he earlier did with the one spoken by the woman in the crowd (11:27–28). The parable of the **great dinner**—referring again to the kingdom banquet—involves a **man** hosting it, a **servant** who is **dispatched** (better, "sent," verb *apostellō*, as in 9:2), those originally **invited** who do not **come**, and two other groups of people who replace them (14:21–23). It is another illustration of God's reversal of the last and the first (13:30).

14:18–20   Those invited **excuse themselves**, beginning with the **first**. They represent those in Israel who are "unwilling" to be gathered by Jesus (13:34), especially leaders like the Pharisee and his guests (see 14:1). As a result, they end up last, not even tasting the dinner (v. 24).

The excuses of those who **purchased a field** and **five yoke of oxen** involve possessions. The third involves a family relationship—the man who **just married a woman**. For similar reasons, the Torah granted an exemption from military service (Deut 20:5–7; 24:5), but that is not the situation here. Moreover, Jesus will presently teach that the radical demands of discipleship in the kingdom involve renouncing "possessions" (Luke 14:33) and even "hating" one's family: "father and mother, *wife* and children" (14:26 [emphasis added]; see comment). The demands are worth it, however. Hence, even if the excuses seem like good ones (see 9:57–62), they pale in comparison to the blessing of dining in God's kingdom (14:15).

14:21   **The servant**—who represents Jesus' disciples sent out on mission—reports the excuses **to his master** (*kyrios*). This **master of the house** (13:25) then twice tells him to find others to come to the banquet. The first group is from **the town** itself, referring to others *from within Israel*: **the poor and the crippled, the blind and the lame**. These are exactly the same categories of people mentioned in Jesus' instructions to the host (14:13), suggesting that Jesus, as the Lord (*kyrios*)

The Great Dinner in Heaven

St. Gregory the Great offers an insightful explanation and application of the parable:

It is now the time for the dinner, and we are being called. As we see that the end of the age has come near [see 1 Cor 10:11], we have all the less reason to excuse ourselves from God's meal. As we reflect that there is no time remaining, we must dread to lose the time of grace at hand. God's meal is not called a lunch but a dinner, because after lunch dinner is still to come, whereas after dinner there is no remaining meal.... Whom does the servant sent by the head of the household ... signify but ... those who preach? ... I am coming to invite you to God's dinner. ... We are invited to God's banquet, and we excuse ourselves.... A supreme Householder is inviting you to a dinner, an eternal banquet, but one person is given to avarice, another to inquisitiveness, another to physical pleasure.... Proud sinners are rejected, so that humble sinners can be chosen.... The poor and the feeble, the blind and the lame, are called, and come, because the weak and the despised in this world are often quicker to hear the voice of God.... Still there is room.... The multitude of Israelites who believed did not fill the space of the heavenly banquet.... Room still remained in the kingdom for the great number of the Gentiles.... You see how he himself calls, how he calls by the angels, by the patriarchs, the prophets, the apostles, by pastors, and even by me; often he calls by miracles, often by calamities; sometimes he calls by prosperity in this world, sometimes by adversity. Let no one treat this lightly: if he has excused himself when he was called, when he wants to come in he may not be able to.... Therefore ... let temporal things be for the journey, and long for the eternal things of your arrival.[a]

a. Gregory the Great, *Homily* 36, in *Forty Gospel Homilies*, trans. David Hurst (Kalamazoo, MI: Cistercian Publications, 1990), 314–23.

and master of the house[14] (as in 13:25–27), is again critiquing the attitude of his host and the other Pharisees.[15] It is precisely those neglected by these Pharisees who end up being invited to the feast. Included among these would also be the tax collectors and sinners with whom Jesus ate (5:29–30; 7:34; 15:1–2; 19:5–7).

With his inclusion of the blind and the lame occurring on his way to Jerusalem, where he is proclaimed king (19:38), Jesus is also presented as a new

14. That the master of the house is angry (**in a rage**) refers to the "wrathful judgment" (Luke 21:23) about which Jesus has repeatedly been warning the people (e.g., 13:35).

15. Whereas the Pharisees here neglect to invite the poor and those with disabilities, the Essenes at Qumran went further in excluding from the community and from the messianic banquet the "paralyzed, ... lame, blind, deaf, dumb," etc.; see 1Q28a (*Rule of the Congregation*) II, 3–22, in *The Dead Sea Scrolls Study Edition*, ed. Florentino García Martínez and Eibert J. C. Tigchelaar, 2 vols. (Leiden: Brill; Grand Rapids: Eerdmans, 2000), 1:103.

David. As earlier he corrected Elijah (9:54–55), he now corrects David, who said, as he went to Jerusalem and became king over Israel, "the lame and the blind shall be the personal enemies of David" (2 Sam 5:8).

14:22–23   **Still there is room**, so the **master** (*kyrios*), addressed as **Sir** (*kyrios*), has a second group brought in, people *from outside* the town—**the highways and hedgerows**. These therefore represent the Gentiles, those outside Israel, who come from all four directions (see Luke 13:29) and will be brought in through the Church's mission (e.g., Acts 11:18).

14:24   The concluding statement blurs the parable with reality since the pronoun **you** is now in the plural, so it is not just the master speaking to his servant, but Jesus warning the guests **invited** (Luke 14:7) to the Pharisee's home that **none** of them will enter the kingdom banquet (13:26–28) and **taste** the **dinner** if they refuse the invitation by rejecting Jesus.

In summary, Jesus' third meal in a Pharisee's home becomes the setting for his extended teaching on the messianic wedding banquet in the kingdom of God. This banquet is not governed by social rules of honor but by the principle of reversal. Jesus has extended his invitation—the verb "invite" or "call" in some form occurs twelve times in verses 7–24—and "everything is now ready" (v. 17). He awaits the response.

Reflection and Application (14:12–14)

Invitation list. "Invite the poor" (14:13). When Mother Teresa was growing up in Albania, her parents by word and example taught her and her siblings this message of welcoming the poor of the community to the family table.[16] Her life gives testimony that she learned the lesson well. How about us? Whom do we invite to dinner?

The Cost of Discipleship (14:25–35)

[25]**Great crowds were traveling with him, and he turned and addressed them,** [26]**"If any one comes to me without hating his father and mother, wife and children, brothers and sisters, and even his own life, he cannot be my disciple.** [27]**Whoever does not carry his own cross and come after me cannot be my disciple.** [28]**Which of you wishing to construct a tower**

16. Kathryn Spink, *Mother Teresa: An Authorized Biography*, rev. ed. (New York: HarperCollins, 2011), 6.

does not first sit down and calculate the cost to see if there is enough for its completion? ²⁹Otherwise, after laying the foundation and finding himself unable to finish the work the onlookers should laugh at him ³⁰and say, 'This one began to build but did not have the resources to finish.' ³¹Or what king marching into battle would not first sit down and decide whether with ten thousand troops he can successfully oppose another king advancing upon him with twenty thousand troops? ³²But if not, while he is still far away, he will send a delegation to ask for peace terms. ³³In the same way, everyone of you who does not renounce all his possessions cannot be my disciple.

³⁴"Salt is good, but if salt itself loses its taste, with what can its flavor be restored? ³⁵It is fit neither for the soil nor for the manure pile; it is thrown out. Whoever has ears to hear ought to hear."

OT: Deut 33:9
NT: Luke 8:8; 9:23; 18:29; John 12:25. // Matt 5:13; 10:37–38; Mark 9:50
Catechism: following Jesus above all else, 1618, 2232, 2544
Lectionary: Luke 14:25–33: Twenty-Third Sunday Ordinary Time (Year C)

Speaking now to the **great crowds** (see 11:29; 12:1) that are **traveling with him**,   14:25–26
Jesus explains the radical commitment required of those who follow him. Three times he sets forth a condition without which a person, he says, **cannot be my disciple** (14:26, 27, 33). First, Jesus demands a commitment greater than one's attachment to family members: parents, **wife**, **children**, and siblings (see 14:20; 18:29–30). Jesus has already led by example in this regard (8:19–21). However, just as there was no incompatibility between Jesus' natural family and the family of his disciples in the early Church (Acts 1:13–14), so too following Jesus does not necessarily lead to a break with one's family. His reference to **hating** one's relatives is a Jewish idiom that uses hyperbole to indicate one's preference (Mal 1:2–3; Rom 9:13). For example, the phrase "Leah was hated" (Gen 29:31 RSV) means that Jacob "loved Rachel more than Leah" (Gen 29:30 RSV). Disciples should thus love Jesus *more than* they love their family, and indeed more than their **own life**. They must of course still love their families—"Honor your father and your mother" (Luke 18:20, citing the Decalogue)—as well as themselves (10:27, citing Lev 19:18).

Second, a **disciple** must **carry his own cross and come after** Jesus. Earlier,   14:27
Jesus had similarly spoken of taking up one's cross and following him (Luke 9:23). Self-sacrifice even to the point of losing one's life for his sake is how one saves it (9:24).

Before mentioning the third condition (14:33), Jesus supports his teaching   14:28–32
with two short parables. Most interpreters apply them to his *disciples*. Because of the commitment involved in following Jesus, potential disciples, according

to both parables, should **first sit down** to deliberate. Following Jesus is not a decision to be made lightly.

In the first parable, about building a **tower**, the issue is **the cost** involved. One must have **enough** financial **resources** to bring the project to **completion**, or else face mockery from **onlookers**. The message of this parable seems to support most closely the third condition of discipleship mentioned in this passage (v. 33), which similarly involves financial resources: deliberation is required before giving up one's possessions to follow Jesus.

In the second parable, about a **king marching into battle** against **another king**, the issue is the number of **troops** needed to win. The stakes are higher than in the first parable since one's life is on the line in the decision whether to fight or to seek **terms** of **peace** (19:42, same Greek phrase as here). The message of this parable especially recalls the first condition of discipleship (14:26), in which Jesus calls his disciples to love him even more than their own lives.

Because of the context of Jesus' journey to Jerusalem, a few scholars interpret these parables as applying in some way to *Jesus*.[17] In Jerusalem, he will be acclaimed king (19:38) and will spend his time in the temple (19:47), which was often symbolized by a tower (see comment on 13:6–9). Although the details of such interpretations are difficult to sort out (e.g., which king in the parable would represent Jesus?), already the reference to the cross in the second condition of discipleship (14:27) suggests some connection to Jesus: it is because of the cross of Jesus that disciples are called to carry their own cross. Interestingly, the verb **laugh at**, or mock, in the first parable is elsewhere used in Luke only to refer to the mockery that Jesus experiences in his passion and on the cross (18:32; 22:63; 23:11, 36).

14:33 Jesus continues with the third condition of discipleship. A **disciple** is ready to **renounce all his possessions**. For example, among the early Christians, there were disciples who freely sold their property and possessions and gave the proceeds to the apostles for distribution among those in need (Acts 2:45; 4:34–37). More generally, Jesus calls all his disciples to be detached from their possessions (see Luke 12:15).

14:34–35 The final saying regarding **salt** that **loses its taste** and is **thrown out** may refer to those who fail to make the radical commitment just described. Such tasteless salt is like the seed that fails to produce fruit (8:7, 14). At the end of that parable (8:8) and at the end of these sayings on discipleship, Jesus gives the same warning: **Whoever has ears to hear ought to hear**.

17. See, e.g., Crispin H. T. Fletcher-Louis, "Jesus Inspects His Priestly War Party (Luke 14:25–35)," in *The Old Testament in the New Testament*, ed. Steve Moyise (Sheffield: Sheffield Academic, 2000), 126–43, from which are also drawn several other ideas in the comment on Luke 14:28–32.

Parables about Repentance and Riches

Luke 15:1–17:10

Jesus teaches mainly through parables in this next unit (15:1–17:10) of the central section (9:51–19:44). He alternately addresses the Pharisees (15:2–3; 16:14–15) and the disciples (16:1; 17:1) in the presence of one another, so that they both may learn what to do and what to avoid. In the three "lost and found" parables of Luke 15, he explains his outreach to sinners and reveals the Father's mercy. Afterward, he gives instruction on the relationship between God and mammon.

The Lost Sheep and the Lost Coin (15:1–10)

¹The tax collectors and sinners were all drawing near to listen to him, ²but the Pharisees and scribes began to complain, saying, "This man welcomes sinners and eats with them." ³So to them he addressed this parable. ⁴"What man among you having a hundred sheep and losing one of them would not leave the ninety-nine in the desert and go after the lost one until he finds it? ⁵And when he does find it, he sets it on his shoulders with great joy ⁶and, upon his arrival home, he calls together his friends and neighbors and says to them, 'Rejoice with me because I have found my lost sheep.' ⁷I tell you, in just the same way there will be more joy in heaven over one sinner who repents than over ninety-nine righteous people who have no need of repentance.

⁸"Or what woman having ten coins and losing one would not light a lamp and sweep the house, searching carefully until she finds it? ⁹And when she does find it, she calls together her friends and neighbors and

says to them, 'Rejoice with me because I have found the coin that I lost.' ¹⁰In just the same way, I tell you, there will be rejoicing among the angels of God over one sinner who repents."

OT: Isa 40:11; Ezek 18:23; 34:4, 11–12, 16
NT: Luke 5:29–32; 7:34; 19:1–10. // Matt 18:12–14
Catechism: Jesus eats with sinners and reveals God's mercy, 545, 589, 1443, 1846; the sacrament of penance, 1465
Lectionary: Luke 15:1–32: Twenty-Fourth Sunday Ordinary Time (Year C); Luke 15:3–7: Sacred Heart

15:1–2   Among those with "ears to hear" (14:35) are **the tax collectors and sinners**, who come **to listen** to (or "hear") Jesus (see 5:1; 6:47; 9:35; 10:39). Ever since Levi's banquet (5:29), Jesus has a reputation as "a friend of tax collectors and sinners" (7:34). He calls them to repentance (5:32), and many who come are undoubtedly moved to repent (see 15:7, 10, 18, 21). They are the "sick" who "need a physician" (5:31). They are among the "poor," "crippled," "blind," and "lame" who should be invited to a banquet (14:13, 21), which Jesus effectively does as he **eats with them**.

However, as before (5:30), **the Pharisees and scribes** object to such table fellowship with those regarded as **sinners**. As members of "this generation" (7:31; 11:29–32), they **complain** or grumble (see 5:30; 19:7), just like Israel's wilderness generation who grumbled against God and Moses (Exod 15:24; 16:7).

15:3–6   Jesus defends his outreach to sinners with a **parable**—probably referring to all three "lost and found" parables in Luke 15. The **lost sheep**, the lost coin, and the lost son correspond to the tax collectors and sinners. The **man** with the **sheep**, the woman with the coins, and the father with the two sons are used to describe how God reaches out to such sinners through Jesus' ministry. Besides the image of finding something or someone lost (15:4, 8, 24, 32), what unites the three parables is the resulting joy (15:5–7, 9–10, 22–24, 32).

In the Old Testament, God is frequently represented as a shepherd of his people (Gen 48:15; 49:24; Ps 23; Jer 23:3). A shepherd who searches for **the lost** sheep more specifically echoes the book of Ezekiel, where God denounces Israel's leaders for failing in this regard—"You did not bring back the stray or seek *the lost*" (Ezek 34:4 [emphasis added])—and so promises to do it himself—"*The lost* I will search out" (Ezek 34:16 [emphasis added]). Moreover, he will set up a good shepherd for them, the Messiah: "I will appoint one shepherd over them to pasture them, my servant David" (Ezek 34:23). By his outreach to tax collectors (like Zacchaeus, Luke 19:1–10), Jesus is fulfilling this plan, "for the Son of Man came to seek and to save *the lost*" (19:10 NIV [emphasis added]).

The shepherd is determined to **find** the lost sheep. To him, it is not inconsequential compared to **the ninety-nine**.[1] It is not just one of an anonymous herd. For him, every sheep counts! On finding it, he carries it **on his shoulders**, an image suggesting Israel's return from exile (see Isa 40:11; 49:22). Indeed, by bringing back sinners, Jesus is accomplishing Israel's true restoration. The resulting **joy** outweighs the time and effort involved. It is a contagious joy that must be shared with **friends and neighbors: Rejoice with me!**

Jesus applies the parable's lesson to his ministry to tax collectors. A sheep **15:7** cannot itself express repentance, so he explains that it represents the **sinner who repents**.[2] In this context, the **ninety-nine righteous people** may correspond ironically to those like the Pharisees (15:2) who *think* they **have no need of repentance** (see 18:9).

The celebration represents the **joy in heaven** of "the angels of God" (15:10) and of God himself: "Have I any pleasure in the death of the wicked, says the Lord GOD, and not rather that he should turn from his way and live?" (Ezek 18:23 RSV).

Like the two earlier parables of the kingdom of God (Luke 13:18–21), the **15:8–9** first parable here involved a man and now the second involves a **woman**. These parables also include male (15:6) and female (v. 9) **friends and neighbors**. The woman's **coins** are Greek silver drachmas, each worth approximately the same value as the Roman denarius (7:41; 10:35; 20:24)—in other words, a day's wage, something worth looking for! Her various actions again express the determination and diligence of the one **searching**, suggesting how God relentlessly seeks out the sinner. The joy when the lost **coin** is **found** is likewise to be shared: **Rejoice with me!**

As in verse 7, Jesus applies the parable to explain his outreach in calling **15:10** sinners to repentance (5:32). The lost and found coin represents a **sinner who repents**. Again, there is also an emphasis on the **rejoicing** that takes place in heaven.

The Compassionate Father and His Two Sons (15:11–32)

> [11]Then he said, "A man had two sons, [12]and the younger son said to his father, 'Father, give me the share of your estate that should come to me.'

---

1. Parables focus on the essentials, so it is pointless to wonder about things not indicated, such as who is taking care of the ninety-nine.

2. The verb "repent" (*metanoeō*) is emphasized in the central section (Luke 10:13; 11:32; 13:3, 5; 15:7, 10; 16:30; 17:3–4).

So the father divided the property between them. ¹³After a few days, the younger son collected all his belongings and set off to a distant country where he squandered his inheritance on a life of dissipation. ¹⁴When he had freely spent everything, a severe famine struck that country, and he found himself in dire need. ¹⁵So he hired himself out to one of the local citizens who sent him to his farm to tend the swine. ¹⁶And he longed to eat his fill of the pods on which the swine fed, but nobody gave him any. ¹⁷Coming to his senses he thought, 'How many of my father's hired workers have more than enough food to eat, but here am I, dying from hunger. ¹⁸I shall get up and go to my father and I shall say to him, "Father, I have sinned against heaven and against you. ¹⁹I no longer deserve to be called your son; treat me as you would treat one of your hired workers."' ²⁰So he got up and went back to his father. While he was still a long way off, his father caught sight of him, and was filled with compassion. He ran to his son, embraced him and kissed him. ²¹His son said to him, 'Father, I have sinned against heaven and against you; I no longer deserve to be called your son.' ²²But his father ordered his servants, 'Quickly bring the finest robe and put it on him; put a ring on his finger and sandals on his feet. ²³Take the fattened calf and slaughter it. Then let us celebrate with a feast, ²⁴because this son of mine was dead, and has come to life again; he was lost, and has been found.' Then the celebration began. ²⁵Now the older son had been out in the field and, on his way back, as he neared the house, he heard the sound of music and dancing. ²⁶He called one of the servants and asked what this might mean. ²⁷The servant said to him, 'Your brother has returned and your father has slaughtered the fattened calf because he has him back safe and sound.' ²⁸He became angry, and when he refused to enter the house, his father came out and pleaded with him. ²⁹He said to his father in reply, 'Look, all these years I served you and not once did I disobey your orders; yet you never gave me even a young goat to feast on with my friends. ³⁰But when your son returns who swallowed up your property with prostitutes, for him you slaughter the fattened calf.' ³¹He said to him, 'My son, you are here with me always; everything I have is yours. ³²But now we must celebrate and rejoice, because your brother was dead and has come to life again; he was lost and has been found.'"

OT: Gen 33:4; 41:42; 46:29–30; Lev 11:7; Deut 14:8; 21:17; Jer 31:18–20
NT: Matt 21:28–32; Luke 6:36
Catechism: conversion and repentance, 1439, 2795; praying like the prodigal son, 2839; the Father's mercy, 1700; the sacrament of penance, 1423, 1465, 1468
Lectionary: Luke 15:1–32: Twenty-Fourth Sunday Ordinary Time (Year C); Luke 15:1–3, 11–32: Fourth Sunday Lent (Year C); Saturday Second Week of Lent

Two Peoples

LIVING
TRADITION

St. Augustine is one of many Church Fathers who interpret the two sons in terms of Israel and the nations: "The man who has two sons is God who has two peoples; the elder son is the people of the Jews, the younger the people of the Gentiles."[a] He reflects on the parable with the help of Paul: "A hardening has come upon Israel in part, until the full number of the Gentiles comes in, and thus all Israel will be saved" (Rom 11:25–26):

> When the fullness of the Gentiles has entered, therefore, his father will go out at the right time so that all of Israel may also be saved. Its blindness was partly caused as though in the case of him who was absent in the field, until the fullness of the younger son, who was living far away in the idolatry of the Gentiles, returned and entered to eat the calf. For the calling of the Jews to the salvation of the Gospel will eventually be manifest. He calls the disclosure of their calling the father's going out to plead with the elder son.[b]

a. Augustine, *Sermon* 112A.2, in *Sermons*, trans. Edmund Hill, 11 vols., WSA III/4 (Hyde Park, NY: New City Press, 1990–97), 4:154.

b. Augustine, *Questions on the Gospels* 2.33.5, in *New Testament I and II*, trans. Roland Teske, WSA I/15–I/16 (Hyde Park, NY: New City Press, 2014), 396.

Like the two previous parables, the familiar story of the "prodigal son" highlights the joy in heaven that results from even one sinner who repents. It thus justifies Jesus' outreach and table fellowship with tax collectors (15:1–2). However, through the accompanying account of the older son, the parable also invites the Pharisees and scribes (15:2) to overcome their grumbling and join in the celebration. Moreover, through the figure of the compassionate father, the parable reveals the merciful Father (see 6:36) who desires all his children to come to the heavenly banquet.

Whereas the parable's immediate context involves Pharisees and tax collectors, the broader context of Luke-Acts suggests another similar scenario that arose in the early Church when certain Jewish disciples objected to Peter's table fellowship with Gentiles (Acts 11:2–3, 18). Applying the parable to this situation, one arrives at the frequent interpretation found among the Church Fathers, where the older son represents Israel (see Exod 4:22) and the younger son—living in a distant country, not observing the law, and tending swine—represents the Gentiles.

The **man had two sons**, and the parable in two parts deals with each individually (Luke 15:12–24, 25–32). In each part, there is a dialogue between one					**15:11** son and the father. The structure thus suggests a comparison between the two sons, but also puts the emphasis on the father, who has the last word.

15:12 An inheritance was typically distributed after death (Num 27:8–11), but it was possible, though not advised, to do so while a person was still alive (Sir 33:20–24). However, **the younger son** takes the initiative here with his demand: **give me** my **share**. For him, the **father** might as well be dead. Under no obligation and despite the shame incurred, the father nonetheless complies out of respect for the younger son's free decision. Since the firstborn son would receive a double portion (Deut 21:17), the younger son apparently received a third of **the property**. The remaining two-thirds is destined for the older son, so the father does not exaggerate when he later says, "Everything I have is yours" (Luke 15:31).

15:13–16 **The younger son** leaves for **a distant country**. There, he **squandered his inheritance**, spending it **on a life of dissipation**—"with prostitutes" (v. 30), the older son will speculate. In order to survive when a **famine** strikes, he finds a job tending **swine**, an unclean animal for Jews (see 8:32–34; Lev 11:7; Deut 14:8). He is living like a Gentile: "far off" and "alienated from the community of Israel . . . without hope and without God in the world" (Eph 2:12–13).

15:17–19 Though he considered his father to be dead to him, now he realizes that he is the one **dying** or perishing. This is the same verb used six other times in the chapter with the meaning "lose" or "be lost" (Luke 15:4, 6, 8–9, 24, 32). Therefore, just as the sheep and coin were lost, the son is lost. The difference is that, **coming to his senses**, he is *aware* that he is lost. Thus, whereas the first two parables need Jesus' explanation about the repentant sinner (15:7, 10), here the son in the parable can express repentance himself: **Father, I have sinned against heaven and against you**. This confession is rehearsed and then repeated (v. 21), giving it emphasis. It echoes confessions in the Old Testament that understand sins against individuals to be offenses ultimately against God (Exod 10:16; Ps 51:6). Though he feels unworthy to be called **son**, he nonetheless still plans to address his confession to his **father**. He remembers his father's benevolence: even the **hired workers have more than enough food** (literally, "bread"). He resolves to **get up** (verb *anistēmi*) **and go** back. The verb "get up" (repeated in Luke 15:20) is one of the verbs used for Jesus' resurrection (18:33; 24:7, 46). Thus, by his repentance, the "dead" son is already coming "to life again" (15:24, 32).

15:20 God's persistent search for the sinner, emphasized in the parables of the lost sheep and the lost coin, is complemented now by his patient waiting: the **father**, on the lookout, **caught sight of** his son from a distance. The father is **filled with**

Figure 13. *Return of the Prodigal Son* by Bartolomé Esteban Murillo.

compassion, like Jesus at Nain (7:13) and the good Samaritan (10:33). He thus **ran to his son**, unconcerned that running was considered beneath the dignity of an old man (Sir 19:30). He then **embraced him and kissed him**. The father's compassion, demonstrated by his actions, teaches how the heavenly "Father is merciful" (Luke 6:36).

　　The **father** interrupts his son's rehearsed confession. With his orders to the **15:21–24** **servants** regarding **robe**, **ring**, **sandals**, and **fattened calf**, he **quickly** restores the **son** to his position in the family. He recognizes that indeed the son **was lost**. However, now that he **has been found**, there is reason to **celebrate**, as the shepherd and the woman did. The son's transformation—he **was dead** but now **has come to life again**—is what Paul describes in Ephesians: "You were dead in your transgressions and sins. . . . But God, who is rich in mercy, because of the great love he had for us, even when we were dead in our transgressions, brought us to life with Christ" (Eph 2:1, 4–5). The first part of the parable ends with the beginning of **the celebration**.

Old Testament Fathers and Sons

BIBLICAL BACKGROUND

The scene of reconciliation between the father and the younger son echoes several Old Testament narratives. For example, when Isaac's younger son, Jacob, returns from a distant country (Paddan-aram), he meets his estranged older brother, Esau. "Esau ran to meet him, and embraced him, and fell on his neck and kissed him" (Gen 33:4 NRSV), details similar to the younger son's return, where the father "ran, and fell on his neck, and kissed him" (15:20 KJV).[a]

The reunion between Jacob/Israel and his son Joseph is described similarly: "Joseph . . . went up to meet his father Israel in Goshen. He presented himself to him, fell on his neck . . ." (Gen 46:29 NRSV). The story of Joseph and his estranged brothers also has parallels in the parable. Like the younger son, Joseph goes to a distant country (Egypt) but ends up receiving a "robe" and "ring" (Luke 15:22; Gen 41:42 LXX). A "famine" (Luke 15:14; Gen 41:54; 42:5) occurs, which leads to the reconciliation of the brothers and the reunion of father and son.

Moreover, a passage from Jeremiah has some similarities to the parable. Ephraim, the son of Joseph (Gen 48:20), becomes the name of the northern kingdom (Isa 7:9) that "seceded from Judah" (Isa 7:17). As a result of the Assyrian exile, Ephraim like the younger son went off to a distant country, from which he prays: "Bring me back, let me come back, / for you are the LORD, my God. / For after I turned away, I repented" (Jer 31:18–19). God responds: "Is Ephraim not my favored son, / the child in whom I delight? . . . / My heart stirs for him, / I must show him compassion!" (Jer 31:20). These Old Testament passages shed further light on the parable's message of reconciliation and God's mercy.

a. See also Tob 11:9, where Tobiah's mother, Anna, acts similarly, after watching for her son's return (Tob 10:7), like the father in the parable.

15:25–28   In the second part, the attention shifts to the **older son**. Apprised by a **servant** about the celebration involving his **brother** and **father**, he becomes **angry** (like the Pharisees who complain, Luke 15:2). The **father came out** to him, as he had done with the younger son.

15:29–30   Whereas the younger son felt he did not "deserve to be called" a "son" (v. 19), the older son ironically speaks to his **father** as if he were not a son but merely a servant: **all these years I served you** or "slaved for you." He never calls him "Father" as the younger son does (vv. 12, 18, 21). Moreover, he does not recognize the younger son as his brother, referring to him instead as his father's

son. He expresses bitterness about how he has been treated in comparison to the younger son. His claim—**not once did I disobey your orders**—may just be false boasting, but some regard it as an allusion to Deuteronomy, where faithful Israel says: "I have not transgressed any of your commandments" (Deut 26:13). Blessings are the promised reward for such fidelity (Deut 26:15–19), but it seems to the older brother that the sinful younger son has received all the blessings. He complains about not receiving **even a young goat**, thus forgetting or ignoring the father's generosity (Luke 15:31). In a sense, he too is lost.

Addressing him as his **son** (or "child"; see 16:25), the father tries to reassure   **15:31–32** him, pointing out that their lives are united: **you are here with me always,** perhaps echoing the psalmist's statement to God: "I am always with you" (Ps 73:23).[3] Hence, "to be near God is my good" (Ps 73:28).

The father also tries to persuade him that the return of the younger son **must** be celebrated. The verb is again *dei* (Luke 2:49; 13:16), indicating in Luke a divine necessity. It is necessary for the father to act in this way because the "Father is merciful" (6:36). This divine logic of grace rises above the jealous comparisons of the older son, inviting reconciliation: **your brother** who **was dead** now **has come to life again.** Like the sheep and the coin, the **lost** son (15:4, 8) **has been found,** so there is cause to **rejoice** (15:5–6, 9)! The father thus wants both sons to come to the feast! The invitation is extended, but the parable's open ending—with no mention of the celebration as in verse 24—gives no indication whether or not the older son was won over by the father's pleading. That decision is left to the Pharisees and scribes—and to the reader.

Reflection and Application (15:11–32)

Children of God. "You are no longer a slave but a child, and if a child then also an heir, through God" (Gal 4:7). Frequent consideration of our Christian dignity as children of God (John 1:12; Rom 8:16; 1 John 3:1–2) can help us carry out our responsibilities with love and joy, not like the embittered older son who considered himself a mere slave and thus viewed others with self-righteous contempt.

Sacrament of reconciliation. "The confession of sins . . . is the act of the prodigal son who returns to his Father and is welcomed by him with the kiss of peace.

---

3. György Geréby, "The Two Sons of the One Father: The Salvation-Historical Interpretation of Luke 15:11–32," in *Religious Apologetics—Philosophical Argumentation*, ed. Yossef Schwartz and Volkhard Krech (Tübingen: Mohr Siebeck, 2004), 356–59.

It is an act of honesty and courage. It is an act of entrusting oneself, beyond sin, to the mercy that forgives."[4]

The Dishonest Steward: Parable and Application (16:1–13)

[1]Then he also said to his disciples, "A rich man had a steward who was reported to him for squandering his property. [2]He summoned him and said, 'What is this I hear about you? Prepare a full account of your stewardship, because you can no longer be my steward.' [3]The steward said to himself, 'What shall I do, now that my master is taking the position of steward away from me? I am not strong enough to dig and I am ashamed to beg. [4]I know what I shall do so that, when I am removed from the stewardship, they may welcome me into their homes.' [5]He called in his master's debtors one by one. To the first he said, 'How much do you owe my master?' [6]He replied, 'One hundred measures of olive oil.' He said to him, 'Here is your promissory note. Sit down and quickly write one for fifty.' [7]Then to another he said, 'And you, how much do you owe?' He replied, 'One hundred kors of wheat.' He said to him, 'Here is your promissory note; write one for eighty.' [8]And the master commended that dishonest steward for acting prudently.

"For the children of this world are more prudent in dealing with their own generation than are the children of light. [9]I tell you, make friends for yourselves with dishonest wealth, so that when it fails, you will be welcomed into eternal dwellings. [10]The person who is trustworthy in very small matters is also trustworthy in great ones; and the person who is dishonest in very small matters is also dishonest in great ones. [11]If, therefore, you are not trustworthy with dishonest wealth, who will trust you with true wealth? [12]If you are not trustworthy with what belongs to another, who will give you what is yours? [13]No servant can serve two masters. He will either hate one and love the other, or be devoted to one and despise the other. You cannot serve God and mammon."

OT: Ezra 7:22; Sir 5:8; 40:28
NT: Luke 12:33, 42; 19:17; 20:34; 1 Thess 5:5; Eph 5:8. // Matt 6:24
Catechism: steward of the Lord's goods, 952, 2402; God and mammon, 2113, 2424
Lectionary: Twenty-Fifth Sunday Ordinary Time (Year C)

4. John Paul II, *Reconciliatio et Paenitentia* (On Reconciliation and Penance in the Mission of the Church Today) 31.

After addressing the "lost and found" parables to the Pharisees to justify his   **16:1–2**
outreach to sinners, Jesus now **also** speaks to **his disciples**. However, the Pharisees are still close by (16:14). With the parables of the dishonest steward (16:1–8)
and the rich man and Lazarus (16:19–31), the focus of Jesus' instruction in the
remainder of the unit is the proper use of wealth.

When Jesus last addressed the disciples (12:22, 41), he spoke about the "faithful" (*pistos*) and "prudent" (*phronimos*) steward (12:42). In effect, he continues
that teaching here with a parable about a **steward** who, though dishonest, acts
"prudently," a point that Jesus highlights by referring to those who are "more
prudent" (16:8). Moreover, in contrast to the steward's dishonesty, Jesus emphasizes the importance of being "trustworthy" (*pistos*, four times in vv. 10–12;
"faithful," NRSV).

The parable has given rise to a wide range of interpretations. The steward
who was accused of **squandering his** master's **property** recalls the prodigal
son who "squandered his inheritance" (15:13). However, whereas the younger
son was considered "lost" and "dead" (15:24, 32), the steward ends up being
"commended" (16:8). This surprising conclusion leads some to argue that he
must have been falsely accused. After all, his master is **rich**, typically not an
attractive characteristic in Luke (6:24; 12:16; 16:19; but see 19:2–10). However,
even assuming that the rich master deserves to hear "woe to you" (6:24), nothing
in the text suggests that what has been **reported** about the steward is untrue.
When told to give an **account** since he is about to lose his **stewardship**, he does
not defend himself against the charges. Though commended at the end of the
parable, he is also called "dishonest" (16:8).

Moreover, **the steward** is not an attractive character either. Unlike the prodi-   **16:3–4**
gal son (15:18), he expresses no repentance when he is talking to **himself**. Rather,
he resembles the rich fool, asking, **What shall I do?** (12:17), and developing a
self-centered plan. He is unable to work hard and too proud **to beg**.

A common interpretation of his plan to reduce the amount owed by **his**   **16:5–7**
master's debtors[5] is that he was simply eliminating his own commission or
the interest on the debt. Charging interest was widely practiced (19:23), even
if the law prohibited it (Lev 25:37; Deut 23:20). However, there is again nothing in the text supporting such a view. Just the opposite. The 100 percent and
25 percent implied interest rates seem random, neither corresponding to the
contemporary 50 percent interest rate on commodities.[6] And everything is

---

5. The two debts mentioned (see Ezra 7:22) are quite large. Estimates for the liquid **measures** (*baths*)
typically range from 6 to 10 gallons each, and 6.5 to 12 bushels each for the **kors**.
6. John S. Kloppenborg, "The Dishonoured Master (Luke 16:1–8a)," *Biblica* 70 (1989): 483.

done **quickly**, suggesting that the steward is simply cheating his master to gain favor with the debtors.[7] Moreover, this view is motivated by the desire to say that the steward's latest behavior is not dishonest but law-abiding, which shifts attention away from the relevant point of the parable.

16:8–9   The **steward** is indeed **dishonest**, but he is **commended** for **acting prudently**. This is like Jesus' command to "be shrewd as serpents and simple as doves" (Matt 10:16). A disciple should imitate how a serpent is "shrewd" (*phronimos*, same word as "prudent" here), but not the serpent's other qualities! The parable involves an argument from lesser to greater, where the lesser part involves someone who exhibits less than upright behavior (as in Luke 11:13; 18:6–7). If the dishonest steward of the **master** (*kyrios*), when asked to give an account (16:2), is prudent enough to plan his earthly future so as to receive a welcome in people's homes (v. 4), how much more ought "the faithful and prudent steward" of "the Lord" (*kyrios*, 12:42), who will have to give an account to God (Rom 14:12; Heb 4:13), prudently plan for a heavenly future so as to **be welcomed into eternal dwellings?**[8] Unfortunately, Jesus points out, **the children of this world** (or "age," Luke 20:34) **are more prudent** in practice **than are the children of light**. The parable thus instructs disciples to take initiative and plan wisely so as to enter God's kingdom. Specifically, it is concerned with the proper use of **wealth** ("mammon," as in 16:13),[9] which eventually **fails** (*ekleipō*) when one dies and therefore no longer retains the stewardship of one's goods. The lesson is thus similar to Jesus' earlier teaching about giving alms so as to be rich in God's eyes (12:21) and store up "unfailing" (*anekleiptos*) treasure in heaven (12:33 NRSV). A disciple who is a prudent steward will paradoxically give away wealth and remit debts, *seemingly* doing what the dishonest steward did but in reality enacting Jesus' jubilee program (4:18–19; 7:41–42).

16:10–13   The emphasis now shifts from being prudent to being "faithful" (12:42) (i.e., **trustworthy**, *pistos*)—thus *unlike* the **dishonest** steward—beginning **in small matters** and then **in great ones** (see 19:17). These verses explain how God expects disciples to use **wealth** ("mammon") so as to receive a **true** reward in heaven. The parallelism between verse 11 and verse 12 (**if you are not trustworthy with . . .**) suggests that one's wealth really **belongs to another**—namely,

---

7. Klyne R. Snodgrass, *Stories with Intent: A Comprehensive Guide to the Parables of Jesus* (Grand Rapids: Eerdmans, 2008), 410–11.

8. "Dwellings" is literally "tents," an image for heaven that recalls the "dwellings" or "tents" (see Luke 9:33) of God's people after the exodus (Lev 23:43), with God dwelling among them in the tent of meeting.

9. The phrase "**dishonest** wealth" (literally, "mammon of injustice") refers not only to wealth acquired unjustly but in general to "worldly wealth" (NIV), which is a trap for those who depend on it (see 1 Tim 6:9–10). See Gary A. Anderson, *Charity: The Place of the Poor in the Biblical Tradition* (New Haven: Yale University Press, 2013), 53, 59.

God. By treating it as one's own, one ends up trusting in it rather than in God. There is a wordplay here, since the word **mammon** likely derives from a Hebrew word meaning that in which one trusts.[10] However, one cannot **serve two masters**. Those who trust in wealth are in effect serving mammon as if it were a god. Faithful disciples will instead **serve** as good stewards of all that **God** has entrusted to them, generously sharing what they have with others.

Reflection and Application (16:2)

Give an account of your stewardship. This phrase has often been used to point us toward the need to be prepared for God's judgment, since we do not know how long our life will last. Meditating on our death can spur us to action, wasting no time to set things right with God and with others.

The Rich Man and Lazarus: Prelude and Parable (16:14–31)

[14]The Pharisees, who loved money, heard all these things and sneered at him. [15]And he said to them, "You justify yourselves in the sight of others, but God knows your hearts; for what is of human esteem is an abomination in the sight of God.

[16]"The law and the prophets lasted until John; but from then on the kingdom of God is proclaimed, and everyone who enters does so with violence. [17]It is easier for heaven and earth to pass away than for the smallest part of a letter of the law to become invalid.

[18]"Everyone who divorces his wife and marries another commits adultery, and the one who marries a woman divorced from her husband commits adultery.

[19]"There was a rich man who dressed in purple garments and fine linen and dined sumptuously each day. [20]And lying at his door was a poor man named Lazarus, covered with sores, [21]who would gladly have eaten his fill of the scraps that fell from the rich man's table. Dogs even used to come and lick his sores. [22]When the poor man died, he was carried away by angels to the bosom of Abraham. The rich man also died and was buried, [23]and from the netherworld, where he was in torment, he raised his eyes and saw Abraham far off and Lazarus at his side. [24]And he cried out, 'Father Abraham, have pity on me. Send Lazarus to dip the tip of his finger

10. Joseph A. Fitzmyer, *The Gospel according to Luke*, 2 vols., AB (New York: Doubleday, 1981–85), 2:1109.

in water and cool my tongue, for I am suffering torment in these flames.' [25]Abraham replied, 'My child, remember that you received what was good during your lifetime while Lazarus likewise received what was bad; but now he is comforted here, whereas you are tormented. [26]Moreover, between us and you a great chasm is established to prevent anyone from crossing who might wish to go from our side to yours or from your side to ours.' [27]He said, 'Then I beg you, father, send him to my father's house, [28]for I have five brothers, so that he may warn them, lest they too come to this place of torment.' [29]But Abraham replied, 'They have Moses and the prophets. Let them listen to them.' [30]He said, 'Oh no, father Abraham, but if someone from the dead goes to them, they will repent.' [31]Then Abraham said, 'If they will not listen to Moses and the prophets, neither will they be persuaded if someone should rise from the dead.'"

OT: Deut 15:7–11; 24:1–4; Prov 21:2; 31:22; Isa 58:7

NT: John 11:1–44; 12:1, 9; 1 Cor 7:10–11. // Matt 5:18, 32; 11:12–13; 19:9; Mark 10:11–12

Catechism: John the Baptist, 523; divorce, 2382; mortal sin, 1859; angels, 336; the particular judgment, 1021; the netherworld, 633; give bread to the hungry, 2463, 2831

Lectionary: Luke 16:19–31: Twenty-Sixth Sunday Ordinary Time (Year C); Thursday Second Week of Lent

16:14   **The Pharisees**, who are still listening close by (see 15:2), **sneered at** or ridiculed **him**, as the Jewish rulers will do at his crucifixion (23:35). They **loved money**,[11] so they may feel that Jesus meant the parable for them (see 20:19). Earlier, he had reproved them for their avarice and encouraged them to give alms (11:39–41).

16:15   In response, Jesus addresses diverse sayings to the Pharisees (16:15–18) and then the parable of the rich man and Lazarus (vv. 19–31). The connecting thread of these seemingly random sayings may be the background involving Herod Antipas (see comment on v. 16). Another proposal is that Luke here arranges Jesus' teaching by using Deuteronomy as a model (see the sidebar, "Old Testament Background of Luke's Central Section," p. 285).

First, Jesus points out the hypocritical disparity (12:1) between the Pharisees' appearance and the reality. Whereas they **justify** *themselves* (see 5:32; 15:7; 18:9), the tax collectors about whom they complain "justified *God*" (7:29 RSV [emphasis added]) by accepting John's baptism. Such tax collectors will be the ones justified (18:14). As lovers of money, the Pharisees have placed their

---

11. Josephus associates the Sadducees with the wealthy and instead describes the Pharisees as living a simpler life and being popular with the people (*Jewish Antiquities* 13.298; 18.12). Nonetheless, the Pharisees likely interpreted wealth to be a blessing for observing the law (see Deut 28:12). Moreover, the Pharisees' reputation for piety and strict observance could be different from the reality (*Jewish War* 1.110–12; *Jewish Antiquities* 17.41).

Old Testament Background of Luke's Central Section

BIBLICAL BACKGROUND

In this central section (9:51–19:44), Luke may at times arrange Jesus' teaching by using Deuteronomy as a model.[a] In several cases, there seems to be a correspondence between material in Deuteronomy and Jesus' teaching on similar subjects. One example is the sequence that includes the parables of the warring king (Luke 14:31–32; Deut 20:1, 10), the lost sheep (Luke 15:4–6; Deut 22:1), and the prodigal son (Luke 15:11–32; Deut 21:16, 18). Another example is the sequence of the parable of the dishonest steward followed by diverse sayings about greed, things that are an abomination, and divorce (Luke 16:1–18). This order is similar to a block of passages in Deuteronomy dealing with slaves who take refuge from their masters, things that are an abomination, usury, and divorce (Deut 23:16–17, 19–21; 24:1–4). Such correspondences may shed light on Jesus' teaching. For example, the injunction to mercy in the parable of the good Samaritan (Luke 10:37) contrasts with Deuteronomy's legislation about unmerciful treatment of foreigners (Deut 7:2, 16). Both teachings follow a discussion about loving God (Luke 10:27, quoting Deut 6:5). Underlying such correspondences is the presentation of Jesus as a new Moses (Luke 9:30–35; Deut 18:15), who gives Moses' teaching its proper interpretation or brings it to fulfillment.

a. See Craig A. Evans, "Luke 16:1–18 and the Deuteronomy Hypothesis," in *Luke and Scripture: The Function of Sacred Tradition in Luke-Acts*, by Craig A. Evans and James A. Sanders (Minneapolis: Fortress, 1993), 121–39.

treasure and hence their heart (12:34) in the wrong place, and **God knows** their **hearts**. They may be held in **esteem** (literally, "high") among people, but they will be brought low in the reversal being worked by God (1:52; 14:11; 18:14). Jesus also describes them with the strong word **abomination**, probably because their love of money leads them to act dishonestly like the steward in the parable: "Everyone who does what is dishonest . . . is an abomination to the LORD, your God" (Deut 25:16). Moreover, the word "abomination" is typically used to refer to the worship of false gods (Deut 7:25; 32:16). The implication is that their love of money is tantamount to idolatry. They are not serving God but mammon (Luke 16:13).

Perhaps because the Pharisees have a reputation for observing the law strictly, **16:16** Jesus continues his response by explaining the role of the law in God's plan: **the law and the prophets lasted until John, but from then on the kingdom of God is proclaimed** (verb *euangelizō*). As he had done earlier (7:28), Jesus indicates that John the Baptist is a bridge figure: "He represents the old, and heralds the new."[12] As a "prophet" (7:26), John belongs to the Old Testament era, but as one who "preached good news" (verb *euangelizō*, 3:18) about the coming Messiah, he also belongs to the new era of the kingdom. Regarding this kingdom, **everyone** is now "urged to enter it" (NET)[13]—compelled, as it were (see 14:23)—not just the righteous but also "the poor, the crippled, the lame, the blind" and "the tax collectors and sinners" too (14:13, 21; 15:1)!

By mentioning John, Jesus may also be alluding to the Pharisees' opposition to the Baptist (7:30). John had been beheaded by Herod Antipas (9:9), with whom some Pharisees were in contact (13:31; see Mark 3:6; 8:15; 12:13). This historical background may explain the sequence of apparently unrelated ideas in these verses, as well as the following parable. The Pharisees' association with Herod may have compromised their fidelity to the law (Luke 16:17). They rejected John, who had rightly criticized Herod regarding the adultery (v. 18) involved in his incestuous marriage to Herodias (3:19; Lev 18:16).[14]

16:17 The result is rather ironic. Despite their claims, the Pharisees are not upholding the law, but Jesus, considered a lawbreaker by the Pharisees, asserts that the **law** cannot **become invalid**. In the new era of the kingdom, the law and the prophets find their authoritative interpretation in Jesus (Luke 24:27).

16:18 As an example of his authoritative interpretation of the law, Jesus refers to marriage with a **divorced** person as **adultery**. In contrast, the Pharisees like other Jews permitted divorce and remarriage (see Deut 24:1–4).[15] Elsewhere, Jesus explains that this was a temporary concession due to their hardness of heart and reaffirms God's original plan regarding the indissolubility of marriage (Matt 19:3–9; Mark 10:2–12; see Gen 2:24).[16] Paul echoes Jesus' teaching on divorce and remarriage: "To the married . . . I give this instruction (not I, *but the Lord*): A wife should not separate from her husband—and if she does separate she must either remain single or become reconciled to

12. Augustine, *Sermon* 293.2, in *Sermons*, trans. Edmund Hill, 11 vols., WSA III/8 (Hyde Park, NY: New City Press, 1990–97), 8:149.
13. The NABRE translates the verb *biazomai* with an active meaning: everyone **who enters does so with violence**. However, the preceding passive verb ("is proclaimed"), Luke's use of a different but related verb for the active meaning (Luke 24:29; Acts 16:15), and the verb's usage elsewhere suggest a passive rendering (NET). See James R. Edwards, *The Gospel according to Luke*, PNTC (Grand Rapids: Eerdmans, 2015), 463–64; Fitzmyer, *Luke*, 2:1117–18. The parallel verse has another passive meaning: "The kingdom of heaven suffers violence" (Matt 11:12).
14. See Simon Perry, *Resurrecting Interpretation: Technology, Hermeneutics, and the Parable of the Rich Man and Lazarus* (Eugene, OR: Wipf and Stock, 2012), 161–71.
15. Josephus, *Jewish Antiquities* 4.253. Later, the †Mishnah describes a debate about grounds for divorce; see *m. Gittin* 9:10.
16. See Catechism 1644–51.

her husband—and a husband should not divorce his wife" (1 Cor 7:10–11 [emphasis added]).

With this introduction, Jesus addresses a parable to the Pharisees about **a rich** **16:19** **man**. The parable begins the same way as that of the dishonest steward (Luke 16:1), but this rich man is further described as a royal figure: he was **dressed in purple garments** (see Judg 8:26; Dan 5:29) **and fine linen** (Gen 41:42). Moreover, he **dined** or celebrated not just on special occasions (Luke 15:24) but **each day**. Earlier, Jesus had implicitly referred to Herod Antipas when giving a similar description of "those who dress luxuriously and live sumptuously" (7:25; see 23:11). Some scholars ancient[17] and modern have therefore seen another allusion to Antipas in this rich man.

A poor man is also introduced. The stark contrast between poor and rich **16:20–21** recalls the Beatitudes (6:20, 24) and Jesus' instructions on banquet guests (14:12–13). Besides being poor, he was hungry (see 6:21), so he longed to eat **his fill**, just like the prodigal son (15:16). He was **lying at** the rich man's **door** or gate, perhaps because he was lame or crippled (see 14:13, 21). He was also **covered with sores** and thus likely considered accursed (Deut 28:35). Adding insult to injury were the **dogs** (see 1 Kings 21:19, 23; Ps 22:17).

Unlike other characters in Jesus' parables, besides the biblical figure Abraham, this one is **named**.[18] "**Lazarus**" is derived from the Hebrew "Eleazar," a very common name meaning "God has helped" (see 2 Macc 8:23). Since Abraham enters the parable next, Lazarus is a fitting name, since Abraham's servant (Gen 15:2) was similarly called Eliezer ("my God is help"). The rich man, however, was of no help to Lazarus (see Ps 146:3–5).

Death comes for both men. **The rich man** can afford to be **buried**. No burial **16:22–23** of **the poor man** is mentioned, yet he receives a greater privilege by being **carried away by angels**. The reversal of their plight thus begins to be seen. **Lazarus** ends up in **the bosom of Abraham**[19]—that is, **at his side** (same word as in John 13:23). The rich man, however, is in **the netherworld**—that is, Hades or Sheol (see comment on Luke 10:15). There, he suffers **torment** (in "flames," v. 24; see Sir 21:9–10), a point repeated several times (Luke 16:24, 25, 28, using two Greek words). Nonetheless, he **saw** (literally, "sees") **Abraham far off**. Jesus' earlier words apply: "There will be wailing . . . when you see Abraham . . . in the kingdom of God and you . . . cast out" (13:28). The poor man, however,

17. Tertullian, *Against Marcion* 4.34.8–10.
18. In Christian tradition, the rich man also acquired a name—Dives—the Latin word for "rich" (Luke 16:19).
19. The phrase signifies the place of comfort (Luke 16:25) for the righteous dead before Christ (see Catechism 633).

is receiving the promised beatitude: "Blessed are you who are poor, / for the kingdom of God is yours" (6:20).

16:24–26   In the first of three exchanges, the rich man asks **Abraham** to **have pity** or mercy on him (verb *eleeō*, related to the noun *eleos*, "mercy"; e.g., 10:37) by sending **Lazarus** to give him a drop of **water**. He calls him **Father**, but John the Baptist had already warned that it was not sufficient to say, "We have Abraham as our father" (3:8), since one also had to "produce good fruits as evidence of . . . repentance." For the rich man, this could have meant giving alms (*eleēmosynē*, "merciful deed"), as Jesus had earlier told the Pharisees to do (11:41). However, he who refused to show mercy to Lazarus by inviting him to a meal (see 14:13) or even giving him "scraps" from his table (16:21) is now refused mercy. Addressing him as **my child**, Abraham kindly but firmly explains why. Having missed the opportunity to repent (see v. 30), the rich man is being **tormented**, the consequences of his own life choices. He has already received his consolation (6:24) during his **lifetime**, and now a great reversal has occurred. **Moreover**, it is impossible to bridge the **great chasm** separating them, **established** by God. The rich man could have bridged the different kind of chasm that separated them in life. He chose not to.

16:27–29   In the second exchange, the rich man asks that Lazarus be sent to **warn** the **five brothers** in his **father's house**. The reply from **Abraham** is brief and once again negative. They have what they need in **Moses and the prophets**—in other words, "the law and the prophets" (16:16)—if they just **listen to them**: for instance, "Open your hand freely to your poor" (Deut 15:11) and "share your bread with the hungry" (Isa 58:7 NRSV). Jesus has repeatedly emphasized the importance of listening to the word of God (e.g., Luke 8:21; 11:28). If the rich man had done such listening, he would have produced fruits of repentance, but his response was "choked by the . . . riches and pleasures of life" (8:14).

16:30–31   He makes one last plea, claiming that **they will repent** provided **someone from the dead goes to them**—meaning Lazarus. That **someone should rise from the dead**, however, points ultimately to Jesus' already predicted resurrection (9:22). For the third time, **Abraham** responds negatively. There is continuity between the Old Testament era and the kingdom of God (16:16), between **Moses and the prophets** and Jesus who fulfills them (24:26–27, 44, 46). Those like the Pharisees who, despite their claims, fail to **listen** to Moses and the prophets will not be **persuaded** even by Jesus' resurrection.[20]

---

20. Some scholars think there is some relationship between the parable about Lazarus and Jesus' raising someone named Lazarus from the dead (John 11:1–44; 12:1, 9–11). Besides the same name,

Abraham and the Rich Man

LIVING TRADITION

St. John Chrysostom drives home the point of the parable to his congregation by having Abraham speak the following words about Lazarus to the rich man:

> When you were living in your wealth, when you were free to see at your own will, you did not choose to see him. Why do you have such keen sight now? Was he not at your gate? How could you avoid seeing him? When he was near you did not see him; and now do you see him from a distance, even across such a chasm? . . . The man whom you passed by a thousand times, whom you did want to see—now do you seek to have him sent to you for your salvation? . . .
>
> And where are your cup bearers? . . . Where are your flatterers? Where is your vanity? Where is your presumption? Where is your buried gold? Where are your moth-eaten garments? Where is the silver which you valued so highly? Where are your ostentation and your luxury? They were leaves—winter seized them, and they are all withered up. They were a dream—and when day came, the dream departed. They were a shadow—the truth came, and the shadow fled away. . . .
>
> When we hear, let us be afraid, my beloved, lest we also see the poor and pass them by, lest instead of Lazarus there be many to accuse us hereafter.[a]

a. John Chrysostom, *Sermon* 6 on Lazarus and the Rich Man, in *On Wealth and Poverty*, trans. Catharine P. Roth (Crestwood, NY: St. Vladimir's Seminary Press, 1981), 111, 116–17.

Reflection and Application (16:14–31)

Rejecting the prosperity gospel. Like some of the Pharisees in Jesus' time, there are some preachers today who falsely regard great wealth as a sign of God's blessing. The corollary would be that being poor is a sign of God's disfavor. Jesus instead charges us, rich or poor, to maintain a clear distinction between God and mammon, so that we may serve God—for example, through our acts of charity to assist those, like Lazarus, who are poorer than we are.

In paradisum. Another act of charity is prayer for the dead. In the chants that may be sung at the end of a funeral Mass, the Church prays, "May the angels lead you into paradise. . . . May the choir of angels receive you, and with Lazarus, who once was poor, may you have eternal rest."[21]

---

other elements common to Luke and John (not found in Matthew and Mark) are the notion of Lazarus's coming back from the dead, and the sisters Martha and Mary (Luke 10:38–42), whom John indicates are Lazarus's sisters. However, that family seems to be rather wealthy (John 12:3, 5), unlike the poor Lazarus here. Moreover, as noted, Lazarus was a very common name.

21. *The Gregorian Missal* (Solesmes: St. Peter's Abbey, 1990), 698 (translation adapted).

Sayings about Discipleship (17:1–10)

¹He said to his disciples, "Things that cause sin will inevitably occur, but woe to the person through whom they occur. ²It would be better for him if a millstone were put around his neck and he be thrown into the sea than for him to cause one of these little ones to sin. ³Be on your guard! If your brother sins, rebuke him; and if he repents, forgive him. ⁴And if he wrongs you seven times in one day and returns to you seven times saying, 'I am sorry,' you should forgive him."

⁵And the apostles said to the Lord, "Increase our faith." ⁶The Lord replied, "If you have faith the size of a mustard seed, you would say to [this] mulberry tree, 'Be uprooted and planted in the sea,' and it would obey you.

⁷"Who among you would say to your servant who has just come in from plowing or tending sheep in the field, 'Come here immediately and take your place at table'? ⁸Would he not rather say to him, 'Prepare something for me to eat. Put on your apron and wait on me while I eat and drink. You may eat and drink when I am finished'? ⁹Is he grateful to that servant because he did what was commanded? ¹⁰So should it be with you. When you have done all you have been commanded, say, 'We are unprofitable servants; we have done what we were obliged to do.'"

OT: Lev 19:17
NT: Luke 12:37; 1 Cor 8:9–13. // Matt 17:20; 18:6–7, 15, 21–22; 21:21; Mark 9:42; 11:22–23
Catechism: scandal, 2284–87; forgiveness, 2227, 2845; faith, 162
Lectionary: Luke 17:5–10: Twenty-Seventh Sunday Ordinary Time (Year C)

17:1–2   After addressing the Pharisees (16:14–31), Jesus resumes instructing his **disciples** (16:1). He speaks about four topics—scandal, forgiveness, faith, and service—which seem unrelated, but which draw concluding lessons from the preceding parables in the unit.

"Scandal" refers here to moral stumbling blocks that lead others to do evil (Catechism 2284)—in other words, **things that cause sin** (*skandalon*), not outrage. For example, seeing the behavior of those who act like the dishonest steward and the rich man who ignored Lazarus, others could be drawn to be dishonest and neglect the poor. Although such things **will inevitably occur**, leading especially **little ones** astray (e.g., the weak in faith, Rom 14:1; 1 Cor 8:9), Jesus pronounces a **woe** against **the person** giving scandal. The terrible punishment described uses a graphic image of **a millstone** for grinding grain or pressing olives (like the basalt millstones found at Capernaum). If it is **put around** someone's **neck**, who is then **thrown into the sea**, death by drowning

Figure 14. Millstone at Capernaum.

quickly ensues. Still, this **would be better** than an *eternity* in torment, as was
the fate of the rich man!

Therefore, **be on your guard!** The Greek phrase is the same as Jesus' earlier   17:3–4
warning—"Beware" (Luke 12:1)—about the Pharisees. He is here similarly
instructing his disciples to take heed not to behave like the Pharisees, who
cause others to sin.

Jesus' next saying about the need to **forgive** serves as a comment on the
relationship between the angry older brother and his prodigal younger brother.
The older brother's attitude expresses how the Pharisees "despised" (18:9) tax
collectors and sinners. Jesus teaches a different approach. Certainly, if a **brother
sins**, one does not ignore it but gives a fraternal **rebuke** or correction (Lev
19:17; 2 Tim 3:16; 4:2). Then, **if he repents**, like the prodigal son did (Luke
15:18, 21; see 15:7, 10), one must **forgive him** (verb *aphiēmi*). This is what the
older brother (and the Pharisees) had difficulty doing. There is no limit to such
forgiveness—even **seven times in one day** (see Prov 24:16)—provided the of-
fender says, **I am sorry** (literally, "I repent"). Underlying this principle is the
petition from the Lord's Prayer: "Forgive us our sins / for we ourselves forgive
everyone in debt to us" (Luke 11:4). Disciples who ask God to grant them jubilee
"liberty" or "forgiveness" (noun *aphesis*, 4:18; 24:47) must extend it to others!

Finding this teaching very challenging, **the apostles**—those chosen disciples   17:5–6
whom Jesus entrusts with leadership responsibilities (6:13; 22:30)—ask **the**

291

Lord for an **increase** in **faith**. They already have faith but consider it to be too weak (see 8:25; 22:32). Jesus' paradoxical reply indicates that even a little **faith**, small as **a mustard seed** (see 13:19), has great power. Similar sayings about faith involve moving mountains (Matt 17:20; 21:21; 1 Cor 13:2), but here it is a **mulberry tree** that is **uprooted and planted in the sea**. Mulberry trees have an extensive root system, and trees are not planted in the sea, so the saying has the general meaning that faith can do the impossible.[22]

17:7–10   Jesus continues with a brief parable, asking his listeners, especially the apostles (Luke 17:5), to compare themselves to a master in relation to a **servant**. The servant returns at mealtime from working **in the field**, and the master is thinking about food more than the servant's well-being. Regarding this scenario, Jesus asks questions in verses 8 and 9 that already contain the expected answers. Instead of inviting him to sit **at table, would** the master **not rather say** to the servant, **Prepare something for me to eat**? Yes, he would. **Is he grateful**? No, he is not. In an earlier parable, Jesus had surprisingly spoken about a master who reverses the roles and waits on his servants (12:37). This time, however, the master simply expects the servant to do his various jobs and carry out **what was commanded**. In the last verse, however, Jesus turns the tables and identifies the apostles not with masters but with **servants** who should carry out what they **have been commanded** to do, without complaint and without a sense of entitlement (see 15:29). Jesus is teaching his apostles what true service means. This lesson particularly applies to the missionary tasks that the apostles as servants (2 Cor 4:5) will carry out: **plowing** to spread God's kingdom (Luke 9:62; 1 Cor 9:10), **tending sheep** as pastors (Acts 20:28; 1 Cor 9:7), being ready to **wait on**—that is, serve—others (Luke 22:26; 1 Cor 9:19), and giving them to **eat and drink** in the Eucharist (1 Cor 11:25–26).[23] Such is the stewardship that Jesus entrusts to the apostles (see Luke 12:42; 16:10; 1 Cor 9:17).

22. Some Old Testament references to the Gentile nations use sea symbolism (Ps 65:8; Isa 17:12; 60:5) and mention uprooting and planting (Jer 1:10). Thus in Christian tradition, Jesus' saying is applied to the faith by which the apostles spread the gospel, such that it was "transplanted into the sea of the Gentiles" (Bonaventure, *Commentary on the Gospel of Luke* 17.17, ed. and trans. Robert J. Karris, 3 vols. [St. Bonaventure, NY: The Franciscan Institute, 2001–4], 3:1640).

23. François Bovon, *Luke*, trans. Christine M. Thomas, Donald S. Deer, and James Crouch, 3 vols., Hermeneia (Minneapolis: Fortress, 2002–13), 2:497.

The Son of Man and the Kingdom of God

Luke 17:11–18:30

As the journey to Jerusalem continues, Jesus' teaching focuses on "the kingdom of God," a phrase that occurs eight times in this unit.[1] The audience includes his disciples (17:22; 18:15, 28) but also Pharisees (17:20), an official (18:18), and others he meets (17:12; 18:15). Jesus teaches using parables (18:1–14) and through a longer speech (17:22–37) that looks to the future coming of the "Son of Man" (17:24, 26, 30). His instruction highlights various conditions for entering the kingdom—in other words, for inheriting eternal life (18:18, 30): faith (17:19; 18:8), humility (18:14, 16–17), and detachment from one's possessions (18:22, 28–29).

Ten Lepers Are Cleansed (17:11–19)

[11]As he continued his journey to Jerusalem, he traveled through Samaria and Galilee. [12]As he was entering a village, ten lepers met [him]. They stood at a distance from him [13]and raised their voice, saying, "Jesus, Master! Have pity on us!" [14]And when he saw them, he said, "Go show yourselves to the priests." As they were going they were cleansed. [15]And one of them, realizing he had been healed, returned, glorifying God in a loud voice; [16]and he fell at the feet of Jesus and thanked him. He was a Samaritan. [17]Jesus said in reply, "Ten were cleansed, were they not? Where are the

---

1. Luke 17:20 (twice), 21; 18:16–17, 24–25, 29.

other nine? ¹⁸Has none but this foreigner returned to give thanks to God?"
¹⁹Then he said to him, "Stand up and go; your faith has saved you."

OT: Lev 13–14; Num 5:2–3; 2 Kings 5:1–19
NT: Luke 4:27; 5:12–16; 7:22; 18:38–39, 42–43
Lectionary: Twenty-Eighth Sunday Ordinary Time (Year C)

17:11   The new reminder that Jesus' destination is **Jerusalem** (see 13:22) marks the beginning of another part of the long section dedicated to the **journey** (9:51–19:44). Jesus is traveling eastward with **Samaria** on his right and **Galilee** on his left, passing "between" (RSV) the two regions, in the small part of the Decapolis west of the Jordan, where the city of Scythopolis was located. Such a route was customary for Galilean pilgrims to Jerusalem, who would then cross the Jordan and continue south along the river valley, before turning west and crossing back at Jericho for the ascent to Jerusalem (18:31, 35; 19:1).

17:12–13   Jesus enters **a village** where he encounters **ten lepers** from **a distance**, since they were required to remain isolated according to the law (Lev 13:46; Num 5:2; see comment on Luke 5:12–16). Humbly addressing **Jesus** as **Master**, the lepers ask for **pity**—that is, "mercy" (RSV). The blind man at Jericho will later make the same plea (18:38–39). These cries, which echo prayers directed to God in the Psalms (Ps 86:3; 123:3), are now directed to Jesus, through whom God's "tender mercy" is being manifested (Luke 1:78). With both the lepers and the blind, Jesus brings healing, thus indicating the advent of the Messiah (7:22).

17:14   Jesus immediately commands the lepers to **go** and **show** themselves **to the priests**, those who can examine them and officially declare that they are clean (Lev 14:1–20). Jesus had similarly instructed the individual leper *after* cleansing him (Luke 5:14). Here, he does so *before* anything takes place. It is by obeying his command—that is, believing that they will be healed—that they are **cleansed** while **going**. The miracle thus recalls Elisha's healing of Naaman the Syrian (4:27), who likewise was cleansed from a distance after obeying the command of the "prophet in Samaria" to "go" (2 Kings 5:3, 9–14).

17:15–16   However, the miracle is only half the story. **One** leper of the group **returned**. Like others whom Jesus **healed**, he is **glorifying God** (Luke 5:25; 13:13; 18:43). Similarly, Naaman had returned and confessed the true God (2 Kings 5:15). Jesus is thus a *prophet* like Elisha. Moreover, the man also **thanked** (Greek *eucharisteō*) Jesus: glorifying God and thanking Jesus are now linked together. In doing so, he literally **fell** "on his face" (RSV)—like the earlier leper (Luke 5:12)—before **Jesus**. This action, given its Old Testament background (2 Sam 9:6; 14:4, 33; 19:19), suggests that Jesus is also to be recognized as a *king* like

Figure 15. Temple inscription prohibiting further entry to foreigners (*allogenēs* in the first line).

David.[2] Indeed, as Jesus continues his approach to Jerusalem, there will be frequent references to his kingship (e.g., "Son of David," Luke 18:38–39), and when he arrives, he will be acclaimed "king" (19:38).

A surprising detail is now revealed: the man **was a Samaritan** (see 9:52–53). The implication is that the others were Jewish.

Jesus expresses disappointment that **the other nine** have not **returned to   17:17–18 give thanks** (literally, "glory") **to God**. He refers to the healed Samaritan as a **foreigner** (*allogenēs*), the only occurrence of this word in the New Testament. This word was part of the Greek inscription that was placed on the wall in the temple courts (called the *soreg*) beyond which non-Jews could not go, on pain of death (see Num 1:51).[3] By his healing work of restoration, Jesus is overcoming the barrier between Jews and non-Jews, thus fulfilling Isaiah's prophecy:[4]

> The *foreigner* joined to the LORD should not say,
>> "The LORD will surely exclude me from his people"; . . .
> And *foreigners* who join themselves to the LORD . . .
> Them I will bring to my holy mountain
>> and make them joyful in my house of prayer . . .

2. Jean-Noël Aletti, *Le Jésus de Luc* (Paris: Mame-Desclée, 2010), 93–94.
3. Josephus, *Jewish War* 5.193–94. Paul alludes to this "dividing wall" in Eph 2:14.
4. David Ravens, *Luke and the Restoration of Israel* (Sheffield: Sheffield Academic, 1995), 86.

> For my house shall be called
>> a house of prayer for all peoples. (Isa 56:3, 6–7 [emphasis added])

Shortly, Jesus will quote this passage when he cleanses the temple (Luke 19:46).

17:19 Jesus dismisses the Samaritan with the same words he spoke to other marginalized people whom he healed or forgave: **Your faith has saved you** (7:50; 8:48; 18:42). The Greek verb for "save" (*sōzō*) also means "heal," pointing on one level to the miracle. However, Jesus' words suggest that the Samaritan received more than the physical healing that all ten lepers received. Luke's readers would thus be reminded that faith in Jesus leads to salvation (Rom 10:9; Eph 2:8). Earlier, a Samaritan in a parable became a model of compassionate, merciful *love* (Luke 10:27, 33, 37). Now a real-life Samaritan has become a model of grateful, saving *faith*. He anticipates the Samaritan people's later response of faith (Acts 8:12).

Reflection and Application (17:11–19)

Gratitude. Am I grateful to God for what he has done in my life? Do I thank (*eucharisteō*) him in the eucharistic celebration and in eucharistic adoration? Am I grateful to the people God has put in my life? How do I express my gratitude?

The Days of the Son of Man (17:20–37)

20Asked by the Pharisees when the kingdom of God would come, he said in reply, "The coming of the kingdom of God cannot be observed, **21**and no one will announce, 'Look, here it is,' or, 'There it is.' For behold, the kingdom of God is among you."

22Then he said to his disciples, "The days will come when you will long to see one of the days of the Son of Man, but you will not see it. **23**There will be those who will say to you, 'Look, there he is,' [or] 'Look, here he is.' Do not go off, do not run in pursuit. **24**For just as lightning flashes and lights up the sky from one side to the other, so will the Son of Man be [in his day]. **25**But first he must suffer greatly and be rejected by this generation. **26**As it was in the days of Noah, so it will be in the days of the Son of Man; **27**they were eating and drinking, marrying and giving in marriage up to the day that Noah entered the ark, and the flood came and destroyed them all. **28**Similarly, as it was in the days of Lot: they were eating, drinking, buying, selling, planting, building; **29**on the day when Lot left Sodom, fire and brimstone rained from the sky to destroy them all. **30**So it will be on the day the Son of Man is revealed. ³¹On that day, a person who is on the housetop and whose belongings are in the house must not go down to get them, and likewise a person in the field must not return to what was left behind. ³²Remember the wife of Lot. ³³Whoever seeks to preserve his life will lose it, but whoever loses it will save it. ³⁴I tell you, on that night there will be two people in one bed; one will be taken, the other left. ³⁵And there will be two women grinding meal together; one will be taken, the other left." ⁽³⁶⁾ ³⁷They said to him in reply, "Where, Lord?" He said to them, "Where the body is, there also the vultures will gather."

OT: Gen 6:1–7:24; 19:1–29
NT: Luke 9:22, 24; 11:2, 50–51; 19:11; 21:5–36. // Matt 24:17–18, 23, 27–28, 37–41; Mark 13:15–16, 21
Catechism: giving one's life, 1889

Two questions **asked** of Jesus begin and end this passage. Here, **the Pharisees** inquire about the *time* **when the kingdom of God** will **come** (see 19:11). Later, the disciples ask about the *place* "where" the things Jesus describes will happen (17:37). **17:20–21**

Between the two questions, Jesus speaks about the future in the first of two speeches about "last things," the so-called †eschatological discourses (17:22–37; 21:5–36).[5] In both speeches, Jesus' words refer to several different events and it is not always easy to distinguish between them. On one level, he announces the impending destruction of Jerusalem and its temple (21:6, 20). However, this event, which took place in AD 70, is "a sign of the last days,"[6] so Jesus also seems to speak on another level about his return in glory at the end of time (17:24; 21:27; see Acts 1:11). Moreover, in this first speech, the context of the journey to Jerusalem suggests that Jesus also refers to his imminent coming to the city, where he will be put to death (Luke 17:25), which will itself signal the city's coming devastation (13:34–35; 19:43–44; 23:28–31).

Perhaps the Pharisees' question was prompted by their having heard about Jesus' instruction on prayer: "Your kingdom come" (11:2). In reply, Jesus explains that **the coming of the kingdom of God** is not an event that can **be observed** (e.g., by seeking after signs, 11:16, 29) or that someone **will announce**. Rather, even now it **is among** them. Because Jesus the "king" (19:38) is in their midst, in some way the kingdom is *already* present (11:20).

However, the kingdom has *not yet* fully come, so one must pray for it (11:2). Jesus thus turns **to his disciples** to explain what will unfold in the future. He **17:22**

---

5. The Greek word *eschatos* means "last." See Matt 24–25; Mark 13.
6. Catechism 585 (citing Matt 24:3; Luke 13:35); see also 673, 675.

Jesus Is Himself the Kingdom

Joseph Ratzinger, who became Pope Benedict XVI, explains Jesus' words about the kingdom with the help of the early Church writer Origen: "The kingdom [*basileia*] of God cannot be observed, yet, unobserved, it is among those to whom he is speaking [Luke 17:20–21]. It stands among them—in his own person. . . . In a splendid coinage of Origen's, Jesus is [the] *autobasileia*"[a]—that is, he is himself the kingdom: "Just as he is wisdom itself and righteousness itself and truth itself, so too is he also the kingdom itself (*autobasileia*)."[b]

St. John Paul II similarly explains the kingdom: "Christ not only proclaimed the kingdom, but in him the kingdom itself became present and was fulfilled. . . . The kingdom of God is not a concept, a doctrine, or a program subject to free interpretation, but it is before all else *a person* with the face and name of Jesus of Nazareth, the image of the invisible God. If the kingdom is separated from Jesus, it is no longer the kingdom of God which he revealed."[c]

a. Joseph Ratzinger, *Eschatology: Death and Eternal Life*, trans. Michael Waldstein and Aidan Nichols (Washington, DC: Catholic University of America Press, 1988), 34.

b. Origen, *Commentary on Matthew* 14.7, quoted in Hans Urs von Balthasar, ed., *Origen: Spirit and Fire: A Thematic Anthology of His Writings*, trans. Robert J. Daly (Washington, DC: Catholic University of America Press, 1984), 362.

c. John Paul II, *Redemptoris Missio* (On the Permanent Validity of the Church's Missionary Mandate) 18 (emphasis in the original).

refers to **the days** that **will come**, when they **will long to see** even **one of the days of the Son of Man**. On one level, they will be tested by the absence caused by his death (17:25), when they do **not see** him anymore and do not yet understand (9:45; 18:34). Indeed, Jesus had earlier spoken of the days that will come (5:35) when he, the bridegroom, is taken away. On another level, the saying applies to the period after Jesus' ascension, when disciples (including readers in succeeding generations) will wish to see his return in glory but will not know the time that the Father has established (Acts 1:7; 3:21).

17:23–24   In any case, disciples should not **run** after **those** claiming he is **here** or **there** (see Luke 21:8). This is because **the Son of Man** will be unmistakably glorious **[in his day]**, like the **lightning** that **flashes and lights up the sky**. This image refers to his second coming in "great glory" (21:27), but it is helpful to remember that by his resurrection Jesus already enters "into his glory" (24:26).[7] A glimpse

---

7. Jesus will thus appear in heavenly glory to Stephen (Acts 7:55) and in a light that flashes around Paul (Acts 9:3; 22:6).

of his glory was already seen at the transfiguration (9:32), where "his clothes became as bright as a flash of lightning" (9:29 NIV).

However, before his glorification, Jesus must **first** be put to death. Using the same words as in the first passion prediction (9:22), Jesus reminds the disciples what awaits him in Jerusalem: **he must suffer greatly and be rejected**. Those rejecting him belong to **this generation**, a phrase that Jesus has repeatedly used (7:31; 11:29–32, 50–51) to compare them to the evil generation in the days of Moses (Num 32:13; Deut 1:35).   **17:25**

Moreover, the phrase recalls the unrighteous generation **in the days of Noah**: "Go into the ark . . . for you alone in *this generation* have I found to be righteous before me" (Gen 7:1 [emphasis added]).[8] In early Jewish and Christian literature, Noah is portrayed as preaching repentance.[9] Heedless of his warnings, however, that generation was otherwise absorbed—**eating, drinking, marrying, giving in marriage**[10] (see Luke 14:20; 20:34–35)—until **the day** the righteous **Noah entered the ark** and so escaped. Then, **the flood came and destroyed them all** (Gen 7:21–23). In Scripture, Noah's generation is considered a prototype of the ungodly who will undergo future judgment.[11]   **17:26–27**

So it will be in the days of the Son of Man. Jesus applies the lesson to the final judgment but also, it seems, to "this generation" (Luke 17:25; 21:32) that will experience Jerusalem's "judgment" (21:23–24). His words are a call to repentance (see 13:3, 5) and vigilance (12:37; 21:36).

Another biblical example is the generation **in the days of Lot**, which was known for its wickedness.[12] They too were absorbed in uninterrupted activity—**eating, drinking, buying, selling, planting, building** (see 12:18–19, 45; 14:18–19; 19:45)—and so were unmindful of God. **On the day when Lot** escaped by leaving **Sodom**, that generation was destroyed by the **fire and brimstone** that **rained from the sky**. Jesus again applies the lesson: **so it will be on the day the Son of Man is revealed** (see 2 Thess 1:7–8).   **17:28–30**

It is crucial therefore to be "prepared" (Luke 12:40) for **that day**. When it comes, **a person** must have priorities in order and not be concerned about losing **belongings** (see 14:33). In such circumstances, being focused on the   **17:31–32**

---

8. Dale C. Allison Jr., *The Intertextual Jesus: Scripture in Q* (Harrisburg, PA: Trinity Press International, 2000), 57–58, 93–94.

9. *Sibylline Oracles* 1.128–29; Josephus, *Jewish Antiquities* 1.74; 2 Pet 2:5; *1 Clement* 7.6; 9.4.

10. The Greek text here (and in v. 28) has no **and** connecting the verbs, creating a dramatic effect. The list may refer to the sins of Noah's generation (Gen 6:1–6).

11. Isa 24:18 (see Gen 7:11); Sir 16:7 RSV (see Gen 6:4 LXX); 2 Pet 2:5, 9; 3:6–7. See also the non-biblical *3 Maccabees* 2:4.

12. Gen 13:12–13; 19:1–29; Sir 16:8; 2 Pet 2:6–8. In *3 Maccabees* 2:5, they are "an example for future generations" (NETS).

kingdom means not turning **to what was left behind** (*eis ta opisō*, as in 9:62), as **the wife of Lot** mistakenly did by looking back (*eis ta opisō* in Gen 19:17, 26 LXX) when fleeing Sodom. In Jesus' other end-time speech, there is a similar instruction: both "those within the city" (i.e., **on the housetop**) and "those in the countryside" (i.e., **in the field**) must "flee" (Luke 21:21).

17:33   The general principle is that disciples should not rely on possessions (17:31) **to preserve** their **life**; otherwise, they **will lose it** (12:19–20). Rather, they should live the paradox of the cross, by which for the sake of Jesus one **loses** one's life through self-denial (9:23–24). In this way, they **will save it** for life eternal.

17:34–35   However, where a person stands may not be readily apparent. As a result, the outcome may be different even for **two people** in the same place and **two women** doing the same thing.[13] God is the one who knows hearts (16:15), and in each case he will distinguish between the **one** and **the other**. **On that night,**[14] those who are spared (as Noah and Lot were) **will be taken** to safety, whereas those who are **left** will experience judgment.[15]

17:37   The speech ends as it began (17:20), with a response to a question: **"Where, Lord?"** The disciples are presumably asking where this judgment will occur. Jesus' response is a riddle: **Where the body is, there also the vultures**—or rather eagles,[16] which are scavengers too—**will gather**. The saying may simply be an example from nature that tells the disciples to be attentive to the signs (see 12:56). However, since each Roman legion carried an eagle standard into battle,[17] it may be another reference to the Roman attack on Jerusalem (21:20), in which many thousands of Jews perished.[18] The parallel verse thus fittingly says "corpse" (Matt 24:28) rather than "body." Another view is that Luke is referring to Jesus' "body" (Luke 23:52, 55; 24:3, 23), which will be raised to glory following his crucifixion. Some thus interpret the question as asking where the righteous will be taken (17:34–35). The eagles would then be the righteous (see Exod 19:4) who will go to be with Jesus' risen body (see 1 Thess 4:15–17; 2 Thess 2:1).[19]

---

13. Drawing on Matt 24:40, some later manuscripts add a verse (17:36) about two men in a field.

14. Some see here an allusion to the night of Passover (Exod 12:12), when people were either smitten or spared.

15. Others, such as N. T. Wright, *Jesus and the Victory of God* (Minneapolis: Fortress, 1996), 366, interpret the phrase the other way around: those taken become captives (Luke 21:24), while those left are spared.

16. James R. Edwards, *The Gospel according to Luke*, PNTC (Grand Rapids: Eerdmans, 2015), 494–95n95; Steven L. Bridge, *"Where the Eagles Are Gathered": The Deliverance of the Elect in Lukan Eschatology* (London: Sheffield Academic, 2003), 57–66.

17. Josephus, *Jewish War* 3.123.

18. Josephus, *Jewish War* 6.420.

19. Bridge, *Where the Eagles Are Gathered*, 49–56; David E. Garland, *Luke*, ZECNT (Grand Rapids: Zondervan, 2011), 702. This interpretation is already found in Cyril of Alexandria, *Homilies on Luke*

The Judge and the Widow (18:1–8)

¹Then he told them a parable about the necessity for them to pray always without becoming weary. He said, ²"There was a judge in a certain town who neither feared God nor respected any human being. ³And a widow in that town used to come to him and say, 'Render a just decision for me against my adversary.' ⁴For a long time the judge was unwilling, but eventually he thought, 'While it is true that I neither fear God nor respect any human being, ⁵because this widow keeps bothering me I shall deliver a just decision for her lest she finally come and strike me.'" ⁶The Lord said, "Pay attention to what the dishonest judge says. ⁷Will not God then secure the rights of his chosen ones who call out to him day and night? Will he be slow to answer them? ⁸I tell you, he will see to it that justice is done for them speedily. But when the Son of Man comes, will he find faith on earth?"

OT: Exod 22:21–22; Deut 24:17; 27:19; Sir 35:15–23
NT: Luke 11:5–8; 21:36; James 5:7–8; 2 Pet 3:9
Catechism: pray always, 2098, 2613; faith at Christ's coming, 675
Lectionary: Twenty-Ninth Sunday Ordinary Time (Year C)

In view of the approaching judgment associated with the kingdom's coming **18:1** (17:20, 26–29), Jesus speaks **about the necessity** that his disciples **pray always**—"your kingdom come"! (11:2)—**without becoming weary**.[20] When Jesus earlier taught them how to pray, he also **told them a parable** (11:5–8) about perseverance in prayer, involving two people. He does the same thing now.

Jesus first introduces **a judge** of dubious character. Rather than "fear God **18:2–3** and keep his commandments" (Eccles 12:13), he **neither feared God nor respected any human being** (repeated for emphasis in Luke 18:4). Second, there is **a widow** who **used to come**—in other words, repeatedly—**to him** asking for **a just decision** in her case. Since widows were in a vulnerable position in ancient Israel, Scripture contains many exhortations to defend them and warnings not to oppress them.[21]

This situation drags on **for a long time** since the judge is **unwilling**. The **18:4–5** **widow keeps bothering** him, like the persistent person at midnight who keeps

---

17:31–37, in *Commentary on the Gospel of Saint Luke*, trans. R. Payne Smith (repr., Astoria, NY: Studion, 1983), 472: "When the Son of Man shall appear, then certainly shall the eagles, even those who fly aloft, and rise superior to earthly and worldly things, hasten to him."

20. Charles H. Talbert, *Reading Luke: A Literary and Theological Commentary on the Third Gospel*, rev. ed. (Macon, GA: Smyth & Helwys, 2002), 197.

21. Exod 22:21–22; Deut 27:19; Isa 1:17; Jer 7:6; 22:3; Mal 3:5.

asking despite his friend's plea, "Do not bother me" (11:7). **The judge**, speaking "to himself" (NRSV) like earlier characters in parables (12:17; 16:3), **eventually** decides to give her **a just decision**. He is motivated only by self-interest: he wants to avoid her **finally** coming to **strike** him.[22]

18:6–8   Further explanation now comes from **the Lord**. The use of the title for Jesus helps to link the parable to the preceding speech ("Lord," 17:37). Like the earlier parable (11:5–8), this one uses a "how much more" argument. If even a **dishonest** or unjust **judge** grants justice to a widow who repeatedly demands justice, *how much more* will **God**, who "executes justice for . . . the widow" (Deut 10:18), **secure the rights** of (i.e., "give justice to")[23] those whom the widow represents—**his** elect or **chosen ones** (see Rom 8:33)? Like God's own "chosen" Son (see Luke 9:35; 23:35), they will ultimately be vindicated, even if the present situation looks hopeless.

The book of Sirach has a similar message: "The prayer of the lowly . . . / does not rest till it reaches its goal; / Nor will it withdraw till the Most High responds, / judges justly and affirms the right" (Sir 35:21–22). It then continues: "God indeed will not delay" (Sir 35:22), which seems to be how Jesus continues here (though the Greek verb is not the same): **Will he be slow to answer** ("delay long," NRSV)? No, for God will render **justice . . . for them speedily**. However, this Greek verb for "delay" (*makrothymeō*) basically means "be patient" (see 2 Pet 3:9). So some translate the question about being slow to answer as a statement: "He is patient toward them."[24] This difficulty in translation reflects the lived tension between the promise of prompt justice and the experience of delay in God's response to prayer. Indeed, many situations of injustice are not set right until the next life (see Luke 16:19–25). However, at the end of the passage, the focus is less on when or how God responds and more on one's own ongoing response of **faith**. In this regard, a good model for those **who call out to him day and night** is the widow Anna, who prayed "night and day" (2:37) for the greater part of a century before having her prayer answered! Nonetheless, because of her faith, she was ready **when the Son of Man** came (to the temple). This concluding reference to the "Son of Man" again links the parable to the previous speech (17:22, 24, 26, 30). Jesus will close his second speech about the end times with a similar

---

22. The verb *hypōpiazō* means to strike or give someone a black eye (see the boxing image in 1 Cor 9:27). The NABRE interprets it literally, while other versions translate metaphorically: "wear me out by continually coming" (NRSV).

23. The Greek text in these verses plays on related nouns and verbs associated with justice.

24. See Klyne R. Snodgrass, *Stories with Intent: A Comprehensive Guide to the Parables of Jesus* (Grand Rapids: Eerdmans, 2008), 458–59.

call to vigilant prayer amid tribulation, in expectation of "the Son of Man" (21:36).

The Pharisee and the Tax Collector (18:9–14)

⁹He then addressed this parable to those who were convinced of their own righteousness and despised everyone else. ¹⁰"Two people went up to the temple area to pray; one was a Pharisee and the other was a tax collector. ¹¹The Pharisee took up his position and spoke this prayer to himself, 'O God, I thank you that I am not like the rest of humanity— greedy, dishonest, adulterous—or even like this tax collector. ¹²I fast twice a week, and I pay tithes on my whole income.' ¹³But the tax collec- tor stood off at a distance and would not even raise his eyes to heaven but beat his breast and prayed, 'O God, be merciful to me a sinner.' ¹⁴I tell you, the latter went home justified, not the former; for everyone who exalts himself will be humbled, and the one who humbles himself will be exalted."

OT: Ezek 33:13
NT: Matt 23:12; Luke 5:33; 11:42; 14:11; 16:15
Catechism: against the self-righteous, 588; humble prayer, 2559, 2613; asking forgiveness, 2631, 2667, 2839
Lectionary: Thirtieth Sunday Ordinary Time (Year C); Saturday Third Week of Lent; Anointing of the Sick

18:9–10 Another **parable** about prayer immediately follows, directed at some who are confident in **their own righteousness** (see Ezek 33:13)—literally, "that they are *righteous*." Fittingly, **a Pharisee** represents such self-righteous people (Luke 16:14–15), who **despised everyone else**. Appropriately, the other character is **a tax collector** (5:30; 15:1–2). The parable compares these **two people**, as earlier parables compared "two people" who "were in debt" (7:41) and "two sons" (15:11). Both have gone **up** to the **temple** mount **to pray**. Thus it is likely a time of public prayer associated with the morning or evening sacrifices, when people gathered to pray (1:10; Acts 3:1).

18:11–12 **The Pharisee took up** the typical posture of standing to pray. His **prayer**, however, is less toward **God** and more **to himself**.[25] In his self-righteousness,

25. Other versions instead say that the Pharisee was "standing by himself" (NRSV). François Bovon, *Luke*, trans. Christine M. Thomas, Donald S. Deer, and James Crouch, 3 vols., Hermeneia (Minneapolis: Fortress, 2002–13), 2:547, indicates that it could be both: "The Pharisee cut himself off from both other persons and God."

he considers **the rest of humanity**—"everyone else"! (Luke 18:9)—including **this tax collector**, to be **dishonest** or unrighteous. The Pharisee's religious practices are exemplary—to **fast twice a week** (Mondays and Thursdays)[26] and **pay tithes on** all that he gets.[27] However, these practices have become his badge of pride. Moreover, in his contempt for others, he neglects weightier matters such as love of neighbor (see Matt 23:23).

18:13 **The tax collector** likewise **stood** to pray, but in a humble manner. He remained **at a distance**, further back in the temple courts. Out of shame, he did **not even raise his eyes to heaven** (see Ezra 9:6). As an expression of his deep sorrow, he **beat his breast** (Luke 23:48). With these gestures, he gave evidence of his repentance, like the woman with her tears (7:38). He also acknowledged that he was **a sinner** and thus asked **God** to **be merciful** (*hilaskomai*) to him. This verb differs from the vocabulary used in Jesus' earlier command to "be merciful" (6:36) or in phrases for having mercy or pity (16:24; 17:13; 18:38–39). It occurs only once elsewhere in the New Testament, where it means to "expiate" or make atonement for sin (Heb 2:17). Such "sacrificial overtones"[28] fit the parable's temple setting, all the more so if the prayer occurs at the time of the daily sacrifice. For Luke's readers, the expression may also call to mind the sacrifice of Jesus, "whom God set forth as an expiation" (Rom 3:25).

18:14 Jesus explains—**I tell you**—the shocking reversal: this tax collector whom the Pharisee held in contempt (Luke 18:11) is the one who **went** down to his house **justified**—considered righteous by God—**not** the Pharisee who considered himself righteous (v. 9). Luke will soon recount the story of a real tax collector, Zacchaeus, who similarly goes down to his house justified, having found salvation (19:5–6, 9).

Jesus concludes with a principle, which repeats verbatim his earlier teaching (14:11). He thus applies the parable to **everyone** and highlights the reversal involving those who are **humbled** and those who are **exalted** (1:52)—by God!

Reflection and Application (18:9–14)

Motivated by love. Jesus' words can serve as an examination of conscience to guard against a self-righteous attitude: "Christians should keep in mind that the value of their good works, fasts, alms, penances, and so on, is not based

---

26. See *Didache* 8.1.
27. The Pharisees practiced fasting (Luke 5:33) to hasten the restoration of God's blessings on his people. Their scrupulosity in tithing (11:42; see Deut 14:22) made reparation for others' failure to tithe (see *m. Demai* 2:2).
28. Snodgrass, *Stories with Intent*, 473.

Justification in Luke

BIBLICAL BACKGROUND

The tax collector goes home "justified" (verb *dikaioō*, 18:14). Thus, as many scholars propose,[a] the roots of Paul's theology of justification—for example, "A person is justified by faith apart from works of the law" (Rom 3:28)—can be found in Jesus' own teaching. Indeed, the Pharisee boasts about practicing works of the law such as fasting and tithing, but Paul reminds us that no one may boast before God (Rom 3:27; 1 Cor 1:29). The Pharisee represents those who are confident that they are just or righteous (Luke 18:9) or who justify themselves (10:29; 16:15) but, in reality, are "ignorant of the righteousness that comes from God . . . seeking to establish their own" (Rom 10:3 RSV).[b] Of course, one brief parable cannot express the whole teaching of the New Testament on justification. For example, the tax collector's faith is not explicitly mentioned (though "faith" is emphasized in the preceding verse, Luke 18:8). Elsewhere in Luke, however, Jesus frequently says that people's "faith has saved" them (7:50; 8:48; 17:19; 18:42), as we find in Paul's letters (Rom 10:9; 1 Cor 1:21; Eph 2:8). Finally, Luke in Acts reports one of Paul's speeches about justification: through Jesus, "forgiveness of sins is proclaimed to you, and . . . everyone who believes is justified from everything from which the law of Moses could not justify you" (Acts 13:38–39 NET).

a. E.g., Joseph A. Fitzmyer, *The Gospel according to Luke*, 2 vols., AB (New York: Doubleday, 1981–85), 2:1184–85.

b. Bonaventure, *Commentary on the Gospel of Luke* 18.14, ed. and trans. Robert J. Karris, 3 vols. (St. Bonaventure, NY: The Franciscan Institute, 2001–4), 3:1718.

on quantity and quality so much as on the love of God practiced in them."[29] True love of God will also find expression in love—not contempt—of neighbor (Luke 10:27–28). Thus Christians will also be careful to avoid falling into the same trap another way—that is, by thanking God that they are not like those self-righteous people!

Children and the Kingdom (18:15–17)

[15]People were bringing even infants to him that he might touch them, and when the disciples saw this, they rebuked them. [16]Jesus, however, called the

29. John of the Cross, *The Ascent of Mount Carmel* 3.27.5; see 3.28.2–3, in *The Collected Works of St. John of the Cross*, trans. Kieran Kavanaugh and Otilio Rodriguez, rev. ed. (Washington, DC: ICS Publications, 1991), 317–18.

Infant Baptism

In the third century, Origen witnesses to the belief that "the Church has received the tradition from the apostles to give baptism even to little children."[a] For his part, St. Cyprian seems to echo this Scripture passage (Luke 18:15–17) when he explains infant baptism: "If, in the case of the greatest sinners and those sinning much against God, when afterward they believe, the remission of their sins is granted and no one is prevented from baptism and grace, how much more should an infant not be prohibited, who, recently born, has not sinned at all, except that, born carnally according to Adam, he has contracted the contagion of the first death."[b] In the fifth century, Pope Innocent, in a letter to the bishops of northern Africa (including St. Augustine), refers to Jesus' words here as a "quick argument" for infant baptism: "Allow the children to come to me, and do not keep them away from me" (18:16; parallels in Matt 19:14; Mark 10:14).[c]

a. Origen, *Commentary on the Epistle to the Romans* 5.9.11, trans. Thomas P. Scheck, FC 103 (Washington, DC: Catholic University of America Press, 2001), 367.
b. Cyprian, *Letter* 64, in *Letters (1–81)*, trans. Rose Bernard Donna, FC 51 (Washington, DC: Catholic University of America Press, 1964), 219.
c. Innocent I, *Letter* 182.5 (to the Council of Milevis), in *Letters* (of St. Augustine), trans. Roland Teske, 4 vols., WSA II/3 (Hyde Park, NY: New City Press, 2001–5), 3:168.

children to himself and said, "Let the children come to me and do not prevent them; for the kingdom of God belongs to such as these. ¹⁷Amen, I say to you, whoever does not accept the kingdom of God like a child will not enter it."

NT: Luke 9:46–48; 10:21. // Matt 19:13–15; Mark 10:13–16
Catechism: accepting the kingdom like a child, 526; little children and the sacraments, 1244, 1261

18:15   The storyline continues without a break, as the preceding parable's lesson on humility is now illustrated.[30]

It is estimated that less than 50 percent of **infants** in ancient Israel survived to reach the age of five.[31] This explains why **people were bringing** them to Jesus **that he might touch them**—in other words, to heal (6:19) or bless them (Mark 10:16). However, **the disciples**, not yet grasping the just-stated principle about the humble (Luke 18:14), **rebuked them**.

---

30. After a long section, much of which is unique to Luke (9:51–18:14), the parallels between Luke and Mark now resume (compare Luke 18:15–43 with Mark 10:13–34, 46–52).
31. Carol Meyers, *Rediscovering Eve: Ancient Israelite Women in Context* (Oxford: Oxford University Press, 2013), 98–99.

As before (9:50), Jesus corrects their misunderstanding: **Do not prevent** 18:16
them. This same verb is used three times in Acts when speaking about people
who should not be prevented from receiving baptism (Acts 8:36; 10:47; 11:17).
Some have therefore suggested that these words reflect the practice of infant
baptism in the early Church at the time Luke was written. Although this cannot be
proven, Church Fathers later interpreted this passage as support for the practice.

Jesus thus invites **the children** to **come**. The reason is that **the kingdom of
God belongs to such as these**. They join others of marginal status (Luke 6:20;
7:28–29) as part of the "little flock" to whom the kingdom is given (12:32).

Jesus emphasizes the point with an **Amen** saying (Luke 4:24). Children not 18:17
only belong in **the kingdom** but actually set the norm to **enter it**, like the
Israelite children who enter to take possession of the promised land (Deut
1:39). Excluded is **whoever does not accept** it by becoming **like a child**. Just
as children rely on others for everything, so one must rely completely on God,
unlike the self-reliant Pharisee (Luke 18:12).

Reflection and Application (18:15–17)

Accepting the kingdom of God like a child. Appreciation for this Gospel truth
has spread through the writings of St. Thérèse of Lisieux, who realized that
she "had to remain *little*" so that Jesus' arms like an elevator could raise her to
heaven, without her having "to climb the rough stairway of perfection."[32] This
little way of spiritual childhood is a solid path to Christian holiness. It involves
placing all our trust in God as his little children, surrendering our lives to him
but also being bold in asking him for what we need. It also involves doing little
things with great love: a ready smile, a kind word, a listening ear, an approach-
able manner, a welcoming attitude, a simple meal shared with someone who
needs company. One strives to carry out the little duties of each day for love of
God, even if unnoticed by others. One also bears with the little crosses of each
day, embracing them in union with Jesus' sacrifice.

The Rich and the Kingdom (18:18–30)

[18]**An official asked him this question, "Good teacher, what must I do to
inherit eternal life?"** [19]**Jesus answered him, "Why do you call me good? No**

---

32. Thérèse of Lisieux, *Story of a Soul*, trans. John Clarke, 3rd ed. (Washington, DC: ICS Publications, 1996), 207–8 (emphasis in the original).

one is good but God alone. ²⁰You know the commandments, 'You shall not commit adultery; you shall not kill; you shall not steal; you shall not bear false witness; honor your father and your mother.'" ²¹And he replied, "All of these I have observed from my youth." ²²When Jesus heard this he said to him, "There is still one thing left for you: sell all that you have and distribute it to the poor, and you will have a treasure in heaven. Then come, follow me." ²³But when he heard this he became quite sad, for he was very rich.

²⁴Jesus looked at him [now sad] and said, "How hard it is for those who have wealth to enter the kingdom of God! ²⁵For it is easier for a camel to pass through the eye of a needle than for a rich person to enter the kingdom of God." ²⁶Those who heard this said, "Then who can be saved?" ²⁷And he said, "What is impossible for human beings is possible for God." ²⁸Then Peter said, "We have given up our possessions and followed you." ²⁹He said to them, "Amen, I say to you, there is no one who has given up house or wife or brothers or parents or children for the sake of the kingdom of God ³⁰who will not receive [back] an overabundant return in this present age and eternal life in the age to come."

OT: Exod 20:12–16; Deut 5:16–20
NT: Luke 1:37; 5:11; 10:25; 12:33; 14:26; Rom 13:9; James 2:11. // Matt 19:16–29; Mark 10:17–30
Catechism: observing the commandments, 2052–53

18:18   The Pharisees **asked** Jesus a **question** earlier (17:20), and now so does **an official** ("ruler," RSV). This word could refer to a civil magistrate (12:58) or a religious leader (8:41; 14:1). Like the scholar of the law (10:25), he calls Jesus **teacher** (adding **good**) and asks: **what must I do to inherit eternal life?**[33] From the earlier dialogue, the reader knows that the answer involves loving God and neighbor (10:27–28). The question is also related to the preceding discussion (18:17), since inheriting eternal life and entering God's kingdom are basically identical (vv. 24–25, 30).

18:19   Before responding, **Jesus** asks: **Why do you call me good?** This detour redirects the conversation so that it focuses on divine initiative rather than human achievement, since **no one is good but God alone.**[34] These last two words subtly recall the †*Shema* prayer[35]—"Hear, O Israel! The LORD is our *God*, the LORD

---

33. The repeated question (Luke 10:25; 18:18) is possibly one signal that Luke's central section (9:51–19:44) roughly follows a ring structure where themes addressed in the first half are taken up in reverse order in the second half. Other indications include the parables about persistent prayer (11:5–8; 18:1–8), rich men who die (12:16–21; 16:19–31), and repentance (13:1–9; 15:1–32). See Craig L. Blomberg, *Jesus and the Gospels: An Introduction and Survey*, 2nd ed. (Nashville: B&H Academic, 2009), 336–37.
34. See Pss 100:5; 118:1; 135:3; 136:1.
35. C. Kavin Rowe, *Early Narrative Christology: The Lord in the Gospel of Luke* (Berlin: de Gruyter, 2006; Grand Rapids: Baker Academic, 2009), 100–101.

alone!" (Deut 6:4 [emphasis added])—which continues with the command to love God with one's whole being (Deut 6:5), precisely the passage used to answer the question the first time (Luke 10:27). However, Jesus' question does not reject the compliment that he is good. Rather, it raises the further issue of his divine identity (see 5:21). Only the fact that Jesus is the *Son of God* (1:35; 22:70) ultimately explains why the answer to a question about inheriting eternal life involves following *him* (18:22).

Jesus now answers directly, indicating five **commandments** from the sec- **18:20–21** ond part of the Decalogue (Exod 20:12–16; Deut 5:16–20)—for example, **you shall not commit adultery . . . honor your father and your mother**. These can be summed up in love of neighbor (Rom 13:9). The commandments thus remain valid. The official asserts that he has kept **all of these** commandments from his **youth**. Some interpret his statement to mean that, like the Pharisee in the parable, he is convinced of his own righteousness (Luke 18:9). However, as he is not there to test Jesus (see 10:25), his response seems sincere and, indeed, typical of what many law-observing Jews might say (see 1:6; Phil 3:6).

Nonetheless, **Jesus** points out that there is **still one thing** that the official is **18:22–23** lacking. He thus tells him to **sell all**[36] that he owns, **distribute** the money **to the poor**, and **follow** him. In this way, he **will have a treasure in heaven**. However, the man becomes **quite sad** because **he was very rich**. Earlier, after the parable of the *rich* fool who stored up *treasure* for himself (Luke 12:16–21), Jesus had similarly commanded: "*Sell* your belongings" so as to have "an inexhaustible *treasure in heaven*" (12:33 [emphasis added]). He had also warned the Pharisees that they neglect love for God (11:42); some of them "loved money" instead (16:14). These earlier passages suggest that Jesus is challenging the official because his riches detract from his love of God (see 16:13) and thus endanger his inheriting eternal life (18:18).

As the official fades into the background,[37] **Jesus** draws the conclusion for **18:24–25** his listeners: **for those who have wealth**, entering **the kingdom of God** is very **hard**. What a contrast to the children, to whom the kingdom belongs (18:16)! Jesus makes it even seem impossible with the memorable hyperbole of the **camel**[38] (the largest local animal) going **through the eye of a needle**[39] (the

---

36. The word "all" is characteristic of Luke's emphasis on radical discipleship (Luke 5:11, 28; 14:33).

37. In the parallel verses (Matt 19:22; Mark 10:22), he explicitly went away.

38. Some later manuscripts read not *kamēlos* but *kamilos*—"rope, ship's cable"—which is less of an exaggeration. See Cyril of Alexandria, *Homilies on Luke* 18:18–27 (trans. R. Payne Smith, 490): "By a camel he means not the animal . . . but a thick cable."

39. There is no historical foundation for the popular interpretation that "needle's eye" meant a small city gate through which a camel, free of its load, could pass through on its knees.

smallest opening). All of Jesus' disciples are thus called to be detached from their possessions (14:33) so as to be more attached to God.[40]

18:26–27   Jesus' words elicit the stunned reaction: **Then who can be saved?** His response, already hinted (18:19), explains that to save is divine: **What is impossible for human beings is possible for God.** Indeed, as the angel Gabriel had said, "Nothing will be impossible for God" (1:37). Moreover, God makes this salvation possible through Jesus, whose mission is "to save" (19:10; see Acts 4:12) even those who are rich, as will soon be illustrated with Zacchaeus (Luke 19:8–9).

18:28   Speaking again for the disciples (8:45; 9:20, 33; 12:41), **Peter** wonders about their future: **We have given up our possessions and followed you**. His words recall how he and his fishing partners had "left" their boats and "followed" Jesus (5:11, same two Greek verbs as here). Though they were not rich like the official, they had left "everything" (5:11).

18:29–30   Jesus' **Amen** reply introduces a general principle (as in 18:17), focusing not on possessions but on family ties that are **given up**. Jesus does not command his disciples to give up these relationships, but rather recognizes the sacrifices that some of his followers will have to make **for the sake of the kingdom**—for example, because of missionary work (Acts 12:12; 13:5; 15:39) and persecution (Luke 21:16). Luke's list differs somewhat from the parallel verses (Matt 19:29; Mark 10:29), most notably by mentioning **wife** (as in Luke 14:26), perhaps so as to include those who remain celibate for the kingdom (see Matt 19:12), such as Luke's companion Paul (1 Cor 7:7–8; 9:5). Jesus promises that the reward **in this present age** for such sacrifices will be **overabundant**—for example, through the new family of believers that gathers together (Luke 8:21; Acts 2:42–47). The reward **in the age to come** will be precisely what the official was pursuing: **eternal life**.

40. From the time of St. Anthony of the Desert (see Athanasius, *Life of Saint Antony* 2), Jesus' words to the rich man (see Matt 19:21) have also been understood as an evangelical counsel directed toward specific members of the Church called to profess a vow of poverty.

The King Goes Up to Jerusalem

Luke 18:31–19:44

The ascent to Jerusalem (18:31) marks the final part of Jesus' journey (9:51–19:44). As the section on Jesus' Galilean ministry (4:14–9:50) led up to the confession of Jesus as Messiah (9:20), so now this central section (9:51–19:44) culminates with the acclamation of Jesus as *king* (19:38). The theme of kingship as well as frequent geographical indications are features of this carefully organized unit.[1] As Jesus begins going up to Jerusalem, he again *predicts* his death (18:31–34). He passes through Jericho, where his two encounters (18:35–19:10) highlight his *kingly role* as son of David (18:38–39) who seeks those who are lost (19:10). A parable on *kingship* falls in the middle of the unit (19:11–28), framed by references to Jerusalem (19:11, 28). Jesus then reaches the Mount of Olives, where in two scenes (19:29–40) he is treated and acclaimed as *king* (19:35, 38). Arriving at the city, he again *predicts* its destruction (19:41–44).

Ascending to Jerusalem, Jesus Predicts His Suffering (18:31–34)

³¹Then he took the Twelve aside and said to them, "Behold, we are going up to Jerusalem and everything written by the prophets about the Son of Man will be fulfilled. ³²He will be handed over to the Gentiles and he will be mocked and insulted and spat upon; ³³and after they have scourged him

---

1. Jean-Noël Aletti, *L'art de raconter Jésus Christ: L'écriture narrative de l'évangile de Luc* (Paris: Seuil, 1989), 120–21, 202–3. For details on the ring structure (*A-B-C-B'-A'*), see Roland Meynet, *Luke: The Gospel of the Children of Israel* (Rome: Gregorian & Biblical Press, 2015), 632–35.

they will kill him, but on the third day he will rise." ³⁴But they understood
nothing of this; the word remained hidden from them and they failed to
comprehend what he said.

OT: Isa 50:6; 53:12
NT: Luke 9:22, 44–45; 13:33; 17:25; 22:37; 24:25–27, 44, 46; Acts 3:18. // Matt 20:17–19; Mark
10:32–34
Catechism: passion prediction, 557

18:31-33   At a solemn juncture, Jesus **took the Twelve aside** (see Josh 4:2) for the third
Son of Man passion prediction (Luke 9:22, 44–45). After journeying south along
the Jordan valley, they are near Jericho (18:35), more than 800 feet below sea
level, and now must turn westward, **going up to** an elevation of about 2,500
feet above sea level in **Jerusalem** (see 10:30). There, as elsewhere in Jesus' life
(4:21), the Scriptures **will be fulfilled** in what takes place (22:37; 24:25–27,
44, 46). Indeed, the details of his passion and resurrection that are mentioned
here allude to texts of **the prophets**. For example, Jesus predicts that he **will be
handed over** (9:44), like Isaiah's †suffering servant: "Because of their sins he was
given over" (Isa 53:12 NETS). This will be fulfilled when the Jewish chief priests
and rulers "hand him over" (Luke 20:20; see 24:20) **to the Gentiles**—that is, the
Romans through their governor Pilate (23:1). Moreover, before they **kill him**,
Jesus **will be mocked** (22:63; 23:11, 36), **insulted** (or "shamefully treated," RSV),
spat upon (Mark 14:65; 15:19), and **scourged** ("flogged," Luke 23:16, 22; see
John 19:1). Again, this is the destiny of the servant described in Isaiah: "I have
given my back to scourges / and my cheeks to blows, / but I did not turn away
my face / from the shame of spittings" (Isa 50:6 NETS). Finally, Jesus' words that
on the third day he will rise (Luke 24:7, 46) echo and embody Israel's hopes
described by Hosea—"On the third day we will rise up" (Hosea 6:2 NETS)—as
well as recall his earlier comparison to Jonah (Luke 11:29; Jon 2:1).

18:34   Only Luke extends the passage one more verse,² commenting that the Twelve
understood nothing of this (as with the second prediction, Luke 9:45). Only
after the resurrection will Jesus open "their minds to *understand*" (24:45 [em-
phasis added]) what is written in the Scriptures and how the Scriptures are
fulfilled in these events. For now, **the word** is **hidden from them** so they do
not **comprehend** or "know what he was talking about" (NIV). At the end of
the unit, something similar will happen to the people of Jerusalem (expressed
with the same two Greek verbs): would that they "knew" how to respond with
peace to Jesus' visitation, but "it is hidden" (19:42) from their eyes.

---

2. Matthew and Mark instead continue with the request of James and John, a passage Luke omits.

The Son of David in Jericho (18:35–19:10)

³⁵Now as he approached Jericho a blind man was sitting by the roadside begging, ³⁶and hearing a crowd going by, he inquired what was happening. ³⁷They told him, "Jesus of Nazareth is passing by." ³⁸He shouted, "Jesus, Son of David, have pity on me!" ³⁹The people walking in front rebuked him, telling him to be silent, but he kept calling out all the more, "Son of David, have pity on me!" ⁴⁰Then Jesus stopped and ordered that he be brought to him; and when he came near, Jesus asked him, ⁴¹"What do you want me to do for you?" He replied, "Lord, please let me see." ⁴²Jesus told him, "Have sight; your faith has saved you." ⁴³He immediately received his sight and followed him, giving glory to God. When they saw this, all the people gave praise to God.

¹⁹:¹He came to Jericho and intended to pass through the town. ²Now a man there named Zacchaeus, who was a chief tax collector and also a wealthy man, ³was seeking to see who Jesus was; but he could not see him because of the crowd, for he was short in stature. ⁴So he ran ahead and climbed a sycamore tree in order to see Jesus, who was about to pass that way. ⁵When he reached the place, Jesus looked up and said to him, "Zacchaeus, come down quickly, for today I must stay at your house." ⁶And he came down quickly and received him with joy. ⁷When they all saw this, they began to grumble, saying, "He has gone to stay at the house of a sinner." ⁸But Zacchaeus stood there and said to the Lord, "Behold, half of my possessions, Lord, I shall give to the poor, and if I have extorted anything from anyone I shall repay it four times over." ⁹And Jesus said to him, "Today salvation has come to this house because this man too is a descendant of Abraham. ¹⁰For the Son of Man has come to seek and to save what was lost."

OT: Josh 2:1; 2 Sam 7:12–16; Ezek 34:16, 22–23
NT: Luke 4:18; 5:29; 7:21–22, 34, 50; 8:48; 15:1–2, 4, 6; 17:13, 19; James 2:25. // Matt 20:29–34; Mark 10:46–52
Catechism: son of David, 439; Jesus Prayer, 2616, 2667; repairing injustice, 549, 2412; reintegrating forgiven sinners, 1443
Lectionary: Luke 19:1–10: Thirty-First Sunday Ordinary Time (Year C)

Jericho was located about seventeen miles northeast of Jerusalem and a mile   18:35
south of its Old Testament counterpart (Josh 6), near the palaces that the †Hasmoneans and Herod the Great had built on account of its mild winter climate. The road (Luke 10:30) that passed near the city was well traveled by pilgrims and traders alike. A **blind man** was **begging** for alms there, **by the roadside.**

His entrance into the story immediately after the mention of the Twelve's incomprehension (18:34) suggests that they too suffer from a form of blindness.[3]

18:36–38   The **crowd** informs the man that **Jesus of Nazareth** (literally, "the Nazorean")[4] **is passing by**. Having likely heard about Jesus—his outreach to the blind (14:13, 21), his restoring their sight (7:21–22)—the man cries out to **Jesus** to **have pity**, or "mercy" (RSV), just as the ten lepers did (17:13). With spiritual insight despite his blindness, and perhaps interpreting the word "Nazorean" to refer to the messianic "branch" (see comment on 1:26–27), he addresses Jesus as **Son of David**. The title indicates that Jesus is king (1:32–33), as indeed he will be acclaimed by the whole multitude of disciples on the Mount of Olives (19:38).

18:39–40   There, some Pharisees will call on Jesus to "rebuke" those who recognize him as king (19:39). Here, those leading the way—perhaps even from among the uncomprehending Twelve—similarly **rebuked** the blind man. Like the disciples who "rebuked" the people who brought infants to Jesus (18:15), they have not yet understood Jesus' mission. However, like the persistent widow (18:3), who represents those who call out (18:7) to God day and night, the man is undeterred: **he kept calling out all the more**. The man is successful in getting a hearing. Jesus commands that he **be brought to him** for healing.

18:41–42   In reply to Jesus' question, the man now addresses him as **Lord** (5:12; 7:6) and asks that he may **see**, or "see again" (NRSV). On account of the mission he announced in Nazareth—"to proclaim . . . recovery of sight to the blind" (4:18; see 7:22; Isa 61:1 LXX)—**Jesus** issues a simple command: **Have sight**, or "Recover your sight" (ESV).[5] He adds a phrase already spoken to three others: **your faith has saved you** (Luke 7:50; 8:48; 17:19). The verb *sōzō* can refer to the physical healing: "Your faith has healed you" (NIV, NET). However, the man's response (18:43) suggests that Jesus has also attended to his spiritual well-being. He has given him more than he requested.

18:43   The miracle takes effect **immediately** (5:25; 8:44, 55; 13:13), and he **received his sight**. Rather than remain "by the roadside" (18:35), his response is to become a disciple: the man **followed him** (18:22, 28). *Jesus* has performed the miracle, but the man gives **glory to God** (5:25; 13:13; 17:15). **All the people** likewise give **praise to God** (2:20; 5:26; 7:16). They recognize that Jesus is carrying out God's work. He is fulfilling his mission and the Scriptures.

---

3. Joseph A. Fitzmyer, *The Gospel according to Luke*, 2 vols., AB (New York: Doubleday, 1981–85), 2:1214.

4. As in Acts 2:22; 3:6; 4:10; 6:14; 22:8; 26:9.

5. The same command is used in Acts by Ananias to heal the blind Saul (Acts 22:13) after "Jesus the Nazorean" (Acts 22:8) appeared to him on the road to Damascus.

Unique to Luke is a second **Jericho** encounter, this time with **a man** whose   **19:1–2**
name is given: **Zacchaeus**.[6] In this town that was near the border between
Roman-controlled Judea and Perea and on an east-west trade route, he worked as
a chief tax collector, overseeing the collection of tolls and duties on transported
goods. On account of his occupation and his collaboration with the Romans,
he was "a sinner" (19:7) in the people's estimation. Nevertheless, readers of
Luke by now are aware that even tax collectors can repent of their sins,[7] as
did the one in the recent parable (18:9–14). As to be expected, Zacchaeus was
wealthy (*plousios*), further complicating his situation in the Gospel,[8] especially
since this word was just used to describe the rich official (18:23) and in Jesus'
warning about the rich (18:25). These two storylines—about tax collectors and
the rich—now come together in this encounter, which also recalls the lessons
from many other passages.

As with the blind man by the roadside, Zacchaeus must first overcome the   **19:3–4**
challenge posed by a personal condition: he **was short in stature**. In both cases,
the crowd also made it difficult (18:36). Hence, the blind man "kept calling
out" to get Jesus' attention (18:39), and Zacchaeus **climbed a sycamore tree** so
as **to see Jesus**.[9] The blind man is like the widow in the parable, representing
those who "call out" to God day and night (18:7), and Zacchaeus is like the tax
collector in the next parable, not only on account of his occupation but also
because of his similar humble disposition (18:14). He is not afraid to make a
fool of himself for Jesus' sake.

As he did for the blind man, **Jesus** stops for **Zacchaeus**, calling him by   **19:5–6**
name and telling him to **come down**. His words indicate that this is no chance
encounter but one that occurs by divine necessity in fulfillment of God's plan.
Visiting Zacchaeus's home is something he **must** do (*dei*; see comment on 2:49),
and the time to do it is **today** (2:11; 4:21; 5:26; 23:43).

The appropriate way to respond to such a divine visitation is "in haste"
(noun *spoudē*, 1:39)—that is, **quickly** (verb *speudō* twice; see 2:16). Abraham
had similarly responded quickly (same verb, twice in Gen 18:6 LXX) after he
welcomed divinely sent visitors (Gen 18:1–5). Zacchaeus, "a descendant of
Abraham" (Luke 19:9), now imitates the patriarch's hospitality. He **received**

---

6. For this Jewish name, see also 2 Macc 10:19; "Zaccai" in Ezra 2:9; Neh 7:14. Richard Bauckham,
Jesus and the Eyewitnesses: The Gospels as Eyewitness Testimony (Grand Rapids: Eerdmans, 2006), 55,
suggests that this passage is based on the recollections of Zacchaeus himself (see Luke 1:2).

7. Luke 3:12–13; 5:27–32; 7:29, 34; 15:1.

8. Luke 1:53; 6:24; 8:14; 12:16–21; 16:13–14, 19–31.

9. The tree in question is the sycamore fig, whose low branches make climbing easy. Moreover, the
situation here recalls that of the man who was paralyzed (5:19): "the crowd" is in the way, so the men
carrying him *go up* on the roof as Zacchaeus *goes up* a tree (same Greek verb).

Jesus, as also another Old Testament figure, Rahab the prostitute, "welcomed" (James 2:25; same verb) the messengers sent from Joshua, in the same town, Jericho (Josh 2:1).[10] Earlier in Luke, Martha had similarly "welcomed" Jesus (Luke 10:38). Moreover, this rich man welcomes him **with joy**, in contrast to the rich official who "became quite sad" in his encounter with Jesus (18:23).

19:7   Jesus goes **to stay** with Zacchaeus, as Joshua's spies went to stay with Rahab (same Greek verb in Josh 2:1 LXX). However, because Zacchaeus is known as **a sinner**, the onlookers in the crowd **grumble**, as did the Pharisees and scribes earlier when Jesus dealt with tax collectors (Luke 5:30; 15:2). They are imitating Israel's wilderness generation that grumbled against God and Moses.[11]

19:8   Addressing Jesus as **Lord**, like the blind man (18:41) and like Abraham speaking to his special guest (Gen 18:3 LXX), **Zacchaeus** responds by resolving that from now on his life will change. From among his **possessions**, he will **give to the poor**—actually doing what the rich official was invited to do (Luke 18:22). Whatever is left he will use to **repay** those whom he has cheated, making restitution **four times over**, going well beyond what the law generally required (Lev 5:24;[12] Num 5:7). His resolution indicates the good fruits that he will produce as evidence of his repentance (Luke 3:8).

Nevertheless, some interpret Zacchaeus's statement not as a resolution about what he will do in the future but as a defense of what he is already doing at the present time, because the Greek verbs translated "give" and "repay" are in the present tense.[13] However, several reasons favor the future view, which interprets the present tense verbs as describing what Zacchaeus is about to do.[14] For example, the other view makes him sound more like the self-righteous Pharisee (18:12) than the repentant tax collector (18:13).

19:9–10 Most importantly, the final words of **Jesus**, which are addressed **to him**, indicate that **what was lost**—that is, Zacchaeus—has been found, like the "lost" sheep, coin, and son in the parables (15:4, 6, 8–9, 24, 32). Meeting Jesus the Savior (2:11) thus marks a turning point in this chief tax collector's life—as it did earlier for the tax collector Levi (5:27–32)—bringing **salvation** to his **house**. Hence, the example of Zacchaeus shows that it is "possible" even for

10. On the allusions to Abraham and Rahab, see Alan C. Mitchell, "Zacchaeus Revisited: Luke 19:8 as a Defense," *Biblica* 71 (1990): 164–71.

11. Same Greek verb as in, e.g., Exod 15:24 LXX; Num 14:2 LXX.

12. Lev 6:5 RSV. On fourfold restitution of sheep, see Exod 21:37; 2 Sam 12:6.

13. E.g., Fitzmyer, *Luke*, 2:1220–21.

14. Dennis Hamm, "Luke 19:8 Once Again: Does Zacchaeus Defend or Resolve?," *JBL* 107 (1988): 431–37. See also Hamm, "Zacchaeus Revisited Once More: A Story of Vindication or Conversion?," *Biblica* 72 (1991): 249–52.

"a rich person to enter the kingdom of God" and "be saved" (18:25–27)! Such is the mission of **the Son of Man**, which explains why it was necessary for him to stay there **today** (19:5). Zacchaeus thought that he "was seeking" Jesus (v. 3), but in reality Jesus had **come to seek** him and **save** him. As Zechariah and Mary had prophesied, Jesus is the horn of salvation whom God has raised up within the house of David (1:69), to bring salvation (1:71) and show mercy to the descendants of **Abraham** (1:55, 73). These include the once-crippled "daughter of Abraham" (13:16) and this once-corrupt "son of Abraham" (19:9 NRSV). Indeed, "God can raise up children to Abraham" (3:8) from those least expected.

In summary, what Jesus taught in the parable, he now teaches by his example. He is revealed as the shepherd who goes seeking the lost sheep. His words allude to and fulfill the shepherd prophecy in Ezekiel: "I will seek the lost" (Ezek 34:16 NETS). And he is once again revealed as the kingly "Son of David" (Luke 18:38–39): "I will set up over them one shepherd, my servant David" (Ezek 34:23 RSV).

Reflection and Application (18:35–19:10)

Kyrie eleison. The pleas for mercy of the blind man and also of the lepers (Luke 17:13) find expression in the penitential act at Mass, in which the faithful pray for mercy, express repentance for their sins, and ask for the help they need to be brought to everlasting life.

Theology of the cross. St. Augustine compares the tree that Zacchaeus climbed to Jesus' cross: "Climb the tree on which Jesus hung for you, and you will see Jesus."[15] This thought can be developed further. Whereas Jesus hung on the tree because he was crucified (23:33), Jesus told Zacchaeus to come down from the tree (19:5). In effect, the sinner is replaced by the Savior. This is the substitution accomplished by Jesus (Catechism 615). He died on the cross in our place, giving us salvation (19:9), which by grace we can begin to experience *today* (19:9; 23:43), and which reaches its fullness in the glory of eternal life.

Shepherds like Jesus. The suggested homily in the Rite of Ordination of priests concludes with an exhortation about priestly ministry that echoes Jesus' words: "Keep always before your eyes the example of the Good Shepherd . . . who came to seek out and save what was lost."[16]

---

15. Augustine, *Sermon* 174.3, in *Sermons*, trans. Edmund Hill, 11 vols., WSA III/5 (Hyde Park, NY: New City Press, 1990–97), 5:259.
16. *The Roman Pontifical*, Ordination of Priests (Vatican City: Vox Clara Committee, 2012), 69.

The Parable of the Returning King (19:11–28)

¹¹While they were listening to him speak, he proceeded to tell a parable because he was near Jerusalem and they thought that the kingdom of God would appear there immediately. ¹²So he said, "A nobleman went off to a distant country to obtain the kingship for himself and then to return. ¹³He called ten of his servants and gave them ten gold coins and told them, 'Engage in trade with these until I return.' ¹⁴His fellow citizens, however, despised him and sent a delegation after him to announce, 'We do not want this man to be our king.' ¹⁵But when he returned after obtaining the kingship, he had the servants called, to whom he had given the money, to learn what they had gained by trading. ¹⁶The first came forward and said, 'Sir, your gold coin has earned ten additional ones.' ¹⁷He replied, 'Well done, good servant! You have been faithful in this very small matter; take charge of ten cities.' ¹⁸Then the second came and reported, 'Your gold coin, sir, has earned five more.' ¹⁹And to this servant too he said, 'You, take charge of five cities.' ²⁰Then the other servant came and said, 'Sir, here is your gold coin; I kept it stored away in a handkerchief, ²¹for I was afraid of you, because you are a demanding person; you take up what you did not lay down and you harvest what you did not plant.' ²²He said to him, 'With your own words I shall condemn you, you wicked servant. You knew I was a demanding person, taking up what I did not lay down and harvesting what I did not plant; ²³why did you not put my money in a bank? Then on my return I would have collected it with interest.' ²⁴And to those standing by he said, 'Take the gold coin from him and give it to the servant who has ten.' ²⁵But they said to him, 'Sir, he has ten gold coins.' ²⁶'I tell you, to everyone who has, more will be given, but from the one who has not, even what he has will be taken away. ²⁷Now as for those enemies of mine who did not want me as their king, bring them here and slay them before me.'"

²⁸After he had said this, he proceeded on his journey up to Jerusalem.

OT: Deut 23:20–21
NT: Mark 13:34; Luke 8:18; 12:35–48; 16:10. // Matt 25:14–30
Catechism: development of "talents," 1880

19:11   Because Jesus is **near Jerusalem**, there is speculation that **the kingdom of God** will **appear there immediately**. On one level, as Jesus earlier explained in response to the Pharisees' question, "the kingdom of God is among you" (17:21) because Jesus is present, and his disciples will soon hail him as "king" (19:38) when he approaches Jerusalem. However, contrary to expectations, he will be crucified, precisely as "King" (23:38).[17] Hence, on another level, as Jesus will indicate in response to the apostles' similar question after his resurrection (Acts 1:6), the coming of God's kingdom in its fullness is still in the future. He must first ascend to heaven before returning, and their mission in the meantime is to be his witnesses (Acts 1:7–11).

In order to convey such a double-level message, Jesus here tells **a parable** that both interprets the events about to take place in Jerusalem and corrects the expectations that the appearance of God's kingdom is imminent.

The parable is about **kingship** (same noun as "kingdom" in Luke 19:11), **19:12** involving **a nobleman** who goes **to a distant country** to become king **and then to return**. The background to this scenario is the recent history of Archelaus, Herod the Great's son, who traveled to Rome after his father's death to be confirmed as the successor to the kingdom by Caesar Augustus.[18]

In contrast to Archelaus who was a cruel tyrant, however, the man in the parable is presented positively as a noble figure. Specifically, the mention of a kingdom in both this verse and the previous one (v. 11) suggests that the nobleman represents Jesus himself. Some scholars even interpret the man's going to a distant country and then returning as a reference to Jesus' ascension into heaven before his second coming.[19]

There is also a second story within the parable. Before leaving, the noble- **19:13** man gives **ten of his servants** the task of trading with **ten gold coins**, sometimes translated "pounds" or, more literally, "minas" (coins worth a hundred days' wages). The servants, who each receive the gift of a coin, may represent the disciples of Jesus who will be entrusted with the gift of the Holy Spirit (Acts 2:38; 10:45)—and his differing gifts of grace (Rom 12:6; 1 Cor 12:4; Eph 4:7)—for the purpose of carrying out their mission (Acts 1:8). Some details about this second story resemble Matthew's parable of the talents, in which three servants receive five, two, and one talent[20] (Matt 25:14–30). However, the first story, about the nobleman becoming king, and the context of Jesus' approach to Jerusalem make the interpretation of Luke's parable somewhat different.

---

17. Klyne R. Snodgrass, *Stories with Intent: A Comprehensive Guide to the Parables of Jesus* (Grand Rapids: Eerdmans, 2008), 539.

18. Josephus, *Jewish Antiquities* 17.202, 208–9, 228. The setting also suggests Archelaus, since he was first proclaimed king in Jericho (Luke 19:1), following Herod's death there (*Jewish Antiquities* 17.173, 194–95). Archelaus restored Herod's palace in Jericho and built a nearby village named Archelais (*Jewish Antiquities* 17.340). Snodgrass, *Stories with Intent*, 537, comments that "it is difficult . . . to think hearers would not have thought of Archelaus."

19. E.g., Fitzmyer, *Luke*, 2:1233.

20. A talent (of silver) was worth about six thousand days' wages, so sixty minas.

19:14   Another element of the first story regards the nobleman's **fellow citizens**, who send **a delegation** as their representatives because they **despised him** and **do not want** him as their **king**. Josephus indicates that fifty ambassadors were sent from Judea to Rome to request that Archelaus not become king, because he had already killed three thousand Jews in quelling an uprising.[21] In the parable, however, the citizens' hatred of the nobleman is unwarranted (see Luke 6:22). Similarly, without having doing anything wrong, Jesus in Jerusalem will encounter those who do not want him as their king (23:2–3; see John 19:15).

19:15   The rest of the parable relates the conclusion of the stories introduced in Luke 19:12–14. Regarding the first story, the nobleman returns with the **kingship**. The historical background is similar. Caesar Augustus compromised by appointing Archelaus not king but ethnarch over half of Herod's kingdom (Judea, Samaria, and Idumea), promising to make him king if he proved worthy.[22] Since the nobleman is now king, he can more readily be understood to represent Jesus, who will be acclaimed as king in the following passage (19:38).

As for the second story, **the servants** are summoned to give an account of their **trading**, a subject that occupies the following eleven verses (vv. 16–26).

19:16–19   Coming **forward**, the servants fittingly address the king as **sir** or lord (*kyrios*; vv. 16, 18, 20), as does the whole group (v. 25). Significantly, both before and after the parable, Jesus is the one called Lord (*kyrios*; 19:8, 31, 34). Something similar occurred earlier with Jesus' dialogue with Peter, inserted between short parables about a master and servants (12:35–48). This connection provides further support for understanding the king in the parable as a figure of Jesus.

The **first** and **second** servants report that the king's gift of a mina **has earned** a profit of **ten** and **five** more minas, respectively. The king thus gives them **charge** of (literally, "authority over") **ten** and **five cities**. They **have been faithful** or trustworthy in a relatively small matter, so the king entrusts them with a greater one, according to the principle of discipleship taught earlier (16:10). Not to be overlooked is the king's generosity in rewarding his faithful servants. Disciples of Jesus who respond faithfully by exercising the gifts entrusted to them will be given further gifts—and the responsibilities that go along with them. For example, the apostles at the Last Supper are given a share in Jesus' kingly authority (22:28–30), which they will then exercise over the new community of believers in Acts.

19:20–21   Only one **other** of the remaining servants is explicitly mentioned. This third **servant** simply returns the **gold coin**, having **kept it stored** safely **in a**

21. *Jewish Antiquities* 17.218, 300–314.
22. Josephus, *Jewish War* 2.93–96; *Jewish Antiquities* 17.317–21.

handkerchief. Surprisingly, he explains his disobedience to the command to "engage in trade" (19:13) by blaming the king for being **demanding** and unfair (taking what he **did not lay down** and harvesting what he **did not plant**), which led him to be **afraid**. However, up to this point, there is no evidence that the king is so severe and unjust. On the contrary, he seems rather generous. Like the fellow citizens' hatred of the king (v. 14), the servant's complaint seems unwarranted. It is rather an excuse for his own failure to respond. He thus may represent those disciples who "fail to produce mature fruit" (8:14) in contrast to the first two servants who bore "fruit through perseverance" (8:15).

In contrast to the first "good servant" (19:17), this one is a **wicked servant**, **19:22–26** whose **words** the king now uses against him. Surprisingly, he does not challenge the servant's description of him, but rather takes it to its logical conclusion. Since the servant **knew** that the king **was a demanding person**, he should have at least put the **money in a bank**—literally, "the table" used by money changers (Mark 11:15)—so as to collect **interest**, which Jews could lawfully do from non-Jews (Deut 23:20–21). The king then orders that servant's **gold coin** to be taken from him and, despite an objection, given to the one with **ten**. This action illustrates another principle of discipleship stated earlier (Luke 8:18): **more will be given** to those who have, while even the little of those who have not **will be taken away**. Of course, this kingdom logic refers not to material possessions but to God's gifts of grace, which disciples should not receive in vain (1 Cor 15:10; 2 Cor 6:1), lest they risk losing those gifts. The third servant loses the mina given to him, but no further punishment is mentioned (compare Matt 25:30).

The parable concludes with a startling reference back to the first story: the **19:27** **king** gives the command to summon the **enemies** who had opposed him (Luke 19:14) and **slay them**. Once again the scenario likely recalls the historical situation under Archelaus. After becoming ethnarch, he remembered who his enemies were and thus continued his barbarous ways before being deposed in AD 6.[23] Since such words are what one would expect from a tyrant like Archelaus but not from Jesus, some scholars deny that the king in the parable represents Jesus in any way.[24] Several points can be made in response. First, it is helpful to remember that this command occurs *within the parable* (12:46), and other parables also contain shocking characters who nonetheless are compared *in some limited way* to Jesus (e.g., the Son of Man appearing unexpectedly like a thief, 12:39–40) or to God (e.g., the unjust judge who hears the widow's plea, 18:5). Second, the context of the journey to Jerusalem is a reminder that the king Jesus

23. Josephus, *Jewish War* 2.111; *Jewish Antiquities* 17.342–44.
24. E.g., David E. Garland, *Luke*, ZECNT (Grand Rapids: Zondervan, 2011), 762–63.

Parables Revisited

BIBLICAL
BACKGROUND

One reason why Luke's central section (9:51–19:44) is so long is that it contains so many parables. Parables have a different function than other kinds of passages.[a] In the parables, the action of the main story—for example, Jesus' journey to Jerusalem—pauses as we hear not a story about Jesus (e.g., some miracle he performed) but a story that Jesus himself tells. In the parables, Luke in a sense allows Jesus to speak to his readers directly, teaching them and persuading them to follow him. Readers thus find themselves in the same situation as the characters in the Gospel who are "listening to him speak" (19:11). In other parts of the Gospel, readers are typically in a privileged position with respect to the characters; in other words, they know more. For example, when the shepherds hear the message of the angel regarding Jesus' identity, readers are not surprised, because Luke has already told them what the angel Gabriel said to Mary. However, in the parables, which are stories within a story, readers to a large extent know just as much—or as little—as the characters in the Gospel. Indeed, Luke does not explain the parables' surprising turns, thus allowing the readers to experience their shock effect. Parables therefore pose a challenge, inviting readers to reflect on their meaning, leading to growth in understanding and to a deeper commitment as disciples of Jesus.

a. For the ideas in this sidebar, see Aletti, *L'art de raconter Jésus Christ*, 150–53.

(19:38) is also different from the king in the parable, since Jesus is the one who is about to be slain. The background regarding Archelaus is thus sharply ironic: some people are rejecting the innocent Messiah as if he were like the wicked Archelaus![25] Third, as he approaches Jerusalem, Jesus will also weep for the city because of the judgment that will befall it for not recognizing God's visitation in his coming (19:41–44). As the encounter with Zacchaeus demonstrated, Jesus has come offering salvation (19:9); however, the flip side is judgment for those who reject that offer. Consequently, the conclusion of the parable is a prophetic warning of the judgment that results from rejection of the king.

19:28   After finishing the parable, Jesus continues going **up to Jerusalem**. The parable is thus framed by references to the *city* at the beginning (v. 11) and at the end, also suggesting that the *citizens* (v. 14) who reject their king are precisely those of Jerusalem. That "king" is about to be identified as Jesus himself (19:38), whose imminent rejection will eventually lead to the city's destruction.

25. Snodgrass, *Stories with Intent*, 537.

The King on the Mount of Olives (19:29–40)

[29]As he drew near to Bethphage and Bethany at the place called the Mount of Olives, he sent two of his disciples. [30]He said, "Go into the village opposite you, and as you enter it you will find a colt tethered on which no one has ever sat. Untie it and bring it here. [31]And if anyone should ask you, 'Why are you untying it?' you will answer, 'The Master has need of it.'" [32]So those who had been sent went off and found everything just as he had told them. [33]And as they were untying the colt, its owners said to them, "Why are you untying this colt?" [34]They answered, "The Master has need of it." [35]So they brought it to Jesus, threw their cloaks over the colt, and helped Jesus to mount. [36]As he rode along, the people were spreading their cloaks on the road; [37]and now as he was approaching the slope of the Mount of Olives, the whole multitude of his disciples began to praise God aloud with joy for all the mighty deeds they had seen. [38]They proclaimed:

> "Blessed is the king who comes
>   in the name of the Lord.
> Peace in heaven
>   and glory in the highest."

[39]Some of the Pharisees in the crowd said to him, "Teacher, rebuke your disciples." [40]He said in reply, "I tell you, if they keep silent, the stones will cry out!"

OT: 1 Kings 1:33; 2 Kings 9:13; Ps 118:26; Zech 9:9; 14:4
NT: Luke 2:13–14; 13:35; 22:8, 13. // Matt 21:1–9; Mark 11:1–10; John 12:12–19
Catechism: Jesus' entry into Jerusalem, 559–60
Lectionary: Luke 19:28–40: Palm Sunday Procession (Year C)

The road leading up to Jerusalem passed by **Bethphage** and **Bethany**, villages   19:29–31
on the eastern slope of the north-south ridge called the **Mount of Olives**, with
Jerusalem about two miles to the west. Bethany, known from John's Gospel as the
village of Martha and Mary (John 11:1; 12:1–3), is later the site of Jesus' ascension (Luke 24:50; see Acts 1:12). Jesus also goes to Bethany at night during his
Jerusalem ministry (Matt 21:17; Mark 11:11–12), although Luke more generally
says the Mount of Olives (Luke 21:37). On the night Jesus is betrayed, he also
goes out to the Mount of Olives (22:39; Matt 26:30; Mark 14:26), specifically
to a place on its western slope, the garden of Gethsemane (Matt 26:36; Mark
14:32; see John 18:1). In the Old Testament, the Mount of Olives appears in a
prophecy: "the Lord will go forth and . . . on that day his feet shall stand on the

Mount of Olives" (Zech 14:3–4 NETS).[26] Indeed, Jesus **the Master**, or rather "the Lord" (*kyrios*, repeated in Luke 19:34),[27] is drawing **near**.

In order to prepare for his arrival, Jesus sends **two of his disciples**—as he does customarily (10:1; 22:8)—to a **village**. The two disciples' task is to fetch **a colt** and **bring it** to him. The animal itself and the specification that **no one has ever sat** on it[28] point to Jesus' dignity as Jerusalem's king:

> Shout for joy, O daughter Jerusalem!
> Behold: your king is coming to you,
>   a just savior is he,
> Humble, and riding on a donkey,
>   on a colt, the foal of a donkey. (Zech 9:9)[29]

Since a king could expropriate animals to do his work (1 Sam 8:16), Jesus instructs the two to respond to **anyone** who questions **why** they are **untying** the colt by saying that the Master—that is, "the Lord" (*kyrios*)—needs it.

19:32–34   The two disciples find **everything just as he had told them**. The same will happen when Peter and John go to prepare the Passover (Luke 22:13). Jesus expresses awareness of how God's plan must unfold not only through his passion predictions (18:31–33) but also in these details. The question about **untying the colt** as well as the answer rehearsed with Jesus (v. 31) are repeated in order to emphasize that Jesus is **the Master**—that is, "the Lord" (*kyrios*). The same title was also used twice in the encounter with Zacchaeus (19:8).

19:35–36   Also the way **Jesus** is treated emphasizes that he is king. For example, when David appointed Solomon to succeed him as king, he ordered his officials to "mount" him upon his own mule (1 Kings 1:33). Similarly, the disciples help **Jesus to mount** the colt. Also, when Elisha's aide anointed Jehu as king over the northern kingdom of Israel, the army commanders spread their garments or cloaks under him (2 Kings 9:13 LXX). Here, they similarly **threw their cloaks over the colt** before Jesus mounted, and **people** likewise **were spreading their cloaks on the road** as Jesus **rode along**.

26. Perhaps motivated by this prophecy, an Egyptian messianic pretender led a multitude of people to the Mount of Olives (Josephus, *Jewish War* 2.262; *Jewish Antiquities* 20.169; see Acts 21:38). His revolt was put down by Felix, the Roman procurator (AD 52–58).

27. C. Kavin Rowe, *Early Narrative Christology: The Lord in the Gospel of Luke* (Berlin: de Gruyter, 2006; Grand Rapids: Baker Academic, 2009), 160.

28. *m. Sanhedrin* 2:5 indicates that no one may ride the king's horse or sit on his throne. Later, Jesus will similarly be laid in a "tomb in which no one had yet been buried" (Luke 23:53).

29. See also Jacob's oracle regarding a king from the tribe of Judah with a **tethered** colt: "He tethers his donkey to the vine, / his donkey's foal to the choicest stem" (Gen 49:11).

Liturgical Coming of the Lord

LIVING TRADITION

"Blessed is he / who comes in the name of the LORD" (Ps 118:26). At Mass, the chant "Holy, Holy, Holy" (*Sanctus*) sung at the beginning of the Eucharistic Prayer includes, since at least the sixth century,[a] these words of Psalm 118 that were addressed to Jesus as he approached Jerusalem (Luke 19:38; see 13:35; Catechism 559). Pope Benedict XVI explains the theological significance:

> Just as the Lord entered the Holy City that day on a donkey, so too the Church saw him coming again and again in the humble form of bread and wine. The Church greets the Lord in the Holy Eucharist as the one who is coming now, the one who has entered into her midst. At the same time, she greets him as the one who continues to come, the one who leads us toward his coming. As pilgrims, we go up to him; as a pilgrim, he comes to us and takes us up with him in his "ascent" to the Cross and Resurrection, to the definitive Jerusalem.[b]

a. Caesarius of Arles, *Sermon* 73.2, in *Sermons*, trans. Mary M. Mueller, 3 vols., FC 31 (Washington, DC: Catholic University of America Press, 1956–73), 1:343: "Shout with trembling and joy: 'Holy, holy, holy, blessed is he that comes in the name of the Lord'" (translation adapted).

b. Benedict XVI, *Jesus of Nazareth: Holy Week; From the Entrance into Jerusalem to the Resurrection*, trans. Philip J. Whitmore (San Francisco: Ignatius, 2011), 10–11.

The repetition of the location, **the Mount of Olives**, begins the second part **19:37-38** of the passage. Jesus is about to descend the mount's western **slope**, and the response to him on this last bit of the journey sums up earlier reactions. Because of **all the mighty deeds**—like the healing of the blind man—that they have **seen** *Jesus* do, **his disciples** begin **to praise God** (Luke 18:43). They do so **aloud**, like the healed leper did (17:15), and filled **with joy**, like those who witnessed his miracles (13:17).

Jesus is acclaimed with the words of a psalm "that was historically understood as featuring Israel's king":[30] **"Blessed is** he / **who comes in the name of the Lord"** (quoting Ps 118:26). John had spoken about one who "is coming" (Luke 3:16; see 7:19–20), and Jesus had prophesied that Jerusalem would not see him until these very words were said (13:35). Now that time has arrived, as he comes into view of the city and everything is being fulfilled (18:31). Moreover, in the middle of this psalm verse are added here the words **the king**, the culminating title of the journey section. This proclamation complements Peter's confession

30. Brent Kinman, "Jesus' Royal Entry into Jerusalem," in *Key Events in the Life of the Historical Jesus*, ed. Darrell L. Bock and Robert L. Webb (Grand Rapids: Eerdmans, 2010), 407.

of Jesus as the Messiah at the end of the Galilean ministry (9:20). Both are titles associated with King David: "the Messiah is the Son of David" (20:41) and "a king" (23:2). However, whereas David captured Jerusalem through war (2 Sam 5:6–8), Jesus comes offering **peace** (Luke 19:42).

Indeed, **the whole multitude** of disciples proclaims peace **in heaven / and glory in the highest**, echoing the "multitude of the heavenly host" who proclaimed, "Glory to God in the highest / and on earth peace," at Jesus' birth (2:13–14), when he was similarly acclaimed as the Davidic and kingly "Messiah and Lord" (2:11).

19:39–40   Amid the acclamation of Jesus as king, **some of the Pharisees**—who are here explicitly mentioned for the last time in Luke—express their disapproval. Perhaps fearing Roman reprisal, they ask Jesus to **rebuke** his **disciples**. Earlier, some people had rebuked the blind man when he called Jesus by the kingly title, "Son of David" (Luke 18:38–39), and Jesus himself had commanded silence about his identity when Peter privately called him "Messiah" (9:20–21). Now, however, Jesus' suffering, which has been repeatedly revealed (9:22, 44; 17:25; 18:31–33), is imminent, so it is proper to proclaim his kingship publicly. One can no longer **keep silent**, else even **the stones** themselves **will cry out** in witness. This saying recalls the "children of Abraham" whom God can raise up "from these stones" (3:8), people like the blind man who "cried out all the more" (18:39 RSV) that Jesus is the kingly "Son of David."

Weeping over Jerusalem, Jesus Predicts Its Destruction (19:41–44)

---

[41]As he drew near, he saw the city and wept over it, [42]saying, "If this day you only knew what makes for peace—but now it is hidden from your eyes. [43]For the days are coming upon you when your enemies will raise a palisade against you; they will encircle you and hem you in on all sides. [44]They will smash you to the ground and your children within you, and they will not leave one stone upon another within you because you did not recognize the time of your visitation."

OT: Deut 29:3; Isa 6:9–10; 29:3; Ezek 4:1–3
NT: Luke 1:68, 78; 8:10; 13:34; 21:6, 20, 24; 23:28–30; Rom 11:8
Catechism: Jesus weeps over Jerusalem, 558

19:41   When this last phase of the journey began, Jesus predicted that he would be killed in Jerusalem (18:31–33). Correspondingly, as he approaches the end of the journey, he predicts Jerusalem's destruction. Thus, when **he saw the city** as

Figure 16. Jerusalem from the Mount of Olives.

he came down the Mount of Olives, he **wept over it**. He weeps on account of
the suffering the people will undergo. Thus, he will also later tell the women
of Jerusalem to "weep . . . for yourselves and for your children" (23:28). His
attitude is very different from that of the king in the parable (19:27).

Jesus addresses his lament to the city itself: **If this day you only knew what**   19:42
makes for peace. However, the thought breaks off without being completed,
implying that Jerusalem will soon fail to recognize him, despite the acclamations
of the present moment. Jesus has come to lead them in "the path of peace" (1:79;
see Acts 10:36), but the city will ultimately reject him and his terms for peace
(see Luke 14:32). On the one hand, this will involve the human responsibility of
those in Jerusalem—that is, the religious leaders—who were "unwilling" (13:34;
see Rom 10:21) to welcome Jesus. On the other hand, it is part of God's plan:[31]
It is hidden from your eyes (see Rom 11:8, 25).[32] Earlier in Luke, when Jesus
referred to "the mysteries of the kingdom," he explained that such knowledge
has been granted to some, but others "may look but not see, and hear but not
understand" (Luke 8:10; see Isa 6:9; Acts 28:27).

Jesus then gives a more detailed prediction of the siege and destruction of   19:43–44
Jerusalem that will take place in **the days** that **are coming** (Luke 21:6; 23:29).

31. I.e., so that the gospel message can reach all the nations during "the times of the Gentiles" (Luke
21:24; 24:47; see Acts 1:8; 28:28; Rom 11:25–26).
32. Jesus' prediction of his death was likewise "hidden" from the Twelve (Luke 18:34).

The vocabulary of Jesus' prophecy echoes passages from the prophets, such as those about the fall of Jerusalem to the Babylonians in the sixth century BC. History would in a sense repeat itself, as Jesus' prophecy was fulfilled when the city fell to the Romans in AD 70.

Your enemies will raise a palisade against you—that is, a barricade fortifying an entrenchment used in a siege on a walled city, as when the Babylonians attacked Jerusalem (Ezek 4:2; 21:27[33]). This statement and another one—**They will encircle you**—also echo a description in Isaiah: "I will circle you with outposts / and set up siege works against you" (Isa 29:3). According to Josephus, the Roman general Titus indeed built ramparts and encircled Jerusalem with a wall as he laid siege to the city.[34]

The city will then be destroyed: **They will smash you to the ground and your children within you**. Similar atrocities were mentioned by the prophets (Hosea 10:14; 14:1; Nah 3:10). The "you" spoken of here continues to be the city of Jerusalem itself, so "your children" are its citizens (Luke 13:34).[35] Likewise, Jesus will later tell the "Daughters of Jerusalem" to weep for their children (23:28). **They will not leave one stone upon another within you**: Jesus will make a similar statement in reference to the temple (21:6). All this will take place **because you did not recognize the time of your visitation**, as Jeremiah had similarly prophesied: "They shall perish in a time of visitation" (Jer 6:15 NETS). God is visiting Jerusalem through Jesus' arrival in the city. The visitation is intended to bring redemption (Luke 1:68, 78; 7:16) but will instead bring judgment to those who do not welcome it.

33. Ezek 21:22 RSV.

34. *Jewish War* 5.466–68, 499–510. Josephus, however, uses vocabulary different from that of Luke and is much more detailed, so no conclusions can be drawn on the basis of 19:43–44 about Luke's use of such historical reports and the dating of Luke's Gospel. See the introduction.

35. François Bovon, *Luke*, trans. Christine M. Thomas, Donald S. Deer, and James Crouch, 3 vols., Hermeneia (Minneapolis: Fortress, 2002–13), 3:18n38.

Ministry in the Temple

Luke 19:45–21:38

Jesus reaches the destination of his journey as he enters the courts of the Jerusalem temple (19:45). This new section about his Jerusalem ministry unfolds almost exclusively in the temple: Jesus cleanses the temple (19:45–46), daily teaches the people there (19:47–48; 20:1; 21:37–38), and speaks about its destruction (21:5–36).

Significant changes of characters mark the end of the travel narrative and the beginning of the Jerusalem ministry.[1] Throughout the journey, Pharisees were frequently Jesus' interlocutors and opponents.[2] However, once Jesus reaches Jerusalem, the Pharisees appear for the last time (19:39). They are never explicitly mentioned in connection with Jesus' temple ministry and subsequent passion.[3] Instead, as soon as Jesus arrives in the temple, the chief priests together with other †Sanhedrin members—not mentioned since Jesus' first passion prediction (9:22)—emerge as his adversaries.[4] Their aim is to have Jesus arrested and put to death (19:47; 20:19–20), so they try to build a case against him by questioning him on various subjects (20:1–8, 20–40). In response, Jesus warns his disciples and the people about the authorities (20:9–19, 45–47) and indirectly reveals his identity as Son and Messiah (20:13, 41). The tense climate will quickly lead to the events of Jesus' passion.

---

1. Jean-Noël Aletti, *L'art de raconter Jésus Christ: L'écriture narrative de l'évangile de Luc* (Paris: Seuil, 1989), 115–16.

2. Luke 11:37–54; 12:1; 13:31; 14:1–6; 15:2; 16:14–15; 17:20; see 18:9–14.

3. This change is likely associated with Luke's generally positive presentation of Pharisees in Acts (Acts 5:34–39; 23:9). Their beliefs (e.g., on the resurrection) were closer to Jesus' teachings than the views of the Sadducees (Luke 20:27; Acts 23:8). Moreover, Luke's companion, Paul, was a Pharisee (Acts 23:6; 26:5).

4. Luke 19:47–48; 20:1–8, 19; 22:4, 52, 66; 23:10; 24:20.

Prophetic Action: The Cleansing of the Temple (19:45–48)

⁴⁵Then Jesus entered the temple area and proceeded to drive out those who were selling things, ⁴⁶saying to them, "It is written, 'My house shall be a house of prayer, but you have made it a den of thieves.'" ⁴⁷And every day he was teaching in the temple area. The chief priests, the scribes, and the leaders of the people, meanwhile, were seeking to put him to death, ⁴⁸but they could find no way to accomplish their purpose because all the people were hanging on his words.

OT: Isa 56:7; Jer 7:11; Zech 14:21; Mal 3:1
NT: Luke 20:19; 21:37; 22:2, 53. // Matt 21:12–13; Mark 11:15–18; John 2:13–16
Catechism: cleansing the temple, 584

19:45–46   As **Jesus entered the temple area**, he also entered the city of Jerusalem, bringing the journey to an end (9:51–19:44). By "temple area" (*hieron*) is meant the whole complex consisting of a number of courts on the temple mount that surrounded the actual sanctuary or temple building (*naos*, 1:9, 21–22; 23:45). Pilgrims could purchase the animals needed for temple sacrifices once they reached the city. Animals had typically been sold at a market on the Mount of Olives. However, around this time, according to some scholars, the high priest Caiaphas permitted vendors to sell animals (see John 2:14) in the outer court of the temple itself, the Court of the Gentiles.⁵ Coming on the scene, Jesus proceeds **to drive out those who were selling things**. His action recalls a verse from the prophet Zechariah: "No longer will there be merchants in the house of the LORD of hosts on that day" (Zech 14:21). Jesus himself explains his action by referring to two other verses from Scripture. First, quoting Isaiah, he says: **My house shall be called a house of prayer** (Isa 56:7). In Jesus' view, selling interferes with the purpose of the temple, and so should be done elsewhere. Second, Jesus quotes Jeremiah, revealing the deeper significance of his action: **you have made it a den of thieves** (see Jer 7:11). This verse is from the prophet's temple sermon, where he foretold the destruction of the first temple (Jer 7:12–14). The corruption of which Jeremiah speaks was also a problem in Jesus' day.⁶ Not surprisingly, Jesus will thus predict the second temple's destruction (Luke 21:5–6).

19:47–48   After driving out the merchants, Jesus' activity **every day** is **teaching in the temple area** (20:1; 21:37),⁷ which recalls his ministry in Galilee of teaching in

5. See the discussion in Klyne R. Snodgrass, "The Temple Incident," in *Key Events in the Life of the Historical Jesus*, ed. Darrell L. Bock and Robert L. Webb (Grand Rapids: Eerdmans, 2010), 450–52.
6. Snodgrass, "The Temple Incident," 455–60.
7. When Luke last mentioned a visit to Jerusalem, the twelve-year-old Jesus was listening to the teachers in the temple (*hieron*), asking questions and giving answers (Luke 2:46–47).

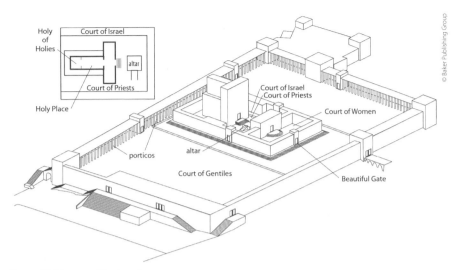

Figure 17. Diagram of the temple.

the synagogues (4:15–16, 31–33; 6:6). His audience is not the undifferentiated "crowd" (Greek *ochlos*) that accompanied him during the journey. Here, it is rather **all the people** (*laos*),[8] a term emphasizing the Jewish people who respond positively to Jesus: they are **hanging on his words**. Opposing Jesus now are not the Pharisees (mentioned explicitly for the last time in 19:39) but **the chief priests, the scribes, and the leaders of the people**. Though he has just arrived in the city, their minds are already made up: they are **seeking to put him to death** (see 22:2). Undoubtedly, they have heard about his being acclaimed as "king" (19:38), and they will use that as a charge against him when they bring him before Pilate (23:2). At present, there is **no way** for them to achieve **their purpose**, because of the people (20:6; 22:2), but they will not stop until they succeed.

The Question about Authority and Parable of the Tenants (20:1–19)

¹One day as he was teaching the people in the temple area and proclaiming the good news, the chief priests and scribes, together with the elders, approached him ²and said to him, "Tell us, by what authority are you doing these things? Or who is the one who gave you this authority?" ³He said to them in reply, "I shall ask you a question. Tell me, ⁴was John's

8. In the central section, "crowd" is used twelve times but "people" just once (Luke 18:43). However, once Jesus reaches Jerusalem, the term "people" predominates.

The Temple

BIBLICAL
BACKGROUND

In the first century, the Jerusalem temple was at the heart of Judaism.[a] It was the place of God's dwelling among his people. The Jewish people would therefore go up to Jerusalem on pilgrimage to appear before the Lord, especially for the great feasts such as Passover, Pentecost, and Tabernacles. The temple was also the place where animal sacrifices were offered in accord with the law of Moses, providing the people with the means to receive forgiveness of sins and ritual cleansing. The sacrificial system contributed to the temple's economic importance—for example, with the purchase of animals. In addition, the temple had political and judicial significance, on account of the roles of the high priest and the †Sanhedrin.

In 19 BC, Herod the Great began his temple renovation project in order to consolidate his position as king of the Jews. Long after his death the work continued (see John 2:20), being completed only a few years before the Jewish revolt against Rome (AD 66). The project's most ambitious aspect was the expansion of the temple mount, whose retaining walls—still largely visible today—surrounded the enormous platform.[b] It also involved the rebuilding of the temple sanctuary, which included the Holy Place (Luke 1:9) and Holy of Holies, separated by a curtain or veil (23:45). In front of the sanctuary was the outdoor altar of sacrifice in the Court of Priests, with the nearby Court of Israel for Jewish men. There was also the larger Court of Women—open to both Jewish women and men (see 2:27)—where the treasury was located (see 21:1). Admittance to these courts was only for Jews, as indicated on the signs on a low surrounding wall (see comment on 17:17–18). Gentiles were permitted only outside this barrier, in the outer Court of the Gentiles, which was likely the place of Jesus' cleansing of the temple (19:45). Jesus' Jerusalem teaching ministry also took place in the temple courts (19:47; 21:37).

a. See, e.g., N. T. Wright, *Jesus and the Victory of God* (Minneapolis: Fortress, 1996), 406–11.

b. The platform is almost rectangular, with the western wall measuring about 485 meters, the eastern wall 470 meters, the northern wall 315 meters, and the southern wall 280 meters. See Ehud Netzer, *The Architecture of Herod, the Great Builder* (Grand Rapids: Baker Academic, 2008), 160.

baptism of heavenly or of human origin?" [5]They discussed this among themselves, and said, "If we say, 'Of heavenly origin,' he will say, 'Why did you not believe him?' [6]But if we say, 'Of human origin,' then all the people will stone us, for they are convinced that John was a prophet." [7]So they answered that they did not know from where it came. [8]Then Jesus said to them, "Neither shall I tell you by what authority I do these things."

[9]Then he proceeded to tell the people this parable. "[A] man planted a vineyard, leased it to tenant farmers, and then went on a journey for a

long time. [10]At harvest time he sent a servant to the tenant farmers to receive some of the produce of the vineyard. But they beat the servant and sent him away empty-handed. [11]So he proceeded to send another servant, but him also they beat and insulted and sent away empty-handed. [12]Then he proceeded to send a third, but this one too they wounded and threw out. [13]The owner of the vineyard said, 'What shall I do? I shall send my beloved son; maybe they will respect him.' [14]But when the tenant farmers saw him they said to one another, 'This is the heir. Let us kill him that the inheritance may become ours.' [15]So they threw him out of the vineyard and killed him. What will the owner of the vineyard do to them? [16]He will come and put those tenant farmers to death and turn over the vineyard to others." When the people heard this, they exclaimed, "Let it not be so!" [17]But he looked at them and asked, "What then does this scripture passage mean:

> 'The stone which the builders rejected
> has become the cornerstone'?

[18]Everyone who falls on that stone will be dashed to pieces; and it will crush anyone on whom it falls." [19]The scribes and chief priests sought to lay their hands on him at that very hour, but they feared the people, for they knew that he had addressed this parable to them.

OT: 2 Chron 36:15–16; Ps 118:22; Isa 5:1–7; 8:14–15; 28:16; Dan 2:34–35, 44–45

NT: Luke 2:34; 3:22; 4:29; 7:29–30; 9:22; 11:49; 13:34; Acts 4:7, 11; Rom 9:32–33; 1 Pet 2:6–8. // Matt 21:23–27, 33–46; Mark 11:27–12:12

Catechism: Church as vineyard, 755; Jesus the Son, 443; stumbling stone and cornerstone, 587, 756

Here begins a series of controversies and other passages in which Luke closely   **20:1–2** parallels Mark's Gospel (Luke 20:1–21:4; Mark 11:27–12:44).[9] It recalls the earlier series of controversies in the Galilean ministry (Luke 5:17–6:11; Mark 2:1–3:6). In this first controversy, Jesus is **teaching**,[10] and the issue is his **authority**, just as in the previous first controversy (Luke 5:17, 24).[11] There the Pharisees opposed him, and here his opponents are **the chief priests and scribes** (20:19), **together with the elders** (see the sidebar, "Jewish Groups and Leaders," p. 82). This trio of groups—making up the †Sanhedrin (22:66; Mark 15:1)—was mentioned in the first passion prediction (Luke 9:22), so their appearance here suggests that

9. The only exception is Mark's passage regarding the great commandment (Mark 12:28–34), a subject already treated in Luke 10:25–28.

10. Jesus is also **proclaiming the good news** (*euangelizō*) here in Jerusalem, just as he did throughout the Galilean ministry (Luke 4:18, 43; 7:22; 8:1).

11. Both passages also begin with the same six Greek words (Luke 5:17; 20:1).

the prediction is about to come true. They are displeased with the **things** he is **doing**: his teaching, driving out the merchants, and kingly entry into Jerusalem. They are the authorities in the temple, so they want to know **what authority** he has and **who gave** it to him.

20:3–4   Like a good rabbi, Jesus responds with **a question**, as he often does (6:3; 10:26; 12:14; 18:19). He asks about **John's baptism** because the people—for example, tax collectors (3:12; 7:29)—who recognize that its **origin** was **heavenly**, not **human**, also tend to recognize Jesus, to whom John witnessed (3:16). In contrast, those who rejected John will likely also reject Jesus (7:30, 33–34). Moreover, it was at John's baptism of Jesus that a *heavenly* voice was heard (3:22)—the voice of God the Father—proclaiming Jesus as his "beloved Son" (see 20:13). Readers thus know what authority Jesus has and who gave it to him!

20:5–7   Neither of the two choices—**heavenly** or **human**—suits the leaders, so they claim **not** to **know**. They did **not believe** the Baptist, so now they cannot **say** his baptism was from heaven. Neither do they dare answer that it was merely human; otherwise **the people** (see v. 19; 19:48; 22:2), who regard **John** as **a prophet, will stone** them to death (see Acts 5:26).

20:8   Since they have not answered his question, **neither** will **Jesus** answer theirs. Their insincerity has been exposed. They are asking about his **authority** not because they are interested in the truth but so as "to trap him in speech, in order to hand him over to the authority . . . of the governor" (Luke 20:20). Hence, Jesus does not directly **tell** them anything that could be used against him.

20:9–13   Instead, he takes an indirect path. In their hearing, he returns to teaching **the people** (v. 1) and uses a **parable**. Like the one about the fig tree (13:6), it involves **a vineyard**, an Old Testament image for Israel: "The vineyard of the LORD of hosts is the house of Israel" (Isa 5:7).[12] Jesus' parable is allegorical, with the details representing specific realities. The **man** who is **the owner** (*kyrios*— literally, "lord") **of the vineyard** stands for God. His going away **for a long time** signifies God's forbearance and patience (see Rom 2:4). In view of the context, the **tenant farmers** to whom the vineyard is **leased** (a common arrangement of the time) represent the religious leaders in Israel—for example, "the scribes and chief priests" (Luke 20:19). God **sent** to Israel one **servant** after another— namely, the prophets, as Jeremiah explains in his temple sermon:[13] "From the day that your ancestors left the land of Egypt even to this day, I kept on sending

12. The image may refer more specifically to the Jerusalem temple—where Jesus is teaching (Luke 20:1). See the discussion of Qumran fragments 4Q500 and 4Q162 in Klyne R. Snodgrass, *Stories with Intent: A Comprehensive Guide to the Parables of Jesus* (Grand Rapids: Eerdmans, 2008), 288.
13. Jesus just quoted this sermon when cleansing the temple (Luke 19:46; Jer 7:11).

all my servants the prophets to you" (Jer 7:25).[14] These were supposed **to receive** the owner's share of the vineyard's **produce** or "fruit" (RSV), which may refer to "repentance" (Luke 3:8), "judgment," and "justice" (Isa 5:7). Instead, the servants got nothing but abuse (Luke 6:22–23; 11:47–51; 13:34). And so, God deliberates—**What shall I do?**[15]—and decides, **I shall send my beloved son.** This refers to Jesus himself, and indeed the same expression was used at his baptism (3:22). Like the baptism scene, it may also recall the sacrifice of Isaac, repeatedly called the "beloved son" (Gen 22:2, 12, 16 LXX), thus shedding light on how Jesus' upcoming death is to be understood.

After tracing the history of God's plan of salvation up to Jesus, the parable now looks forward to the two events that Jesus has frequently predicted: his upcoming passion when he will be **killed** (Luke 9:22; 18:33) and the subsequent destruction of Jerusalem (13:35; 19:43–44; 21:20). With regard to the first, before killing the son, **they threw him out** (see 4:29). This detail may point to Jesus' crucifixion "outside the gate" of Jerusalem (Heb 13:12). Though the son was the **heir**, they wanted the **inheritance** to be theirs, not his. Paul, however, will explain that it is precisely by recognizing the Son that people become "joint heirs" with him (Rom 8:17; see Gal 3:29; 4:7). As for the second event, the time for patience will give way to the time for judgment, when **the owner** will finally **come**. Indeed, the Romans will come—as agents of God's judgment, like the Babylonians before them (2 Chron 36:15–20)—**and put those tenant farmers to death.** As a result, **the vineyard** will be given **to others**, a reference especially to the apostles, who will replace the temple authorities in looking after God's vineyard (see Luke 22:29–30). *(20:14–16)*

By using the parable, Jesus has given an indirect answer to the question about authority. His authority is that of the beloved Son, given to him by the one who sent him, God the Father. He has also sounded a warning against the religious leaders who are questioning him. Understanding the gist of what Jesus is saying about the vineyard, **the people** (20:9) plead that **it not be so.**[16]

Jesus then **looked** at them intently (22:61) to explain the parable. He cites a **scripture** verse (Ps 118:22) taken from the same psalm that he earlier quoted (Luke 13:35) and that was also used to acclaim him as he approached Jerusalem (19:38; Ps 118:26). He, the beloved Son, is also **the stone**[17] that is **rejected** (Luke *(20:17)*

---

14. See 2 Kings 17:23; 24:2; Jer 25:4; Amos 3:7.

15. In Greek, this question matches the beginning of the question in Isaiah's song of the vineyard (Isa 5:4 LXX).

16. This exclamation (*mē genoito*) is found fourteen other times in the New Testament, all in letters of Luke's companion, Paul (Romans, 1 Corinthians, and Galatians).

17. The images of son and stone are related by a Hebrew wordplay—*ben* (son) and *'eben* (stone)—underlying the Greek text; see, similarly, "children" and "stones" in Luke 3:8. See Snodgrass, *Stories with Intent*, 290.

9:22; 17:25) by **the builders**—in other words, the Jewish leaders. However, whereas the temple's stones will be thrown down (19:44; 21:6), this stone "will rise" (18:33) and **become the cornerstone**.[18] Indeed, Peter in Acts refers to Jesus' resurrection and quotes this same psalm verse (Acts 4:10–11; see 1 Pet 2:7), before concluding that "there is no salvation through anyone else" (Acts 4:12).

20:18   Jesus makes a further statement using **stone** imagery: **everyone who falls on** it **will be dashed to pieces**. In other words, those who reject the stone will suffer punishment. Underlying this saying is a verse from Isaiah about "a stone for injury, / A rock for stumbling" (Isa 8:14).[19] The final phrase, about the stone's effect when it **falls** on **anyone**, is illuminated by a passage from Daniel: after the rise of a series of earthly kingdoms, the "God of heaven will set up a kingdom"—depicted as a stone—and "it shall **crush** all these kingdoms and bring them to an end, and it shall stand forever" (Dan 2:44 NRSV). Hence, the same stone will bring judgment to some (Luke 20:18) and salvation to others (v. 17). As Simeon had foretold, Jesus is "destined for the fall and rise of many" (2:34).

20:19   **The scribes and chief priests** understand enough of what Jesus was saying to know **that he had addressed this parable to them** as the tenant farmers. They may also perceive that he claims to be the beloved son, as they will later ask him if he is "the Son of God" (22:70). Though they wish to arrest him, they are again restrained because **they feared the people** (19:48; 20:6).

The Question about Tribute to Caesar (20:20–26)

[20]They watched him closely and sent agents pretending to be righteous who were to trap him in speech, in order to hand him over to the authority and power of the governor. [21]They posed this question to him, "Teacher, we know that what you say and teach is correct, and you show no partiality, but teach the way of God in accordance with the truth. [22]Is it lawful for us to pay tribute to Caesar or not?" [23]Recognizing their craftiness he said to them, [24]"Show me a denarius; whose image and name does it bear?" They replied, "Caesar's." [25]So he said to them, "Then repay to Caesar what belongs to Caesar and to God what belongs to God." [26]They were unable to trap him by something he might say before the people, and so amazed were they at his reply that they fell silent.

18. In Ephesians (Eph 2:11–22), Christ is the cornerstone that brings together Israel and the Gentiles.
19. See also Rom 9:33 and 1 Pet 2:6–8, passages that cite Isa 8:14 together with Isa 28:16.

OT: Gen 1:26–27
NT: Luke 6:7; 11:54; 14:1; Rom 13:1–7. // Matt 22:15–22; Mark 12:13–17
Catechism: paying taxes, 2240; civil disobedience, 2242

Looking for another opportunity, **they watched him closely**, like the Pharisees 20:20–21
did earlier (6:6–7). They send **agents** to Jesus **to trap him in speech** (11:54).
Their goal is **to hand him over to** Pilate, the Roman **governor** (3:1; 23:1), which
would fulfill one aspect of Jesus' passion predictions (9:44; 18:32). Since these
"spies" (RSV) are **pretending to be righteous**, they introduce their **question**
with effusive praise of Jesus' **correct** teaching and lack of **partiality**, perhaps
thinking that he will let down his guard.

They ask whether it is permitted for them **to pay tribute to Caesar**. When 20:22
Rome took direct control of Judea (AD 6), its inhabitants had to begin paying tribute (a poll or head tax as well as a land tax) as an acknowledgment of
their dependence on the emperor. At that time, a census was taken for such
tax purposes, which led to an unsuccessful revolt led by Judas the Galilean
(Acts 5:37). He viewed paying tribute to Rome as a sign of slavery for a people
who should serve God alone.[20] So, if *Jesus* the "Galilean" (Luke 23:6) now
tells them **not** to pay, he can similarly be accused of opposing the payment of
taxes and inciting the people to revolt (23:2, 14). In contrast, if he complies,
he will lose credibility with the people, who expect a king (19:38) to liberate
them.

Staying one step ahead of **their craftiness**, Jesus tells them to **show** him a 20:23–24
silver **denarius**, the amount of the annual head tax, equivalent to a day's wage
(7:41; 10:35). Apparently, he does not have such a coin, but they do! Their hypocrisy thus begins to be exposed: if they were really "righteous" (20:20), they
would not be carrying such a coin in the temple area (20:1). Unlike the coins
of Herod Antipas in Galilee, which only had plant images (see comment on
7:24–25), thus following the Jewish practice of not portraying people, the denarius bore a human **image** (Deut 4:16 RSV) of the emperor,[21] together with his
abbreviated **name**—in other words, an "inscription" (RSV) that also promoted
Roman emperor worship: TI CAESAR DIVI AUG F AUGUSTUS ("Tiberius
Caesar, son of the divine Augustus, Augustus").[22] Jesus draws attention to these
uncomfortable details by asking **whose** features the coin has. They are forced
to admit: **"Caesar's."**

---

20. Josephus, *Jewish War* 2.118, 433; *Jewish Antiquities* 18.4.

21. Josephus, *Jewish War* 2.169–74; *Jewish Antiquities* 18.55–59, reports how Pilate brought military standards with Caesar's image on them into Jerusalem, but ongoing Jewish protests convinced him to remove them.

22. David Hendin, *Guide to Biblical Coins*, 5th ed. (Nyack, NY: Amphora, 2010), 485–88.

Figure 18. Denarius of Tiberius Caesar.

20:25   Jesus then issues a pronouncement that begins: **Then repay to Caesar what belongs to Caesar**. The question (Luke 20:22) had asked whether one should "pay" (literally, "give" [RSV]). Jesus' response is slightly different: one should "repay" (see 10:35)—literally, "give back" (NIV)—what is Caesar's. If they use Caesar's coin, they should have no problem giving it back to him in payment of the tax. Jesus' words eventually were understood to sum up the Christian principle of giving civil authorities their due (see Rom 13:7; Catechism 2239–40). Thus, Jesus is no Zealot.

However, neither is he like the unpopular Sadducees[23] who collaborated with the Romans. The second half of Jesus' pronouncement makes this clear, as it puts the first half in proper perspective: repay **to God what belongs to God**. This unexpected addition creates a parallel, inviting them to recall what bears not Caesar's image but *God's*—namely, human beings, who are created "in his image" (Gen 1:27). Hence, the things of God that they are to give back to God include their very selves.[24] The two do not necessarily conflict with each other, but ultimately the obligation to give our whole selves to God takes precedence over the demands of civil authorities.

20:26   The spies have failed in their effort **to trap him** in speech (Luke 20:20). Instead, they are **amazed** with his answer (see 4:22) and fall **silent** as a result. However, out of malice the leaders will later distort Jesus' answer so as to accuse him falsely before Pilate: "He opposes the payment of taxes to Caesar" (23:2).

---

23. Josephus, *Jewish Antiquities* 13.298.

24. Tertullian, *On Idolatry* 15.3, in *De Idololatria: Critical Text, Translation and Commentary*, trans. J. H. Waszink and J. C. van Winden (Leiden: Brill, 1987), 53: "Consequently you should render to the emperor your money, to God yourself."

Reflection and Application (20:20–26)

Give back to God what is God's. Many Christians throughout history and still today in some parts of the world have accepted martyrdom rather than render to the civil authorities what belongs to God. Most Christians do not have to face such extreme trials, but nonetheless they may face situations—for example, regarding basic human rights and Gospel teachings—where they may be forced to practice civil disobedience (Catechism 2242), in a peaceful manner, thus accepting the sufferings that may result while also seeking recourse so as to remedy the situation.

The Sadducees' Question about the Resurrection (20:27–40)

²⁷Some Sadducees, those who deny that there is a resurrection, came forward and put this question to him, ²⁸saying, "Teacher, Moses wrote for us, 'If someone's brother dies leaving a wife but no child, his brother must take the wife and raise up descendants for his brother.' ²⁹Now there were seven brothers; the first married a woman but died childless. ³⁰Then the second ³¹and the third married her, and likewise all the seven died childless. ³²Finally the woman also died. ³³Now at the resurrection whose wife will that woman be? For all seven had been married to her." ³⁴Jesus said to them, "The children of this age marry and are given in marriage; ³⁵but those who are deemed worthy to attain to the coming age and to the resurrection of the dead neither marry nor are given in marriage. ³⁶They can no longer die, for they are like angels; and they are the children of God because they are the ones who will rise. ³⁷That the dead will rise even Moses made known in the passage about the bush, when he called 'Lord' the God of Abraham, the God of Isaac, and the God of Jacob; ³⁸and he is not God of the dead, but of the living, for to him all are alive." ³⁹Some of the scribes said in reply, "Teacher, you have answered well." ⁴⁰And they no longer dared to ask him anything.

OT: Exod 3:1–6, 15–16; Deut 25:5–6
NT: Luke 14:14; 17:27; 18:30; Acts 4:1–2; 5:17; 23:6–8. // Matt 22:23–33, 46; Mark 12:18–27, 34
Catechism: resurrection of the dead, 575, 993; virginity a sign of the coming age, 1619; angels, 330
Lectionary: Luke 20:27–38: Thirty-Second Sunday Ordinary Time (Year C)

Some Sadducees (see the sidebar, "Jewish Groups and Leaders," p. 82) now **20:27** enter into controversy with Jesus. It is not surprising to encounter them in the temple area (20:1), since the group included leading priests and often the high priest himself (Acts 4:1–2; 5:17). In contrast to Jesus (Luke 14:14) and the Pharisees, they **deny that there is a resurrection** (Acts 23:6–8).[25] Both Sadducees and Pharisees originated in the second century BC. At that time, belief in the resurrection was becoming more widespread among Jews after the experience of the Maccabean martyrs (2 Macc 7:9, 11, 14, 23, 29). However, the Sadducees were opposed to this trend. In matters of belief, they accepted only those teachings clearly written down in the Torah, the law of Moses,[26] regardless of other passages in the Old Testament that lent support to such a belief.[27]

20:28–33   In their view, **Moses** actually teaches *against* the resurrection. The law of levirate marriage (Deut 25:5–6) states that the **brother** of a man who **dies leaving a wife but no child** should marry the widow and thus **raise up descendants for** the deceased (see Gen 38:6–11). So the Sadducees present a test case, taking inspiration from Tobit (Tob 3:8–9, 15) and 2 Maccabees (2 Macc 7): **seven brothers** successively **married a woman**, but **all the seven died childless**; then **the woman also died**. Their question about the hereafter—**whose wife** is she?—makes **the resurrection** look absurd and therefore false.

20:34–36   **Jesus** gives a two-part answer. First, he rebuts their argument by pointing out that life in **the coming age** is *not* the same as life now, as they are assuming. It does not involve **marriage**. The purpose of the levirate law, besides providing for the widow, was that "the name of the deceased" would continue through a descendant (Deut 25:6). However, in **the resurrection of the dead**, people **are like angels** in that **they can no longer die**, so there is no need for marriage to perpetuate one's name. So, whereas **the children of this age marry** (Luke 17:27), those in "eternal life" (18:30) are characterized above all by their relationship with God: they are **children of God**. The further description that **they are the ones who will rise** is more literally translated "they are children of the resurrection" (NIV). Jesus' words also imply that not all **attain to** this blessing, so people, including the Sadducees questioning him, should focus on doing what is necessary to be **deemed worthy** by God to receive it.

20:37–38   Second, Jesus shows that the resurrection of **the dead** is indeed taught by the law of **Moses**, thus arguing on the basis of the authority the Sadducees accepted. At the burning **bush**, the **Lord** revealed himself to Moses as **the God of** the patriarchs **Abraham**, **Isaac**, and **Jacob** (Exod 3:6, 15–16). Though they died centuries before Moses, to God they are **living. He is not God of the dead**,

---

25. According to Josephus (*Jewish War* 2.165; *Jewish Antiquities* 18.16), Sadducees deny an afterlife involving rewards or punishments and hold that the soul perishes at death along with the body.
26. Josephus, *Jewish Antiquities* 13.297; 18.16.
27. 2 Macc 12:43–44; Job 19:25–26; Ps 16:10–11; Isa 26:19; Ezek 37:1–14; Dan 12:2.

which means that belief in the resurrection is actually necessary for having a proper understanding of God.[28]

But how are they **alive**? The resurrection of the body has not yet taken place, as the Sadducees could point out by referring to the cave of Machpelah in Hebron, where the patriarchs were buried (Gen 49:31; 50:13),[29] for which Herod the Great had constructed a massive enclosure that still stands. Hence, if Abraham is alive, as the parable about Lazarus also assumes (Luke 16:19–31), there must be some "intermediate state,"[30] as Christian teaching has affirmed with respect to the immortal soul (Catechism 1023).

Some of the scribes (see Acts 23:9) acknowledge that Jesus has **answered** the Sadducees **well**. However, the Sadducees will later take up the issue again with Jesus' disciples, who are proclaiming the resurrection of the dead *in Jesus* (Acts 4:1–2), who is "the first to rise from the dead" (Acts 26:23). 20:39–40

As a result of Jesus' skill in fending off three questions (Luke 20:2, 21–22, 28–33), his opponents **no longer dared to ask him anything**. From now on they will simply seek how "to put him to death" (22:2).

Jesus' Question about David's Son (20:41–44)

[41]Then he said to them, "How do they claim that the Messiah is the Son of David? [42]For David himself in the Book of Psalms says:

'The Lord said to my lord,
"Sit at my right hand
[43]till I make your enemies your footstool."'

[44]Now if David calls him 'lord,' how can he be his son?"

OT: Ps 110:1
NT: Luke 2:11; 9:20; 24:44; Acts 2:33–35. // Matt 22:41–45; Mark 12:35–37
Catechism: son of David, 439; Jesus is Lord, 202, 447

Now it is Jesus' turn to pose a question. He asks about the **claim that the Messiah is the Son of David** (see the sidebar, "Messianic Expectations," p. 179). The title "Messiah" (*christos*) occurs here for the first time since Peter's confession (9:20). 20:41

28. Joseph Ratzinger, *Eschatology: Death and Eternal Life*, trans. Michael Waldstein and Aidan Nichols (Washington, DC: Catholic University of America Press, 1988), 114.
29. Josephus, *Jewish War* 4.529–32.
30. Ratzinger, *Eschatology*, 124. Indeed, Josephus (*Jewish War* 2.163; 3.372–74; *Jewish Antiquities* 18.14) explains that the Pharisees believed in both an immediate life after death because of the immortality of the soul and a future resurrection of the body.

Psalm 110 and Jesus' Priestly Authority

BIBLICAL BACKGROUND

Psalm 110 is the Old Testament text most frequently used in the New Testament, either in direct quotations (e.g., Luke 20:42–43) or in allusions (e.g., 22:69). In one of Peter's speeches in Acts, verse 1 of the psalm ("Sit at my right hand") is used to describe Jesus' ascension and heavenly exaltation at God's right hand (Acts 2:33–35).[a] Paul in 1 Corinthians likewise refers to this verse when speaking about the period of Jesus' heavenly reign following his ascension until his second coming (1 Cor 15:23–25). The Letter to the Hebrews also quotes this verse (Heb 1:13) and alludes to it (Heb 1:3; 8:1; 10:12–13), and it also extensively uses verse 4 of the psalm to explain Jesus' priesthood in relation to that of the priest-king Melchizedek from Genesis (Gen 14:18): "You are a priest forever / according to the order of Melchizedek" (Heb 5:6; 7:17).[b] The origin of this description of Jesus in priestly terms, so developed in Hebrews, may be Jesus' own use of Psalm 110 in the Gospels (Luke 20:41–44 and parallels): "By citing the psalm that promises priestly office to the Davidic line and thereby the Messiah, Jesus is suggesting his own priestly authority."[c] Indeed, "there should be little doubt what Jesus was thinking. Psalm 110 is the *only* biblical text that *explicitly* speaks of a king who is also a 'priest.' . . . Did Jesus think he was that priest-king? If he did, . . . this would get him into trouble. In the first place, it obviously entails a direct attack on the Sadducean high priesthood."[d] Later, it is precisely when Jesus again refers to Psalm 110 (together with Dan 7:13–14), during his interrogation by the chief priests and the †Sanhedrin (Luke 22:69), that they decide to hand him over to Pilate.

a. See Mark 16:19; Rom 8:34; Eph 1:20; Col 3:1.
b. See also Heb 5:10; 6:20; 7:3, 11, 21.
c. Timothy C. Gray, *The Temple in the Gospel of Mark: A Study in Its Narrative Role* (Grand Rapids: Baker Academic, 2010), 87.
d. Crispin H. T. Fletcher-Louis, "Jesus as the High Priestly Messiah: Part 1," *Journal for the Study of the Historical Jesus* 4 (2006): 173–74 (emphasis in the original).

There, Jesus had told his disciples "not to tell this to anyone" (9:21) because it needed clarification, as his suffering had not yet been revealed. However, after his passion predictions and with his suffering now imminent, he uses the title himself, but he does so indirectly, with a question.[31] He is not denying his Davidic lineage, which Luke's Gospel has repeatedly mentioned (1:32; 2:4; 3:31; 18:38–39). Rather, he is clarifying the title "Messiah."

31. This is similar to the indirect way he just referred to himself as the "beloved son" (of God) using a parable (Luke 20:13).

He does so by quoting from **the Book of Psalms**. After his resurrection, **20:42–44**
Jesus will explain: "Everything written about me in the law of Moses and in the
prophets and psalms must be fulfilled" (Luke 24:44; see Acts 13:33). Here it is
Psalm 110—a psalm of **David**—that must be fulfilled, as it announces that the
Messiah, who is also **lord**, will be glorified at the **right hand** of **the Lord** God.
The question is **how** the Messiah is both David's **son** and **lord**. The question
is left unanswered here, but Luke has already given his readers the tools for
answering it themselves by using the title "Lord" (*kyrios*) almost equally for
God and for Jesus, thus pointing to his divinity (see the sidebar, "Jesus the
Lord," p. 115). In Acts, Luke will give a more direct answer through one of
Peter's sermons: Jesus, by his resurrection and ascension, is exalted as "Lord
and Messiah," bringing the psalm to its fulfillment in his enthronement "at the
right hand of God" (Acts 2:33–36).[32] Here in Luke's Gospel, Jesus will again
allude to the psalm, at his questioning before the †Sanhedrin, at which point
they will understand his claim to divinity as the Son of God (Luke 22:69–71).

In summary, in the series of controversies with his opponents, Jesus has not
only answered their questions and posed his own, but has also pointed to his
identity as Son of God, Messiah, and Lord.[33] Moreover, in indirect ways, he has
made reference to the saving events that are about to unfold: his death (20:15),
resurrection (20:36), and ascension (20:42).

Of Scribes and Widows (20:45–21:4)

[45]Then, within the hearing of all the people, he said to [his] disciples,
[46]"Be on guard against the scribes, who like to go around in long robes
and love greetings in marketplaces, seats of honor in synagogues, and
places of honor at banquets. [47]They devour the houses of widows and,
as a pretext, recite lengthy prayers. They will receive a very severe
condemnation."
   [21:1]When he looked up he saw some wealthy people putting their offerings into the treasury [2]and he noticed a poor widow putting in two small
coins. [3]He said, "I tell you truly, this poor widow put in more than all the
rest; [4]for those others have all made offerings from their surplus wealth,
but she, from her poverty, has offered her whole livelihood."

NT: Luke 11:43; 12:1; 14:7; John 8:20. // Matt 23:1, 6–7; Mark 12:38–44
Catechism: Jesus' concern for the poor, 2444; the widow's example, 2544

32. Richard B. Hays, *Echoes of Scripture in the Gospels* (Waco: Baylor University Press, 2016), 233.
33. These three titles were all proclaimed in the infancy narrative (Luke 1:32; 2:11).

20:45–47   Jesus has finished speaking with his opponents and now addresses the **disciples**, as **all the people** listen. As earlier he warned them to "beware" of the Pharisees (12:1), he now similarly warns them about **the scribes** (19:47; 20:1, 19), pointing out the same weaknesses of pride and vanity: they **love greetings in marketplaces, seats of honor in synagogues** (11:43), **and places of honor at banquets** (14:7). Also criticized are their ostentation in walking about **in long robes** and their false piety in reciting **lengthy prayers** as a show. An even more serious fault is the scribes' insatiable and unscrupulous greed as **they devour the houses of widows**. Jesus in a parable had spoken about the difficulties widows have in obtaining justice, and Scripture is filled with warnings not to oppress them (see comment on 18:2–3). The judgment on those who do such things will be **very severe**. Since pride and greed are recurring temptations (9:46; 12:15; 22:24), the disciples need to be reminded to avoid such behaviors. They should instead conduct themselves in simplicity (12:22), humility (14:10), and generosity (Acts 4:34). A model for such behavior is the widow who now appears on the scene.

21:1–4   Having just mentioned widows, Jesus sees **a poor widow** as well as **some wealthy people** depositing their monetary **offerings** in the temple **treasury**, in the area where Jesus taught (John 8:20). The treasury was located in the Court of Women, where there were thirteen trumpet-shaped collection boxes for both general and specific purposes.[34] The widow contributes **two small coins** or pennies (*lepton*; see comment on Luke 12:59). Despite the small amount, Jesus recognizes that, relative to her means, she has given **more than** those with **surplus wealth**. She has given everything, **her whole livelihood** (see 12:33; 14:33; 18:29–30). In contrast with the greed and hypocrisy of the scribes, Jesus is praising her generosity and true piety.

Some scholars instead say that Jesus laments the widow's gift, seeing her as a passive victim of the corrupt religious leaders. Jesus indeed denounces the Jewish leaders' exploitation of the people (19:46) and of widows in particular (20:47) and is also about to prophesy the destruction of the temple to which the widow has contributed (21:6). Nonetheless, he praises her as a model of self-giving to God. She is among the pious poor, the †*anawim*, to whom the kingdom belongs (see comment on 6:20, 24). The reader recalls the generosity of the widow of Zarephath (4:26; 1 Kings 17:10–16) and the piety of the widow Anna in the temple (Luke 2:37). In Acts, Luke will indicate how the early Christians strove to tend to the needs of widows (Acts 6:1).

---

34. *m. Sheqalim* 6:5.

Prophetic Word, Part 1: The Desolation of Jerusalem and Its Temple (21:5–24)

⁵While some people were speaking about how the temple was adorned with costly stones and votive offerings, he said, ⁶"All that you see here— the days will come when there will not be left a stone upon another stone that will not be thrown down."

⁷Then they asked him, "Teacher, when will this happen? And what sign will there be when all these things are about to happen?" ⁸He answered, "See that you not be deceived, for many will come in my name, saying, 'I am he,' and 'The time has come.' Do not follow them! ⁹When you hear of wars and insurrections, do not be terrified; for such things must happen first, but it will not immediately be the end." ¹⁰Then he said to them, "Nation will rise against nation, and kingdom against kingdom. ¹¹There will be powerful earthquakes, famines, and plagues from place to place; and awesome sights and mighty signs will come from the sky.

¹²"Before all this happens, however, they will seize and persecute you, they will hand you over to the synagogues and to prisons, and they will have you led before kings and governors because of my name. ¹³It will lead to your giving testimony. ¹⁴Remember, you are not to prepare your defense beforehand, ¹⁵for I myself shall give you a wisdom in speaking that all your adversaries will be powerless to resist or refute. ¹⁶You will even be handed over by parents, brothers, relatives, and friends, and they will put some of you to death. ¹⁷You will be hated by all because of my name, ¹⁸but not a hair on your head will be destroyed. ¹⁹By your perseverance you will secure your lives.

²⁰"When you see Jerusalem surrounded by armies, know that its desolation is at hand. ²¹Then those in Judea must flee to the mountains. Let those within the city escape from it, and let those in the countryside not enter the city, ²²for these days are the time of punishment when all the scriptures are fulfilled. ²³Woe to pregnant women and nursing mothers in those days, for a terrible calamity will come upon the earth and a wrathful judgment upon this people. ²⁴They will fall by the edge of the sword and be taken as captives to all the Gentiles; and Jerusalem will be trampled underfoot by the Gentiles until the times of the Gentiles are fulfilled."

OT: Gen 19:17; Hosea 9:7

NT: Luke 6:22; 8:15; 12:11–12; 13:34–35; 17:31; 19:42–44; 23:29; Acts 6:10; 27:34; Rom 11:25; Rev 11:2. // Matt 10:17–22; 24:1–21; Mark 13:1–19

Catechism: the temple's destruction a sign of the last days, 585; the Church persecuted, 675; times of the Gentiles, 58, 674

Lectionary: Luke 21:5–19: Thirty-Third Sunday Ordinary Time (Year C)

21:5   **Some people** are admiring the beauty of the **temple**. Indeed, Josephus remarks that no one had **adorned** it like Herod the Great. It had massive white **stones** that made it appear from a distance like a snow-covered mountain. Moreover, the façade of the sanctuary was covered with gold, and its entrance had a golden vine from which hung **votive offerings**, gifts dedicated to God such as golden grape clusters.[35]

21:6   In response, Jesus, who has been teaching *in* the temple (19:47; 20:1), now teaches *about* the temple—about its impending destruction. Jeremiah similarly had prophesied the fall of the first temple in his "temple sermon" (Jer 7:1–15), which Jesus has already made his own by calling the temple "a den of thieves" (Luke 19:46; Jer 7:11). Echoing also his earlier words about the city's devastation (Luke 19:43–44), he speaks of **the days** that **will come when** not **a stone** will **be left** standing **upon another stone** in the temple. Everything will **be thrown down**. Josephus details the total destruction of the temple during the siege of Jerusalem by the Roman general Titus in AD 70. The temple and its surrounding courts were consumed by fire, and indeed on the same day and month—the ninth of Av—as when the Babylonians destroyed the first temple.[36] What remained of the temple as well as large parts of the city were then demolished.[37]

21:7–11   Asked **when** and after **what sign** such events will **happen**, Jesus responds with his second major speech about "last things" (21:5–36; see 17:22–37). As in the first discourse, this one includes prophecies regarding the fall of Jerusalem (21:8–24) as well as others about the world's judgment at his second coming (vv. 25–36).[38] The former event is a sign of the latter (Catechism 585), since the temple was considered to represent the universe (Ps 78:69): the Holy of Holies signified heaven while the other parts represented land and sea; the four colors of the veil symbolized the four elements; the seven-branched lampstand (menorah) symbolized the number of the "planets" known in the ancient world; and the twelve loaves of the presence represented the months of the year.[39] Hence, events like those leading up to the fall of the temple (e.g., in Luke 21:10–11) will also mark the onset of the end times.

Before describing Jerusalem's **end** (vv. 20–24), Jesus refers to events (vv. 8–11), including persecutions (vv. 12–19), that **must happen first**. As he did earlier (17:21, 23), Jesus gives a warning not to **follow** or **be deceived** by the **many** who

---

35. Josephus, *Jewish War* 5.208–23; *Jewish Antiquities* 15.391–96; see *m. Middot* 3:8.

36. Josephus, *Jewish War* 6.260–84.

37. Josephus, *Jewish War* 7.1–4.

38. Joseph A. Fitzmyer, *The Gospel according to Luke*, 2 vols., AB (New York: Doubleday, 1981–85), 2:1334.

39. Josephus, *Jewish War* 5.212–17; *Jewish Antiquities* 3.123, 180–83. See G. K. Beale, *The Temple and the Church's Mission* (Downers Grove, IL: InterVarsity, 2004), 45–50.

Figure 19. Temple ruins (southwest corner).

will purport to **come in** his **name**, claiming **I am he**. One such messianic pretender was the Egyptian Jew who around the year AD 56 led thousands of followers in a rebellion that was put down by the Roman governor Felix (Acts 21:38).[40] There were also many false prophets who promised deliverance at the time of the Roman siege.[41] Many others have made similar claims in succeeding centuries.

Jesus also mentions **wars and insurrections,** as one **nation** or **kingdom** rises up **against** another. Such phrases are a fitting description of the decade preceding Jerusalem's fall, as the Zealot revolt against Rome began in AD 66, and Rome itself experienced turmoil with the succession of four emperors following Nero's death in AD 68.

40. Josephus, *Jewish War* 2.261–63.
41. Josephus, *Jewish War* 6.285–88.

Using language often found in the Old Testament to express divine judgment, Jesus also speaks of natural disasters such as **earthquakes** (Isa 29:6) and **famines** (Isa 51:19). In Acts, Luke records a prophecy about a famine, which then happened about AD 45–48 while Claudius was emperor (Acts 11:28).[42] Moreover, Jesus mentions **awesome sights** as well as **mighty signs** in **the sky**. Josephus indeed describes many strange signs that preceded the fall of Jerusalem.[43] Such signs in the heavens will also occur before Jesus' second coming (Luke 21:25–27).

21:12–19   During the time of upheaval before Jerusalem's fall, those in authority will **persecute** Jesus' disciples. In God's plan, this will give the disciples the opportunity to give **testimony** to Jesus. In Acts, Luke describes the fulfillment of these words (Acts 4:8–13, 20; 5:29–32), with the apostles even rejoicing that they suffer on account of Jesus' **name** (Acts 5:41). The disciples will be tracked down in **synagogues** (Acts 9:2; 22:19; 26:11), put into **prisons** (Acts 5:18; 8:3; 12:4; 16:23), and **led before kings** (Acts 9:15; 25:23) **and governors** (Acts 23:33; 24:1; 25:6). As they make their **defense** (Acts 24:10; 25:8; 26:1–2), they will be given **a wisdom** that their opponents cannot withstand (Acts 6:10; see Acts 4:13–14). In such circumstances, the disciples will be taught by the Holy Spirit, as Jesus earlier said (Luke 12:11–12). Persecution will divide families (12:52–53), as disciples are **handed over** even by **relatives** and **friends**. For **some**, it will lead to **death** by martyrdom (Acts 7:60; 12:2). Paradoxically, by being **hated** in these ways on account of Jesus' **name**, disciples will receive the blessing promised in the Beatitudes (Luke 6:22–23)—a great reward in heaven. Hence, God's providential care for them will extend even, so to speak, to the **hair** on their **head** (12:7), if not here on earth (Acts 27:34), then hereafter. Their **perseverance** will bear fruit (Luke 8:15) in eternal life.

21:20–24   Jesus' speech now predicts the fall of **Jerusalem** itself, in response to the original question (21:7).[44] The events that will fulfill Jesus' prophecy will also fulfill the **scriptures**. For example, as in the past, Jerusalem will be **surrounded** (Isa 29:3).[45] In particular, as in the events leading up to the Babylonian exile, enemy **armies** will come against the city (Jer 34:1), leading to **its desolation** (2 Chron 36:21; Jer 7:34; 22:5). Those will be **days** of divine **punishment** (Hosea 9:7), and the people will die **by the edge of the sword** (Jer 21:7) or be **taken**

42. Josephus, *Jewish Antiquities* 3.320; 20.101.

43. Josephus, *Jewish War* 6.289–310.

44. As with Luke 19:43–44, no conclusions can be drawn on the basis of these verses about the dating of Luke's Gospel.

45. In the †Septuagint version of all the Old Testament examples given in this paragraph, the same Greek words are found as those used here in Luke.

as captives (2 Kings 24:14). It will be a time of great suffering, especially for **pregnant women and nursing mothers**, as Jesus will again say when he addresses the women lamenting him (Luke 23:28–29).

However, Jesus also signals a way of **escape** for the people of the **city**. When these things happen, **then those in Judea must flee to the mountains**. This instruction, including the command not to **enter the city**, is similar to Jesus' earlier reference to Lot's flight to the hills away from Sodom, where he stressed the importance of not turning to the things left behind (17:29–31; see Gen 19:17). According to two Church Fathers—Eusebius and Epiphanius—the Jewish-Christian community in Jerusalem heeded such prophecies and fled the city before the war, settling in Pella, a city of the Decapolis bordering the region of Perea.[46]

The result is clear: **Jerusalem will be trampled** on **by the Gentiles** (see Isa 5:5; Dan 8:13; Rev 11:2). However, the duration is unspecific: **until the times of the Gentiles are fulfilled**. The Letter to the Romans, after speaking about "a hardening" that "has come upon Israel in part," similarly gives as the duration: "until the full number of the Gentiles comes in" (Rom 11:25; see Acts 28:28). These phrases point to events leading up to the time of Jesus' second coming, which is the focus of the following verses.

Prophetic Word, Part 2: The Coming of the Son of Man (21:25–38)

[25]"There will be signs in the sun, the moon, and the stars, and on earth nations will be in dismay, perplexed by the roaring of the sea and the waves. [26]People will die of fright in anticipation of what is coming upon the world, for the powers of the heavens will be shaken. [27]And then they will see the Son of Man coming in a cloud with power and great glory. [28]But when these signs begin to happen, stand erect and raise your heads because your redemption is at hand."

[29]He taught them a lesson. "Consider the fig tree and all the other trees. [30]When their buds burst open, you see for yourselves and know that summer is now near; [31]in the same way, when you see these things happening, know that the kingdom of God is near. [32]Amen, I say to you, this generation will not pass away until all these things have taken place. [33]Heaven and earth will pass away, but my words will not pass away.

[34]"Beware that your hearts do not become drowsy from carousing and drunkenness and the anxieties of daily life, and that day catch you

46. Eusebius, *Ecclesiastical History* 3.5.3; Epiphanius, *Panarion* 29.7.7–8; 30.2.7.

by surprise [35]like a trap. For that day will assault everyone who lives on the face of the earth. [36]Be vigilant at all times and pray that you have the strength to escape the tribulations that are imminent and to stand before the Son of Man."

[37]During the day, Jesus was teaching in the temple area, but at night he would leave and stay at the place called the Mount of Olives. [38]And all the people would get up early each morning to listen to him in the temple area.

OT: Dan 7:13–14
NT: Luke 17:22–37. // Matt 24:29–35; Mark 13:24–31
Catechism: second coming, 671, 697; watchfulness, 2612
Lectionary: Luke 21:25–28, 34–36: First Sunday Advent (Year C)

21:25–28   Turning the attention from Jerusalem to **the world,** Jesus announces the cosmic upheaval that will accompany the end times. There will be **signs** that cause **people** to be **perplexed** and even to **die** or faint **of fright** (the Greek verb can mean either). These events are described in a general way using imagery often found in the prophets concerning the **heavens,** the **sun,** and the **moon**—for example, the passage from Joel that Peter will later quote in his Pentecost sermon: "I will set signs in the heavens and on the earth . . . / The sun will darken, / the moon turn blood-red, / Before the day of the Lord arrives" (Joel 3:3–4; see Acts 2:19–20).[47] Jesus' second **coming** will **then** follow, which he describes here by drawing from Daniel, as elsewhere in the Gospel (Luke 9:26; 22:69): **the Son of Man** will come **in a cloud with power and great glory** (Dan 7:13–14). In response, Jesus' disciples should not cringe in fear (Luke 21:26) but rather **raise** their **heads,** knowing that the day of **redemption is at hand** (Eph 4:30). When he comes as "deliverer" from heaven (Rom 11:26), "the times of universal restoration" (Acts 3:21) and of the resurrection of the body (1 Cor 15:22–23, 51) will come to pass.

21:29–33   Jesus illustrates his teaching with **a lesson** (literally, "parable") about a **fig tree.** Earlier, a parable about a barren fig tree indicated that the time for producing fruit was running out for Jerusalem (Luke 13:6–9). This parable is also about **all the other trees,** recalling other sayings that likewise emphasize bearing good fruit (3:8–9; 6:43–44). When the trees begin to sprout leaves, it is a sign that **summer** and the time for fruit is **near.** Similarly, when these signs occur, **the kingdom of God** in its fullness **is near,** bringing either judgment or redemption, and answering the petitions of those who have prayed for its coming (11:2).

---

47. See also Isa 24:19; 34:4; Joel 2:10; Hag 2:6, 21.

Jesus adds two related sayings. The first emphasizes just *how near* the **things** are that he has prophesied—that is, regarding Jerusalem's fall, which is the sign of the end times. They will take **place** within the lifetime of **this generation**, a phrase that as elsewhere in Luke (7:31; 11:29–32, 50–51; 17:25) must refer to Jesus' contemporaries. A biblical generation is forty years (on account of the wilderness generation, Num 32:13). Indeed, Jesus preached these words around AD 30 (or 33), and Jerusalem fell in AD 70. The second saying emphasizes just *how certain* Jesus' **words** are. More firm even than **heaven and earth** (Luke 21:25–26), they **will not pass away** and are thus worthy to be believed.

Recalling what he has taught elsewhere in the Gospel, Jesus concludes with **21:34–36** a call to **be vigilant** (12:37) so as not to **become drowsy** (9:32; 22:45–46), for reasons such as **drunkenness** (12:45) or **the anxieties of daily life** (8:14), and thus be caught **by surprise** by the **day** of the Lord's coming. This can be applied to **everyone**—those of Jesus' generation, those alive at his second coming, and all those in between. All must **pray** for **the strength to escape** (see 21:21) the judgment and **to stand** (v. 28) for the redemption that **the Son of Man** will bring.

Following the conclusion of Jesus' discourse, a brief summary serves to frame **21:37–38** the Jerusalem ministry section (19:45–21:38). The mention of Jesus' routine of **teaching in the temple area** by **day** and of the eagerness of **the people** to go **to listen to him** echoes the description back at the beginning of the Jerusalem ministry (19:47–48). However, there is also a new piece of information that looks forward in the narrative: **Jesus** goes **at night** to **the Mount of Olives**. Other Gospels specify further that he would go to Bethany (Matt 21:17; Mark 11:11–12), on the mount's eastern slope (see Luke 19:29). Luke's more general reference provides a hint of what is to come. On the night of his arrest, Jesus will go, as is "his custom, to the Mount of Olives" (22:39).

These two verses are the calm before the storm. The very next verse (22:1) announces the feast of Passover, beginning the narrative of Jesus' suffering and death (22:1–23:56).

The Passover of the Messiah

Luke 22:1–71

The approaching feast of Passover signals the arrival of the Messiah's "exodus" (9:31)—namely, his suffering and death (22:1–23:56) followed by his resurrection and ascension into heaven (24:1–53). Now the Scriptures and Jesus' predictions will be fulfilled (18:31–33), thus accomplishing God's plan of salvation in Jesus.

The Plot to Hand Jesus Over (22:1–6)

---

¹Now the feast of Unleavened Bread, called the Passover, was drawing near, ²and the chief priests and the scribes were seeking a way to put him to death, for they were afraid of the people. ³Then Satan entered into Judas, the one surnamed Iscariot, who was counted among the Twelve, ⁴and he went to the chief priests and temple guards to discuss a plan for handing him over to them. ⁵They were pleased and agreed to pay him money. ⁶He accepted their offer and sought a favorable opportunity to hand him over to them in the absence of a crowd.

OT: Exod 12; Lev 23:5–8; Deut 16:1–8
NT: Luke 2:41; John 11:53; 13:2, 27. // Matt 26:1–5, 14–16; Mark 14:1–2, 10–11

22:1 **Passover** is the annual celebration of Israel's liberation from slavery in Egypt through the exodus (Exod 12). It is followed by the weeklong **feast of Unleavened Bread** (Lev 23:5–8; Deut 16:1–8), all of which was also **called** Passover by the time of Jesus. Unleavened bread—"the bread of affliction" recalling the "hurried flight" from Egypt (Deut 16:3; see Exod 12:39)—is eaten with the Passover lamb the first night and throughout the following week (Exod 12:8, 18). Luke earlier mentioned the Passover when Jesus was twelve years old (Luke 2:41–42), which foreshadowed the events taking place now.

With the feast approaching, **the chief priests and the scribes** continued   22:2
their efforts to find **a way to put him to death** (19:47; 20:19). However, since Jesus had the support of **the people** (19:48; 21:38), they were **afraid of** them and sought to do it covertly.

The breakthrough came when **Judas**, called **Iscariot**, turned traitor even   22:3–6
though he was one of **the Twelve** (6:16; Acts 1:16–17, 25). **Satan**—that is, the devil—who was awaiting the opportune time (Luke 4:13), now **entered into** him (see John 13:2, 27) as an instigator to sin, though Judas still remained free and responsible for his actions—and hence blameworthy (Luke 22:22; see Catechism 407). He went **to the chief priests and temple guards** (a police force, see 22:52–54; Acts 4:1, 3; 5:24) and conferred with them about **handing Jesus over. They were pleased** (literally, "they rejoiced") but "over wrongdoing" (1 Cor 13:6). One of Judas's motives was **money** (Matt 26:15; John 12:6); he thus failed to heed Jesus' words "to guard against all greed" (Luke 12:15). From then on, he looked for an **opportunity to hand him over**, when no **crowd** of supporters would be present. Jesus' prediction is about to be fulfilled: "The Son of Man is to be *handed over* to men" (9:44 [emphasis added]).

Preparing for the Passover (22:7–13)

[7]When the day of the feast of Unleavened Bread arrived, the day for sacrificing the Passover lamb, [8]he sent out Peter and John, instructing them, "Go and make preparations for us to eat the Passover." [9]They asked him, "Where do you want us to make the preparations?" [10]And he answered them, "When you go into the city, a man will meet you carrying a jar of water. Follow him into the house that he enters [11]and say to the master of the house, 'The teacher says to you, "Where is the guest room where I may eat the Passover with my disciples?"' [12]He will show you a large upper room that is furnished. Make the preparations there." [13]Then they went off and found everything exactly as he had told them, and there they prepared the Passover.

OT: Exod 12:6, 18; Lev 23:5–6
NT: Luke 19:29–32. // Matt 26:17–19; Mark 14:12–16
Catechism: celebrating Passover, 1096; Passover and Eucharist, 1151, 1339–40

22:7 **The feast** that "was drawing near" (22:1) has now **arrived**, specifically, the **day for sacrificing the Passover lamb,**[1] the fourteenth day of the Jewish month of Nisan (falling in March or April). Prior to the temple's destruction in AD 70, tens of thousands of lambs were sacrificed that afternoon in assembly-line fashion to accommodate the hundreds of thousands of pilgrims to Jerusalem (with one lamb for every ten or so people). The lambs were slaughtered near the altar by those who brought them to the temple, with priests collecting the blood in basins that were poured out at the base of the altar.[2] Pilgrims then returned with their lamb to their place of lodging to roast it for the meal. After sundown (hence, after the beginning of the fifteenth of Nisan), the lamb was eaten with **unleavened bread** and bitter herbs (Exod 12:8; Lev 23:5–6).

22:8–13   As the Jewish leaders and Judas were getting ready, so was Jesus. Aware of the significance of this Passover, Jesus **sent** two disciples (as in Luke 19:29–30) to **make preparations** for both the sacrifice and the meal. As observant Jews, **Peter and John** understood *what* needed to be done. The key question was: **Where?** Perhaps Jesus, knowing that he was a marked man, had quietly made prior arrangements that he now communicates to them, and thus the location of the meal was unknown to Judas beforehand. Another possibility is that by special foreknowledge, Jesus explains how events will unfold (see 19:30–31). Once they **go into the city**, they will be met by **a man** who is **carrying a jar of water**. The rendezvous may thus occur near a pool, such as the Pool of Siloam in the southeastern part of the city that collected the waters from the Gihon spring. They are to **follow him into the house that he enters**, perhaps not too far away in the southwestern part of the city, the traditional location of the Last Supper. **The master of the house**, though unnamed, is a trusted acquaintance of Jesus, whom he knows as **the teacher**.[3] In his hospitality, he makes available **the guest room** (Greek *katalyma*), the same word earlier translated "inn" (2:7), where Jesus at his birth did *not* receive hospitality. Here it is a **furnished**, **large upper room**, perhaps the same place later used by the early Christians (Acts 1:13). Just like the two disciples who were sent to fetch the colt (Luke 19:32), Peter and John **went off and found everything** just **as he had told them.**

---

1. Because of the reference to sacrifice, the Greek word *pascha* is here translated "Passover *lamb*" (see 1 Cor 5:7). Elsewhere in Luke, *pascha* is translated simply "Passover" but may refer to the weeklong feast (Luke 22:1), the meal on its first night (22:11, 15), or both the sacrifice and the meal (22:8). See Brant Pitre, *Jesus and the Last Supper* (Grand Rapids: Eerdmans, 2015), 339–40, 395.

2. Pitre, *Last Supper*, 396–98. See Josephus, *Jewish War* 6.423–24; *m. Pesahim* 5:5–7.

3. The title "teacher" is typically used in Luke by those who are not close disciples (7:40; 8:49; 9:38; 10:25; 11:45; 12:13; 18:18; 19:39; 20:21, 28, 39).

Last Supper, Part 1: Institution of the Eucharist (22:14–20)

---

¹⁴When the hour came, he took his place at table with the apostles. ¹⁵He said to them, "I have eagerly desired to eat this Passover with you before I suffer, ¹⁶for, I tell you, I shall not eat it [again] until there is fulfillment in the kingdom of God." ¹⁷Then he took a cup, gave thanks, and said, "Take this and share it among yourselves; ¹⁸for I tell you [that] from this time on I shall not drink of the fruit of the vine until the kingdom of God comes." ¹⁹Then he took the bread, said the blessing, broke it, and gave it to them, saying, "This is my body, which will be given for you; do this in memory of me." ²⁰And likewise the cup after they had eaten, saying, "This cup is the new covenant in my blood, which will be shed for you."

OT: Exod 24:4–11; Jer 31:31–34

NT: Luke 9:16; 1 Cor 11:23–26. // Matt 26:20, 26–29; Mark 14:17, 22–25

Catechism: Eucharist and the kingdom, 1130, 1403; institution of the Eucharist, 1337–40; the Eucharist as sacrificial memorial, 610–11, 621; 1365; the Eucharist means thanksgiving, 1328; the Eucharist is the body and blood of Christ, 1381

Lectionary: Luke 22:14–23:56: Palm/Passion Sunday (Year C); Luke 22:14–20, 24–30: Holy Orders

After nightfall,[4] the **hour** (see John 13:1) arrives for the meal and Jesus reclines **22:14**
at table with the apostles. He gives a farewell address (Luke 22:14–38),[5] which begins with the announcement of his upcoming suffering and death (vv. 15–18) and the institution of the Eucharist (vv. 19–20). All this is part of an unfolding plan that "has been determined" (v. 22) and "must be fulfilled" (v. 37). However, Jesus is not passively resigned to his destiny but actively takes the initiative to accomplish his purpose (19:30; 22:8).

His comment—**I have eagerly desired to eat** (literally, "with desire I have **22:15–20**
desired to eat," reflecting an underlying Hebrew expression)—is another indication that he acts with intention. The significance of what he says and does here can be examined by focusing on three interrelated key words.

1. **Passover:** This Passover night is different from all others. The Jewish Passover is a *memorial* of God's liberation of the people of Israel from slavery in Egypt through the *exodus* (Exod 12:14; 13:3). Those who observe the annual Passover feast do not simply recall the exodus as a past event but, in a sense, relive it at the present time and thus experience the Lord's saving power (see

---

4. *m. Pesahim* 10:1.

5. William S. Kurz, "Luke 22:14–38 and Greco-Roman and Biblical Farewell Addresses," *JBL* 104 (1985): 257–58, 262. Paul's farewell address in Acts 20:17–38 has many of the same elements (e.g., final instructions, warnings).

Exod 13:8).[6] However, at this Passover,[7] Jesus institutes *his memorial*, saying: **in memory of me** (or "in remembrance of me," 1 Cor 11:24–25; Greek *anamnēsis*). Likewise, he is about to accomplish *his "exodus"* (Luke 9:31)—his death and resurrection—which will bring to those who believe in him a different kind of liberation: forgiveness of their sins (24:47). Thus his apostles who observe the new Passover memorial in obedience to his command will experience the saving power of this new exodus.

In instituting this new Passover, which was prefigured at the multiplication of the loaves with its similar actions (9:16), Jesus **took the bread, gave thanks,**[8] **broke it, and gave it to** the apostles. His accompanying words provide the interpretation. The bread is not the expected "bread of affliction" of the exodus (Deut 16:3) but becomes his very self: **This is my body**. In this new Passover, it will be Jesus' body, not that of the lamb, that **will be given** in sacrifice.[9] Like the sacrifice of the lamb (Exod 12:13, 23, 27), this will be done **for you**, he tells the apostles—in other words, on their behalf and for their benefit. Moreover, this body is **eaten** (see Matt 26:26), as was the lamb (Exod 12:8–11).[10] Bread that has become the Eucharist through these words is not merely a symbol. Just as the lamb is real, so the Eucharist is really his body, as indeed Christians have understood from the beginning.

Likewise, Jesus' words provide the interpretation of **the cup** taken **after** supper (1 Cor 11:25), the third of the four cups of wine in the Passover meal, the "cup of blessing" (1 Cor 10:16):[11] the wine in the cup becomes **my blood** (see Matt 26:28; Mark 14:24). By drinking the cup, his apostles thus have communion in his blood (1 Cor 10:16). Jesus is referring to his imminent, violent death: his blood **will be shed**[12] like "the blood of all the prophets *shed* since the foundation of the world" (Luke 11:50 [emphasis added]). However, "he transforms his

6. *m. Pesahim* 10:5.

7. Matthew, Mark, and Luke present the Last Supper as a Passover meal, but John seems to present Jesus' death as occurring at the time the Passover lambs are being slain—hence, before the meal. For a discussion of the various proposals for explaining this difference, see Pitre, *Last Supper*, 251–373.

8. The Greek verb *eucharisteō* appears in both Luke 22:17 and v. 19. The NABRE translates "gave thanks" in v. 17 but **said the blessing** in v. 19 (see Matt 26:26; Mark 14:22, which use a different verb). Paul also uses *eucharisteō*: "after he had given thanks" (1 Cor 11:24). From this usage comes the name of the new rite that Jesus institutes: the Eucharist (Catechism 1328).

9. These words and the rest of Luke 22:19, as well as v. 20, are missing in one fifth-century Greek manuscript and some Latin manuscripts; some thus consider them a later addition based on 1 Cor 11:24–25. However, since all other Greek manuscripts, including those from the third and fourth centuries, include them, most scholars consider them to be original.

10. For the ideas in this paragraph, see Pitre, *Last Supper*, 405–11.

11. *m. Pesahim* 10:1, 7. See Joseph A. Fitzmyer, *The Gospel according to Luke*, 2 vols., AB (New York: Doubleday, 1981–85), 2:1390; Pitre, *Last Supper*, 483–84n124.

12. Using the same verb, Jesus had earlier spoken of "new wine" that "will be spilled" (Luke 5:37).

violent death into a free act of self-giving for others and to others."[13] In other words, as he already indicated in speaking of his body, his death becomes a sacrifice, offered **for you**—he again tells his apostles—in other words, on their behalf, for the purpose of atonement. Hence, a better translation is that his blood is not just shed, but "poured out" (22:20 NIV; see Catechism 610). Indeed, the blood of the Passover lamb (see 2 Chron 30:15–16; 35:11) and of sacrifices in general (Deut 12:27) was poured out at the base of the altar (Lev 8:15).[14]

2. **Kingdom**: Prior to the two statements about his body and blood, Jesus announces in two statements (Luke 22:16, 18) that this is indeed his "last supper" because of his imminent death. After this meal,[15] he will thus **not eat** the Passover meal nor **drink** its cups of wine[16] **until** the time of **fulfillment** of the coming **kingdom of God**. With these words, Jesus looks ahead to his resurrection and entrance into kingly glory (24:26; Acts 2:32–33). After his resurrection, he will once again eat and drink with his disciples (Luke 24:30, 41–43; Acts 10:41), a sign of the kingdom banquet (Luke 13:29), where he will eat and drink with his apostles (see 22:30).[17] Certainly the kingdom has *already* come among them in Jesus (11:20; 17:20–21), yet its future coming in power has *not yet* occurred. Thus, just as the Jewish Passover not only looked back to the exodus but also forward to God's saving action in the future, so too whenever his disciples celebrate the Eucharist they will do so not only in memory of Jesus' death but also in anticipation and as a foretaste of the kingdom banquet.

3. **Covenant**: Following the first Passover and the exodus, Moses at Mount Sinai had thrown the blood of sacrifices against the altar (Exod 24:6) when God established the covenant with the twelve tribes of Israel. He also "splashed it on the people, saying, 'This is the blood of the covenant'" (Exod 24:8), before taking part in a sacred meal in which "they ate and drank" (Exod 24:11). Here, in the context of the Last Supper with the twelve apostles, Jesus' reference to a covenant in his blood recalls this event.[18] However, it also indicates something **new**. Indeed, if there is a new Passover and a new exodus, there will also be a "new covenant" (1 Cor 11:25), as Jeremiah had prophesied: "See, days are

13. Benedict XVI, *Jesus of Nazareth: Holy Week; From the Entrance into Jerusalem to the Resurrection*, trans. Philip J. Whitmore (San Francisco: Ignatius, 2011), 130.

14. *m. Pesahim* 5:6. See Pitre, *Last Supper*, 413–14.

15. Some interpret Jesus' words to mean that he abstains from the Passover meal, but the context suggests otherwise (Luke 22:8, 11, 15).

16. The blessing for wine—said at Passover (*m. Pesahim* 10:2)—uses the expression **the fruit of the vine** (*m. Berakhot* 6:1).

17. John Paul Heil, *The Meal Scenes in Luke-Acts: An Audience-Oriented Approach* (Atlanta: Society of Biblical Literature, 1999), 226.

18. Pitre, *Last Supper*, 94–95.

The Eucharistic Real Presence

LIVING
TRADITION

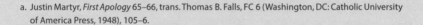

Writing in the second century, St. Justin Martyr explains the celebration of the Eucharist and Christian belief in the real presence of Jesus in the Eucharist:

> Bread and a chalice containing wine mixed with water are presented to the one presiding over the brethren. He takes them and offers praise and glory to the Father of all, through the name of the Son and of the Holy Spirit, and he recites lengthy prayers of thanksgiving to God. . . . And when he who presides has celebrated the Eucharist, they whom we call deacons permit each one to partake. . . . We call this food the Eucharist, of which only he can partake who has acknowledged the truth of our teachings, who has been cleansed by baptism for the remission of his sins . . . and who regulates his life upon the principles laid down by Christ. Not as ordinary bread or as ordinary drink do we partake of them, but just as, through the word of God, our savior Jesus Christ became incarnate and took upon himself flesh and blood for our salvation, so, we have been taught, the food which has been made the Eucharist by the prayer of his word, and which nourishes our flesh and blood by assimilation, is both the flesh and blood of that Jesus who was made flesh. The Apostles in their memoirs, which are called Gospels, have handed down what Jesus ordered them to do; that he took bread and, after giving thanks, said: "Do this in remembrance of me; this is my body." In like manner, he took also the chalice, gave thanks, and said: "This is my blood." [Luke 22:19; Matt 26:28; Mark 14:24][a]

a. Justin Martyr, *First Apology* 65–66, trans. Thomas B. Falls, FC 6 (Washington, DC: Catholic University of America Press, 1948), 105–6.

coming . . . when I will make a new covenant with the house of Israel and the house of Judah" (Jer 31:31).[19]

Moreover, under the Mosaic covenant, the bread of the presence (see comment on Luke 6:3–4) was offered (not just set out) each sabbath (Lev 24:7) by the Levitical priests as a kind of grain offering (see Lev 2). It was an unbloody sacrifice. These unleavened loaves were a "memorial" (*anamnēsis*, Lev 24:7 LXX) of the covenant made at Sinai (Lev 24:8).[20] Here, Jesus' command to his apostles to **do this** in "memory" of him (Luke 22:19, same Greek word) means that the eucharistic bread that the apostles will offer will serve as a memorial that represents the New Covenant established by Jesus through his bloody sacrifice.

19. Hebrews quotes this verse (Heb 8:8, 13) and also discusses other elements found in Luke's institution narrative (Luke 22:19–20): Jesus' body given in sacrifice (Heb 10:10), ritual memorial (*anamnēsis*, Heb 10:3), "new covenant" (Heb 9:15; 12:24), references to Exod 24:8 (Heb 9:20), and blood poured out (Heb 9:22; see Heb 12:24).

20. Pitre, *Last Supper*, 126–36.

Thus, the role of the apostles in the New Covenant was in a sense prefigured by that of the Levitical priests in the Mosaic covenant. Because of Jesus' command, the Church understands the Last Supper as the institution of the Eucharist and also the institution of the New Covenant priesthood (Catechism 611).

Last Supper, Part 2: Predictions and Instructions (22:21–38)

[21]"And yet behold, the hand of the one who is to betray me is with me on the table; [22]for the Son of Man indeed goes as it has been determined; but woe to that man by whom he is betrayed." [23]And they began to debate among themselves who among them would do such a deed.

[24]Then an argument broke out among them about which of them should be regarded as the greatest. [25]He said to them, "The kings of the Gentiles lord it over them and those in authority over them are addressed as 'Benefactors'; [26]but among you it shall not be so. Rather, let the greatest among you be as the youngest, and the leader as the servant. [27]For who is greater: the one seated at table or the one who serves? Is it not the one seated at table? I am among you as the one who serves. [28]It is you who have stood by me in my trials; [29]and I confer a kingdom on you, just as my Father has conferred one on me, [30]that you may eat and drink at my table in my kingdom; and you will sit on thrones judging the twelve tribes of Israel.

[31]"Simon, Simon, behold Satan has demanded to sift all of you like wheat, [32]but I have prayed that your own faith may not fail; and once you have turned back, you must strengthen your brothers." [33]He said to him, "Lord, I am prepared to go to prison and to die with you." [34]But he replied, "I tell you, Peter, before the cock crows this day, you will deny three times that you know me."

[35]He said to them, "When I sent you forth without a money bag or a sack or sandals, were you in need of anything?" "No, nothing," they replied. [36]He said to them, "But now one who has a money bag should take it, and likewise a sack, and one who does not have a sword should sell his cloak and buy one. [37]For I tell you that this scripture must be fulfilled in me, namely, 'He was counted among the wicked'; and indeed what is written about me is coming to fulfillment." [38]Then they said, "Lord, look, there are two swords here." But he replied, "It is enough!"

OT: Isa 53:12
NT: Luke 9:3, 46, 48; 10:4; John 13:21–30, 36–38; Acts 20:17–38. // Matt 19:28; 20:25–28; 26:21–25, 33–35; Mark 10:42–45; 14:18–21, 29–31
Catechism: authority and service, 894, 1570; the Twelve share in Christ's authority, 551, 765; faith tested, 643, 2600; Peter strengthens his brothers, 552, 641
Lectionary: Luke 22:24–27: Blessing of Abbots and Abbesses

22:21–23   Jesus' farewell address now continues with a series of predictions and instructions for the apostles. First, he announces that **one** of them will **betray** him (6:16; 22:3–6). The verb "betray" (22:21–22; also 22:48) is elsewhere rendered "hand over" (e.g., 22:4, 6) when referring to Judas's treachery. The betrayal is particularly distressing coming from one who at **table** "ate . . . bread" with Jesus (Ps 41:10; see John 13:18). Jesus' suffering is part of a divine plan that **has been determined** in advance (Acts 2:23), but that does not excuse individuals like Judas who are involved in the human "plan" (Luke 22:4; 23:51) that brings it about. Thus Jesus pronounces a **woe** on Judas, warning him of the consequences (see Acts 1:18).[21] Of course, the other apostles know nothing of Judas's plan, so they discuss **who** it might be.

22:24–27   Their discussion leads to **an argument** about who is **the greatest**. It is not the first time (Luke 9:46)! Indeed, it happened on another occasion when Jesus spoke about being betrayed ("handed over," 9:44). Unwittingly, the disciples are imitating the Pharisees and scribes who love and vie for seats of honor (11:43; 14:7; 20:46). In response, Jesus gives the apostles instruction in **servant** leadership (see 17:7–10). To enter the kingdom of God, one must become "like a child" (18:17); hence **the greatest** must become **as the youngest**—the ones who are "least" (9:48) in terms of status. This is a reversal of the way **the kings of the Gentiles** operate, who **lord it over** people. Their rulers exercise **authority** by becoming **benefactors**, but their gifts have strings attached, as they expect social status and public honor in return. Jesus is a benefactor of a different kind, going about "doing good" (Acts 10:38) without such worldly expectations. He is the model of servant leadership since he is **the one who serves** (see Luke 12:37).

22:28–30   Now that he has explained what kind of leadership is required, Jesus as a benefactor can reward his loyal apostles **who have stood by** him,[22] not with worldly kingdoms (see 4:5–6) but by conferring on them a special position in the **kingdom** of God. The word rendered **confer** (*diatithēmi*) is the verb form of the noun "covenant" (*diathēkē*, 22:20); the two words are often used together in the †Septuagint when a covenant is made (e.g., Exod 24:8 LXX). The verb's use here emphasizes the relationship between covenant and kingdom already suggested in the institution narrative. In the Old Testament, God's covenant with David involved granting him a kingdom forever (2 Chron 13:5; Ps 89:4–5, 29–30). As the "Son of David" (Luke 18:38–39; 20:41), Jesus is the heir who has had the kingdom **conferred** on him (i.e., "covenanted" to him) by his **Father**.

---

21. Luke does not narrate Judas's departure from the supper (see John 13:30). It is nevertheless implied, since Judas next appears leading those who will arrest Jesus (Luke 22:47).

22. Jesus refers to his **trials**, as does Paul in his farewell address (Acts 20:19).

He now "covenants" his **kingdom** to the apostles, giving them a share in his authority over the New Covenant community. He promises them that in the heavenly banquet they will **eat and drink at** his **table** in his **kingdom** (see 13:29) and **sit on thrones**. However, the task of **judging the twelve tribes of Israel** begins already on earth,[23] with their ruling—as servant leaders—over the Church community of restored Israel and the Gentiles. This is what takes place in Acts,[24] as expressed, for example, in Paul's similar farewell address: "Keep watch . . . over the whole flock of which the holy Spirit has appointed you overseers, in which you tend the church of God that he acquired with his own blood" (Acts 20:28).[25]

A special mission is reserved for one apostle, last but not least,[26] whom Jesus **22:31–34** here calls twice (see Luke 10:41) by his original name: **Simon, Simon** (4:38). Earlier, Jesus referred to a foundation laid on "rock" (*petra*, 6:48). Now he spells out Simon's rock-like task—**strengthen your brothers**—and addresses him (for the first and only time in Luke) as **Peter** (from *petros*; see Matt 16:18). However, this solidity is not Peter's own, despite his boasting that he is **prepared** for anything. Rather, as an individual, Peter remains fragile, especially on account of the onslaught of **Satan**. The devil goes after the whole group of apostles—**you** plural—having **demanded** (see Job 1:11–12; 2:5–6) **to sift** them **like wheat**—that is, to shake their faith so completely as to take away the seed of the word from their hearts (see Luke 6:48; 8:12). Peter will indeed experience a fall—the **three** denials **before the cock crows** (22:54–62). In anticipation of this fall, Jesus has **prayed**[27] for Peter—**you** singular—that his **faith may not fail**. Hence, on that basis Peter will be enabled to fulfill his task of confirming the faith of the others. After he has **turned back**, he will also encourage others to "repent . . . and turn back" (Acts 3:19 ESV). At that point, not now, Peter will be ready **to go to prison** (Acts 5:18–19; 12:3–5) and eventually **to die** (see John 21:18–19) on account of Jesus.

In view of the present crisis but also the future mission of the apostles, Jesus' **22:35–38** final instructions in his farewell address repeal the earlier restrictions about not taking **a money bag** or **a sack** when **sent** out (Luke 9:3; 10:4). In the more

23. Hence, the necessity of replacing Judas with Matthias before the day of Pentecost so as to have twelve apostles (Acts 1:20–26).

24. For the ideas in this paragraph, see Scott W. Hahn, *Kinship by Covenant: A Canonical Approach to the Fulfillment of God's Saving Promises* (New Haven: Yale University Press, 2009), 227–29.

25. The Greek word for "overseer" is *episkopos*, from which the English word "bishop" derives.

26. At the Last Supper, Jesus deals with Judas Iscariot first and Simon last, but in the list of apostles (Luke 6:14–16), Simon ends up first but Judas last (see 13:30).

27. Jesus prays before choosing Peter and the rest of the Twelve (Luke 6:12–16), before Peter's confession (9:18–20), and now before Peter's temptation. See Catechism 2600.

hostile environment they will face, they will have to provide for their own needs, as Paul explains in his similar farewell address: "I have never wanted anyone's silver or gold or clothing. You know well that these very hands have served my needs and my companions" (Acts 20:33–34).

Likewise, Jesus' puzzling command to purchase **a sword** is best understood as referring to the hostile response that lies ahead. Indeed, this is confirmed by the **scripture** passage that Jesus gives as a reason for his command: **He was counted among the wicked** (see Isa 53:12). Mistakenly, **they** take his words literally by pointing to **two swords**, which they conclude could be useful in self-defense. Consequently, Jesus replies, **it is enough!** or "That's enough!" (NIV), bringing an end to the discussion and indicating that his command was meant to be taken metaphorically, as an injunction to be ready for the worst. They will nevertheless persist in their misunderstanding (Luke 22:49–51).

Coming at the beginning of the passion narrative, Jesus' quotation from Scripture also again emphasizes that his suffering, death, and resurrection are things that **must** (9:22; 24:7) happen in order to bring **to fulfillment** all that **is written about** him (18:31–33; see 24:26–27, 44–46). Moreover, this specific quotation from Isaiah comes from the fourth song of the †servant of the Lord (Isa 52:13–53:12; see comment on Luke 3:22), which Luke also quotes elsewhere (Acts 8:32–33, citing Isa 53:7–8). That passage explains Jesus' mission as the †suffering servant who gives his life as a sacrifice for the sins of many (see Luke 22:19–20).

Reflection and Application (22:32)

Strengthen your brothers. The Catholic Church understands certain words of Jesus to Peter as conferring a special authority not only on him but also on his successors (see Catechism 552, 880–82). Throughout history, disagreements on this issue and on how popes should exercise the office of Peter have caused divisions among Christians. However, in recent years, ecumenical dialogue has led to some progress in overcoming these differences between Catholic, Orthodox, and Protestant Christians.[28] Scripture study also plays a role in this regard. For example, the non-Catholic Scripture scholar Markus Bockmuehl notes: "The principle of a continuation of the Petrine ministry *as such* seems clear . . . beginning perhaps with classic 'Petrine primacy' texts such as Matt. 16:17–19;

---

28. See, e.g., the "Ravenna Document" of the Joint International Commission for the Theological Dialogue between the Roman Catholic Church and the Orthodox Church, October 13, 2007; and the document "Gift of Authority" of the Anglican-Roman Catholic International Commission (ARCIC), September 3, 1998.

Luke 22:31–32; and John 21:15–17. All three texts imply a post-Easter continuation of Peter's task that seems intrinsically permanent in nature and not tied to the identity of the one apostle."[29] All Christians should pray for further progress leading to greater unity.

The Agony and Arrest on the Mount of Olives (22:39–53)

[39]Then going out he went, as was his custom, to the Mount of Olives, and the disciples followed him. [40]When he arrived at the place he said to them, "Pray that you may not undergo the test." [41]After withdrawing about a stone's throw from them and kneeling, he prayed, [42]saying, "Father, if you are willing, take this cup away from me; still, not my will but yours be done." [[43]And to strengthen him an angel from heaven appeared to him. [44]He was in such agony and he prayed so fervently that his sweat became like drops of blood falling on the ground.] [45]When he rose from prayer and returned to his disciples, he found them sleeping from grief. [46]He said to them, "Why are you sleeping? Get up and pray that you may not undergo the test."

[47]While he was still speaking, a crowd approached and in front was one of the Twelve, a man named Judas. He went up to Jesus to kiss him. [48]Jesus said to him, "Judas, are you betraying the Son of Man with a kiss?" [49]His disciples realized what was about to happen, and they asked, "Lord, shall we strike with a sword?" [50]And one of them struck the high priest's servant and cut off his right ear. [51]But Jesus said in reply, "Stop, no more of this!" Then he touched the servant's ear and healed him. [52]And Jesus said to the chief priests and temple guards and elders who had come for him, "Have you come out as against a robber, with swords and clubs? [53]Day after day I was with you in the temple area, and you did not seize me; but this is your hour, the time for the power of darkness."

OT: Gen 3:19; 4:10–11
NT: Matt 6:10; Luke 11:2, 4; 21:37; Acts 1:16; 21:14; 27:23; Col 1:13; Heb 5:7. // Matt 26:30, 36–41, 47–56; Mark 14:26, 32–38, 43–49; John 18:1–11
Catechism: watchful prayer, 2612; Jesus at prayer, 2600; divine will and human will, 475, 2605, 2824; Jesus with angels, 333; Jesus' agony, 612; Judas's betrayal, 1851

After the meal, despite knowing that he would be betrayed (22:21), Jesus led   22:39
the way **and the disciples followed**. **He went** across the Kidron Valley (John

29. Markus Bockmuehl, *Simon Peter in Scripture and Memory: The New Testament Apostle in the Early Church* (Grand Rapids: Baker Academic, 2012), 183 (emphasis in the original).

Figure 20. Olive trees in Gethsemane on the Mount of Olives.

18:1) **to the Mount of Olives**, according to **his custom** (Luke 21:37)—Judas would thus be able to find him (22:47). On Passover night, pilgrims to the festival were obliged to remain within the greater Jerusalem area (see Deut 16:7), whose boundary included Bethphage (Luke 19:29).[30]

22:40   **The place** is unnamed in Luke, but the other Gospels specify a "garden" named "Gethsemane" (Matt 26:36; Mark 14:32; John 18:1–2).[31] The first scene there (Luke 22:39–46) is framed by Jesus' words to the disciples to **pray** so that they **may not undergo the test** (vv. 40, 46; "enter into temptation," RSV). This directive recalls the last petition in Luke's version of the Lord's Prayer: "Lead us not into temptation" (11:4 RSV). Indeed, that prayer will be especially urgent now as they continue facing trials (see 22:28).

22:41–42   Likewise echoing the Lord's Prayer, Jesus **prayed** by addressing his **Father** (11:2). The details regarding his prayer—that he withdrew **about a stone's throw** and was **kneeling**—are recalled at the martyrdom of Stephen, who prays while kneeling as stones are thrown at him (Acts 7:58–60). Moreover, Jesus' insistence that the **will** of the Father **be done** is echoed in Acts when a group of disciples recognize Paul's similar resolve that "the Lord's will be done" (Acts 21:14). Jesus

---

30. *m. Menahot* 11:2.

31. The traditional site is marked today by the Church of All Nations, built over the remains of an earlier fourth-century church. See Jerome Murphy-O'Connor, *Keys to Jerusalem: Collected Essays* (Oxford: Oxford University Press, 2012), 104.

Jesus' Human Will and Divine Will

LIVING TRADITION

The Third Council of Constantinople (AD 681) taught that because of Jesus' two natures, divine and human, there are in Jesus two wills, divine and human, and the human will acts in conformity with the divine will: "His human will is compliant; it does not resist or oppose but rather submits to his divine and almighty will."[a] With his human will, Jesus exercises his human freedom to obey the divine will. The Council thus ratified the teaching of St. Maximus the Confessor, who reflected on the words of Jesus' prayer—"Not my will but yours be done" (Luke 22:42)—and drew from them a practical lesson for Christians "of setting aside our own will by the perfect fulfillment of the divine."[b] Pope Benedict XVI comments on these teachings and makes a similar application: "The human will, as created by God, is ordered to the divine will." In other words, human beings attain their fulfillment by accomplishing God's will. However, sin introduced opposition to God's will, so that we experience obedience to God's will as a threat to our freedom. Through his prayer, Jesus has overcome this opposition and "transformed humanity's resistance, so that we are all now present within the Son's obedience."[c] By our union with Jesus (Gal 2:20), obedience to God's will becomes possible.

a. Denzinger 556; see John 6:38; Catechism 475.
b. Maximus the Confessor, *Opuscule* 7.80D, in Andrew Louth, *Maximus the Confessor* (London: Routledge, 1996), 186.
c. Benedict XVI, *Jesus of Nazareth: Holy Week*, 160–61.

in his suffering and death is thus presented as a martyr, like the prophets of old (Luke 11:49–51; 13:34) and as the model for his own disciples. However, Jesus' death also goes one step further because it is sacrificial: **this cup** that God is giving him is the sacrifice of the New Covenant in his blood that will be poured out in his death (22:20; see Catechism 612).

Verses 43–44, accepted as canonical by the Catholic Church, are found in **22:43–44** some of the oldest manuscripts (from the fourth and fifth centuries) but are missing from many others (including some from the third century). The NABRE thus puts them in brackets, as scholars are divided as to whether they are original to Luke's Gospel or are a later addition to it based on an ancient tradition. However, St. Justin Martyr in the middle of the second century refers to the passage and says that it comes from the Gospels (probably Luke).[32] The verses also have several phrases typical of Luke (e.g., compare Luke 1:11 and 22:43).

32. *Dialogue with Trypho* 103.8.

For these and other reasons, there are many noted scholars who argue in their favor.[33] The verses may have been intentionally omitted from manuscripts because of fears that they detracted from Jesus' divinity.

As Jesus **prayed, an angel**[34] came **to strengthen him** (see 4:10; Mark 1:13). The angel **appeared to him** (see Luke 1:11) to confirm him at a crucial point in his mission—right before his passion—as did the voice **from heaven** at his baptism at the beginning of his public ministry (3:22) and the similar voice at the transfiguration right before his journey to Jerusalem (9:35). On those two occasions, Jesus was praying as he is doing here (3:21; 9:28–29).[35]

During this "test" (22:40, 46), Jesus experiences **agony** (*agōnia*), meaning "anguish" or "distress" (2 Macc 3:14, 16; see Heb 5:7), though some understand it more in the sense of "struggle" (see Luke 13:24 for a related verb). He continues praying (22:41) **so fervently** that **his sweat** becomes **like drops of blood falling**. This phrase is often interpreted figuratively to mean profuse sweating, but others point out the rare medical condition, known in the ancient world, in which sweat becomes tinged with blood.[36]

The test that Jesus here undergoes recalls how the devil earlier put him to the test ("temptation," 4:13). There, Jesus proved to be the new Adam, in contrast to Adam who fell to temptation (see comment on 3:38 and 4:2). Because of his disobedience, Adam was punished, forced to survive "by the sweat" of his brow (Gen 3:19). Here, despite the sweat of this intense experience, Jesus remains obedient.[37]

22:45–46   Strengthened by **prayer** and the angel, Jesus **rose** (the verb is often used for his rising from the dead; e.g., Luke 18:33; 24:7, 46), suggesting that he has emerged victorious from the test and is ready to face the sufferings that lie ahead. In contrast, the disciples—with their strength sapped by **grief** (see Sir 38:18)—are **sleeping**, as were the three disciples at the transfiguration (Luke 9:32). They should instead **get up** ("rise," RSV) like Jesus. After Jesus' resurrection, Peter and the disciples at Emmaus will do just that (24:12, 33) on their journey of faith. Here, despite Jesus' repeated exhortation to **pray** (see 22:40), they are not ready for the unfolding **test**.

As he is **still speaking, a crowd** led by **Judas** approaches. In this arrest scene   22:47–48
(vv. 47–53) as at the Last Supper, his **betraying** Jesus is portrayed as especially grave, not only because he is **one of the Twelve** apostles (22:3, 14) but also because he perverts signs of friendship such as table fellowship (22:21) and **a kiss**.

Seeing that Jesus is about to be arrested, **his disciples** ask him about using   22:49–51
the **sword** (22:38). Not waiting for an answer, **one of them** cuts off the **right ear** of **the high priest's servant**.[38] In response, Jesus repairs the damage done: he **healed** the severed **ear**. His words—**Stop, no more of this**—put an end to the violence (Matt 26:52; John 18:11) and allow God's plan to unfold through his arrest (Matt 26:54).

Those in the crowd accompanying Judas (Luke 22:47) are now identified as   22:52–53
the chief priests and temple guards and elders—that is, many of those who have been plotting Jesus' arrest (19:47; 20:1, 19; 22:2, 4). Jesus reproaches them for treating him as **a robber**, fulfilling the scripture passage he earlier mentioned (22:37), though he was with them **in the temple area** teaching each **day** (21:37). What they are doing is the work of the devil: their **hour** is associated with **the power of darkness**. However, through Jesus' suffering, his followers will be "delivered . . . from the power of darkness" (Col 1:13).

Jesus Is Denied by Peter and Mocked by Guards (22:54–65)

---

[54]**After arresting him they led him away and took him into the house of the high priest; Peter was following at a distance.** [55]**They lit a fire in the middle of the courtyard and sat around it, and Peter sat down with them.** [56]**When a maid saw him seated in the light, she looked intently at him and said, "This man too was with him."** [57]**But he denied it saying, "Woman, I do not know him."** [58]**A short while later someone else saw him and said, "You too are one of them"; but Peter answered, "My friend, I am not."** [59]**About an hour later, still another insisted, "Assuredly, this man too was with him, for he also is a Galilean."** [60]**But Peter said, "My friend, I do not know what you are talking about." Just as he was saying this, the cock crowed,** [61]**and the Lord turned and looked at Peter; and Peter remembered the word of the Lord, how he had said to him, "Before the cock crows today, you will deny me three times."** [62]**He went out and began to weep bitterly.** [63]**The men**

---

38. John's Gospel identifies the individuals as Peter and Malchus (John 18:10).

who held Jesus in custody were **ridiculing and beating him**. ⁶⁴They **blind-folded him** and questioned him, saying, "Prophesy! Who is it that struck you?" ⁶⁵And they **reviled him** in saying many other things against him.

NT: Luke 12:9; 18:32. // Matt 26:57–58, 67–75; Mark 14:53–54, 65–72; John 18:12–18, 24–27
Catechism: Peter's tears of repentance, 1429

22:54 From the garden on the Mount of Olives, Jesus is taken to **the house of the high priest**.³⁹ Caiaphas was the high priest in office (see Matt 26:57), though his father-in-law, Annas, a former high priest, remained influential (Luke 3:2; John 18:13, 24; Acts 4:6). **Peter** is **following** Jesus, seemingly "prepared" for the worst (Luke 22:33), though he remains **at a distance** (like the disciples at the cross, 23:49).

22:55–60 Jesus and his captors momentarily remain in the background, as the story focuses on **Peter**, who has joined a group seated by **a fire in the middle of the courtyard**. He cannot escape notice, however, as all eyes appear to be fixed on him. First a staring **maid** and then **someone else saw him**, recognizing that he was **one** of those **with Jesus**.⁴⁰ For **another** person, it was Peter's **Galilean** accent that gave him away (see Matt 26:73). Confronted by their comments, each time he **denied** any association with Jesus. After the third denial, **the cock crowed** in fulfillment of Jesus' prediction (Luke 22:34).

22:61–62 Precisely at that moment, Jesus happens to be standing within view. Turning, he **looked at Peter, and Peter remembered the word** spoken by Jesus that he would **deny** him. Remembering Jesus' words always leads to greater understanding (24:6–8; Acts 11:16). Moreover, Jesus is here twice called **Lord**, which is what Peter called him not only when the denials were predicted (Luke 22:33) but also when he was aware of being "a sinful man" (5:8) and when Jesus spoke to him about being faithful (12:41–42). Realizing that he is a sinful man who has not been faithful to his Lord, Peter goes out **to weep bitterly**, perhaps remembering Jesus' other words as well: "Whoever denies me before others will be denied before the angels of God" (12:9).

However, when Jesus **turned** toward Peter, hope was reborn for Peter's own *turning back* in repentance, on account of Jesus' prayer (22:32). Indeed, Peter's sinning against Jesus **three times** in one day is more than covered by Jesus' offer of sevenfold forgiveness for those who *turn back* (17:4). Later, Peter will thus preach to others that they should repent and "turn back" to God (Acts 3:19 ESV).

39. The twentieth-century Church of St. Peter in Gallicantu (meaning "cock crow") commemorates the event, but the actual location of the high priest's house is disputed. Most scholars favor other sites.
40. In Acts 4:13, Peter will similarly be recognized (along with John) as among those who were with Jesus. There he no longer denies him but rather confesses him with boldness.

With Peter's departure, attention shifts back to **Jesus**. Whereas the other   22:63–65
Gospels refer to his being questioned by a high priest during the night (Matt
26:57–68; Mark 14:53–65; John 18:12–13, 19–24), Luke here just recounts the
mistreatment he received from **the men** guarding him. They were **ridiculing**
or mocking him, fulfilling his passion prediction (Luke 18:32) and giving a
foretaste of things to come (23:11, 36). They also kept saying **many other** in-
sults to **him** (see 23:39). In addition, there is physical abuse: they were **beating
him**,[41] precisely what the wicked tenants in the parable did to the servants—in
other words, the prophets (20:10–12; see 11:49; 13:34). Indeed, deriding Jesus'
reputation as a prophet (though it was just verified by his accurate predictions
regarding Judas and Peter), **they blindfolded him** and asked him to **prophesy**
who **struck** him. Unwittingly, they fulfill what he earlier prophesied concerning
his suffering (9:22; 17:25).

Jesus before the Sanhedrin (22:66–71)

[66]**When day came the council of elders of the people met, both chief
priests and scribes, and they brought him before their Sanhedrin. [67]They
said, "If you are the Messiah, tell us," but he replied to them, "If I tell you,
you will not believe, [68]and if I question, you will not respond. [69]But from
this time on the Son of Man will be seated at the right hand of the power
of God." [70]They all asked, "Are you then the Son of God?" He replied to
them, "You say that I am." [71]Then they said, "What further need have we
for testimony? We have heard it from his own mouth."**

OT: Ps 110:1; Dan 7:13–14
NT: Luke 9:20; Acts 7:55–56. // Matt 26:63–65; Mark 14:61–64
Catechism: Jesus before the Sanhedrin, 591, 596–97; Son of God, 443; Jesus at God's right hand,
  663–64

When day came (Matt 27:1; Mark 15:1; see John 18:24, 28), Jesus was **brought**   22:66
in for questioning **before** Judaism's judicial body in Jerusalem—namely, **the
council of elders** with **chief priests and scribes** (see Luke 9:22; 20:1; Mark
15:1), also called the †**Sanhedrin.**

The leaders, wanting to know who Jesus claims to be, ask him two questions.   22:67–69
First, is he **the Messiah** (*christos*)? The angel first announced to the shepherds
that Jesus is the Messiah (Luke 2:11), and Peter confessed him as Messiah in
the presence of the disciples (9:20). Moreover, while teaching in the temple,

41. Later, the disciples will receive similar treatment (Acts 5:40; 13:45; 16:22–23; 18:6).

Jesus had referred to "the Messiah" in his question about David's son (20:41). However, Jesus' earlier experience when discussing authority with the Jewish leaders indicates that they **will not believe** it (20:5) nor will they **respond** if he asks them a **question** (20:3, 7). Nevertheless, he answers the question by interpreting the title for them: **from this time on the Son of Man will be seated at the right hand of the power of God**. The emphasis here is not on Jesus' second "coming" (21:27) *from* God's right hand (see Matt 26:64; Mark 14:62) but rather on his imminent exaltation following his death and resurrection *to* God's right hand, to which Peter and the apostles, and also Stephen,[42] will soon bear witness (Acts 2:33–34; 5:31; 7:55–56). The words about sitting "at the right hand" are from the psalm Jesus quoted earlier (see Luke 20:42; Ps 110:1), and the Son of Man title here refers to Daniel's prophecy of a divine-human figure who receives everlasting dominion (Dan 7:13–14; see Ps 80:18). With these biblical allusions, Jesus declares himself to be a messianic king with a divine identity.

22:70–71   None of this is lost on those interrogating him, who thus follow up with a second question: **Are you then the Son of God?** It was again an angel who first announced this title (Luke 1:35), and the voice from heaven confirmed it at key moments in Jesus' ministry (3:22; 9:35). In response, Jesus indirectly affirms: **You say that I am**. That Jesus is again staking a claim to divine status is apparent to them. No more **testimony** is needed to charge him with blasphemy, since they **have heard it from his own mouth**. They can now hand him over to the Roman governor, as they have been hoping to do (20:20).

42. Details of the hearing that are found in Matthew and Mark—e.g., false witnesses and the charge that Jesus would destroy the temple (Matt 26:60–61; Mark 14:56–58)—are absent here in Luke but reappear in the account of Stephen's martyrdom (Acts 6:13–14).

Trial, Crucifixion, and Death

Luke 23:1–56

"We adore you, O Christ, and we praise you. Because by your holy cross, you have redeemed the world." With these words, the faithful introduce each of the Stations of the Cross, which are prayed in churches throughout the world, especially on Good Friday. Pilgrims to Jerusalem pray these Stations on the *Via Dolorosa* through the city's crowded streets.

The biblical events commemorated in the Stations are now unfolding in Luke's Gospel—for example, the verdict of Pilate, the journey of Jesus to the site of crucifixion, the assistance of Simon of Cyrene, the encounter with the women of Jerusalem, the crucifixion, the death on the cross, the taking down from the cross, and the burial in the tomb. "Blessed be the Lord, the God of Israel," who through these events has "brought redemption to his people" (1:68; see 2:38; 24:21).

Trial, Part 1: Jesus before Pilate and Herod (23:1–12)

[1]Then the whole assembly of them arose and brought him before Pilate. [2]They brought charges against him, saying, "We found this man misleading our people; he opposes the payment of taxes to Caesar and maintains that he is the Messiah, a king." [3]Pilate asked him, "Are you the king of the Jews?" He said to him in reply, "You say so." [4]Pilate then addressed the chief priests and the crowds, "I find this man not guilty." [5]But they were adamant and said, "He is inciting the people with his teaching throughout all Judea, from Galilee where he began even to here."

⁶On hearing this Pilate asked if the man was a Galilean; ⁷and upon learning that he was under Herod's jurisdiction, he sent him to Herod who was in Jerusalem at that time. ⁸Herod was very glad to see Jesus; he had been wanting to see him for a long time, for he had heard about him and had been hoping to see him perform some sign. ⁹He questioned him at length, but he gave him no answer. ¹⁰The chief priests and scribes, meanwhile, stood by accusing him harshly. ¹¹[Even] Herod and his soldiers treated him contemptuously and mocked him, and after clothing him in resplendent garb, he sent him back to Pilate. ¹²Herod and Pilate became friends that very day, even though they had been enemies formerly.

NT: Luke 9:9; 20:22–25; Acts 4:27. // Matt 27:1–2, 11–14; Mark 15:1–5; John 18:28–38
Catechism: Trial before Pilate, 596, 600

23:1 Following the early morning hearing, the **whole assembly** of Jewish leaders now **brought him before Pilate**, thus fulfilling Jesus' prediction that he would be handed over to the Gentiles (18:32). Jesus' trial before Pilate is well remembered in the early Church: besides the four Gospels, there are references to it in the Acts of the Apostles (Acts 3:13; 4:27; 13:28) and one of the epistles (1 Tim 6:13), and it even finds its way into the creeds.

The Roman governors normally lived in Caesarea Maritima (see Acts 23:33),[1] where an inscription with Pilate's name was found in 1961. However, they would go up to Jerusalem for feasts such as Passover to secure public order. According to the other Gospels, Jesus' trial before Pilate took place in the "praetorium," which Mark also describes as a "palace" (Matt 27:27; Mark 15:16; John 18:28).[2]

23:2 The †Sanhedrin's religious concerns about Jesus are now translated into political **charges**. First, **this man** is **misleading** or "perverting" (RSV) their nation. Ironically, the leaders are the ones perverting the truth. Their second charge—that Jesus **opposes the payment of taxes to Caesar**—twists his earlier response (Luke 20:25), as if Jesus were "inciting the people to revolt" (23:14; see Acts 5:37). Their third accusation is even more dangerous: he **maintains that he is the Messiah** (see Luke 20:41; 22:67). Jesus is a suffering Messiah (9:20–22; 24:26), but nonetheless the title means that he is **a king**, which they

---

1. E.g., Josephus, *Jewish War* 2.171; *Jewish Antiquities* 18.57.
2. Most scholars locate the praetorium at Herod the Great's upper palace in the western part of the city. Others favor the older †Hasmonean palace near the temple mount's southwest corner or the Antonia Fortress, the army barracks at the temple mount's northwest corner. See Bargil Pixner, *Paths of the Messiah*, ed. Rainer Riesner, trans. Keith Myrick, Sam Randall, and Miriam Randall (San Francisco: Ignatius, 2010), 266–94; Jerome Murphy-O'Connor, *Keys to Jerusalem: Collected Essays* (Oxford: Oxford University Press, 2012), 108–9.

Figure 21. Pilate inscription
at Caesarea Maritima.

interpret as one who "opposes Caesar" (John 19:12). The acclamation—"king" (Luke 19:38)—has become an accusation.

The actual interrogation of Jesus by **Pilate** is presented in summary form (see 23:3–4 John 18:33–38). Pilate, taking up the last charge, asks Jesus (in all four Gospels): **Are you the king of the Jews?** This title will be used to mock him (Luke 23:37) and will appear as the inscription on the cross (23:38). Jesus answers the question indirectly, as he did when asked by the †Sanhedrin if he is the Son of God (22:70): **You say so.** As before, the reply is affirmative, but there is an ambiguity in the indirect response because it emphasizes the questioner's understanding of the question. The Sanhedrin understood Jesus' indirect response as proof of blasphemy (22:71), but **Pilate**—who has a different understanding of kingship than Jesus—judges that Jesus is not claiming to be a political, military king.[3] He thus finds him **not guilty.** This is the first of three such statements by Pilate (see 23:14, 22).

With the verdict pronounced, the trial should now be over, if it were a just 23:5 process. However, "the issue throughout the trial is not one of justice but one of power."[4] The Jewish leaders are **adamant**, again taking up their first charge (v. 2) by insisting that Jesus is **inciting the people with his teaching** wherever he goes in **all Judea** (see 4:44; 7:17), beginning from his own region of **Galilee**.

---

3. Jean-Noël Aletti, *L'art de raconter Jésus Christ: L'écriture narrative de l'évangile de Luc* (Paris: Seuil, 1989), 162–64.
4. James R. Edwards, *The Gospel according to Luke*, PNTC (Grand Rapids: Eerdmans, 2015), 671.

23:6–8   The issue of proper **jurisdiction** gives **Pilate** a possible way out. Since Jesus is **a Galilean**, **he sent him to Herod** Antipas, tetrarch of Galilee (3:1), who had also come to **Jerusalem** for the Passover.

The emphasis in their encounter is on seeing: **Herod** is **glad to see Jesus** and **had been wanting to see him** and **had been hoping to see him**. Previously, he had "kept trying to see him" (9:9), but without success. His interest in Jesus, however, does not spring from a good motive. He merely seeks a **sign**, and Jesus characterized such people as "an evil generation" (11:29).

23:9–10   Despite being **questioned** by Herod **at length** as **the chief priests and scribes** are **accusing him harshly**, Jesus does not **answer**.[5] Apparently, he said enough in his earlier message for Herod, given through the Pharisees who told him that Herod wanted to kill him: "Today and tomorrow, and on the third day I accomplish my purpose" (13:32). Strikingly, Jesus now meets Herod "today" on the day of his death, and after "tomorrow," on "the third day" (24:7, 46) he will accomplish his purpose with his resurrection.

23:11–12   Answering nothing, Jesus is **treated** literally as counting for nothing—that is, **contemptuously**. He is again **mocked** (see 18:32; 22:63), with **Herod** even **clothing him** like a king, **in resplendent garb** (see 7:25; 16:19; Acts 12:21). However, rather than pronounce on the case, the tetrarch **sent him back to Pilate**. As a result of the exchange, the two rulers overcome their enmity (see Luke 13:1) and become **friends**. Their collaboration in Jesus' death fulfills Scripture: "The princes gathered together . . . against his anointed" (Acts 4:26, quoting Ps 2:2). "Indeed they gathered in this city against your holy servant Jesus whom you anointed, Herod and Pontius Pilate" (Acts 4:27).

Trial, Part 2: Pilate Hands Jesus Over to Be Crucified (23:13–25)

[13]Pilate then summoned the chief priests, the rulers, and the people [14]and said to them, "You brought this man to me and accused him of inciting the people to revolt. I have conducted my investigation in your presence and have not found this man guilty of the charges you have brought against him, [15]nor did Herod, for he sent him back to us. So no capital crime has been committed by him. [16]Therefore I shall have him flogged and then release him." [17]

[18]But all together they shouted out, "Away with this man! Release Barabbas to us." [19](Now Barabbas had been imprisoned for a rebellion

---

5. Some interpret the silence as an allusion to the †suffering servant: "Though harshly treated, he submitted / and did not open his mouth" (Isa 53:7).

that had taken place in the city and for murder.) ²⁰Again Pilate addressed
them, still wishing to release Jesus, ²¹but they continued their shouting,
"Crucify him! Crucify him!" ²²Pilate addressed them a third time, "What
evil has this man done? I found him guilty of no capital crime. Therefore I shall have him flogged and then release him." ²³With loud shouts,
however, they persisted in calling for his crucifixion, and their voices
prevailed. ²⁴The verdict of Pilate was that their demand should be granted.
²⁵So he released the man who had been imprisoned for rebellion and murder, for whom they asked, and he handed Jesus over to them to deal with
as they wished.

NT: Acts 3:13; 13:28. // Matt 27:15–16, 21–26; Mark 15:6–7, 12–15; John 18:39–40; 19:4–16
Catechism: Responsibility for Jesus' death, 597

Addressing Jesus' case once again, **Pilate** calls together **the chief priests** (who   23:13
appear, often first, in virtually every list of Jesus' opponents in Jerusalem)⁶ as
well as **the rulers** (23:35; 24:20; see 19:47)—for example, other members of
the †Sanhedrin (see Acts 4:5–6). Also **summoned** are **the people**. When Jesus
taught in the temple, "all the people" listened (Luke 19:48; 20:6, 45; 21:38), and
thus the leaders feared arresting him (20:19; 22:2). Now, however, at least some
of "the people" have joined with Jesus' opponents (see 23:18, 23; Acts 3:12–13).
Nevertheless, "a large crowd of people" will follow Jesus on his way to the cross,
mourning and lamenting him (Luke 23:27). "The people" will then watch as
he is crucified (23:35), before returning home as a repentant crowd (23:48).

Summarizing the process in legal terms, Pilate for the second time declares   23:14–16
that he has **not found** Jesus **guilty of the charges** (23:4). Moreover, this second
judgment has the backing of **Herod**, who likewise did not condemn Jesus. Thus
Jesus has **committed** nothing meriting death—in other words, **no capital crime**.
With these words, Pilate expresses his awareness that, beneath the accusations,
the Jewish leaders have their own reasons for wanting to put Jesus to death
(19:47; 22:2; see Matt 27:18; Mark 15:10) and have turned to him to carry out
such a punishment (see John 18:31). However, based on his findings, he plans
to **release** Jesus. He will just **have him flogged** first, in order to give him a
warning and in an attempt to appease the insistent Jewish leaders.

However, Pilate's decision is soundly rejected, as **all together** the Jewish   23:18–19
leaders and even the people **shouted: Away with this man!** In Acts, when Paul
is arrested in Jerusalem, those who want to kill him will similarly shout, "Away
with him!" (Acts 21:36).

---

6. Luke 19:47; 20:1, 19; 22:2, 4, 52, 66; 23:4, 10, 13; 24:20.

Parallels between Luke and Acts

BIBLICAL BACKGROUND

Many events of Jesus' life in Luke correspond to events in the life of the Church in the Acts of the Apostles. For example, as the Holy Spirit descends upon Jesus at his baptism (Luke 3:22), so too does the Spirit descend on the early Church (Acts 2:1–4). By highlighting such historical similarities, Luke shows that Jesus' life is the model for the Church's life and the lives of individual Christians (Catechism 520). Christians thus imitate Jesus, but in addition, their lives are lived in him and his life is lived in them (Catechism 521). Thus when Saul is persecuting *Christians*, Jesus appears to him and asks, "Saul, Saul, why are you persecuting *me*?" (Acts 9:4 [emphasis added]). He reiterates: "I am Jesus, whom you are persecuting" (Acts 9:5).

In particular, Acts shows how the lives of Stephen, Peter, and Paul mirror Jesus' life in various ways. As Jesus asks the Father to forgive those who crucified him, and then commends his spirit into the Father's hands at his death (Luke 23:34, 46), so Stephen prays to Jesus to receive his spirit and asks the Lord not to hold the sin of his stoning against those who did it (Acts 7:59–60). As Jesus gives an important speech explaining the fulfillment of Scripture (Luke 4:16–30), so do Peter and Paul (Acts 2:14–40; 13:16–41). As Jesus heals the paralyzed (Luke 5:24–25) and raises the dead (7:14–15; 8:53–55), so do Peter and Paul (Acts 3:2–8; 9:40; 14:8–10; 20:9–12). As Jesus finds faith in a centurion (Luke 7:9), so do Peter with the centurion Cornelius and Paul with the Philippian jailer, leading to their baptism (Acts 10:43–48; 16:31–34).

Moreover, many events of Paul's imprisonment recall those of Jesus' passion.[a] Both Jesus and Paul travel to Jerusalem knowing that they will suffer there and be handed over to the Gentiles (Luke 18:31–33; Acts 21:11–13). Both give farewell addresses (Luke 22:14–38; Acts 20:17–38). Both break bread in the Eucharist (Luke 22:19; Acts 20:7, 11). In Jerusalem, they are arrested (Luke 22:54; Acts 21:30) and struck (Luke 22:63-64; Acts 23:2). There are four phases to their trials, as Jesus is brought before the †Sanhedrin, Pilate, Herod Antipas, and Pilate again (Luke 22:66; 23:1, 7, 11), and Paul is brought before the Sanhedrin, Felix, Festus, and Herod Agrippa II (Acts 22:30; 24:1; 25:5, 23). Both are declared innocent three times (Luke 23:4, 14, 22; Acts 23:9; 25:25; 26:31). During their trials there are shouts of "Away with this man!" (Luke 23:18) and "Away with him!" (Acts 21:36). In both cases, a centurion reacts favorably (Luke 23:47; Acts 27:1, 3, 43). Through these and other parallels, Luke confirms what Paul says in Galatians: "I live, no longer I, but Christ lives in me" (Gal 2:20).

a. E.g., see Charles H. Talbert, *Reading Luke: A Literary and Theological Commentary on the Third Gospel*, rev. ed. (Macon, GA: Smyth & Helwys, 2002), 218–20.

Moreover, an additional demand is made of Pilate: **Release Barabbas to us**. This request refers to the custom of a Passover amnesty for a prisoner, mentioned in the other Gospels (Matt 27:15; Mark 15:6; John 18:39).[7] The situation is highly ironic: they ask for one whose name means "son of the father," but they reject the true Son of the Father.[8] They press their case against Jesus for "inciting the people to revolt" (Luke 23:14), yet they ask for **Barabbas**, who is in prison precisely **for a rebellion** and **murder**. Since the people (v. 13) who allegedly are being incited to revolt are themselves calling for his execution, the falsehood of the charge against Jesus becomes evident.[9]

The trial has deteriorated into a contest of whose voice is the loudest and whose will is the strongest. In response to their shouts, Pilate **addressed** or called out to **them**, trying to assert his voice. He expressed his will, **wishing** (literally, "willing") **to release Jesus** (v. 16). However, they continue **shouting** over him, indicating their will: **Crucify him!** For the **third time** (23:4, 14), **Pilate** says that he has **found him guilty of no capital crime**, and he wonders aloud **what evil** Jesus has **done**. He repeats that he will **release him** after he is **flogged**. A scourging was earlier predicted by Jesus (18:33), but the actual scourging mentioned in the other Gospels (Matt 27:26; Mark 15:15; John 19:1) is not recounted by Luke, who emphasizes more the mockery of Jesus than his physical sufferings.[10] However, it was typical Roman practice to precede crucifixion with other punishments such as a severe scourging. · 23:20–22

More **loud shouts** demand that he be crucified, and **their voices prevailed**. In accord with what **they asked** (23:18) and contrary to what he said (see vv. 16, 20, 22), **Pilate** decides to have Barabbas **released** while **Jesus** is **handed over** to be crucified (Acts 3:13–14). The leaders thus get what **they wished**—in other words, their will. The way of the cross has begun. · 23:23–25

Jesus Is Led Away to Be Crucified (23:26–32)

---

²⁶**As they led him away they took hold of a certain Simon, a Cyrenian, who was coming in from the country; and after laying the cross on him, they**

---

7. Verse 17 ("For of necessity he must release one unto them at the feast," KJV) is missing from many early manuscripts and is omitted in most modern Bibles. It is considered a later addition to Luke based on the verses in Matthew and Mark that explain the Passover amnesty. Among Jewish sources, a possible, later witness to this custom is *m. Pesahim* 8:6.

8. E.g., Ambrose, *Exposition of the Holy Gospel according to Saint Luke* 10.100, trans. Theodosia Tomkinson (Etna, CA: Center for Traditionalist Orthodox Studies, 1998), 424.

9. Aletti, *L'art de raconter Jésus Christ*, 168–69.

10. Luke also does not mention the crown of thorns (Matt 27:29; Mark 15:17; John 19:2, 5).

made him carry it behind Jesus. [27]A large crowd of people followed Jesus, including many women who mourned and lamented him. [28]Jesus turned to them and said, "Daughters of Jerusalem, do not weep for me; weep instead for yourselves and for your children, [29]for indeed, the days are coming when people will say, 'Blessed are the barren, the wombs that never bore and the breasts that never nursed.' [30]At that time people will say to the mountains, 'Fall upon us!' and to the hills, 'Cover us!' [31]for if these things are done when the wood is green what will happen when it is dry?" [32]Now two others, both criminals, were led away with him to be executed.

OT: Hosea 10:8
NT: Luke 9:23; 14:27; 19:41–44; 21:23. // Matt 27:31–32; Mark 15:20–21; John 19:16–17

23:26   After Pilate's verdict, the soldiers (see 23:36) **led** Jesus **away** through the streets of Jerusalem and out one of the city gates[11] (Heb 13:12). According to the typical Roman practice, **Jesus** carried the horizontal crossbeam[12] (see John 19:17), which would be attached to the vertical post at the site of the crucifixion. However, lest Jesus die along the way on account of his earlier beating and flogging, they compel **a certain Simon**, originally from Cyrene in Libya, who is **coming in** at the time, to **carry** Jesus' **cross** (Matt 27:32; Mark 15:21). He thus fills in where another Simon should be—that is, Peter (Luke 22:31, 34)—who left the scene after denying Jesus (22:62). As the **Cyrenian** carries the cross **behind** Jesus, he does what the model disciple is called to do: "If anyone wishes to come after me, he must deny himself and take up his cross daily and follow me" (9:23). And again: "Whoever does not carry his own cross and come after me cannot be my disciple" (14:27).[13]

23:27–29   Luke, who often mentions a man and a woman in pairs, now complements Simon with **many women**, whose encounter with **Jesus** is not recorded in the other Gospels. They are part of a large multitude of the **people**, probably of those who listened to him teaching in the temple (19:48; 21:38) and who now **followed** him, as indeed disciples are called to do (5:27; 9:23, 59; 18:22). Though these **Jerusalem** women **mourned and lamented him**, **Jesus** is instead concerned about **them** and their **children**. Indeed, their city will be destroyed in **the days** of judgment that **are coming** (17:22; 19:43; 21:6, 22). Corresponding to his earlier "woe" for "pregnant women and nursing mothers in those days" of "terrible calamity" (21:23) is the beatitude he now pronounces: **Blessed are**

11. The Gennath gate (see Josephus, *Jewish War* 5.146), so named because there was a garden nearby (John 19:41).
12. Latin *patibulum*.
13. The Greek word *opisthen* ("behind," Luke 23:26) is similar to *opisō* ("after," 9:23; 14:27).

the barren, the wombs that never bore and the breasts that never nursed.[14] In the case of the barren Elizabeth (1:7, 36), her condition was considered a disgrace and the Lord took it away from her (1:25). Now, in view of the looming crisis, such a condition itself becomes a blessing (see Jer 16:1–4).

A prophetic word from Hosea confirms Jesus' prophecy: to end such suffering, people will wish that **the mountains** would **fall upon** them and that **the hills** would **cover** them (Hosea 10:8). Jesus finishes with an analogy that argues from bad to worse: they are putting an innocent man to death in a time of "peace" (Luke 19:42)—that is, **when the wood is green**. So **what will happen** in a time of war? The whole city will go up in flames, like wood that **is dry**.   23:30–31

Also **led away** are **two others** who are **criminals**, who will **be executed** with Jesus (23:33). Scripture is being fulfilled in him, as he earlier said: "He was counted among the wicked" (22:37, quoting Isa 53:12).   23:32

Jesus Is Crucified (23:33–43)

[33]**When they came to the place called the Skull, they crucified him and the criminals there, one on his right, the other on his left.** [34]**[Then Jesus said, "Father, forgive them, they know not what they do."] They divided his garments by casting lots.** [35]**The people stood by and watched; the rulers, meanwhile, sneered at him and said, "He saved others, let him save himself if he is the chosen one, the Messiah of God."** [36]**Even the soldiers jeered at him. As they approached to offer him wine** [37]**they called out, "If you are King of the Jews, save yourself."** [38]**Above him there was an inscription that read, "This is the King of the Jews."**

[39]**Now one of the criminals hanging there reviled Jesus, saying, "Are you not the Messiah? Save yourself and us."** [40]**The other, however, rebuking him, said in reply, "Have you no fear of God, for you are subject to the same condemnation?** [41]**And indeed, we have been condemned justly, for the sentence we received corresponds to our crimes, but this man has done nothing criminal."** [42]**Then he said, "Jesus, remember me when you come into your kingdom."** [43]**He replied to him, "Amen, I say to you, today you will be with me in Paradise."**

OT: Ps 22:8–9, 19; 69:22; Isa 53:12
NT: Luke 22:37; Acts 7:60. // Matt 27:33–44, 48; Mark 15:22–32, 36; John 19:17–24
Catechism: Jesus prays on the cross, 597, 2605, 2635; Jesus as king, 440; the good thief, 1021, 2616
Lectionary: Luke 23:35–43: Christ the King (Year C); Luke 23:33, 39–43: Masses for the Dead

14. This beatitude is virtually the opposite of the one spoken earlier by a woman to Jesus (Luke 11:27).

23:33   Once outside the city, **they came to the place** and **there** Jesus was fastened to the wood of the cross. Interestingly, the phrase here in Greek occurs only one other time in the Bible, in the story of the sacrifice of Isaac, where it too is followed by the word "there": "*They came to the place* that God had mentioned to him. And [Abraham] built the altar *there* and laid on the wood, and when he had bound his son [Isaac] hand and foot, he laid him on the altar atop the wood" (Gen 22:9 NETS [emphasis added]).[15] According to Jewish understanding, this event in Genesis occurred basically at the same place (Mount Moriah) and at the same time of year (Passover) as Jesus' crucifixion.[16] Luke has already prepared the reader for such an allusion with the earlier references to Jesus as the "beloved son" like Isaac (Luke 3:22; 20:13; see Gen 22:2, 12, 16 LXX) as well as the earlier comparison between their mothers Mary and Sarah (Luke 1:37; Gen 18:14 LXX). The allusion's purpose is to indicate that Jesus' death is a sacrifice. Jesus explained this in another way at the Last Supper, saying that his body will be given and his blood will be poured out "for you" (Luke 22:19–20). As a result, the blessing promised to Abraham in the story of Isaac's sacrifice comes through Jesus, as Luke later says through Peter's speech that quotes the same passage (Acts 3:25–26; see Gen 22:18). Jesus' death thus has saving significance.

The crucifixion occurs at an abandoned rock quarry that is **called the Skull**, probably on account of its shape. The other Gospels also give its Aramaic name, Golgotha. Early Christian veneration of the site and of the nearby site of the empty tomb led the Romans under the emperor Hadrian in AD 135 to build a pagan shrine in an effort to eradicate the memory.[17] The result was just the opposite, as the shrine preserved the exact location. Later, under the patronage of the emperor Constantine, the Church of the Holy Sepulchre was dedicated in AD 335 marking both sites.[18]

Jesus is **crucified** "among the wicked" (Luke 22:37, quoting Isa 53:12)—in other words, between the two **criminals**. Indeed, crucifixion was a Roman penalty frequently imposed on brigands, political rebels, and slaves who revolted.[19] Though some were fastened with ropes, others, including Jesus himself, had

15. This seems to be another example where Luke quotes verbatim a unique string of words from the †Septuagint (see Luke 7:15; 13:17; 24:31), in order to highlight how Jesus brings an Old Testament figure or text to fulfillment.

16. Mount Moriah (Gen 22:2) was identified as the site of the temple (2 Chron 3:1), and the Passover time of year (Exod 12:2–6) was linked to the sacrifice of Isaac (*Jubilees* 17.15–18.3). See Edward Kessler, *Bound by the Bible: Jews, Christians, and the Sacrifice of Isaac* (Cambridge: Cambridge University Press, 2004), 90, 151.

17. Jerome, *Epistle* 58.3.

18. See Murphy-O'Connor, *Keys to Jerusalem*, 159–218.

19. John G. Cook, *Crucifixion in the Mediterranean World* (Tübingen: Mohr Siebeck, 2014), 216–17, 398.

their hands and feet nailed to the cross (Luke 24:39–40; see John 20:25),[20] and death followed slowly, as a result of asphyxiation, blood loss, and trauma.

Jesus' response is to "pray for those who mistreat" him (Luke 6:28): **Father,**   23:34
forgive them (verb *aphiēmi*). Only Luke records this saying,[21] one of the seven last words from the cross gathered from the four Gospels. The "liberty" (4:18; related noun *aphesis*) proclaimed by Jesus in Nazareth is here offered to his enemies, preparing also for the disciples' proclamation of "forgiveness" (24:47; same Greek noun) to all the nations. Jesus also provides his executioners with an excuse—**they know not what they do**—which will later be echoed by Peter, when he observes that they "acted out of ignorance" of Jesus' true identity (Acts 3:17; see 13:27). Presumably, "if they had known it, they would not have crucified the Lord of glory" (1 Cor 2:8).

After crucifying Jesus, **they divided his garments by casting lots**. This phrase indirectly refers to the Roman custom of crucifying people naked or wearing just an undergarment.[22] Moreover, it alludes to Psalm 22: "They divide my garments among them; / for my clothing they cast lots" (Ps 22:19). This psalm (echoed again in Luke 23:35) details the unjust sufferings of a righteous man. References to it are found in the crucifixion account in all four Gospels. Thus, "what is written about" Jesus is "coming to fulfillment" (22:37), including what the psalms say about the sufferings of "the Messiah" (23:35; see 24:26, 44, 46).

Indeed, the same psalm also says: "All who see me mock me" (Ps 22:8). As   23:35–39
the people there **watched**, Jesus is taunted by three sets of characters: among those who **sneered at him** were **the rulers**, but **the soldiers** also **jeered at him**, and even **one of the criminals hanging there reviled** or insulted him.

The scorn of the rulers and the criminal focuses on Jesus' title of **Messiah** (Luke 23:35, 39). If that is really who he is, **let him save himself**—again echoing the same psalm (which refers to God as the one who saves): "Let him deliver him" (Ps 22:9). The emphasis on the verb **save**, occurring four times in these verses, paradoxically explains the significance of Jesus' crucifixion: by not saving himself, **he saved others**. Indeed, Jesus is the "savior" (Luke 2:11) who has

20. Josephus, *Jewish War* 2.308; 5.451. In 1968, in a tomb in the Giv'at ha-Mivtar neighborhood of Jerusalem, the heel bone of a first-century man was discovered with a nail still through it, physical evidence of such a form of crucifixion.

21. Because the evidence of the manuscripts is divided, the NABRE puts this verse in brackets. However, by considering other evidence—such as the similarities to the Lord's Prayer (Luke 11:2, 4) and the parallel prayer of Stephen (Acts 7:60)—many recent commentators hold to the verse's authenticity. For a thorough discussion and defense, see Nathan Eubank, "A Disconcerting Prayer: On the Originality of Luke 23:34a," *JBL* 129 (2010): 521–36.

22. Cook, *Crucifixion*, 427.

come to bring "salvation" (19:9) and "to save what was lost" (19:10). This is his mission as Messiah (2:11; 9:20)—that is, as a Messiah who suffers (24:26, 44).

The rulers also derisively refer to Jesus as **the chosen one** (see 9:35), a title pointing to another biblical passage that sheds light on the crucifixion: "Here is my servant whom I uphold, / my *chosen one* with whom I am pleased" (Isa 42:1 [emphasis added]). Jesus is this †servant foretold by Isaiah (Isa 52:13) who at his crucifixion is "counted among the wicked" (Luke 22:37, quoting Isa 53:12). Moreover, Moses was also called God's "chosen one" (Ps 106:23). At the transfiguration, Jesus spoke with Moses about his "exodus" to take place "in Jerusalem" (Luke 9:31), and the voice from heaven referred to him as the "chosen Son" (9:35). This exodus of God's chosen one is now being accomplished.

The mocking by the Roman soldiers focuses on another title—**King of the Jews**—which is how the title "Messiah" was earlier explained to Pilate (23:2–3). Bearing the same title of **King of the Jews** is an **inscription** on the cross. According to the Roman practice, it was likely carried in front of Jesus on his way to the site in order to announce his crime and was then affixed to the cross for the same reason.[23] As part of their mockery, the soldiers **offer** Jesus a drink of sour **wine** (*oxos*). They unwittingly fulfill another psalm associated with Jesus' passion: "For my thirst they gave me *vinegar*" (Ps 69:22; *oxos* in the LXX).

23:40–41   **Rebuking** the criminal's mocking of Jesus (see Luke 17:3), **the other** one urges him—especially since they are about to die—to have **fear of God** (see 12:5), which is necessary for obtaining God's mercy (1:50). He confesses that they **have been condemned justly** on account of their **crimes** but recognizes that Jesus **has done nothing** wrong. He thus echoes Pilate's threefold assertion that Jesus is not guilty (23:4, 14, 22).

23:42–43   He next addresses **Jesus** and directs a plea to him: **remember me when you come into your kingdom**. His moment of conversion comes just in time. His appeal recalls biblical prayers to the Lord God—for example, "Remember me according to your mercy" (Ps 25:7; see Luke 1:54)—yet it is addressed to Jesus, whom Luke has frequently presented as Lord. His prayer expresses the hope that he will be saved not from the cross (see Luke 23:39) but from his sins, and so enter after his death into Jesus' kingdom.

Jesus' final **Amen** saying (see 4:24) solemnly grants the appeal. He promises him that he will soon be **in Paradise**, which was commonly understood in Jewish literature of the time as the realm of blessedness for the righteous after death.[24] Now, however, this blessedness comes from being *with Jesus*: **you will**

23. Cook, *Crucifixion*, 427.
24. E.g., *4 Ezra* 7.123; 8.52.

be with me. Originally, the garden of Eden was the earthly paradise (Gen 2:8, 15 LXX) where God placed Adam. However, Adam was driven out of paradise because of the fall (Gen 3:23–24 LXX), and it remained closed to sinners. Now, Jesus the new Adam (see comment on Luke 3:38 and 4:2) reopens paradise[25]— actually, a greater paradise of eternal life. Moreover, as seen throughout Luke, the fulfillment of the promise occurs not in some distant future, but **today** (see 2:11; 4:21; 19:9).

Reflection and Application (23:42)

Jesus, remember me. These words are brought to mind by a line from the eucharistic hymn *Adoro te devote*, attributed to St. Thomas Aquinas: "I ask for what the repentant thief asked" (*Peto quod petivit latro paenitens*). "Jesus, remember me." What a beautiful short prayer! Each day and throughout the day we can ask Jesus for the many things we need, summing up our prayers of petition by asking Jesus to remember us, according to his mercy, remembering not our sins (Ps 25:7). And, like the good thief, let us ask at the moment of our death: "Jesus, remember me when you come into your kingdom" (Luke 23:42).

Jesus Dies on the Cross (23:44–49)

[44]It was now about noon and darkness came over the whole land until three in the afternoon [45]because of an eclipse of the sun. Then the veil of the temple was torn down the middle. [46]Jesus cried out in a loud voice, "Father, into your hands I commend my spirit"; and when he had said this he breathed his last. [47]The centurion who witnessed what had happened glorified God and said, "This man was innocent beyond doubt." [48]When all the people who had gathered for this spectacle saw what had happened, they returned home beating their breasts; [49]but all his acquaintances stood at a distance, including the women who had followed him from Galilee and saw these events.

OT: Exod 26:31–33, 36–37; Ps 31:6; Amos 8:9
NT: Luke 8:2–3; 18:13; 24:10; Acts 7:59. // Matt 27:45–56; Mark 15:33–41; John 19:25–30
Catechism: Jesus' death, 730; Christian death, 1011
Lectionary: Luke 23:44–46, 50, 52–53; 24:1–6: All Souls; Masses for the Dead

25. Jerome Neyrey, *The Passion according to Luke: A Redaction Study of Luke's Soteriology* (Mahwah, NJ: Paulist Press, 1985), 179–92.

23:44–45   The penitent thief experienced the saving significance of the crucifixion. Now its cosmic implications are manifested in signs, which also bring the Scriptures to fulfillment. For three hours on that first Good Friday, from **about noon** till **three in the afternoon, darkness** came **over the whole land**, because the light **of the sun** "failed" (NRSV).[26] At Pentecost, Peter appears to refer to this sign as the fulfillment of the prophet Joel: "And I will work wonders in the heavens above. . . . The sun shall be turned to darkness . . . before the coming of the great and splendid day of the Lord" (Acts 2:19–20, quoting Joel 3:3–4).[27] The darkness is thus a warning about the coming day of the Lord (see Luke 17:24).[28] The three hours are a sign of God's judgment, like the plague of three days of darkness over the land of Egypt before the exodus (Exod 10:21–22).

A second sign occurs around three o'clock: **then the veil of the temple was torn down the middle**. On the one hand, this is likewise a sign of judgment, similar to Jesus' cleansing of the temple (Luke 19:45) and his temple prediction (21:6): the era of seeking atonement through the temple's animal sacrifices will soon come to an end. However, in contrast to the restricted access to God symbolized by the veil,[29] the torn veil also indicates that access to God is now readily available through Jesus' atoning sacrifice: "Through the blood of Jesus we have confidence of entrance into the sanctuary by the new and living way he opened for us through the veil, that is, his flesh" (Heb 10:19–20).

Though Matthew and Mark also note these two signs (Matt 27:45, 51; Mark 15:33, 38), only Luke mentions them together, suggesting a joint interpretation.[30] Since Jesus' crucifixion is accomplishing his "exodus" (Luke 9:31),[31] the key may lie in recognizing that similar signs occurred at the original exodus: "there was darkness" and "the water was divided,"[32] giving God's people open access to salvation through the middle (Exod 14:20–22 NETS).

---

26. Though the NABRE refers to a solar **eclipse**, such an event can only happen at a new moon, when the moon is between the sun and the earth, and not at a full moon as at Passover. Rather, the darkness could be caused by "thick black clouds" (Zeph 1:15) or by a dust storm (see *Sibylline Oracles* 3.800–802).

27. Joel 2:30–31 RSV. See also Amos 8:9: "On that day . . . / I will make the sun set at midday / and in broad daylight cover the land with darkness."

28. See Ezek 30:3; Joel 2:1–2; Amos 5:20; Zeph 1:14–15.

29. Scholars are divided as to which veil is meant: the outer one at the entrance to the temple sanctuary (the Holy Place; see Exod 26:36–37), or the inner one in front of the Holy of Holies (Exod 26:31–33). The tearing of the outer veil would have been visible to people outside, not just the priests inside. However, the tearing of the inner veil would have greater significance. See Heb 6:19; 9:3.

30. Whereas Matthew and Mark say the veil was torn from top to bottom, Luke says it was torn in the middle.

31. Joseph A. Fitzmyer, *The Gospel according to Luke*, 2 vols., AB (New York: Doubleday, 1981–85), 2:1502, 1514.

32. The verb for the "tearing" of the veil and the "dividing" of the sea is the same (*schizō*). See Daniel M. Gurtner, *The Torn Veil: Matthew's Exposition of the Death of Jesus* (Cambridge: Cambridge University Press, 2007), 177–78.

The Suffering and Death of Jesus

LIVING
TRADITION

Blessed John Henry Newman reflects on how Jesus intentionally and completely gave himself on the cross:

> He took a body in order that he might suffer . . . and when his hour was come, that hour of Satan and of darkness [Luke 22:53] . . . he offered himself wholly . . . as the whole of his body, stretched out upon the cross, so the whole of his soul, his whole advertence, his whole consciousness, a mind awake, a sense acute, a living cooperation, a present, absolute intention, not a virtual permission, not a heartless submission, this did he present to his tormentors. His passion was an action; he lived most energetically, while he lay languishing, fainting, and dying. Nor did he die, except by an act of the will; for he bowed his head, in command as well as in resignation, and said, "Father, into thy hands I commend my spirit" [23:46]. He gave the word, he surrendered his soul, he did not lose it.[a]

a. John Henry Newman, "Mental Sufferings of Our Lord in His Passion," in *Discourses Addressed to Mixed Congregations* (repr., Notre Dame, IN: University of Notre Dame Press, 2002), 330–31.

Crying out **in a loud voice, Jesus** speaks his last word from the cross: **into**   23:46
your hands I commend my spirit (*pneuma*). Whereas Matthew and Mark record a saying drawn from the beginning of Psalm 22 about the experience of feeling forsaken by God (Matt 27:46; Mark 15:34), this saying comes from another psalm (Ps 31:6) and emphasizes trusting abandonment to God, whom Jesus again addresses as **Father** (Luke 10:21; 11:2; 22:42; 23:34). At his martyrdom, Stephen will follow Jesus' model but will address his prayer to Jesus himself: "Lord Jesus, receive my spirit" (Acts 7:59). Through these prayers, as well as the penitent thief's plea (Luke 23:42), Luke teaches Christians how to prepare for death.

The death of Jesus follows, as he **breathed his last**. The verb here is related to the noun *pneuma*, which can mean "breath" or "spirit." In dying, Jesus thus carries out what he just prayed, in control and fully intent on his mission right to the end.

Three sets of people react to Jesus' death. First, the Roman **centurion**,   23:47
seeing Jesus' death, **glorified God**. Throughout Luke, such a response indicates recognition that God is at work in Jesus, bringing his plan of salvation foretold in the Scriptures to fulfillment.[33] The centurion also affirms that Jesus

---

33. See Luke 2:14, 20; 5:25–26; 7:16; 13:13; 17:15; 18:43; 19:38. Peter Doble, *The Paradox of Salvation: Luke's Theology of the Cross* (Cambridge: Cambridge University Press, 1996), 46–47, 66.

undoubtedly **was innocent** or "righteous" (NIV; *dikaios*).[34] This confirms Pilate's repeated declaration that Jesus was not guilty (23:4, 14, 22), as well as the penitent thief's similar statement (23:41). However, Luke also intends a further meaning. The word *dikaios* elsewhere in the Gospel describes those who are righteous or upright before God—for example, Zechariah and Elizabeth (1:6), Simeon (2:25), and Joseph of Arimathea (23:50). In this regard, Jesus is the foremost "Righteous One" (Acts 3:14; 7:52; 22:14), whose coming was foretold (Jer 23:5; 33:15). Despite being "the righteous one" (Wis 2:12, 18), Jesus is condemned "to a shameful death" (Wis 2:20). He thus also fulfills the mission of the †suffering servant: "A righteous one . . . shall bear their sins" (Isa 53:11 NETS).[35]

23:48   Second, **all** the crowds **who had gathered** (Luke 23:4, 27, 35) now **returned home beating their breasts**. Their gesture is a sign of mourning (23:27) over Jesus' death. It also suggests repentance (see 18:13), inasmuch as they regret their own role in having him condemned to death (23:13, 18, 21, 23). Later, Peter will explicitly call them to such repentance (Acts 2:38; 3:19).

23:49   Third, also present are **all** of Jesus' **acquaintances**, presumably including some of his disciples (see John 19:26), though the only ones mentioned are **the women who had followed him from Galilee** (Luke 8:2–3). These women will play a significant role in the following accounts of Jesus' burial (23:55–56) and resurrection (24:1–10). They **stood at a distance**, perhaps because they could not or were afraid to get closer (see 22:54). Their stance may also suggest humility and reverence, like that of the tax collector who "stood off at a distance" and prayed for mercy (18:13). He went home from the temple "justified" (18:14). Now, on account of Jesus' death, there is a new means of atonement: sinners "are justified freely . . . through the redemption in Christ Jesus, whom God set forth as an expiation" (Rom 3:24–25).

Jesus Is Buried (23:50–56)

[50]Now there was a virtuous and righteous man named Joseph who, though he was a member of the council, [51]had not consented to their plan of

34. In Matthew and Mark, the centurion instead calls Jesus "Son of God" (Matt 27:54; Mark 15:39). Raymond E. Brown, *The Death of the Messiah: From Gethsemane to the Grave; A Commentary on the Passion Narratives in the Four Gospels*, 2 vols. (New York: Doubleday, 1994), 2:1165, explains that a verse from Wisdom provides the bridge between the two descriptions: "If the righteous one is the son of God, God will help him" (Wis 2:18).

35. References to the †suffering servant of Isa 53 thus frame Luke's account of the events of Jesus' passion and death (Luke 22:37; 23:47). See Acts 3:13–14; 8:32–35.

action. He came from the Jewish town of Arimathea and was awaiting the kingdom of God. ⁵²He went to Pilate and asked for the body of Jesus. ⁵³After he had taken the body down, he wrapped it in a linen cloth and laid him in a rock-hewn tomb in which no one had yet been buried. ⁵⁴It was the day of preparation, and the sabbath was about to begin. ⁵⁵The women who had come from Galilee with him followed behind, and when they had seen the tomb and the way in which his body was laid in it, ⁵⁶they returned and prepared spices and perfumed oils. Then they rested on the sabbath according to the commandment.

OT: Exod 20:8–11; Deut 5:12–15
NT: Luke 8:2–3; 19:30; 24:10; Acts 13:29. // Matt 27:57–61; Mark 15:42–47; John 19:38–42
Catechism: sabbath rest on Holy Saturday, 624

As a **man named Joseph** (1:27) cared for Jesus in his infancy, so also at his **23:50–51** death. This Joseph is **a member of the council**, the †Sanhedrin (22:66), but **had not consented** to **their plan of action** of seeking to put Jesus to death (22:2–6; 23:1). He was originally from **Arimathea**, which is likely Ramathaim—that is, the Ramah of the prophet Samuel (1 Sam 1:1, 19).[36] Like Simeon at the presentation in the temple, Joseph is **righteous** and is **awaiting** the fulfillment of God's plan (Luke 2:25). Simeon had prophesied that Jesus was coming for both Gentiles and Jews: "a light for revelation to the Gentiles / and glory for your people Israel" (2:32). Despite Jesus' being put to death by Gentile and Jewish leaders (Acts 4:27), Simeon's prophecy now has a measure of fulfillment in the Roman centurion and Joseph.

Going **to Pilate**, he **asked for the body of Jesus**. Since **the sabbath was about** **23:52–54** **to begin** at sunset, it was necessary to bury him immediately (Deut 21:23). Having obtained Pilate's permission (Matt 27:58; Mark 15:45; John 19:38), he took **the body down** from the cross and **wrapped it in a linen cloth**.[37] Jesus was then **laid**, according to a burial custom common among Jews of the area, **in a rock-hewn tomb**—that is, a chamber cut out of the limestone, with a shelf on which the body was laid—and a disc-like stone was rolled into place at the entrance (Luke 24:2). Jesus was buried in a new tomb (Matt 27:60), one **in** **which no one had yet been buried**.[38] This detail recalls the colt "on which no one has ever sat" (Luke 19:30), used by Jesus when he entered Jerusalem and

---

36. The **town** is **Jewish**, perhaps meaning "of the Judeans," thus distinguishing it from towns with the same name in other regions.

37. For a recent discussion of the possibility that this linen cloth is the well-known Shroud of Turin, see Robert J. Spitzer, *God So Loved the World* (San Francisco: Ignatius, 2016), 343–91.

38. According to Jewish burial custom (for those who could afford a tomb), once the flesh of the deceased decomposed, the bones would be placed in a smaller ossuary, and the larger tomb reused.

Silvano Kim

Figure 22. Church of the Holy Sepulchre.

was acclaimed as "king" (19:38). Despite dying like a criminal, "the King of the Jews" (23:38) is buried with royal dignity.

23:55–56   Besides Joseph, **the women who had come from Galilee** are eyewitnesses attesting that Jesus was really buried. They saw not only **the tomb** but also **the way in which his body was laid in it**. These details anticipate a possible objection that Jesus' tomb was later found empty because he was never buried. Paul will likewise affirm: "I handed on to you as of first importance what I also received: that Christ died for our sins in accordance with the scriptures; that he was buried . . ." (1 Cor 15:3–4).

These women **followed behind** Joseph to the tomb. They in turn have been followed by millions of pilgrims over the centuries who have visited the tomb of Jesus, over which the Church of the Holy Sepulchre was constructed.

Because of the lack of time on Friday to complete the burial customs, the woman then **prepared spices and perfumed oils** with which to anoint Jesus' body after **the sabbath** (Luke 24:1). On that Holy Saturday, **they rested** in faithful observance of **the commandment** (Exod 20:8–11; Deut 5:12–15),[39] while Jesus' body rested in the tomb.

---

39. Like the individuals in the infancy narrative—Zechariah and Elizabeth (Luke 1:6), Mary and Joseph (2:22–24, 27, 39)—the women are exemplary in fulfilling the commandments of the law.

Fulfillment in Jesus' Resurrection

Luke 24:1–53

Faith in Jesus is possible because of his resurrection. Without it, faith would be worthless (1 Cor 15:17). Therefore, so that readers may know that the event of Jesus' resurrection is true (Luke 1:4), Luke, like the other evangelists, first testifies to the fact of the empty tomb and then recounts a selection of appearances of the risen Jesus. Moreover, he emphasizes that Jesus' resurrection was necessary in order to bring to fulfillment God's plan in the Scriptures (24:7, 26, 44). Luke's Gospel then concludes with Jesus' ascension (24:51), which looks forward to the sequel in the Acts of the Apostles. Strengthened by the Holy Spirit (24:49), the disciples will carry out their mission to all the nations (24:47), knowing that Jesus is still among them "in the breaking of the bread" (24:35).

The Resurrection (24:1–12)

¹But at daybreak on the first day of the week they took the spices they had prepared and went to the tomb. ²They found the stone rolled away from the tomb; ³but when they entered, they did not find the body of the Lord Jesus. ⁴While they were puzzling over this, behold, two men in dazzling garments appeared to them. ⁵They were terrified and bowed their faces to the ground. They said to them, "Why do you seek the living one among the dead? ⁶He is not here, but he has been raised. Remember what he said to you while he was still in Galilee, ⁷that the Son of Man must be handed over to sinners and be crucified, and rise on the third day." ⁸And they remembered his words. ⁹Then they returned from the tomb and announced

all these things to the eleven and to all the others. ¹⁰The women were Mary
Magdalene, Joanna, and Mary the mother of James; the others who accompanied them also told this to the apostles, ¹¹but their story seemed
like nonsense and they did not believe them. ¹²But Peter got up and ran to
the tomb, bent down, and saw the burial cloths alone; then he went home
amazed at what had happened.

NT: Luke 8:2–3; 9:22; 18:32–33; 23:49, 55–56. // Matt 28:1–8; Mark 16:1–8, 10–11; John 20:1–10
Catechism: the Lord's day, 1166, 2174; empty tomb witnessed by the holy women and Peter,
     640–41; the living one, 625–26; Jesus' prediction, 652; apostles' disbelief, 643
Lectionary: Luke 24:1–12: Easter Vigil (Year C)

24:1–3 Very early on that Easter Sunday morning, **the first day of the week**, the women
from Galilee who were present at the crucifixion (23:49) and burial (23:55)
bring **the spices they had prepared** (23:56) and go **to the tomb**. However, they
discover that **the stone** covering its entrance has been **rolled away**. Once inside,
they do **not find the body** that they had observed lying there in the same tomb
only two days earlier (23:55). The tomb is empty!

Though Luke has not yet narrated the explanation for this circumstance,
he tips his hand by referring to the body as that **of the Lord Jesus** rather than
simply "the body of Jesus," as he did just a few verses ago (23:52). In Acts, the
combination of the title "Lord" with the name "Jesus" occurs frequently and at
times refers explicitly to the *risen* Jesus (Acts 1:21; 4:33). The use of the combination here (its only occurrence in Luke's Gospel) suggests that Luke is already
pointing to the resurrection: Jesus is Lord of life and death.[1]

24:4–8 Indeed, such is the explanation that follows: Jesus **has been raised!**[2] He is
the living one and therefore is not to be found in the tomb **among the dead**.
The women needed to hear this message because **they were puzzling over** the
empty tomb, which in itself could admit of other explanations (see Matt 28:13;
Catechism 640). Making the proclamation to the women are two witnesses
(Deut 19:15) **in dazzling garments**, a scenario similar to the two witnesses
at the transfiguration (Luke 9:30) and later at the ascension (Acts 1:10). In
fact, the Greek phrase introducing the witnesses—here rendered **behold, two
men**[3]—occurs only in these three passages (in Luke-Acts but also in the whole
Bible). These similarities suggest that Luke intended to link them together. For

---

1. C. Kavin Rowe, *Early Narrative Christology: The Lord in the Gospel of Luke* (Berlin: de Gruyter,
2006; Grand Rapids: Baker Academic, 2009), 182–86. Of course, the title "Lord" by itself is applied to
Jesus many times in the Gospel (see the sidebar, "Jesus the Lord," p. 115).
   2. The passive voice indicates that *God* raised Jesus from the dead (Acts 2:24, 32; 3:15, 26; 4:10; 5:30;
10:40; 13:30, 33–34, 37).
   3. They are later described as "angels" (Luke 24:23).

example, the risen Jesus now possesses the glory that the three disciples saw in him on the mountain (Luke 9:29, 32). His body has not merely been resuscitated like those of the widow's son and Jairus's daughter (7:15; 8:55). Rather, he lives to die no more (Rom 6:9).

Similar to the reaction of others who received such heavenly messengers (Luke 1:12, 29; 2:9; Acts 10:4), the women **were terrified and bowed their faces to the ground**. However, so that they can make sense of what they heard, they are further told to **remember** Jesus' predictions **while he was still in Galilee**— namely, **that the Son of Man must** not only **be handed over** (Luke 9:44) **and be crucified** but also **rise on the third day** (9:22; see 18:32–33). Despite their fear, the women **remembered his words**. With remembering comes understanding (see 22:61; Acts 11:16; 20:35), which here leads to faith.

The women who received the Easter proclamation then **announced** it **to the apostles** (now reduced to **eleven** on account of Judas's departure) and **the others**. These women were present at all the key events: crucifixion, death, burial, empty tomb, and proclamation of resurrection (Luke 23:49, 55; 24:1–10). They thus have an important role as eyewitnesses testifying to the certainty of these events recorded in the Gospel (1:2–4). For this reason, Luke now specifies the names of three of them: **Mary Magdalene** (8:2) and **Mary the mother of James**, both of whom other Gospels attest as being present,[4] and also **Joanna**, whom only Luke mentions. Earlier, he had introduced her as one of the women who accompanied Jesus along with the Twelve (8:3). She is included here—indeed, at the center of these verses—perhaps because she is Luke's eyewitness source for this information.[5] *(24:9–10)*

The women's words, however, are dismissed as **nonsense**. In general, the apostles and other disciples **did not believe them**. Elsewhere in this chapter, Luke will point out the disciples' difficulty in believing in the resurrection (24:25, 37–38, 41). Luke's emphasis on their doubts also answers a possible objection that the resurrection was some scheme invented by the disciples (see Matt 28:13). Rather, the truth is that they did not believe it themselves! *(24:11)*

However, **Peter**, who has not been mentioned since his departure following his denial of Jesus (Luke 22:61–62), now appears as one who considers the women's report worthy of further investigation. He therefore **ran to the tomb**, *(24:12)*

---

4. Matt 27:56, 61; 28:1; Mark 15:40, 47; 16:1; John 19:25 (mentions Mary wife of Clopas); 20:1 (mentions only Mary Magdalene).

5. Richard Bauckham, *Jesus and the Eyewitnesses: The Gospels as Eyewitness Testimony* (Grand Rapids: Eerdmans, 2006), 48–51, 129–31. See also Bauckham, *Gospel Women* (Grand Rapids: Eerdmans, 2002), 186–94, who notes how Luke seems to highlight Joanna's role by putting her at the center of the ring structure of Luke 24:9–11: *A* the eleven; *B* other disciples; *C* a person named Mary; *D* Joanna; *C'* a person named Mary; *B'* other women; *A'* the apostles.

bent down to peer into its entrance, **and saw the burial cloths alone** (John 20:3–10). This last phrase gives a further piece of information about the empty tomb: still present is the linen cloth that Joseph of Arimathea wrapped around Jesus' body (Luke 23:53), but the body itself is missing. If the body had been stolen (Matt 28:13), would the robbers have gone to the trouble of unwrapping it?

Peter then returns **home amazed,**[6] a frequent reaction to the marvelous workings of God (Luke 2:18; 8:25; 9:43; 11:14). It is not said that Peter believed yet (see John 20:8), but on account of Jesus' prayer that Peter's "faith may not fail" (Luke 22:32), it looks like he is headed in that direction. Peter's faith will soon be confirmed by Jesus' appearing to him (24:34).

Appearance at Emmaus (24:13–35)

[13]Now that very day two of them were going to a village seven miles from Jerusalem called Emmaus, [14]and they were conversing about all the things that had occurred. [15]And it happened that while they were conversing and debating, Jesus himself drew near and walked with them, [16]but their eyes were prevented from recognizing him. [17]He asked them, "What are you discussing as you walk along?" They stopped, looking downcast. [18]One of them, named Cleopas, said to him in reply, "Are you the only visitor to Jerusalem who does not know of the things that have taken place there in these days?" [19]And he replied to them, "What sort of things?" They said to him, "The things that happened to Jesus the Nazarene, who was a prophet mighty in deed and word before God and all the people, [20]how our chief priests and rulers both handed him over to a sentence of death and crucified him. [21]But we were hoping that he would be the one to redeem Israel; and besides all this, it is now the third day since this took place. [22]Some women from our group, however, have astounded us: they were at the tomb early in the morning [23]and did not find his body; they came back and reported that they had indeed seen a vision of angels who announced that he was alive. [24]Then some of those with us went to the tomb and found things just as the women had described, but him they did not see." [25]And he said to them, "Oh, how foolish you are! How slow of heart to believe all that the prophets spoke! [26]Was it not necessary that the Messiah should suffer these things and enter into his glory?" [27]Then beginning with Moses and all the prophets, he interpreted to them what referred to him in all the scriptures. [28]As they approached the village to

---

6. The phrase translated "home" literally means "to himself," so that the end of the verse may also be translated "he went away, wondering to himself what had happened" (NIV).

which they were going, he gave the impression that he was going on farther. ²⁹But they urged him, "Stay with us, for it is nearly evening and the
day is almost over." So he went in to stay with them. ³⁰And it happened
that, while he was with them at table, he took bread, said the blessing,
broke it, and gave it to them. ³¹With that their eyes were opened and
they recognized him, but he vanished from their sight. ³²Then they said
to each other, "Were not our hearts burning [within us] while he spoke
to us on the way and opened the scriptures to us?" ³³So they set out at
once and returned to Jerusalem where they found gathered together
the eleven and those with them ³⁴who were saying, "The Lord has truly
been raised and has appeared to Simon!" ³⁵Then the two recounted what
had taken place on the way and how he was made known to them in the
breaking of the bread.

NT: Luke 9:16, 22; 17:25; 18:31; 22:19, 37; John 20:3–10; 1 Cor 15:4–5. // Mark 16:12–13
Catechism: Jesus' risen body, 659; disciples demoralized by Jesus' death, 643; Jesus reveals and
    fulfills Scripture, 112, 555, 572, 601, 652, 1094; from the Scriptures to the Eucharist, 1346–47;
    Jesus appears to Simon Peter, 641; breaking of the bread, 1329
Lectionary: Third Sunday Easter (Year A); Wednesday Easter Octave; Institution of Acolytes;
    Masses for the Dead; Luke 24:13–16, 28–35: All Souls

The first resurrection appearance recounted by Luke occurs later that same   24:13
Easter **day**, as **two** disciples are **going to a village**. They were among the "others" who had heard the news of the empty tomb from the women but had not
believed (24:9–11). They see no reason to remain in **Jerusalem** and are thus
headed, probably back home, to **Emmaus** about **seven miles** away—literally,
60 stadiums,⁷ though some manuscripts read 160 stadiums (about eighteen
miles). Though the location is disputed, corresponding to the latter distance
is the Emmaus mentioned in 1 Maccabees (1 Macc 3:40, 57; 4:3; 9:50), later
renamed Nicopolis.⁸

As they are **conversing and debating** about the events in Jerusalem—   24:14–16
undoubtedly a lively discussion—the risen **Jesus** appears and joins them on
the journey. However, **their eyes were prevented from recognizing him** (see
Mark 16:12)—that is, by God. The divine purpose is to reveal the risen Jesus to
them gradually, through the Scriptures and the breaking of the bread. In this
way, their eyes will be opened (Luke 24:31) not only in sight but also in faith,
thus overcoming their lack of faith (v. 11).

7. A stadium is a unit of measure equal to 607 feet.
8. Eusebius, *Onomasticon: The Place Names of Divine Scripture*, trans. R. Steven Notley and Ze'ev
Safrai (Leiden: Brill, 2005), 88. Josephus mentions this Emmaus (e.g., *Jewish War* 2.71; 3.55) but also
another Emmaus located thirty stadiums from Jerusalem (*Jewish War* 7.217), which some scholars
identify as the site, taking Luke's sixty stadiums as the round-trip distance.

24:17–24   When the unrecognized stranger asks them **what** they are **discussing**, their sad and **downcast** faces signal their disillusionment as a result of Jesus' death. Ironically, they consider themselves to be more knowledgeable than this **visitor**, who seems ignorant **of the things that have taken place**. They proceed to tell him their understanding of what happened. Whereas the other traveler is unnamed, **one of them** is identified as **Cleopas**, who may be Luke's source for this event and also the Clopas whose wife, Mary, stands by the cross in John's Gospel (John 19:25).[9]

In their summary about **Jesus the Nazarene**, they first identify him as **a prophet** (Luke 4:24; 7:16, 39; 13:33). This is correct, since Jesus is the prophet **mighty in deed and word** like Moses (Acts 7:22) and foretold by Moses (Deut 18:15; Acts 3:22; 7:37). However, it is not the full truth of Jesus' *identity*—for example, as Messiah (Luke 24:26) and Lord (24:3). Second, since Jesus was **crucified**, their hopes that he would **redeem Israel** (1:68; 2:38) are lost. They thus lack proper understanding of Jesus' *mission*. They fail to recognize that by his death he has accomplished a different kind of redemption, ransoming captives enslaved to sin by bringing them liberty (*aphesis*, 4:18)—that is, forgiveness (*aphesis*, 24:47). Third, they remain unconvinced by the report of the **women** (24:9). Though some of the disciples—like Peter (24:12)—have confirmed the empty **tomb, him they did not see**. The two disciples thus lack *faith* that Jesus is **alive**, risen from the dead.

24:25–27   Now there is a role reversal regarding who is knowledgeable and who is ignorant, as it is the stranger's turn to give an explanation. Regarding *faith*, he upbraids them for being **slow of heart to believe** Scripture. If they truly believed **all that the prophets spoke**, then they would have believed what the women spoke. Regarding Jesus' *mission*, the crucifixion should not have made them lose hope since, in accord with God's biblical plan, it was **necessary** (see comment on 2:49) **that** Jesus **should suffer** (9:22; 17:25; Acts 3:18) and die before rising to **his glory**. Regarding Jesus' *identity*, Jesus is not only a prophet but **the Messiah**.[10]

So that the two disciples might understand who Jesus is and what has taken place, the stranger then **interpreted to them** the things about Jesus **in all the scriptures**. Looked at the other way, the key that unlocks the meaning of these biblical passages is provided by the events of Jesus' life, death, and resurrection.

---

9. Bauckham, *Jesus and the Eyewitnesses*, 47. Eusebius, *Ecclesiastical History* 3.11; 4.22.4, explains that the second-century writer Hegesippus identified Cleopas as the brother of St. Joseph and father of Simon, who became bishop of Jerusalem after James.

10. Jesus used the more enigmatic title "Son of Man" when he predicted his sufferings, but now he speaks more directly about himself as the "Messiah."

Moreover, it is Jesus himself (here still unrecognized) who provides the authoritative interpretation of Scripture, **beginning with Moses and all the prophets**. Later, he will similarly instruct the apostles in Jerusalem (Luke 24:44–46). The apostles' preaching in Acts gives an idea of which Scripture passages Jesus may have explained to the disciples.[11]

The decisive juncture occurs when they reach their **village**. Captivated by the   24:28–31
insights of the stranger who appears to be **going on farther**, the two disciples **urged** him (the verb indicates strong insistence) to **stay** as their guest. When Jesus had gone to "stay" at Zacchaeus's house (19:5), he brought with him the blessing of salvation (19:9). Here he will similarly bring blessing because their welcoming invitation (see 10:8) is an opening to faith. So Jesus goes **to stay with them**, though he will again reverse the roles, becoming the host of the meal.

By now, **the day is almost over**, just as in the feeding of the five thousand when "the day was drawing to a close" (9:12). Jesus sits **with them at table**, just as there the people were made to "sit down" (9:14–15). Jesus **took bread, said the blessing, broke it, and gave it to them**, just as there, "taking the five loaves . . . he said the blessing over them, broke them, and gave them to the disciples" (9:16). Whereas the feeding of the five thousand looks ahead to the Eucharist at the Last Supper, now the Emmaus account looks back to it, as four similar actions also occur there: "He took bread, and when he had given thanks he broke it and gave it to them" (22:19 RSV). At the Last Supper, Jesus instituted the Eucharist by which he would be recognizably present to his disciples. This was foreshadowed at the feeding of the five thousand, which in Luke's account is immediately followed by Peter's recognition of Jesus as Messiah (9:20). Likewise at Emmaus, following the similar actions, **they recognized him**.

Whereas previously "their eyes were prevented from recognizing him" (24:16), now **their eyes were opened**. This exact expression (of three consecutive words in Greek) occurs elsewhere in Scripture only in the account of the fall in Genesis, which similarly occurs during a meal involving taking and giving and results in the recognition of a hidden reality: "The eyes of the two were opened, and they knew . . ." (Gen 3:7 NETS).[12] St. Leo the Great comments that "the eyes of these men were opened far more happily when the glorification of their own nature was revealed to them, than the eyes of those first parents of our race on whom the confusion of their own transgression was inflicted."[13] Through this allusion, Jesus is presented once again as the new Adam (see Luke 3:38; 4:1–13;

11. See, e.g., Gen 22:18; Deut 18:15; 21:22–23; Pss 2:2, 7; 16:10; 110:1; 118:22; Isa 53:7–8.
12. Also, the Greek verbs translated "recognize" (Luke 24:31) and "know" (Gen 3:7 LXX) are related.
13. Leo the Great, *Sermon* 73, in *Sermons*, trans. Jane P. Freeland and Agnes J. Conway, FC 93 (Washington, DC: Catholic University of America Press, 1996), 323 (translation adapted).

Figure 23. *Supper at Emmaus* by Caravaggio.

22:44; 23:43), who here gives the food that brings not death but life. "This meal at Emmaus is the first meal of the new creation."[14]

Thereupon, Jesus **vanished from their sight**, disappearing as quickly as he had appeared (24:15). It is an indication that after his resurrection Jesus' body has not returned to normal, earthly existence but has been transformed into a glorified body, whose properties include the ability "to be present how and when he wills."[15] Moreover, after his ascension, Jesus will indeed vanish from the earthly sight of his disciples. Nonetheless, he will stay with them (Matt 28:20), especially "in the breaking of the bread" (Luke 24:35), the Eucharist. That is where disciples can recognize him.

24:32   As at the beginning of the passage (v. 13), the two disciples find themselves alone, again conversing with **each other** (v. 14). However, the encounter has led them to faith, radically changing their perspective. They are no longer downcast (v. 17), and their once "slow" **hearts** (v. 25) are now **burning** because Jesus—the one who baptizes "with the holy Spirit and fire" (3:16; see 12:49; Acts 2:3)—has **opened** to them **the scriptures**.

14. Arthur A. Just Jr., *The Ongoing Feast: Table Fellowship and Eschatology at Emmaus* (Collegeville, MN: Liturgical Press, 1993), 67. See also N. T. Wright, *The Resurrection of the Son of God* (Minneapolis: Fortress, 2003), 652.

15. Catechism 645 (citing Matt 28:9, 16–17; Luke 24:15, 36; John 20:14, 17, 19, 26; 21:4).

Having regained their hope (see Luke 24:21), they now have plenty of reason to return to **Jerusalem, so they set out at once** (literally, "that same hour"
[RSV]).[16] Their hurried journey recalls the haste and excitement of the shepherds to share what they had experienced (2:16, 20). In the city, the two find
the eleven and all the others **with them** (24:9).

However, before they can communicate their own news, they receive an
update on events that have happened there: **The Lord has truly been raised
and has appeared to Simon!** This apparition of the risen Jesus to Simon Peter
is also attested by Paul: "He appeared to Cephas" (1 Cor 15:5). Though it is not
explicitly narrated in the Gospels, it can be understood as a confirmation following Peter's visit to the empty tomb (Luke 24:12). It is mentioned here, before the
testimony of the two disciples, so as to indicate that the truth of the resurrection
is entrusted above all to Peter and the other apostles, those to whom Jesus has
given authority (9:1; 22:28–29) and who will become its chief witnesses (Acts
1:22). Moreover, the name "Simon" (rather than Peter) recalls the first mention
of "Simon" early in Jesus' Galilean ministry (Luke 4:38). Simon Peter is thus
the first disciple of Jesus named in the Gospel as well as the last. This framing
device, which Luke may have adapted from Mark (Mark 1:16; 16:7), is another
indication of the importance of Simon Peter's authoritative testimony as an
eyewitness of the events of the Gospel (Acts 1:21).[17] The name "Simon" further
recalls Jesus' words at the Last Supper—"Simon, Simon" (Luke 22:31)—where
he announced that Peter, once he turned back after denying Jesus, would be
the one to strengthen his brothers. Indeed, that time has come, and Peter will
thus take up this role in Acts (Acts 1:15; 2:14; 4:8).

Then the two report their own encounter with Jesus and how **he was made
known to them in the breaking of the bread.** The phrase "breaking of bread"
is shorthand for the four actions occurring at the feeding of the five thousand,
the Last Supper, and Emmaus—he took bread, blessed or gave thanks, broke,
and gave. In Acts, Luke uses this phrase to refer to the celebration of the Eucharist (Acts 2:42; 20:7, 11).[18] Jesus continues to make himself known to his
disciples in the Eucharist, where they can recognize him. As St. Augustine
says: "Where did the Lord wish to be recognized? In the breaking of bread.
. . . It was for our sakes that he didn't want to be recognized . . . because we
weren't going to see him in the flesh, and yet we were going to eat his flesh.
So if you're a believer . . . you may take comfort in the breaking of bread. The

---

16. I.e., the same hour as the Emmaus meal, which took place in the late afternoon, when it was
"nearly evening" (Luke 24:29). Therefore, there is still time to return to Jerusalem that same night.

17. Bauckham, *Jesus and the Eyewitnesses*, 126–27.

18. See Catechism 1329.

The Word and the Eucharist

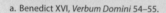

LIVING TRADITION

The Emmaus pattern of opening the Scriptures followed by the breaking of the bread is repeated in every Mass, with the Liturgy of the Word leading to the Liturgy of the Eucharist (Catechism 1346–47). Pope Benedict XVI explains:

> Luke's account of the disciples on the way to Emmaus enables us to reflect further on this link between the hearing of the word and the breaking of the bread. . . . The presence of Jesus, first with his words and then with the act of breaking bread, made it possible for the disciples to recognize him. . . . From these accounts it is clear that Scripture itself points us towards an appreciation of its own unbreakable bond with the Eucharist. . . . Word and Eucharist are so deeply bound together that we cannot understand one without the other: the word of God sacramentally takes flesh in the event of the Eucharist. The Eucharist opens us to an understanding of Scripture, just as Scripture for its part illumines and explains the mystery of the Eucharist.[a]

a. Benedict XVI, *Verbum Domini* 54–55.

Lord's absence is not an absence. Have faith, and the one you cannot see is with you."[19]

Appearance at Jerusalem (24:36–49)

[36]While they were still speaking about this, he stood in their midst and said to them, "Peace be with you." [37]But they were startled and terrified and thought that they were seeing a ghost. [38]Then he said to them, "Why are you troubled? And why do questions arise in your hearts? [39]Look at my hands and my feet, that it is I myself. Touch me and see, because a ghost does not have flesh and bones as you can see I have." [40]And as he said this, he showed them his hands and his feet. [41]While they were still incredulous for joy and were amazed, he asked them, "Have you anything here to eat?" [42]They gave him a piece of baked fish; [43]he took it and ate it in front of them.

[44]He said to them, "These are my words that I spoke to you while I was still with you, that everything written about me in the law of Moses and in the prophets and psalms must be fulfilled." [45]Then he opened their minds

19. Augustine, *Sermon* 235.3, in *Sermons*, trans. Edmund Hill, 11 vols., WSA III/7 (Hyde Park, NY: New City Press, 1990–97), 7:41.

to understand the scriptures. [46]And he said to them, "Thus it is written
that the Messiah would suffer and rise from the dead on the third day
[47]and that repentance, for the forgiveness of sins, would be preached in his
name to all the nations, beginning from Jerusalem. [48]You are witnesses of
these things. [49]And [behold] I am sending the promise of my Father upon
you; but stay in the city until you are clothed with power from on high."

OT: Hosea 6:2

NT: Luke 4:18; 18:31; 22:37; Acts 1:2–8; 2:3–4; 10:39–43; 1 Cor 15:5. // Mark 16:14–15; John
20:19–20

Catechism: Jesus appears to the disciples, 641; Jesus' risen body, 645, 999; the disciples' disbelief,
644; Jesus reveals and fulfills Scripture, 108, 112, 572, 601, 652, 702, 2625, 2763; the third day,
627; the Church's mission, 730, 1120, 1122; forgiveness of sins, 981; witnesses in confirmation
by the Spirit's power, 1304

Lectionary: Luke 24:35–48: Third Sunday Easter (Year B); Thursday Easter Octave; Luke 24:44–48:
Institution of Readers

Another appearance of the risen Jesus immediately takes place **while they**   24:36–38
were still speaking. Jesus stands **in their midst** and greets them with **peace**
(John 20:19), as indeed he had instructed his disciples to do when entering a
house (Luke 10:5). However, it is not merely a greeting, since Jesus is the one
who brings universal peace, on earth and in heaven (2:14; 19:38). In particular,
through his death and resurrection, "we have peace with God" (Rom 5:1; see
Eph 2:14).

In response, they are **terrified, troubled,** and filled with **questions,** recalling
the common reaction to an angelic apparition by Zechariah (Luke 1:12), Mary
(1:29), the shepherds (2:9), and the women at the tomb (24:5). They think they
are **seeing a ghost**—that is, a "spirit" (RSV) separated from the body.

After asking why they doubt, Jesus proceeds in three ways to demonstrate   24:39–40
the reality of his *bodily* resurrection.[20] Such a truth was difficult not only for the
apostles but also for other early Christians to believe (see 1 Cor 15).

First, Jesus invites the eleven and the others to use their sense of sight: **Look
at my hands and my feet.** He then **showed them his hands and his feet,** so
that by seeing the marks of the nails from his crucifixion (John 20:25, 27), they
could affirm **that it is** Jesus—**I myself**—standing before them. Significantly, this
shows the continuity between Jesus' crucified body and his risen body.

The second proof involves another one of the senses—**Touch me and see**—so
that they can feel that unlike **a ghost** he is made of **flesh and bones.** This event
may stand behind a phrase in the first letter of John (which uses the same rare
Greek verb translated "touch"): "What we looked upon / and touched with

---

20. Acts 1:3: "He presented himself alive to them by many proofs after he had suffered."

our hands / concerns the Word of life" (1 John 1:1). Moreover, St. Ignatius of Antioch, writing around AD 107, is familiar with this event, which he uses to defend the truth of Jesus' bodily resurrection: "For I know and believe that he was in the flesh even after the resurrection. And when he came to those with Peter he said to them: 'Take, handle me and see that I am not a phantom without a body.'"[21]

24:41–43   Their response is one of **joy** (John 20:20), yet in a sense they are **still incredulous** (literally, "disbelieving" [NRSV]). It all seems too good to believe! Clearly, belief in Jesus' risen body was not something contrived and then spread among a group of gullible individuals. However, their doubts help the faith of future generations of Christians, as St. Augustine says: "It was incredible, and they had to be persuaded of the truth of it, not only by their eyes but by their hands too, so that through the bodily senses faith might come down into the heart, and faith coming down into the heart might be preached throughout the world, to people who neither saw nor touched, and yet believed."[22]

    Jesus thus follows up with a third demonstration of his bodily resurrection. He asked for something **to eat**, received from them **a piece of baked fish**, and **ate it** in their presence. Later, when witnessing to the resurrection, Peter will similarly say that they "ate and drank with him after he rose from the dead" (Acts 10:41; see Acts 1:4 NIV, NJB). Moreover, this meal with *fish* complements the Emmaus meal with *bread* (Luke 24:30), the two elements eaten at the feeding of the five thousand (9:13, 16), to which these two meal scenes refer in various ways. Now, however, it is the apostles who act as hosts of the meal, a sign of their role in the early Church, when they will be the ones who celebrate the Eucharist, "in memory of" Jesus (22:19).[23]

24:44–46   In the next part of the scene, Jesus instructs his disciples about the fulfillment of Scripture and then announces their future mission. First, he reiterates how it was necessary that **everything written about** him in the Old Testament come to pass (18:31; 22:37). The two verbs used—**must** and **fulfilled**—have been repeated throughout the Gospel[24] and here emphasize one last time that all the events of Jesus' life have unfolded in accord with God's plan, especially as revealed

21. Ignatius of Antioch, *Smyrnaeans* 3.1–2, in *The Apostolic Fathers*, trans. Kirsopp Lake, LCL (Cambridge, MA: Harvard University Press, 1912), 255.
22. Augustine, *Sermon* 116.3, in *Sermons*, trans. Edmund Hill, 11 vols., WSA III/4 (Hyde Park, NY: New City Press, 1990–97), 4:204.
23. For the ideas in this paragraph, see John Paul Heil, *The Meal Scenes in Luke-Acts: An Audience-Oriented Approach* (Atlanta: Society of Biblical Literature, 1999), 221–26.
24. For the verb "must" (*dei*) in reference to Jesus' life, see Luke 2:49; 4:43; 9:22; 13:33; 17:25; 19:5; 22:37; 24:7, 26. For verbs indicating that Jesus has come to "fulfill" (e.g., *plēroō*, *teleō*), see Luke 1:1; 4:21; 9:31, 51; 12:50; 18:31; 22:16, 37.

in Scripture. As he did with the two disciples on the road to Emmaus (24:32), **he** thus **opened their minds to understand the scriptures**. Whereas there he referred to two parts of the Old Testament ("Moses and all the prophets," 24:27), here he indicates three parts: **the law of Moses, the prophets**, and the **psalms**.[25] In particular, he highlights that the Scriptures foretold **that the Messiah** (24:26) **would** both **suffer** and **rise from the dead on the third day** (Hosea 6:2).

Second, he explains **that repentance, for the forgiveness** [*aphesis*] **of sins,**   24:47–48 will be **preached** [*kēryssō*] **in his name**. This is the mission now announced to the apostles and the other disciples. Indeed, in Acts, repentance and forgiveness of sins through the name of Jesus will become the core message of the apostles' preaching ("kerygma").[26] The **beginning** of the apostles' mission in **Jerusalem** will thus recall the beginning of Jesus' public ministry in Nazareth, when he read from Isaiah and announced a jubilee, explaining that he was sent to *proclaim liberty* (Luke 4:18; *kēryssō* and *aphesis*). Now this jubilee is being extended in time and space: **from** Jerusalem the liberty that is forgiveness will be preached **to all the nations** (Acts 1:8).[27] The apostles and disciples will be the **witnesses**[28] of all **these things** about Jesus: his words and deeds (Acts 1:1)—his life, death, and resurrection.

One last instruction is that they should **stay in the city** until they are **clothed**   24:49 **with power from on high** to enable them to carry out their mission (Acts 1:4–5, 8). This power, which Jesus also describes as **the promise of** his **Father** whom he is **sending upon** them, is the Holy Spirit whom the disciples will receive at Pentecost (Acts 2:1–13, 33). As Jesus carried out his ministry "in the power of the Spirit" (Luke 4:14; see Acts 10:38), so too will his followers be filled with the power of the Spirit in order to carry out their mission of spreading the gospel (see Rom 15:19; 1 Cor 2:4; 1 Thess 1:5).

Reflection and Application (24:48–49)

You are witnesses. The *apostles* carried out their mission, "with great power" bearing "witness to the resurrection of the Lord Jesus" (Acts 4:33). However, all Christians are entrusted with the *apostolate* in one way or another (Catechism 900). In other words, we are called to be witnesses to Jesus in our lives and thus

---

25. The Jewish Bible is similarly divided into three parts: the law of Moses (Torah), the Prophets, and the Writings (which include the Psalms). Such a division is already suggested in the prologue or foreword to Sirach.

26. Acts 2:38; 3:19–20; 5:31; 10:43; 11:18; 13:38; 17:30; 20:21; 26:18, 20.

27. Thus fulfilling Simeon's prophecy (Luke 2:32) and Jesus' own words (4:24–27).

28. Acts 1:8, 22; 2:32; 3:15; 4:33; 5:32; 10:39, 41; 13:31; 22:15; 26:16.

advance his mission. "Clothed with power from on high" (Luke 24:49)—the power of the Holy Spirit received through baptism and confirmation—we can bear witness to Jesus by our deeds and by our words. This is what the early Christians did, and thus the faith spread quickly, despite persecution, to every part of society. This is what Christians today can and ought to do, joyfully sharing their faith with family members, friends, and coworkers.

The Ascension (24:50–53)

⁵⁰Then he led them [out] as far as Bethany, raised his hands, and blessed them. ⁵¹As he blessed them he parted from them and was taken up to heaven. ⁵²They did him homage and then returned to Jerusalem with great joy, ⁵³and they were continually in the temple praising God.

OT: Lev 9:22; 2 Kings 2:11; Sir 50:20
NT: Luke 1:22; 2:34; 4:8; 9:31; 19:29, 38; Acts 1:9–12. // Mark 16:19
Catechism: Ascension, 659
Lectionary: Luke 24:46–53: Ascension (Year C)

24:50–51 Luke's Gospel concludes with an account of Jesus' ascension into heaven (see Mark 16:19), in which he elegantly presents Jesus the Messiah (Luke 2:11; 24:26, 46) as priest, prophet, and king.[29] Moreover, as Lord (2:11), Jesus is to be worshiped. Though the timing of the event is not made explicit here, Luke indicates in Acts—where he also recounts Jesus' ascension (Acts 1:9–11)—that it took place "forty days" after the resurrection (Acts 1:3).

After giving his final instructions, Jesus **led** his disciples **[out]** of Jerusalem. The Greek verb *exagō* (lead or bring out), which occurs only here in Luke's Gospel, is the verb typically used in the †Septuagint—and even by Luke himself in Acts—to describe the exodus from Egypt under Moses.[30] At his transfiguration, Jesus had discussed with Moses and Elijah his own "exodus" from Jerusalem (Luke 9:31). As a *prophet* like Moses (see 9:35; Deut 18:15, 18; Acts 3:22–23), Jesus now completes his exodus from Jerusalem to heaven. Moreover, as a *prophet* like Elijah (Luke 4:25–26; 9:8, 19), Jesus is **taken up to heaven**, and his followers will then receive his Spirit (Acts 2:4; 2 Kings 2:9, 11, 15).

29. See John T. Carroll, *Luke: A Commentary*, New Testament Library (Louisville: Westminster John Knox, 2012), 495; and James R. Edwards, *The Gospel according to Luke*, PNTC (Grand Rapids: Eerdmans, 2015), 740.
30. Exod 3:8; 12:17, 42; 13:3 LXX; Acts 7:36, 40; 13:17.

Jesus takes them **as far as Bethany**. This village on the Mount of Olives was earlier mentioned only when Jesus was drawing near to Jerusalem (Luke 19:29). It was then and there that he was acclaimed "king" (19:38). His triumphal entry then is now completed by his "triumphal exit"[31] as he ascends to heaven, taking his place at the right hand of the Father, as the son but also as the lord of King David (20:41–44; 22:69; Acts 2:33–35; Ps 110:1).

Jesus also **raised his hands, and blessed them**. These actions are those of a *priest*, such as Aaron, who "raised his hands over the people and blessed them" (Lev 9:22), or Simeon, son of Jochanan (Onias) (Sir 50:1), who "would raise his hands / over all the congregation of Israel" and "the blessing of the LORD would be upon his lips" (Sir 50:20). Jesus' priestly blessing of his disciples at the end of the Gospel provides a frame with the Gospel's beginning, as it recalls the blessing of Mary and Joseph by Simeon (Luke 2:34) and supplies for the missing blessing of the speechless Zechariah (1:22). After giving his blessing, Jesus **parted from them** and ascended into heaven.

Before they **returned** to the city, his disciples **did him homage**—that is, 24:52–53
they "worshiped him" (NRSV). When earlier the devil had tempted Jesus to worship him (4:7), Jesus had responded by quoting Scripture: "You shall worship the Lord, your God, / and him alone shall you serve" (4:8; see Deut 6:13). Now his disciples worship Jesus, but not in violation of Scripture, since by his resurrection Jesus has been vindicated as "Lord" (Luke 24:3, 34) and "Son of God" (1:35; 22:70; see Rom 1:4).

Jesus' departure could seem like a sad ending, but it is rather a new beginning marked by **great joy**. Moreover, as at the beginning of the Gospel (Luke 1:9), so also now the setting for this new beginning is **the temple**. From there in **Jerusalem** the Church's mission will unfold in the Acts of the Apostles and will then continue down throughout history, as the gospel spreads even "to the ends of the earth" (Acts 1:8). The disciples' mission—then and now—is to be "witnesses" to Jesus (Luke 24:48), spending their time and their eternity **praising** and blessing **God**.

---

31. Mikeal C. Parsons, *The Departure of Jesus in Luke-Acts: The Ascension Narratives in Context* (Sheffield: Sheffield Academic, 1987), 104, 112.

Suggested Resources

From the Christian Tradition

Bonaventure. *Commentary on the Gospel of Luke*. Edited and translated by Robert J. Karris. 3 vols. St. Bonaventure, NY: The Franciscan Institute, 2001–4. Bonaventure draws on earlier works, such as the commentaries of Ambrose and Bede and the homilies of Gregory the Great.

Just, Arthur A., ed. *Luke*. Ancient Christian Commentary on Scripture: New Testament 3. Downers Grove, IL: InterVarsity, 2003. Excerpts of interpretations from patristic writers.

Scholarly Commentaries

Bovon, François. *Luke*. Translated by Christine M. Thomas, Donald S. Deer, and James Crouch. 3 vols. Hermeneia. Minneapolis: Fortress, 2002–13. This massive commentary in the Reformed tradition includes discussion of the history of interpretation of passages.

Edwards, James R. *The Gospel according to Luke*. PNTC. Grand Rapids: Eerdmans, 2015. Insightful, recent commentary by a Presbyterian scholar.

Fitzmyer, Joseph A. *The Gospel according to Luke*. 2 vols. AB. New York: Doubleday, 1981–85. A wealth of information by a noted Jesuit scholar. The lengthy introduction also covers Luke's theology.

Garland, David E. *Luke*. ZECNT. Grand Rapids: Zondervan, 2011. Thorough treatment with extensive pastoral applications by a Baptist scholar.

Popular Commentaries

Gray, Tim. *Mission of the Messiah: On the Gospel of Luke*. Steubenville, OH: Emmaus Road, 1998. An engaging overview of Luke's main sections and major themes by a well-known Catholic author.

Martin, George. *Bringing the Gospel of Luke to Life: Insight and Inspiration*. Huntington, IN: Our Sunday Visitor, 2011. Lengthy, easy-to-read commentary intended to aid personal *lectio divina*, by a veteran Catholic writer on Scripture. It provides helpful background information and reflection questions.

For Special Study

Snodgrass, Klyne R. *Stories with Intent: A Comprehensive Guide to the Parables of Jesus*. Grand Rapids: Eerdmans, 2008. In-depth treatment of Gospel parables, useful for preaching and teaching, by an evangelical scholar.

Glossary

anawim: Hebrew word meaning those who are poor, lowly, humble, meek, and afflicted (Pss 10:17; 25:9; 37:11; 69:33; Zeph 2:3), who thus depend on God and put their trust in him.

Dead Sea Scrolls: a collection of ancient manuscripts dating from around 250 BC to AD 70, discovered beginning in 1947 in the caves near Qumran, close to the northwest shore of the Dead Sea. Besides biblical texts, they include many other texts that shed light on Jewish belief and practice of the time.

eschatological (Greek *eschatos*, "last"): having to do with the last things accompanying God's decisive intervention in history. The last times have *already* begun with Jesus' first coming, but during the time before his second coming they have *not yet* reached their definitive fulfillment.

Hasmonean: the family of Jewish priests who led the Maccabean revolt (167–164 BC) and eventually ruled Judea from 135 to 63 BC, when it came under Roman control. After various power struggles, the last Hasmonean king was defeated by Herod the Great in 37 BC.

incarnation: "the fact that the Son of God assumed a human nature in order to accomplish our salvation in it" (Catechism 461). Thus, "Jesus Christ is true God and true man" (Catechism 464).

Mishnah: a collection of Jewish teaching compiled at the end of the second century AD, giving written expression to the oral traditions of the rabbis.

nazirite: an Israelite man or woman consecrated to God for a set time or for a lifetime. The vow involved abstaining from alcohol and not cutting one's hair (Num 6:1–21).

Sanhedrin: the Jewish people's supreme judicial council in Jerusalem, made up of the high priest and seventy other members, drawn from the leading priests, elders, and scribes.

Septuagint: Greek translation of the Hebrew Bible that was begun in the third century BC. The name means "seventy" in Latin (thus the designation LXX), from the tradition that there were seventy translators. Old Testament quotations in the New Testament often follow the Septuagint, since it was used by Greek-speaking Jews and Christians.

servant of the Lord: The figure portrayed in four passages of Isaiah that are identified by scholars as servant songs (Isa 42:1–9; 49:1–7; 50:4–11; 52:13–53:12). In particular, the third and fourth passages describe a suffering servant. These passages are applied to Jesus in the New Testament (Luke 3:22; 9:35; 22:37; Acts 8:32–35).

servant songs: *See* **servant of the Lord**

Shema (Hebrew for "Hear!"): Israel's confession of faith in one God, which begins with Deut 6:4: "Hear, O Israel! The LORD is our God, the LORD alone!"

suffering servant: *See* **servant of the Lord**

synoptic (Greek: "seeing together"): term applied to the Gospels of Matthew, Mark, and Luke, because they can be viewed in parallel since they contain much common material that at times even uses the same wording and appears in the same order.

type: a person, place, thing, institution, or event in an earlier stage of God's plan that prefigures a greater reality (called an antitype) at a later stage. "Typology" refers to the use or study of such type-antitype pairs (e.g., Adam-Christ).

typology: *See* **type**

Vulgate (Latin: "common"): the fourth- and early fifth-century Latin translation of the Bible by St. Jerome, used widely and declared to be the official Latin text at the Council of Trent.

YHWH: transliteration of the four Hebrew consonants of God's holy name revealed to Moses (Exod 3:14–15). Out of reverence, Jews do not pronounce the name when reading Scripture aloud, substituting instead the title "Lord" (Hebrew *Adonai*, Greek *Kyrios*).

Index of Pastoral Topics

This index indicates the location in Luke of topics that may be useful for evangelization, catechesis, apologetics, or other forms of pastoral ministry.

Index of Sidebars

N

SEA

SYRIA

Sidon

Damascus

PHOENICIA

Tyre

Caesarea
Philippi

GAULANITIS

Trachonitis

Batanea

MEDITERRANEAN

GALILEE

Chorazin
(Korazin)

Bethsaida

Capernaum

Gergesa

Cana

Magdala

Sepphoris

Sea of
Galilee

Auranitis

Tiberias

Nazareth

Mt. Tabor

Gadara

Nain

Scythopolis

Caesarea

DECAPOLIS

SAMARIA

Jordan River

Samaria

Mt. Ebal

Gerasa
(Jerash)

Mt. Gerizim

PEREA

Joppa

Emmaus
(Nicopolis)

Jericho

Jerusalem

Qumran

Bethlehem

JUDEA

Hebron

Dead
Sea

IDUMEA

Masada

NABATEA

Herod Antipas

Philip

Archelaus and
successors

0   5   10 mi

0   5   10 km